3RD EDITION
GUNSMITHING
PISTOLS & REVOLVERS

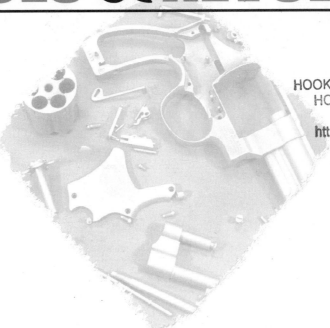

by Patrick Sweeney

©2009 Krause Publications, Inc.,
a subsidiary of F+W Media, Inc.

Published by

Gun Digest®Books

An imprint of F+W Media, Inc.

700 East State Street • Iola, WI 54990-0001
715-445-2214 • 888-457-2873
www.gundigestbooks.com

Our toll-free number to place an order or obtain
a free catalog is (800) 258-0929.

Cover photo courtesy of Yamil R. Sued
hotgunshots.com

Library of Congress Control Number: 2009923230

ISBN 13: 978-1-4402-0389-3
ISBN 10: 1-4402-0389-X

Designed by Dave Hauser

Edited by Dan Shideler

Printed in the United States of America

CONTENTS

DEDICATION

First I'd like to thank you, the readers, for sticking with me for all these years. In all modesty I must be doing something right, or else you'd have left me behind. That you're still reading my efforts is encouraging. That I have not burned myself out, as I've done in so many hobbies, careers and avocations before now is perhaps a clue that I've figured out how to balance my life.

In the course of my working career, I've not just had a bunch of jobs, but a string of careers. One of those was a stint in radio broadcasting, where in short order I had shuttled through stations big and small, top and bottom of market, and equivalent to, as I put it then, "WKRP without Loni Anderson." One thing we all knew back in the days of vinyl was that last year's smash hit album would be followed by something less interesting. As one rock 'n roller put it; "You've got your whole life to do your first album, but you have to have the second one done in eighteen months."

Eleven or so years ago the staff at DBI Books wanted me to re-write their Gunsmithing series. But while I was a very interesting speaker, getting it down on paper wasn't always so easy. In fact, at times it was downright ugly. Felicia came to the rescue. She not only saw to it that I paid attention to such mundane details as connecting the proper verb to the correct noun, and spelled each word correctly, but kept me on path to deliver the intended book, on time, and in a format my editors could work with. "Did you know that there was a famous gun writer who sent articles to his editor single-spaced, typed top to bottom, edge to edge, on both sides of the paper?" I once asked her. "I'm not surprised," she said. "I have no doubt that you guys were all dreaming up diagrams of guns and ammo in English class instead of diagramming sentences."

In many things I much prefer to learn from the mistakes of others. It can be so much less expensive, and potentially less scarring (physically and mentally) to pay attention to the mistakes of others, than not paying attention and doing it all over again yourself. To that end, I paid attention. I also married her. A well-tuned handgun can be very comforting in a dangerous situation. But a well-suited life partner is very comforting in times good and bad. Me, I have both.

So, if you can read this and keep it straight, thank your grade school English teacher. And for its being written in a format your teacher would recognize, thank Felicia. I do.

ACKNOWLEDGMENTS

Producing any book requires teamwork. An author writes it, but the editors look it over and point out mistakes, disagree over the proper structure of gerunds, and lash the page layout proles to produce a good-looking manuscript. I have lately been lucky to have had Dan Shideler as my Editor, who corrects my errors while not changing my prose. (Is it presumptive of a mere gunwriter to speak of prose?) He does yeoman work for little recognition.

Part of writing in a technical book is knowledge, and part is equipment. For the knowledge, I'd like to thank the many gunsmiths who have helped me through the years with their tips, hints, secrets and hard-won information. Their names are scattered through the book, but the formative ones are Dan McDonald and Tom Stone. Dan, for a gunsmith with no time at college (that I ever heard of) had a better grasp of the Scientific Method than many graduates of top-notch engineering schools I've met. He could ignore the extraneous details of a firearms problem, home in on the essentials, and figure out how to test his hypothesis. All while keeping in mind that the customer wanted it fast, cheap and pretty.

Tom Stone founded the gun shop where I learned much gunsmithing. His brother Irv went on to form Bar-sto, the now-famous and original match handgun barrel making company. Tom knew not only the dimensions and tolerances of every surface on a 1911 (and Browning Hi-Power) barrel, but he knew what that surface did, and how it interacted with the rest of the pistol.

I learned a great deal from both men, information that I have found to be useful to this very day.

In the course of writing this book I received parts, tools and guns from many manufacturers. The help from Brownells was essential. I cannot say enough good things about Frank Brownell and his employees. If you buy anything from them, parts, tools, books, and have a question of any kind, they are more than happy to track down the answer. Or tell you straight; "We don't know." Dave Skinner has been no less helpful. I'm pretty sure if I showed up at the front door of STI with word that my truck was dead, my camera was busted and my horse was sick (why I'd have both truck and horse is confusing, but I live in Michigan, and STI is in Texas) he would loan me all three and not ask for them back for several years. He would even smile and ask how the work was going when I complained that the loaner truck was a Chevy, the camera a Nikon, and the horse, well, what do I know about horses? (I drive a Ford, shoot with a Canon, and haven't ridden horses since the peanut farmer was in the Oval Office.)

I'd be remiss if I did not thank Gary Smith of Caspian. He has answered questions for years, sent me samples, product and the transparent and cutaway models you see here.

And even after all these years and many books, they're still answering my phone calls and e-mails. Updating this book once again was an interesting challenge, between the first and second editions I'd gone from film to digital, updated through two computer platforms and five generations of software, a change in publisher, and learned a whole lot more. Between the second and third I shuffled through three more computing machines, upgraded camera systems twice, and talked to a whole lot of other gunsmiths about just what-all goes into wrenching on firearms, I hope it is as fun to read as it has been to write, and that you find it useful, informative and worth your time. And for those who ask, at matches and industry get-togethers "Is it as much fun as it seems?" I can only reply: You betcha.

Patrick Sweeney
Spring, 2009

CHAPTER

PISTOLSMITHING FOR FUN

The idea of working on your own equipment seems to be very much an American one. In traveling to three World Shoots, a bunch of National Championships and in talking with shooters from around the world, I find that "do-it-yourself" is very much an American trait. Overseas shooters are much more like American shooters in that regard than their own non-shooting compatriots, but not to the degree that American shooters are. And there is a lot more home gunsmithing in some shooting disciplines than in others. Every other IPSC shooter you encounter will have done something to his handgun. Not so many Glock Sport Shooting competitors will have. (Partly the rules, partly the people.) But for those of you who want to do things yourself, here you go.

You should keep clear in your mind your choices: you can do pistolsmithing for fun, or as a route to a new career. It is entirely possible to start out just wanting to do "a few things for myself" and soon find yourself with a new career anyway. The purpose of doing things yourself is not to deny the professional a living income. Unless you are an absolute whiz at it, you aren't going to deprive the area pros of a living just by working on handguns on evenings and weekends. No, the best reasons for doing gunsmithing yourself are to understand how the mechanism works, and to maintain control over the work, the time it takes, and the results you get.

There is no secret body of knowledge in pistolsmithing, no set of mysterious "tricks" handed down from one generation of pistolsmiths to another. This isn't some branch of Shaolin Temple Gung-fu. Yes, much of what is done by professional pistolsmiths is done behind closed doors, but not to be mysterious. The door is closed to keep the customer from jostling the pistolsmith's elbow or asking distracting questions. Well, it is also done to keep the customer (sometimes) from seeing just how easy a particular task is, and then trying it himself.

But if it isn't all a really big secret, and if you could look behind that door, what would you see? What do you

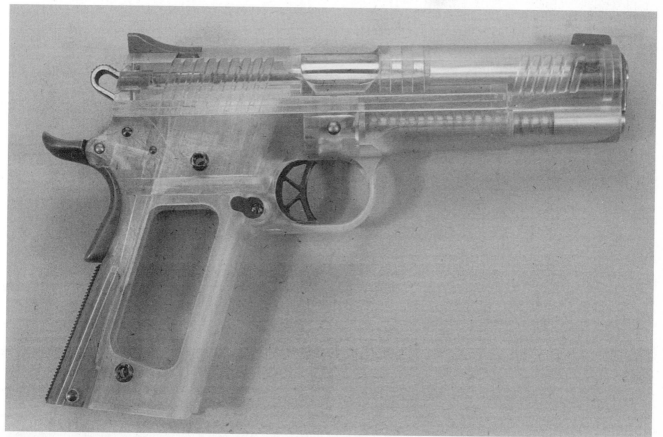

If the slide and frame were clear, you could watch everything as it happens. Unfortunately, steel is not transparent.

Handguns are expensive and you do not have the luxury of experimenting. If you make too great a mistake, you may have to buy a new handgun. Go slowly.

A messy workbench is an invitation to damage tools, lose parts and hurt yourself. Keep the bench clear of extraneous parts and tools.

need to work on your own handguns?

You need patience. Unless you have a large budget you will not have the luxury of scrapping a few pistols in order to learn the tasks quickly. You have to learn "on the job." As the late Dean Grennell, long-time author and reloading expert, pointed out in the past, skeet and trap shooters seem to have large amounts of cash to drop into their shotguns. Handgun shooters do not. In order to learn as you go, patience will be your constant companion.

As a professional, I had the luxury of a supply of "dead guns" to work on. In the course of buying and selling, the shop (we, the staff and the business) bought and sold many guns. Sometimes in order to get a good gun or guns, we had to buy the bad one or two as part of a package deal. The incremental cost of the "bad gun," the extra $20, $30 or $50, was simply tacked onto the cost of the good one when a retail price was calculated. The bad gun was stripped of useful parts and set aside for experimentation. It would bring tears to your eyes to see the guns I learned to stipple, checker, solder and file on. If they were particularly unuseful models, they wouldn't even be stripped for parts. Once they were used up in practice, the wrecked results were turned over to the State Police for disposal. You may have the option of practicing on scrap guns bought at a gun show for a mere pittance. If you do, jump at the chance. If, however, the paperwork requirements of firearms ownership are so onerous in your home state that the dead-gun option is not open, do not despair. You can practice on rifles or shotguns or just bars of steel. If you want to practice checkering a frame, or milling a slide for sights, bars will do. Shotgun barrels will do. Select a bar or barrel with the same radius, and work out your technique on that instead of an expensive-to-replace frame or slide.

You need the right tools. The kinds of tools usually found in the home workshop are not at all suited for the task of pistolsmithing. While you may have files out in the garage, they are probably too coarse, too rusty and too worn to be of any use in working on a pistol. Your screwdrivers are probably sized wrong and ground incorrectly, and the faithful claw hammer you used to frame your garage is a poor substitute for the hammers

you will need. What do the professionals use? Almost always they use the best. The cost difference between the best file and a file that is "good enough" is small. The best file will last longer and cut cleaner than the average or low-cost file. The same goes for parts: a top-quality part lasts longer and requires less work to fit to your handgun because it is made to tighter tolerances than its cheaper competitors.

Do you need a fully-equipped machine shop to do good or even excellent pistolsmithing? Not really. For decades at the National Matches in Camp Perry, the various factory armorers and service teams have had all their needs handled by the tools and equipment that would fit into a small trailer. If you do have a machine shop in your basement or garage, or if your uncle has just left you one in his will, great. But don't go out and buy a bunch of power tools just because you think you must have them to do any pistolsmithing. After all, the cost of power tools will pay for a lot of gunsmithing done by other people.

What do you need besides patience and the right tools? In all modesty, you need this book. Many texts directed at professional pistolsmiths assume the reader already has a large base of knowledge and experience. If you do not have such an education, random experimentation on your guns can be expensive, frustrating and painful. While I have made a few mistakes in my nearly 20 years of professional work, I have seen thousands more brought in by my customers after unguided do-it-yourself efforts. This book can pilot you through those dangerous rapids on your rafting trip to pistolsmithing rewards. For the shooters and readers who want to get the job done right the first time, this book is the beginning of your adventure. You can also, if you are of a mind, simply read this book and use it as a guide to talking to your gunsmith. Knowing how things are done, and what works and doesn't, can save you from expensive and needless work, and might also keep your guns out of the hands of a hack.

What can you do at home, working on your own? Provided you have the right tools, more than you might think. Replacing parts such as sights and barrels, checkering and stippling metal work, delicate stoning of

There is no such thing as too much information. This is only part of the author's firearms and gunsmithing library.

trigger parts for a better trigger pull — all are within the ability of the shooter who wants to do his or her own work. A small torch will give you all the heat needed to do soldering of all types. The right basic tools make cleaning and polishing a cinch. With a few specialized tools you can do much more advanced work. For example, with the right fixture you can thread your own barrels to install a compensator. With a large drill press you can drill and tap holes for a scope base. With a mill you can do any type of sight installation, including the popular Novak Low mount on a Colt 1911 pistol.

Still, there are jobs beyond the range of the small home workshop. Every year many optimistic shooters decide they can drill the holes for a scope base with a variable-speed drill. Even with a small drill press this takes patience and a bit of practice. With a hand-held drill you are simply asking for disaster. Usually those optimists give up after the first, crooked, hole. Armed with their new knowledge that the steel of firearms is tougher than the steel they are accustomed to drilling around the house, they bring their project in. By then it's too late. Repairs sometimes only involve some solder-

The Brownells catalog is a great read, even if you never order anything from it. If you do order, you won't be disappointed.

ing, filing and polishing. Sometimes the part has to be replaced. If the part under consideration is the frame, the serial-numbered part, a replacement is expensive and the paperwork can be onerous. Without a mill you cannot install a low-mount Novak rear sight. I suppose if you were trained to use a file under the British gunsmith system you could, but why would you want to? An experienced gunsmith with a mill and the correct cutters can mill a slide for a Novak (or other sight) in half an hour or less if the machine is set up for that and only that. Doing it by hand? How about a day or two? Does that sound good to you? I thought not.

Take all your welding tasks for handguns to a professional. Always, and to the correct professional. Welding for handguns is an entire level of skill above welding a broken footpedal back onto the garden tractor. Properly done welding requires expensive equipment that you have to use on a regular basis in order to keep "the touch." Buying a welding rig to weld on our handguns is even more of an optimistic choice than buying a mill and lathe.

Additional jobs best left to the professional include many surface finishes and heat treatments. These processes require dedicated space, expensive and elaborate tanks, and chemicals. Nasty chemicals. The chemicals themselves are expensive, dangerous and require correct professional disposal when they are exhausted. Disposing of them incorrectly can make you ill or land

you in prison, or both. Other than bluing, you could do a baked-on epoxy finish. And this only if you are scrupulous about cleaning the oven afterwards. Some Parkerizing is within your efforts. But traditional blueing and the new exotics? Fugeddaboutit,

In the old days the aspiring pistolsmith had to make almost everything that was needed, from drawings of the proper dimensions to screwdrivers; from files to fixtures. That is not the case today. Oh, you can still make everything you need if you want to. Some of them you should, for the practice and to know how the tools work. Many shooters and pistolsmiths do so for those and other reasons. They may have budget restraints or an immediate need for the tool. They may not have found the toolmaker who makes the gizmo they want. If you love to tinker, make your own tools. If you want to better understand how something is made, or works, or can be improved, make your own tools. That is another book entirely. Right now we'll concentrate on tools that are readily available.

When it comes to catalogs of pistolsmithing tools, parts, fixtures, and knowledge, the Brownells catalog is by far the best. Starting right after WWII, Frank Brownell began dealing in gunsmithing tools. He didn't limit his catalog to just the tools he made, but also became a dealer for other makers of tools and fixtures. Starting as a rather thin publication, the basic motto of Brownells catalog seems to be "If we don't have it, we'll find it for

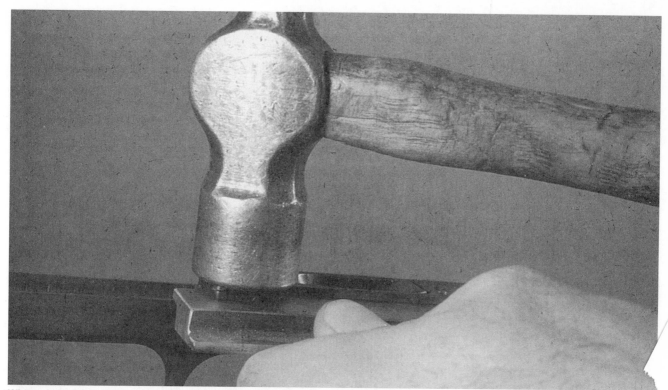

With only forming rails and a ball peen hammer, you can tighten the slide-frame fit.

you." Were it any larger, the Brownells catalog would rival a volume of the Encyclopedia Brittanica, if that prestigious title is even being printed any more. One "drawback" to the Brownells catalog is their impressive business sense. While they will gladly stock and place in the catalog anything they feel has a chance of selling, or being useful, if it doesn't deliver, it gets dropped. Thus, old catalogs list products no longer available, and you have no way of knowing that your old catalog has non-stocked items until you ask. If you want to know what is currently available, you need the latest catalog. Getting the latest catalog is simple. Just ask for it. It will be the best few-dollars purchase you ever made. Or go on-line and search the Brownells web page (www.brownells.com).

The Brownells catalog is very well laid out and organized. Every item has a clear photograph of the part in question so you can easily see what it is. If you wanted to buy a barrel for your 1911 just look up "Barrels, 1911." Like items are grouped together. Flip to any other section and you can see all the specifications for the different manufacturers' offerings there in a group. You won't have to flip back and forth to compare two or three of them.

Looking at the catalog for the first time, you will be tempted to start ordering all kinds of stuff: things you must have, things you want to have, and things that look like they would save you lots of time. Unless you are working with someone else's credit card, I would advise restraint. (And if you are using someone else's credit card, stop right now. I do not want to encourage unlawful behavior.) You need a little to get started, and the rest can be ordered when you need it. If it is in the current catalog, Brownell's most likely has it on the shelf.

If you need something, it is only a few days away. You needn't order something you "might need" or will "need in the future" just to be sure you'll have it then. While drawing up a wish list is a nice way to spend an evening or two, remember you are equipping your own shop, to work on your own gun, not a professional's shop. It would be relatively easy to max out a credit card going crazy with a Brownells catalog.

Have fun. But exercise some restraint. We don't want to read about you in the latest issue of whatever, after you've had to join or start some new 12-step program. "Hi, my name is Bob, my wife can't pry the Brownells catalog out of my hands." The idea is to use the catalog to make your life easier. Not make the catalog your life. But if you do, we've all been there for at least an afternoon.

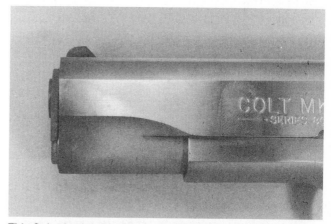

This Colt 1911 is very dirty from a range trip, and has a large thumbprint right on the "C." Depending on the owners perspiration, this thumbprint may be a cause of rust. The pistol should be cleaned.

CHAPTER

A PLACE FOR EVERYTHING AND EVERYTHING IN ITS PLACE

Now that I've warned you against a messy work environment, I'm reluctant to show you the bench of a professional. Yes, it looks messy, but there is a clear spot in the middle where he is working.

There is no such thing as too much shelf or drawer space. You won't have to keep track of this many jobs, but you could end up needing this much space.

Just how much room are you prepared or able to devote to your pistolsmithing? While you don't need to have a full-sized shop for working on your handgun, you do need a dedicated space. Struggling to assemble your handgun as you reach past the chainsaw, trying all the while not to knock the motor oil off the shelf above your head, is not conducive to concentration. It can also get you hurt. Trying to install the recoil spring on your handgun, and failing to avoid getting oil on the linens your wife has just folded, will get you more than just hurt.

If you have to do your pistol work in the same place as the rest of your work around the house, at the very least dedicate an end of the bench exclusively to it. Keep the small engine repairs separate from the large pistol repairs. In the course of moving several times, I've relo-

cated my shop, my reloading, my gun and ammo storage and my library. More than once I've felt so frustrated about the move that I swore I'd take a different tack on the next move: burn and buy. I'd burn or sell everything that could be replaced, and buy new when I arrived at the new locale. The trouble is, I can never put anything in the "burn" pile, not even mentally, and every time I turn around the "buy" option gets more painful. One way to avoid the "moving a mountain of gun stuff" dilemma is to not let the mountain build up in the first place. By keeping a neat and orderly workspace, you avoid the buildup of debris that plagues every pack rat. When you build a new space, avoid the temptation to build the Taj Mahal of reloading, work or gun space. Extra storage invites gear to be stored. Despite my having lead a wan-

A clean and neat workbench is a must. This workbench not only has fluorescent lights in the ceiling, but a flexible lamp on the bench itself. On the left is a vise, and on the right is a bench grinder. Drawers in the back hold parts and small tools.

dering life, I had accumulated a lot of stuff. One painful at first but useful in the long run piece of advice my wife gave me was this: recall the last time you used that tool/part/gizmo. Was it six months ago? A year? If you use it so rarely, why do you have it? After that, I spent a week in my shop looking at things. There were literally drawers which I had no recollection of having opened for more than a year. I started tossing stuff, which caused a bit of mild panic among those who had known me.

A garage can be a great place to do your work, provided it is tight enough from the weather and heated, so the tools and chemicals will not freeze or bake. It also must be wired, so you have electricity for lights and power tools. With a large enough garage you can build a separate bench for the pistol work, away from the area devoted to lawn and garden tools and auto maintenance. Garages can, however, have security problems. Cleaning your pistol in clear view of the neighbors walking by is bad manners and the police may drop by to discuss this habit with you. This happened to one of the members of our gun club, fortunately to no bad result. However, in the modern era of heightened law enforcement response to possible terrorist activity, you may not be so lucky. If your open garage door leaves a clear view of your workspace, then you must add completely closeable and lockable cabinets and drawers. It is also a good idea to install a screen to block outside viewing of the bench. Otherwise, you may receive a visit by somewhat nervous public servants, in response to your neighbor's phone call. The screen can also do double duty as a

block to drafts or errant breezes when you've opened the door for ventilation. If those are not options, and you must keep the door closed, then you must add proper ventilation to the project of building your space. Some of the solvents used in cleaning are not just noxious, but hazardous.

Basements are a big favorite. Without X-ray vision your neighbors can't just walk by and look in. (And if one of them is lying outside your house, peering into your basement windows, another neighbor is likely to phone the police on them.) Curtains or glass-block window replacements would be a useful addition. A full basement will already be wired for electricity, and will most likely stay warm enough in the winter and cool enough in the summer for all gunsmithing work. Basements with exterior entrances are not as secure as those with only interior entrances, but the exterior door can be reinforced, deadbolted and cross-barred.

The main problem with basements is that they are often damp. Dampness is a disaster for your tools and parts. The quickest way to dull a file, even faster than misuse, is to let it rust. Ditto other delicate gunsmithing tools. The tools you use and all the steel parts of your pistols are subject to rust, even the stainless ones. You must keep them dry. On a personal note, I find basements a bit tight as a site for work because damn few of them are high enough. At 6 feet, 4 inches tall, I find most basements a maze of plumbing pipes, heating ducts, and lighting fixtures that I must maneuver around or risk banging my head. To deal with moisture, you can inves

Efficient Machinery Co. makes a modular workbench that can be a portable unit, or a starter bench. (photo courtesy Efficient Machinery Co.)

Your bench must be sturdy. If it can't hold 200 pounds without creaking, maybe you shouldn't put a $1,000 worth of guns and tools on it.

in a dehumidifier. Either the dump-pan or a tube to the floor drain lets you get rid of the moisture it has sucked out of the air. Seal the walls cracks if any, paint the walls, and once dry you have a great potential space.

A small spare room or large closet can be used as a pistolsmithing space, without the potential poor security of a garage or the dampness of a basement. The closet may require re-wiring to get enough outlets for all of your lights and tools, and in hot weather may be a bit stuffy. I built a workroom for pistolsmithing in a small room at home that measures 5 feet by 8 feet. The bench runs away from the door the full 8 feet, with shelves above, drawers below and sufficient elbowroom. It is plenty large enough for all but the most involved work. A larger room of 8 feet by 10 feet would be spacious enough to do everything except machine work with large machines. If you have a miniature lathe or mill even those would fit into a room this size. If you do not live alone, a small room or closet may be noisy to the other occupants when you are using power tools. In this case you may have to install additional soundproofing. Ask if you are making too much noise, and they will tell you. Be sure to always wear ear protection and keep the door closed.

ONCE YOU HAVE SELECTED A LOCATION, WHAT DO YOU NEED THERE?

First, you have to have sufficient working light. Strain-

ing your eyes and struggling in the dark with your pistol can damage the pistol and hurt you. Large fluorescent fixtures over your workspace will ease the eyestrain and make your work pleasant. You cannot get too much light unless you have so many bulbs strung in the room that the heat drives you out. While a multiplicity of light fixtures can be just what your tomato seedlings need, you probably do not. However, do not work in the gloom. To avoid casting a shadow on your work, buy a flexible desk lamp. Get one with a heavy base or with a base that can be clamped to the bench. Swivel or position it to shine directly where you are working, and form a direction your body does not block.

Along with the light you will need physical comfort. A bench that is too high or low or in the wrong location is a ticket to torture, back pains and repetitive-motion injuries. A work chair that doesn't offer back support or is uncomfortable will give you leg cramps or a backache in short order.

How high should your bench be? It depends on your height and your reach. If you are starting from scratch try a simple disassembly and reassembly of your pistol on different benches, tables or counters in your house. You will quickly find out which ones are the wrong heights. If you have more options at the gun club, do it there. If you are working with a bench already installed and find it is too high, make shallow boxes to stand on or get a higher chair and sit down. A low bench can be

You must store your tools where they are out of the way, organized and ready. The Kennedy box on the left runs $500, the plastic one on the right is $50. Both get the job done.

useable if you work from a low chair. You have to try it a few times. Unlike shoes, where if you have the incorrect size you'll know it in a few steps, you can probably work "OK" on a wrong-height bench. Only a bit of time will tell you if the bench is good, or off by a few inches.

Of course you may not need a bench at all. One shooter I know used to have a sumo-like physique. His comfortable working position was in a recliner, his magnifying work hood on, and the parts resting on his belly. He could do his work for long periods of time this way, provided he didn't need to use a vise. While I would make a very skinny sumo, I have occasionally done some work on my lap, only because I had to at that moment, and not by choice. Barring such a large and stable belly, you must have a bench and it must be solid. (The other guy later took up competitive bicycle racing, and shed the sumo-like belly.) When starting from scratch the best way to make sure your bench will be solid enough is to make it out of 2X4s with 4X4 legs, and a plywood top at least 5/8 inch thick. You can test the solidity of an existing bench by sitting on it. If you can't climb up on it and sit down without creaks and groans (the bench, not you) then it needs reinforcing. An extra support leg in the center, with an extra layer of plywood laminated to the top, will stiffen up even a wobbly bench. Add diagonal bracing to a bench that doesn't have any. In order

to keep the bench from walking around the room with you, secure it to the wall if you can. This way, if you are wrestling with a particularly recalcitrant part, you won't be wrestling with the bench too. If bolting the bench to the wall isn't an option, then bricks, sandbags or bags of lead shot on a lower shelf will keep the bench from moving. If all you do is pistol work, 200 lbs. should be enough, but keep in mind the rock 'n roll motto: "some is good, more is better, too much is not enough."

If the prospect of constructing a bench from scratch is more than you care to contemplate, kits are available. Efficient Machinery Co. in Bellevue, Wash. makes benches originally intended for reloading that double as fine workbenches. If you order one you will be greeted with the phrase "some assembly required," as they are shipped disassembled. The benches are available in three heights: 33 inches, 36.5 or 41 inches, and in two sizes of tabletop.

The local big-box hardware store will have work benches for sale. While attractive, they do have some drawbacks. All the current ones will have particle-board tops and sheet-metal frames. In order to make it solid enough, you may have to laminate a sheet of plywood to the particle board, and you may have to bolt the bench top to the frame. It has been quite a few years since I've seen all-lumber workbench kits at any big-box hardware store.

If there is one thing all professional shops have in common, it is that they have many shelves, drawers, benches and cabinets.

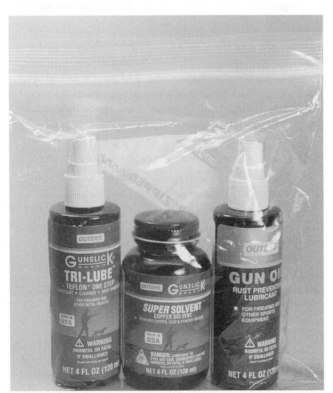

When you store your solvents and lubricants, place them in a plastic bag. Otherwise, the inevitable leaks will ooze and drip someplace undesirable.

With a well-lit workspace and well-placed bench you now need to turn an eye toward organizing your tools.

WHERE TO PUT THINGS?

Simply tossing your tools into a pile on top of the bench is messy and a good way to damage them. Do not do this. The five places to put your tools are shelves, cabinets, racks, drawers and toolboxes.

Shelves are easy to make and easy to install. If you don't mind taking a step or two when you need something the shelves don't even have to be right over your bench. If you do install shelves right over the bench, store objects on those shelves that cannot be damaged by falling, and can't damage anything if they fall: light, non-fragile things such as masking tape, instructions for your tools, packets of steel wool, cleaning patches and cleaning rods, and other stuff. Seal your epoxy, solder, cold blue, cleaning solvents and other chemicals in individual plastic bags to keep leakage from making a mess, and put them up there too. Shelves under the bench are the place for heavy objects. This way you cannot drop a heavy object onto yourself or a valuable firearm while trying to put something on an overhead shelf. The weight also acts to stabilize the bench. Shelves do not offer any security because they cannot be locked, and objects on shelves will gather dust. Put a hook on your

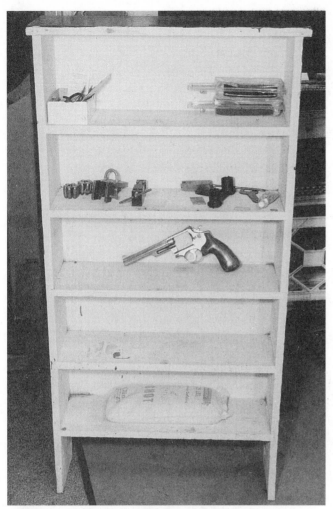

A small set of shelves are handy for holding tools, parts, fixtures and the occasional handgun in process.

shelves where you can hang your cleaning apron after you take it off.

Current shelving material has gone the way of all things: particle board. Particle board shelves, with a vinyl coating, are good enough for some things, but gun stuff tends to be heavy. Bowed shelves from the weight are a disaster waiting to happen. When you make shelves, anchor them securely to the wall. (A bolt pulled from the wall due to weight means tools and parts all over the floor.) Build for the max anticipated weight, and use lumber or construction boards as shelving material.

If you can obtain cabinets they will offer more secure storage of your tools and parts. Just remember that cabinets are designed for dishes and cooking utensils. If you overload them they will fall apart or off the wall. If you are using salvaged cabinets, study the design to see if you can reinforce them to hold more weight. I once pulled a set of cabinets away from the wall by storing nothing more in them than handguns. A standard-sized kitchen cabinet shelf can hold 24 pistols, and this is more weight than it was designed for.

If your bench is large or deep enough, store the tools used frequently in racks on the bench top. Place the screwdrivers and drift pins here, where they are out of the way but easy to reach. A rack at the back of the bench can hold the hammers.

When I built the latest location for my shop, I resisted the urge to build deep benchtops. What I found over time was that a bench any deeper than the workspace simply attracted debris at the back. Once it piled up enough, the debris then "crept" forward. If there's no room at the back of the bench to just leave stuff, you won't leave stuff there and will more likely put it away where it belongs.

Objects that need protection go into the drawers. Here are the files, the dial calipers, a micrometer if you have one, and any fixtures for fitting or cutting parts. Taps and dies should also be offered the protection of drawers and not left on the bench. If your bench isn't large enough to keep the punches and hammers out on top, keep them in drawers separate from the delicate things.

If building cabinets or drawers sounds like work that will keep you from pistolsmithing, go to your local tool warehouse store. There you can find toolboxes of the kind mechanics use, and for a lot less money than they pay.

When you aren't using a tool, put it back where it belongs. Dumping all of your files into a drawer may keep them out of sight, but it is a good way to nick and dull them, too. The digital dial calipers you paid $150 for will last a whole lot longer if you don't leave them out on the bench where the ball-peen hammer can be dropped on them.

TOOLS ARE IMPORTANT

The finest bench in the world is not sufficient by itself. You need tools to work with, and only the right ones will do.

Central to your use, but not always centered on the bench, is your vise. A vise is your third hand, holding objects so you can see them, work on them, assemble them. Buying a vise smaller than you need is false economy. It will not securely hold large parts, no matter how firmly you tighten the handle. A large vise, however, can hold small parts, provided it is precisely fitted. For pistol work you need a vise with jaws at least 5 inches wide, and an opening of not less than 4.5 inches. While bigger is better, there is a limit. Don't go out and buy a vise large enough to hold an engine block just to show off to your shooting buddies. Such a vise may break both your wallet and your bench.

Before you attach the vise to your bench you'll need to find the best spot for it. Place it on the bench and pretend you are working on a part. Can you get to the part from every angle? Position your light and look at the part. Are you working in your own shadow? Move the vise from time to time to check a new location. Find what works for you. I need at least 3 feet between my vise and the wall for my comfort. This distance will be different for you. Make it comfortable. Before you mark and drill, take a look at the underside of the bench. Make sure you aren't positioning one of the bolts right at a support beam. Then pull out your drill to install the vise bolts.

A solid vise is a must. This vise is over twenty years old and works as well today as the day it was bolted to this bench.

A drill press is nice. A power buffer is a luxury. A fire extinguisher is a must. In all three cases, bigger is better.

A bench grinder is useful, noisy and dirty. Do not get a little one, it will disappoint you.

Should you have a bench grinder? A bench grinder allows you to sharpen or alter tools, modify parts, and remove stock fairly quickly. It is also noisy and dirty. It can get you in trouble. With too heavy a hand, you can take off much more metal than you intended. You can overheat a part and draw the temper from it. You can burn yourself. I have seen people using a bench grinder lose hold of the part they were grinding and launch it across the room.

For many, things however, such as quickly grinding down the frame of a pistol to fit a beavertail grip safety, a bench grinder is just the ticket to save you several evenings of filing by hand.

If you decide you must have a bench grinder, get one with a 1/4-horsepower or larger motor and at least a 6-inch wheel diameter. More horsepower means you are less likely to slow down the grinder by pressing a part against the wheel. Large wheels give you a larger surface area for wear of the wheel, and a larger ground surface on the part. A larger bench grinder does cost more, and requires more electricity than a smaller one, but is worth it. My grinder, a 1/2-horsepower Sears grinder with 6-inch wheels is still running smoothly nearly 20

years after I bought it used. If the noise and the mess are too much in the house or basement, then banish the bench grinder to the garage. It will do fine out there.

Most of the hand tools you will need for your work are simple and common. A few are somewhat specialized.

You'll need several types of hammers. Most important is the ball peen hammer. The ball peen hammer is alloyed and tempered for the job of banging against metal. The more common claw hammer is not. Use the claw hammer for peening and it is likely to suffer damage from repeated use. You could even injure yourself. Hammers are not so expensive that you need to be cheap about this. Buy a 12-ounce ball-peen. Yes, a heavier hammer can strike a harder blow, but you will become tired using it and make more errors. You definitely don't want to peen the wrong spot on a part, or your thumb.

Next buy yourself a plastic and rubber mallet. This has one face made of a tough plastic, while the other is softer rubber. Be sure and get one with replaceable faces. With some jobs such as lapping a slide onto a 1911 frame you may end up chewing the plastic end to bits after a few slides. Replacing the face is cheaper than buying a new hammer. You'll use the rubber end when you want to tap something on or off without leaving marks.

Some pistolsmiths use a smaller hammer than the 12-ounce ball peen or the large plastic mallet, but I only keep small hammers in my emergency tool kit. The larger hammer on my bench will do all the work of a smaller one. The only advantage of the smaller hammer is less weight to lug around in your shooting bag.

The screws used in firearms are traditionally different from the screws found around the house, and need slightly different screwdrivers. Pick up one of your screwdrivers and take a close look at the tip. A standard screwdriver has a tip that is ground with the flats at a slight angle towards each other. In a cross-section it looks wedge-shaped. This angle of the blade lets the tip fit into the slot of a screw regardless of the slot's tolerances. While it isn't exactly a "one size fits all," it is a method to get a whole lot of screws handled by just a few screwdrivers. Firearms screws are different: the slots of the screws are machined parallel. You need a screwdriver that has parallel faces, not the tapered household screwdriver. Use a household screwdriver in the screws on your pistol and you will round the corners of the slot. Not only is this unsightly, it is also the obvious mark of an amateur. The tip on the standard screwdriver is tempered to be softer than you need. The softness keeps the tip from breaking. When working on firearms we would rather break the tip of the screwdriver than mar the screw slot.

Firearms screwdrivers have a hard tip, and the tip is ground so the flats are parallel. The screws on firearms come in a much greater variety of slot sizes than common household screws do. In order to properly fit a screwdriver to each screw you will encounter, you either have to have dozens of screwdrivers, or be willing to modify the ones you have. Professionals do both. At last count, my drawers and shelves held 47 screwdrivers, not counting the overflow drawer that holds the "to be modified" screwdrivers, and the various screwdriver kits with replaceable tips. A good way to start is to buy one of the many replacement tip screwdriver sets. The hollow shaft is magnetized and will hold the tips in place until you pull them out to replace them. If you have to modify one of them, a new tip is cheap to buy. While there are some scope rings and such that use allen screw or torx-head screws, we can all be thankful that there are very few known instances of Phillips-head screws being used on firearms (with some buttplates and recoil pads being obvious exceptions).

You won't need much in the way of pliers. When reassembling after cleaning, a narrow needle-nose pliers can be handy.

Buy a bushing wrench for your 1911, so you can remove tight fitting bushings. In the 1911 chapter I'll show you how to fit a bushing so it is accurate and still removable with your fingers. As for other wrenches, I haven't found a use for them in pistol work.

A constant companion at the bench will be a top-qual-

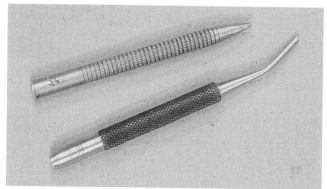

You will eventually bend a drift punch. Use your bench grinder to cut the bent shaft off and turn the punch into a tapered punch, so you won't bend the next one.

A good set of screwdrivers such as these from Dillon are a must-have item.

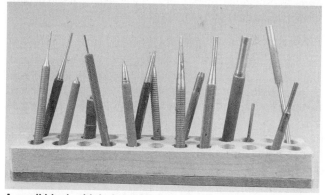

A small block with holes drilled through it will organize your punches. Make another one for your files.

You'll need cleaning brushes. Some handguns come with a brush. This one from Glock has plastic bristles and will last quite a long time.

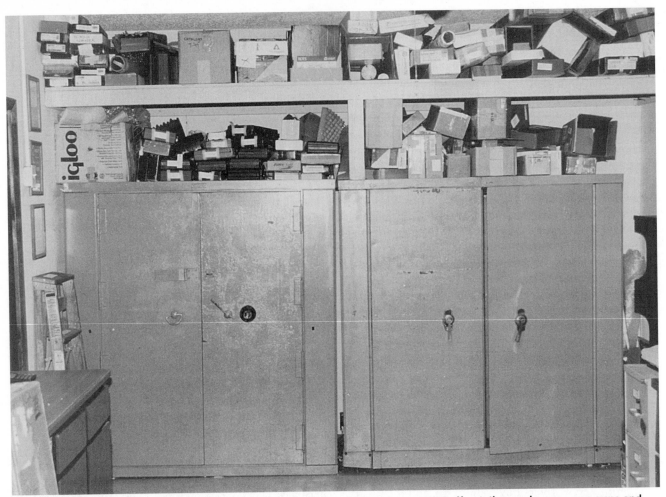

Safes are comforting, heavy and expensive. If you can get a safe into your home, great. If not, then make sure your guns and workspace are in a locked room.

ity calipers. Either dial or digital, you will use it almost all the time. When you're fitting parts, calipers will tell you how much metal you have removed and how much more you have to go. In the professional's shop, the dial or digital calipers are used a hundred times a day. You can spend as little as $30 for the dial type, and $120 for the digital type. Take care of it, keep it clean and stored safely, or you may be buying a new one too soon.

Buy two types of punches, steel and brass. The brass ones are for drifting sights, or pressing parts together when you don't want to leave a mark. A 1/4-inch rod long enough to hold onto without hitting your hand with the hammer works well. Even though it is brass you still have to be careful. Too heavy a blow with the hammer will leave a mark on a soft steel part from the brass rod. Some pistolsmiths prefer nylon to avoid this, but I have found nylon flexes just a bit, and makes removing tightly bound sights tougher. Use steel drift punches to remove pins that hold assemblies together, like the safety on a Beretta M-92 or the ejector on a 1911. If you plan to do a lot of work on a pistol with roll pins, and you don't want to mar the pins, buy drift punches specifically for roll pins. The steel punches come in sets or individually. A good basic set is the Brownells Gunsmith Professional punch set. This contains ten punches: a selection of drift punches, a center punch and a staking punch. It cov-

ers most everything you'll need. Or measure the pins on your handguns with your calipers and then trek off to the tool store to pick up just the sizes you need. Of course you'll have to do it again for the next handgun, and the next....

With the workspace finished and stocked, you now have to secure it. Back in the really "old days," shooters left their firearms in glass-fronted display cases, for their friends to admire. Now, the consideration of many shooters is "to safe, or not to safe?" If you have a specific room that is used for nothing but your pistol work, then putting a deadbolt lock on the door is a good idea and a good start. If you have a part of the garage or basement devoted to your work that is not separate from the rest of that space, the best approach is to build or install cabinets above and drawers below that can all be locked. When you are done and clean up your workbench (and you will clean up, right?) there is nothing left out in the open to be seen as "gun stuff." The pistols themselves can either go into locked cabinets or into a small gun safe. For extra security, put gun locks on each of your handguns. You can also arrange your handguns on a rack, and then thread a plastic-coated steel cable through the trigger guards, bolted at one end and locked on the other. Rather than trying to keep track of a large ring of keys, use the Speed Release brand gun lock. It

Moisture tarnishes and rusts metal. A desiccant in the safe or cabinet can protect your valuable tools and handguns. Handled carefully it will serve as a protectant for years.

uses lighted buttons that you press in the correct combination. If someone tries several incorrect entries the lock shuts down and won't respond until it has waited long enough.

If you built your bench into the corner or end of the basement, you can install French doors to block the view of visitors to your basement. Make sure the safe is hidden by the doors, too. I am not saying that your neighbors are waiting and once you go on vacation they will descend upon you and strip the house of everything of value, but people talk. And by the time the fourth or fifth person down the conversational line has heard about your "walk-in vault full of guns and cameras," they may not be so law-abiding. And the tale will also have "grown in the telling" and thus your firearms will be even more enticing to the unlawful.

Security is not just a matter of keeping guns out of the hands of kids or thieves. What if you don't secure your workroom, and out of curiosity a party guest who has wandered off turns on your lathe? If your luck is good, they will only turn it on. If your luck is bad his tie will get sucked up by the chuck and the next thing you know his face is being hit by the edges of the chuck at 400 rpm. Lock the cabinets and drawers, use a master power switch, and then lock the door!

All these tools, and the handguns themselves need protection from moisture. If you lock everything up in a closet, cabinets or a gun safe, you may be locking moisture in there with them. Invest in a canister of dessicant.

If you live in a humid climate, or a wet house, a room dehumidifier can keep your guns and gear dry.

You may also want to consider a gun lock, even if your handguns are in a safe or locked cabinet.

The dessicant sucks moisture from the air, protecting your guns and tools. When it has had its fill, bake it in your oven to dry it out and start again. Or invest in a power dehumidifier. I have a floor model that I bought from Sears. When the climate is humid, I'm dumping the fill pan once a week. In the wintertime I only use it for extra heat and as a fan, as the winter indoor humidity usually hovers around 30 percent: dry as the Sahara.

As a last item, you may want to talk to your insurance agent about the coverage for your tools. It would be a shame to spend a chunk of money and have a ball learning to do your own pistolsmithing, only to find out that the insurance company won't replace the tools when your basement floods. Do not try to be cute with your agent, and declare that you have a "home workshop of woodworking tools" when what you want to cover is all your specialized gunsmithing tooling. Tell him what you have. If he is uncomfortable about your gear, find a new agent or a new insurer. Document the tooling with photographs, invoices and serial numbers if possible. I had all kinds of insurance problem tales brought in to the old shop. We'd get people coming in at least once a week (Detroit is everything the news stories make it out to be) asking if we could tell their insurance company what their guns were worth. And the unpleasant truth

was: after the fact, we couldn't. Not in good conscience, we couldn't, and not without breaking a multiplicity of laws. As a result, regardless of what firearm they may have had, their .30-06 rifle or .45 pistol was worth what the lowest value of a decent-shape item listed in the *Standard Catalog of Firearms* said it was. A custom piece? Too bad. Your Dad's WWII bring-back Luger, with papers, photographs and the German officers identity card? Just another Luger. So, if your house gets broken into, just how are you going to convince your insurance agent that you a) actually owned a Powers stoning jig, and b) that it cost you $150? Or any of the other tools, fixtures or parts you've invested in? And while you're taking care of the insurance paperwork, make sure your will is in order. It is hard enough on the rest of your family to be taking care of matters, without wondering: "What is this thing? What is it worth? And what should I do with it?" In many cases, your expensive firearms and tools will simply be dropped off at the nearest State Police post for disposal. Said disposal usually involves a smelter. Or, a steady stream of sad-looking "friends" who offer their condolences and the phrase "He always said he wanted me to have...." And for $100, too.

Save your loved ones the hassle. Do the paperwork ahead of time.

CHAPTER

THE LONG AND SHORT OF REMOVING METAL

Just as pencils have erasers to remove excess letters and words, so the pistolsmith must have something to remove excess metal. The bench grinder and mill are your large erasers. Using power tools you can remove large amounts of metal readily, or small amounts quickly. The mill also allows you to remove exactly-known amounts. Files, stones and emery cloth are your small erasers for fitting parts, smoothing engagement surfaces or polishing. They can be found in every gunsmithing shop as well as other machine shops in the country.

If you already have these hand tools at home, they are likely to be of the common household variety. The file is coarse and usually rusty. The sandpaper is rough and made for sanding wood. Most stones I have seen around friends' houses are worn, uneven and clogged with gunk. Suitable perhaps for sharpening a hunting knife (but often not even that) and entirely unsuited to the task of stoning a firearms part.

Files for your handguns must be much finer than the files intended for sharpening the lawnmower blade. Pistolsmithing files are precision tools. As such, you should treat them kindly, and never loan them. You will find that files and rasps intended for cabinet making, stock making and other woodworking tasks are too coarse. The finest-cut common wood file is too coarse for much use on metal. However, if you buy files that are too fine, you'll have to do more work (each pass will remove less metal than a coarser file would) but on the plus side you will be hard-pressed to file off too much metal. At a bare

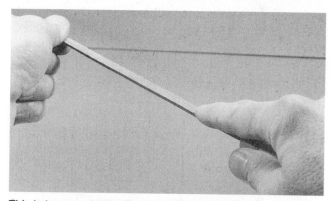

This is how you hold a file for power and control.

The tips of two files. On top is the extra narrow #2 Swiss pillar file. Underneath is a 10-inch American Second Cut.

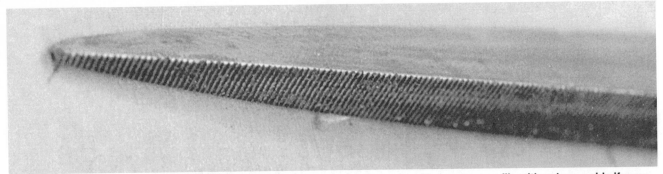

A three-sided file with one edge safe. The file teeth have been ground off on one side, so you can file with only one side if you want to.

minimum you will need two large files, one medium file and a set of small ones. First, purchase an extra narrow pillar file in the Swiss #2 cut. This file, 8 inches long and just over 1/4-inch wide, is narrow enough to maneuver into and around your work, large enough to hold comfortably, and cuts smoothly enough that with the right touch will produce a near-finished or finished surface. If you cannot find them at a tool store in your hometown, Brownells carries them. I have used so many and been so pleased with each of them that I refer to it as "the perfect file." It does have a drawback, and that is its flexibility. It will bend while you work with it and you have to watch out for unwanted rounding of your cut surface because of this flex.

While you could limit yourself to "the perfect file," why should you? For your other large file, get an American 10-inch 2nd Cut file. The Swiss don't make one the size and cut you need. The teeth are coarser than the #2 Swiss, and the file is wider, longer and stiffer than the pillar file. All these features let you remove stock faster

The best source of practice parts is at a gun show. Buy obviously abused parts (like these bulged barrels) and practice to your heart's content.

than the pillar file. When you are making large cuts you want a big file so you can keep your cut surface flat. If you use a small file to level a large area, you will have to work harder to keep "bite marks" out of your work. These are unsightly creases where the edge of the small file has cut into your surface. An example of its utility is where the 10-inch 2nd Cut file lets you blend the compensator body to the slide on your pistol, or carefully square the face of a revolver frame when you install a new barrel. A smaller file would not be so useful.

For your medium file, purchase a 6-inch tapered, triangular file in either the American Smooth or Swiss #2. It is important to get one with a safe edge (that is one face without cutting teeth). If you cannot find one with a safe edge, then the first use of your bench grinder will be removing the teeth from one face of the file. Use a light touch and many passes, to minimize heat buildup, and work slowly and carefully to keep the ground face level. Excessive heat will draw the hardness out of the file. Later you will use the triangular file to fit certain rear and front sights. The tip will get into places the larger files can't.

Purchase your needle file set in a fine cut. These files — flat, round, half-round, triangular and beveled — are perfect for reaching into small areas. Also use them for light work when you simply can't risk cutting past the needed depth. The finest files of all are diamond files. You need them only for the hardest metals, and then rarely. The advanced armorer's course for Glocks requires diamond files to fit slides. Glock slides are treated by the Tenifer process, creating a very hard surface. Regular files will just slide off. However, unless you are doing a lot of Glock work and need to file the slide, you won't need diamond files. Put them in the "nice but not necessary" category.

Buy a file card and file chalk; you will need them as soon as you start filing.

Files have been referred to as "hand-held mills" for good reason. You can remove impressive amounts of metal with the right file, even when the file isn't specialized. The right file can also save time. And they are fun to use. A professional pistolsmith often has drawers full of files for all these reasons.

The pistolsmith from whom I learned the trade had

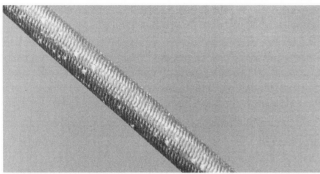

This file has many pins in it, and needs to be cleaned. This is caused by not using file chalk.

to make compensators from bar stock. Back in the old days, there were no pre-made compensators you could simply screw onto a pre-threaded barrel. Dan had to not only make a comp from scratch, he then had to thread the barrel. After boring the comp on the lathe, threading and fitting it to a slide, he would then file them down from their rectangular profile to the slide profile. For the first hour of filing he used a 12-inch American Bastard cut file. Very coarse, this file can remove large amounts of metal relatively quickly. With the heavy work done, he'd switch to finer files. Compensators are now available already profiled, and today there is no reason to make a comp from a rectangular block. You probably won't need a 12-inch Bastard cut file, but if you really want one they cost about $15. Go ahead and splurge.

SPECIAL TOOLS

Specialized jobs require specialized files. For example, some hammers on the 1911 are so rough that you need to use a hammer hook squaring file even before you start using stones. In all fairness, I have to point out that those are the really, really cheap ones, and if you simply splurge on a good-quality hammer, you can save yourself a whole lotta work. When you fit a barrel to your 1911, a barrel lug file is the only one that will fit in the locking lug slot. Both of these files are absolutely square on cross-section, with two opposing faces as cutting edges. The other two edges are "safe.

Another specialized file for 1911 barrel fitting is the bottom lug file, a circular file .200 inches in diameter. This is the diameter of the slide stop pin, which is not an even fraction of an inch.

For some reason, the rear sight dovetail on the 1911 has traditionally been 65 degrees. There is a specialized file for this, a safe-edge 65-degree file. The regular three-sided file cuts at an angle of 60 degrees. In an emergency you could fit a 1911 rear sight with a three-sided file, but do yourself a favor and spend the $12 for the proper file and save yourself the work.

Back in junior high shop class my teacher, Mr. Braisted, had a collection of photographs of mistakes in shop procedures, and the often-messy results. The one that sticks on my memory is of the fellow who had been filing on the lathe without a file handle. The large, color glossy photo was of that poor sod standing in the infirmary with the tang of a 10-inch bastard file sticking through his hand. Put a handle on all of your files! Even if you are not using your files on a lathe, handles will be more comfortable and give you more control.

You will have to make the even more specialized files

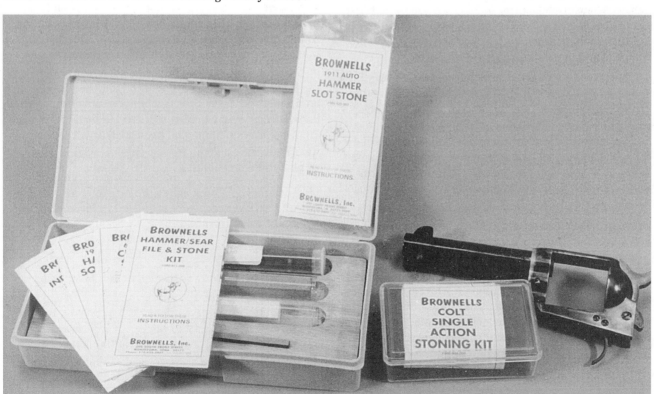

It takes some special stones to do a proper job on the single-action revolver.

yourself. For example, I have yet to find in a catalog just the right file for adjusting the extractor ratchet when timing the double-action trigger pull of a Smith and Wesson revolver. If anyone makes this file, other than Smith & Wesson, I didn't see one when I needed mine, so I made it. For this you will have to take one of your needle files and modify it with the bench grinder. Select the tapered one with a cutting face and a safe-edge back. Grind the left side of the cutting edge down until the file is a narrow strip. Grind the back to thin the file just enough to fit between the ratchet teeth on the extractor star. This file will then let you file just the right spot on the ratchet to time your cylinder.

Just as important as selecting the right file is knowing the correct method of using it or any file. Pick up your file and look at the teeth. You will see a series of serrated lines, pitched towards the front of the file. These are what cut the metal. A file cuts only on the forward stroke, and dragging it backwards over the work will only prematurely dull it. Each time you stroke forward when pressing the file against the part, some of the metal you file falls off of the file, while other bits remain in the file teeth.

When a row of teeth is full of metal, that row will not cut any more. You can feel this. The file will seem to float across the work surface, and only bite when you reach the end of the loaded section. Most of these filings will simply fall out if you tap the file against a hard object, or wipe it against your shop apron. There are filings, however, that will not fall out. If you do not remove these bits of metal (called "pins") they will mar your work, gouging the surface as they are dragged along in the file against the part you're filing. This is where your file card comes in. A file card is a brass brush with very short and stiff bristles. With it, you can brush, or "card" the collected metal out of the file teeth.

File chalk is a soft, white, talc-like material. Apply it by rubbing the file over the block as if you were filing the chalk. Liberal use of file chalk makes the metal filings easier to remove and reduces the number of pins you have to pry out of the file teeth. It extends the life of the file, reduces pinning, and gets all over the place. Filing is messy if done right. Be sure to clean up afterwards or you will be tracking filings and chalk all over the house.

The last addition to your file drawer is a chemical solution called Dykem. It is a dye in an evaporative base, and when you brush or spray it on Dykem coats metal and dries like a very thin paint. When you have coated a part, any work you do shows through the dye coat where the coat has been rubbed off. You can see right where you are filing. A small bottle should last years if you keep it tightly closed. In large machine shops Dykem and its competitors are used in aerosol cans. You don't need this much, unless you really want the part, the vise jaws, part of the bench, and maybe even your hands to be a nice, even, dark blue. The company also makes red Dykem.

Now you are ready to file. Apply Dykem to the area of the part you will be filing. Secure it in your vise. Take your clean file and chalk it. Grasp the file by the handle and its tip. This gives you the maximum control over the depth and direction of the cut. Place the file against the working surface, check the angle to make sure it is correct, and press the file down and forward. At the end of the stroke, pick the file up and start over.

Check the file and your cut surface regularly. At the first sign of a pin on your file, stop, clean and re-chalk the file. To check your filed surface, remove the part from the vise. Examine the Dykem coating. Are you filing the correct spot? Check the angle. Does it look right? More importantly, does it fit right? Check the fit every couple of passes. Files are great for removing metal, but very bad at putting metal back. File off too much and you'll be visiting the welder.

ABOUT STONES

Cutting finer than even the finest file, stones have been used even before there were pistols to work on. My oldest reference books all mention using stones to work on parts for fitting and smooth functioning. In the old days stones were just that, chunks of rock carved out of a mountain, graded as to their grit and hardness, and more or less ground to the shape you needed. You've probably read about them: the finest stones were expensive and fragile. They had to be stored soaked to keep them from becoming brittle. They had to be used with lots of oil, the oil acting to keep the stoned-off particles of steel from clogging the pores of the stone. If you wanted stones that were square you had to grind them flat on a piece of glass using grinding compound. If you didn't grind them, the corners of your new stone would quickly be rounded, and the edge of your cut would always be round, too. You can't imagine the aggravation of trying to do a proper trigger job with a newly ground stone only to find that you had hit a soft and crumbly spot on the edge, and either had to re-grind another edge, or get another stone. Even for a number of years after I started gunsmithing we gunsmiths still used India and Arkansas stones soaked in honing oil because that was all there was. They were a great, messy, painful hassle and we are all glad to be done with it.

Properly stoning the sear requires a fixture such as this Series 1 from Powers.

Now, you can buy synthetic stones that not only are more consistent, but also come ground square. As an additional bonus, the synthetic stones use water as a lubricant, and clean up with soap and water. Buy synthetic and don't look back. Trust me, no one uses the old stones anymore if they have any choice at all. Having said all that, it is my sad duty to tell you that you can't get synthetic stones in all the sizes and shapes you might need or want.

You don't need stones in all cutting grades for the simple reason that you don't need a stone that cuts any coarser than the finest file you own. This means you need stones only in medium-fine and extra-fine grade. The Brownells ceramic stones are color-coded: the medium-fine is black; the extra-fine is white. They are large stones, 6 inches long by 1/2 inch square. While intended for trigger work, they make great general-use stones as well. You must keep separate stones for trigger work and general work. Otherwise you will be regularly grinding new corners on your stones for trigger work, because the general work has rounded them off.

For smaller sizes and other shapes, Brownells and Spyderco both make a set of smaller synthetic stones. Triangular, round and square, these are great for getting into areas that the larger stones won't reach.

Stoning and filing are different processes. In a file, the teeth cut small pieces off the surface. These filings can be brushed out of the files teeth. A stone abrades the metal off, in much smaller pieces. These pieces fill the pores of the stone, and have to be washed out. If you do not wash them out, the clogged stone surface cuts less and less until it is not cutting at all, but simply riding across a slurry of metal and stone particulates. Stoning is done with two hands whenever possible. On a large stone you hold the ends, on a smaller one or in cramped work you get both hands on the back end of the stone.

Lubricate the stone, and work it smoothly and evenly across the work surface. Unlike files, stones cut in both directions. Some pistolsmiths will not use a stone back and forth because the motion tends to round the cut. By only pushing the stone they keep the cut level. If you are using a stoning fixture you can't round the cut. The problem is that only a few specialized jobs lend themselves to using a fixture.

To stone, cover with Dykem the area you will stone. Realize that the Dykem will also clog the stone's pores, but it is an acceptable cost that lets you monitor the cutting process. Firmly secure the part in your vise. Take a clean stone, and lubricate it. With a hand at each end if possible, or both at the back end if that is all you can do, gently rub the stone across the surface a few times. Check the part to make sure you are stoning on the correct spot, and at the correct angle. Check the fit of the part. Once you have the location and angle of your stoning established, press harder on the next set of passes. Continue until the stone is too loaded to work with, or you have finished the job. As you use stones you'll find they get loaded up with stoned off metal faster than a file, and are harder to clean.

With a synthetic stone, a basin of soapy water at hand lets you clean the stone easily. Dip your fingertips in the soapy water, and rub the stone surface to remove the filings. Swish the stone in the water and rub again until the metal is gone, then rinse with clear water and continue stoning. When you are done, a synthetic stone needs to be cleaned and dried before being put away.

For natural stones, you have to use more of the honing oil. You need a basin of oil, and a small brush to scrub the stone instead of your fingertips. Once it is clean, re-oil with the honing oil and get back to work. The natural stones should be cleaned and left oiled. Place them in the plastic tubes they were shipped in and label each tube for future reference.

WORKING THE POLISH

Polishing, the process of creating a uniform and desired surface texture, can be cosmetic or functional. In polishing you do not remove or reshape metal the way you do in grinding. Instead, you create a smooth and consistent surface texture. Well, that's what you should be doing. If you actually intend to remove metal or change contours, polishing is an inefficient way to go about it. And if you aren't planning on major metal reshaping, you can still make a lot of trouble for yourself if you lose track of what you're doing, say by using the wrong grit or pressing too hard. Correct polishing requires a careful and attentive touch.

Examples of bad "polishing" are everywhere. 1911s often have their original sights removed. The front or rear of the slide then gets welded up and "polished" down. Some shooters think coarse emery cloth, used without any lubricant, and with a heavy shoe-shine motion, is just the ticket for dressing down that weld. Not only does this method produce an unsightly repair, it also

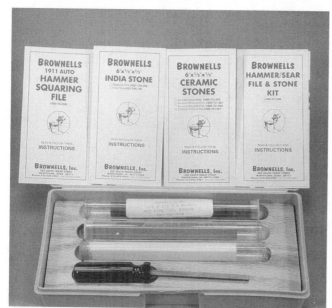

You will need stones for polishing and fitting. The best are ceramic stones. The Brownells hammer/sear stone kit is also useful as a general-purpose set of stones.

turns the straight line between the sides and top of the slide into a wavy mess. Do not ever "polish" this way.

For polishing larger areas, or blending surface finishes, emery cloth is just the ticket. While there is some overlap in the grit ranges of carpentry, cabinet-making, and pistolsmithing, you should buy paper or cloth-backed abrasives intended for use on metals, and rated for wet sanding.

I buy my cloth in two types, rolls and sheets. E-Z Flex Metalite cloth comes in rolls 1-1/2 inches wide and up to 50 yards long. Brownells carries it. This cloth can be torn to the length and width you need, and with a little mineral spirits as a lubricant can polish rounded surfaces easily. If you want to polish a flat surface, use an old file as a backer or lay the cloth on a hard flat surface and draw the part across it. Rolls are available in grits

Abrasive cloth comes in a wide variety of paper and cloth sizes, and abrasive grits.

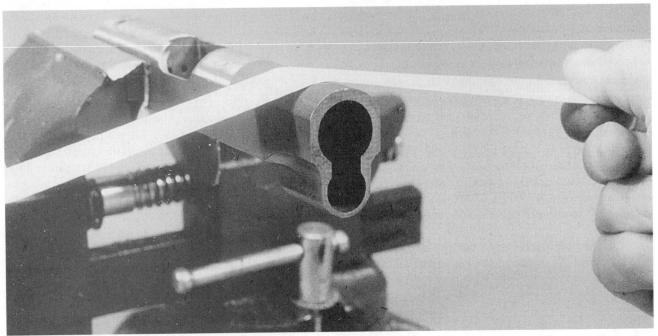

Holding the abrasive cloth taut limits the area sanded to a small part of the curve.

Holding the cloth down on the sides sands the entire radius of this slide.

from 120 to 500. You'll need 600 or finer grit for a mirror finish. Buy sheets for this final polishing.

Composition of the grit is not a big deal. I have tried both Aluminum Oxide and Silicon Carbide, and do not see any difference between them.

Dry sanding is not very useful in firearms. Firearm steel is so hard that you will quickly rub the grit off the cloth or paper, leaving an expensive bit of rag. Use only cloth or paper intended for wet sanding, or "wet and dry" grades. Wetting the cloth or paper with mineral spirits extends its life. (In the interests of not having to type "cloth and paper" the next 100 times, please understand that from here on I am referring to both when I use "cloth", and talking specifically of paper when I use "paper.") The mineral spirits and the rubbed-off grit form an abrasive slurry, which keeps cutting the steel. When you want to inspect the surface you will have to rub this slurry off. Be careful, and only use a dedicated cloth to wipe the slurry off. If you use a general cleaning cloth, and then use that cleaning cloth to rub down a firearm, you will scratch this firearm with the slurry held in the cleaning cloth.

I use mineral spirits as a solution for keeping my abrasive paper or cloth wet. Be sure to buy 100 percent pure odorless mineral spirits because the mineral spirits will get all over your hands. The smell will get in your hair and into your clothes. Odorless mineral spirits will cost more than the industrial mixes that have a percentage of reclaimed content, but the reclaimed mineral spirits will have a definite kerosene odor that you may find objec-

tionable. If you do not live alone, your co-resident may also find the odor offensive. Buy the good stuff.

It can take a little extra work to find pure, odorless mineral spirits. Look in your phone book for "machine tools" or "machine tool suppliers." These people provide tools to the small manufacturing shops in your town. When you call to inquire, don't be surprised if they tell you the pure mineral spirits cost $6 or $7 per gallon. A gallon will last you a long time, and the extra cost over the stuff that has an odor is well worth it. If your hands dry out from using the mineral spirits, a good hand lotion will put the moisture back in your skin.

Using abrasive cloth on metal is not a mystery, but you must keep a few things in mind. You have to follow the order of the grit, going from one to the next. The

You can see the difference in the amount of area sanded.

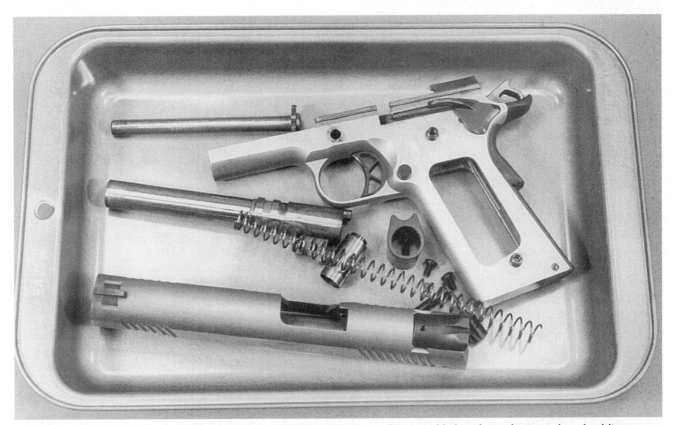

If you don't have a parts tank, a small pan can do to clean your handgun. Disassemble it and pour in your mineral spirits or Brownells d'Solve.

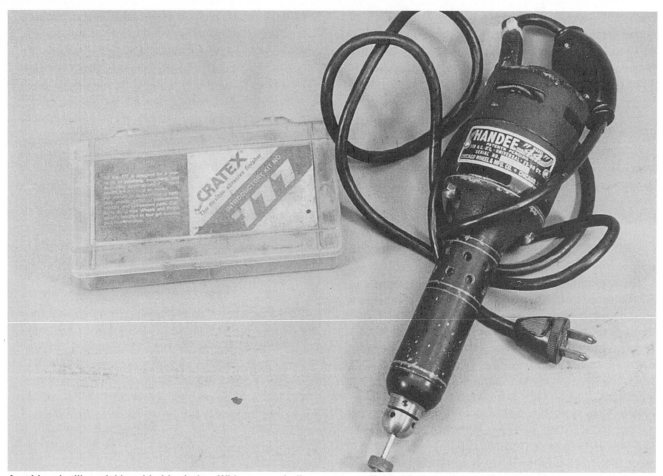

An old and still-useful hand-held grinder. With some grinding stones, polishing bobs and a sanding drum or two, you can fit anything.

coarsest cloth to use is 180-grit. It will quickly cut down a high spot on a slide or frame. You can use it to blend a welded repair, or adjust the curvature of a compensator body to match that of the slide.

The next grit, 220, is probably the best general-purpose grit. It will not cut as quickly as the 180. If you use a light touch, it will not alter angles, lines, or the edges between two surfaces. It is smooth enough that you can leave it as your final surface preparation before bluing or plating. The 220-grit delivers an even, satiny look to your surface, but with a definite grain to it. When you switch to the next-finer grade, you should work at an angle to the grain of the 220, to polish out that grain. Change back to the previous angle for the next grit. If at all possible, with each change of grit I work at an angle to the previous grit. This way I can easily make sure I have polished out the grain of the previous grit. The final polish grit is done in the direction I want the finish to be oriented, removing the marks from the next-to-last grit.

There are some situations where it simply isn't possible to change directions very much, or at all. Polishing a compensator is one case. Here I make use of liberal amounts of Dykem, and closely examine the surface to make sure I remove all of the previous grain. An awkward place to polish is blending the back of a frame during the installation of a something like the Ed Brown grip safety. I alternate between the hand-held grinder and the

If you do not brace your hand when using a hand-held grinder, the stone may slip. If you are lucky, you may only mar your handgun, as on this 1911 slide. You may hurt yourself.

emery cloth. A light touch with the grinder and a polishing bob buffs up the high spots, letting me see the areas that need more attention from the emery cloth.

The most versatile and arguably the most useful power tool is a Dremel or Foredom hand-held grinder. It is also the one most often blamed for problems. Some of my compatriots like to joke about requiring a fifteen-day waiting period before getting permission to dremel. While the bench grinder operates at 1,200 to 1,800 rpm, the smaller stone or polishing bob of the hand-held grinder can run at 5,000. This high speed allows you to cut, grind or polish just about anything. There is a risk. It also means that if you aren't careful you will inadvertently cut, grind or polish anything else the wheel touches. The unit is so handy that it is easy to get caught up in a task and go too far. Or your hands may slip and you'll find that the grinding stone you were using to level a lowered ejection port has just ground a swooping line across the side of the slide.

With a little care you can minimize the risks and maximize the advantages of a hand-held grinder. Have the part you are working on securely fastened in your vise. Brace your hands. Wear eye and ear protection. Remember, you'll be using the grinder inches from your face and you will find it impressively loud. The grit and metal chips being thrown into the air make quite a mess. Wear a breathing mask. Stop frequently to check your work.

The wheels, or stones, for your grinder come in a bewildering variety of sizes, shapes and grits. Standard wheels of silicon carbide work for most every application. The regular wheels vary from 1/4 inch to 1-1/4 inches in diameter, and come in wheel, barrel, cone and ball shapes. They will wear down as you use them. After a few uses you'll have a larger choice of diameters for later work. You may want to get a special tapered stone for use on 1911 slides. Buy one made of Aluminum Oxide impregnated with Cobalt, the tapered shape of which cuts that flare at the back of the ejection port that some shooters love. Other compositions are available in the tapered shape, but they will not last as long against the hard steel of the 1911 slide. You will spend more time polishing the flare. If you want the flare, buy this stone.

Next get a sanding drum. A sanding drum starts life as a standard grinding shaft with a shoulder attached

The author, getting ready to do some grinding. Protective glasses, magnifiers, earmuffs and a breathing filter are standard for grinding, if you want to keep your eyes, ears and lungs.

to it. Pressed over the end of the shaft to the shoulder is a rubber cylinder, called a drum. The sanding sleeve passes over the drum. When you tighten the screw on the top, the drum is squeezed and bulges out, holding the sanding sleeve in place. I find the sanding drum particularly useful when fitting the Ed Brown grip safety onto a 1911. This safety requires a great deal of blending of the frame and safety. The sanding drum speeds up this blending.

Unlike grinding stones, the sanding drum does not change its diameter as you use it. Instead of wearing down, it wears out and becomes duller and duller. When the sleeve becomes too dull to be of any use, take it off and replace it. Sometimes you can get more life out of a sleeve. If your drum is slightly oval, one part of the sleeve will wear out faster. Loosen the screw, rotate the sleeve and retighten. You will have a new or newer surface on the cutting face of the drum.

You'll also need Cratex polishing bobs. These rubber tips are impregnated with a grinding compound. I use only the fine and extra-fine bobs for polishing. Cratex makes a kit of all the various sizes and shapes, in all four grits. While convenient, I prefer to buy only the points I need. I also buy extra shafts. Once you have a bob installed, and ground to the size you want, leave it on that shaft. If you need another polishing bob, rather than switching from your one-and-only shaft, simply set up another bob on a shaft.

Pistolsmithing sometimes requires small work on hardened steel parts. For these applications you'll need solid-carbide cutters. Carbide cutters retain their shape. Stones do not. If you start with a small stone for a small job, the stone can wear completely away before the job is done. Carbide won't do this. Carbide can cut even the hardest steel if you are willing to be patient about it. If you are impatient you'll overheat your cutter, burning and dulling it.

I have found that using a carbide cutter on steel creates the most curious metal flakes. They aren't filings; they are almost miniature scales, and they are magnetized. If you make the mistake of trying to wipe them away with your hand you will have these annoying little shavings stuck in the skin of your fingertips for a couple of days until they work their way out. Instead, after cutting with carbide, take the part to your wastebasket and give it a shot from one of the aerosol gun cleaners. If you have had to do a lot of cutting and the shavings are really balled up you may have to give the part several of these shots. Don't use your fingers.

To complete your hand-held grinder ensemble, get a set of cut-off wheels. You can use them to make saw-like cuts into even the hardest metals. If you are removing the hammer spur from your revolver use a cut-off wheel. While you can grind the whole spur off, doing so creates a lot of heat that can draw the temper out of your hammer. With the cut-off wheel you put the hammer in the vise. The mass of the vise draws off the heat, protecting your hammer as you make your cuts. Make sure you

This bench has the luxury of two vises. There are also drawers under the bench, to hold larger and heavier items.

wear some sort of mask when using a cut-off wheel, as the dust it creates is particularly fine. You DO NOT want to inhale this stuff.

Always keep two things in mind when using the hand-held power grinder. First, the machine is meant for light cuts. You cannot "lean into" your work. Pressing harder does not speed things up; it slows down the motor, overheats the cutting tool (or the part being cut) and eventually grinds up the stone or polishing bob itself. When you see a plume of dust arc up from the work, you are pressing too heavily. The only warning you will get with carbide is a slight change in pitch. If you persist in pressing too hard until the carbide cutter changes color, it is already too late. Take it easy. Use light, even passes with the cutting stone. Your hands should move steadily during the cut. Don't stop. The tool keeps cutting and the stone, cut-off wheel or carbide will cut a small trough in your slide if you do. Use a file for the final cosmetic touches.

Second, the cutting tool will grab the metal and yank your hand in the direction of rotation. If you do not have your hands braced when the stone, carbide or cut-off wheel grabs, your hand will be pulled into the direc-tion of rotation. If this doesn't sound unsafe to you, you haven't had a grinding wheel race across a finger, a finger being used to keep the grinder properly located on the job. I did that, a long time ago, and recommend against it. Not only is using an unbraced hand-held grinder unsafe, you can mar the pistol.

A grinder may seem like a lot of hassle. Goggles. Mask.

Hearing protection. Bracing your hands. Grinding down stones and polishing bobs to just the right diameter before using them. Why do this? What is the advantage of the Dremel/Foredom? You gain power and reach. You save time and effort. For example, modifying the ejection port of a 1911 by filing takes forever, since the longest stroke is less than half an inch. With the Dre-mel/Foredom you grind right to the line you marked in your Dykem. A grinder lets you do the heavy work with power.

THE INS AND OUTS OF DRILLING AND MILLING

Drilling on handguns is a delicate operation. When drilling holes at home for installing lamps, shelves, or who-knows-what, plus or minus a quarter-inch (.250) is probably good enough. On a pistol, that is practically the next zip code. If you are off .010 inches drilling a hole for a scope mount, you may not be able to get the base to work at all. Even if you can attach it, the scope will be pointed three targets over rorm the one you want to hit. Drilling holes in handguns with a variable-speed drill is definitely out.

Only with the drill press can you properly drill on your handgun. Why drill? The primary reason is the installation of sights. A sight may use more than the holes the factory drilled and tapped. The Bo-Mar rear sight requires a hole drilled and tapped for the eleva-tion adjustment screw. (Let us take a moment to mourn the passing of the Bo-Mar sight.) The Millett Dual-Crimp

This Smithy CB 1220 XL is large enough to handle any handgun milling need. It is also a lathe. The mill head can be used as a drill press. Three tools on one, for less cost and less floor space than three separate tools.

Jim Clark Jr., of Clark Custom Guns, firing up a surface grinder. This is an expensive piece of equipment that only a full-time professional needs. But it is a really neat toy.

front sights must have two holes drilled at the front of the slide. Mounting a scope on a handgun often means drilling and tapping holes for the scope base.

You will need drills and taps of the correct sizes, a tap wrench and tapping fluid along with your drill press. You do not need to buy a free-standing drill press. A bench-top drill press will be large enough for handgun work. Any of the hardware stores carry a large selection. You will not need a drill press with a chuck larger than half inch. Removing more metal than half-inch calls for a mill.

The big boy of the metal-removing family is the mill. Some surface grinder enthusiasts argue that for taking off large amounts of even hardened metal, the surface grinder is the king. To which I reply, "Can a surface grinder cut a dovetail?" No, but a mill can. If all you need are flats or plain notches you don't need a mill, a bench grinder and files are fine. Don't spend the large amounts of money that even a modest mill will cost if you don't need dovetails and lots of them. If you do, then consider a mill.

MINI PROJECT

In order to work on handgun frames you have to clamp them securely. When you try this you will run into several problems. Clamping isn't always easy or possible, since the rounded surfaces often prevent you from getting a purchase with the vise. Or you may find that having finally, somehow, clamped the frame, you can't get into the area you want to modify. Worst of all, if you clamp too tightly you may squeeze the receiver and distort it. Your 1911 frame won't do you any good at all if you can't get the magazine into it because you squeezed part of the receiver.

Superbar to the rescue! A bar that slides into the magazine well and locks in place, the superbar prevents frame crush. Brownells offers one for the 1911 that does exactly this, but you can make one that does much more. At the industrial tool supply store, pick up a mild steel bar. Get a piece at least a foot long, sized .500 inch by 1.500 inches. If the store doesn't have this size, have them mill down a slightly larger one. You'll also need a relatively small piece of steel plate 1 inch by 6 inch by quarter-inch. When you get your bar, see if they have any scraps close enough to cut or file to size. If the industrial store doesn't have one then order an 18 inch length of 3/16 inch by 1-1/2 inches mild steel from Brownells. Complete your shopping list with three cap screws 1-1/2 inches long of 1/4 inch X 20 thread, a 1/4 X 20 tap, a #7 and a 17/64 inch drill.

Clamp the bar in your vise, narrow edge up. Leave a few inches sticking out to the side. With your 10-inch American 2nd Cut file, start filing a radius on the long edge of the bar. You want to match the contour of the magazine well of your pistol. Radius the first inch, checking the fit to the frame until the frame will start onto the bar. Once you have the radius established, make a rough cut bevelling the bar for 6 inches. Now, radius the bevel for an inch or so, and check fit. As the frame gets close

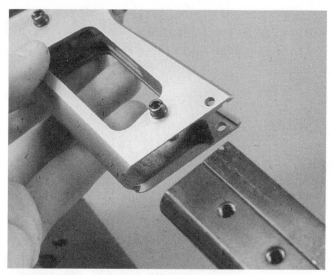

Insert the frame holder into the magazine well.

to sliding on, use Dykem to find the high spots of your radius and dress them down. Once the receiver can be wriggled on, use the E-Z Flex Metalite cloth to make it a smooth sliding fit. Polish the radius in a shoeshine manner until the bar and frame fit is snug but smooth.

Measure 1 inch down the bar on the right side, and with a cut-off wheel in your Dremel or Foredom grinder, cut a magazine catch notch. On the left side, put this notch at 3 inches down. The magazine catch will hook onto the bar at either of these. The right-hand notch is for locking the frame upright. The left-hand notch is for putting the frame on the bar up side-down. In both directions you can work on the receiver without the vise getting in the way.

Starting 1 inch from the end of the bar, mark and drill five holes, each an inch apart center to center, with the #7 drill. Tap these with the 1/4 X 20 tap. Drill the cap screw clearance holes in the mild steel plate with the 17/64-inch drill. These are also 1 inch apart center to center. Deburr all the holes with the #2 pillar file.

To hold a revolver frame, place the butt opening over the holes in the bar. Clamp the holding plate down with the screws to keep the frame in place. Now you can hold the revolver in any position, and work on it without the vise being in the way. With the farthest holes being 5 inches apart, you can also clamp the revolver through the frame opening. If you need unrestricted access to the grip area of the frame, this bar is the only easy way to securely hold the frame.

The Wilson frame holder is a solid piece of steel that allows you to hold your frame in the vise without damage. You can also make your own frame holder.

Slide the top of the holder fully into the frame.

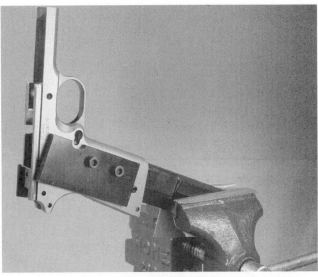

On the Wilson frame holder, the sideplate clamps the frame to the bar. You can work in the top, front, back and left side without interference.

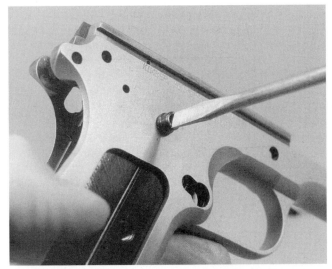

You have to remove the top grip screw bushing to clamp on the side plate.

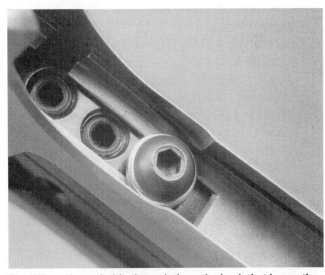

The Wilson frame holder has a bolt on the back that keeps the frame secured while you work on the front or sides.

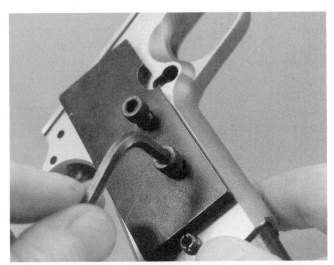

Once the bar is inserted into the frame, clamp the sideplate down.

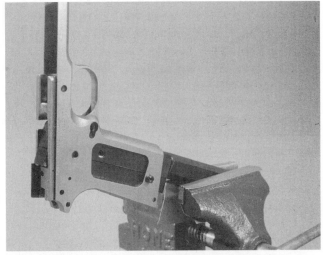

A frame holder allows you to both clamp the frame of your 1911 and work on it. Without the holder, securing the frame and still getting to it can be impossible.

USING A MILL TO ADJUST YOUR SIGHTS

A neat trick you can do with a mill is to adjust front and non-adjustable rear sights. Say your pistol is hitting low and you want to adjust it. The calculation involves four figures: the amount you need the bullet moved on the target, the distance to the target, the sight radius of your handgun, and the amount of correction of the sight blade. The ratio of the bullet correction to the distance to the target is equal to the ratio of the sight correction to the sight radius. An example: a pistol with a sight radius of 6 inches is hitting two inches low at 25 yards. Convert the yards to inches, and we have $2/900 = C/6$, where "C" is the correction to the front sight. Multiply both sides by 6, and we get $6 \times 2/900 = C$. Thus we find that our correction will be to mill 0.013 inches off of the top of the front sight.

Another way to do the same thing is what a friend of mine does: he checks all handgun sight-in at 28 yards. Why 28 yards? Because it is close enough to 1,000 inches (1008, to be precise) to make the math easy. Simple, any error on the target, in inches, times the sight radius, is his correction on the sights. A one-inch error at 28 yards, on a six-inch sight radius means .006 inch of correction.

Now to make the correction: Clamp the slide in your mill vise, level it, and then dust off the top of the front sight by the calculated amount. De-burr, cold blue and you are done.

If you are hitting too high, and your fixed rear sight has enough metal, you can do the same thing to the rear sight with one extra step. After you have dusted off the top of the rear sight with your end mill, switch to another end mill the same size as rear sight notch (usually .125 inch) and deepen the notch by the same amount you had just lowered the top of the rear blade. If you didn't do this the notch in your rear sight would be shallower than it was before you started. When you de-burr the edges of the rear sight, be sure to slightly round the corners on the outside, so you won't cut your hands handling the pistol. Cold blue the exposed steel, and you are done.

You can do the same job with a file, but you must be very careful. Even the slightest tip in your angle of filing will leave the front sight top angled. A visible angle on the top of the sight makes aiming difficult. If you plan to file, file to a depth short of the required depth. Then carefully, and with the finest file you have, file down to the required depth. Check your work regularly, to make sure you are filing evenly.

BASIC METALWORKING AND MINOR REPAIR

POLISHING AND FILING

You're probably ready to dive in and start working on your pistols, right? Wrong. Before you begin using the cutting tools described above, it's a good idea for you to practice on something a little less expensive than your handguns.

Open up your Brownells catalog, and order some steel — a bar and some large flats will do. Brownells sells both in 18-inch lengths. Buy one bar in the 1-inch diameter. Buy two flats, both 1/8 by 1 inch. These will be your filing, polishing and grinding practice pieces. Each time you want to work on your handguns, you can pull these out of the drawer and warm up, refresh your memory, and get your touch back.

If your area has large gunshows, start cruising the aisles looking for a dead slide. Emphasis on dead; you are not looking for a replacement slide for your 1911 (the most common one out there), but a slide that has been used up and can no longer serve its original purpose. Look for a slide that's just too rusted, or bent, or cracked. You may see one with the locking lugs set back from too many hot loads or an incorrectly fitted barrel. In such a case the engagement surfaces on the locking lugs will look notched, rounded or somehow damaged. See Chapter 18 for a complete explanation

Expect to spend around $20, far less than the $200 a perfectly good new replacement slide would run. You can practice on this slide (even if you don't have a 1911) to your heart's content, safe in the knowledge that any mistakes you make are to a $20 investment, and will never see the light of day.

Your first polishing drill will be on the rod. Place it in your vise. Start with a 1-inch strip of 180-grit cloth. Pick an area somewhere in the middle of the rod, and hold the cloth taut to begin polishing. Use a gentle shoeshine motion. How you hold your polishing cloth determines how much of the rod (or the top of your slide, when you get one) gets polished. With the cloth taut you should be polishing only the very top of the curved surface of the rod. Check your work. You are using a shallow angle of departure — the cloth, held taut, barely deviates from the 180-degree plane running along the top of your bar and parallel to the floor. Polish until the area is bright. Observe the difference between the original surface and your polished surface.

Now move to an unpolished area and change your grip. This time hold the ends of the cloth down below the edge of the rod, at about a 45-degree angle of departure. Gripping the cloth this way will allow you to polish a third of the rod's diameter. Use the same shoeshine motion and polish again until the area is bright. Stop and compare the two spots you've polished. The second one will be much bigger than the first.

Stay with this larger polished surface. Coat it with Dykem and move up to 220-grit. Take a few light passes, and then wipe the surface clean. Notice how the Dykem remains in the deepest marks of the 180 grit cuts. Apply more Dykem, move one hand forward of the other, and polish at an angle to the previous work.

Try different grits, and change angles each time. Work your rod until it approaches a mirror finish.

For your second drill, fire up your bench grinder and cut a shallow gouge in the polished surface of your rod. Place your rod in the vise. Start on the gouge with the 180-grit cloth. To polish only the gouge and its near vicinity you will need to use a shallow angle of departure. Hold the cloth taut. Polish the gouge out. Change grits and angles as necessary to achieve a finished surface. Now look at your work, including the areas adjacent to the polished-out gouge. See how the surface is dished? Look for this dishing when checking used handguns for quick (and poor) repairs.

Gouge a different part of the rod. This time, take the rod to your welder, and have him fill the gouge with soft steel. With your 10-inch 2nd Cut file, file the weld down. This filing should be done in a series of flat motions. You should not file the entire weld at any time. Do not tilt the file or flex it over or around the weld. Do not file the original rod. Instead, create a series of flat surfaces in the weld, each at an angle to the next, with the aggregate of the small flats approaching the radius of the rod. Once your series of filed flats is just about down to the rod surface, change to your Swiss pillar file. Now start using a rounding motion to blend the flats together. When the flats are blended, switch to the 220-grit cloth. Begin polishing, in a shoeshine manner, and an angle of departure just deep enough to cover the weld plus 1/4 inch of rod

surface. Polish with the 220 until the weld outline disappears, then switch to finer grits until you reach the level of shine you would want on your slide. Done properly, the surface will not be dished.

The lesson of our exercises here: Weld up gouges and dress them down! If you simply polish out the gouge, the surface will be dished and wavy.

Some drills you do, and some drills you buy. Before doing any flat stock polishing drills, let's look briefly at drills that go in the drill press.

There is no such thing as a "standard" firearms thread, and you cannot buy any firearm screws you may need at the local hardware store. There are common threads used in the firearms industry: The most common thread sizes used in firearms are, in order, 6-48, 8-40, 10-32. What do these numbers mean? Some people would say "Just about anything!" and they'd almost be right. The 6-48 thread, (pronounced "six, forty-eight"), refers to a number 6 screw, with 48 turns to the inch. Because the system of naming screws and pairing drills with screws is so (sorry, I can't help myself) screwy, the designers of firearms have tried as much as possible to not use screws. Still, you will find screws on your pistols, and you will occasionally need to drill them. The 1911 has four screws, (and, true to form, they are not among the three most common sizes mentioned above) each threaded into a bushing screwed into the frame. You will have to deal with these, and others.

In order to tap a hole for any screw, you have to make just the right diameter hole. Too narrow, and you can't get the tap started. Too wide, and the threads will not hold. For a 6-48 you use a number 31 drill. Why are they named that way? I have no idea. Whoever came up with this arcane system must have been out of his mind,

Holding the abrasive cloth taut limits the area sanded to a small part of the curve.

because no one in his right mind would assume that for a "number 6" screw you would use a "number 31" drill. Check the chart for what drills go with what screws. Don't assume you can pick the right drill by eye. Don't bother trying to memorize the chart. Just follow it.

Place one of your steel flats on the bench. Mark a location, 1 inch from the end, and in the middle of the 1-inch flat. Mark the spot with a centerpunch. Clamp the flat in the drill press, and drill the hole with the number 31 drill. Put the flat back in your vise. Pick up the 6-48 tapered tap and lock it in the tap wrench. With the fingers of your left hand hold the body of the tap wrench upright on the steel. You must hold the wrench straight up. To check your position, move your head from one side of the steel to another, and adjust the tap until it is vertical. With your right hand, simultaneously press the tap wrench down as you rotate it. Use your left fingers to guide the tap and keep it vertical.

If, as you turn the tap, you do not use enough downward force, the tap will simply ride along the edge of the hole, instead of biting in. Once you press hard enough you will feel the teeth of the tap cutting the steel. After a couple of turns, stop. The teeth have been cutting steel and the spirals of cut steel have been building up in the flutes of the tap. Turn the tap backwards half a turn to break these spirals, and then continue rotating clockwise again, cutting steel. On a deeper hole, or on harder steel, you will have to back the tap up several times before you finish tapping the hole.

Use the tapered tap for holes that go completely through. The tapered tap has the first 8 or 10 teeth tapered. Blind holes, which are holes that do not go completely through, require a plug tap and then a bottoming tap. The plug has the first 3 to 5 teeth tapered, and the bottoming tap has only the first tooth tapered.

Look closely at your tapped hole. Notice the shoulder around the hole. That shoulder was not created by the drill. It was the tap that forced the shoulder up. If you are going to bolt something to the hole, say a scope mount, the shoulder can get in the way. Take your Swiss pillar file, and attempt to file the shoulder down. Unless you have superhuman patience, and an unbelievable touch, you'll find you can't. You may also find that you have filed the flat surface around the shoulder, something you do not want to do. Instead, take a drill larger in size than the hole you drilled (the size isn't really important) and, using only your hands, turn the drill in the hole. You can get rid of the shoulder and very slightly bevel the hole with only a few turns of the drill bit. If you use a very light touch, you can even do this in the drill press. However, it is best if you perform this particular step by hand. It only takes a slight slip with the drill press in beveling the hole and you'll suddenly have a deeply-dished hole. Oops.

Another way to eliminate a shoulder is to prevent it from coming up at all. After drilling your hole, and before tapping, switch to a larger drill and very lightly "kiss" the hole with the larger drill. You want to do this just enough to offset the shoulder that your later tapping will kick up.

Take your flat steel and clamp it in the vise vertically. Leave two inches sticking up above the top of the vise. With your 10-inch file, file the top edge of the steel. You will feel some vibration as the file cuts the steel. The 2 inches of steel sticking out of the vise makes proper filing impossible. If you press harder you will start cutting a striped pattern in the steel. Because of the vibration and the force you are applying, the file is jumping along its teeth and cutting the striped pattern. Ease up in the force you use, and the pattern (but not the vibration) will go away.

Unclamp the steel, and move the top edge down so only 1/2 inch protrudes from the top of the vise. Now there is no vibration when you file, and no matter how hard you lean, the pattern you saw before will not reappear. When the part you are filing is clamped correctly in your vise, it is the force of your pressure, and the rigidity of the part, which determine the finished surface of your cut.

With your hacksaw, cut 3 inches off one of your flat pieces of steel. Bevel the edge with any file. You want to knock off the burrs. Tape a piece of 220-grit cloth to a hard, flat surface. You'll be wetting the cloth with mineral spirits, and, unfortunately, the mineral spirits will dissolve the glue on most tapes. I find large pieces of duct tape hold together long enough to allow me to finish a job. The best surface to tape to is a large piece of steel. If you don't have one, glass will do. Be careful, as the glass will break if you do not support it fully. Wet the cloth. Pick up your de-burred 3-inch steel, and put it down flat on the cloth. Push it away from you. Pick it up again and push it away again.

Simply wiping the steel back and forth, and back and forth, instead of lifting and placing and pushing, will produce a curved grain to your polishing.

Look at the surface you have just correctly polished. It probably looks uneven. The "flat" steel you've been working on is not flat. Unless the manufacturer used a surface grinder to finish the surface, there is no such thing as a "flat" piece of steel. We just call it flat for our own convenience.

You must remember that flat surfaces are not flat when you go to polish your slide. I refer to this as "Hibbert's Law," named after the shooter at our club who, after an exasperating session trying to polish his 1911, exclaimed, "Nothing is straight, nothing is flat, and nothing is where it's supposed to be." He had used a surface grinder, a very good tool for making dead-flat surfaces, to "clean up" the sides of his slide. On the first pass, he was screwed: the rollmarker had dished the slide, and they were so far below level that his first pass has simply made a flat-sided slide with a deep and wide dished section. His choices at that point were to try and polish it out, or surface grind the whole thing flat. Either way, it was going to be a lot of work and remain ugly afterwards.

A standard front sight, soon to be changed to a Millett Dual-Crimp front sight.

Clamp the sight and rotate the slide to one side or the other.

The front sight has broken free, sight is in the vise and the foot of the tenon still in the slide.

Use a narrow tapered punch to drive the foot of the tenon out of the slide.

Take out your dead slide. Even if you are going to be working on a Beretta or Glock, using a 1911 slide for practice will work just fine. Plus, they are easy to get. At any gun show you will see 100 dead 1911 slides for every deceased Beretta or Glock slide.

Take a drift punch and your hammer, and drift the rear sight out. Depending on how long it has been assembled, this may take some hammering. Scrub and clean the slot and sight. Re-insert the sight and drift it back to center on the slide. When, in Chapter 13, you go to change sights on your operating 1911 (or other pistol) you can check the fit, and practice filing the slide sight slot on this dead slide.

Look at the front of the slide. The front sight, if original, will be a small blade staked into a slot in the slide. You cannot remove this sight without destroying it. The fast way to get rid of it is to clamp the sight in your vise with the slide upside down, and then rotate the slide to twist the sight off. If the spectacle of a twisted lump of metal that used to be your sight lying on your bench disturbs you, you can use the sight to practice filing. It takes a delicate touch to file the sight off without touching the slide.

Either way, you will be left with the sight stub in the slot. Take a narrow drift punch and punch the stub, called a tenon, out of the slide from the top.

Tenons come in three sizes. The original, or narrow tenon, held sights just fine when sights were tiny little

thumbnail-sized things. Larger sights were prone to come off the slide when secured by a narrow tenon. When Springfield Armory began production of 1911 pistols, they increased the tenon to the medium tenon. Colt stayed with the narrow tenon until they began production of the Series 80 pistols, when they went to the wide tenon. The wide tenon is the full width of the sight; .125 inches.

When modifying the sights on your slide you must pay attention to the width of the new sight's tenon and the width of the original slot. They must match. It is not possible to stake a sight to a slot larger than the sight's tenon. Nor can you widen a slot that is too narrow for a tenon.

Now, practice polishing using your dead slide. Apply Dykem to the sides. Begin by polishing the slide's sides with 220-grit cloth taped to a hard, flat surface. Once you have polished the high spots, you will have to take a separate piece of the same cloth and polish by hand. To do this, clamp the slide in a padded vise with the flat up. Use your thumb, wrapped in cloth, to polish the areas the flat surface polishing could not reach. Apply more

The traditional front sight on a 1911 has a tenon that sticks through a slot cut in the slide. The tenon fits into the slot and the bottom of the tenon, inside the slide, is swaged to wedge the sight into place.

Dykem and switch to a finer grit. Repeat the process, polishing flat, and then polishing by hand to get the lower areas.

When using cloth, remember that it has one great strength. Properly supported and backed, cloth will conform to the general shape of whatever you are polishing. In this case, your thumb is the backer. If your thumb becomes tired, use a narrow piece of wood with the end rounded.

You may be thinking that's a lot of work — switching from flat-backed to thumb-backed cloth, and steadily moving to finer and finer grit as you polish your slide. You may wonder why you shouldn't just use a coarse grit and polish the slide side until it is truly flat. The truth is, it is more work to use a coarse grit and polish flat. And you would be removing way too much

Once the sight is inserted in the slot, the MMC swaging tool is placed on the slide, and the sight protector is placed onto the sight. Tighten the top screw to hold the sight in place.

Place the swaging bar into the fixture.

And drive the swaging bar through the fixture.

metal from the slide. The slide stop hold-open notch is not the full thickness of the slide side. If you take too much metal off the sides of the slide, this notch will be too shallow. It will not long withstand the impact of stopping on the hold-open lever. Eventually it will round off, and your slide will not lock open when the magazine is empty. That was the dilemma faced by Glenn Hibbert back then: make it truly flat and thinner, or leave it wavy (but not seen) and polished.

Before starting any project on your good slide, take out the dead slide first. Practice on it. If you decide to lower the ejection port of your operating 1911, practice on the dead slide. If you want to hard-fit the slide and frame, practice squeezing the slide on your dead one, not the good one. If you chew up your practice slide until there's nothing left to it, just go out and get another. Use it as a sacrificial practice lamb to protect your good slide.

PROJECTS:
SAFETY AND SLIDE STOP ENGAGEMENT

On the left side of the frame of a 1911 just above the grip panel is the plunger tube. Inside it rest the plungers and spring that hold the slide stop and thumb safety in their places. Unfortunately, they don't always work as well as we'd like. Every time you fire, and the slide cycles, the slide stop and thumb safety vibrate and bounce. On some pistols the slide will lock back before the ammunition is expended. On these particular pistols the slide stop will pop or vibrate up and hold the slide open before you are out of ammo. On other pistols the safety will bounce up enough to just barely engage the sear or interfere with its movement. This can be dangerous. When you release the trigger, the sear may not return to rest. I once had to repair a pistol whose safety

would pop up and bind the sear in such a way that if you pushed the safety off, the sear released, firing the pistol. To say this was startling is an understatement.

If the slide stop and safety do not behave on your pistol, you must fit them properly.

Let's start with a malfunctioning slide stop. Make sure the pistol is empty. Take the slide off of the frame. Remove the thumb safety, plungers and spring. Now put the slide stop back in the frame. Clamp the frame in a padded vise, or slide it on your holding bar. (Or place it on the 10-8 frame block we'll discuss in the 1911 chapter.) Take the Krieger dimpling drill, and chuck the fat end in your variable-speed drill. Snake the narrow end into the plunger tube, and be sure it comes out the other end. If it doesn't, you'll be drilling on the internal shoulder of the plunger tube. This does not help your situation.

Hold the dimpling drill tip against the slide stop face, and push the slide stop down, both into the frame and down from where the slide would be, with your left thumb. Press the stop down with a good amount of

Dimple just enough to keep the slide stop from bouncing up and locking the slide open too soon.

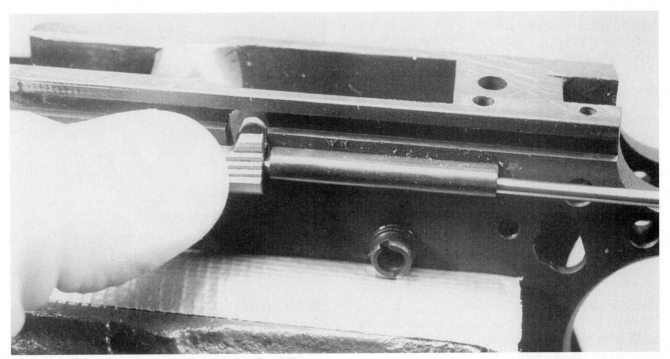

Hold the slide stop down while you use the dimpling drill.

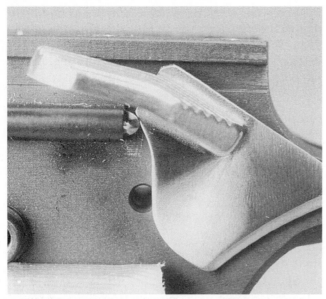

If your thumb safety comes off too easily, pull the dimpling drill through the plunger tube and attach the drill to the other side. Carefully drill the safety until it is harder to push off, but not too hard.

force, as you want to hold it in place when you turn on the drill. Drill for no more than a couple of seconds. It is much better to under-drill than to over-drill the slide stop. Pull the drill out, pull out the slide stop and look at the end of it. On the end of the slide stop you should have a small dimple, no larger in diameter than .070 inch.

This operation, like any others in gunsmithing, is a "cut and try" task. You don't have a set measurement you will drill to, you have an operational requirement. On the next trip to the range, check to see if your slide stop is fixed. If it isn't, and your pistol is still locking open prematurely, you have to repeat the process and

drill the dimple slightly larger and deeper. Don't make the dimple too deep on your first try, or the pistol will fail to lock open even when it is empty. A deep dimple can be corrected, but you will have to prevail upon your dentist for used dental drills. To correct an over-dimpled stop, take a cylindrical dental drill. Install it in your Dremel tool. Work from below the dimple. Position the drill at a shallow angle and cut a ramp out of the dimple. The ramp will let the slide stop ride out of the dimple, and up into the path of the slide when the empty magazine presses the slide stop up.

The thumb safety that pops up can be more than irritating. It can be dangerous. To fix this problem, again remove the slide assembly from the unloaded 1911. Cock the hammer, and remove the thumb safety, and the spring and plungers from the plunger tube. Either clamp the frame in a padded vise, or use your frame-holding bar to secure the frame. Put the narrow end of the Krieger drill through the plunger tube, and pull that end all the way forward. The drill should now be sticking past the front of the frame, with the fat end completely inside the plunger tube. Reinstall the thumb safety. Chuck your variable speed drill onto the end of the drill bit. Hold the thumb safety down, turn on the drill, and push the drill into the safety. Again, it is better to under-drill than over-drill.

Turn the drill off. Remove the thumb safety, unchuck the drill and pull it out of the plunger tube. Brush the drilling chips off the safety, reassemble the pistol, and on your next range trip check the thumb safety function. If it still pops up, you need to drill more. If you over-drill, the safety will be difficult to press into the safe position. Correct over-drilling with a round needle file, filing the bottom of the dimple you have drilled. By breaking the bottom edge of the dimple you ease the work your thumb must do in pushing the safety up.

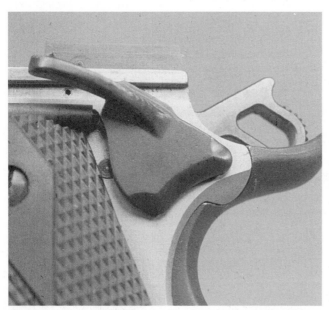

To remove the thumb safety, cock the hammer and place the safety at the halfway point between "on" and "off." Then lift the safety out from the frame.

When you pull the thumb safety out of the frame, keep a fingertip over the back of it. This prevents the spring and plungers from leaping to freedom.

1911 GRIP SCREW BUSHINGS

The grips on a 1911 are held on with screws, and these screws thread into bushings that are themselves screwed into the frame. Why not simply screw the grip screws right into the frame? Good question. My suspicion is that John Moses Browning was in one of his "belt and suspenders" moods. If you lose the screws, the bushings still keep the grips from shifting, and a piece of string or tape will keep them from falling off the frame. Without the bushings, lose the screws and you can't keep the grips on. Also, the threads fastening the grip screws have to be somewhat coarse. Given the thin wall section of the frame, the coarse threads of the grip screws may not find much joy. I'd love to know if it was a matter of try and fail, or so obvious to him that he never tried to do without the bushings.

There will come a day when you go to remove the grip screws on your 1911 and find that you have unscrewed one of the bushings right along with it. In your hands will be a screw-grip-bushing sandwich. You can ignore the attached bushing and just screw it back into the frame when you put the pistol back together, but it's better to fix it. The bushing threads are very fine, and if you continue to screw the bushing in and out you will eventually damage them. The trick is to remove the bushing without destroying it. I've talked to a number of gunsmiths who simply mangle the old grip screw bushing off, replace the bushing and the screw or screws, and simply bill the customer. Me, I figured if I could take an extra minute of time, and save my customer $20, they'd be appreciative. In any case, I figured a way to salvage the situation instead of simply replacing everything.

You will need your largest pliers, a screwdriver that fits the grip screw slot properly, a screwdriver that fits the bushing slot properly, your Swiss pillar file, Loctite, and two taps. A grip screw bushing driver or wrench is useful, but not an absolute must. As long as you have a screwdriver that properly fits the small slots cut in the bushing itself, you're good to go. The first tap is a grip

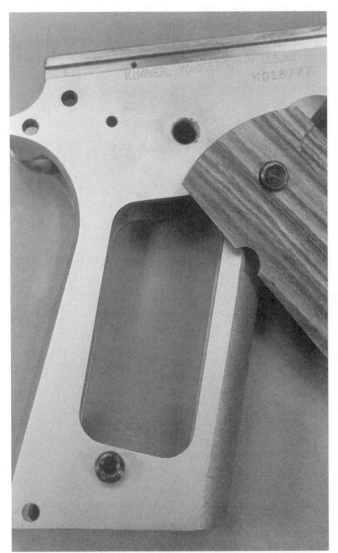

Sometimes when you remove the grip screws, a bushing will come with one of them. Don't worry, we can salvage this without having to buy a replacement.

Use a large pair of pliers to hold the bushing for removal from the grips.

Hold the bushing tightly. If it slips in the pliers you will not be able to salvage it. Remove the screw from the bushing.

screw bushing tap, size .236-60. The second tap is the grip screw thread size, .150-50. Both are available only through gunsmithing supply houses such as Brownells. (Yes, threads, taps and screws that are non-standard even by firearms standards. Welcome to the wacky world of gunsmithing.)

Take your pliers and grasp the bushing by its exposed (threaded) end. Even though you will mar the threads with the pliers clamping teeth, hold the bushing as tightly as possible. If the pliers slip, you'll have to replace the bushing. Better to mar the threads instead. With a properly-fitting screwdriver, turn the grip screw out. It will resist. (It is stuck, after all.) These screws almost always come free with a snap. As soon as you feel the screw release, relax. Ease your death-grip on the bushing, and remove the screw without further struggle.

The pliers will mar the threads where the bushing was held.

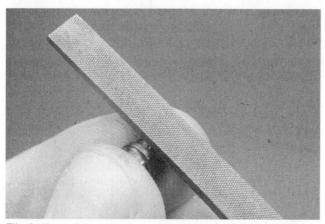

File the burred threads so you can screw the bushing back in.

This is what the filed bushing will look like. Don't worry, there are enough threads to keep it in the frame. You can only do this to a bushing once. The second time it is stuck you must replace it.

With the screw out, you'll have to repair the bushing. Use your swiss file to remove the marred portions of the bushing threads, and just those marred areas. You'll create a couple of flat areas in the threads, but if you're careful you will not remove enough threaded area to be a problem. With your frame-thread tap, the .236-60 tap, clean out the threads in the frame. You will find that an amazingly large amount of years-old gunk and crud can come out of a very small recess. Try the bushing in the frame and make sure it screws in smoothly. If it doesn't, either you haven't fully filed off the marred portions of thread on the bushing, or you haven't completely cleaned out the frame threads.

Once the bushing will screw down all the way without requiring force, unscrew the bushing, and degrease both it and the frame threads. Carefully place a small amount of the highest grade of Loctite you have on the threads. Blue is OK, but you will end up having to do all this again in a few years. Red is better, and dark green is the best Loctite for this situation. Screw the bushing in and snug it down firmly. The traditional method of securing the bushing is to stake it in. For this, a star-shaped wedge is placed on the inside of the bushing. By sliding a punch through the other bushing and striking it with a hammer, the back of the bushing is peened to the frame. I have had a staked bushings come loose. I have never had a Loctite-ed bushing come loose, so I Loctite and don't bother staking.

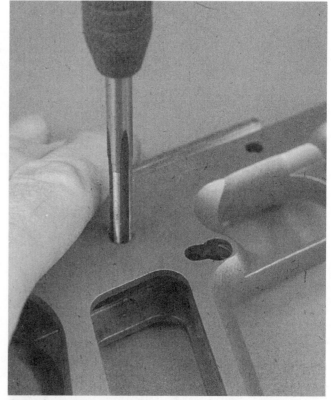

Clean the frame threads with a tap before replacing the bushing.

Be sure to wipe the Loctite out of the inside of the frame! If you use too much, whatever is leftover on the inside of the frame can run into other parts. You can literally glue the trigger bar in its slot, or other parts together. Not good. I have even encountered 1911's with their magazine glued into the frame, from just a stray drop of Loctite!

Give the Loctite a few minutes to set before working on the inside of the bushing. You'll find a lot of gunk in there, too, since this is where the screw was stuck. Use the grip screw tap to clean out the crud. If you don't clean out the threads you'll just have the screw stuck again the next time you go to clean your pistol. Once the inside threads are clean, take a moment to dress down the inside of the frame. Use your swiss file, and remove any protrusions or lip that might have been kicked up at the back of the grip screw bushing.

When you reassemble, put a drop of oil on the

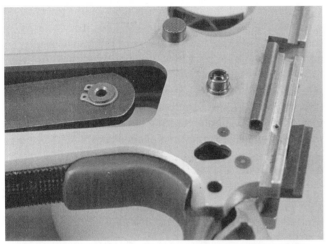

The grip screw bushing staking tool slides into the magazine well and rests against the lower bushing. Then slide a drift punch through the upper bushing and rest it in the cup in the bushing staking tool. Strike the punch with a hammer.

If the frame threads are stripped you will have to replace the old bushing with a new over-sized one. The frame has to be re-tapped to the new thread size.

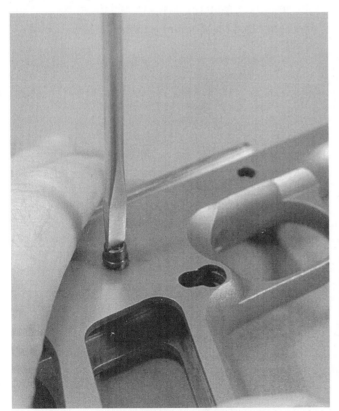

Replace the bushing, using some Loctite to secure it.

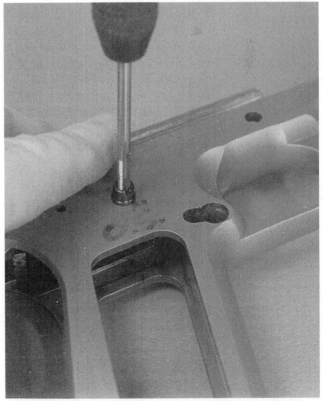

Once you have replaced the bushing, clean the screw threads with a tap. Otherwise, you'll be faced with the same problem again soon.

threads of the grip screws. As a final step, use the file again with the grip screw installed. If the screw protrudes into the frame it can bind a magazine. You want it flush instead.

Sometimes, when a bushing accidentally comes out along with its screw, it strips the bushing threads. You remove the bushing from the grip screw the same way, but you can't re-use the bushing. The threads on the bushing, and in the frame, will most likely be destroyed. You'll have to re-tap the hole. Buy an oversize bushing and a size .255-60 oversized tap.

Place the stripped frame on a flat padded surface. Start the tap, and using considerable force, re-cut the threads. The frame steel is relatively hard, the hole is oversized, and the tap has a short taper to it. You will have to lean on the tap handle. Take extra care at the start to make sure the tap is straight. A cocked hole will not help your cause. Once you have cut the threads, check the fit of the new bushing by threading it in. When you can screw it all the way down, unscrew it, degrease and Loctite it, and screw it back in. Snug it down. Then finish with the same finish steps as above.

What if 1) you go to remove the grips, 2) the bushing comes out along with the screw, 3) it strips the threads as it comes out, and 4) you realize it's an oversize bushing already? This is a tough repair. You can't go up another thread size — no one makes an over-over sized bushing and tap. In 15 years as a Professional Gunsmith and 12,000 guns, I have run into this problem just once. You probably won't, but for the three people who do, here is how to fix it. Jump ahead to Chapter 8, and read

up on silver-soldering. Take the stripped bushing, disassemble the frame, and degrease the frame and bushing. Flux the bushing and its frame hole. Heat and silver-solder the bushing into the frame. With care you will not have to clean up excess solder, but you will have heated the frame enough to ruin its bluing or plating. (That's life, get used to it.)

The bushing will now withstand the force of a grip screw. Be sure to use your grip screw tap to clean out the inside of the bushing, or the screw will bind and stick. Those aspiring pistolsmiths who want the extra credit can file down the bushing, drill out its center to the proper hole size for the standard bushing threads, and re-tap the hole for a new, original-sized bushing. You must Loctite this new bushing in. If you try to stake it you will break out your silver-soldered repair. You'll also have to measure the hole locations with precision, or you will end up slightly shifting the grip on the frame. It may not be noticed, and then again it may.

S&W CRANE POLISHING

The crane is the axis of rotation of the cylinder in your revolver. Drag on the crane can increase the force needed to pull the trigger, and make for a gritty feeling trigger pull.

Polishing the crane is one part of your revolver trigger job. Remove the front sideplate screw of your S&W revolver, and pull the cylinder and crane out of the frame. Pull the crane out of the cylinder. Scrub and degrease the crane, and then clamp the base of it in a padded vise.

The barrel that the cylinder rotates on should be hori-

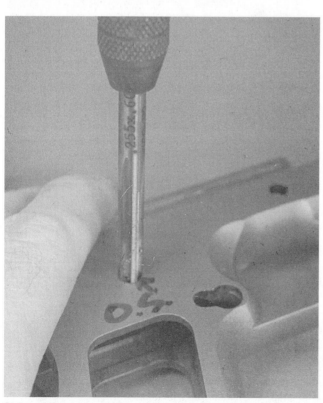

Stripped threads must be re-tapped to the next size larger.

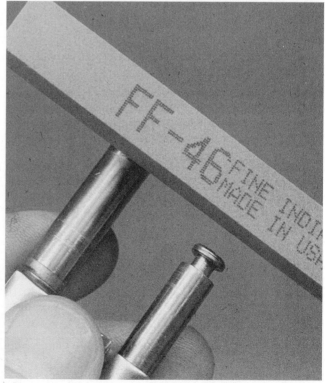

Use a stone to dress down the edges of the line if the crane will not re-enter the cylinder.

zontal, and sticking forward out of the vise so you have clearance all around it.

Do not use coarse cloth for this job! Coarse cloth would even out the whole surface of the crane, reducing the diameter of the barrel, and introducing wobble into the rotation of the cylinder. A wobbly rotation can harm accuracy. If the crane is dragging, you want to polish only the high, or bearing, spots. Apply Dykem to the barrel. Install the cylinder and spin the cylinder on the crane. Compressed air will help turn it fast enough to rub the Dykem. Take the cylinder off and see the high spots. Use your 400-grit cloth (600 is better) in a shoe-shine manner, with the ends of the cloth coming off the barrel parallel to each other. Polish all around the barrel just enough to wipe off the Dykem. Inspect the surface closely. You should be able to see the areas you have

polished. Do not worry that you have not gotten all of the surface. These low spots are not the problem. Switch to your 600 or finer cloth, and polish the high spots to a mirror finish. Scrub, degrease and reassemble.

ENDSHAKE IN THE S&W REVOLVER

If your Smith & Wesson revolver has seen a lot of use it may have developed a condition known as endshake. Does the cylinder, after being closed and locked in place by the locking bolt, move forward and back on the crane? In extreme cases the cylinder can actually bind on the back of the barrel extension, or move so far forward that the firing pin cannot fully strike primers,

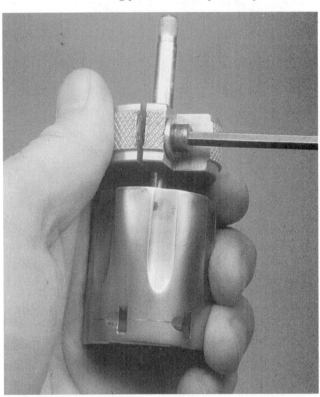

Tighten the Wessinger ejector rod clamp firmly. If it slips you will not be able to unscrew the ejector rod.

When buying a used firearm, look for signs of dropping. This dented barrel may not have harmed the crown, but it might have lead to the barrel being bent or the frame twisted. Look, check, and get a return guarantee if you can.

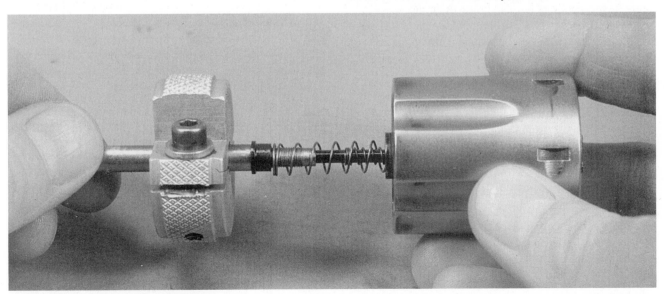

Use the clamp to unscrew the ejector rod.

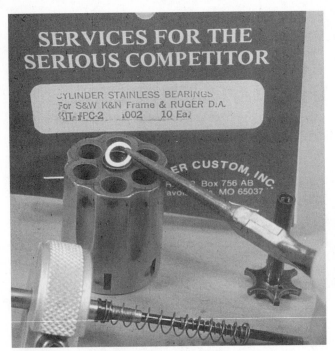

Place a Power bearing washer in the cylinder to remove endshake.

Use the crane to press the washer to the bottom of the tunnel.

causing misfires.

Endshake is not good.

Years of use and thousands of rounds have loosened the fit of the crane to the cylinder, causing play. On each shot, recoil has accelerated the frame back, and the cylinder slams against the end of the crane. While it isn't much, the high spots can get ironed down and eventually create endshake. In order to remove endshake, you must remove this play. There are two methods. You can shorten the hole, or you can lengthen the crane. For the first method, you need a set of feeler gauges, headspace gauges, crane bushings or shims, and your Swiss pillar file or medium-fine stone. If you do not have headspace gauges you can get by with unfired or once-fired empty cases. The factory-approved second method, of lengthening the crane, does not use crane bushings or shims. Instead, a crane stretcher, which looks very much like a modified pipe-cutter, and a crane alignment gauge are used to squeeze the crane, stretching it and making it longer.

With either method, begin by removing the crane and cylinder from the revolver. Pull the crane from the cylinder. Unscrew the ejector rod, and pull the rod, centerpin and springs from the cylinder. Pull the ejector star out of the cylinder. As you take each part out, look at it closely to remember how it fits with the others.

For the first method, take one of your .002-inch Power crane bushings and drop it down into the cylinder center hole. Push it to the bottom and make sure it is flush. Put the ejector star back in the cylinder. Make sure the ejector star slides through the bushing without pushing it out of place.

Put the crane back into the cylinder, and put the crane

and cylinder into the frame. Attempt to close the cylinder. If you can close the cylinder, check endshake. Still there? Pull the cylinder apart and put another bushing in. If you need more than two .002 inch bushings, pull them out and put in a .004 bushing, then another .002. Continue putting in bushings and checking fit until you cannot close the cylinder. Pull the last .002 bushing out. You should be able to live with this fit. Reinstall the centerpin, ejector rod and their springs. Tighten the ejector rod. Check cylinder rotation. It should rotate smoothly, without binding.

If you find that a full stack of bushings eliminates endshake when the cylinder is closed, but that the cylinder no longer rotates easily, or, that when the cylinder rotates easily, you still have too much endshake, you'll have to do additional work. In these cases the fit needs .001 inch of adjustment. You can stone the crane's barrel end to gain this. Take the cylinder and crane out, pull the crane from the cylinder and use Dykem on the end of the crane barrel. If you have left the cylinder short one bushing, put that last one back and reassemble the cylinder.

Rotate the cylinder once. Pull the crane back out and look at the end of the barrel. Almost always, you will find that the Dykem on the crane barrel end has not been worn off evenly. One part of the end is higher. Carefully stone or file the bright spot where the Dykem was worn off. Apply more Dykem and when the Dykem is dry, try again. In a couple of tries, you should have the cylinder rotating smoothly and free of endshake. If you have filed religiously on your practice bar and have acquired a good touch, a single pass with the file will do the work of two, three or four passes with the stone. If you file too much, though, you will have to add another bushing to the stack.

Turn the crane swager until a line appears.

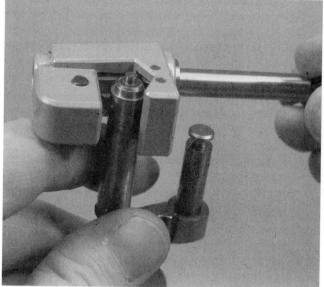

Place the Power crane swager on the crane near the end. Be sure the alignment tool is inserted, or you will collapse the crane.

The factory method does not depend on bushings. Slide the crane alignment tool into the crane barrel. This tool prevents the crane stretcher from crushing the barrel, and forces the crane to lengthen. If you forget the alignment gauge, you will squeeze the crane barrel, the ejector rod will not pass through the narrower section, and you'll have to send the revolver back to the factory. Put the crane stretcher over the crane barrel and tighten the adjustment nut. Rotate the crane stretcher once around the barrel.

Take the stretcher off, the alignment gauge out, and check the crane fit. If there is still endshake, put the alignment gauge back in, put the stretcher back on, and after tightening, give the stretcher one turn. Do not go too far, or you will have to stone the barrel end back. When you get to the point that the cylinder closes, but binds on turning, apply Dykem to the end of the crane barrel as before, and see if it has stretched unevenly. Stone it even, until the cylinder rotates freely.

With either method, once you have a cylinder that rotates freely without endshake, you must measure the clearance of the cylinder, front and back. Begin with the front. Reassemble the cylinder and re-install it in the frame.

With the feeler gauges, check the gap between the front of the cylinder and the back of the barrel. Removing endshake has expanded this gap. You have forced the cylinder to the rear, and kept it firmly there, when you removed the endshake. If the endshake you removed was .002 inch, then that is the theoretical amount you increased the barrel gap. The factory specifications for the minimum gap have been constant for decades: it cannot be less than .003 inches for continued reliable function. Less than this, and the powder residue buildup on the front of the cylinder and back of the barrel will cause the cylinder to bind. The maximum has varied. An S&W factory representative once (back in the mid-1980s) informed me that a gap less than .013 inches was acceptable. I told him in indignation that if he shipped that revolver back to me with a gap of .012 inches, both the customer and I would reject it and send it right back to him. It showed up with a gap of .006.

S&W now considers a gap of .003 to .007 inches perfect. If you set back your endshake and the gap falls in this range you are going to be a happy shooter, indeed. Up to .010 inch you will still do fine, although the blast of powder out of the sides of the gap can scorch your shooting bench or mats. Beyond .010 inch, you will find that other shooters may object to the blast, and they may experience particles being blown their way from your now-excessive gap. A revolver with so many rounds through it that you had to remove endshake and ended up with a gap this large, probably has serious wear in the forcing cone. In this case, you must set the barrel back, a job covered in Chapter 20.

Removing endshake does not always increase cylinder gap. After all, if there was .007 inch (to pick a number at random) of gap, and your cylinder had .005 of endshake, it was simply flopping back and forth in the amount of space it had before it would touch the rear of the barrel. When you reduce the endshake to zero, you simply restore the pre-existing .007 gap.

Now measure the rear of the cylinder. If you are using headspace gauges, the cylinder should close and rotate on all the chambers, with the "go" gauge in place. It should not close or rotate on any chamber with the "no-go" gauge in place. Without headspace gauges the job is a bit more difficult. Measure the rims of a bunch of de-primed cases, and find six that are the same thickness. Put these in the cylinder, and then rotating each chamber in line, measure with your feeler gauges. The total of case rim thickness and feeler gauge you can fit between the rim and the firing pin plate must not exceed the maximum headspace figure. The .38 Special, for example, has an allowable headspace range of .060 to .066 inches. If you have a case with a rim of .061 inch, you must not be able to fit more than a .005 feeler gauge between the case and the firing pin plate. This hardly ever happens. Usually, when you remove endshake you end up with a headspace range of .059 to .063 inches. Since the cartridge rims are slightly undersize, .056 to .060 inches, things work out fine. You just want to measure to be sure.

REMOVING FROZEN SCREWS

If you work in firearms long enough, you will run into screws that refuse to budge. With the correct screwdriver and the proper force, a screw should move. If it doesn't, stop. Go through this checklist: Is the screw a properly fitting screw? When was the last time this screw was moved? Has Loctite been applied? If you don't know, is it a screw that is likely to be locked in place? (The most common places you will run into screws locking in place will be on scope mounts. People who don't know how to properly tighten a screw will use Loctite when it's not needed.)

You must proceed with caution or you will mar or strip the screw slot, making a difficult job that much more difficult. Do not let anything slip. The screw or even the firearm will be damaged. In extreme cases you can hurt yourself.

Double-check that you are using a properly fitting screwdriver. If the screw is locked in placed with Loctite, use a propane torch to break down the Loctite. You must be careful. The strongest grades of Loctite will withstand 400 degrees Fahrenheit. At 600 degrees you will heat-damage the bluing, but the steel itself will not be harmed.

If the screw is frozen, but not locked in with Loctite, heat will have no effect. Put the firearm on your bench so the screw is level, and place a drop of penetrating oil, such as Liquid Wrench, on the screw head. Let the oil work into the screw for an hour, a day, or a week, if you can. Now try again with a screwdriver.

Some people prefer to work horizontally, others vertically. I'm a vertical person. I set the handgun on top of the padded vise, with the jaws open enough to let the frame fit in the droop of the padding. I hold the screwdriver vertically and place it into the slot. My chin rests against the end of the screwdriver's handle while I use both hands to turn the screwdriver. In this way I can exert maximum force and still feel for any movement of the screw. The screw usually lets go with a small snap. Sometimes it doesn't. A variation of this involves the drill press. Clamp the firearm to the drill press table. Put a driver bit that fits the screw in the drill press chuck. Make sure the drill press is not just turned off, but unplugged. Lower the drill press head, line the blade of the screwdriver up with the slot. Using the drill press to keep the screwdriver blade firmly in the screw slot, turn the drill chuck by hand. You can also, if there is room, get a wrench on he screwdriver shaft, for extra leverage. If the screw is completely immovable, or the screw slot has already been damaged enough that you cannot get the screwdriver to purchase, you must now resort to extreme measures.

EXTREME MEASURE #1: RE-CUT THE SCREW SLOT

Position a cutoff wheel in your Dremel tool. Grind the wheel down to a diameter small enough that you can re-cut the screw slot without touching the frame of the firearm or the base of the scope mount. This method works better with large screws than with small.

EXTREME MEASURE #2: DRILL THE SCREW

Clamp the handgun in your drill press. DO NOT attempt this with a hand-held variable speed drill. If you simply attempt to drill, the drill will flex against the screw slot, "walk" and drill places you don't want drilled. Clamp the handgun in your drill press. Use only a center drill. Drill the center of the screw down just far enough to drill off the head. You do not have to match the drill to the screw head diameter. So long as the drill is larger than the threaded portion of the screw, when you get down to the threads the head will come off. This method is most useful when the firearm is plated, or the part being held by the screw is aluminum.

You can now remove whatever the screw was holding on, and the screw shaft will turn out easily with a pair of pliers.

EXTREME MEASURE #3: WELDING

Take the firearm to your welder. (And for goodness sake, let him know you are coming, and why!) He can build up a post of weld on the screw, and then either weld a section of welding rod to the stub, or weld a nut to the post. Either way, the screw will turn out, and it will be intact. The screw, having been welded on its head, can be turned, polished, and have a new slot cut. You won't need to replace the screw. What you will need to do is repair anything damaged by the heat of the welding process. Any bluing or plating will be torched off around the screw. If the screw was holding down something made of aluminum, the torch will have destroyed it.

STUCK CYLINDERS: UNSCREWED EJECTOR RODS

Very rarely the cylinder on a revolver won't open. Sometimes it won't even rotate. A squib round may have stopped right in the forcing cone, jamming the cylinder. To check, first look at the gap between the cylinder and the barrel. If there is a bullet across the gap, use your range rod to force it back into the chamber. Now you can open the cylinder, remove that cartridge and the others, and never, ever, use that brand of reloaded ammunition again. (In ever instance I've seen of this, it was a case of reloads, not factory ammo, that caused the problem.)

When the cylinder jams on a Smith and Wesson revolver, it could be that the ejector rod has unscrewed itself from the ejector star, and now the additional length will not allow the front end of the rod to clear the front locking bolt. Push the cylinder latch forward and look at the forward end of the ejector rod. The centerpin will still be recessed in the end of the ejector rod. Unfortunately, the ejector rod sometimes unscrews when the revolver is loaded. You must exercise extreme caution!

The messy and unprofessional method of screwing the rod back is to reach in with a small screwdriver and rotate the rod. This mars the knurling on the rod's end.

Instead, take your chamber scraper, and wedge the sharp end of it into the gap between the ejector rod and barrel. With your feeler gauges, reach under the cylinder and push the locking bolt down out of its slot in the cylinder. You can now rotate the cylinder, and screw the ejector rod back in.

A complication: Smith and Wesson has changed its mind about whether the threads on the ejector rod should be right-hand threads or left-hand. There is a chart, but it is easier to simply try one direction and then the other. If you rotate the cylinder until it stops, but it still won't open, you went the wrong way. Wedge the scraper on the other side of the ejector rod, and rotate the cylinder the other way. Now, when it stops

rotating, you should be able to open it.

If the cylinder was loaded, remove the cartridges. Unscrew the ejector rod completely. Degrease the threads. Put at least two EMPTY cases in the cylinder, more if you have them, to support the extractor star. Screw the ejector rod back into the cylinder, and tighten it as tight as you can with your bare hands. Do not use Loctite. Do not use a pair of pliers. If experience teaches you that your hand strength is not sufficient to tighten the rod against future loosening, buy a rod-tightening tool. The tool is an aluminum cylinder with a hole though it and a locking screw on the hole. Slide the tool over the ejector rod, tighten the screw, and using the tool as a wrench, tighten the ejector rod. Again, use support cases to take the strain off the extractor star, and do not use Loctite.

To screw a loosened ejector rod back into the cylinder, wedge the front of the rod. Slip a feeler gauge between the locking bolt and the cylinder locking slot. Rotate the cylinder to tighten the rod.

REPAIRING/REPLACING REAR SIGHT BLADES

If you drop your revolver, odds are whatever part of it hits the ground first will be marred. If the sights hit first, you will bend or break the blade. Since adjustable rear sights are more fragile than fixed rear sights, dropping can damage the entire rear sight assembly.

If the assembly is damaged, replace the whole thing. Remove the screw on the front of the sight assembly and slide the sight out backwards. To put the new assembly in, slide the sight foot on the bottom of the assembly into the slot milled into the top of the frame. You need to watch the foot as you slide it. Because it is square, it often needs some fussing before it will fit. Tighten the front screw down. Take your revolver to the range, and zero in the sights.

If only the blade is damaged you can replace it without having to buy a whole new assembly. You'll need a new

Modify a spare screwdriver to fit the rear sight locking nut.

Hold the lock nut with the pronged screwdriver while you unscrew with the regular screwdriver.

With the lock nut free, pull it out of the sight.

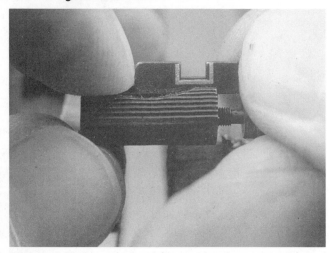

Keep your fingers over the plunger and spring as you slide the sight out.

The rear sight assembly on a Smith & Wesson adjustable sight. The largest part is half an inch long. If you drop the spring or plunger, or allow them to leap to freedom, you will have a devil of a time finding them.

blade and three screwdrivers. The first, an adjustment screwdriver, must fit the windage adjustment screw properly. The second, a small eyeglass screwdriver, will re-stake the sight-locking nut at the very end of the process. You must buy these two screwdrivers. The third screwdriver fits the sight-locking nut. You can buy or make this third screwdriver. I made mine 25 years ago, and it has served me through more than 100 rear sight repairs.

To make one, take a medium screwdriver, and grind or file the blade to a thickness of .045 inches and a width of .165 inches. Now clamp the screwdriver in your vise with only the tip sticking out, and with a cutoff wheel in your Dremel tool, grind the center out of the blade. Check the fit as you go, as you do not have a whole lot of leeway here. You will end up with a horned, or two-tipped screwdriver. The two tips will fit into the slots of the sight-locking nut, and over the sight screw that protrudes from the nut. Take the screwdriver out of the

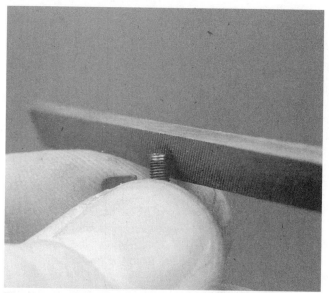

File the end of the shaft to remove the staked portion of threads. If you do not, you will not be able to either screw the blade on, or install the lock nut.

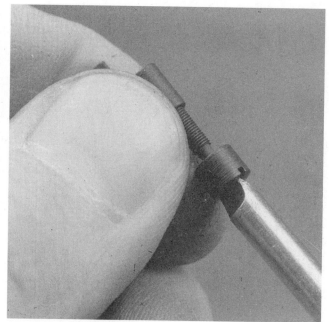

Screw the adjustment screw into the blade.

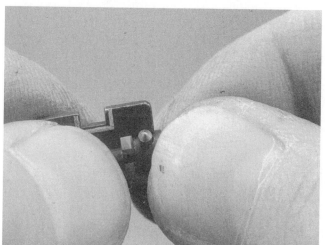

Place the spring and plunger into their hole in the shaft.

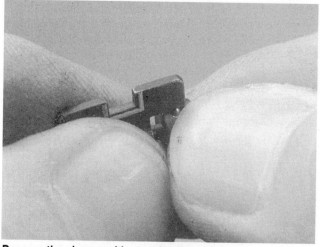

Depress the plunger with your thumbnail and rotate the nut until the plunger is held in place by the blade.

Slide the blade assembly into the housing.

Press the lock nut against the shaft and turn the screw just enough to get the nut started on the threads.

Hold the adjustment lock nut in place while you turn the adjustment screw.

vise, put your padding back in, and put the unloaded revolver in the vise.

There are two methods of removing the old sight blade and replacing it. The factory method destroys and discards all the internal sight parts. Those parts cost money, and the method is wasteful when the only one broken is the blade. My method only requires a new blade.

Place the modified screwdriver in the left side of the sight locking nut and the regular screwdriver in the adjustment slot on the right. Hold the modified screwdriver tight, and back the adjustment screw out. In three or four counterclockwise turns, you will have turned the locking nut free. Stop. Switch to the regular screwdriver to unscrew and remove the locking nut.

The adjustment screw has a detent spring and plunger, which cause the clicks you feel every time you adjust your sights. You must find the plunger. Rotate the adjustment screw. Look to the right of the blade. The plunger will come into view through the slot. When it does, stop. From the left side, push the adjustment screw out of the sight body, and use your fingertips to keep the plunger from escaping.

Pull the plunger and its spring out of the adjustment screw. Set them aside. To secure the screw to the locking nut, the factory stakes the end of the screw. You must remove these swollen threads. Bevel the end of the screw with your file, until the threads are gone. Now you can remove the adjustment screw from the broken blade. Screw the adjustment screw into the new blade. If you are using a white outline rear blade, the screw goes into the blade from the right.

Rotate the screw into the blade until the plunger hole can pass under the end of the blade. Insert the detent spring and plunger into the hole, and turn the screw so the blade holds the plunger in place. This way you will not have to compress the spring and plunger at the same time you insert the screw and blade into the sight body.

Insert the screw and blade and push them all the way to the left. Start the locking nut onto the end of the screw. Use the modified screwdriver to turn the locking nut down until it contacts the sight body, and then back it out one-quarter turn.

Take the revolver out of the vise, and lay it on the bench on its right side. For support, put a copper, brass or plastic block under the adjustment screw. Don't use steel, as it may peen the sight slot. With the eyeglass screwdriver, stake the ends of the adjustment screw into the slots of the locking nut. Pick the revolver up and

The replaced sight, with the adjustment shaft re-staked.

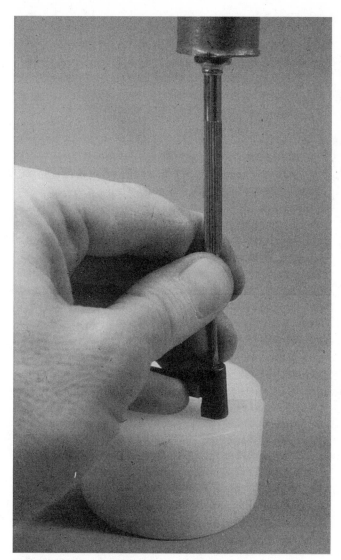

Use an eyeglass screwdriver or a tapered punch ground to a flat tip to stake the adjustment lock nut to the adjustment shaft.

use the regular screwdriver to adjust the sights. Watch the locking nut. If the screw moves and the nut doesn't rotate with it, your staking was not strong enough. Line the slots up with the stake marks, and stake again. When the locking nut rotates with the adjustment screw, you are done.

The factory method? Turn the adjustment screw counterclockwise until the broken sight bottoms out on the left. Continue turning until you break the screw. Turn the locking nut to unscrew the screw shaft from the blade, and pull the broken screw out from the left. Use the now-loose blade to push the adjustment screw head out of the sight body. Buy and assemble a new screw, blade, locking nut, spring and plunger into the sight body.

HOW THEY WORK AND WHAT TO LOOK FOR

The action of most pistols is simple: They are a balance of Newtonian forces. When you fire the round, the cartridge case is almost instantly pressurized, and that pressure forces the bullet to leave. (Which is, after all, the purpose of the pistol.) According to Newton, every action has an equal and opposite reaction. The weight and speed of the bullet (and powder) leaving the handgun are going to be balanced by the weight and speed of the handgun going in the opposite direction.

However, the handgun is not a single unit (except for a T/C contender) and that is where the fun begins. Each part is accelerated in turn according to how much energy it takes to move it. A heavier slide moves slower, a lighter one faster. Add weight to the barrel, and you slow down the pre-unlocking motion without changing the post-unlocking motion much.

Let's take two examples, common pistols that all of you will have at least one of: the 1911 and the Glock. The initial reaction to firing of both is the same, the pistol

jolts back into your hand. Recoil velocity and momentum of the bullet and powder gases must be matched by recoil velocity and masses of the pistol and your hand-arm-shoulder (until the energy is dissipated.)

But a planned thing happens: The slide and barrel are free to move on top of the frame. As the energy is being absorbed by the pistol and dissipated into your hands and arms, some of that energy is used to move the slide and frame. There is additional resistance to opening/ slide movement offered by the hammer. The spring tension of the hammer in its down position (obviously not a factor in Glocks) adds resistance to slide movement. Some pocket pistols use the force of a heavier than normal hammer spring to control slide movement on a pistol that would otherwise have a light slide. And blowback pistols obviously use hammer resistance to control slide movement.

The slide and barrel move backwards on the frame until the unlocking cam or link engages. On the 1911,

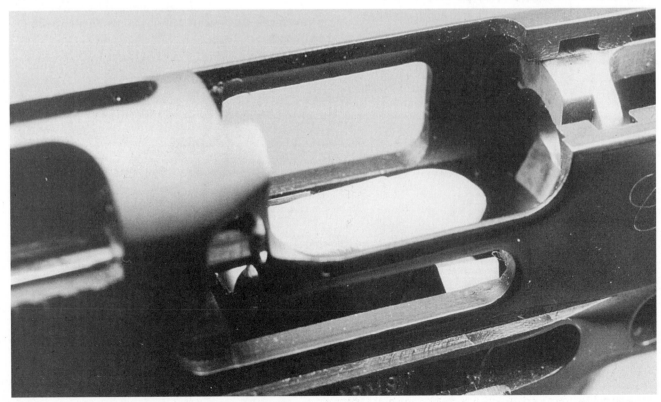

Feeding in the pistol. The slide pushes the round forward.

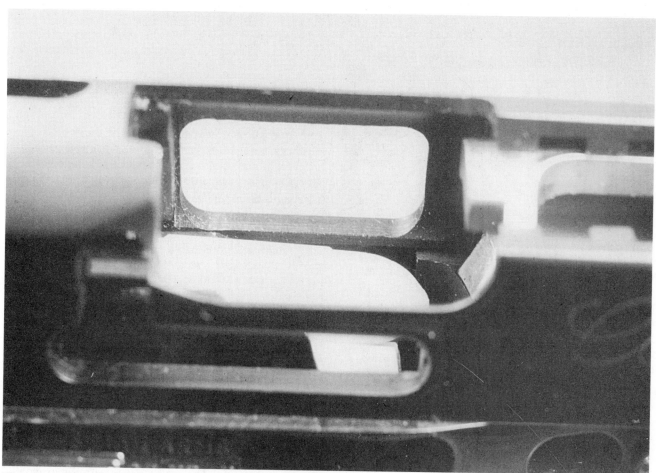

When the slide first pushes it, the round noses down to the feed ramp.

The ramp guides the round up until it strikes the top of the chamber.

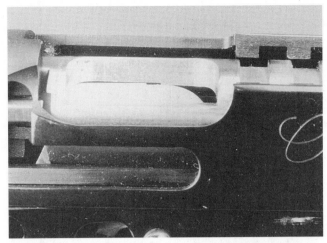

Until the round is fully forward, and the slide begins pushing the barrel towards lockup.

the link pulls the barrel out of the slide. On the Glock (and many other designs derived from the same Browning source, the P-35) the barrel cam strikes the locking block, and the angled surfaces cause the barrel to be pulled down from the slide.

From that point back, the slide is cycling against the force of the recoil spring. The last portion of the felt recoil is the slide striking the frame. In a pistol with a heavy slide, the impact can be significant. If the slide is light, or the recoil force almost dissipated before impact, the stop may not be noticeable. Slide mass also has an effect on this force. A light slide will have less force when it bottoms out, but it will have a necessarily higher slide velocity. At a high enough velocity, the sights may suffer. (That was a problem my friend Brian Enos had with his EAA pistols: the slide velocity was so high that adjustable sights could not survive the experience. But I digress.)

As soon as the slide clears the top round in the magazine, that round pops up to the feed lips. Prior to the slide clearing it, the round had been held down in the magazine by the center portion of the slide. It, and the others in the magazine, have also been bouncing back and forth, as well as rattling up and down, due to the effects of recoil. If the recoil spring is too heavy, the slide may be propelled forward before the round is lifted high enough, or settled firmly against the feed lips. Yes, it is possible to have too heavy a recoil spring, as well as too light a magazine spring.

Moving forward, the round is stripped out of the magazine by the slide. Some pistols are very easy on the round. The Beretta M-92, for example, holds the round quite high, and you could almost use a barrel lacking a feed ramp. The 1911 is hard on rounds. The round strikes the feed ramp, gets cammed up, snapped out of the feed lips, and then cammed up and over the other way from its previous motion, over the corner between feed ramp on the barrel and the chamber.

Once the round is going forward, the slide contacting the barrel moves the barrel forward on its cams or links to close and lock.

THE SINGLE-ACTION REVOLVER

THEY MIGHT ALL LOOK THE SAME, BUT THEY ARE NOT AT ALL THE SAME

Anyone who has ever seen one of the thousands of Westerns turned out by movie studios and television production houses has seen a single-action revolver in use. Originally designed by Samuel Colt in the 1830s, the single-action revolver was a technical tour-de-force. Before Colt, pistols were either single-shot, requiring the shooter to reload after each round, or, even more complicated, not just single-shot but single-shot/single barrel — with each separate shot requiring its own separate barrel (a design known as the pepperbox). Needless to say, such a pistol was very clumsy, heavy and expensive to use. And as a method of defense, neither type of pistol was very practical. Samuel Colt's single-action revolver forever changed that. With its advent any man or woman could possess a light, durable package that was not just easy to use, but extremely useful against attackers.

Despite drawbacks that were obvious from the start, single-action revolvers reigned supreme for decades. In the 1950s they even enjoyed a renaissance that continues to this day, and the renewed interest has helped work out some of the safety problems with the original design.

What were the drawbacks? Most significant was safety, for under certain conditions the revolver could fire seemingly at will. The mechanism itself was fragile, containing parts and springs that failed under minor stresses. Not counting an accidental discharge, there was no way to fire the revolver without first thumb-cocking the hammer. And, because the cylinder stays in the frame for loading and unloading, they were clumsy to use.

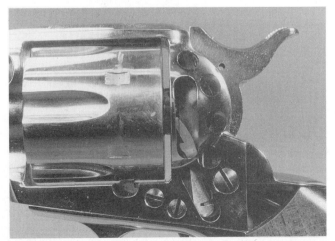

The first notch, or so-called safety notch of a single-action revolver holds the firing pin away from the primer. Don't trust it! Load old-style single-action revolvers so the hammer rests on an empty chamber. A blow to the hammer can fire the round if it is under the firing pin.

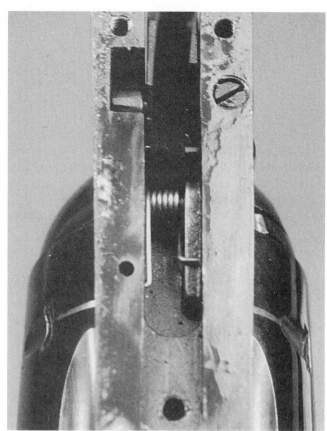

The flat two-leaf spring in the Colt is replaced with a coil spring in the Old Model Rugers and a spring and plunger in the New Model Rugers.

Unloading and reloading each chamber one at a time is a fussy operation even at a range. In the cold, or dark, or under stress, it becomes very difficult. Cocking the hammer to fire each round is a slow method of shooting. Neither of these problems, though, was serious enough in the 19th century to send people back to old single-shot pistols or get them itching for even better guns. Instead, they found an easy way around both difficulties:

they simply carried a second, loaded revolver. Far from being the mark of a paid gunslinger, carrying two guns was the act of a prudent man.

Despite its apparent sturdy looks, the design of a single-action revolver contains some fragile parts. The trigger/cylinder lock spring is a flat piece of spring steel that ends in two fingers, where it is prone to breaking. Replacing a spring is not a big deal, generally, except that with this particular one the operation requires removing and replacing no fewer than eight screws. Another flat spring, the hand spring (so named because it presses the hand into the ratchet, and its base is staked into the hand), breaks easily. When it does, or when it simply comes loose, the hand will not bear against the cylinder, and the cylinder won't rotate. The so-called "safety" notch on the hammer tends to break at its shoulder. When this happens the hammer rests directly on the cartridge beneath it, and the revolver will fire as a result of a sharp blow.

With his internal redesign of the single-action revolver in the early 1950s, Bill Ruger replaced the flat springs with coil springs. These springs do not break or wear out. There are, however, still an awful lot of screws in there. There's only so much anyone can do and still keep the flavor of the revolver.

With proper care you can expect years of use from even the fragile Colt or its clones. But if you abuse them, they complain. Fanning is a major source of trouble. We all know what fanning is: on his fast-draw, the movie hero holds the trigger down and slaps at the hammer with his left hand. Fanning is very hard on the revolver, battering the locking bolt and slots and peening the hand and ratchet. Along with fast-draw, fanning is also a major risk factor for dropping the revolver, which is really hard on it. Dropping a revolver can bend the barrel, sight, and cylinder pin or grip straps. It can also bend or break the screws that hold the grip frame to the receiver.

The main problem with an old-style single-action six-

The Ruger firing pin is in the frame.

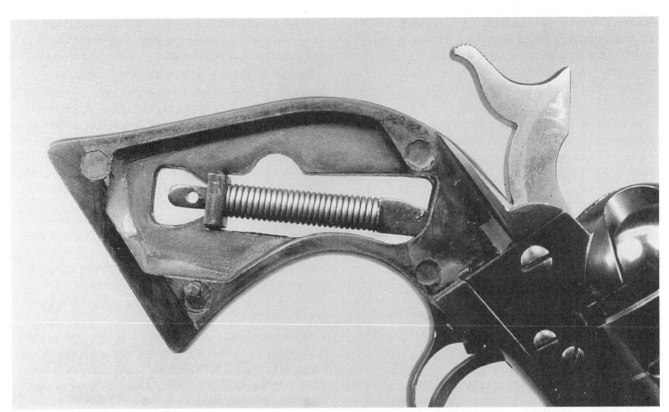

The Ruger re-design of the single-action revolver replaced the flat mainspring with a coil spring that works over a shaft.

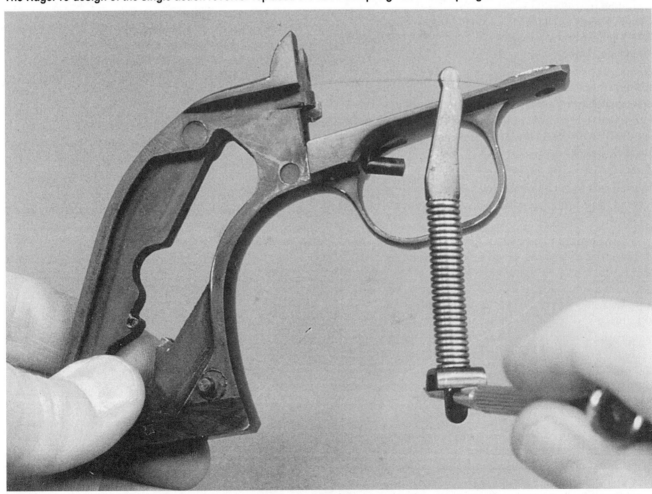

After cocking the mainspring, place a punch or small screwdriver through the hole in the shaft. Remove the five screws, and the grip frame comes off in one piece. The plunger in the trigger guard is the trigger return spring and plunger.

shooter, then and now, is safety. If the hammer is rested not on an empty chamber but on a loaded round, any blow to the hammer can cause the revolver to fire. There is a simple solution. Rest the hammer on an empty chamber, effectively turning your six-shooter into a five-shooter.

As legions of cowboys learned, it doesn't take much force to set off that 12 o'clock round in a fully loaded six-shooter. The classic "cowboy limp" was often the result of simply saddling a horse. The cowboy would pick up the saddle, swing the nearside stirrup over the top and then place the saddle on the horse. Tossing the stirrup up onto the saddle allowed him access to the cinch. If the horse moved while the cowboy was bent over tightening the cinch, that stirrup could slide off the saddle and fall right onto the cowboy's exposed hammer spur. The rest would be painful history. Stirrup would hit hammer, hammer would discharge primer, exploded primer would send bullet down barrel, and bullet could hit cowboy in leg or foot. With bad luck, lack of medicine, or a long ride back to help, the cowboy could die from such an accident.

The essential "unsafeness" of single-action revolvers is so well known to some that it earned a mention in John Wayne's last movie, *The Shootist*, when our hero told his would-be protégé that revolvers were only carried safely with five rounds. Unfortunately, this safety drill was not so familiar to the numbers of people who were buying single-action revolvers in the 1950s and 1960s during the cowboy movie-inspired fast-draw era. Competition required single-action revolvers, and since there were six chambers in the revolver, many shooters assumed they could load all six. Not so. Loud and unexpected "Bangs!" taught them quickly: always load five, and only five.

The traditional method of making an SA revolver safe was to load one round, skip the next chamber, load four more, cock the hammer and lower it. If you haven't missed the count, the hammer now rested on an empty chamber.

Bill Ruger wanted a better way, so when he redesigned the mechanism he moved the firing pin from the hammer to the frame. He lightened the firing pin, and spring-loaded it away from the primer. The redesigned firing pin was so light that its own weight could not overcome the spring and strike the primer, even if the revolver is roughly handled. This was not enough. The Old Model SA Rugers could still fire inadvertently. So, in the second redesign, he cut away the face of the hammer. This change rendered the revolver inoperable, as the hammer could no longer engage the firing pin. To make it possible to fire the revolver, Ruger then attached a transfer bar to the trigger. When pressed, the trigger moves the transfer bar into the gap between hammer and firing pin, filling it and allowing the force from the blow of the hammer to transfer to the firing pin. As soon as the trigger is released, the transfer bar slides out from between the hammer and firing pin, breaking the connection.

These improved SA revolvers are called "New Model"

Rugers. You can tell at a glance if a Ruger is a New Model. Just look for the cross pins with which Bill Ruger replaced the hammer and trigger screws. No screw slots? It is a New Model, and safe to carry with six.

As an even more impressive design improvement, Bill Ruger figured out how to retrofit safety bars in his earlier revolvers. If you have a single-action Ruger revolver that pre-dates the safety bar design, you can send it back to Ruger for a free installation of the new parts. Other than allowing you to load six rounds safely, the new parts don't change your SA's function, they don't alter its look, and you even get your old parts back. If your revolver is of some historical significance, you can always reinstall the old parts. To check an Old Model Ruger for the transfer bar, cock the hammer on an unloaded revolver and look into the hammer slot in the frame. The flat safety bar will be obvious.

Current production single-action revolvers fall into two groups. The first are the Colts and all their clones, including the early Rugers that have not had the safety bar retrofit. None of these revolvers have a transfer bar and if fully loaded the hammer sits right on the primer of the 12 o'clock round. Even the Italian clones, shipped with Federally mandated mechanical safeties, are not safe with six rounds. I don't trust them because the safeties only work if you move the centerpin, or shift a stud on the hammer, or some such other safety mechanism. If you forget to work the new parts, the revolver is still unsafe. My personal rule with any of these revolvers is to load only five rounds in them. I never break this rule. The consequences are just too serious.

The second group are all Rugers built since the "New Model" design change, and old Rugers retrofitted with the safety bar. These can be carried with all six rounds chambered.

One nostalgic loss in the New Model Ruger was the loss of the "four clicks." In order, they were: The so-called safety notch, which isn't, and shouldn't be trusted as such, the unloading notch, the locking bolt clicking back into place against the cylinder, and the hammer full-cock notch. The New Model has two clicks: the locking bolt snapping against the cylinder, and the hammer going to full cock. Ah, the sound of progress.

By the turn of the century handgun designers had figured out how to overcome the shortcomings of the SA revolver, and what they came up with we know as the double-action revolver. Iver Johnson had an advertising campaign entitled "hammer the hammer," showing someone pounding on the hammer spur of one of his revolvers with a claw or ball-peen hammer, without firing the round under the revolver's hammer. Even so, for decades after double-action revolvers came into use, shooters carried their revolvers with the hammer down on an empty chamber. The Pennsylvania State Police even went so far as to make it regulation. Through the 1950s their officers carried their Colt double-action revolvers with only five rounds, despite being safe with six.

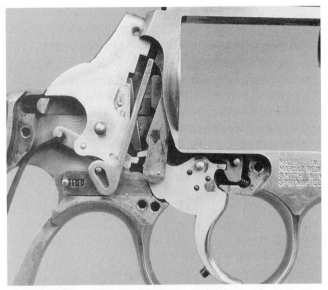

The lockwork of a Smith & Wesson revolver.

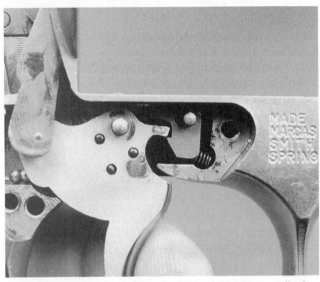

At the beginning of the action, the front of the trigger pulls the cylinder bolt down, releasing the cylinder to rotate.

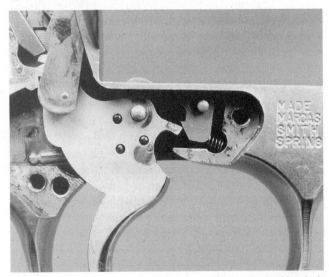

Once the hand has begun rotating the cylinder, the locking bolt pops back up, ready for the next locking slot of the cylinder.

DOUBLE-ACTION REVOLVERS:

IT'S ALL IN THE TRIGGER

A DA revolver uses linkage somewhat different than the SA does. The double-action revolver in single-action mode is pretty much the same as the SA revolver, with the locking block usually being out in front of the trigger rather than alongside. The hammer cams the trigger, unlocking the cylinder bolt. Then the hand turns the cylinder. The locking bolt is quickly released, and rides along the outside of the cylinder until it encounters the locking slot. If correctly timed, the hand stops rotating the cylinder as the locking bolt drops into the slot. Immediately after, the single-action sear clears the single-action notch, and you can stop cocking. Pulling the trigger drops the hammer without releasing anything else.

In double-action mode, things are a bit different. The trigger starts three operations almost simultaneously. It releases the locking bolt, lifts the hand, and contacts the double-action sear. The unlocked bolt is released as soon as the hand has lifted the cylinder past the initial locking slot. (If it doesn't, the bolt snaps back into the initial slot, and the cylinder won't rotate.) The released bolt rides on the cylinder until it encounters the locking slot. The hand stops rotating the cylinder just as the bolt drops in the slot. And then the trigger rotates out of contact with the double-action sear, dropping the hammer.

A problem revolvers fired a lot in DA-only mode might have that would not be uncovered is poor carry-up. The inertia of the DA rotation will carry a cylinder past where the hand might lift it. If you shoot a very slow DA trigger pull, the hand might not lift the cylinder fully to the locking position, the cause of which can be 1) the hand is too short, 2) the ratchet worn, 3) the sideplate loose, or 4) any combinations of the preceding. Lack of carry up is why you check DA revolvers with a very slow DA trigger pull, and lightly dragging a thumb on the cylinder.

BUYING USED

There is nothing wrong with buying a used handgun. Assuming, of course, that there is nothing wrong with the used gun you are buying. But how to tell? The first thing to do is buy from a reputable gun shop, one with a clear return policy. The best chance of buying a good used gun is from a shop with a gunsmith in residence. With a 'smith on premises, you can be pretty sure every used gun that came in went through his hands. And any used one you buy can be returned for an inspection to see if the problem you are encountering is real, or caused by an outside force.

The process is simple: look, feel and listen. Look for things out of place; wear that is odd, or signs of abuse. Feel for the way it functions, compared to a new model or a known-good used one. (Obviously, experience

No external safeties, only a magazine release and a slide stop lever. This is a "Double Action Only" pistol available from Smith & Wesson. Think of it as a magazine-fed revolver.

When you buy a new handgun now, it will come with some sort of warranty. If a part breaks, and the manufacturer is at fault, and you haven't modified it, you'll get it fixed. Put a couple of hundred rounds through a brand-new handgun before starting to work on it. If anything breaks, it is still under warranty.

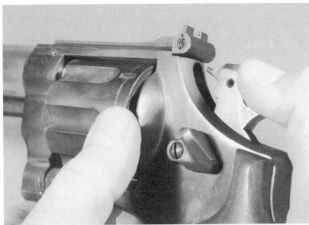

Test the cylinder carry-up by using your thumb to drag the cylinder. If the hammer cock doesn't bring the cylinder completely up to lock, then you need to advance the timing a bit.

helps, and already owning or having owned a similar handgun also helps.) Listen to the noise of the springs, the clicks, the slide cycling. They can all tell you something.

And ask. What does the owner/merchant know about it? Its history, previous owners, performance or reputation? Buying a competition gun can be good, and it can be bad. Was it the backup gun of a Grand Master that spent most of its time lounging in his range bag waiting its turn? (Can you say "tuned, low-mileage cream puff?") Or was it the experimental subject of an aspiring gunsmith or competitive shooter? (Can you say "ridden

hard and hung up wet?") Be careful, ask, listen, and get the return policy in writing.

ETIQUETTE OF BUYING USED

There are a few things you have to know about buying a used firearm. First of all, remember that until you hand over the money, it is someone else's firearm you're handling. It is entirely within the performance parameters of many handguns to be dry-fired from now until the end of time and suffer no damage. However, some people don't believe it and will be very grumpy if you dry-fire their handgun. Ask before you dry-fire. If they refuse, then you have to either move on, or do your pre-purchase due diligence without dry-firing.

Ask before you disassemble, as, again, some people just don't like having their handgun yanked apart. They may be cranky, and they may simply have had too many bad experiences with people who didn't know what the frak they were doing.

Also, keep in mind that everything is negotiable. Point out details that ngiht lower the price. If the price can't be lowered, ask about extra magazines, speedloaders, ammo, holsters, anything that improves the deal for you. Properly done, a purchase and negotiation is a social event, and not a dental visit.

BUYING A USED 1911

When you're considering a used 1911, start with a good visual inspection. Has the exterior been abused? Hammer marks or rough file marks on the outside

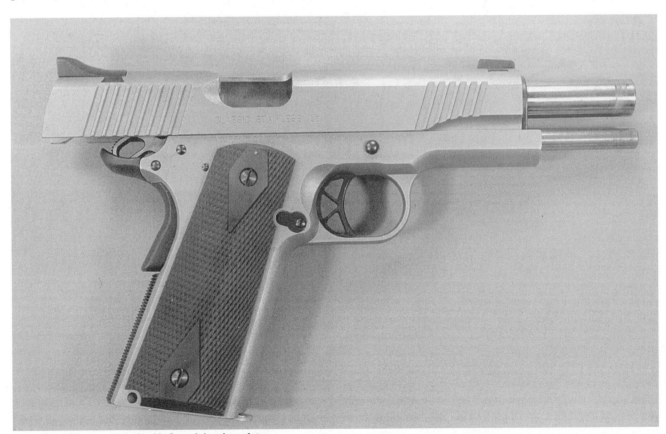

Here is the Kimber, with the McCormick grip safety.

Some "problems" are cosmetic. This crack in a 1911 has been the same size for over 10 years and 5,000 rounds. There isn't any real need to weld it up and re-finish the frame.

should make you wonder how careful the previous owner was with the inside. If the original blued surface is now gray from years of use and carry, but the owner never dropped it and fired it seldom, you have a great opportunity. The looks are likely to bring the price down, but mechanically it can be just fine. If it is a pistol used in competition you might be able to find some answers by asking about its history with other competitors. Did the previous owner have a reputation of always shooting unreliable guns? Or were his pistols always reliable, just ugly?

After the visual inspection, start checking the operation. If you haven't already done so, make sure the pistol is unloaded, and tell the clerk at the store that you want to perform some safety checks. Cock the pistol and dry fire it. Was the trigger pull very light? A very light trigger pull will have to be made heavier to be safe and durable. Or was it very heavy? Did it feel as if it was crunching through several steps before it finished its job? A very heavy or gritty trigger pull will have to be made smoother and lighter.

Execute a "pencil test." Cock the pistol and drop a pencil down the bore, eraser end first. Point the pistol straight up, and dry fire it. The pencil should be launched completely out of the pistol. If it isn't, something is keeping the firing pin from its assigned duties. Find out what before you buy.

You must perform a mechanical safety test. Cock the hammer again and push the thumb safety on. Holding the pistol in a firing grip, press the trigger a bit harder than you would to fire it. Seven or eight pounds of pressure is sufficient. Let go of the trigger, and push the thumb safety off. Now hold the pistol next to your ear, and slowly draw the hammer back. You should not hear anything. If you hear a little "tink" when you draw back the hammer, the thumb safety is not engaging fully.

If you heard the "tink," here's what happened. When you pulled the trigger with the safety on, the sear moved a tiny amount until it came to bear against the safety lug. It shouldn't have moved at all. The hammer tension

kept the sear from moving back into position when you pushed the safety off, leaving the sear partially-bearing on the hammer hooks. When you held the pistol close to your ear and drew back the hammer, that tension on the sear was removed. The sear spring pushed the sear back in place, causing the tink you heard. If the hammer stayed cocked, the sear only moved a tiny amount. The fix is easy. What if you never got to the "tink?" If the hammer fell when the safety was pushed off, before you even tried to listen, the thumb safety fit is very bad and you will have to buy and fit a new safety. In the worst case, the hammer falls even when the safety is on. These also need a need thumb safety. Considering the amount of work needed, and the possibility of other things being badly fit, you might just want to pass on this particular 1911. Unless, of course, you can get it for a very good price, and want to do the work yourself anyway.

Next test the grip safety. Cock the hammer, and, holding the frame so you do not depress the grip safety, pull the trigger. Release the trigger, and, now grasping the pistol so you do depress the grip safety, hold the pistol up to your ear again and draw the hammer slowly back. If you hear that tink again, the grip safety is barely engaging. Look at the grip safety. Because some competitive shooters don't feel the need for one, they grind the

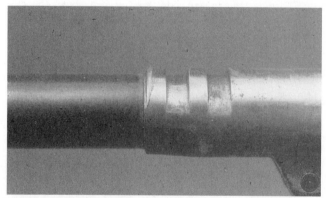

This is a soft, cheap barrel that was improperly fitted. The slide peened the barrel until the upset metal bound against the inside of the slide enough to crack the barrel on the bottom. Buy good parts and fit them properly.

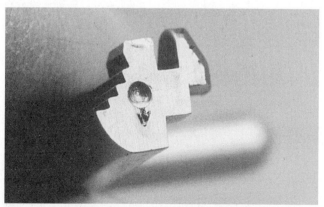

Custom guns will have custom features. Check to see that they are properly done. This slide stop has been dimpled for correct function, a sign of good work.

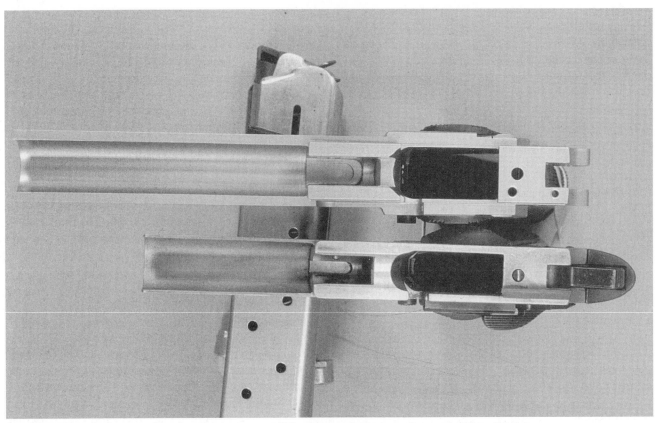

The STI frame has a longer, wider, heavier dust cover. This changes the balance for competition shooters.

The STI Short Block has all the hard work done. The slide, frame and barrel have all been fitted. You need to put sights and internals in it. A great deal, and a great pistol.

tip of the grip safety off where it blocks the trigger. If this has been done to the 1911 you're thinking of buying, you will have to have the tip welded back up, and fit it to the trigger. If the tip hasn't already been ground off, or otherwise altered, you're looking at an easy fix. It is probably just a simple mis-fit, which you can correct with careful peening.

The last test you need to perform is hammer/sear engagement, or hammer flick test. There's a good way and a bad way to perform this test. In the caveman days we would lock the slide open empty. Then we would release the hold-open lever and let the slide crash home on an empty chamber. This is more like abuse than a test, especially since it doesn't fairly test the hammer sear engagement. Continued "testing" this way can actually do harm to your hammer and sear. In the modern, improved "flick" test, you cock the hammer, grip the pistol so the grip safety is depressed, and hold down the thumb safety. With your other hand, flick the hammer back against the grip safety, and let the hammer go forward to sear engagement. This non-destructive test can be performed until the cows come home, or your fingers bleed, and will not harm the sear and hammer hooks. If, however, during this test the hammer falls — even once — the hammer/sear engagement will require work. You cannot depend on this pistol to stay cocked when firing. The pistol may simply require re-stoning the engagement surfaces, or it may require a new sear, or both new sear and hammer. Until you look at the engagement through a magnifier, there is no way to tell.

Aside from the grip safety check, which is unique to the 1911, these tests can be performed on any other pistol you might be considering for purchase, though double-action pistols require a modification of the thumb safety test. With the DA pistol unloaded and the hammer cocked, again place your pencil down the bore eraser end first. Point the cocked pistol up, push the hammer drop safety down to its safe position, and drop the hammer. The pencil had better not move at all. If it does, something is seriously wrong with the safety, and the future travel plans of that pistol include a trip to the factory. Push the safety off. With the muzzle pointing up, dry fire the pistol. Pick the pencil up off the floor, or investigate the firing pin's malfunction.

With the safety checks out of the way, look for signs of abuse or experimentation. Take the slide off the frame and look at the frame rails. Have they been peened to tighten the fit? Even an ugly peening job can be fine, if the parts have been lapped for a smooth fit. If you're looking at an after-market frame and slide combination like the Caspian, put the slide back on the frame without the barrel and recoil spring assembly. Such combinations left the manufacturer as a tight fit and were lapped to slide smoothly. If the pistol is now very loose, it has had many, many rounds through it. The barrel may need to be replaced. The price had better reflect this.

With the slide off, look at the feed ramp. Has it been polished? Polishing is fine. Has it been re-ground, altered

or subjected to an incorrect "feed" job? These alterations can be a problem. If the ramp has been incorrectly altered, the pistol will feed poorly, and if the top of the feed ramp has been rounded off, the pistol will not feed at all. Take the barrel and place it on the frame in its unlocked seat, ahead of the feed ramp. Push it all the way back into the cutout, and check the relationship of the barrel to the feed ramp. There should be a small gap between the bottom of the barrel and the top of the feed ramp. A gap of 1/32nd of an inch is about right. A smoothly rounded and blended fit is the indication of a bad feed job. Such a pistol will feed only with round-nose, full-metal-jacket ammunition, if at all. Anything else will hang up. The fix, which involves welding the frame and re-cutting the surfaces is expensive. Unless you can get the pistol for a song, pass on it.

Look closely at the barrel. The feed ramp of the barrel should not be altered, only polished. Ramping the barrel deeper into the chamber was a prehistoric method of ensuring reliable feeding, and is not an acceptable practice anymore. An over-ramped barrel has to be replaced. Look at the locking lugs. Are they clean and sharp? They should be. If they are rounded, or show a set-back shoulder or burred edge, the barrel was improperly fit to the slide. If only the barrel is damaged, a new barrel properly fitted will solve the problem. If the slide locking lugs are also damaged, then you have to replace the top end. Putting a new barrel into a slide that has rounded, set-back or otherwise damaged locking lugs will only damage the new barrel, wasting your money.

Look at the barrel bushing. Some bushings are cast of soft metal, and the locking lug will deform against the harder slide. If it hasn't already, then in short order the wear will harm accuracy. A new bushing solves this problem at low cost.

Are there cracks in the frame? Many shooters worry about visible cracks, though some do not matter. A crack in the dust cover over the recoil spring is not a concern unless it is extensive, or you are planning to mount a scope right there. This common crack results from contact between the top edge of the dust cover and

If at all possible, get a trial period on a used handgun. If it doesn't perform as advertised, return it.

the slide. Many shooters feel that since the stress between the dust cover and the slide has been relieved by the crack, any problem has been solved. If, however, you still want to eliminate the crack, you must first file down the top of the dust cover to keep it from contacting the slide. Then have the crack welded. Another common crack, through the left rail at the slide stop cutout, is so normal and harmless that Colt actually incorporated it into the design when they began machining the cutout hole completely through the rail.

BUYING A USED GLOCK

What with every police department on the planet going to the Glock (or so it seems) there are large numbers of used Glocks for sale everywhere. Every wholesaler flyer I get has used Glocks listed, sometimes pages of them. So, you're peering through the glass at your local gun shop, or cruising a gun show, and you see a used Glock offered at a good price. What to look for? First, give it a good visual external inspection. Look to see if there are any signs of abuse, neglect and/or experimentation. External abuse would be things like the corners of the slide being chewed up and or dented from being dropped. Dropping the slide when it is off the frame can bend the recoil spring retaining tab. Neglect would be rust (rare) or a cracked slide from too many hot reloads (even rarer). Experimentation would be something like the slide being machined to take some other sight system than the factory one. Or milled for ports other than factory. The good news is that the cracked slide might be replaced by the factory for free or at little cost. The other cosmetic problems or experimentation done by previous owners are items that Glock will likely leave you on your own cover. Glock isn't going to help you with a dropped slide, and the one that was machined will have a voided warranty. Don't worry about what sights might be on it; sights are cheap and easily replaced. At the current pricing, an armorer's cost for a new set of sights is only $5! You can get good replacements other than Glock polymer for around $20 to $30.

A scarred and chewed-up frame can be cleaned up but Glock won't be replacing it just because it got scraped along a curb during a fight. Glock will replace it, regardless of condition, if it is one of the E-series Glocks that were made from September 2001 through May 2002 that they deem needs replacing. If you aren't sure, give Glock a call. One way to tell is the serial number of the frame. The E series will be marked (as an example) EAA123US. If the frame has been recalled and replaced, the slide and barrel will still have the original serial number, while the frame will be marked "1EAA123US." The numeral 1 indicates replacement.

With the permission of the owner, cycle the slide and dry fire it. Try firing it without depressing the trigger safety. It should not fire. Try pulling the trigger normally and then hold it back and cycle the slide. Does the trigger return? If not, it may be due to a broken/bent trigger spring or a "trigger job" gone awry. The parts don't cost much, so bargain the price down as much as you can but don't expect the owner to budge much.

Disassemble and inspect the slide and barrel. Is the barrel clean? Un-marred? Look down the bore. Do you see dark rings? "Smoke rings" are bulges in the barrel from lodged bullets being shot free. A new barrel costs money. At the armorers cost, a Glock barrel runs $95 to $125, with compensated barrels running up to $140. Aftermarket Match barrels can run up to $200. If the barrel is bulged, bargain hard, for a replacement won't be cheap.

Look at the slide, in the breech face area. Inspect the area around the firing pin slot. In a very high-mileage 9mm, fed many rounds of +P or +P+ ammo (as some police departments use) you may find the area around the firing pin slot eroded or even peened back. The erosion comes from pierced or blown primers jetting hot gases back at and through the firing pin slot. In those you should check the firing pin to make sure it is in good shape. The peening comes from the high-pressure setback of the primer. The wall between the breechface and the firing pin tunnel isn't thick (it can't be) and the repeated hammering from a steady diet of +P or +P+ loads can peen it back. Yes, the Tenifer makes the slide hard, but the substrate isn't hard. If the area is too hard, it may break. If it is too soft, it may peen. It must keep Glock engineers awake at night, worrying about it.

If a Glock with a peened or eroded breechface still works fine (you won't know until you test-fire it), then you can use it. But the drag on the empty case from the primer expanding into the bulge or erosion can create malfunctions. Glock may or may not replace the slide. If they do, and they charge you, it can get expensive. The old armorer's manual listed slides and frames as parts that could be ordered. The new manual does not, so I cannot look up the expected price. You will know only after you ask Glock. Aftermarket slides can cost as much as the barrels do, up to $200. Check the underside of the slide for peening from impacts with the locking block. A small amount is OK, but very heavy peening indicates something is wrong. Peening happens mostly with the .40 Glocks, as they have a relatively high bullet mass/velocity ratio. 9mms rarely have it, and the 10mm/.45s do not show it much at all. Perhaps the previous owner fired a great many hot loads through it. Other parts of the Glock may have been stressed. Look at the front of the slide. The excessive recoil may have stressed the front of the slide where the recoil spring assembly bears on it. A crack there is very bad, and cannot be repaired. The slide must be replaced. Bargain the price down. Also, the slide is thin on the ejection port side, and a steady diet of +P or +P+ loads may have cracked it there. (If you're lucky, a peened breechface also has a cracked slide, and Glock will likely replace it at low or no cost. A bargain!)

If you have a Glock with a cracked slide, I'd suggest a letter and some photos first. If Glock is willing to replace the slide for free, ship it. If they want to charge you for it, find out how much. A replacement Caspian slide can be had for $140 for a G-17, and you may want to go that route if Glock will charge you more. But if they already have your pistol, and won't ship it back without repairing it, you won't be able to exercise the Caspian option.

Check the firing pin safety for function. Press the striker back, then try to push it forward. If it goes forward past the firing pin safety, the firing pin and its safety need inspection and replacement.

The extractor needs a look. A chipped extractor may not function 100 percent, but a replacement isn't very much, $10 at armorer's cost. What you may need is the armorer to replace it, as Glock needs to know serial number and caliber to use the correct one.

Look at the trigger parts. Black? Silver? Black is old and must be replaced, but Glock will do it for free. Check the trigger safety engagement. With the slide off, press the trigger bar forward, and listen for the safety clicking in place. While still pressing forward, pull the trigger and ease the bar back. If there is a problem, it may be very dirty. Then again, it may have been polished, ground, filed or otherwise experimented on. Internal parts for Glocks are inexpensive, easy to replace, and common. At a good enough bargain price you can replace all the guts and still be in for not much money.

Inspect the frame forward of the locking block. Gently flex the recoil spring housing right and left, up and down. Some guns, especially the major-caliber compacts and subcompacts, have been known to crack near where the serial number plate is inserted. A cracked frame will be replaced by Glock, but gives you an opportunity to bargain the price down. It also gives you an opportunity to create a collector's piece. If Glock returns the gun with a new serial number, keep the paperwork. You have a factory mis-match, and it may bring a bit of a premium at some future time. But only if you have the paperwork to prove it.

Recoil springs on Glocks don't give up the ghost very easily, so looking at the spring won't tell you much. Unless you have a Glock so old that it pre-dates the switch to the captured recoil spring assembly. (It probably has the old trigger parts, too.) A new recoil spring assembly is inexpensive, so don't worry about it, but keep bargaining.

One way to have fun and get your used and abused Glock upgraded is to go to a GSSF match. There, the factory armorer will as a matter of routine upgrade all the free stuff, and repair at low cost the mangled and abused stuff. He can also tell you what the other repairs will cost (if any) and can tell you how long it takes to get such a repair turned around. And, you can shoot the match, have fun, and maybe even win yet another Glock.

Magazines are almost always part of a handgun purchase. Pistols don't work very well without magazines. Inspect the magazines to make sure they are as stated. Old-style or drop-free? If they are drop-free, do they? Insert them in the Glock in question and see. Make sure they are Glock, especially if you are paying a premium

for honest to goodness Glock mags. Check the feed lips to see if the polymer is still attached. We've been seeing more Glock magazines delaminating, that is, having the polymer separate from the steel feed lips. Glock won't replace magazines that have delaminated but still function. If they're ugly but still work, Glock doesn't see it as a problem. The internals and baseplates can easily be replaced, so your main concern is the tube itself. If it is in good shape and correct for the pistol you're buying, then shake over a price and have fun with your new toy.

BUYING A USED BERETTA 9MM

The first things you have to be careful of are military "surplus" parts. As a relatively controlled item, there are no surplus items released from government stores. Second, it is current government policy that no useable parts are allowed out for civilian sale. Yes, that's right, they torch everything. Why? Some say spite, others say fear of liability lawsuits. (Me, I lean towards the "spite" option.) Buy government-marked items with caution, or not at all. A manufacturer may well have deliberately made a production over-run, to have "surplus" items for sale. Then again, they might be parts that were spirited out of government ownership. Check a used Beretta to make sure the safety operates properly. Make sure it is unloaded. Cock the hammer. Drop a pencil (eraser first) or dowel down the bore, and use the safety to drop the hammer. If the pencil does more than bounce, the safety is not blocking the firing pin. Check that the trigger returns smoothly when released after dry-firing. Check that the magazines drop free. Look down the bore for bulges. A Beretta barrel is just as pricey as any other barrel. You could easily drop another $150 on a replacement barrel, so if you see a bulged barrel, bargain the price down accordingly.

A heavily used Beretta should have all the small springs and some parts replaced. You can get the stan-

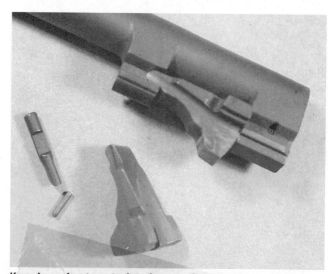

If you're going to put a lot of ammo through your handgun, stock spares. For example, if your Beretta M-92 has the original locking block, get the 4th-generation one from Langdon Tactical. It will last forever.

dard replacement kits from Langdon Tactical Technology. A high-mileage Beretta may need a new locking block. If the block shows as much wear as the barrel does, and the finish on both is heavily worn, get a new block. You could even use the need for a new block as a bargaining lever. However, if you've already bargained down from everything else, you may find the seller is at his or her price limit.

BUYING A USED REVOLVER

Buying a revolver, single- or double-action, involves pretty much the same process as buying a used pistol. First, assess the exterior to see if the revolver shows signs of hard use or abuse.

Look at the finish. Is it heavily worn or scratched? A used blued revolver will show white steel at the corners of the frame and cylinder. This wear is caused by holstering and drawing, and is normal. If the scratches look as if a sidewalk instead of a holster caused them, pass on this revolver. Or if you see scratches down to copper on a nickel revolver, pass again. A used revolver with a shiny new finish may have been re-blued or re-nickeled and needs close examination to determine its condition. Look at the screw holes. Are they oval? Not good. Incor-

rectly used, the fabric of a polishing wheel will reach down into the screw hole and dish it out. The proper, factory method of re-polishing requires fitting sacrificial screws to the frame. After the frame is polished, these screws are thrown away and new ones are fitted. Look also at the letters and markings. Do they look as if they are blurry? Blurry letters and markings in an otherwise shiny and good finish with good screw holes tell you that the polisher was careful. While he didn't dish the screw holes, he couldn't avoid "pulling" the markings. Blurry markings do not harm function, but should lower the price.

To determine if the revolver was ever dropped, check the muzzle, sights and hammer spur for dents and dings. In extreme cases, the sights will have been bent or broken completely off. A revolver with a dinged muzzle but a new front sight was dropped hard enough to break the sight, which was then replaced. Unless you can check barrel straightness and cylinder alignment before you buy, pass.

Look at the cylinder for these same dents and dings. If you see marks, gently open and close the cylinder. A dropped double-action revolver that lands on its cylinder can end up with a sprung crane. If you have to press

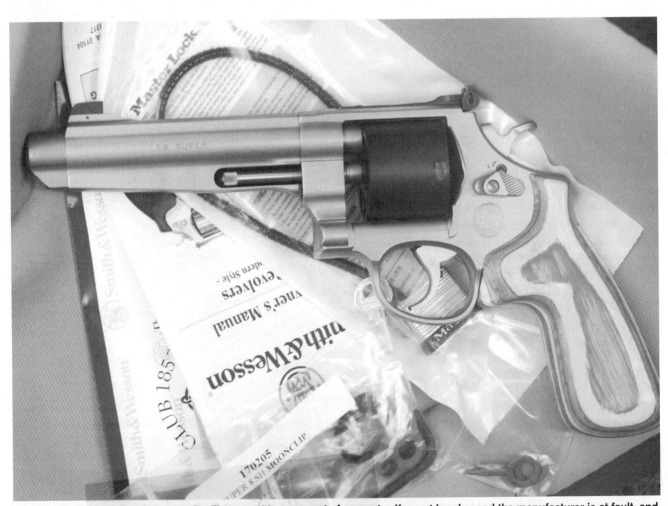

When you buy a new handgun now, it will come with some sort of warranty. If a part breaks, and the manufacturer is at fault, and you haven't modified it, you'll get it fixed. Put a couple of hundred rounds through a brand-new handgun before starting to work on it. If anything breaks, it is still under warranty.

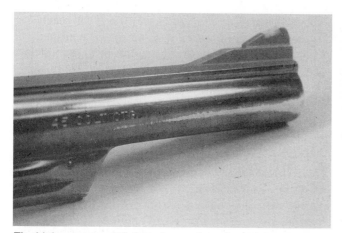

The bluing wear on this barrel came from the holster. A better holster will prevent this in the future. If it really offends you, have the revolver re-blued. It is just as accurate whether you blue it or not.

When buying a used firearm, look for signs of dropping. This dented barrel may not have harmed the crown, but it might have lead to the barrel being bent or the frame twisted. Look, check, and get a return guarantee if you can.

firmly with a thumb on the cylinder to get the centerpin to click into its seat in the frame, the crane needs alignment. Straightening it is an easy operation.

To check function on the single-action revolver, first make sure it is unloaded. While holding the revolver with your firing hand, grasp the cylinder with your other hand and try to move it back and forth. A very small amount of movement is okay. If the cylinder moves more than the smallest fraction of an inch, however, you may have to adjust endshake after you buy it. Not a big deal. If the cylinder moves so much you can actually hear it clacking back and forth, buy this revolver only if it is cheaper than dirt, or you like a good re-building challenge.

Gently cock the revolver. In the old-style single-actions, (direct copies of the Colt SAA), you should hear four distinct clicks. Odd, tinny sounding clicks could mean weak springs or modified parts. Muffled clicks usually mean the action is over-oiled or greased. Gently cock the revolver through all six chambers. As you do this you must be sure to move the hammer slowly and deliberately to eliminate any momentum in the cylinder. As an additional test, lightly press a thumb or fingertip against the cylinder, to add drag. Did the revolver fully

The bottom chamber is bulged, right at the notch for the locking bolt. A hot load that was over pressure has just cost this shooter a new cylinder.

The front sight insert on this revolver is slightly dinged, but doesn't impair shooting. A front sight with bent and gouged metal has been dropped and should be inspected carefully before you buy it.

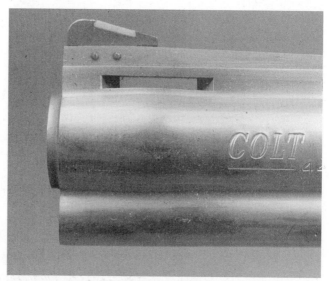

The owner of this Colt saved some money on some cheap reloads. A new barrel will cost many times his "savings."

carry-up, that is, did the cylinder come all the way up and lock? If it did not, the revolver may have a short hand or a worn ratchet. Though these problems are easy to fix, try to bargain the price down.

Do the pencil/firing pin test again, to make sure the firing pin is striking hard enough.

Look at the locking slots on each chamber. If they are burred or chewed up the revolver has probably seen too many sessions of fast-cocking shooting, or god forbid, fanning. Pass on the revolver.

Pull the center pin out, remove the cylinder, and look at the locking bolt. Is it beaten up? Are its edges peened? Heavy use, or just a bit of fanning and fast-draw practice will wear the locking bolt. While the bolt is cheap to replace, the cylinder is not. Heavily worn locking slots on the cylinder mean an expensive repair. Pass on the revolver.

Finally, look at the back of the barrel. If the forcing cone is caked in powder residue and lead, ask if it can be cleaned up. You need to see it. Check that the edges of the forcing cone are sharp. A worn or rounded edge means the revolver has seen lots of shooting. Is the rifling clean and distinct? Heavy use erodes the rifling as well as the edges of the forcing cone. Setting the barrel back and re-cutting the cone can rectify a barrel with heavy wear in the forcing cone.

Cracks in the forcing cone cannot be fixed. Uncommon outside of magnum revolvers, these cracks result from the high pressure of the magnum ammunition stressing the edges of the forcing cone. Unlike wear, you cannot easily set the barrel back enough to fix a crack. With a cracked forcing cone it's much simpler just to replace the barrel.

With double-action revolvers you do all the same external checks that you did with the single-action revolvers. A significant percentage of the double-action revolvers available on the used market are ex-police revolvers. When police departments switched to automatics, they traded in or sold their revolvers. Pay attention to the details and you can get a good deal on a used double-action .38 or .357.

Many ex-police revolvers have the bluing rubbed off where they rode in a holster, but otherwise have little wear. Since many police departments qualify only annually, your revolver may have had only a couple of hundred rounds a year put through it! The grips, if original, will probably be very ugly. While rest of the revolver was protected by the holster the grips were outside, getting banged by car doors, signposts, and who knows what. Grips are cheap and easy to replace.

To begin your mechanical checks, first release the cylinder latch and swing it open. Is the revolver loaded? No? Good. Swing the cylinder in and out several times. Make sure it swings smoothly, and closes easily. Smith & Wessons binding while swinging usually means the sideplate screws have been switched. In other brands, it means the crane is dirty. If you have to press the cylinder to make it click when closing, the crane is out of alignment.

There are two checks for carry-up, one for single-action cocking and one for double. Single is simple. Slowly cock the action while watching the cylinder, just as you would for a single-action revolver. I do my double-action check very, very slowly, with my left thumb against

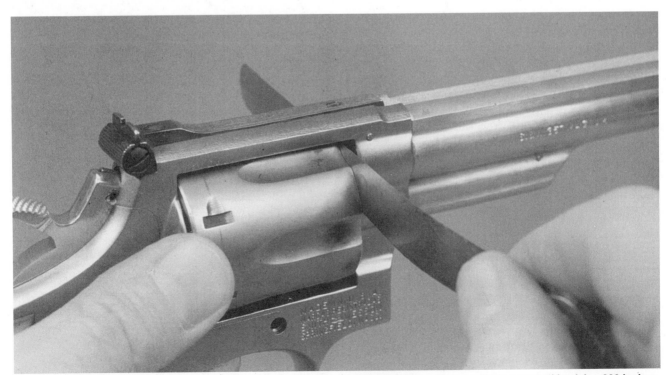

Check cylinder gap while pushing the cylinder forward. If this is less than the gap with the cylinder pressed back by .003 inches or more, remove the endshake.

the hammer, so when the trigger releases the hammer, the momentum of my trigger finger doesn't throw the cylinder into lockup. You can also use a fingertip to drag against the cylinder. Although failure to carry-up can be fixed, you should bargain for a lower price because of it.

Open the cylinder and look at the forcing cone, on the back of the barrel. Give it the same thorough exam described for a single-action revolver.

Now look into the cylinder. At the front of the chamber is the shoulder. A magnum revolver that had a lot of .38 Specials put through it would have developed a crusty ring just in back of this shoulder. You may also see such a ring in single-action revolvers, where many competitors use shorter cases for lighter loads. It may be that the .357 Magnum you are looking at has been fired extensively with cases not much longer than a 9mm Parabellum, and the forward half of each chamber is sheened with lead. There can be corrosion under the crusty buildup. Ask to have any visible grunge scrubbed out, and check the area for the pits that indicate too much time between cleanings. Pits can make extraction harder when you fire magnum ammunition, and continue to rust if you use Specials. If the revolver has pits, don't buy it.

Check the back of the cylinder, at the openings to each chamber. If the revolver was used for competition, the chamber openings may have been chamfered to allow faster reloading during matches. Poorly done, however, chamfering makes ejection uncertain. Look at the work closely. Only the cylinder itself should be beveled. If the extractor star is also beveled, ejection may suffer. To check, you need to fire the revolver and eject the empties for at least 100 rounds. Since the cure for a bad chamfering job is fitting a new extractor, an expensive factory job, if you can't shoot the revolver beforehand or get a warranty pass on it.

During your test-fire you may find that the sights are off slightly. On a revolver with adjustable sights, just crank them over. (Indeed, this is a good time to find out if the adjustable sights actually adjust.) In a fixed-sight revolver a small amount of "off" is OK. After all, you'll want to be able to adjust your new revolver to you and your ammo. However, if the sights are off more than a few inches at 25 feet, or the groups with standard ammo for the caliber, are hitting high, you may have problems. A few inches is about all you can correct by turning the barrel. A high bullet strike means a low front sight, and it is difficult to add height to a fixed sight. Take a quick look and see if the sight has been filed or machined. If it hasn't, the frame may be bent, and only the factory can correct that. And not for free. You must make a choice: is this a project gun, for experimentation in fitting a new front sight, or is it a returned gun, for your money back? Only you can decide.

CHAPTER

KEEP IT CLEAN

Do you want to know the best-kept secret of the professional gunsmith? No deep learning, no years of practice, just one little thing to keep in mind: Ninety percent of the handguns that show up for work simply need a good thorough cleaning and proper lubrication, and their "problems" were solved. And the rest of the problems? Most of them could have been avoided with one good cleaning each year after hunting season. In fact, it was the lack of cleaning on the part of hunters that drove me out of general commercial gunsmithing. It got to the point where I just couldn't stand the thought of another season spent hosing the gunk out of an endless parade of Remington 1100s and 742s. At that time I was working on nearly a thousand firearms a year, and I could count on seeing a couple of hundred 742/7400 and 1100/11-87 Remingtons in each pre-season rush. Yes, the money was good, but not if it drove me to drink. I now clean only my own firearms, and am much the happier for it. As a bonus, I now write about firearms, and manufacturers send me ones to test. Those I don't clean at all.

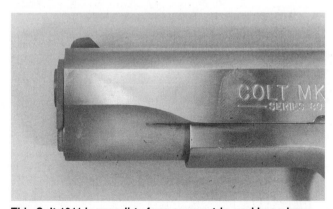

This Colt 1911 is very dirty from a range trip, and has a large thumbprint right on the "C." Depending on the owners perspiration, this thumbprint may be a cause of rust. The pistol should be cleaned.

Rusted surface that requires re-bluing? Cleaning it after the rainstorm the last day of hunting season would have prevented that.

Broken extractor? Maybe, if the chamber hadn't gotten so crusty that the extractor was stressed, it never would have broken.

Failure to feed in an auto? Groups getting so large that scores are dropping off? Scrub out the pistol, keep the bore clean and these problems won't occur.

WHEN TO CLEAN? MORE OFTEN THAN THIS...

In the early 1990s, when the Federal Bureau of Investigation went looking for a new pistol for their Hostage Rescue Team, they knew what they wanted. Custom gunsmiths who felt up to the challenge received a set of specs the size of a large paperback book and began toiling away, hoping to get the Bureau contract.

Each handgun had to pass a rigorous set of tests. One, naturally enough, was an accuracy test. Only it had a twist. After a normal check for accuracy, the FBI fired 20,000 rounds of Remington Golden Saber .45 ACP through each pistol — without stopping, and without cleaning. Whenever the pistols became, no kidding, too hot to handle, the testers sloshed them around in a trough of water, lubed them up, and continued shooting. At the end of the 20,000 rounds, they tested the pistols for accuracy again. Not all made the cut.

You are not likely to need a pistol this sturdy or accurate, nor are you likely to try this test. Should you want to, be warned! At current wholesale the ammunition alone will cost you nearly $20,000 and generate a dumpster full of empty brass, boxes and cartons!

And the abuse will also contribute to the early demise of your handgun. Those 1911 pistols would probably have lasted 100,000 rounds if treated properly. As it was, after those 20,000 they were probably scrapped. At the very least they needed an overhaul. (Knowing the Federal government, they were probably required to be scrapped, fed into a shredder or melted down.)

Yes, you can have someone else do it. But it will cost you. I always charged as much as I could. And if you do dump it off at a shop, you may be contributing to the depression and despair of some poor unfortunate gunsmith out there who faces the same dilemma I had. Take pity on the poor guy, and scrub your handguns now and then.

So, how to clean it, and when to do it?

A friend of mine, who stayed in the Marine Corps long enough to buy a set of gas stations when he was discharged, believes in cleaning firearms every time they are used. Seems like a lot, but the Marine Corps training he received, combined with his own biology, convinced him that every time was the way to go. His biology? Yup. He is one of those unlucky individuals whose perspiration corrodes steel right away. He once rusted a 1911 through a hard-chrome job. If I hadn't seen it, I wouldn't have believed it. With sweat like that it isn't any wonder he believes so thoroughly in cleaning. I only wonder how he managed to survive 12 years in the Corps. We solved his problem by telling the plater to run his frame through the process twice. Yep, double-plated.

Since I am one of the lucky ones whose perspiration doesn't seem to rust firearms at all, my cleaning habits are a little less compulsive. If I have the time, and remember to do so, I'll clean my pistols as soon as I get back from shooting them. But quarterly and annually, depending on how much I shoot a pistol, they all get a check, and cleaning if needed. In season, the competition guns get cleaned a couple of times a week. That schedule works for me. Only you can determine the right schedule for you and your guns, but keep in mind that very first fact we discussed: Most "broken" pistols just need a good, thorough cleaning. (OK, I lectured and you patiently read.) You can hardly clean too often.

Before we discuss the specifics of disassembly and cleaning, let's begin with an overview. If you've made a workspace in a well-ventilated corner of the basement or the garage, you can set up a basin and tub arrangement right by your workbench. If you're using a closet or a

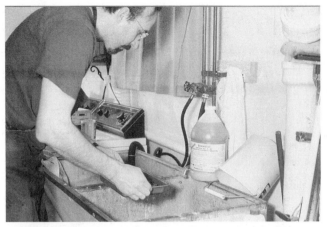

Put the plug in your laundry sink, and scrub away to your hearts content.

corner of commonly used room, you will have to clean your guns elsewhere. Gun scrubbing chemicals, even "odorless" mineral spirits, have some smell. "Elsewhere" means out of the house. Don't think you'll scrub a gun in the kitchen sink "just this once." Don't tell yourself no one will know because there's an open window right over the sink. What if you spill chemicals onto the floor inside your home? Or drop a part down the garbage disposal? Not good.

You need a bench on which to disassemble the handgun. This can and should be the same bench on which you plan to do the rest of your pistolsmithing. For the regular pistolsmithing you need a hard surface, to prevent your bench from soaking up oils, solvents and God knows what. For cleaning, though, you want to have a padded work surface. Simply get a separate mat that can be rolled or hung up out of the way of your regular work. Outers makes a soft mat that's perfect, as does Brownells. Available in two sizes, it is soft enough to keep from scratching the pistol and its parts, but tough enough it won't get torn to shreds from use.

You can get by with carpet samples, edged so they won't unravel, but the coarser weaves let the smallest gun parts disappear into the carpet. You'll be more suc-

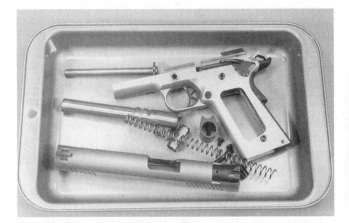

If you don't have a parts tank, a small pan can do to clean your handgun. Disassemble it and pour in your mineral spirits or Brownells d'Solve.

The only drawback I have found to the laundry sink method is the bending over. Shorter shooters may not have this problem.

A soft mat on the workbench will protect your handgun's finish. The dark matte finish of this Outers mat will also protect your eyes from the glare of bright lights.

cessful with the right tool/bench mat for the job.

You'll also need a large basin or old sink, braced at a convenient working height. If you're using a sink put a stopper in the drain. The stopper prevents a dropped part from disappearing down the drain.

I have found that using a small basin inside the larger sink is the best way to clean handguns when you have to clean them other than in gunsmiting-specific basins. With a small basin I can use a small amount of solvent and still be able to immerse the parts. The larger sink contains any splashes while I'm working, and afterwards I just scrub the sink clean. I save and reuse the mineral spirits, pouring them back into their gallon can. If you're doing high volume cleaning, you might find this method hard on your back, but for once a month or even once a week, it works just fine.

A parts washer with a pump to send solvent through, and a compressor. Essentials for the professional, luxuries for the home.

If you'll be cleaning a lot of handguns an auto parts washer works very well. The washer consists of a sink which sits on a drum of solvent (generally mineral spirits) and filtering water. An electric pump brings the solvent up into the sink. You dump the parts into the sink, grab a brush and start scrubbing. Check with your local waste carrier for disposal of the exhausted solvent. The drain drains the mineral spirits down to the bottom of the drum, where they rise (organic solvents are less dense than water, and thus ride on top if they are insoluble) and filter out impurities. The pump sucks up solvent from the top layer, providing you with mostly clean mineral spirits. However, there will be a small amount of water in the solvent, so you must, absolutely must, re-lube after cleaning.

With either the high-volume or low-volume home systems, if you have to use other solvents on the bore, apply them and let them soak in while you are scrubbing the rest of the pistol. Scrub the bore in the mineral spirits last.

Though it may seem like a big job, devising a basin and sink combo for cleaning your handgun (or entire collection) is pretty straightforward. Police departments, on the other hand, have to clean really large numbers of firearms on a regular basis.

To clean in large volumes quickly and easily, L&R has developed a series of ultrasonic cleaning tanks. Police departments love them, and no wonder; they work almost like magic. You just take the grips off your pistol, so the solvent can get to all the parts, open the action, and place the handgun in the tank. Close the lid, flip a switch, and come back after the paperwork and coffee have been finished. Presto, a clean pistol.

Sound too good to be true? Close.

The cleaning tank is great, no doubt about that, but what it produces is a pistol that is degreased, not one that is completely clean. There may still be copper in the bore, even if the department uses the ammoniated solution instead of the plain. It is also very likely there will be lead fouling. Any copper or lead deposits must still be removed by brushing.

There's another catch, not significant for a police department, but big for a home shop. A tank that will handle one handgun runs just over $700. The concentrated solution, enough to make 8 gallons, costs just over $50.

Finally, since the tanks thoroughly degrease anything put in them, if after cleaning you don't properly and immediately oil your handgun, it will rust. L&R includes a water-displacing lubrication bath to re-lubricate the now-dry pistol.

The unit comes with complete instructions for setup and operation. You will need four or five feet of bench space to set up and operate the system. If you don't have this much room always available, you will have to store the units on a shelf or in a closet.

Mix your solution. Should you use the ammoniated cleaner? No. It cleans slightly faster, but the heavy ammonia odor requires much greater ventilation than the standard cleaner. The extra cleaning isn't worth the hassle of the odor. The cleaning solution comes as a concentrate. Mix one part of the concentrate to seven parts clean fresh water. The easiest way to do this is to take a used water bottle and measure the side. Divide its height by eight, and mark the side of the bottle that far up from the bottom. Pour in concentrate to the mark, and then fill with water.

Pour enough cleaning solution into the tank to cover your handgun when it is in the basket.

Take the grips off. For pistols, remove the slide and recoil spring. For revolvers, remove the grips and the crane and cylinder. The vibrations of the ultrasonic cleaning may cause smaller parts to shift. To prevent this, if you remove the sideplate for a thorough cleaning also detail strip the action of your revolver.

Place the parts in the cleaning basket and suspend the basket in the solution. If your parts are not completely covered, add more solution. Put the lid on it. Turn the unit on and clean for 10 minutes. Some models have timers and a heating unit. Set the timer for 10 minutes. For units with a heater, turn the heat on when you start, and turn the heat off when you are done. You do not need to pre-heat the solution.

When done, pull the basket out of the pan and drain it in your sink. Rinse with hot water. If you have compressed air, blow dry.

Put the parts back into the basket and place the basket in the auxiliary pan. Add enough water-displacing lubrication solution to cover your parts. Take the pan and basket, and place it on top of the ultrasonic tank so the pan bottom is slightly immersed in the solution of the main tank. This provides contact to transfer the ultrasonic vibrations form the main tank to the auxiliary pan.

Turn the machine on and run it without heat for 10 minutes.

The L&R lubricant will displace the water left in the nooks and crannies of your handgun. When done, drain the lubricant back into the pan. The more you drain, the faster the handgun will dry. Allow the handgun to air dry, Do not blow dry. To speed drying, place the parts on a towel, and position a lamp a foot away.

The L&R ultrasonic cleaning did not remove metal fouling, it only loosened it. Once dry, use a brush and patches on the bore to remove the fouling. Lubricate as usual.

There is no arguing with the convenience of the L&R Ultrasonic cleaning system. If you are willing to pay the going rate, you can save lots of time and hassle.

Whatever method you use, the scrubbing part of cleaning leaves you with dripping-wet gun parts. You will have to dry them. Wipe the parts down with a dry towel, shop rag or paper towel, and leave them disassembled on the bench until they air-dry. Or, after wiping them down, set them in the sun – inside and out of sight, of course so they can dry even faster. Professional gunsmiths use compressed air. A compressor with a hose and nozzle will blow the surface dry in a few seconds. A compressor, though, is noisy and expensive. Also, you cannot "blow off" mineral spirits indoors – even in the garage – without a hood and exhaust fan. Back in high school and college chemistry we used hoods to control the vapors we regularly produced. A "chem hood" is a lighted cabinet with sliding doors at the front and a fan at the back to draw the vapors into a filtration system, and those hoods were great. But they are way too much for home use. If, working in a shed or garage in the country, you want to use compressed air, it's easy enough to step outside and dry your parts. However, in the city, or a cluster of condominiums, stick with ordinary air-drying.

One fellow I know figured a way to "blow dry" his guns. For a couple of bucks he picked up a fan and a blow dryer at a yard sale. He built a drying chamber and hooked the blow-dryer to one side of it. On the other he connected the fan, orienting it to exhaust right out of his garage. After scrubbing guns, he puts the parts in the chamber, closes the door and flips the switches. The blow dryer pumps hot air in to the parts, and the fan sucks the solvent-laden air outside. His parts are dry in five minutes.

Another way to blow parts clean, more expensive than do-it-yourself-blow-drying but cheaper than a compressor, is a used scuba tank with a nozzle attachment. One of the members of my gun club uses one to dry his handguns. Apparently when scuba divers buy tanks, they only buy new. No one wants to risk their continued breathing and continued existence on used tanks. Used tanks are thus common and inexpensive and cheaply filled. The catch is, you have to be scuba-certified, like my friend, to get tanks filled. Instead, go to a welding supply shop. They can fill tanks with compressed air or nitrogen for you to use. The pressure will not be as high as the scuba tanks, but it will be high enough. The welding supply shop can also provide valves, hose and a nozzle. You must, however, secure your tank to the wall. Compressed air exits a broken-off valve with enough velocity to propel the tank. If it gets knocked over and the valve breaks off, it will scoot away at a high enogh velocity to break things and hurt people. Chain your tanks!

Once the handgun is clean and dry replace the lubricants removed by the cleaning solvents and reassemble the parts.

What Tools and Chemicals Do You Need To Get Started?

Get a cleaning rod, long enough to go all the way through your longest pistol barrel. Buy patches and brushes in your calibers. Buy cleaning solutions and lubricants. In really dirty firearms you may need some specialized cleaning tools that you will have to make. We'll discuss these in detail later.

"NOT CLEANING" AS A CHOICE?

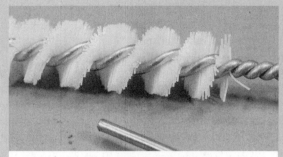

You'll need cleaning brushes. Some handguns come with a brush. This one from Glock has plastic bristles and will last quite a long time.

There are some barrel makers who tell you to go easy on cleaning. Irv Stone III of Bar-sto barrels is one. His reason is that he has seen too many barrels prematurely wasted due to excessive cleaning. In particular, worn-out barrels due to the use of stainless steel bristle brushes. The stainless brush (bristle, not the looped kind) can scratch and gouge the bore. Given the choice between a stainless bristle brush and no cleaning at all (do barrels have choices?) your barrel will likely last longer uncleaned than so abused. However, in some instance a stainless brush may be your only option.

Others tell you not to clean at all. Hmmm. The reasoning goes like this: the pressures and velocities of handgun ammunition are so low that little, if any jacket material is deposited. The wear of cleaning is greater than the wear of fouling. So, no cleaning. I find some problems with this, namely, the "jacket" part and the "fouling" part. If all you shoot is jacketed bullets, fine. Maybe. And as long as you only use the same bullets, fine. Maybe. But those using cast bullets do not have such an option. And I'd worry about problems with differing kinds of fouling built up, from different brands of bullets. Lead can build up, even when you use correctly sized and properly hardened bullets. And if you use something that is already at the top end of pressures, like .38 Super, .40 S&W, 10mm or others (especially the .40) then any fouling buildup can increase pressures, perhaps too much.

Clean your bore. Clean it at least once a year. Clean it from the breech end. And do not use stainless steel bristled brushes.

The manufacturers of many pistols ship new handguns with some kind of cleaning rod. These work fine. The material of the rod doesn't matter. Aluminum is popular because it is light, rust-proof, and cheap. If you feel you need to use a steel rod because your aluminum ones bend when you use them, you have brushes and patches that are too tight.

If you don't have a cleaning rod just buy a kit. Inexpensive kits, either caliber-specific or universal, come with everything you need to start cleaning. I buy universal kits for my home and shop work, and range kits for my shooting bag. Since I never know when I will need one, I keep kits at almost every location I will be shooting, or working on, guns.

There are two styles of handgun brushes, bore brushes and action brushes. Both can be purchased in plastic, brass and stainless steel. Because Glock ships a plastic-bristled brush with their pistols some people believe that brass or stainless steel brushes damage the Glock rifling. To the contrary, Tenifer, the surface hardening

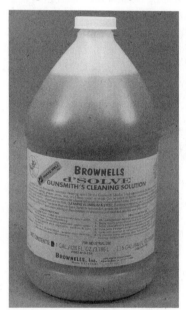

If the odor of even "odorless" mineral spirits are too much for you, Brownells d'Solve is a water-based cleaning concentrate. Completely odorless, this gallon will make enough solvent to scrub a hundred handguns.

Aerosol penetrating oils specifically formulated to remove tight bolt and nuts are great for loosening screws, bullets stuck in the bore and tight-fitted parts.

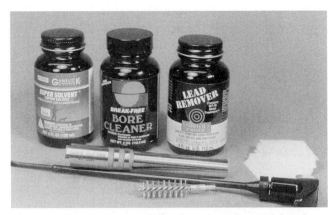

The old-fashioned way to clean a barrel requires rod, brush, patches and solvent. It still works, and it still takes time and elbow grease.

of the Glock manufacturing process, is so hard it actually wears out brass or stainless steel brushes. Glock ships plastic brushes because they last longer. They're cheaper, too.

For really heavily leaded barrels, stainless steel brushes clean the bore more quickly than brass, and much more quickly than plastic. Some shooters are concerned that the stainless steel bristles wear the bore, but after many conversations with manufacturers I've found only a few barrel-makers don't like the idea of using the stainless brushes. Others don't think it makes any difference. Personally, I've used stainless brushes for decades, and I haven't seen any wear on my pistol barrels that I can blame on the brush. If you want to try stainless, but find yourself nervous, I recommend the Tornado brush. Instead of bristles, the Tornado brush is looped. The loops scrape the bore without poking it, reducing the possibility of any wear. One shortcoming of the Tornado brush, due to its wound design, is that it doesn't scrub the corners of the grooves very well. After a few passes I switch to a brass-bristle brush to make sure I get into the corners.

Bore brushes should be the correct size for your caliber. Using a .44 caliber brush on your .357 will not clean the pistol faster, but it will wear the brush out faster because you will be bending and breaking the bristles while cleaning. You can also bend your cleaning rod. The one exception to matching your brush size to your bore size used to be with a .40 caliber pistol. When I first wrote this book the .40 S&W was new, and .40 caliber brushes were not made. Since then, the makers of cleaning products have made them, and if you shoot a .40 S&W or 10mm pistol, you should buy and use them instead of settling for some other caliber that is "close enough." Looking very much like a toothbrush, the action brush is used on all the other parts of the handgun. If you want, you can even use an old toothbrush. Like using a carpet sample for a bench mat, though, using a toothbrush for an action brush has a drawback. The bristles of a toothbrush are not as stiff as the bristles of the real gun-cleaning brush. Again, the right tool is a good investment, and in this instance cheap and long-lasting.

Cleaning requires patches. Little pieces of cloth that are used once and thrown away, patches, like brushes, need to be sized for your bore. I remember, as a kid, sitting up late at night after a day at the range, cutting old bed sheets into just-the-right-size cleaning patches. I have to assume that my father, having grown up in the depression, was reluctant to pay good money for little throw-away cleaning rags. As a result, it was a good long time before I actually bought patches. Store-bought patches are easy to use. You don't have to worry about hammering a too-big patch through the bore, which risks bending an aluminum cleaning rod, or, worst of all, poking a steel rod through the patch and marring the bore. Commercial patches are specifically designed to provide proper scrubbing action against the bore. Cleaning is much easier when you buy patches the right size for your bore.

Brushes and patches by themselves are not sufficient

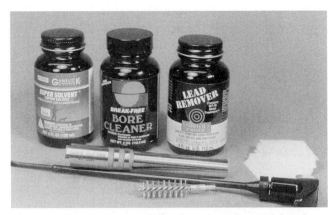

Shooter's Choice makes a full line of solvents and lubricants. The Quick-Scrub III cleans and de-greases. While expensive, it works fast. Use it at the range, not at home in the rec room.

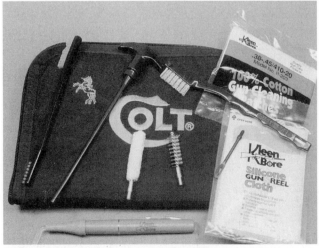

For a trip to the range, stuff a compact cleaning kit in your range bag. This way you can handle minor cleaning problems without having to cut short your range trip.

to properly clean your handgun. You must also use cleaning solvents of some kind. The simplest solvents act to wash away what you have scrubbed free.

For a basic cleaning solvent I go through gallons of mineral spirits every year. Whether you've decided on a basin and tub or a pumped parts washer, mineral spirits do a good job of dissolving powder residue and gummy oil. As discussed in Chapter 3, always buy the pure, odorless mineral spirits, even if they are more expensive than the reclaimed industrial stuff. The odor of the "odorless" spirits is much less objectionable and much easier to wash off, justifying the higher cost. While mineral spirits are safe to use, they will dry out the skin on your hands. You may want to use hand lotion when you are done cleaning. Other industrial solvents are not so safe, and many of the ones we old-timers used to use "in a pinch" have since proven to be unhealthy to use. Yes, in a combat environment you might use avgas to clean, and hydraulic fluid as a lubricant. But we aren't in a combat environment, are we?

Basic solvents such as mineral spirits don't do anything for the lead or copper in your bore. For these you need a bore solvent. There have always been cleaning solvents formulated to dissolve the lead, copper, plastic and powder residue left behind in your bore and chamber. In the old days, the solvent of choice was Hoppes #9, with its distinctive smell and load of chemicals that we later discovered to be harmful to your liver. Now we have chemicals that are much friendlier to our body parts. They work better, too. Still, sometimes I wax just a little nostalgic for the old odor of Hoppes.

The reformulated Hoppes works just fine most of the time, but if you find that you have a particularly persistent bore-leading or copper-fouling problem, then a dose of an even more specialized solvent may be needed. Highly specialized solvents can come in liquid or aerosol form. Although the aerosol solvents, like the aerosol cleaners below, are easy (but expensive) to use, don't confuse the two. Many specialized solvents can cause etching. I recommend Shooter's Choice Copper Remover, Shooter's Choice Lead remover and Outers Super Solvent Copper solvent. They do a great job of removing deposits and do not etch the surface of your bore if you leave them in too long.

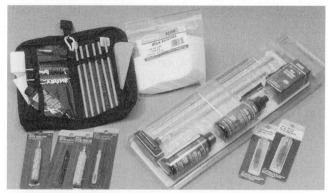

For home cleaning, a full-size cleaning kit is best. You can keep all of the items handy and ready to use.

After using any bore solvent, you must put a light film of protective lubricant back on the bore. To do this, take a clean patch and put two drops of your lubricant on it. Run this back and forth through the bore for a couple of passes.

In the last 10 years, aerosol cleaners have joined the arsenal of maintenance gear. With an aerosol you can scrub and degrease all in one shot. At the Second Chance shoot, which is alas no more, where clean guns were a must, high ammunition consumption was a social necessity, and shooters spent the week outdoors, cases of Gun-Scrubber, One-Shot and other cleaners disappeared every day down barrels and into actions. The operative word with aerosols is "outdoors". Using these in the house is a really bad idea. Whenever they expect to shoot hundreds (or, in the case of Second Chance, thousands) of rounds, most shooters take a can along with them to the range, or to a match. Aside from their smell, the major drawback to aerosols is their cost. At home or in the shop, you can clean a hundred handguns with a gallon of mineral spirits. The same money spent on aerosols may clean a dozen.

An approach to cleaning with aerosol cleaners to save money is to go to an auto parts store and buy "brake cleaner." Yes, it is cheaper, but be careful and test it

If you do not restrain the spring and plunger, it will leap free. This unit jumped under the furnace, and had to be swept out. Between the lint, dust, dirt and ant attached, I wasn't really sure I wanted it back.

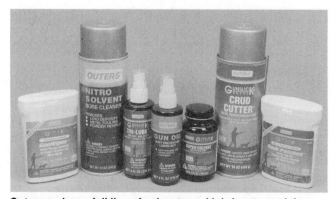

Outers makes a full line of solvents and lubricants, and the neatest item: Gunslick Redi-Patches and Gunwipes. These are pop-up patches already soaked with either a cleaning solution or an exterior wiping solution. Pull the patch out, use it and toss it in the trash. No need to drag bottles of solvent to the range!

before you go hosing. Spray a test squirt on the back of grips, or on an unobtrusive part fo the frame or slide. The "brake cleaner" may be (more likely is) more aggressive than the firearms aerosols. It may attack your plastic grips. It might dissolve your fiber-optic sights. Test, and be careful.

Remember, if you use mineral spirits, solvents, or an aerosol cleaner any time in the cleaning process, you must lubricate all the now degreased parts.

An ideal firearms lubricant reduces friction, prevents water from reaching the steel, and keeps dust, crud and powder residue from adhering to the handgun. It does not react to the hot gases produced by the burning powder, or come off on your hands, your clothes, paperwork, or anything else you touch. And it does not chemically change over time.

If you're thinking "I know, I'll use WD-40," stop right there. Do not, repeat, do not, use WD-40 as a firearms lubricant. I know that it is found in millions of homes around the country, and we all have countless uses for it, but lubricating handguns should never be one of those uses. WD-40 is a formulated mixture of lubricants, designed to be a water-displacing oil mixture. It's in the name: Water-Displacing #40, or WD-40. The more volatile portions of the mixture gradually evaporates, so if you lube a handgun with it, and leave it alone long enough, the remaining oils in the mixture harden over time. The hardening WD-40 glues small parts together so tightly that they cannot freely work, rendering the firearm inoperative. If this were not bad enough, the hardening

mess collects any dust and lint around, and incorporates these into the solidifying gunk. If you've abused your handguns with WD-40, you'll need paint thinner to dissolve the lacquer between the parts. Don't use paint thinner inside. The odor is just too strong.

WD-40 has many useful functions, but not for firearms.

I have found two very useful lubricants in Break Free and FP-10. Break Free is a teflon-based lubricant. It has a liquid teflon base, and teflon microspheres that act as mechanical lubricants. I use either one on all my firearms. Inside, on the bearing surfaces, both keep the parts well lubricated. Outside, after degreasing, they protect the exterior from water and prevent rust.

FP-10, a lighter lubricant, is useful during our Michigan winters. If you hunt, FP-10 will keep parts ready to go during a cold-weather deer chase, or a frigid afternoon out in a goose blind. If you compete all winter, as we do at my club, switch to FP-10 when you start having trouble keeping your hands warm. Just as we once changed oils in our cars from summer to winter, using lighter lubricants in our guns during colder weather assures their continued good performance.

When you oil, you need to know how much oil and where to use it. Between the wars, Smith & Wesson had an advertising campaign for their revolvers, entitled "Seven Drops of Oil." Diagrams showed seven spots, and told how often each one needed its drop. I tend to use more than seven drops, but my handguns come out of a solvent tank, and are completely dry.

Break-Free makes bore solvent, and Break Free CLP. This is a cleaner, lubricant, preservative that I find so useful I have used nearly a gallon a year since it came out.

CLEANING

In all the explanations of cleaning, I will start out by telling you to make sure the handgun is unloaded. I know, I know. I am being repetitive to the point of growing tiresome. But I know something else, too: With 20 years' experience behind the counter at various gun shops, I have lost count of the number of loaded firearms that have been handed to me. In almost every case, the hand-off was accompanied or preceeded by the phrase, "Don't worry, it isn't loaded." I have always checked. I will always check. Seeing the chambered cartridge clatter across the counter at the gun shop generally gives the careless owner some of that ol' time religion, but for how long, I don't know. Even if you are sure, absolutely and completely, that your handgun is not loaded, check it anyway. It only takes a moment. And the time you save not checking will be small comfort, when you do encounter that loaded, "unloaded" gun. The least you can expect is a scare, and perhaps a hole in the wall.

A simple cleaning is like a trip to the fast-lube oil shop. You wipe or scrub the powder residue off of the frame and slide, without taking the frame apart. The only thing you do to the frame in the way of disassembly is to take the grips off. You scrub the bore of your barrel, and the cylinder if you are cleaning a revolver, until they are clean. If you are using dirty ammunition that leads your bore, even a simple cleaning will involve lots of barrel scrubbing. You should do a simple cleaning after every trip to the range. One new aspect of the simple cleaning is the Bore Snake. It is a thick section of rope-like fabric, with a series of caliber-specific brass bristles in one end. You open the action, drop the Bore Snake down the bore, and then pull the bristles and thick cleaning section through the bore.

It scrubs and wipes clean the bore, and if you run the bore snake up the magazine well of a pistol, when it runs across the feed ramp it cleans that too.

A detailed cleaning is your trip to the service station. Instead of simply having your oil changed, you have your mechanic (in this case, you) look over all the fluid levels, check the brakes, the battery and rotate your tires. The detailed cleaning of your firearm involves completely dismantling the slide and frame. Some parts of your handgun, such as the firing pin of a double-action pistol, you will leave assembled, partly because they never need service, but mostly because it takes specialized tools to dismantle them. You should do a detailed cleaning of your firearms on a schedule, just as you do your car. Every 1,000 rounds is a good rule of thumb.

An aside here. Barrels are not alike in their cleaning requirements. A match barrel will be easier to clean than a factory barrel because of its harder and smoother bore surface. The rougher surface of a factory barrel will build up lead and copper deposits more quickly, and require more scrubbing to come clean. A lightly pitted bore will lead quite quickly, and require a good deal of scrubbing to clean.

CLEANING THE 1911

Before you begin cleaning your 1911, check to see that it is not loaded. You'll have to decide whether your pistol needs a detailed cleaning or a simple cleaning. Remember the mantra, "Simple every time, detail every 1,000." Have you fired 1,000 rounds since the last detailed cleaning? If not, then a simple cleaning will be sufficient.

In this cleaning description, and all those that follow, I will be describing how a right-handed person handles the handguns when cleaning. The process of disassembly, cleaning and reassembly involves juggling the parts, and rotating them on almost every axis. If you are a left-handed shooter, you will have to make adjustments during cleaning, as you do in the rest of the dextrous-oriented world around you.

In a simple cleaning of the 1911, dismount the slide assembly from the frame. Pull the recoil spring and assembly if any, out of the slide, and remove the barrel and bushing. Scrub the bore with a bore brush for several passes, starting with a Tornado brush if the leading is severe. Swab the bore with a bore solvent and set it aside while you work on the rest of the parts.

Wipe the powder residue off of the bushing, the recoil rod if you have one, and the slide. On the breechface and around the extractor the powder residue gets packed hard enough that you will have to use your action brush to loosen it.

Check the barrel once you are done with the slide. Brush the bore again, run a dry patch through it and inspect it. Is there still lead in the corners of the rifling? Scrub it again. Use a bore solvent. When done, set the barrel down while you clean the frame.

Take the grips off the frame. Wipe the powder residue from the frame. Around the barrel seat (the part of the frame where the underside of the barrel rests when unlocked) the powder residue may be packed in place, as it was on the breechface. Brush here with the action brush to loosen the powder residue, and wipe it away. Wrap a cleaning patch around your action brush and wipe the inside of the magazine well clean.

If you had to brush the barrel out and soak it a second time, check it again. Does it still need scrubbing? If the answer is yes, and it hasn't been very many rounds since your last cleaning, you may be wondering why. The fault may not lie with your scrubbing, or your bore.

Have you recently switched brands of bullets? Some shooters find after a practice session of only several hundred rounds that a new brand of bullets will lead significantly more than the old brand. In a severe case the bore can look more like a section of sewer pipe than a pistol barrel. Start out with the tornado brush, and brush for a dozen passes or so. Run a patch of specialized lead solvent into the bore and let it sit for 10 minutes. Run a dry patch down the bore, and then brush with the tornado brush again. Once the lead is mostly scrubbed out, and remains only in the corners of

Starting with an empty pistol, hook the left thumb in the trigger guard and pull the slide back until the smaller notch lines up with the slide stop.

If your pistol does not have a recoil spring guide rod, curl your fingers underneath and control the spring as you pull the slide off.

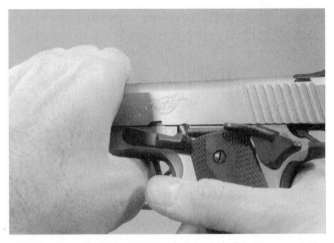

With the disassembly notch lined up to the slide stop, push the slide stop out of the frame with the tip of your right forefinger.

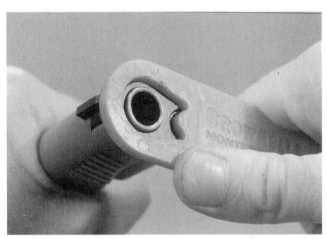

Use the bushing wrench to push the retainer down, and rotate the bushing to the right side of the slide.

1911 pistols such as this Kimber, that have a recoil spring guide rod, are easy to pull apart. The rod will keep the spring under control until you later turn the bushing.

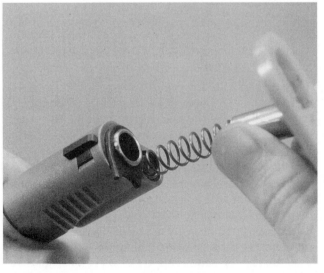

Use the bushing wrench to keep the recoil spring under control. Ease the spring and retainer forward.

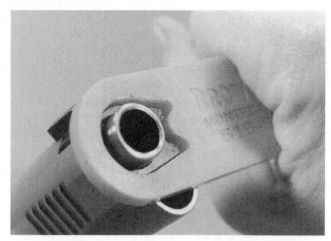

Turn the bushing to the left side of the slide before removing the barrel.

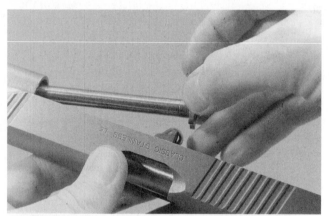

One piece rods are removed from the rear, after the recoil spring and its retainer have been slid out of the front of the slide.

the rifling grooves, switch to a bristle brush. Alternate between the wet and dry patches, and the bristle brush, until the bore is clean. And switch back to the previous brand of bullet.

If you're noticing heavy copper fouling, use the plastic brush to loosen powder residue, then wet a patch with a copper-solvent bore cleaner and run it through your bore. Let it sit for 10 minutes, then run a dry patch, plastic bristle brush and a wet patch again. As it dissolves and reacts to any copper deposit on the bore, copper solvent turns the patch blue or green. This is why you must use a plastic, or, in the case of very heavy copper fouling, a stainless steel brush. If you use a copper or brass brush, the solvent will react to the presence of the brush, and you will never see a "clean" patch. Continue the process until the patches come out without any green or blue on them. Copper solvents are very aggressive. You must not leave them soaking in your bore for more than the recommended time or they can etch it. While the etching may not have any affect on accuracy, longevity or service life of the barrel, who wants to find out the hard way?

Once the barrel does not need any more attention, you are ready for oil and reassembly.

Oiling should be done sparingly. You need a drop of oil on the barrel at the muzzle, the link and the upper lugs. If you have a recoil spring guide rod, place a drop of oil on it after the spring is in place. Before you put the slide assembly back on the frame, put a drop of oil into each rail on the frame.

After reassembly, wipe the exterior with an oily cloth.

GETTING DETAILED

In the 1911, a detail cleaning starts in earnest after you have finished with the barrel. Secure the front of your slide in the padded vise in order to remove the firing pin. Push the firing pin in with a drift pin, and, while holding your hand over the end of the slide, slide the retaining plate down. If you don't cover the end of the slide you will launch the firing pin across the room. Use a small

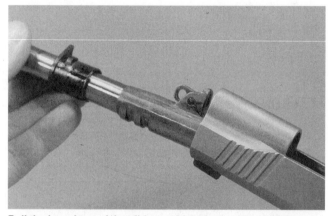

Pull the barrel out of the slide, pushing the bushing with it.

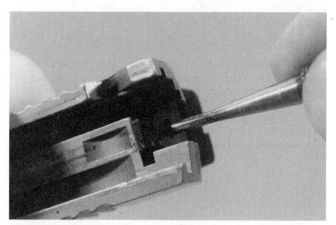

To remove the firing pin and extractor, push the firing pin into the slide.

screwdriver to pry the extractor out of its tunnel. Pull it completely free and set it down on the mat next to the other slide parts.

This job is a bit more detailed for the Colt Series 80 pistols. Hold the slide upside-down in the vise. Use one drift pin to push the safety plunger into the slide, and then use another to push the firing pin into the slide. Let go of the safety plunger. Let go of the firing pin and let it go forward against the plunger. The firing pin is now held in the slide. Remove the firing pin retainer. Push the

A box of cotton-tipped swabs are great for getting crud out of otherwise inaccessible places. A few strokes and the tunnel is clean.

safety plunger down, and the firing pin will come out. Take your small screwdriver and pry the extractor out a small amount. The plunger is now free, and you can lift it and its spring out with your hemostat. Finally, pull the

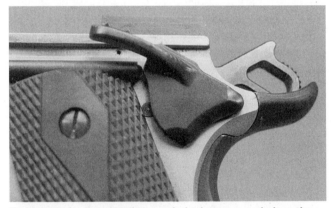

To remove the thumb safety, cock the hammer and place the safety at the halfway point between "on" and "off." Then lift the safety out from the frame.

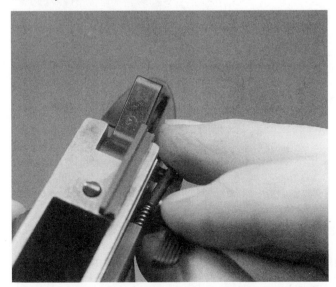

When you pull the thumb safety out of the frame, keep a fingertip over the back of it. This prevents the spring and plungers from leaping to freedom.

extractor out of the slide.

Now that the firing pin and extractor tunnels are empty, you can scrub out the powder residue. Cut a bore patch into a small square, and use a drift pin to push it through the extractor tunnel. Take a .22-caliber brush and scrub out the firing pin tunnel. Wipe off the firing pin, its spring, the extractor, and in the Series 80 pistols, the safety plunger.

On the frame, cock the hammer and turn the thumb safety to a position halfway between "safe" and "fire" and lift the safety out of the frame. The safety won't come out if you don't first cock the hammer. Grasp the plunger that bears against the safety, and pull it out of its tube. This assembly consists of two plungers, one on each end of a coil spring, and it should be one unit. If the plungers come off of the spring the function of the pistol does not suffer, but it's awfully easy to lose track of the parts. Carefully set the assembly where you will find it again, and do not set other parts on it.

Ease the hammer fully forward. For cosmetics, grind a drift pin to match the cupped end of the mainspring housing retaining pin, located at the bottom rear of the frame. With your modified punch, drift this pin out. Slide the housing down and out of the frame. Lift the grip safety out of the frame. Push the hammer pin out, and lift the hammer out. Push the sear pin out of the frame, and lift the sear and disconnector from the frame. Turn the frame on its left side, and with a small screwdriver, push the magazine catch partially out of the frame from the left side with your left hand. At the same time, turn the screw on the right side a quarter turn counterclockwise. When you hit the slot, the screw will turn and the magazine catch will pop out of the frame. Pull the trigger out of the frame.

Scrub the powder residue out of the now bare frame. Be sure you reach down into the trigger slot with the narrow end of your brush, and scrub the powder, dust,

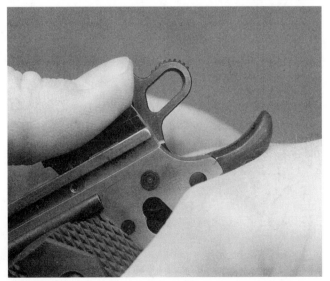

Ease the hammer down to remove tension from the mainspring.

and lint out of the hammer and sear recesses. Wipe or scrub the powder and dirt off all the parts you have pulled out of the frame.

If you have used mineral spirits or an aerosol scrubber on the frame or parts, you will have to lubricate on each part as you re-insert it.

All the internal parts that move, including the hammer, sear, disconnector and trigger, get a drop of oil.

In the slide, place a drop of oil in the locking lugs if there are any, or on the edges of the ejection port if there aren't. The top inside of the slide, where the barrel rubs as the slide cycles back and forth, gets a drop of oil. The cam surfaces or link get another drop of oil.

To begin reassembly put the trigger back into the frame. With the trigger in, insert the magazine catch, and turn the screw clockwise while holding the mag catch slightly out of the frame. When you turn the screw into the frame slot, the magazine button spring will snap the magazine button back in place. To insert the sear/disconnector, hold the disconnector with a hemostat or needlenose pliers, and place the sear in its correct position on the disconnector. Then reach into the frame and put the top of the disconnector in its hole and the

bottom against the trigger bow. Let go of the pliers, and pick up a dental pick. With the pick, align the disconnector and sear pivot holes with the frame hole, reaching in from the right side. Finally, insert the sear pin from the left side.

For the Series 80 pistols, after you have pushed the sear pin through the frame far enough to hold the sear and disconnector, stick your left pinky down into the magazine slot. Approach from the top. Turn the pistol on its left side and hold the sear pin in place with your left thumb. With the hemostat, position the firing pin safety lever in place. Looking through the pivot hole on the right side, use the dental pick to line the lever up with the hole, and then push the pin through. Use your pinky finger to keep the lever from falling into the magazine slot while doing all this juggling.

Turning the frame back onto its left side, place the hammer in the frame, line up the hole and push the hammer pin through. Series 80 pistols, as usual, need a bit more juggling. Push the hammer pin in only far enough to catch the hammer, and then turn the frame upright. Check the trigger lever, just installed, to make sure it is down and bearing against the trigger. If you don't check, and the trigger lever is misaligned, you won't know until

Drift the mainspring housing retaining pin out of the frame.

With the mainspring housing slightly lowered, lift the grip safety out of the frame.

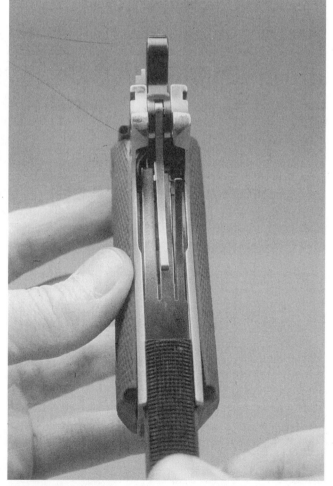

Slide the mainspring housing down out of the frame.

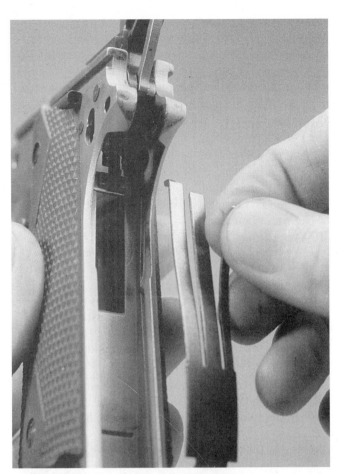

Lift the three-leaf spring out of the frame.

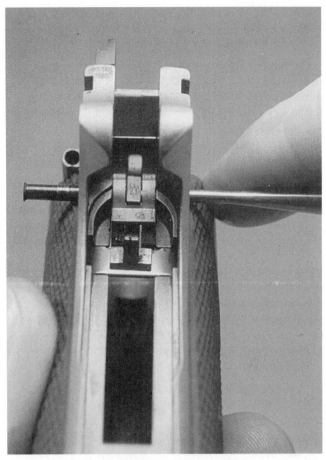

Push the disconnector-sear pin out of the frame.

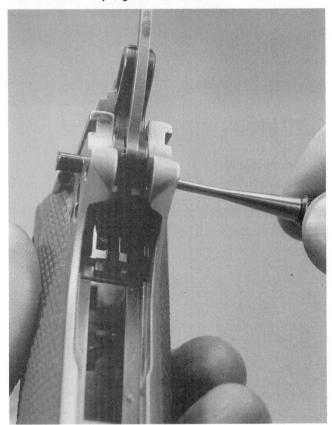

Push the hammer pin out of the frame.

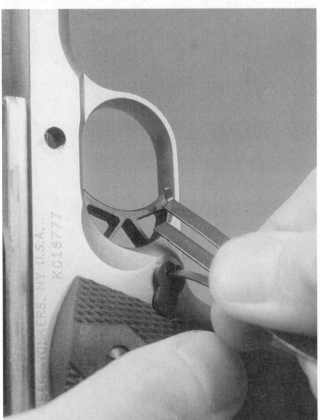

If you don't have a small screwdriver, the third leaf, the grip safety one, can be used to turn the magazine catch retainer.

you try to fire the pistol. It won't fire. Insert the upper safety lever, and lining it up with the hole for the hammer pin, push the hammer pin through it.

Holding the frame with the front end down, flip the hammer strut up. You should now have enough clearance to install the three-leaf spring. Place its bent tab in the slot near the bottom of the frame, and check to see that the left hand leaf rest on the sear foot, while the center leaf rests on the disconnector bevel. Slide the mainspring housing up just far enough to capture the three-leaf spring. Swing the hammer strut down and place the grip safety into the frame. Make sure the hammer strut fits into the notch in the grip safety. There is a cup on the top of the mainspring housing. Slide the housing to capture the strut in this cup. Take a moment for a visual check of the back of the frame. Does everything look like it did when it was together? If so, then push the mainspring housing all the way up, and place the retaining pin into the frame and partially into the mainspring housing. You should be able to place the pin far enough into the holes by hand to keep the mainspring housing from falling out.

Check to see if you can cock the hammer. If you can, let it back down and drift the mainspring-retaining pin in all the way. If you can't you probably have the strut

out of line and jammed against the top of the mainspring housing. Pull out the retaining pin, pull the mainspring housing down a bit, and line the strut up again. Push the mainspring housing up, and try again. Cock the hammer again, insert the thumb safety plunger assembly into its tube, and start the thumb safety into the frame. As in removal, the hammer must be cocked to insert the safety. The plunger assembly will prevent the safety from fully seating. Use your dental pick to push the safety plunger far enough into its tube to clear the safety, and push the safety all the way home.

Reassemble the slide. Check the extractor for cracks or chips on the hook. Install the extractor. Look at the firing pin spring. Is it short, or broken? The minimum length for the spring is 1.650 inches. Is the firing pin straight? If not, get a new one. Although the bent one has been working, firing pins are not expensive, and there is no need to risk stressing the pin more by trying to straighten it. Install the pin and spring, push them into the tunnel and slide the retainer in behind them. Once together, check to see that the firing pin moves freely through the retaining plate's hole.

The Series 80 takes more work. Put the slide back in your vise upside-down. Push the extractor in place. Look through the plunger hole until you see the little shoul-

Lift the magazine catch clear.

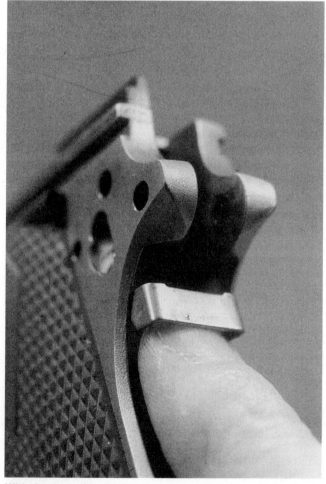

With the magazine catch out, pull the trigger out of the frame.

der on the extractor. Push the extractor back out until this shoulder clears the hole. Insert the safety spring and plunger in the hole, and holding the plunger down, push the extractor forward again to capture the plunger. Check to see that the plunger moves freely in and out. Pushing the plunger into the slide, insert the firing pin and spring. With a drift pin, push the rear end of the firing pin past the plunger. Let go of the plunger. Let go of the firing pin. The firing pin should now be captured by

the plunger. Insert the retaining plate. Push the plunger in one last time. The firing pin should snap out to the retaining plate. Check the firing pin. You should not be able to push it past the plunger. Pushing in the plunger allows you to push the firing pin forward. The slide assembly is finished.

Assemble the barrel into the slide. Before you put the slide on the frame, place a few drops of oil on the rails. Perform the mechanical checks on buying a used 1911, explained in Chapter 4, to make sure you have put things back together properly.

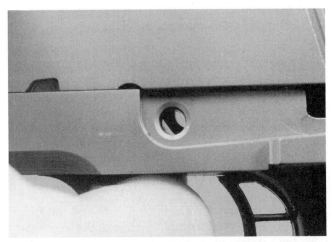

With the link out of alignment you cannot reassemble the 1911.

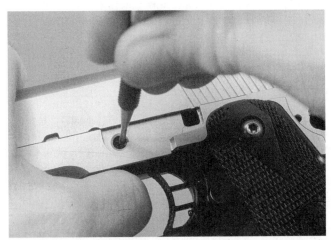

Use a drift punch or small rod to catch the link and line it up.

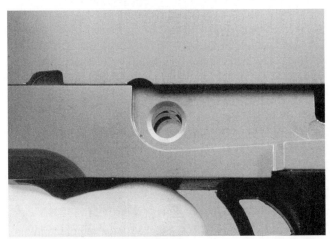

Now the link is properly positioned.

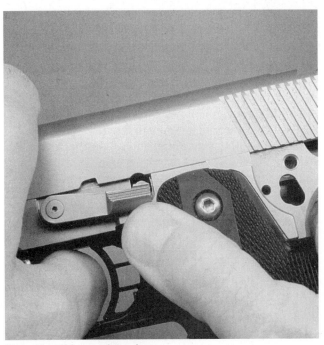

With the link lined up, place the slide stop in the frame.

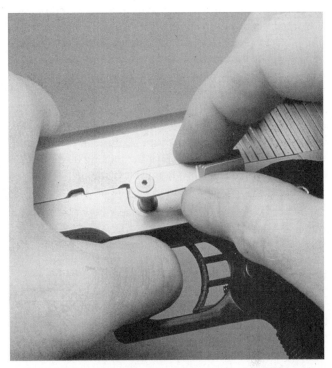

Press the slide stop into place.

CLEANING THE BERETTA M-92

The Beretta 92 is quite easy to strip for simple cleaning. It is issued to the Armed Services, and the last thing a G.I. needs is a pistol he can't quickly and easily clean the mud from. After you check to make sure it isn't loaded, use the safety to de-cock the hammer. Remove the magazine. On the right side of the frame ahead of the trigger guard is a small button. On the left side of the frame is a lever. Press and hold the button into the frame. Pivot the lever down from the slide. You can now remove the slide and barrel from the frame.

Grab the rear of the recoil spring guide rod and push it toward the muzzle, lifting it from its seat. Since the rod and spring are not one unit, be careful not to launch the rod. With the spring out of the slide, look at the rear of the barrel. Find the small plunger. This unlocks the barrel from the slide. Push this plunger in, and lift the barrel up and out of the slide.

For a simple cleaning wipe off the powder residue, brush and use solvent in the bore. Lubricate the Beretta with a drop of oil on the front of the locking block. On the slide, lubricate the firing pin safety plunger. Once everything is clean and oiled, reassemble.

I have to confess that a detailed cleaning of the Beretta M-92, like any other double-action pistol, is a pain in the butt, and I skip it if I can. When your pistol needs more than just a simple cleaning, but does not yet require a detail cleaning, try the following: Take the slide off and remove the grips from the frame. Immerse the frame in mineral spirits and let it soak for 20 minutes. Allow it to drip-dry and, if you can, finish drying with compressed air. Lubricate with Break Free. Break Free acts as a solvent for, among other things, powder residue. Work the action, and immerse the frame for another twenty minutes. Dry the frame, re-oil it and reassemble.

I admit this is not as thorough as a detail cleaning, but it will save you more than an hour of stripping, cleaning and reassembly. It will also postpone your need for a detail cleaning.

Eventually, you will need to do the dreaded detail cleaning. Take the grips off. When you removed the slide, you rotated the disassembly lever down. Now, push the disassembly button into the frame and turn the lever the other way. Rotate it until the tip of it points straight up. Lift the disassembly lever out of the frame on the left side, and the disassembly latch button and spring from the right side.

Place the frame on its left side. With a small screwdriver, unseat the upper part of the trigger bar spring from the trigger bar. Lift the spring from its hole in the frame. Pull the trigger bar straight out from the frame. The trigger spring is difficult to replace once it has been removed. You do not need to remove the trigger, so don't.

The hammer must be down to disassemble the hammer and sear. Take a 1/8-inch punch. Hold the frame in one hand and press the lanyard loop against your bench. Use the punch to push the retaining pin from the frame. Ease the lanyard loop and mainspring out gently.

Push the hammer pin out from right to left. Lift out the hammer and hammer strut. For cleaning, you do not need to remove the sear. Removal of the hammer gives you room to scrub the sear and the other parts. If you are going to do a trigger job to the Beretta, you must remove the sear. The hole for the sear pin is the one directly behind the upper grip screw bushing. With a 3/32-inch punch, press the pin out of the hole and let the sear drop free.

To reassemble, reverse the order. Hold the frame in a padded vise. Use a pair of needle-nose pliers to position the sear, and push your 3/32-inch punch through from the right side to hold the sear in place. Use the pliers again to position the sear spring, and push the punch through enough to capture the spring. Press the sear pin into the frame form the left side, and catch the spring and sear while using the sear pin to push the punch out of the frame.

Place the hammer strut in the frame, kinked end towards the muzzle. Place the hammer in the frame, and push the hammer pin in from the right. Push the hammer forward to the uncocked position. Slide the mainspring into place, and make sure you have the top end of the hammer strut in its seat in the hammer. Grasp the frame, and pressing against the bench push the lanyard loop into the frame and slide its retaining pin into the frame.

CLEANING THE GLOCK

The Glock is different, and in some major ways. Make sure the gun is not loaded, and, to begin the disassembly, dry-fire it. Hold the slide back 1/10th of an inch to take the recoil spring tension off of the disassembly lever, and pull this lever down on both sides of the frame at the same time. If you pull the slide back too far you will re-set the mechanism and must dry fire the pistol again and start over. With the disassembly lever down, the slide assembly slides off of the frame.

Older Glocks have their recoil spring and guide rod separated, and you have to be careful prying the rear of the guide rod out of its seat in the barrel. If you lose your grip, you'll launch the rod and probably lose track of the spring, too. Newer Glocks have the recoil spring and guide rod assembled as a unit at the factory, and they stay together.

Before you scrub the barrel and slide, you must know two important details. If your Glock is brand-new it will have copper gunk on the underside. This gunk, an anti-seize compound, is placed there by the factory so the slide and disconnector can properly burnish against each other. Though it will gradually wear away, you should not clean it away. (This is one way to tell if a Glock really is "brand new." If it doesn't have this compound, it isn't new, no matter how clean it looks.)

The second detail? The Glock striker (firing pin) and its tunnel should not be oiled. Not at all. To reduce friction the striker tunnel is lined with a plastic sleeve. The striker spring is assembled to the striker with two little plastic cups. If you oil the tunnel, the oil will attract grit, dust and powder residue, which will act as a lapping compound to grind up the plastic.

For a simple cleaning of your Glock proceed as in the 1911.

A detail cleaning of the Glock first requires stripping the slide. Look at the front end of the striker slot, under the slide. Find the edge of the plastic cup. With a punch, press and hold it towards the muzzle. With the cup held in place, work a small screwdriver into the gap between the back of the slide and the striker retainer plate. Pry the plate down part way. Let go of the punch holding the striker cup. Remove the striker retainer plate, using your fingers to keep the extractor plunger from launching itself out of the slide. With the plate off, pull the striker assembly and the extractor plunger assembly out. Depress the firing pin safety and lift the extractor out of its slot. Remove the firing pin safety.

Scrub everything clean. Check the extractor for chips or breaks. If your extractor is chipped but still works, keep using it, but write the Glock factory Service Department to get a new one. Place a drop of oil on the firing pin safety spring and the foot of the extractor. To reassemble the slide, push the firing pin safety into its hole, and hold it down while you insert the extractor in the slide. The extractor plunger, spring and cap, and striker assembly go in next. The edges of the striker retainer get a drop of oil before you start sliding the striker retainer in place. Depress the extractor cap to clear the retainer. Once the cap is down, push the striker spacer cup down, and slide the retainer plate all the way in. Before replacing the barrel in the slide, oil the top inside surface of the slide.

Now disassemble the frame. Original Glock 17s only had one pin holding the locking block in place. With the start of Glock 22 production, the locking block gained another pin called the locking pin. This pin, if present, should always be the first pin out on disassembly, and the first pin in on reassembly. Push it out from left to right. The trigger pin, common to all Glocks, and held into the frame by the slide stop lever, requires a bit of fussing. Press on the pin. At the same time, wiggle the slide stop lever until the pin shoulder clears the edge of the hole through the lever. Remove the pin.

Lift the slide stop lever out of the frame. Stick a small screwdriver or drift pin under the locking block and pry the block out of the frame. It will lift up along guide slots cast into the frame.

Turn to the back of the frame and push the trigger mechanism housing pin out. Since it is not locked in it should slide out easily. Remove the trigger assembly by sticking your same small screwdriver or drift pin under the ejector. Use the ejector to pry the trigger assembly out. Carefully lift the entire assembly out of the frame without further disassembly.

Look closely at how the trigger bar and trigger housing fit together. With the housing in your left hand, and the trigger in your right hand, give the trigger and trigger bar a turn counterclockwise, and pull them up out of the housing. The spring should stay attached. Before you clean these up, practice putting the end of the trigger bar back into the housing. Twist it clockwise to reassemble it. Do this a few times until you have a good feel for how the parts fit. It's ingenious, and not obvious if you don't closely observe and practice it.

Scrub these parts clean, except for the anti-seize compound on the connector. Remember, leave that alone.

Begin reassembly by inserting the trigger assembly into the frame. Push the rear pin in place. Push the locking block into the frame. Insert the locking block pin through the frame and block. Insert the slide stop lever, and start the lower (trigger) pin. Wiggle the slide stop until the trigger pin slides through its hole in the slide stop.

Before putting the slide assembly back, oil the top front corner of the locking block. Slide the assembly on. You do not have to hold down the disassembly levers. Just run the slide back far enough to re-set the mechanism. The disassembly lever locks in place. In general, the less oil you put on an in your Glock, the better.

CLEANING THE SINGLE-ACTION REVOLVER

A simple cleaning of the single-action revolver is easy. I have described the Colt and Old Model Ruger simple cleaning together, as they are identical. The detailed cleaning of Colt, Old Model Ruger and New Model Ruger have their own niceties, so I have separated them. The demonstration revolver is an EMF Dakota.

COLT, COLT CLONES AND OLD RUGER SIMPLE CLEANING

First, check that your Colt or Ruger is not loaded. Draw the hammer back to the second click, which lowers the locking bolt and allows the cylinder to be rotated. Open the loading gate. Press the spring-loaded plunger (located in the front of the frame) crossways, and pull the centerpin out of the frame. Lift the cylinder out of the frame through the loading gate opening. Scrub the powder residue, and brush each of the chambers just as much as you do the barrel. Get everything clean.

For reassembly, make sure the hammer is still at the second click. Place the cylinder into the frame. You may want to put a drop of oil on the centerpin. Hold the cylinder in place as you juggle the revolver to reseat the plunger and insert the centerpin, sliding it in from the front.

COLT AND EMF SINGLE-ACTION DETAIL CLEANING

The detailed cleaning of the Colt single-action revolver involves as many as a dozen screws. Check your screwdrivers to make sure they are a proper fit or you will chew up a lot of screw slots. Begin by removing the backstrap. Remove the screw in the butt of the frame, and the two screws below the hammer. When you set the backstrap aside, put the screws back through their holes. By doing this, you will not only keep the screws where they belong in the frame, you'll also avoid misplacing them. The large flat spring you see is the mainspring. Unscrew the mainspring retention screw.

On the bottom of the trigger housing are three screws. Remove these. On the Colt, the locking bolt and spring are worked by the flat, two-leaf spring in the bottom of the frame. Remove the screw holding this spring in, and while you have the spring in hand give it a thorough inspection. The fingers are prone to cracking and breaking off. If you see even a small crack replace the spring.

Now find the three screws on the side of the frame. Unscrew the two smaller ones, and after you pull them out remove the trigger and locking bolt. Unscrew the bigger one, and draw the hammer down out of its slot, guided by the hand riding in its slot.

Scrub everything, and reassemble in the reverse order. Note: you should tighten the three screws holding the trigger guard in place before you tighten the mainspring screw. Otherwise, you will be holding the trigger guard in place against the tension of the mainspring. It is strong. You will lose.

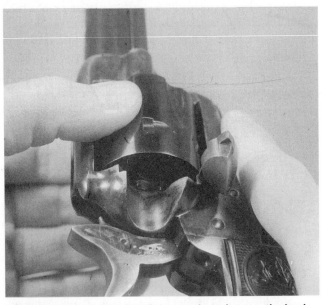

Thumb the hammer back to the second notch, open the loading gate and rotate the cylinder.

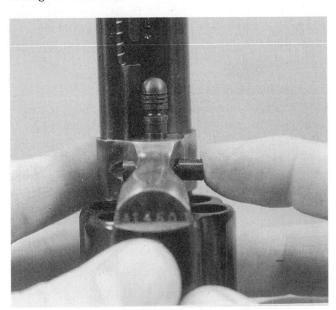

The retaining catch is spring-loaded.

Make sure the revolver is unloaded.

Push the retaining catch to the side and pull the center pin out of the cylinder and frame.

Remove the cylinder.

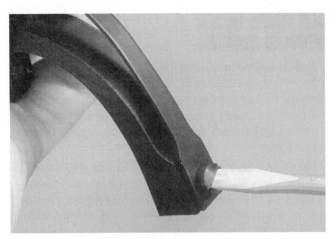

The mainspring screw must be removed before you can remove the lower half of the grip straps.

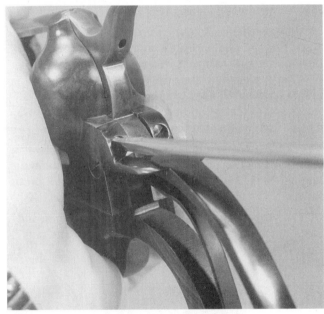

And two at the top on either side of the hammer.

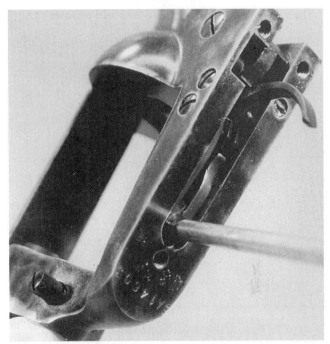

The Colt single-action has a trigger-locking bolt spring with two leaves. Remove the screw and inspect the spring.

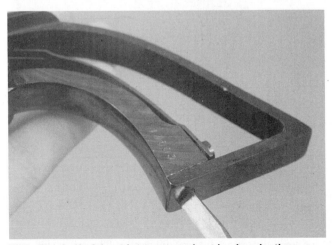

The upper half of the grip straps are kept in place by three screws, one at the bottom of the frame.....

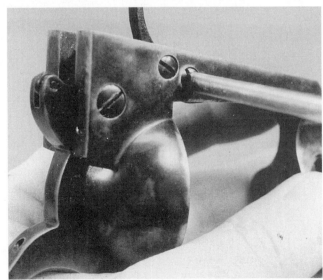

Remove the trigger, locking bolt and hammer screws.

OLD MODEL RUGER DETAILED CLEANING

Remove the grips on the Ruger. The Ruger mainspring is a coil spring over a strut. Cock the Ruger and put a pin through the hole in the bottom of the strut. Lower the hammer. The Ruger grip frame is a single piece. You will remove the mainspring assembly when you pull the grip frame loose.

Loosen the two screws below the hammer, and the three screws around the trigger guard. On the Colt the two screws under the hammer are identical. On the Ruger the left-hand screw holds in the hand spring, so keep this one in the left side of the backstrap when you set it down. Pull the hand spring and plunger out of the hole, and set them aside.

The trigger return spring is hooked and pivoted

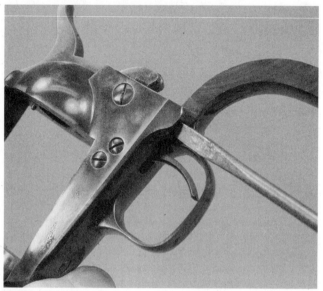

Remove the three screws from the bottom half of the grip straps.

behind the trigger. Unhook the legs from their posts. The trigger housing contains the locking bolt spring and plunger. These are small parts. Be careful!

You can now pull the entire grip frame away from the main frame. Scrub everything clean.

Clamp the frame upside down in a padded vise for reassembly of the lower frame to the upper. To make reassembly a little less difficult, place a drop of oil on all moving parts before beginning. Place the mainspring strut assembly in the housing. The top of the strut rides in a slot cut into the back of the hammer. Align the top with the slot. You will have to juggle the grip frame onto the cylinder frame, and keep the locking bolt spring and plunger in place, while aligning the strut and slot (see above), and the trigger return spring and hand spring (see below). Hook the trigger return spring over its shelf on the trigger. Check to make sure the mainspring strut assembly is still in its bearing slot. Be careful not to crush the hand spring when sliding the grip frame in place. There are a lot of little things to watch for in this procedure. I wonder where the Ruger factory finds six-fingered people to hire as assemblers.

With your thumb, hold the grip frame down. Check to see that the mainspring assembly is still properly aligned. If it isn't, realign it. You can't do this after the grip frame is secured. Start the three bottom (trigger guard) screws. You need to snug one of these down before you can let go of the grip frame. Tighten all three screws. Tighten the two screws below the hammer.

Cock the hammer and remove the capture pin. To check the function of the hammer and trigger, thumb the hammer back. Watch the locking bolt to see that it drops down into the frame and pops back up.

If everything appears to work, put the cylinder in and check function again. Wipe down the exterior and put the revolver away.

The EMF reduced-power mainspring on the right. Simply switching from your full-power mainspring to this one will ease the work of cocking your single-action Colt or clone.

DETAIL CLEANING THE RUGER NEW MODEL

The re-design of the Ruger single-action revolver that culminated in the New Model changed the revolver's safety features, and some aspects of the disassembly. The New Model has no screws for the hammer, trigger and locking bolt, which are held in by crosspins. Because the loading gate now unlocks the cylinder for rotation, you no longer have to partially cock the hammer to load, unload or disassemble the revolver.

For a simple cleaning, open the loading gate and make sure the revolver is unloaded. Press the centerpin plunger. Draw the centerpin out of the frame. The cylinder now drops free of the frame. Wipe off the powder residue and scrub the bore and chambers clean.

For detailed cleaning, follow the Old Model disassembly up to the removal of the trigger, locking bolt and hammer.

Once you have removed the lower frame, turn the revolver upside down and clamp it in a padded vise. The spring that activates the locking bolt also works the loading gate and keeps the trigger pin from falling out. Use a drift pin to push down the leg of this spring where it passes through the slot in the trigger pin. With the spring held down out of the way (and it is a strong one!) push the trigger pin out of the frame. Lift the spring, trigger and locking bolt out of the frame. Push the hammer pin out of the frame. Lift the hammer and hand out of the frame.

Scrub everything.

To reassemble, put the hammer in place. Push the hammer pin into the frame. Place the locking bolt, loading gate and trigger in the frame, and start inserting the trigger pin. Begin from the side opposite the spring. Slide the pin up to the spring. Push the spring down to clear the pin. Slide the pin the rest of the way over. Release the spring. Check the locking bolt, loading gate and trigger to see that the spring is bearing on them properly. If the tip of the spring does not correctly engage the loading gate, the gate will not work. If you do not discover this until you do your final reassembly check, you will have to remove all the parts to get back to the spring. Save time, and check now.

With the spring in place, reassembly follows the Old Model pattern.

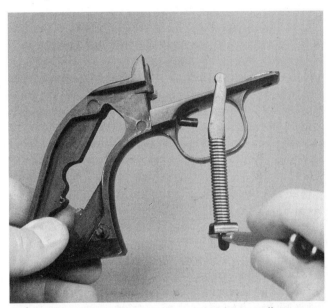

After cocking the mainspring, place a punch or small screwdriver through the hole in the shaft. Remove the five screws, and the grip frame comes off in one piece. The plunger in the trigger guard is the trigger return spring and plunger.

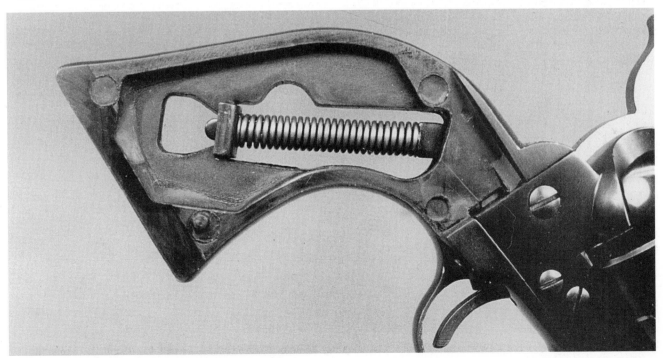

The Ruger mainspring is a coil spring, riding on a shaft.

CLEANING THE DOUBLE-ACTION REVOLVER

Double-action revolvers fall into two camps: revolvers with sideplates, and Rugers.

On the Smith & Wesson, Colt, Taurus, Rossi and any revolvers that have sideplates, remove the front screw and the cylinders for a simple cleaning. With the cylinder removed, scrub the bore and chambers, and wipe the powder residue off of the frame. Replace the cylinder. On the Ruger DA revolvers leave the cylinder in place. Wipe, scrub, and you're done.

In a detailed cleaning of revolvers with a sideplate, remove the screws. Carefully set them aside in the order they came off the frame. Handling screws carefully is especially important in older S&W, Taurus and Rossi revolvers. Front sideplate screws on these models are precisely fitted to hold the crane without binding. If you inadvertently switch screws you can cause the crane to bind on opening and closing. On new S&W's and Colts the crane retention screw is a spring-loaded plunger assembly, and is too large to mix up with the sideplate screws.

Hold the frame in your left hand, with your thumb over but not touching the sideplate. With a hammer handle or a wooden block in your right hand, whack the grip straps. You want to pop the sideplate out with inertia. Aim for your bench, and do not let the sideplate hit the floor. Do not pry the sideplate to remove it. Prying will burr the edge and run the risk of bending it. A bent sideplate can interfere with proper function.

There are two ways to remove the mainspring on S&W, Taurus and Rossi revolvers. If it is a flat spring, back out the strain screw at the bottom of the front grip strap. Pull the bottom of the spring out of its slot in the frame, and unhook the top from the hammer stirrup. If it is a coil spring, cock the revolver and put a capture pin through the hole at the bottom of the strut. Release the hammer. The capture pin will keep the spring compressed, allowing you to remove the strut and spring together. Lift out the safety bar.

With a tapered screwdriver, pry up the back end of the trigger rebound bar. Don't let the spring launch itself out. With the rebound bar out, cock the hammer before lifting it from the frame. Pull the hand back from its slot, and lift the trigger and hand out of the frame together.

On Colts, we again have two methods to remove the mainspring. On the Python, Detective Special, and other Colt revolvers with a "V" spring, clamp the spring with a pair of needle-nose pliers and work it out from under the hammer stirrup. Lift the hand out of the trigger. Drift out the action bar pin and remove the action bar. Cock the hammer and lift it out. Look at the trigger assembly; make sure you understand how its parts fit. Now lift it out.

Newer Colts have a coil mainspring. Cock the hammer. Put a capture pin through the strut, as per the S&W and Taurus. The newer Colt revolver internals lift out without having to lever against any springs.

Remove the locking bolt. On the S&W, Taurus, and Rossi revolvers, a spring pushes the locking bolt up. Use a small drift pin or dental pick to push the locking bolt down against the spring. Wedge another dental pick under the bolt. Slide the bolt up its shaft. Be patient. There isn't a lot of room here. On the Colt "V" spring models a small screw holds the locking bolt in. Unless you are replacing the bolt, do not remove the screw. Check it for tightness, and then leave it alone.

Scrub all the parts and the frame.

Last parts out, first parts in. On the S&W, Taurus and Rossi revolvers, place the locking bolt on its shaft. Insert

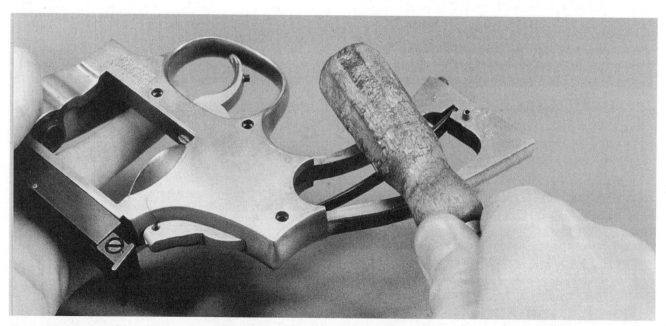

Once the sideplate screws are out, rap the frame with a wooden bar, hammer handle or large screwdriver handle to loosen the sideplate. Do not pry the sideplate out, you may bend or mar it.

the spring in the bolt. Slide the bolt down the shaft until the spring binds against the frame. Use a small screwdriver to compress the spring into the bolt, and shove the bolt and its spring the rest of the way down into the frame.

Take the trigger and hand, and tilting the hand back, slide the trigger down onto its shaft. Once it is down, tilt the hand forward into its slot. Hold the frame in your left hand. Use your left index finger to pull the cylinder release back. Continue holding it down. Pull the trigger with your left middle finger, and hold it back. Put the hammer on the hammer shaft, in its full-cock position, and push it down into the frame. Release the trigger and push it and the hammer to their forward, resting position. Start fitting the front of the rebound block into the back of the trigger. Compress the rebound slide spring until you can push it down behind the rebound bar retaining stud. Place the safety bar onto its pin on the rebound block.

On the Colt V-spring revolvers, reassembly starts with the trigger linkage. Hook the long end of the flat bar onto the trigger, positioning ring down. Hook the safety bar onto the short end of the flat bar. Come from underneath the flat bar. The whole assembly must fit over the hammer shaft boss and trigger pivot pin as one piece. Put the hammer on its shaft. Place the action bar into the frame and drift its pin through. Put the hand onto the trigger. Make sure it is down all the way. The action bar point must cam against the hand's internal shoulder. With your needle-nose pliers compress the V-spring and hook it under the hammer stirrup.

On all the revolvers, place a drop of oil on all the internal parts, either where they rotate or where they engage other parts. On the hammer, oil the pivot hole, the pivot of the DA sear, the mainspring stirrup, and the SA notch.

On the trigger, oil the pivot hole, the hand spring and slot, and the bolt tip. On the cylinder bolt, oil the spring and the pivot hole. On the rebound block, oil all four sides, as well as the trigger return spring.

In the cylinder, place a drop of oil on the center pin at both ends. Lift the extractor star and place a drop of oil at its base. Let the extractor slide back in place.

On the crane, place a drop of oil on the outside. Rub the oil around with your fingers. Place a drop of oil inside the crane, place the cylinder into it, and give the cylinder a spin.

Secure the sideplate. Wipe down the exterior first with an oily rag, then with a dry one. You should be able to see an oily finish, but not feel it when touching the surface. Too much oil will attract lint and dust.

DETAIL CLEANING OF RUGER DOUBLE-ACTION REVOLVERS

At first glance, the Ruger double-action revolver seems strange. There is no sideplate, and the only screw to be seen is in the grips. How to disassemble it?

Take the grips off. You'll find a pin in a recess inside the grip. This is the mainspring capture pin. Cock the hammer, put the pin through the hole at the bottom of the strut, and release the hammer. Pull the base of the strut to one side, and pull the mainspring assembly down out of the frame.

Look at the hammer pin. On one side the pin has a flat tail. Push from the other side to remove the pin. Lift the hammer out of the receiver.

The plunger that holds the trigger assembly in the receiver is located at the top of the grip frame cutout. Use a drift pin to push the plunger towards the trigger. When the plunger clears the frame the rear of the trigger

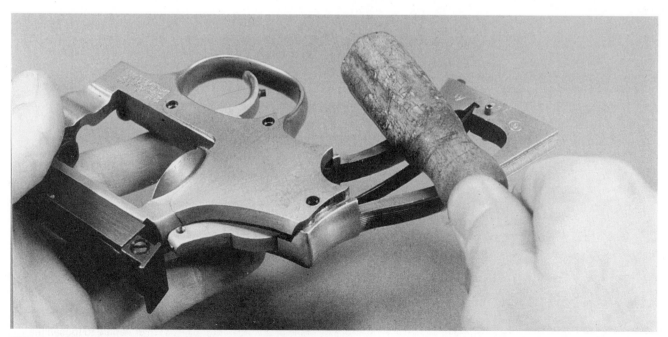

With the sideplate loose you can begin removing the internal parts.

assembly will move down from the frame. The trigger guard assembly is hooked into the frame at the assembly's front. Grasp the trigger guard. Pivot the rear of the assembly down as you pivot it free of the frame.

Open the cylinder and pull it forward out of the frame.

Before disassembling the trigger assembly any further, look at it carefully. The parts, pushed by small springs and plungers, pivot in their seats in the trigger guard body. If, for example, you snatch the safety bar out, you will launch its spring and plunger. Work each part out carefully and set it aside with its respective spring and plunger. If you think you'll clean the entire assembly without handling the small parts, think again. Simply blasting the assembly with aerosol, or scrubbing it as one piece and finishing with compressed air, will scatter all the little parts all across the room. Be patient. It works better in the long run.

As with the Ruger New Model single-action revolvers, oil all the clean parts before assembly.

Replace the cylinder and close it in the frame.

Hook the front of the trigger guard assembly into the frame. Pivot the rear up. If you feel some resistance, stop and look down through the hammer slot. Find the top of the safety bar. It may be binding against the cylinder release. Reduce the pressure on the trigger guard and, with a small screwdriver, pivot the safety bar back from the cylinder release. Continue pressing on the trigger guard until the plunger at the rear snaps in place in the frame.

Insert the hammer into the frame from the top. Line

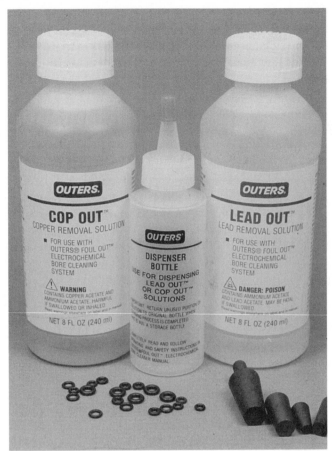

The Foul-Out comes with separate solutions for lead and copper. Also included are bore plugs and o-rings to keep the rod from touching your barrel. If the rod touches the barrel the unit will not work.

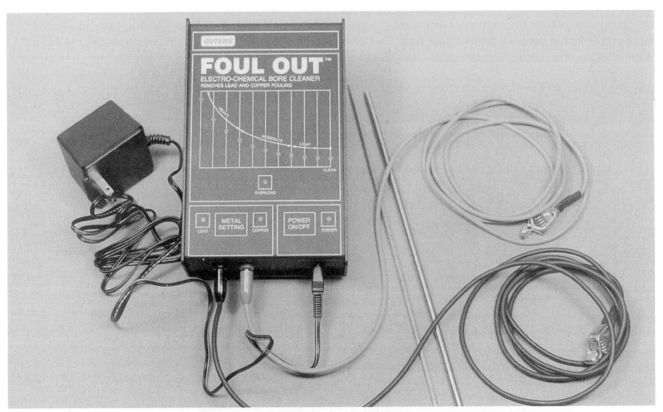

The Outers Foul-Out makes bore cleaning such a snap, you won't believe it.

the hammer pivot hole up with the hole through the frame. Push the hammer pivot pin into the frame; making sure the tail of the hammer pivot pin is in the slot cast for it on the side of the frame.

Work the mainspring strut up into the frame. Put the base on the frame seat and cock the hammer. Remove the capture pin. Be sure to put the pin into its storage slot in the grips! Finally, reinstall the grips.

THE OUTERS FOUL-OUT™

A heavily lead- or copper-fouled bore can require a great deal of elbow grease to clean, and take a lot of time in the process. An easier way is to use the Outers Foul-Out™.

It removes the lead and copper by reverse electroplating. With a chemical solution and a sacrificial rod in the bore, and electricity, you plate the lead or copper off the bore and onto the rod.

There are some catches. You can't use the same solution for both lead and copper. If you have a bore with lead and you use the copper solution, you don't get any result. The same is true with copper fouling and lead solution. If you have a bore with both, you have to use both, one after the other.

There's a second catch. If you do not follow the instruction exactly, you can begin eating up your barrel.

Read the instructions that come with the unit. The booklet may seem thin, but it has lots of information, information you need to know. What doesn't come with the unit is a method of holding your barrel. You need to hold the barrel firmly and vertically. Simply standing it in a corner will not do. I went to the local hardware warehouse and found a small stand and an insulated clamp.

The important things to keep in mind, after you have read the instructions, are these;

You must de-grease thoroughly. The barrel and the rod must be clean of lubricants, or the solution may not reach the surface of the fouling.

The o-rings are there to prevent the rod from touching the barrel. If you select a ring that is too large, the unit cannot clean the bore at the point the o-ring is pressing against it.

Scrub the rod between cleaning cycles with dry abrasive cloth. Do not use steel wool. Steel wool contains oil as an anti-rusting agent. The oil will prevent proper cleaning.

The first time you clean a barrel, check for corrosion. After the first fifteen to thirty minutes, stop the unit and pour the solution out. If the solution has become yellowed, corrosion is present. If you continue using the Foul-Out™, you will attack the steel of the barrel itself. Pour out the solution and use patches and brush on the bore. Brush vigorously and use patches until they come out clean. Degrease the bore and start over again with fresh solution. Repeat until the Foul-Out™ solution does not yellow. Then you can begin removing the fouling.

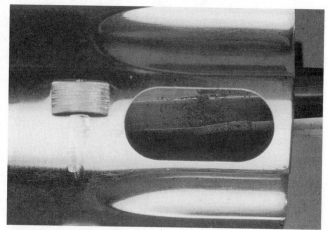

The reamer removes the lead, but does not cut the steel of the chamber.

Here is the Outers Foul-Out cleaning up a Smith & Wesson .44 Magnum. After an hour, there is no more lead or copper in the bore. Quick, painless and difficult to do wrong, this is a neat tool.

The Outers Foul-Out lets you know when you are done. When only the "clean" light is lit, there is no more of that metal left in the bore.

As with all cleaning solutions, the solvents used in Foul-Out™ can be hazardous to your health. Wash thoroughly if you spill any on yourself. Of course you will not be doing this in the kitchen, nor will you be eating lunch while cleaning your handguns, right?

The Outers Foul-Out™ will ease your cleaning chores. A clean bore in your handgun means greater accuracy, a longer service life and less chance of a gunked-up bore causing a malfunction.

How much do I like the Foul-Out™? When I was done with the testing, Outers did not get the unit back. It resides in a corner of my shop, waiting patiently each day for the handguns that return from the range.

SPECIALIZED CLEANING TOOLS

Some cleaning jobs on your handguns will require specialized tools. Without them you will spend more time cleaning–time you could have devoted to reloading ammunition, or to your family. Specialized cleaning tools you may need are: chamber reamer, collared chamber brush, slide hoe, and a range rod.

Some revolver calibers are designed to allow shorter caliber rounds to be fired in them. You can fire .38 Specials in a .357 Magnum, .44 Russian or .44 Specials in a .44 Magnum, and .45 Schofields in a .45 Colt. In all these situations, the lesser-powered case is simply a shorter version of the Magnum round.

You cannot use a .38 Smith & Wesson in the .38 Special, nor can you use 9mm Kurz in the 9mm Parabellum. These are not simply short versions of the longer cartridge, but a different cartridge entirely.

A cylinder leaded-up, or with crusty chambers from using short brass, requires aggressive cleaning. This chamber cleaning reamer from Clymer will scrape the gunk out.

The problem with using a short cartridge in a long chamber is the powder build-up. At the front of the chamber there is a shoulder stepping from the case diameter to the bullet diameter. The shoulder guides the bullet into the forcing cone. If you use a shorter case, you end up with a gap between the end of the case and the start of the shoulder. This gap gets caked with powder residue. When you load a longer case into the crudded-up chamber, it may slip into place just fine. On firing, however, the case expands against the crud and locks the empty in place. Extracting locked-in empties is no fun.

If you are in the habit of shooting short cases, get a reamer. Clymer makes one that scrapes most of the crud out. You can brush out the rest. Brushing alone takes a good, long while.

Powder residue builds up differently in pistol chambers. Because the empty cases are yanked out after each shot, powder residue is shaken out of the case and left in the chamber. Each successive round pushes some of this residue forward against the front edge of the chamber. The rest stays in the chamber and gets hammered flat by the expanding case. The just-fired case takes some of the powder residue it has hammered flat out of the pistol, and deposits still more.

Eventually you end up with flat sheets of powder residue packed hard against the sides of your chamber. The powder residue pushed forward creates a crusted ring at the chamber front. The tighter the chamber, the sooner the buildup becomes a problem.

To remove the buildup, buy a brass bar at least six inches long and 1/4-inch in diameter. Brass cannot harm the steel of your barrel. File the end on a sharp angle, so you have a curved point on it. Use the point to scrape the flat powder out of the chamber, and to dig the packed crud out of the front of the chamber. Since the powder residue is very abrasive, you will have to sharpen this rod frequently, and keep it clean. Otherwise the abrasive residue may harm your barrel.

As an aid in cleaning the chamber, dedicate a rod and brush to each caliber. If you take a brand-new brush for your caliber, it has just enough extra diameter to scrub the chamber. But the first time you push it through the bore it will flatten just a bit, and lose its bite in the chamber. To keep your dedicated chamber brushes from flattening, put a collar between the brush and rod to prevent running the brush any deeper into the barrel than the chamber. The size and thickness of the collar don't matter. Drill a hole through the collar just large enough to pass the threaded end of your brush. Use an oversized cleaning rod that is large enough in diameter to stop your collar from sliding away from the brush. Slip the threaded end of the brush through the hole, screw the brush into the rod, and now your chamber brush won't get flattened.

Powder also builds up on the slide. On all pistols the slots behind the breechface, where the ejector rides, will get coated with powder. Brushes can only get so far into these slots. On the 1911, the locking slots of the slide will collect crud that has to be removed.

Large amounts of powder residue will collect where the barrel rests on the frame. The residue may even get packed into a hard, flat mass similar to that found in the chamber.

To make a "slide hoe," use a broken aluminum cleaning rod. If you don't have one of your own, go to your local gunshop, where broken cleaning rods collect like tangled hangers in a closet. Or buy a section of aluminum rod of a similar diameter. Don't break a cleaning rod just to make this tool. File the end of the rod to a square cross-section. File the tip to a chisel point. Being aluminum, your hoe can't harm any steel. Scrape the crud out of the nooks and crannies where brushes can't easily reach.

RANGE RODS AND BORE OBSTRUCTIONS

A range rod is a brass or aluminum rod (never steel!) that is just small enough in diameter to fit down your bore. Put it in your shooting bag, along with your range cleaning kit. If you run into a squib round, one that leaves a bullet in the barrel, you want to be able to remove it without going home. If you have what you think is a squib, you can run the rod up the bore (AFTER you have unloaded the handgun!) and check. If the rod stops, hammer on it to drive the bullet out. A rod too small in diameter will flex and break, or wedge against the bullet, possibly scoring the rifling.

For .40 caliber or larger, a 3/8-inch diameter brass rod works nicely. For .38/.357/9mm, use a 1/4-inch diameter rod. For a better fit, use your lathe to turn down the 3/8-inch (.375 inch) rod to .340 inch for your .38s. For the .44 or .45 turn down a 1/2-inch rod to .430 or .440, respectively. Or call Brownells and order one already turned to the correct diameter. It is also helpful if you use some penetrating oil on the bore to decrease friction between the bore and jacketed bullets. Lead bullets rarely need oil.

One job I encountered in removing a bullet involved a S&W M-19 but could happen with most any handgun. The owner had lodged a jacketed bullet halfway up the bore. In trying to push it out he had used a cleaning rod, and the smaller than the bullet diameter of the rod simply drove the core of the bullet and the base of the jacket back out of the bore. (I have to assume it was a jacketed hollow-point or softpoint, and the cleaning rod locked in the exposed lead. When he hit the rod with a hammer, the core drove against the jacket base, breaking it.) The jacket remained behind, still stuck in the bore. Brushes wouldn't budge the jacket. I was reluctant to use the Outers Foul Out due to the amount of copper I'd need to remove. An hour taking out some jacket fouling is one thing. Days spent running the machine, changing goop every couple of hours, did not seem prudent.

The wrong bullet-removal method caused this jacket to be stuck in the bore. Getting it out was easy once I'd figured out how.

S&W said it was a simple fix; replace the barrel. When I told him of the offer from S&W, the customer was not too keen on a $200 fix, for a $300 revolver. But he wanted it fixed, and was willing to have me mull things over until I figured a way. Then I hit on an idea. I spent a week soaking the bore with penetrating oil. I turned a short section of brass rod on the lathe until it was a snug slip fit on the rifling and bored a hole in one end big enough for a steel rod. My plan was three steps: try the snug header. If that failed, use a rimmed pistol case, with the rim filed to match and engage the rifling. If that failed, I'd use Cerrosafe to make a full-length casting of the bore, and yank the jacket out with the Cerrosafe. I need not have worried, the machined header pressed the jacket

out without a problem. The good news of a problem solved was dampened by the news I received from the family when I contacted the customer: he had died. (Nearly 20 years, over 15,000 firearms worked on, and he was the only customer of mine to die with a gun in the shop. Other professional gunsmiths I've talked to remark on how I've only had the one; they've had several.) The family was surprised to hear from me, as they had no idea he owned the M-19. The family had no interest in receiving the repaired firearm, and requested that I retain it in exchange for services rendered. The story thus has two lessons: how to remove really obstinate bullets, and the need for having a will and keeping it up to date.

CHAPTER

POWER TOOLS FOR THE AMBITIOUS

Large enough to work hard, small enough to be out of the way.

The allure of lathes and mills is understandable. Large, powerful, precise and able to do in a short time what would be hours of laborious hand filing, lathes and mills are what every gunsmith "needs." Or at least desires. The lust for power tools of the "stand in their own rooms" category definitely falls into what my brother Mike calls "confusing needs with wants." You want the power. But do you need the capability? I'm not trying to steer you away, just to make things clear.

For those with the burning desire, or the clear need, one of each is a must for the complete gunsmithing shop. There are a number of jobs that can only be done on a mill or a lathe. Even considering doing them by hand is lunacy. If you plan to, or must do, the jobs that require a mill or a lathe, then plan your purchase and get what you need.

When considering the purchase of one, you should look carefully at what you plan to do, how much it will cost, and how often you plan to do it. The two competing temptations when buying either a mill or a lathe is to get one that is too small, or get one that is too large. On the small end are the machine tools suitable for use in making model railroad equipment and the like. A lathe big enough to turn a brass rod a 1/4-inch in diameter for use in a railroad engine or a radio controlled plane is not big enough for gunsmithing. Oh, you could get some work done, but it wouldn't be fun. You couldn't work very large pieces (by gunsmithing standards) you couldn't work hard materials, you couldn't do work quickly. On the other hand, too much can be just as bad. At my old shop, I had the good luck to be next door to the machine shop of Tom Stone, brother of Irv Stone of Bar-sto. In addition to answering my questions on things related to barrel fitting and metalworking, Tom showed me a few lathe tricks. He had a pair of Clausing 1300s, huge turret-lathes suitable for production work and precise enough for tool room work. Oh, how I lusted after those machines. And how quickly I dropped the idea of getting one when I learned what they cost. The lure of a small machine is that it "only costs as much as a few barrel fittings" or whatever measure you care to use. The price of the big machines (and getting them wired to your power) is the drawback of going too big.

How much should you spend? In today's markets, you

can get a suitable, if limited machine for $1,000 each. At the $2,000 level you get a much more capable machine, but now you have to start asking yourself, "How much work can I get done, that these machines could do, for $4,000?" Quickly followed by "Should I let someone else do that, and concentrate on other parts of gunsmithing?" The answer to that is something only you can provide.

To learn machine tools, you have two options. You can get lucky and learn from someone who already does the machine work you are interested in, and learn from or apprentice with them. But, if you are interested solely in pistolsmithing (a reasonable assumption, since you are reading this book) then learning machine tool procedures from a machinist who spent his entire career milling, grinding and lathe-turning malleable cast iron, or is a specialist in titanium, won't help you much. If his career as a machinist consisted solely of working a lathe or mill in a production shop/assembly line, doing the same operation over and over, he won't be much help with other tasks. The other route is to enroll in classes at the local community college, and learn the basics of machine tool work.

What can be so hard, you ask? Let's take one example; turning threads on a barrel. How deep a cut do you make on each pass? (And do you do it all at once, or in several passes?) What is the starting diameter of the shank for your threaded section? At what RPM do you turn the barrel? In the old days we all had our "secrets." The truth is, you look up the accepted feed rates for the material of your barrel (4140, 416 Stainless, etc.) and go with that. With one proviso: the accepted feed rates are for production work. They will have you feeding at high rates, and the chips coming off will sometimes be red-hot. (A good thing, heat taken away by the chip is not heat left in the part.) You may want to ease up on the rates a bit just so you can monitor what is going on, and let your tools last a bit longer.

The classes at the community college will teach you how to find the accepted values, and how to apply them. You'll get good experience at basic machining. Just don't expect to be able to bring your guns into the class and work on them. It has been a long time since that was accepted practice. Those of you in a machine shop class out West might still be able to bring firearms in for work, but those of us in the East, or near a big city, don't have the option. Heck, in today's PC environment, simply wearing a firearms-related t-shirt to class might be enough to get you tossed.

A lathe turns cylindrical parts, nearly or mostly cylindrical parts, or bores holes in non-cylindrical parts. The most common use for a lathe in pistolsmithing is barrel fitting. With a good lathe, you can turn down and thread barrel blanks for installation in a revolver. You can adjust the hood length quickly on many pistol barrels. You can fabricate recoil spring retainers for a 1911, and make them just the way you want them. For handgun work, a lathe can be very useful. But it is not required

for as many jobs, as a mill would be. A 9 x 20 lathe (The first number is the "swing over bed," the largest piece that can fit in the chuck and clear the rails. The second number is the maximum length between center, chuck and tailstock.) is large enough to handle handgun work. The problem is not with the costs plus shipping but the extra costs as well. Where will you put it? It (the smallest we're discussing) weighs 250 pounds. It requires a solid, stable bench or cabinet. You cannot just clamp it to an old kitchen table. The support must be solid to avoid vibration, and heavy enough not to tip with 250 pounds on top of it. So, the smallest lathe and a cabinet or bench to perch it on will come in around 400 to 500 pounds. Then there are the tools. You'll need several hundred dollars worth of cutting and measuring tools. Calipers, cutting tools, lubricant, it all adds up. A lathe will have power feed. The big threaded shaft on the front is the power feed (at least longitudinal feed) for thread cutting and surface turning. For cross-cutting you have to get to production machines before you get to power cross-feed, the smallest machines won't have that option. One thing you managed to avoid by getting the smallest is power: it will probably only come wired for 110/120V. You needn't worry about getting 220/250V service into your house. If you move up in size, then the problems become worse. A 12 x 36 machine will weigh half a ton by itself, and the steel cabinet it sits on is likely to add a couple of hundred pounds to that. And it would be a good idea to anchor such a machine to the floor. How will you negotiate that into your shop? If your shop is your garage, great. But don't plan on getting that, or any larger machine, into your basement. The larger the machine, the more likely it is to run on 220/250V power. You can use a phase converter to jump your electrical feed from 110/120V to 220/250V and even three-phase, but at a cost. The converter costs money to obtain, to wire in, and it costs to run it. And using such a big machine and the converter to feed it may void your homeowner's insurance.

In the end, you can have a bunch of barrels fitted, for the cost of acquiring and learning a lathe. Just buying a good lathe, the tools to cut with, and some practice stock, costs as much as 10 fitted barrels. If we assume you'd be buying the barrels anyway, and only consider the labor, you could have 50 barrels fitted for the cost of the lathe.

Lust, but calculate before you buy.

WHAT CAN YOU USE A MILL FOR?

Installing a Novak front sight on a 1911 or Browning Hi-power slide is simple enough that I have seen the dovetail cut done with files. I would not do this. Using files takes too long. Filing the rear of the slide for a Novak rear sight installation is something I would recommend only to enthusiastic masochists or impoverished 18-year-olds. For the detailed cutting that a BoMar sight installation needs, not even files and enthusiasm will do. You must have a mill for this.

The checkering on the front strap of many 1911 pistols is not hand-cut in many custom gunsmiths shops anymore. With the right fixture and cutting tool, the checkering is now machine cut. A mill, this fixture and the correct cutting tool can save you many hours of hand-cramping filing time. And your checkering lines will be straight the first time, and every time.

A drill chuck for your mill allows the mill to be used as a drill press, with the hole spacing precisely controlled by the table movements. Once the work is positioned on the centerline, you position each hole with the mill table, and measure with your calipers just to be sure. You can drill holes for a scope base with confidence, knowing the holes will be the exact distances apart required for your base and handgun.

Slides are basically rectangular, and easy to clamp in the mill vise. Some operations go faster if you have a slide fixture. The D&J slide fixture lets you easily clamp the slide and gives plenty of room between the mill table and the tool head. You can watch the cutter in its work, and reach in to measure the work without lifting the cutter completely away from the working area. This fixture is great for cutting the scallop on the back of ejection ports. Once you have the angle worked out for the best look and performance, scribe a line on the fixture along the top of your mill vise to position the fixture the same way each time.

For work on the 1911 receiver, Evolution Gun Works makes a frame fixture that allows you to position and clamp the frame for a number of operations. You can position it for machine-checkering the front strap, removing the front strap to weld in a pre-checkered panel, and turn the frame on its side to drill for scope mounts. Positioning the frame upright, the fixture lets you mill for a ramped barrel installation. When the frame is upside down you can mill off the bottom preparatory to welding on or silver-soldering a magazine funnel.

A modest mill requires either a very sturdy bench or its own stand. It, along with the necessary cutters and tools to go with it will set you back nearly $2,000. Miniature mills, while wonderful for applications such as model railroad parts or slot cars, cannot handle a large enough vise for handguns. Their motors will not be up to the heavier tasks of pistol work. The first time you run into a hard slide when you go to install a rear sight (Colt slides are well-known for being hard-skinned) you are stopped cold. You will beat up and prematurely dull your cutters cutting through the hardened areas around soldered inserts. The hard spots around welded areas will be impossible to cut on a small mill. Remember, you don't need a mill, so if you really want one, get one that will do all the work you may encounter. For the kind of money a mill represents you can have a lot of work done to a dozen pistols. The basic bench mill weighs 700 to

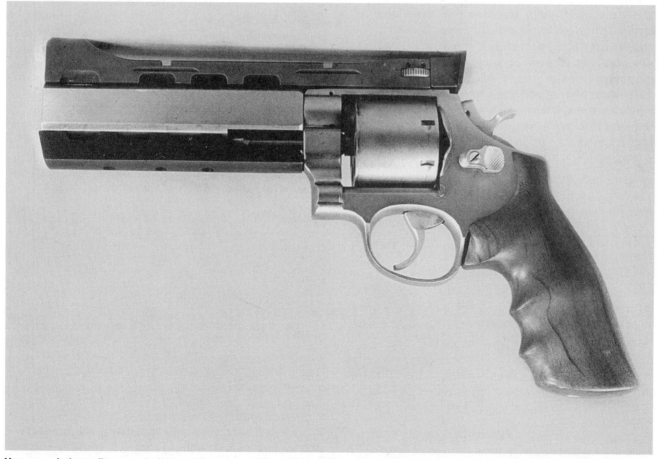

You use a lathe to fit a new, bull barrel, but you need a mill or drill press to drill the holes to secure the rib and weight. Good gunsmiths have both.

With a mill you can easily lower an ejection port so the brass will clear even a scope mount.

The mill makes easy work (relatively speaking) of a low-mount sight installation. Here a Caspian slide is being cut for a Bo-Mar rear sight.

900 pounds, and must have a sturdy bench. A step up to an 8 x 30 knee mill brings the weight to nearly 1,500 pounds, the cost over $2,000, and if you are lucky still runs on 110/120V electrical power. If you aren't lucky, it runs on 220/250, and you'll have to get you work space properly wired for it. As with the lathe mentioned before, the initial cost doesn't include the cutting tools. An additional cost for mills that you don't have for lathes are vises. Not the kind that risk social censure, but the kind that clamp objects. You must have a vise large enough and suited to the job, or you can't cut well. A small vise is often a poor choice, where at the least it exposes the job to the risk of movement. A part that slips will not be milled accurately. And at the worst, the part can be snatched out of the too-small vise and thrown across the room. If you happen to be in its path, peering closely at the work as you cut it, well.....

On both lathes and mills, the "must-have" item for production is digital readout. With digital readout, you greatly reduce the possibility of an incorrect operator

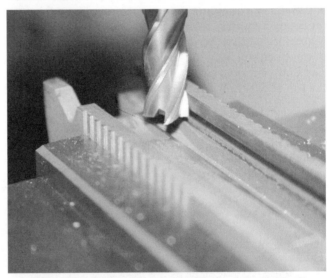

A mill also lets you clean up irregularities in a slides' rails. If the rails were warped in the heat-treat process, or are just a few thousandths narrow, the mill can open them up.

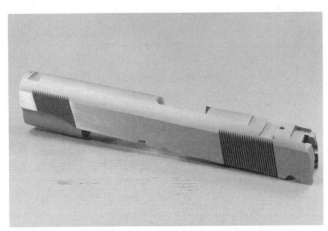

All the work you see on this slide can be done with a mill. While you might be able to do some with a set of files, I'd recommend against it.

To fit a hybrid barrel you simply must have a mill. Any good slide will be hard to file with any comfort or chance of success before you die of old age or give up from exhaustion.

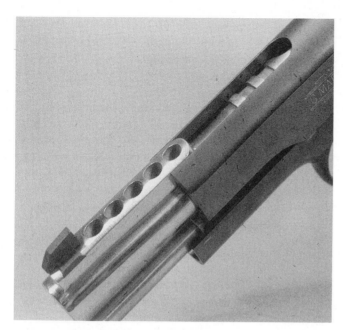

The mill allows you to fit the barrel precisely. Anything less than precision is a waste of time, effort and money.

read of the cutting location. (It isn't impossible, just much less likely.) You can also come back to zero without risk of the gear backlash causing an incorrect tool position. Think of backlash as slack in the gears. Let's say you go to the right, stop, and come to the left back to where you started. Your cutting tool is actually to the right of the start position by the amount of backlash (slack) in the gears. For a good machine, the backlash will be a thousandth of an inch or two. In a bad machine, or one poorly maintained or operated, the backlash can be much greater. Do you need digital readout for gunsmithing? You might. However, for the more than $1,000 it costs, you might want to re-think digital readouts. If you do expect to use digital readout, invest in a machine that can be retro-fitted. It would be a shame to buy a small machine, and then have to upgrade to a larger machine just to add the digital readout you couldn't afford earlier. Power feed on a mill is not standard. You will double the cost of a basic machine by adding digital readout and power feed. (You should not get power feed without digital, but you can use digital without power feed.) Power feed is a production necessity, not a gunsmithing one. If you will be milling slides for Novak sights eight hours a day, then get the digital and power feed. Otherwise, wait.

In the end, $2,000 is a lot of Novak sights fitted to a lot of pistols. It is a warehouse full of old 1911 slides with lowered ejection ports. Think long and hard before investing.

TOOLS FOR YOUR TOOLS

Looking through the Brownells or machine industry tooling catalogs, you'll wonder what all the various modifiers and designations mean. "Tool steel" "Carbide" "TiN" ceramic, what do they all mean? When you go to cut a piece of steel, you either move the part or

you move the cutting tool. Lathes move the part, and mills move the cutting tool. You must use a cutting tool harder than the piece you are cutting. Were you to try to lathe-turn a cylinder which was composed of steel harder than your cutting tool, you'd simply create heat, a marred part, and a dulled tool. Luckily, tooling manufacturers have known about the problem for centuries. The choices you have are cost and tooling durability.

TOOL STEEL

Tool steel, which differs somewhat from "high-speed steel (HSS)," means that the steel the cutting tool is made of has (usually) a higher carbon content, and is heat-treated to be harder than what you're cutting. Tool steel and HSS will not last as long as the harder substances other tools are made of, but offer one real advantage: they can be relatively easily sharpened and shaped. (Compared to shaping a chunk of carbide, tool and HSS cutters are a piece of cake.) A tool-room machinist will often make a bunch of prototype cutters from tool steel or HSS simply to try various shapes and to determine what works. Once the final dimensions are worked out, then the drawings are sent off to fabricate carbide cutters or other-substance cutters. If you have a bench grinder with a fine grit wheel, and the time, you can shape and re-sharpen your own cutting tools. (At least lathe tools. Shaping milling tools is an art and requires more than just a bench grinder.) A carbide tool for a lathe might cost four dollars, while a tool steel blank (that you must shape and sharpen) is $2. For most of what you'd do as a gunsmith, the pre-shaped carbide cutter is worth the two dollars extra.

CARBIDE

A super-hard metal, carbide lasts a lot longer than tool steel or HSS. It also costs more. You have two choices: solid carbide, or carbide inserts. Solid is just what you think, a solid chunk of carbide shaped into a cutting tool. A carbide insert tool is one that has the cutting surfaces composed of inserted pieces of carbide, which are shaped to the desired cutting edge and then inserted in a steel shank. Insert tools are often much larger than you'll need for gunsmithing and are meant for production work. The cost savings of a large tool with carbide inserts compared to solid carbide can be significant when the cutter is 2 inches across its cutting face. For our work, where you'll be buying 3/8-inch or 1/2-inch cutters as "big" cutters, solid carbide is a viable choice. Get the size you need, and then worry about the cost difference between solid and inserts. Inserts come two ways, inserts soldered to the shank to form the tool, and inserts that can be clamped into the tool. The advantage of cost for replaceable carbide again matters only for production. For a milling machine, a 3/8-inch HSS end mill can be had for as little as $8. A solid carbide tool of the same size will run over $20. However, the carbide, properly treated, will last more than three times as long, for a cost savings and for a longer clean-cutting service life. Abused tool or HSS cutters get dull. An abused car-

Cutting tools come in High Speed Steel, carbide and TiN coated. Here are a carbide (right) and a TiN-coated carbide (left) milling cutters. Don't waste money on HSS, buy carbide or TiN-coat carbide.

bide cutter chips or breaks. If you are regularly chipping your carbide cutters, you are working them too hard.

CERAMIC

One problem with high-speed cutting is heat. Heat can quickly dull or destroy a tool steel or HSS cutter. Even carbide cutters will give up if the cutting speed is so high that the heat produced overheats the cutting tool. Ceramics are much more resistant to heat than are metals. A ceramic cutter can continue to work in a production environment even under extreme heat. I've seen cutting operations where the chips being produced came off the part in a red-hot stream. (The sight of red-hot, properly broken and thrown chips coming off of a huge lathe-turned part that was to be the exterior tube of a naval gun barrel is most impressive. Photographs were expressly forbidden, so I can offer you none.) Under such extreme circumstances, ceramics are the only cutting tools that will survive. However, ceramics can't be shaped, as steel or carbide can. Ceramic cutters come as pre-shaped insert "lozenges" of squares, diamonds, circles, or rectangles. The inserts are then clamped in the tool holder, and positioned in the machine to cut. Mills of enough horsepower to swing such a cutter can even use cutters that clamp four, six, eight or more ceramic tips in a cutting head, to be used to mill the parts being shaped. Ceramic tips are of the replaceable type only, and not soldered to a shank to form the cutting tool.

TITANIUM NITRIDE

"TiN" coating of the cutting tool leaves it with a shiny gold coating. The titanium nitride is a hard coating on the cutting tool (commonly done to tool or HSS cutting tools) that extend their life and keep them cutting clean longer than bare steel. A "tin-coat" tool lasts longer than HSS, but not as long as carbide or ceramic. It also costs

in between those other choices. TiN is great for drill bits, but for lathe and mill cutting tools I usually jump right to solid carbide or carbide insert tools.

LATHE COMPONENTS

The nickel tour: A lathe holds a turns an object (not necessarily a cylindrical object) so that you can turn the outside or inside creating a cylindrical surface. In order to perform this function, a lathe needs at an absolute minimum a head and a bed. The head turns, and the bed guides the cutting tool. You will be hard-pressed to find such a basic lathe outside of a museum or antiques store. The basic lathe you can buy today will have a head with interchangeable chucks or faceplates. Inside the head is the motor and gearing or pulleys to adjust turning speed. You need to adjust the turning speed to match the material you are cutting, and the type of cut you will be performing. The chuck is just like the chuck on a drill or drill press. It closes and opens in an even fashion so as to clamp a cylindrical object more-or-less centered. Three and six-jaw chucks open and close automatically. The four-jaw chuck closes either automatically with individual adjustments, or each jaw closes independently. Why? So you can clamp an irregular object with the desired turning location centered on the machine axis. The faceplate is a flat plate to which you clamp even more irregularly shaped objects in order to turn them. You might have need of a four-jaw chuck to be able to turn the exterior of a barrel centered on the bore. You'll probably never need a faceplate.

The bed is comprised of the two rails on which the cutting tools ride. Most new machines are "gap-bed" lathes, where you can remove the portion of the bed closest to the head in order to swing an object that would otherwise strike the bed. Needless to say, there are no such objects in pistolsmithing.

The tool carriage has the toolpost on top, the carriage, and the crosspiece or crossfeed. The toolpost holds the cutting tool. Older lathes might have the means of only holding one cutting tool. The first machine I used was such a lathe, and I dreaded changing from one tool to another. Newer machines have a four-position toolpost.

A lathe turns the part, and the stationary (except for threading) cutting tool then cuts. Left is the chuck, center the toolpost, right, the tailstock.

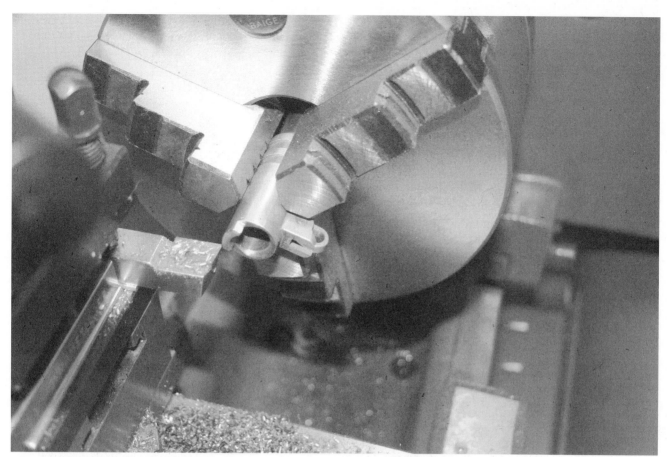

Here we see a lathe being used to shorten a too-long hood on a 1911 barrel. What the lathe can't do is adjust the hood width. For that you need a mill or a file and a steady hand.

You can fix four tools, and quickly change from one to another. The type you have would depend on the jobs you are doing. At the least you'd have a turning/facing tool to remove metal and create a shoulder, and a 60-degree cutting tool with which to thread. The carriage moves left and right, cutting parallel to the object surface. The crosspiece or crossfeed moves in and out, cutting perpendicular. You use the crossfeed to set the amount to be cut, and move the carriage left and right to remove metal. Underneath the carriage is a threaded shaft. That is your power feed. On the head end of the lathe are controls for the feed rate. You can set a fast or slow feed rate. (You also use the feedrate to cut threads.) The carriage and crossfeed have indicator dials on their handles, so you can keep track of where you are and how much you are cutting. The head will have

To hold a long piece while turning, you fix one end on the center with the tailstock, using a centerpiece. The center can be live (moves to adjust) or dead (fixed in place) depending on what you need to cut.

In threading, the lathe pulls the cutting tool across the part at the selected rate, cutting threads on the surface. Here a barrel is being threaded for fitting to an S&W revolver.

a plate attached telling you what settings provide what feed rates or thread pitches, and there will also be a plate somewhere telling you what gear or pulley setting provide what turning rates.

On the right end is the tailstock. The tailstock is to be centered on the machine axis. In the tailstock you can place a live or dead center, to hold a long object on center. When you cut metal on a lathe the object being cut flexes away from the cutting tool. The center can hold it in place. You can also replace the center with a chuck, install a drill in the chuck, and drill on the lathe.

Production machines have what is called a "turret" or the lathe itself is called a "turret lathe." The tailstock is a four-, six- or eight-faced affair. Each face can hold a tool. Each tool is centered on the machine axis. By quickly switching from one face to another, you can perform multiple operations on a single piece.

LATHE WORK FOR THE HANDGUN

Lathe work is all barrel work. For a revolver, you don't have many options unless you're using a barrel blank, or you have centers you can fit to muzzle and forcing cone that allow you to turn the barrel. With lathe centers you

The chuck holds the part. The three-jawed chuck (shown) automatically centers the part. There are also four-jawed chucks, for holding irregularly shaped parts.

The lathe is the tool you need (or desire) to set back the shoulder on a revolver barrel. Set back the shoulder a thread or two, and you can re-cut the cylinder gap and forcing cone. Many barrels can be made like new by being set back.

are not depending on the exterior of the barrel being concentric to the bore, you use the bore itself as the centering dimension.

For a revolver, you cut threads and set the shoulder back. With a pistol you turn muzzle diameters to fit bushings, fit bushings themselves, and adjust the hood length to fit the slide.

MILL COMPONENTS

Unlike the lathe, which turns the object and holds the tool still, the mill holds the object still and turns the cutting tool. On top of the mill is the gearbox or pulleys for adjusting speed. Underneath is the chuck or spindle, which holds the cutting tool. Beneath that is your table, which can move on three axes, up and down, left and right, and in and out. You can tilt the head, or use a sine vise to hold an object at an angle, should you need to make an angled cut. The controls for the table have indicator dials to show you how much you are moving the table, and in what direction. There is a plate somewhere to tell you what gear settings or pulley combinations provide what rotational speed.

With a machinist's vise clamped to the table, and the proper cutting tool in the spindle, you are ready to begin cutting. A useful addition is a dial indicator to read part movement as you make your cut. The dials on the control wheels are good, but you can't be too careful when removing metal.

MILLING WORK FOR THE HANDGUN

First, the Weigand fixture and a 1911 barrel. Fitting a 1911 barrel requires work on a lathe and mill. The lathe work is in fitting the barrel muzzle to the bushing and the bushing to the slide. We've done that. Now, the hood and bottom lugs. (There will be some hand-fitting before you finish.) The mill work requires the Weigand fixture, your new barrel and pistol being fitted, a 3/8-inch end mill, a 3/16-inch end mill, and the chucks to hold them. As I've mentioned before, a practice barrel is a very good thing when learning, or refreshing your memory. A scrap barrel, or a welded-up rusted, pitted or trashed barrel is a perfect one to learn on. Five dollars spent at a gun show for a pitted barrel, and another $10 at your welder for welding the hood and bottom lugs, and you've got a perfect test tube to machine.

Start with the hood. The Weigand fixture has detailed instructions on measuring your barrel, so I'll cover the highlights. Use the fixture to locate and level the hood sides, so you can mill them down (rather than hand-filing and trying to keep the sides parallel) so the hood clears the slide opening. Unlike the hood length distance, you want the hood width to be a snug but free-running fit to the slide. Making it a force-fit will not improve accuracy and will decrease reliability. The hood sides guide the barrel into place, and adding friction on the sides only increases the likelihood of malfunction. As the Weigand fixture allows you to return the barrel to it's exact location, you can mill the sides, check the fit

Here a slide is locked in the mill, ready to have a dovetail cut for a rear sight.

The mill turns the cutting tool, and moves the part up and down, left and right, and in and out in order to make the cuts desired.

and re-mill if needed.

Once you have the sides cut, use your same 3/8-inch end mill to trim the hood length to a snug or press fit to the slide. While it is possible to machine the hood length to a firm but free-sliding fit to the slide, the master gunsmith method involves hand fitting. (It always does.) Once your hood is a snug or press fit (requiring the use of one or two thumbs to press into place) use Dykem to mark the hood or slide breechface. Once the Dykem is

dried, press the barrel into place several times. (Bushing installed, no recoil spring, barrel to slide only, no frame involvement) Stone only the high spots rubbed on the barrel or slide (whichever you've marked) to remove the binding.

Once the hood is a snug fit (you'll shoot it in later, and can always deal with high spots again if need be) check the barrel rise. In the old days we'd take the simple way and install a sized but unprimed case in the chamber, install the barrel to the slide and look through the firing pin hole. If the flash hole lined up, we were high enough. (Oh, the good old days!) Rather than take the old and easy way, measure the lug engagement using modeling clay. You should have not less than .040 inch engagement on the lugs, and they should contact uniformly across the face of the lug that takes the main load. More engagement is better. To "lift" the lugs in match barrels you need to stone or file the stop pads. On Kart barrels the stop pads are visible between the lugs. On Bar-sto barrels and others, the rear shelf is cut at a different location so the ends bear in the slide to stop barrel lift. If you find you have insufficient barrel lift, Dykem the stop areas, press the barrel in place and then stone/file the pad that bears. Fit to have the barrel stop on both pads evenly, and the barrel high enough to get the engagement you need. Once the barrel lifts high enough, bears evenly on the hood rear and does not bind on the sides you are ready to fit the bottom lugs.

The bottom lugs prop the barrel on the slide stop bar to lock it into the slide. You should not be using the link to prop the barrel. Many do, and many guns last a long time using "link lock" as the locating mechanism, but it is asking a lot of a small part. To fit the bottom lugs of your barrel with the Weigand fixture, replace your 3/8-inch end mill with the 3/16-inch end mill. (You may have to change the taper chuck as well, depending on how your machine is set up.) To determine how much to start taking off the lugs, you can use diameter gauge pins, or a set of numbered drills, to measure lug overage. Install a lose bushing to allow for barrel movement. Install the barrel and slide on your frame, and insert the gauges or drills through the frame slide stop hole. Check the barrel lockup until you find a drill/gauge that allows the slide to close. Measure the diameter of the drill, and subtract that diameter from the diameter of your slide stop. Subtract another .005 inch, and you now have your cutting dimension. Install the barrel in the fixture and with the 3/16-inch end mill remove your calculated amount from the bottom lugs. Do not cut to the rear of the lug radius. Check the fit of the barrel on the frame using your slide stop. If you have followed the instructions your barrel bears evenly but will not close. Put the barrel back into the fixture, move your cutter .005 inches more, cut and re-test. Once the barrel locks up, replace it in the fixture. Do not change the cutting dimension up

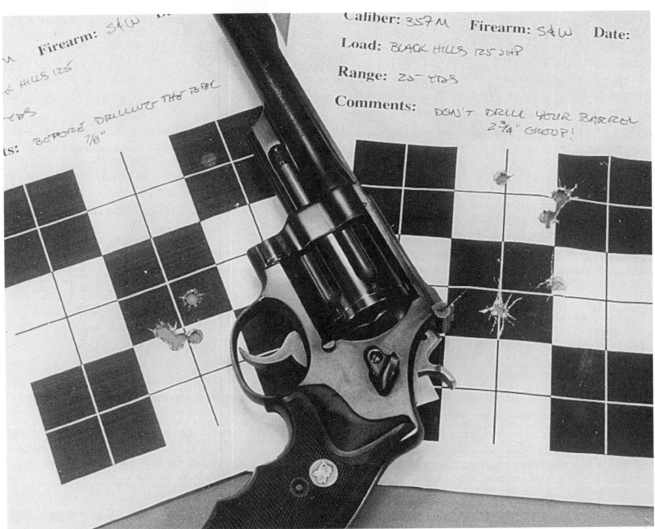

This Smith & Wesson revolver had its barrel drilled for recoil reduction. Before, it shot well but not spectacular groups of less than an inch. After, the groups rarely were smaller than three inches!

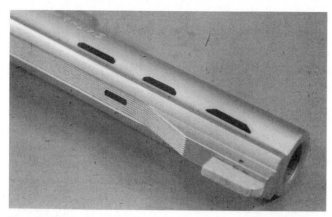

Mag-Na-Port can put ports in your barrel with Electrical Discharge Machining. It does not alter the finish, harm accuracy or decrease velocity. Well, it doesn't if you only get one or two sets. The seven slots in this barrel have decreased measured velocity about 2 percent. 20 fps off of a load that delivers 1,000! No problem.

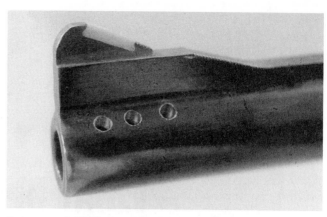

Some people think that drilling their own holes for recoil reduction is a cheap alternative. Actually, it ends up being an expensive one, after you replace the barrel you have ruined.

towards the top of the barrel. Cut the lug engagement surface back to the rear of the radius, removing .005 inch. Check fit. The first set of cuts created the gap to allow barrel lockup. The cuts you are making now have the effect of moving the slide forward on the frame. Do not cut until the slide is flush to the frame, leave the slide slightly rearward of the frame. The cut creates "dwell time" allowing the barrel to stay locked to the slide longer during the unlocking sequence. Do not cut more than a total of .010 inch out of the rearward portion of the locking radius during this step of the milling.

Once you've finished the milling, you're ready for the hand-fitting of the link, up in the 1911 chapters.

MILLING OR DRILLING?

You can also use a mill to drill holes. You'll need a drill chuck in place of your R8 taper chuck that you've been using for the end mills. You can drill holes on revolver topstraps for mounting scopes. Or on a slide for mounting a rib or scope mount. You can also drill frames for scope mounts. While a drill press can also drill holes (and if you're only drilling one, work as well) the advantage of a mill is simple: the mill measures hole spacing for you. Lets say you're drilling for a scope mount, and the base pattern calls for holes every 1/4-inch. (Each scope mount will have different hole spacings, and will be accompanied by a drawing showing the hole pattern.) Once you have located the first hole, and made sure your frame is fixed square or with the desired offset, you move the table 1/4-inch and drill each hole in turn.

A mill is also very useful in re-drilling repaired holes. As an example, the replacement grip-screw bushing repair mentioned in Chapter 3 is a lot easier in the silver-solder final stage if you are using your mill to located and drill the hole. Once the bushing (or a lathe-turned filler plug) is sliver-soldered in place, you can use the mill to locate the exact spot for the new bushing hole. Then using a carbide drill you drill the hole. Using the chuck (don't move it while changing cutting tools) as your centering handle, then hand-turn the tap to cut the threads. Done properly, the repair will be noticeable only when the grips are off, and be cause for admiration at your elegant work.

CHAPTER

WHAT IS INVOLVED IN TESTING?

How do you know your handgun is in need of accuracy work? Is it really malfunctioning? The first thing you must keep in mind is that you cannot properly test with bad ammo or magazines. To truly know, you must either have a source of absolutely reliable reloaded ammunition (tough, if you're not a reloader or you are a reloader, but one with poor habits) or factory ammo. Second, pistol shooters must have reliable magazines. How can you tell if your ammo is the problem? Feed your handgun factory ammo. While there may be some poor or even bad factory ammo, the chances are very good that any you select is better than the average reloads. If you find that your handgun is unreliable, and you want to eliminate the ammunition factor, invest in a couple of boxes of plain ammo for your caliber. Now, not all of the plain ammo will be the same. In particular, the Winchester white box load for 9mm with 115-grain FMJ bullets is well-known to be wimpy. If you have reliability problems because your feeding is rough, or the recoil spring too heavy, the W-W ammo will simply aggravate them. But barring that, factory ammo can be counted on to give you more reliable information than most reloads. If, however, you are or know a reloader who crafts superb ammo, you can glean as much information from using his (or her) ammo for your testing as you can form using factory ammo.

Accuracy and reliability testing is not a "have the most of everything" exercise. Ideally you want it all, but sometimes you have to make tradeoffs. It may be that the most accurate load is not the most powerful. A maximum power load may have only "average" accuracy. You cannot give up reliability for anything else, not accuracy, not power, and not cost. Cheap ammo that is unreliable will only waste your match entry fee, your hunting license fees or your patience. Or risk you rlife. How much of one you give up for another is something only you can decide. And if you must have it all, only you can decide if the cost you pay (time, effort, money, experimentation) is worth the gain you get.

You need test two things, reliability and accuracy. As accuracy is the harder to test, we'll cover it first.

ACCURACY: HOW MUCH?

Beware of someone who tells you that such and such a level of accuracy is "good enough for defensive purposes." There is no such thing as "too much" accuracy. (Or power, or reliability, either.) You want all you can get. But what you have to consider is your ability to shoot, and the statistical variance of any manufactured product. Ideally, you check accuracy by clamping your handgun in a Ransom rest and plugging groups into the target until you find the perfect load. And I have done just that. More than once I tried various factory loads in my carry guns until I found what would shoot best. Currently, it means my 1911 Lightweight Commander in .45 gets fed a hoarded stash of Hornady 200-grain XTP ammo. It shoots those rounds like a Bull's-eye load. I once tested a customer's carry gun, and found that for him, the most accurate load was CCI Blazer .45 ACP 200-grain JHP. (No kidding.) He kept my report and the test group, in case he ended up in court (he was a private investigator) and anyone wanted to know why he was using such "cheap" ammo. The Ransom rest is the Terminator of testing: It won't get tired, distracted, learn to flinch or whine about the weather. But you must use it in a consistent manner. Do not use the handgun itself to lever the rest down out of recoil. Use a solid bench or post, and do not change what rests on the bench or post. If you use sandbags to add dampening mass to the table, do not move them until you are finished. Scrub the bore between types of ammo (brands, different powders, going from lead to jacketed, etc.) and re-shoot "settling groups" to get the gun settled in and the bore reconditioned to the new load.

If you do not have access to a Ransom rest, you have to use sandbags or a rest. Ideally every shot will have a perfect sight picture and perfect trigger release/break. As we are all human, such is not likely to be the case. The question is what do you use to measure the group size? With the Ransom it is easy; every shot fired. If you are shooting over sandbags or a rest, do you shoot five and throw out the widest one? Six and throw out two? Seven? Do you throw out any? The problem with the "best X shots" approach is that you don't know those shots were your fault, and you may be applying a crude statistical machete to a finer problem. Also, you are more likely to throw bad shots at the very beginning and as your testing session goes on too long, more so than once you are "in the groove."

I use five, five-shot groups from the Ransom as the measure of a load or handgun. Five-shot groups are easy to manage, and five of them gives me a good statistical base (relatively speaking) to work with. A single group tells you nothing except how that particular group shot. That sole group could have been the best or the worst group that gun shot that day, with that ammo, and you have no way of knowing otherwise. For shooting over a rest, I shoot the same five, five-shot groups, but I only compare like to like. I do not compare a Ransom tested gun to a hand-held one (on paper) for I know I am no Ransom rest. I also do not throw out shots. I shoot five. I measure five. When I get tired I quit.

If you are not sure of your own shooting skills, have the best shooter at your gun club have a try with your gun and ammo.

HOW MUCH ACCURACY?

The better question is: how much should you settle for? That depends on the application. For hunting, I insist on groups half the size of the kill zone of what I'm hunting, at the maximum range I plan to shoot. Let us assume a whitetail deer has a kill zone of 8 inches. At the distance a gun and load reaches a 4-inch average group out of the Ransom, that is as far as I'd hunt with it. If it means a 100-yard maximum range, great. If only 50, fine. First, is the load powerful enough, and have a proper bullet? Then, what is the max range for that load/gun/sight combo? For competition, your acceptable accuracy depends on the match you are shooting. For PPC, you have to have a handgun that is capable of placing every single shot inside the "10" ring at the maximum distance fired. Outdoors, that means 50 yards. Indoors, 50 feet. For IPSC shooting, you want something that will keep every shot inside the "A" ring to 50 yards. At 6 inches wide for the A zone, that means a gun capable of under 6 inches at 50 yards, 2 inches at 50 feet. (Still smaller than the "10" ring in PPC.) More accuracy is better.

For me, a competition gun has to deliver groups smaller than 2 inches at 25 yards out of the Ransom rest. If it doesn't, I'll either use another or rework it until it does. For a defensive gun, I work from the ammo first. With a selection of appropriate ammo, I'll go with what is the most accurate, or if there is not enough to have a ready supply for a few years, the next most available ammo. As I mentioned, my LW Commander currently gets fed Hornady 200 XTP. My LE 1911s are all capable of shooting 2 inches with plain old hardball (230-grain JRN) so I either take the Wilson CQB or the Springfield Government out of the safe for classes and training. My S&W ICORE .357 revolver shoots groups around an inch at 25 yards with its special competition load of Rainier or West Coast plated round-nose bullets and Hodgden Titegroup. The only one I settle for less from is my IPSC revolver. It is an old S&W 25-2 in .45 ACP, and with jacketed round-nose bullets it shoots "only" about 2-1/4 inches at 25 yards. As the JRN bullets reload faster than any other, I'm willing to settle for a bit less accuracy in favor of the faster reloads. The same gun and load, with Hornady XTP bullets instead of the JRN's, shoots like the ICORE revolver. But I'd rather have the faster reloads than the better accuracy.

RELIABILITY

The reliability tests are more involved, less demanding, and can actually be fun. You can do your reliability testing as part of your practice or plinking. More than one shooter I know does reliability testing simply by setting up targets and doing drills. Or plinking at chunks of target holder wood tossed up onto the backstop. First, for a revolver shooter. One advantage revolver shooters have over their pistol-shooting compatriots is that you can uncover a lot of problems by dry-firing. If a revolver is mistimed, skipping or failing to carry up, you can see it without the need for ammo. We'll assume yours has passed the basic dry-fire tests. Fire a few cylinders to make sure it functions properly. Inspect the primers to make sure they are struck on the center, and that they aren't cratered, pierced, blown or otherwise looking in poor health. (This test must be done with proper-pressure factory ammo or reloads, not your brother-in-laws "bear hunting" ammo.) Then test to see that your wheel-gun can shoot 50 rounds double-action. If the cylinder gap is too tight (or the load too dirty) you may find that the cylinder rubs against the rear of the barrel before you can go 50 rounds. Dirty ammo may also cause a problem with crud or unfired powder granules trapped under the extractor star on a DA revolver. Once yours has proven it can go at least 50, try accuracy testing again. If accuracy noticeably drops off, you may have ammo or dimensional problems that manifest themselves in severe leading and accuracy loss.

A too-small cylinder gap must be opened up to allow proper function. A tight gap of .002 inch may be great, but many competitors will gladly go with .005 inch and a very slight velocity loss in order to have reliability enough to get through a match without problems. The crud under the star can only be taken care of with better ammo or religiously reliable cleaning.

If you have changed barrels and not gotten the new one tight enough, you will probably find out by the end of the 50-round test session. If the barrel is going to unscrew it probably will have done so by then. But if in the course of several practice sessions you find your groups have drifted farther to the left, the barrel may need tightening. You'll have to either re-cut the shoulder and set it back, or peen the barrel shoulder to tighten the fit. Do not use Loctite to secure the barrel. If you ever want to remove that barrel in the future, the thread-locking compound will make it real work.

PISTOL RELIABILITY

With good ammunition and good magazines, testing is relatively simple. You'll need 200 rounds for a basic reliability test. Start with a single round in the mag. Fire it. Does the magazine lock open? Great. Now load two. Fire them. Why such caution? If you've done any trigger work (or even reassembled your pistol incorrectly) you don't want it running away with a full magazine. A double is exciting enough; you needn't be hanging on through seven, eight or 15 rounds. (Although it doesn't take long!) Once you know it works with two and doesn't double, load up your mags. Check the feel of the feed as you strip off the first round. Is there a catch or hitch in the feed? Does the slide hesitate? You may have too much extractor tension, a rough feed ramp, or a marginal magazine. If the barrel has just been replaced, you may have a tight chamber or sharp edge on the tip-over line. Watch empties as they exit. Do they fly consistently, or is each one headed in a different direction? If they differ you may have too little or too much tension. The ejector may be loose, broken or missing. Pick up a few of the first you fire. Is the brass bent, dinged, or marred? Are the case mouths knocked in? They may be hitting the slide. The sidewall may be too high, or the recoil spring may be too weak or strong. A weak spring allows too-high slide velocity on the backstroke, a too-strong one too much speed on the forward stroke. A weak spring also has "tadpole" primer hits, where the firing pin hasn't had time to retract before the barrel begins unlocking from the slide.

You should be able to get 50 rounds out of the tightest gun ever made and still have it work reliably. If you can't, you'll have to go back and re-do your work until you find the dimension that is too tight and correct it.

In the event of a malfunction, stop. Do not perform an immediate action drill to clear the problem. In a class or match, you clear it and get on with things. In reliability testing you stop and observe. What is the exact nature of the problem? Where is the brass, the magazine, and your hands? Have you made any ammunition changes? Magazine changes? Did you hold it differently? Write down the problem: What kind of problem is it, how many rounds in the magazine, which magazine are you using (you do have them marked, don't you?) what ammo, what in particular were you doing? If you have the same problem, you can track the variables. Maybe it is just that ammo. Maybe it is just that magazine. Maybe it is just you shooting weak-handed. Memory can fail. Write it down. If the problem is too frequent, stop and shoot something else. Otherwise, keep going. Expend all your planned testing ammo and see what malfunctions you had if any, and what kind they were.

Long-term testing requires keeping track of the type and frequency of malfunctions, if any. It doesn't do any good to have a "gut feeling" that a particular handgun is unreliable, if you can't remember how often, and of what type, malfunctions occurred.

Unlike the FBI testing pistols, you do not want to simply be knee-deep in brass as your testing method and the excess shooting is simply an invitation to premature wear on your handguns and a flinch for you. Make note of what is going on so you can correct the problems.

CHAPTER

WELDING AND METAL JOINING

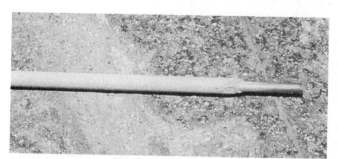

Coated welding rod. The coating creates a layer of gas around the weld, preventing atmospheric oxygen from reaching the bead and contaminating it.

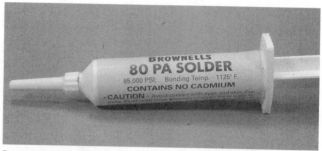

Brownells makes a high-temp silver solder that is in paste form with its flux mixed in. Very convenient in use, it is a high-strength solder.

When you want to join two metal parts permanently, duct tape simply will not do. Granted, duct tape has many uses. Pistolsmithing is not one of them, regardless of what you may have learned from the movie Aliens. For handguns, we need something with a lot more style and strength.

Joining metal means welding or soldering. There are two differences between these processes. Welding will always require a higher temperature than soldering. Also the "glue," or intervening metal between the two parts being welded, will be the same as the two parts and actually become part of them. In soldering this "glue" will always be a different metal, and will bond to them but not become part of them.

The metals used in gunsmithing work just like any other solid, only at a higher heat. A solid is a material that maintains its form. A liquid takes the shape of its container. Think of liquid water and solid ice, and you can understand steel. Water is a solid below 32 degrees F, and boils off to vapor at 212 degrees F. In between those two temperatures, it is a liquid. Soldering and welding use the same principle, just at higher temperatures. Depending on the alloy tested, solid steel melts to liquid somewhere between 2,450 to 2,780 degrees depending on the alloy. The boiling point? Over 6,000 degrees Fahrenheit!

As metals get hotter they change their color. This change is especially marked with steel and allows you to roughly gauge the temperature simply by looking. However, there are limits to using the "Eyeball, Mk 1" as a temperature gauge. The old low-numbered Springfield rifles were brittle because the old hands at the armory

prided themselves on being able to judge the temperature of the receiver and barrel steels in the forging process by looking at them at-heat. However, their eyes were not as accurate as they thought, and many barrels or receivers were over-heated and "burned" as a result. What the armory found was that the difference between a sunny and a cloudy day made a measurable difference in steel temperature from looking. And looking can cause injury. Looking without goggles works fine for soldering. At the hottest welding temperatures, though, the light given off by the steel, the torch, or the electric spark will damage your vision. Buy and use industrial-rated goggles before you begin, or begin watching, welding. Sunglasses will not do.

Three different welding guns, MIG, heli-arc and stick. Each requires a different technique to use, and delivers different results.

A typical welding shop has bare walls, high ceilings and lots of ventilation. It is cold in the winter and hot in the summer. You can't prevent this without lots of insulation, which increases the fire risk.

In a welded joint, you melt the edges of the two parts to be joined and feed in additional metal of a similar composition from a filler rod. The two parts and the added metal become one part, with no clear border between them. The added metal fills gaps between the parts, and replaces metal that is lost from the intense heat. Excess filler puddles on the surface, and is called the "bead." After the welded part has cooled, you grind, file and polish the bead flush, creating a smooth surface at the joint. Without the bead, refinishing is much more difficult. Despite your best efforts, or rather, the best efforts of your welder, there will still be visible traces. Even if the filler rod alloy exactly matches that of the two pieces, the welded area will have undergone a different history of heating than the rest of the part. The crystalline grain structure will be different. The bead area may take a slightly different polish when buffed, or a slightly different color when blued. If sandblasted for plating, the bead may "rough up" a bit differently. A good welder can minimize the differences and a good refinisher can adjust for them.

There are a number of ways to weld. The oldest, forge welding, is what the blacksmith does. Two pieces of metal are heated. Instead of melting the metal to create a joint, the blacksmith hammers the hot pieces together. While hammering gives a blacksmith strong arms and hands, useful in reducing the shock of felt recoil, there is little else about forge welding that is useful for handguns.

The first improvement in welding came near the end of the 19th century. Called gas, or oxy-acetylene, welding, this improved process mixes two gases in a welding torch nozzle and ignites them. The resultant (and very hot) flame is used to melt the parts being joined as well as the filler stick.

Now we have electric welding, where a large electrical charge creates a spark that is used to heat the parts and the filler stick. Machine shops use electric welding because it is cheap and precise.

In every type of welding, the creation of so much heat in the presence of atmospheric oxygen creates a large amount of burnt metal, called "scale." Scale is bad for the weld, and can weaken it. To reduce scale, welders use coated filler rod. When the coating ("flux") melts and then evaporates from the heat, it generates a gas that floats on the surface of the weld, insulating it from atmospheric oxygen. The coating oxidizes and forms slag on the surface. Once the metal cools, the resultant "slag" can be cleaned off. Another way to reduce scale is to bathe the area being welded in an inert gas, shielding the weld from the outside air, a process known as TIG or MIG welding.

Welding requires temperatures well above the melting points of the metals involved, or the metals will not flow together and create a strong joint. While the welded area must be heated past the melting point, it cannot be made so hot as to burn up, or vaporize, the metal. The amount of heat you can pump into a small part without vaporizing it is very limited. The amount needed to weld it is only a bit less than that. You can burn up a number of expensive handgun parts before you learn the exact amount of heat needed. Good welding comes through experience, which is a good reason to find a good welder and stick with him.

A welded joint, properly done, is as strong as the metal itself. A bad weld, with voids and slag in the bond,

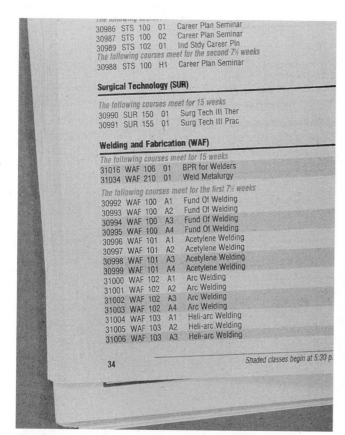

Your local community college may have classes on welding. If you are really curious about trying to weld, learn in a classroom rather than through trial-and-error. A mistake with a welding torch can cause serious injury.

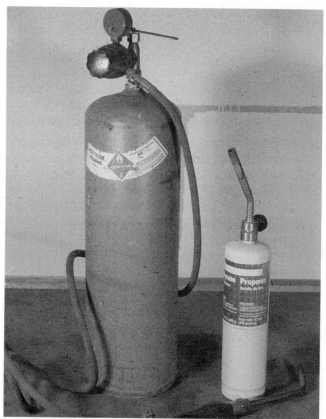

For soldering, you can use propane, the small tank, or acetylene, the large tank. I often use both, with one in each hand to evenly heat large parts.

is not. A weld that does not penetrate into the parts, but joins only at the surface, will be weak. The heat from any weld can also affect the heat-treatment of the parts joined. If you are welding near a critical area, such as the locking lugs of a slide, you must instruct the welder to use a "heat sink" to protect the temper in that area. The heat sink is a block of metal that draws off heat before it can reach an important area.

In a soldered joint, you place the two cleaned and degreased parts together, apply a protective layer of flux (not the same flux used in welding) and heat the parts enough to melt the solder that will join them. Once heated, you apply solder to the joint, and the solder will wick into the gap. You don't heat the solder. After cooling, the parts are a single piece, but the joint, being made of a different metal, is visible. The metals of the two parts are not mingled.

Solders are referred to by their metal compositions. The softest, lead solder, is commonly referred to as "soft solder," and usually has a melting point around 600 degrees F. The low working temperature makes soft solder very useful for electronics and electrical applications. The very low melting point, however, comes at a price. Low-temp soft solder has a bond strength of only 4,000 pounds per square inch. While 4,000 psi will work for a long gun, handguns require much higher bond strength.

When considering the use of a soft solder alloy you

must keep in mind that soft solder alloys, while easy to work with, have a very poor record of surviving the caustic solutions used for bluing. Old double-barreled shotguns have been known to come out of the bluing tanks in pieces, as the soft solder used to hold the ribs to the barrels commonly gets dissolved by the bluing salts.

Introducing silver into solder mixtures increases their strength and makes them very useful for handgun purposes. Called, not surprisingly, silver solder, the hottest mixtures melt at 1,125 degrees and have a bond strength

The area being soldered must be clean and free of grease. Spray and dry several times with an aggressive aerosol such as this Brownells TCE.

of 85,000 psi. Use a silver solder for anything that will be blued or plated.

Firearm manufacturers fasten parts together with a slightly different alloy, one that contains copper or bronze instead of silver. The process is called brazing. The reason is cost. When you are attaching gas cylinders to thousands of shotgun barrels a year, the cost difference between a solder that contains copper and one

that contains silver can be significant.

Solder can be used to create durable and effective joints. However, be aware that solder can be adversely affected by bluing solutions. It is softer than steel, and will be eroded faster when a part is sand blasted for plating. If you solder a part or parts, and do the job so well the joint cannot be seen, let your refinisher know. If he doesn't notice the joint, the refinishing process might undo your work.

Silver-soldering with an acetylene torch.

Once the area being soldered is up to temperature, the solder is touched to the joint.

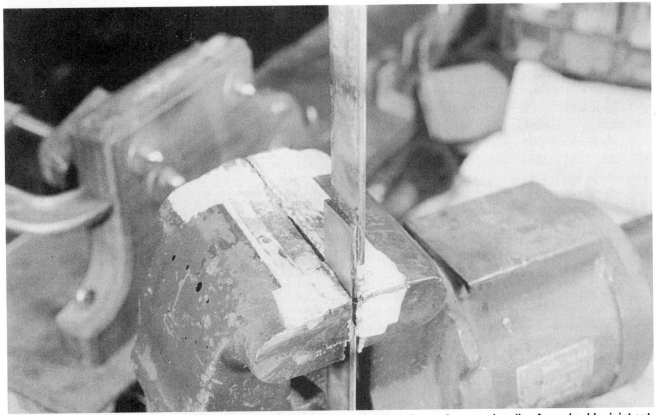

Practice on flat steel, and test your work. Clamp one flat and bend it using the other end as your handle. A good solder joint out of high-temperature silver-solder should break the steel before the joint lets go.

ALL THAT GEAR

The equipment for welding is expensive, and you must weld on a regular basis to keep your touch. If you are considering home welding, the minimum equipment you'll need is a set of oxygen and acetylene tanks or an electrical welder, hoses or power cables, nozzles or electrical tips, heavy gloves, an apron, and a welder's mask.

Expect to wear long sleeves and long pants for welding regardless of the weather — the temperature of the torch and the steel is so hot, and the light given off is so bright that you can get "sunburn" on exposed skin. The frequencies of the light given off by the arc on electrical welding equipment are in the ultraviolet range. Even though it doesn't come from the sun, what you end up with is real sunburn, only much worse. Like the light from an eclipse, the light generated by welding can cause blindness. That's why, even on the hottest days of the year, welders wear long-sleeved shirts, gloves, aprons and a mask.

To hold the parts being welded, you need a heavy gauge steel table (you can't weld on wood) and a machinist's vise with copper jaws. The copper provides both a heat sink and a non-adhering surface. If a bit of bead flows off the part onto the copper, it will not stick. Use a steel-jawed vise, and you can easily end up with your part welded to your vise.

Not only is this is a lot of expensive equipment; it also must be properly handled and serviced. Some precautions, like securely fastening the tanks so they don't fall, should be obvious. If a tank is left unsecured, and falls, it can break off its valve and regulator and turn — quite literally — into a rocket. That's no exaggeration. Oxygen is bottled at 2,200 psi. If a 200-pound tank falls and breaks off its valve, that 2,200 pounds of thrust will propel the 200 pounds of tank right through a brick wall, a car, or you.

You must be sure your tanks do not leak, and are not exposed to any unintended sparks or flames. Acetylene is highly flammable. A slight leak can create a cloud of vapor. Light a match, and you can ignite the cloud. The results can be fatal.

Other precautions are not so obvious. You must never use any kind of oil or grease on the threads of the oxy-

Gas, electric, and wire welders. The wire welder feeds wire from a spool, for continuous welding. All are expensive, hard to use without constant practice, and dangerous.

gen tank. The oxygen is so pure, and its pressure in the tank is so high, that any grease the oxygen contacts can spontaneously burn. This is not merely inconvenient; it is catastrophic.

Electrical welding machines require electricity in large amounts. The bigger the machine, the faster the welding job it permits, and the greater the power requirements it has. The smaller ones will work on household current, 110/120V service. Larger ones will require 220/250V or three-phase.

Welding is best done in a building with a bare concrete floor, block or sheet metal walls, and an uninsulated high ceiling. Besides the great heat generated, welding throws off a large number of sparks. These sparks must not contact anything flammable or they will start a fire. With the oxygen and acetylene tanks nearby, you might soon have an explosion.

Welding is a job that is hot in the summer and cold in the winter. You must invest a great deal of money and time in order to do it well. You must have a dedicated space. You must be very safety conscious. And you must practice to be any good at it.

I hope I have persuaded you away from personally welding your handguns. If you are still curious, sign up with the local community college for courses on welding. There, you can find out if you have the knack for it without spending a small fortune on the equipment. You will also get instruction from people who do it for a living. You will find out quickly if you have the welding touch.

If you aren't going to do the welding yourself, how do you find a welder? Pick up the yellow pages and start calling. Be prepared with a few questions. Ask if they regularly weld on firearms. Do they do work for local gunshops or gunsmiths? If they do, then you have found as much of an endorsement as you will need. A welder who regularly works on guns for a professional gunsmith will already know more about welding handguns than you will ever need to know.

If no one in your area already welds on firearms you will have to find a welder who is willing to try. Look for someone who works regularly with small parts. A welder accustomed to repairing tools for tool and die shops would be a better choice than a welder who repairs semi-trucks and trailers. No insult intended, but welding on big parts versus small parts is more than just a matter of scale.

Once you have found a welder you must know how to "talk welding." The first and most important thing to keep in mind is that you must describe results, not methods. Tell your welder what you want done, not how.

1) Describe where the welding goes. Do not be embarrassed if you have to draw a diagram. Include dimensions. "A little bit here" does not help the welder. "Add 3/32nds from here to here" does. In determining just how much you want added, remember that you cannot weld up to exactly the finish size you need. You must

weld past that size and file or grind the welded metal back down to fit.

2) Explain what the part will be subjected to. A weld on a part that withstands repeated impacts, like a frame or a slide, must be tough, or it will crack. How tough is tough can be tricky. A weld that is too hard will crack from the repeated vibrations of cycling. Too soft, and it will peen and deform. The better your description of the part's function, the more likely your welder will give you the right weld. (And let me add right here that welding a cracked slide is bad idea. No, let me re-phrase that, it is a BAD IDEA. Weld frames to repair cracks, to build up worn or damaged areas, or to create the beginnings of an integral mag funnel. If you have a cracked slide, retire it and buy a new one.)

3) Tell him how hard the weld must be. If you have him weld with harder metal than you need, you will have a tough time filing or grinding the bead. I tell my welder what method I will be using to fit the part: filing, grinding, or machine cutting with a lathe or mill. When I have to file a part, I ask for "just hard enough, but not too hard."

4) If you know, tell him the composition of the parts. It can be difficult to get a good weld between two parts made of dissimilar steels. If the welder has to guess at the alloys, he may be wrong, and your parts may not stay together. The manufacturers of handguns and parts often give a steel industry standards number describing the composition of the steel. Look for a four-digit number such as 4140, 1020, or 1030 in either the manufacturer's catalog or Brownells. The number is a shorthand code for the exact steel alloy used. Knowing the alloy, you know how to heat treat, and how to weld, the parts.

Stainless steels use a different numbering system. What matters to the welder with stainless, though, is not the exact alloy used but whether your parts are ferrous, or magnetic. A stainless alloy with so much chromium or nickel in it that it does not attract a magnet requires a filler rod of a different composition than a magnetic stainless.

Don't worry about what the numbers mean. Just find them out, if you can, and tell your welder. He'll take it from there.

5) Is there any additional information the welder has to know? European American Armory pistols, for example, are heat-treated to be very hard. If you have your EAA pistol welded, and the welder does not anneal (soften) the parts and the weld he has put on, you will never be able to mill, drill, tap, or file the repair. The hardness of the steel will also affect how your welder welds, and the filler rod he uses.

Back in the "good old days" everything could be welded, and, due to the scarcity of parts selection, often had to be. When I started shooting competitively there were just two choices for thumb safeties: the old, original, really small design, or the new, improved, somewhat larger size. (By today's standards, the somewhat larger one is still really small.) If you wanted anything other than these two, you had to weld up a spare thumb safety and file it down to the shape you wanted. These days Brownells has almost four full pages of thumb safeties. Unless you want the practice, do not weld up a thumb safety. Just buy it.

Back then match barrels were few and far between, and always very expensive. Rather than pay all that money only to wait months to get one, then wait again while it was fitted, shooters customarily would have a pistolsmith weld up and re-fit the barrel they already had. Welding offered a cheaper, if not always successful, alternative.

Grip safeties were also welded larger. Sights were welded into their slots and the slide remachined for new sights. I have even heard of cases where shooters had a welder build up the rails of a frame, so the slide could be lapped to fit without play. That takes a welder with a delicate touch, indeed!

One pistolsmith by the name of Claudio Salassa was so good at artistically welding and sculpting old parts to look like new parts that he was lured from South Africa to Texas by the Briley company. He arrived in the United States right at the beginning of the expansion of the aftermarket parts field. Luckily for Claudio he was equally skilled at designing new parts and re-fitting existing parts. Today there are so many parts available that no one welds to build parts, only to repair them.

For example, the grip safety on a 1911 sometimes does not fit correctly. The grip safety pivots in the back of the frame, and when properly fitted must be depressed to allow the trigger to move.

The safety bar must engage the trigger bow, or the pistol may fire even when the safety is not depressed. In the past, some shooters found that their hand did not fully depress the grip safety. Before the improved grip safeties that are larger at their lower ends were available, shooters who couldn't fully depress the grip safety would file or grind off the tip of the safety lug, allowing the pistol to fire without the grip safety being depressed. You'll sometimes encounter this on a used competition pistol, where the previous owner didn't want the safety to work.

To repair such a situation, you can either buy and fit a new safety, or have the tip of the old one welded up, and re-fit the safety bar/trigger bow engagement.

Sometimes an experimenting shooter files or grinds his frame to take a new, beavertail safety. If he gets a little carried away it can create a different kind of problem. I once saw a grip safety "fitted" to the frame of a Colt 1991 which had such large gaps I was afraid to fire the pistol for fear of being pinched by the safety and bleeding all over the gun. This repair requires welding the edges of the frame to fill the gaps, and then filing down the weld until the space between the safety and the frame is a thin line, and not the Grand Canyon.

Welding can repair cracks on the frame. As mentioned in Chapter 4, in the section "Buying a Used 1911," some cracks (such as the crack commonly found on the left side of the 1911 frame rail) should just be ignored. Others, either because of function or aesthetics, should be fixed. Some shooters find a cracked dust cover on a 1911 objectionable. Welding it is easy. Do not be surprised if your best welding efforts are in vain. I have had welded-up dustcovers re-crack in short order. Every gunsmith I have talked to has done it at one time or another, all with little success. Some have welded frames that have

Some "problems" are cosmetic. This crack in a 1911 has been the same size for over 10 years and 5,000 rounds. There isn't any real need to weld it up and re-finish the frame.

stayed welded. Most haven't. And those that have will be the first to tell you it isn't a guaranteed job.

Welding a poorly ground feed ramp can be a headache. Some shooters, eager to improve the feeding of their 1911s but disinclined to read up on the proper method, sometimes just round off the top of the frame ramp. This "improvement" makes feeding worse. If you find yourself in possession of a firearm that's been damaged this way, your only option is to weld up the top of the frame ramp and re-cut the frame to the proper dimensions. You'll probably make several trips to the welder before you've completely filled and smoothed the repair. You'll also have to refinish the frame once you're all done, as the welding will have discolored it.

A trigger body over-filed to fit into the frame will rattle around in its slot. Welding to re-fit can salvage it. Since a new trigger is a only few dollars more than welding the old one, a trigger repair can offer some good, cheap practice for you and for a new welder.

One thing you absolutely must not repair is a cracked slide. A cracked slide must be replaced. Welding a slide for new sights is fine. If the old sights have been replaced too many times the steel can require repair. Or if they are an obsolete design, the old dovetail slots may need some welding up and filing down before your new sights will fit.

Outside of 1911s there are very few pistols that crack and require welding. I have seen some Beretta M-92s with many, many rounds through them whose frames were cracked. Each time, the frames were already so worn that welding the cracks would have been a waste of time. In one case, the pistol was unserviceable due to a chunk broken out of the frame — clearly not a candidate for welding. I have never seen a Smith & Wesson pistol crack, even after being dropped. One, dropped from such a height that the frame was twisted and could not be reassembled, still had no cracks.

Sometimes Smith & Wesson revolvers crack at the thinnest part of the frame, where the barrel screws in. The very thin steel here cannot take the stress of unscrewing the barrel without proper support. It may also crack if the barrel is screwed on very tightly. The crack is not a design fault. If you replace barrels the proper way you will never crack a frame.

Welding this crack is somewhat involved, but easy compared to filing down the weld and re-tapping the frame. Leave that particular repair to a professional pistolsmith.

DOING YOUR OWN SOLDERING

Unlike welding, soldering does not require elaborate equipment and a dedicated wing of the fallout shelter. I've yet to have a soldering job spark at me. As long as you keep flammable materials at a safe distance, you can solder in a frame building. Try to avoid carpeting. If your space is already carpeted, and you'd like to keep it that way, invest in a sheet of thin plywood or one of those hard plastic mats designed for the wheels of an office chair. Either will protect your carpet (or good wood floor, for that matter) from the occasional, but inevitable, drips of molten solder. Drip on your carpet, or drop a hot part on your wooden floor, and just try to repair the damage. You can't, and trust me, your wife will notice. The plywood or plastic mat will clean up pretty easily, if you want to bother.

As a heat source for professional silver-soldering you can use a pair of propane torches, available at the local hardware store. I have found the "Bernz-o-matic" brand works just fine. If you plan to do many soldering jobs with large pieces of steel you should consider an acetylene torch. An acetylene torch for soldering is different from the oxyacetylene used in welding. An acetylene torch uses the air around the torch as a source of oxygen, instead of the tank of pure oxygen required for oxyacetylene. Acetylene torches are not nearly hot enough for welding, but for soldering, acetylene has one big advantage over propane: It commonly comes in tanks much larger than propane. That means acetylene torches can take a larger nozzle and heat a larger area than a propane tank can.

You will need gloves and your work apron. Also wear safety glasses. You don't need welding goggles, but you should have some protection for your eyes. Your shooting glasses will do.

You will need solders and fluxes. Buy solder designed for the job you're doing, and the strength your repair needs. Buy the flux specific to that particular solder. While you may be able to do all your work with one type of solder, you will never make all types of solder work with one flux.

Buy soldering talc. This white talc bar looks similar to your filing chalk. Since solder will not adhere to it, apply the talc to areas you do not want soldered. Suppose you want to solder a front sight base onto a barrel or slide. How do you prevent solder from flowing out of the heated joint and hardening on an adjacent area? Talc that outside area first. The solder still will flow out, but it will not longer adhere. The talc prevents the solder from sticking.

Rather than experimenting with solders from the local hardware store, use your Brownells catalog. Their solders will all be suited for use on firearms. All you'll have to do is decide which one is best for your application and which flux goes with it.

When buying solder, use only high-temp silver solder. It comes in wire, sheets, and a really neat homogenized mixture. The mixture is a paste of the solder and its flux, packaged in a plastic syringe and ready to apply. While each of these requires a slightly different method of soldering, the preparation for all is the same. In welding you can meld together parts whose initial fit was poor. Not so in soldering. Because a strong joint depends on a thin film of solder rather than a large glob of it, a strong solder job depends on a tight mechanical fit of the parts. After you check your parts for fit, (and file, if necessary) you must be sure they are cleaned of dirt, all surface finishes and any oxidation. A thorough de-greasing is essential. While a good, clean surface is important in welding, it is imperative in soldering. Solder cannot bond through contaminants, including bluing, plating, or your fingerprints.

Soldering practice is easy. To start, clamp the largest part firmly in your vise. Use the flat bars you filed and drilled in Chapter 6. If the largest part is not held firmly, you can make a great mess and even burn yourself. Spend some time arranging the part so that it is level, you can get to it easily and the direction of the flame is not pointing at something flammable, including you. If the largest part is not held level in your vise, the smaller part can shift when the heat is applied. It may even fall off the rest, and onto something you'd rather not dam-

age. Like your carpet, for example. Or your leg, or hand, if you forget and try to catch the hot, falling part. Let the plywood or other covering you've put down catch the hot part. That's what it's there for. A few minutes spent planning will save you starting all over again.

Since excess solder will run out of the joint, you must apply soldering talc to prevent it adhering to the surrounding area. Rub the talc around the area you will be soldering. When soldering a barrel, add talc not just next to the sight base, but all the way down under the barrel. Otherwise, the solder can run right past the talc, and stick to the barrel below the talc you applied. Talc the sides of the sight base, or the solder can wick up the base. If you are using the homogenized mixture, your preparations are complete here. Do not flux. With wire or sheets of solder, continue. On your practice bars, clean and flux 1/2 an inch of the ends.

Silver-soldering with an acetylene torch.

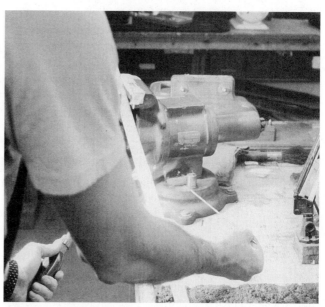

Once the area being soldered is up to temperature, the solder is touched to the joint.

Practice on flat steel, and test your work. Clamp one flat and bend it using the other end as your handle. A good solder joint out of high-temperature silver-solder should break the steel before the joint lets go.

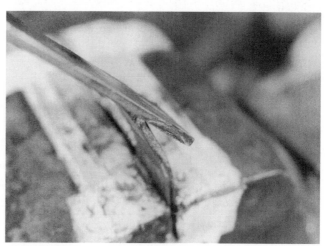

After a small bend, this joint fails.

A post-mortem reveals a lack of heat. The solder was not melted enough to form a good bond, and failed.

Brush your flux where you will solder, and only there. Do not use too much! Solder will follow excess flux.

The most common mistake for a person new to soldering is insufficient heating of the parts to be joined. You cannot heat the solder, let it run into the joint, and call it a solder job. You must heat the juncture of the parts past the melting point of the solder, and then introduce the solder. Once bonded, you must leave the repair untouched until hardened. As with any glue, if you shift it while the solder is cooling the joint will be weak and crooked.

Your preparations for soldering are now complete. What you do next depends on the type of solder you have. Wire is the standard, and oldest, method. Place the prepared and fluxed parts together, and begin heating them. Heat the largest part first. Let the heat flow to the smaller or thinner parts. Watch the color of the steel (see chart). Once the parts are up to the solder's melting point, hold the flame on one side of the joint, and touch the solder wire to the other side. The solder will melt and flow into the joint. Keep feeding wire into the edge. The solder will wick through the fluxed joint towards the heat. When you see solder come out on the flame side evenly across the joint, pull the solder away and remove the flame.

With sheet solder, cut a piece to the size and shape of the joint. Place this piece between the fluxed parts, and then start heating. The color of the steel will let you know when you've reached the solder's melting point. You will see the edge of the solder melt. Remove the heat.

The homogenized solder comes in a syringe. Squeeze enough of the solder/flux paste to cover most of the surface, but don't overdo it. Not only is the mixture expensive, the joint will be stronger with a thin layer of solder. Press the parts together briefly, pull them apart, and look. If you have most of the surface covered with solder paste, you're all set. Put the parts back together. If the surface is not mostly covered with solder, add more. If you've added too much, carefully scrape away the excess solder that oozes out when you press the parts together. Once the gap is completely filled with a thin layer of solder paste, heat the joint to the solder's melting point. Check the color of the steel against the chart. Remove the heat.

You've soldered your practice bars together. Let them cool, and then test your soldering abilities. Clamp one of the bars in the vise, just under the soldered joint. Flex the other bar back and forth, stressing the joint and the steel just under it. You should be able to flex the steel until you break the bar. The soldered joint should hold. If your soldered joint lets go, practice some more.

Common reasons for weak solder joints include lack of solder flow into the joint, insufficient flux, and too much solder. The first is caused by insufficient heat. Do not be afraid of heating the job past the indicated melting point by 100 degrees to 200 degrees. If you were stingy with flux, try again and use more. A joint with too much solder usually means you rushed your preparations. Start over, and check each stage of your work.

PROJECTS

EXTENDED MAGAZINE BUTTON

Our first silver-solder job is the easiest, but requires a lathe to clean up and finish. Find someone who will turn your part once it is soldered. If you want an extended magazine button, but do not have access to a lathe, go to Chapter 18. That's where we cover the drill and tap method of extended magazine button installation.

The magazine release button on the 1911 is rather short, and some shooters find it hard to press. By making the button longer, you can make releasing the magazine during a match easier. Remove the button from the frame, and the spring and plunger from the button. File the ridged end smooth. Some buttons will be slightly

The extended button on the left, with a standard button on the right. You don't need much extension to make a difference as you reload.

surface hardened, and your file may have a tough job of it. You can use the bench grinder to clean off enough of the ridges to make your filing easier.

Take a 3/8-inch diameter mild steel rod, and file an end of it smooth and square to the rod's length. Hacksaw a piece off this end about 3/8 inches long.

Clamp the magazine release in your vise with the end to be soldered sticking up. Do not clamp too much of the release in your vise or the vise will act as a heat sink, and you will not be able to get the parts hot enough. I prefer to use the homogenized high-temperature solder for this job. Squeeze a small circle of the solder paste onto the release, and press the extension down onto the release, and heat the parts. For this solder, the melting point is 1,125 degrees, and I heat the joint up to a medium cherry red, 1,250 degrees.

Once the part is cool, turn on a lathe to bring the extension diameter down to that of the button, and checker the end. Do not make the button too long. I find that a long button gets in the way of my left hand, and I can actually drop the magazine while shooting. Also, if you have to shoot in a match where the pistol starts lying on a table, a magazine button that is too long can press against the table, and you may find your magazine dropping out as soon as you pick it up.

SOLDERED GRIP SCREW BUSHINGS

Grip screw bushings on the 1911 occasionally come loose. Rarely, loose bushings strip their threads. Rarest of all, a stripped thread bushing is one that has already been replaced with an over-sized bushing. There is not

Here the extended magazine button is being turned down on the lathe.

an over-over-sized bushing. Take the bushing, and once you have it free from the grips, set it aside. Strip the frame. Check the bushing fit in the frame. It cannot be loose; there must be some mechanical fit. Place your frame bar in the frame of the pistol, and using the frame bar as a backer, stake the edges of the hole until the bushing can barely be pressed into place. Pull the bushing out, degrease the bushing and frame, flux the hole and bushing, and press the bushing in place. Remove the bar. Clamp the frame so you can easily get to the bushing with your torch. Heat the bushing and frame, and when you are up to temperature, touch the solder to the bushing/frame juncture.

When cool, scrub the frame clean and check to see that a magazine will freely enter and drop from the frame. If it doesn't then solder inside the frame is binding the magazine. File the solder until the magazine drops freely. Run a grip screw tap into the bushing to clean out the threads, and attach your grips after you have assembled the pistol.

ADDING A RAISED PALM PAD TO A GRIP SAFETY

Some shooters find that the grip safety on a 1911 does not always release the trigger. This is because of the way the shooter is holding the pistol. The grip safety was designed in 1911 to work with a single-handed, thumb under the safety grip. With the thumb on the thumb safety and a higher two-handed grip, the bottom of the safety is not always pressed down enough to release the trigger bar. The answer is not changing your grip, but filling the gap. One way is to switch to a new grip safety that already has a palm pad. If you already have a safety that feels good, why buy another?

Remove the safety from the pistol, and clamp it in the vise with the lower end sticking out to the side. With your 10-inch 2nd cut file, file a notch on the end, starting 1/2 inch from the end. Do not file this notch so deeply into the safety that you come to the hammer strut clearance slot. File until you have gotten down 1/4 inch. Take a piece of mild steel, and file a chunk that will fit the notch you have filed in the safety. The top of the chunk should stick up from the safety enough to fill the gap between the safety and your hand, at least 1/4 inch. Degrease and flux the safety and the chunk, and silver-solder the two together. When cool, round the edges of the safety extension so they do not abrade your hand. Polish and refinish.

SOLDERED-ON MAGAZINE FUNNEL

The bolt-on magazine funnel is covered in Chapter 18. If you want the simple approach, skip ahead. The elegant and permanent method takes more work and should be left to the professional. It involves soldering a magazine funnel onto the frame of your 1911. There are two styles of funnel, a pre-machined one-piece funnel, or a two-piece funnel. Each uses a different method of attachment. I explain the process for those who are curious, but recommend you wait until you have much experience with soldering and with grinding, filing and polishing.

For the one-piece funnels, you must file, grind or machine off the bottom 1/4 inch of the frame. You lose the holes your mainspring housing pin goes through, and must re-drill them. To do this you must have a locating fixture. The new funnel attaches over a small surface area. If your soldering is not precise the funnel will fall off. The one-piece can also be welded in place, but this requires work of a different kind. To weld thin-wall sections takes a light touch. To machine the frame precisely calls for a milling machine. To locate the funnel for welding (your welder will probably start with a couple of "tack" welds before he then starts running a bead) you have to have a holding fixture that keeps the funnel and frame clamped and aligned.

Last, your welder has to have a light touch. I cannot over-emphasize this. If he uses too much heat, he will blow-through the thin frame wall. If he pumps too much heat into one section, he risks warpage. A warped frame doesn't improve your reload speed.

The two-piece magazine funnel does not require elaborate equipment, and you do not lose (and then have to re-locate) your mainspring housing holes.

It does require a delicate touch when soldering, and hours of grinding and polishing. I use mild steel "gauge stock" that I obtain from my local machinists' supply store. If you use 1/4 inch stock, your funnel will not be quite as high as the thickness of most grips. If you use 3/8-inch stock, you will have to do more grinding and filing to bring the widest section down to the width of the grips, but when you are done the funnel will be flush

The end-product of a two-piece magazine funnel. The result of at least ten hours of soldering, grinding, filing, polishing and fussing.

The magazine-view of a magazine funnel. If you miss this, you need a white cane. Or more practice.

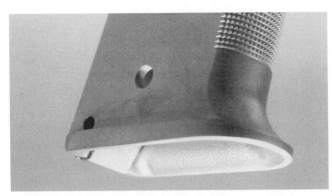

You can avoid the hassle of trying to solder on a magazine funnel, one piece or two. Just order a Caspian frame with integral magazine funnel.

with your grips. Cut two pieces of the gauge stock just a bit longer than the frame at the bottom. Strip the frame and remove the lower grip screw bushings. Polish the frame where the funnel will be soldered on, and one side of one of the pieces. Degrease and flux the polished surfaces. Clamp your frame in the holding bar, sticking out of the vise, with the side of the frame level with the floor. Place the gauge stock piece on the frame, at the bottom, and heat and solder. You do one side at a time. When one side has cooled, remove the frame from the holding bar and clamp it in the drill press, soldered side down. Using the mainspring housing hole from the other side as a pilot hole, drill your new piece through with a #21 drill.

Polish the other side of the frame, and the other gauge stock. Solder these together. You can solder the second piece without loosening the first piece if you heat the second piece from below and at a slight angle. Done properly, the flame will be split by the inside edge of the frame, with half the flame going up the inside of the magazine opening. The torch will not heat the first piece enough to affect the solder. You can also prevent loosening of the first piece by resting the frame, on the fist soldered-on piece, on its side on a metal benchtop. The metal benchtop will act as a heat sink, and errant heat from the second soldered piece will be drawn off by the benchtop. If however you heat the second piece from above instead of below, the flame going past the second piece will heat the first piece enough to loosen it. With the second piece cool, drill the second hole using the first one as a pilot.

Now you've done the easy part. The hard part is to grind, file and polish the exterior flush to the grips, and then the interior as a funnel. This is advanced work, and best left as either a job for the professional, or our next pistolsmithing volume.

For those considering it, and who have a milling machine handy, the answer is yes: you can use the milling machine to do a lot of the heavy work. You can use a mill to remove a lot of the metal on the inside (a bench grinder works fine for the heavy lifting on the outside) and establish the general contours of yru mag well funnel.

But sooner or later you're going to have to be work-

ing on it with a Dremel and grinding tip, wearing a mask, goggles and hearing protection. However, there is one advantage that a soldered ro welded mag funnel gives you: the funnel is flush with the frame. That is, the new funnel aids in reloading, but does not add height to the pistol. This is an advantage how, you're asking? In some competitions your pistol has to fit a box of a certain size, or it isn't allowed. If you add size at the bottom, with a bolt-on mag funnel, then you are reducing your options on top, with sights.

Also, if you are doing this to a carry gun, you are gaining a reloading advantage without making your carry gun larger. Yes, a reload is probably not necessary. But if we start looking at the probabilities, the likelihood of needing that gun are pretty small, too. Before any police officers think of using this as a reason to deny citizen CPL/CCW, if we follow the probabilities, police officers probably don't need guns either. So don't go there. In any case, the welded/soldered-on mag funnel gains an advantage without adding bulk to your pistol.

THE MEDIUM-OLD DAYS: WELDING A BARREL

As an experiment and demonstration I welded and re-fit a barrel as we did in the old days. The test pistol was

A 1911 barrel with the hood and bottom lugs welded and re-fit to the frame and slide. This used to be common in the old days, but now is a complete waste of time.

The barrel on this Springfield Armory 1911A1 was welded and re-fit, for not much results. Groups went from three inches to two and a half inches.

a Springfield Armory 1911A1 in .45 ACP. I used it only because it was available, and not to pick on Springfield. The cost savings over a new, match barrel were appreciable. The welding cost $25. A match barrel runs $125 to $200. The amount of work to fit the welded barrel was only a little more than the work needed to fit a match barrel. The accuracy gained? Almost none. Out of the Ransom rest, the factory barrel before welding delivered 3-1/2-inch groups at 25 yards. After welding, group sizes "shrank" to 3 inches on average. I say "shrank" because the groups still varied in size. Largest to smallest, the groups varied from 2-1/2 to 5 inches. Only by averaging the sizes of a number of test targets could I determine that the welded barrel had improved. I would have had a greater improvement in accuracy from installing a match bushing instead. My experience with the combination of welded barrels and match bushings is that the welding doesn't help at all, but the bushing does. But the real lesson is to avoid welding a barrel, and to simply replace it when warranted.

The current experiment is in agreement with one I inadvertently conducted 30 years ago. At the first National Championship I attended, the TargetWorld in Cincinnatti, I won a gun. A Colt Series 70 1911A1. Out of the box it would not reliably feed, fire, extract or eject. (And Colt wondered back then why Springfield was able to take the market away from them!) It didn't take long to have it working properly. But it was not very accurate. I sent it off to a big-name gunsmith to have the barrel welded and re-fit. Luckily I acquired a Ransom rest just before sending it off, and was able to fire some groups before and after. Before, 50-yard groups were only slightly smaller than the typing paper I used as targets. (Yes, 8-inch groups at 50 yards!) After? Not enough better to be statistically significant. And lest you think that the

The owner of this barrel was not so lucky. The barrel was heated too much in welding, and the hood broke off after a few thousand rounds. He wasn't hurt, but he was very angry.

problem lay with my reloaded ammo, I conducted the test with Federal 185 match Wadcutter ammunition.

Why did the welding show no improvement? Because tightly-fitting a barrel that is not particularly accurate will show no increase in accuracy. If the barrel is accurate or potentially accurate, but not well fitted, then re-fitting it will allow it to shoot up to its potential.

The current experiments included plugging Olympic, Bar-sto and Kart barrels into the Springfield. The match barrels? The Olympic barrel delivered 2-inch groups with very little change in group size from target to target. Groups from the Bar-sto and Kart barrels hovered around 1 inch. Lesson learned: Do not bother welding barrels except as a means of producing practice barrels for you to fit to your pistols. A welded barrel (especially a rusted one bought cheap at a gun show) can be the perfect test tube to practice your barrel fitting skills before you take file or milling machine to the $200 match tube.

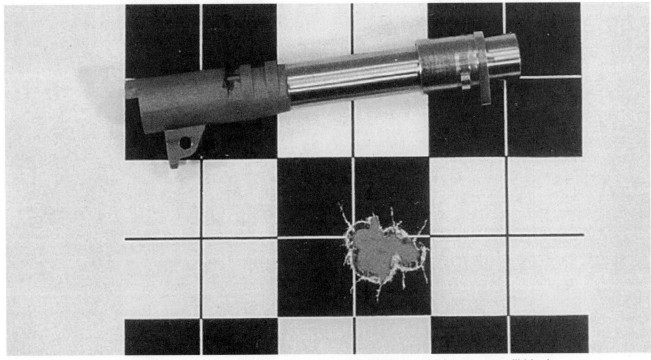

A correctly fitted Kart barrel delivers accuracy like this. Any better, and people would think you were fibbing!

CHAPTER

REFINISHING

"This new stuff rusts."
Anonymous, 1000 BC

The newest high-tech wonder weapon has just hit the agora, or marketplace. All over Greece and Persia, sport hunters and would-be Olympians are clamoring to get their chance to try a great new metal. Iron, they hear, will change everything. It's stronger, harder, all around better. It has just one itty, bitty, little problem. But then, it's always something, isn't it?

Iron was a definite step up from bronze. It was also more difficult and more expensive to manufacture. When blended with other elements, iron becomes an alloy (as do all metals). The alloy we call steel is iron with a certain small percentage of carbon in it. Carbon imparts strength and hardness. Other trace elements in the steel can improve machinability, allow forging, or change its response to heat-treating. A "hardening" steel is one that can be heated and then quickly cooled, thus changing its crystal size, and as a result its hardness. A "stainless" steel has chromium and nickel mixed in it. Many people believe stainless steel does not rust, but it does. Takes a long time, though.

Not merely an aesthetic affront, rust can impede proper function and destroy an iron/steel mechanism.

This is the cleaner being applied.

Oddly enough, the very first protective finish "applied" to iron was rust. By carefully controlling the process, a somewhat preservative rust layer can be built up. For almost 3,000 years, it, and the choice of scouring the iron bright and keeping it bright, were the only finishes available for iron implements.

Right up past the American Civil War, scouring rifle barrels bright with a wet application of campfire ashes was considered an appropriate method of cleaning and maintenance. The barrel steel of those rifles are barely steel by today's standards. It was not until the Bessemer process came into common industrial use right after the Civil War that good-quality steel could be produced in volume and cheaply.

Steel is much stronger than iron. It is also amenable to chemical protective finishes.

For a quick touch-up of blued handguns, Outers makes a felt-tip pen applicator set. Clean the steel, touch it up, and give it a final wash.

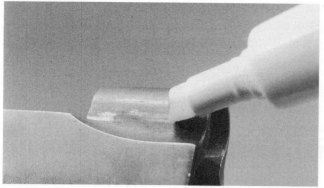

Now the bluing solution. You can see that some of the bright metal is already reacting.

The touched-up slide. The only way to see the cold-blued area is to angle the light.

The question always arises: Do you really need to have some kind of finish on your handgun? Well, no. A stainless handgun, for example, will rust only if exposed to severe conditions and massive neglect. But it will rust. With some regular work, carbon steel also can be left bare, but it will rust more quickly than stainless. One of the competitive shooters in our area was such a compulsive parts experimenter that trying to keep his pistols in any kind of finish was impossible. Rather than have his pistol a patchwork of parts, all differently finished, he simply bead blasted his pistols clean. Mark was well known for shooting "bare" guns. He also kept them coated in oil, to protect the steel from oxidation.

Most shooters do not constantly experiment. Even fewer have a bead-blasting cabinet in their basement. While you are making modifications to your handgun, go ahead and leave the steel mismatched or bare. Once you're set, protect your work with a good finish. The whole point of a protective finish, of any kind, is to seal your firearms surface away from the oxygen in the atmosphere. You could leave it stored in a vacuum, except that would cause the oil on it to boil off. That, and getting your safe open would be tough.

Protective finishes for your handguns come in two types. The first and oldest — browning, bluing, color case-hardening, and Parkerizing — result from a chemi-

Brownells baking lacquer is available in several colors, gloss and matte, and is easy to apply. While not greatly durable, it is better than standard blueing and can be touched-up when it shows wear.

cal reaction with the surface of the steel itself.

Instead of merely browning when treated to a controlled rusting process, steel takes on a deep blue color when rusted with the appropriate chemical mixtures. Steel also can be heated to oxidize the surface. When heat-soaked in ovens at the right temperature, the resulting "fire blue" is very striking. Colt, in their 1936 centennial celebration book, described their then state-of-the-art heat-bluing process. It would give the EPA and OSHA of today an attack of the vapors. Then, as now, a good finish required a completely degreased surface. To secure this, Colt would dunk racks of polished handguns into tanks of boiling gasoline! Then, right out of the tanks, off they'd go to the bluing ovens. The finish sure looked nice when they were done!

Heat bluing of small parts offered manufacturers a one-step way to draw the temper of heat-treated or forged parts, give them color, and protect them from the elements. The small parts on Luger pistols are a yellow color, called "straw." The manufacturer heat-blued them, but the process called for stopping short of bringing the steel to the full blue color and left it simply yellow, or straw in color. You will be heat-bluing small parts in the projects to come.

As attractive as these finishes are, they are not any more durable than the old browning method. Firearms manufacturers looked for a more lasting method, and their customers insisted on it. Hot bluing, a boiling solution of caustic salts, proved more durable than browning, rust-bluing or fire bluing. By the standards of yesterday, it was a big advance. By the standards of current coatings and platings, even hot-dip blue is hardly effective against corrosion.

The second type of finish includes chrome, nickel, gold, or even paint. These coatings or platings adhere to the steel and seal it away from oxidation. Firearms manufacturers and aftermarket firearms refinishers are constantly developing combinations and improvements of these finishes.

Before WWII, if you wanted to blue your handgun, you bought the assorted chemicals and mixed the bluing solution yourself. In his book *The Modern Gunsmith*, last updated in 1941, James V. Howe listed over 50 formulae for various firearms finishes, none of which could be purchased over the counter. The raw ingredients needed to mix the formulas included nitric acid, hydrochloric acid, sulfuric acid and copper sulfate, combined with alcohol and chased with a whiff of distilled water. One formula, my favorite, used potassium cyanide to touch up color case-hardening! I'm not sure you could today even buy a lot of the chemicals he called for.

Today, any finishing that can be done at home is done with pre-mixed chemicals. Brownells offers pages of solutions and tanks, ready for you to set up and start the work. You might be tempted to try. But should you?

No. Except for a few finishes that you can apply without going to the trouble of setting up a separate room for the process, re-finishing work should be left to the professionals. The first one that you can do yourself is chemical cold blue. The second is heat blue of small parts with a propane torch. The third is Brownells bake-on epoxy finish. The fourth is cold rust blue. The last is Brownells Amer-Lene Parkerizing. Any other finish that you may be tempted to apply to a firearm requires tanks, chemicals, heat or electricity, and ventilation. The cost of the equipment alone easily exceeds that of a dozen bluing jobs done for you by a professional. And you still need a dedicated space. Remember that bare, empty room we talked about for welding in Chapter 8? You need the same kind of room for hot-dip bluing or plating, and it can't be the same room you use for welding.

COLD BLUE

Cold bluing, or chemical bluing, is used to touch-up slightly worn or nicked blued finishes. It is suitable for covering up the holster wear on the muzzle of a revolver, or a spot on a slide where your sweat lifted the blue. It is not nearly as durable as a hot-dip blue finish. Some cold-blue formulas contain sulfides, and a handgun that has been touched-up too much can have a very slight, but noticeable, smell of rotten eggs. Sniffing a used firearm, to see if there has been any use of cold blue to hide wear, is an old trick in the gun business.

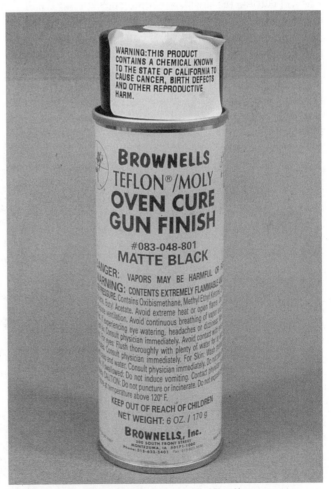

The Brownells Teflon/Moly oven cure finish offers greater durability than the baking lacquer.

My standard cold-blue solution is Brownells Oxpho-Blue. It gives a reasonably durable finish and can be applied repeatedly until the color is dark enough to match the existing finish. To use a cold-blue solution, first scrub the area to be blued with 0000 steel wool and light oil. Clean the surface of powder residue, mild oxidation and any pre-existing finish that is ready to lift off. Obviously, you don't cold blue a handgun with a plated surface, or a stainless steel handgun. Once scrubbed, thoroughly degrease the area. Clamp the handgun in a padded vise, and bring your work lamp close to the surface. Use the lamp to warm the area you're working. With a cotton swab, brush the Oxpho-blue onto the steel. Leave it on the surface for a minute, and then polish with dry 0000 steel wool. Degrease, and apply the Oxpho-blue again. Repeat until you get the color you want. Oil the surface to finish the process.

HEAT BLUE

To heat-blue small parts requires a propane torch and oil. You must use a petroleum-based oil. A modern synthetic lubricant will not do. Have the oil in a small cup or jar. Polish the surface of your part to a texture that will match the rest of the handgun. Degrease the part, and holding it with a pair of needle-nose pliers, play the propane torch on the surface to be blued. As the part heats up, you will see the surface turning colors. First you'll see the straw color of a Luger, followed by violet, light blue and finally Colt fire blue. If you heat too quickly the part will pass right through all four colors and turn white again. If you let that happen,you'll have to let the part cool, buff the surface to remove oxidation, and begin the heating process all over again. When the part is hot enough that the surface has turned a light blue, drop it in the oil. The oil will darken the blue finish. Remove the part and let it cool. To finish, buff the surface with 0000 steel wool and oil.

Practice will let you easily gauge the right moment to drop the part into the oil. If you don't want a dark finish, let the part air cool without the oil bath. For the darkest finish, immerse the part in the oil when hot, fish it out of the oil with pliers, and use the torch to briefly burn the oil off the part.

You can only heat-blue small parts. To heat-blue a slide evenly takes a temperature-controlled heat furnace, which costs as much as a dozen or more blue jobs on your handguns.

BAKE-ON FINISHES

The Brownells baked-on epoxy finish is simple, reasonably durable, and does not require a large investment in equipment. It turns a bright stainless or plated handgun an even black, brown or green. If you want to, you can even get all three colors, and apply your own camouflage pattern. The final finish looks like paint. It smells bad when you bake it.

Brownells offers two finishes, with pretty much the same application process. One is the matte or gloss Baking Lacquer. The other is their Teflon/Moly Oven Cure.

In order to hold the parts while you spray them and bake them, you should make supports. For the slide, I

This is Amer-lene Parkerizing covered with Brownells baking lacquer. After five years of daily carry, 5,000 rounds of ammunition, and two trips to Gunsite, this is all the wear that shows.

take scrap pieces of steel that fit under the slide. I wrap them in aluminum foil, to make cleanup easier. For 1911 frames, I just use my holding bar. Since you are heating only to 350 degrees, you could even cut supports from wood. Brownells suggests that you can apply the baked-on finish right over a blued finish. I prefer to apply it to bare metal for better bonding. Rub the parts with 0000 steel wool to remove all of the old blue finish that will come off. Degrease. Take a blow dryer and gently heat the parts you will be spraying. Hold your hand close to the part to check its warmth, but don't touch it. Spray the finish onto your parts, and let dry for 30 minutes. Spray the finish on in even, thin coats, passing smoothly from end to end. For the lacquer, give the parts three thin passes, for the Teflon/Moly, only two. While the parts air-dry, pre-heat a clean oven to 350 degrees. Also open the windows. Remember, the process smells. Bake the parts for 30 minutes. (Don't use any regular cooking pans for baking on your finish!) Cool. When done, wipe the oven with warm water and detergent. The finish is not poisonous, but do you want dinner tasting like it? I think not.

The resulting finishes are unaffected by oils and solvents. It will take some doing before they start wearing through. When they do, wet-sand only the worn area with your finest grade of cloth, degrease and apply a new "patch."

Another approach, not firearms specific, is to use a baked-on automotive engine paint. These are available in a variety of colors as well as basic black. A candy-apple red handgun? Hmmm.

RUST-BLUING

Cold rust-bluing, used more in the past than today, does not require the kind of equipment needed for hot-dip bluing, but is a labor-intensive process that takes at least four days. Some of the old formulas even suggested ten days or two weeks!

In a cold-rust bluing process, the gunsmith polishes the steel, degreases it, and swabs on the bluing solution. The firearm is then suspended over a tank of warm water, which rusts the steel. After rusting, any crusty sections are carded off with a wire wheel or brush, leaving the surface of the steel darkened. This process is repeated daily, with each day's start a dip in a boiling water bath. The finish on the steel becomes darker and darker. It took four days to get a good finish with the fastest formula. With some formulas the process could be continued until you got tired of it, and just couldn't wait to shoot the firearm. Oiling halted the rusting process and protected the finish.

Modern improvements in chemistry have shortened the time, and reduced or removed the need for the warm water tanks to keep the surface humid. They have not removed the need for a tank of boiling water, or the carding of the steel over several days of waiting.

On a handgun for presentation or exhibition, a rust-blued surface can be gorgeous. To get that gorgeous finish requires lots of practice, patience and skill.

AMER-LENE

The standard professional parkerized finish requires tanks of boiling phosphoric acid laced with dissolved filings of steel, zinc or manganese. Big, obviously hot tanks. Amer-lene is a zinc-phosphate process. With Amer-lene you still need a source of heat, but you can manage on a camp stove or a gas burner in the garage. I am specifically counseling against trying this on the kitchen stove.

Amer-lene, available as a concentrate, produces a dark gray color on the steel. This is the standard color of Parkerizing. You can make the parts black, or dark green, before or after you use the Amer-lene. Wear rubber gloves to protect your skin from the solutions. Mix into a stainless steel basin, according to the directions on the bottle. Since Amer-lene is a one-shot solution, mix only enough to cover the parts you are parkerizing. Once the solution cools the chemistry degenerates, and cannot be reversed or refreshed. Heat the mix. Place the stripped and degreased parts in the solution, and leave them there for five minutes. Every minute or so, gently stir the solution to get complete coverage of your parts.

If you want a black finish, Amer-lene offers a pre-dip blackener. Pour the blackener into a fiberglass pan, and after you have cleaned and degreased the parts, dip them into the blackener, and then into the heated Amer-lene.

After five minutes, pull the parts out of the solution and immediately rinse them under cold running water for 30 seconds. Wipe the parts completely dry, or blow dry them. Spray with Amer-lene stop/seal. Because the spray stops the chemical reaction and seals the surface, adding corrosion resistance, make sure you soak the parts with spray. The parts are now ready for assembly.

The Amer-lene Parkerizing kit is one of the few finishes that can be applied at home.

Clean with mineral spirits, oil and assemble. If you want your gray finish to be darker, vigorously rub dark grease into the surface. The porous Parkerizing will trap and hold the grease, adding corrosion resistance as well as color.

Amer-lene etches the surface of steel, so you should not treat the barrel. If you must treat the barrel's exterior, use neoprene plugs to block the muzzle and chamber.

FINISHES APPLIED BY PROFESSIONALS

The most important part of any refinishing job is the polishing of the surface. Only baked-on epoxies or teflon finishes will hide flaws. Flaws in the polishing of the steel will show up in a blue or color-case job. Hard chrome or nickel will highlight any polishing errors. Polish out the flaws before you ship, as we discussed in Chapter 6.

If you do not want to polish out flaws in the surface of your handgun yourself, you can have the refinisher do it. Think about it first. Good polishing takes time, and the refinisher will be charging for his time. At the highest hourly rate I have seen, two hours of polishing will equal the cost of the plating job itself. With polishing, a plating job can quickly become very expensive. Some finishing houses do not accept "no polish" jobs. You tell them what ou want, and they do it. What they have told me is that they have had too many unhappy customers who sent in a "no polish" job and were later not happy that their home polishing efforts showed so badly once the hard chrome or whatever was applied.

This is a S&W M-65 in .357 Magnum. Coated with Accurate Platings Enduracoat, this locking notch shows no chipping or wear after 2,000 times of dry-firing.

To save headaches and heartaches, those refinishers do the polishing you ask for, but don't plate unpolished firearms.

Whether or not you do your own polishing, try to see a sample of the refinisher's work beforehand. Look for pulled letters or dished screw holes. If you find any signs of these, go somewhere else. Check with local gunsmiths to find an established refinisher who declares he goes to all reasonable lengths to prevent pulling and dishing.

Unlike the home-applied finishes described

Firearms refinishing requires tanks, chemicals and lots of ventilation. This plating room at Accurate Plating uses the natural breezes of the Gulf of Mexico for ventilation.

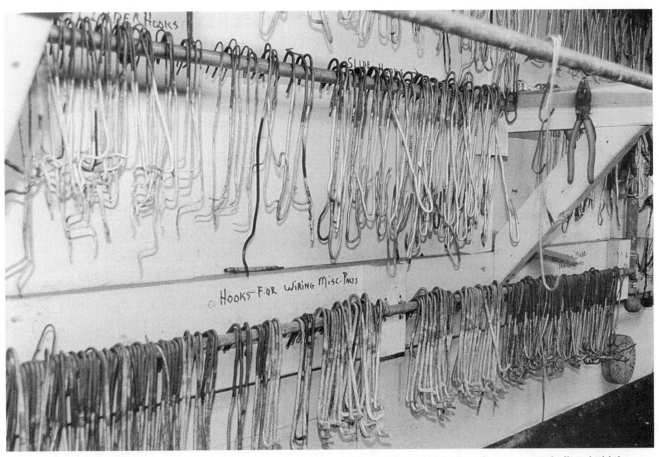

Proper refinishing also requires a means of holding the parts or handguns. These hooks have been custom-built to hold the frames, slides and cylinders.

earlier, which can be touched up or repaired, all of the professional finishes must go on whole. Once done, they're done. They cannot be touched up, and if you change your mind about what you want, too bad. For hot-dip blued handguns the cost of later "corrections" is not terribly high, because the process is simple: through the strip tank, into the hot dip, back to you. But if your handgun is plated and you make a change to it, the handgun must be stripped completely (think hydrochloric acid and sand-blasting) and then re-plated. It gets pricey very quickly.

Look at getting your handgun plated as having it carved in stone. The very last thing you do to a handgun — because once you get it plated there are no chances to try more modifications, no more changes to see if it'll be perfect now — is get it plated.

HOT-DIP BLUING

The blue finish on your handgun is the best finish the factory can apply at a reasonable cost. Not everyone wants a nickel- or chrome-plated handgun, or one in stainless. Shooters' tastes have been firmly in favor of blued steel for a century. Using a solution of caustic chemicals heated to temperatures from 270 degrees to 285 degrees, hot-dip bluing is considered the standard of the industry.

The process begins with a dip in a boiling cleaning

If the hooks and racks are not kept separated by process, they may contaminate other tanks.

solution to remove oil, gunk, wax, and fingerprints from the steel. Then, if necessary, the parts are polished or bead blasted. Next is an acid etching solution to remove any oils or oxidation accumulated during the polishing. This also removes any remaining blue finish.

Now the parts are ready to be blued. They go into and out of the caustic bluing salt solutions several times. When they reach the desired color, the parts go into a stop bath to neutralize the bluing salts. Finally, they go through a hot oil bath, to remove any water left behind by the stop bath.

If you want to take up bluing as a hobby, or yearn for

a career change, I must warn you that over nearly 20 years of gunsmithing, I have used seven different bluing professionals. I don't know, maybe it wasn't from the chemicals, but they all seemed an unhealthy lot, and retired or even died at an alarming rate.

I strongly recommend against hot-dip bluing at home. Blueing requires more than adequate ventilation, and simply propping a fan in the corner of the garage is not nearly enough to be "adequate" let alone sufficient.

The particular chemical solution used by a factory or a re-finisher really doesn't matter. Any hot-dip solution can be used on all carbon steels, including springs. Tossing a stainless part in the solution is a waste of time, as the part will come out looking dirty, not blued. On anything but stainless, all hot-dip methods produce a dark blue, almost black finish. While attractive, this finish will not cover pits or errors in polishing. It is not durable. If neglected, it will quickly rust.

If you have a pitted handgun that you want to blue, have the refinisher use a relatively coarse medium to bead blast the surface. A coarse bead blasting will diminish the look of the pitting, without creating the ripples seen with buffing.

Color case-hardening is an old method of both protecting the surface and hardening the iron. While attractive, it doesn't do either very well.

COLOR CASE HARDENING

In color case hardening, the finish most commonly found on the frames of Colt single-action revolvers, the "color" is actually a by-product of attempts to harden the steel. While the malleable iron or mild steel available in the 19th century was easy to machine, it was not as durable as the manufacturers wanted. They decided to try to harden it.

The process starts by packing the bare frames in a carbon-containing medium, usually bone meal, or bone meal with strips of scrap leather, and heating the bins of packed parts in ovens to 1,400 degrees for 2 to 4 hours. The temperature drives carbon from the bone meal into the surface of the iron or steel. To stop the heating, the frames are quenched in clean, soft water, agitated by bubbles, which fixes the carbon in the surface. The colors that result can be very attractive. Unfortunately, the hardness is only .005 inch thick. Longer soaking times in the oven, or higher temperatures, drive the carbon deeper into the surface. The color, however, rapidly diminishes as the carbon penetrates deeper. Harder was good from an operational standpoint, but not so from a sales viewpoint. So, they got less-deep hardness, but really good looks.

Very few professionals use this process anymore. The heat-and-water-quench warps too many parts unless your workers are very skilled and experienced, and both end up making the process too expensive.

Like many Colt SA revolvers, the Ruger Vaquero is available in a color finish. The alloys Ruger uses in their revolvers don't need to be case hardened, and wouldn't change color even if you tried. Ruger's color finish, a trade secret, is the result of a chemical reaction, vaguely similar to hot-dip bluing.

PARKERIZING

The process of phosphate coating in use since the late 1800s found itself refined around 1910 and trade-named Parkerizing. Later, the trade name came into common usage to describe the general process. Parkerizing is a very durable finish that is not very appealing to civilian hunters and sportsmen.

The firearm is first dipped in a cleansing, mild acid bath. Once clean, the parts are immersed in a boiling solution of phosphoric acid containing iron and either zinc- or manganese-phosphate. Depending on the particular steel and the precise solution, the surface reacts to form either manganese phosphate or zinc phosphate. The color of the final finish is dark gray. The manganese phosphate is a heavier, thicker and more durable finish than the zinc.

Because a rough surface is larger than a smooth one, and provides more area with which the phosphate can react, Parkerizing is best done to a surface that has been bead-blasted or brushed with a coarse wire wheel. After Parkerizing, a firearm is even rougher than it was going into the tanks as any previous polishing gets matted both when the steel is dipped in acid and during the Parkerizing process itself. A tightly-fitted pistol may require re-lapping the slide and frame until they slide smoothly.

The newly rough surface traps and holds oil, and an oiled Parkerized surface is very rust resistant. Unfortunately, it is just not pretty enough for some hunters and sportsmen. Now that the military is using aluminum instead of steel in their rifles, they no longer Parkerize.

In an effort to cut costs and increase durability, many manufacturers offer an alternative: lower-cost models of firearms with an even less-polished, but still Parkerized finish. Some shooters do not like the much-rougher surface, and others are happy with the lower cost.

NICKEL

Near the end of the 19th century, nickel began showing up as a protective finish. First available in mirror-bright, and later in brushed or bead-blasted, nickel finishes did offer protection from corrosion.

The first nickeling processes involved a tank full of nickel dissolved in metallic cyanide salts. The parts to be plated were suspended at one end of the tank, while at the other was a sacrificial bar of nickel. An electrical current was pumped into the tank, through the nickel bar and the gun parts. The current removed nickel atoms from the bar and deposited them on the parts.

Pistols so treated soon became the hallmark of the low-class criminal in big cities, handicapping nickel finishes from wider acceptance elsewhere. The attitude in many circles was that one simply didn't do that sort of thing to one's firearm if one had any taste at all. The only way to have a handgun nickeled and still maintain social status was to have it engraved and then nickeled.

Electrolytic nickel plating is a complicated and costly process, involving electricity, expensive chemicals, and the expensive disposal of those chemicals when exhausted. A firearm that isn't plated properly will easily chip or flake. Firearms manufacturers gradually phased out nickel, replacing the finish with stainless steel.

Because some shooters desire a shiny finish, nickel

Large tanks of chemicals require good ventilation. Those aren't windows in the background, that's open air.

is available from refinishing shops. Even properly done, electrolytic nickel can peel and crack away from the underlying steel. The finish is also susceptible to the old formula of Hoppes #9; there were reports of long-term soaking in it sometimes caused flaking. Even though new formula Hoppes does not cause flaking, the finish still cracks, and flakes, anyway on its own.

The social stigma of shiny guns has faded a great deal in the last couple of decades. The advent of stainless first made a white handgun acceptable. Now, extremely durable finishes such as hard chrome (see below) are accepted and not exceptional. For about the same cost as electrolytic nickel these new finishes leave the handgun both bright and protected.

HARD CHROME

Using the same metal as decorative chrome, hard chrome (or "industrial hard chrome") was developed to plate the cutting edges of milling and drilling tools, affording them longer life in industrial applications. At first, the large, very hard steel parts became brittle during their rather long plating process. "Hydrogen embrittlement," which was never much of a concern for the machine tools, was a big deal for the much softer steel and much thinner plating needs of handguns, and has been solved both for the machine tool industry and firearms plating.

When hard chroming had grown common enough, in the mid- to late 1970s, shooters started treating their handguns. Hard chrome, a bright white plating with a thickness of less than .001 inch, commonly .0004 inch, is very stark. It will not hide anything. Any flaw you have left behind in preparing the surface will jump right out.

The surface hardness of hard chrome is between 65 and 70 on the Rockwell C scale, much harder than the approximately 30 of a handgun's frame and the 40 of its slide. The bond is so good that a blow hard enough to dent the underlying steel does not break the chrome away. Properly done, hard chrome will not crack, chip or flake. To remove it your refinisher must use an acid bath.

Hard chrome also has a very low coefficient of friction, and two chromed surfaces sliding on each other rub less than two steel pieces do. The harder surface and decreased friction greatly increase the service life of any moving parts.

In many regards hard chrome comes very close to being an ideal firearms finish. Although it is not the ultimate in corrosion resistance, (steel will rust through, though very slowly), it is very popular with competitors whose firearms see a lot of use.

Here in the Detroit area, we occasionally see old handguns that we call "bumper chrome" guns. With so many auto plants in the area, all making chrome-plated

A good reason to mark your parts before shipping them. Eight trays, eight handguns, eight different states of the union. You want to get your parts back.

bumpers, it was not a big deal for one worker to ask a couple of his buddies to chrome the occasional pistol. Stripped, degreased, and dipped in hydrochloric acid to remove the blue, the parts were dropped into the moving tanks of bumpers and fished out at the other end by another fellow autoworker. Bumper chrome, applied to firearms, is not very durable. It flakes easily. The typical lack of polishing leaves a shiny but rough finish, and the fish-belly white color to the plating is not only a dead giveaway to the origin of the finish, it's pretty unattractive, too. If you don't live near an auto plant, you'll probably never see this "finish."

With the advent of hard chrome, and more and more stainless steel handguns available, interest in developing new handgun finishes surged in the late 1970s and early 1980s. Since then a number of processes have emerged. All offer advantages and disadvantages. The perfect firearms finish has not yet been developed.

ARMOLOY

In addition to electroless nickel plating and industrial hard chrome, the Armoloy company offers a specialized application of chrome. Called Armoloy, it is a nodular thin dense chrome application. The thickness applied is .0002 inch! As with all hard chrome, it is hard stuff, 70 on the Rockwell C scale. (A file measures in the low 60s.) The plating is a slightly darker gray than regular hard chrome, resists salt and acids, and is a snap to clean up. You can plate any kind of steel, carbon or stainless. You should not put Armoloy on springs, and they will not plate aluminum or plastic. Armoloy is a plating company, and does not offer any pistolsmithing services. You must ship your handgun completely disassembled, with a list of the parts. Also, they cannot plate composite parts.

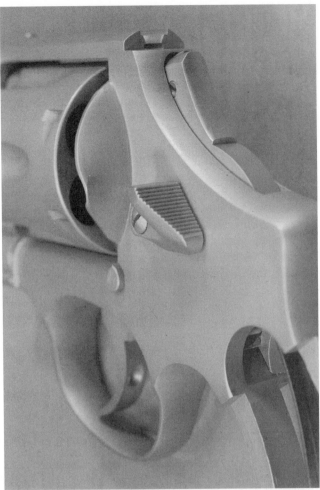

Hard chrome is a white plating that shows the texture of the surface finish. This is Enduraguard from Accurate Plating, and they did a very nice job of bead-blasting the surface before plating it.

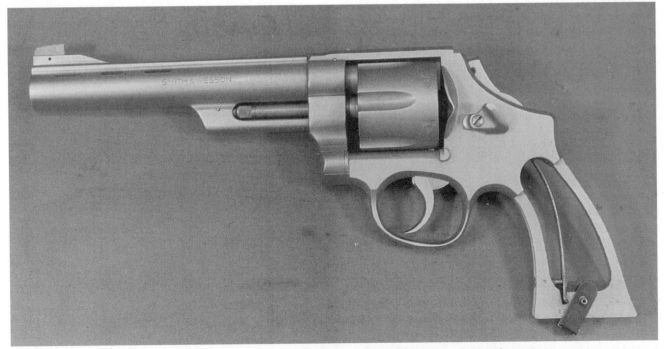

This is a Smith & Wesson 25-2, .45ACP revolver that was plated by Accurate Plating. Powder residue wipes off, and the surface shows no wear even after many practice sessions and thousands of rounds of hot bowling pin ammunition.

This Armoloy finish shows all the markings, good or bad. The caliber designation is needed, and the small dimple is a reminder. Both stayed, and both show.

Armoloy does not have a gunsmith on the premises, you must ship your handgun to them completely disassembled. It will come back the same way.

That is, they cannot plate an aluminum frame with steel parts attached to it.

TEFLON

Teflon started appearing on handguns in the 1970's. Just like the early Teflon frying pans, the first Teflon-plated guns weren't very durable. A few months of daily carry in a holster could wear the Teflon right through, exposing the steel underneath. The finish tended to fade. The process has improved greatly in the years since.

Accurate Plating can put a Teflon finish right over electrolytic nickel. Called "Ebony T," because of its black color, the finish does show wear. For greater durability of the underlying plating, Accurate can first do an electroless nickel finish, then the Ebony T. Not surprisingly, this process is 50 percent more expensive.

Rambear Enterprises also offers a Teflon finish, called Bearskin, which can be applied over other platings, aluminum, steel and stainless steel. They use a Kevlar binder to increase the durability of the Teflon, without decreasing its resistance to chemicals and solvents. Bearskin adheres to the base metal much better than previous Teflon finishes. I took a test disk of sheet metal coated with Bearskin, and bent it in half. The Bearskin did not flake off at the bend.

Bearskin also acts as a lubricant. Pistols treated with it do not need lubrication. If you want to lube you can.

A Teflon finish can be used in applications where other finishes won't work. A revolver with an aluminum frame, for example, cannot be otherwise plated. Solutions to plate the aluminum will attack the steel pivot pins of the hammer and trigger, as well as the steel barrel and cylinder. Solutions to plate the steel will dissolve the aluminum frame. Before Teflon, plating a gun like this required prying the steel parts out, and reinstalling them later. Now Teflon, applied with an airbrush, protects the revolver — with much less disassembly required. As a bonus you can have a camouflage pattern brushed on. They can probably sign your name, as well.

If you are going to have a revolver Teflon-coated, do not have the inside, or any of the interior parts coated. Teflon is applied in a thicker layer than the metal platings, and this can cause problems with tightly fitted revolver parts. If you send a pistol with a snug slide-frame-rail fit, after the Teflon is applied over the rails the pistol may not go back together. You can end up lapping the rails again, until the slide moves freely. You'll scrub most of your Teflon off the rails. I have seen a number of rusted pistols through the years, and the last place they rust is on the rails. By the time that happens, you will definitely notice the rest of the pistol getting shabby.

ELECTROLESS NICKEL

Electroless nickel is a definite improvement over the old nickel process. For one thing, it offers a matte finish, with a slight gold or yellow tinge to it instead of the old

The Bearskin finish on this Gunsite ATP 1911 shows all the markings, and does not dull the forward grasping grooves.

Rambear Enterprises makes a teflon-kevlar finish called Bearskin. You can have it in a spectrum of colors, and even applied in a camo finish.

bright nickel. A chemical deposit which provides a very uniform plating, electroless nickel starts off as a heated solution containing nickel. When the solution is driven through the proper temperature ranges, the nickel precipitates onto the firearm. While it is not as hard as hard chrome, "only" 53 to 56 Rockwell C, electroless nickel does not build up the slightly thicker deposits on corners and edges that electrically-driven plating processes such as hard chrome can. A properly applied electroless nickel plating will not peel away from the underlying steel, even if the part is bent through 180 degrees. There is even a government test for this, MIL-C-26074A. And you wondered where your tax dollars went.

ELECTROLESS AND TEFLON

As icing on the cake, the Robar company developed a process that combines electroless nickel with Teflon. Called NP3, the electroless nickel solution incorporates sub-micron particles of Teflon throughout the plating. If the nickel wears, fresh Teflon-bearing surface is exposed. The plating is extremely even, and only .0002 inch thick. It is slightly less hard than straight electroless nickel, measuring 48-51 on the Rockwell C scale.

The finish is a silver-gray and shows the texture of the base metal. If you have the surface of your handgun sandblasted, you will end up with a dark gray finish. A curious aspect of NP3 is that if you scratch the surface

down to the bare steel, any rust that forms does not seem to spread under the edges of the plating that remains. If we could get it to grow back, then we'd really have something!

Because of the Teflon trapped in the nickel, NP3 has a very high lubricity, and the friction between parts is just about as low as you can get. NP3 is a very popular finish for desert applications. Because of the low friction, you don't really have to oil the parts. Without oil to attract and hold the grit of the desert, the NP3 actually lasts

This 1911 came back from Robar in protective layers of plastic wrapping film. If it gets scratched, it won't happen at Robar, or coming back from Robar.

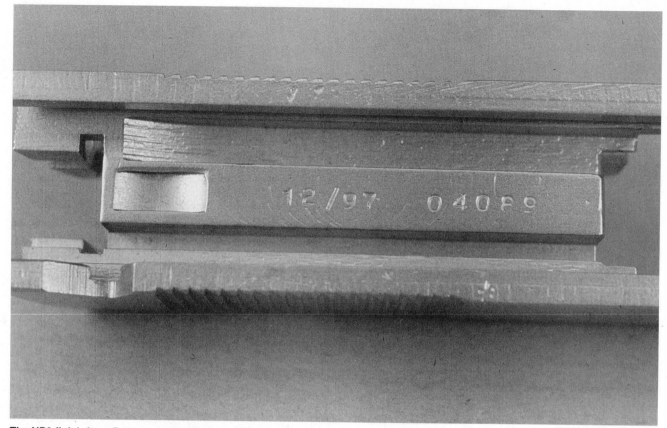

The NP3 finish from Robar is an electroless nickel that incorporates teflon in the plating. It is less than .001 inches thick, and clearly shows the markings on the bottom of this slide.

longer dry than it would if oiled. For non-desert uses, I still oil NP3. The combination of a light film of oil and the natural lubricity if the NP3 makes cleaning up a simple wipe-clean operation.

STAINLESS STEEL BLACKENING

Robar also offers a blackening process for stainless steel. The chrome already in the stainless alloy is oxidized in a chemical treatment solution, resulting in a Chrome-sulfide surface. Since the surface is not plated, the dimensions of parts are not changed. While not changing the heat-treatment or durability of the steel, the process does increase resistance to corrosion.

Stainless steel blackening depends on the treatment plant knowing the alloy being treated. Robar has a chemistry lab right on site. If you ship them something they haven't seen before they can test it before treating it. If you want to send your stainless handgun to someone else for blackening, ask if they have treated that model before you ship it.

BLACK CHROME

Back in the 1980s, black chrome was thought to be the next, great leap forward in firearms finishes. With a black chrome finish, it was thought, shooters could have the durability of hard chrome and the black color of bluing. Unfortunately, black chrome is not very durable. Accurate Plating applies it over a base coat of nickel or

electroless nickel to increase durability and adhesion. It does not reach into the internal spaces of a handgun, so the magazine well of a pistol may not be fully blackened.

While the jet-black finish is quite attractive, for the same durability, at a lower cost, and the ability to patch-repair the finish, you are better off with a baked-on epoxy.

GOLD PLATING

Flashy, expensive, and very soft, gold plating offers no durability. In very expensive custom firearms, gold can be inlaid into the surface of the steel. As inlaid wire gold is slightly more durable. The most frequent use for gold plating is on small parts of a presentation handgun, to accentuate the bluing of the frame, slide, barrel, cylinder, or other larger parts.

BAKED-ON FINISHES

Paint to protect metal has been common for the last couple of centuries. In the early attempts, the paint quality was so poor that a painted metal surface wasn't really protected. Maintaining the paint was more work than maintaining the metal.

While modern paints are far more effective, they are still not durable. Epoxies provide the needed durability. A reaction between two or more chemicals, epoxy forms a tough and lasting coating. The epoxy finish for a handgun doesn't fade, and is very scratch- and chip-resistant. Paint dries, epoxy reacts. Epoxy, unfortunately, also costs. And it has the same large choice of colors that Henry Ford supposedly offered his early customers: black.

One of the best epoxy finishes for your handgun is Roguard, from Robar. Robar is so confident of Roguard's ability to resist peeling and corrosion that they offer a lifetime warranty on it. If Roguard peels, or if your firearm corrodes through the finish, Robar will replace the finish. Obviously, tire tracks and hammer marks would negate the warranty on the parts of your handgun so marred.

Roguard goes on in a layer only .001 inch thick, so you do not lose any of your markings. Any mars and blemishes will likewise be sealed in but not covered up if you do not first prepare the surface and remove them. Roguard can be patched, unlike the other platings already discussed. If you do wear the high spots of your handgun down to the bare metal, you can ship it back to Robar for a touch-up session.

Accurate Plating also does a baked-on epoxy finish,

called Enduracoat. When I was testing various finishes, I discovered an interesting thing about Roguard and Enduracoat: their feel. The finishes are smooth without being slick, and they feel soft. Not spongy-soft, but just soft enough to take the hard touch from the base metal. When I first pulled the handguns with these coatings from their shipping packages, I could hardly put them down!

Another coating that provides good results is Techkote by Spradlins. They coated my Springfield "stealth CQB," and it has held up under use in a number of classes, matches, and as a loaner while teaching. I had it done in the current tactical fashion, black slide with OD Green frame and associated parts, and even after a couple of years of use it is showing very little holster wear.

ANODIZING

"Airweight" handguns have frames made of aluminum alloys. Aluminum can be finished with electro- and electroless nickel, hard chrome, Teflon and any of the epoxy finishes. The caustic solutions of a hot-dip blue, intend-

Back from Robar, this 1911 was covered with Roguard. It is a semi-gloss black that promises great durability, and is curiously soft to the touch.

ed to work on steel, will dissolve aluminum. Do not rust, heat or caustic blue a firearm with aluminum parts.

The factory anodizes the aluminum to finish it. A heat and chemical treatment of the surface, anodizing forms a hardened skin out of the surface layer of the metal. Properly done, anodizing is amazingly hard. If you have to file anodized aluminum, you'll find your file sliding off the surface until you bear down and scuff through it. Bear in mind that the aluminum scope rings used for rifles are often not anodize-hardened, just blackened.

The Enduracoat faithfully reproduces all the markings on this M-65.

The Roguard finish reproduces the serial number stamped on this mainspring housing, as well as the stippling.

Depending on the dye used near the end of the process, you can have aluminum anodized a whole series of colors, including the ever-popular black. Over time and under use, however, anodizing will fade. The black dyes commonly used turn a blue-ish or purple color. Sweat and wear will leave the front and back of the frame of a well-used Colt Lightweight Commander significantly lighter in color than the rest of the firearm.

An aluminum frame being re-anodized must have all

This is a S&W M-65 in .357 Magnum. Coated with Accurate Platings Enduracoat, this locking notch shows no chipping or wear after 2,000 times of dry-firing.

of the steel parts removed, or they will contaminate the chemical solutions. If you have to repair an aluminum revolver frame, you have two choices for a new finish. One, send it back to the manufacturer. They can properly remove the steel parts without damaging the frame, re-anodize it and reassemble it. Two, use some other finish that is compatible with both steel and aluminum.

Re-anodizing an aluminum 1911 frame is easy. Pull the grip screw bushings and the plunger tube off, get the frame re-anodized, and then reinstall the bushings and tube. The hard part is in finding an anodizer who will do your firearms. Chemical plants that do anodizing do batches of it for manufacturers. They are accustomed to treating large batches of identical parts at once. Those parts are made of the same alloy by the same machinist, from batch to batch. The anodizer knows exactly what to expect. Your part may not be (probably isn't) the same alloy as anything they treat. And if it is, which alloy is it? The gun maker certainly isn't going to tell them. As a result, if the anodizer will hard-coat anodize your frame, they will do it by itself in the smallest treatment urn they have. They aren't going to risk contaminating an entire production batch of one of their regular customers, just to slide in your part. So, you'll bear the full cost of a treatment run in their smallest urn, for your one part.

As a result, many aluminum-alloy frames are treated to something other than a new anodize coat after they've been worked on.

FACTORY-AVAILABLE FINISHES

In many cases, the choice of finishes available from the factory is pretty limited. Hot-dip blue or stainless steel are generally offered. Sometimes you can get a mix, such as a blued slide and a stainless frame. Some manufacturers will electroless nickel parts on a stainless handgun to match the finish. You cannot ask the manufacturers to hard-chrome or electroless nickel a handgun before they ship it to you.

GLOCK

When Glocks appeared, they brought with them a new, uncommonly hard finish. Called Tenifer, the finish made the surface of Glock slide so hard it would resist a file. Tenifer is not a plating, but a treatment of the surface of the steel for hardness and corrosion resistance. At Rockwell C 69 or 70, you need to use a carbide drill or end mill to do any major metal removal. Use a diamond file on a Glock slide; it's the only thing that will stand up to the Tenifer.

Glock only offers a black finish. The black is an oxide coating applied over the Tenifer for aesthetics. Buff off the black, and the underlying steel will still be protected by the Tenifer. Buffing a Glock slide and then plating it with hard chrome or electroless nickel is gilding the lily. You will be plating the steel with a layer that is slightly softer than the steel itself, and will add only the smallest extra measure of corrosion resistance.

SIG SAUER

As a factory option, SIG offers a polymer finish on their handguns. This baked-on epoxy coating reduces friction and adds corrosion resistance.

The bulk of SIG pistols are shipped with black oxide steel parts and hard-anodized aluminum frames. Occasionally the factory releases a batch done in hard chrome or electroless nickel, but this happens without any fanfare or warning. Miss the batch, and you have to wait until the next one.

SMITH & WESSON

Smith offers the widest line of stainless steel pistols and revolvers. When the popularity of stainless rose in the early 1990s, Smith dropped the nickel finish. Between the environmental regulations, and nickel's declining sales, Smith could no longer justify the costs for

If you think you might want to take up re-finishing as a hobby, look at the tanks, lights and ventilation needed for one room.

nickel-plating on a production basis. You can still have a nickeled Smith & Wesson re-finished in nickel, but you cannot get a new one, with a very few rare exceptions such as the "Classsic" revolvers.

Smith offers some two-tone models, with black oxide slides and stainless frames. They do not offer hard chrome.

The rest of the handgun manufacturers for the most part offer only blue and stainless. Occasionally you can get your blue or stainless in a high polish, and sometimes even a two-tone blue and stainless mixture is offered. Mostly, though, you don't get a choice, and will end up sending your handgun off to a re-finisher after you have done the modifications you feel are necessary.

WHICH FINISH SHOULD YOU USE?

Base your choice of finish for your handguns on the availability and benefits of each finish, the cost, your expected use, and your own taste. If you just can't stand the thought of a nickel or nickel-like finish on your handguns, then don't let anyone talk you into a decision you will end up hating. In the end, you have to go with what you like.

I am somewhat embarrassed to say that my competition revolvers have the original finish on them. That is, where they have a finish. My uncomped Smith & Wesson 25-2 in .45 ACP used for bowling pin and USPSA/IPSC shooting, is mostly factory blue. I say "mostly" because in places the bluing is worn off from years of practice and competition. Sooner or later, when the experimentation has stopped, I will have it hard chromed. My radically-ported "pseudo 25-2" pin gun (ported with seven slots by Mag na Port) is hard-chromed. I settled on the configuration years ago, and Mag Na Port can port right through hard chrome, so I had it gussied up. My International Revolver Confederation competition handgun is a seven-shot Baumannized .357 Magnum. It started life as a blued Smith & Wesson Model 28, and since leaving Springfield it has acquired a stainless S&W model 627 barrel. I haven't decided on a finish yet.

My two PPC revolvers are both mixtures. One is a stainless S&W M-66 with a carbon steel barrel that I have never gotten around to bluing, and an Aristocrat rib in blue steel. The other one is an S&W Model 27 that was electroless nickeled before I put a stainless barrel and a Powers rib on it. The previous owner had gold-plated

Call me old-fashioned, or conservative, but for a single-action revolver I think that a mixture of blueing and color case-hardening is the only appropriate finish. I also think the earliest T-birds are the most attractive cars ever made.

the hammer and trigger. Not for me! I replaced the gold with a Cylinder & Slide hard-chromed roller-action hammer and trigger.

Starting over, I would build a PPC revolver on a stainless frame and fit a stainless barrel to it. The rib would be an Aristocrat or Powers rib made of blued steel. For bowling pin competition, I would use an S&W 625-2, again in stainless steel. In these applications the finish doesn't matter. Any money spent should be spent on improving performance.

If I were starting from scratch for a hunting revolver, just like the competition revolvers I would start with stainless steel. However, once I had done all the custom work that I needed, I would send it off to Accurate Plating, or Robar, and have the stainless blackened. While hunting, the flash or gleam of a polished, or stainless steel revolver can startle the game. I might even consider a camouflage pattern, if one were available.

For Cowboy Action I would stick with tradition: a case-hardened and blue finish. Yes, hard-chroming makes it easier to clean, and improves its long-term durability, but, heck, it's just not right. I will confess to owning at least one bright-nickel-plated single-action revolver. In my own defense, I won it at a match and was not offered a choice of finish. I know I could have traded it for one more suited to my tastes, but I do not trade or sell guns I have won. I know, I know. It's a failing on my part, but, except for duplicates, I just can't bear to part with prizes.

For daily concealed carry for personal defense I would select a stainless revolver and have it blackened. Blackening affords an extra measure of corrosion resistance, and makes the handgun less obvious.

My preference on pistols is to leave many of them "in the white," that is, stainless or plated. For practical shooting, or a competition handgun that will fire many thousands of rounds, both service life and ease of cleaning are important. After finalizing the custom work, I would go with an NP3, hard chrome, or electroless nickel coating. Any of these finishes makes cleaning up easier, and increases service life. I would leave the sights black.

Thinking of shooting in the National Matches at Camp Perry? The social imperative here seems to be for a blued or black pistol. Hardly anyone shoots a hard-chromed handgun. Not that the rules forbid it, but who wants to stand out too much?

In the case of building a pistol for bull's-eye, I would be sorely tempted to have the pistol plated for longevity, and then have the exterior coated with black epoxy. Or even black paint.

An all-steel pistol for daily concealed carry could use any one of several strategies. Your goal should be to improve corrosion resistance without drawing attention to the firearm. You could start with a coating of NP3, hard chrome or electroless nickel followed by either the Brownells bake-on lacquer finish in black, or Roguard. Another approach is to nickel plate the firearm and

have Accurate Plating give it an Ebony T coating. Or, for the best combination, try a hard chrome or electroless nickel covered with the Rambear Bearskin. You could even NP3 plate your handgun, and then Bearskin coat it, to build up two layers of Teflon protection.

All of this is expensive. The pistol, the custom work, the two finish jobs, they add up. But you could wear the pistol all day, depend on it 100 percent, and know that rust would never attack it. Your only maintenance problems would be brushing out any dust bunnies and swapping ammunition on a regular basis.

A less expensive method of protecting your concealed carry pistol is to take the Brownells route for both layers of protection. First, Amer-lene black and Parkerize the surface, obviously not an option with a stainless steel. Then, use a baked-on finish to further seal it away from corrosion.

A carry pistol with an aluminum frame would get the steel parts plated, and then the whole thing would be Roguarded, Bearskin or covered with bake-on epoxy.

Exceptions to all the above? A Glock needs no extra finish at all.

PREPARING YOUR HANDGUN FOR THE PLATER

First, consider how much work you want to do yourself to prepare the surface. The process of plating is exactly like the process of painting a car. If you turn your car over to the paint shop with dirt, bugs and scratches on the surface, you'll either get back a paint job with dirt, bugs and scratches under it, or a bill for the labor to clean the surface before painting. If you don't care that tool marks, casting lines and scratches will show through the plating on your pistol, fine. Your plater, though, may have a different idea.

Some platers are so concerned with their work, and the image of their plating, that they insist on polishing out the more egregious marks. They'll charge you for that work, too. Do your homework. Get catalogs. Along with the request for a catalog, find out their shop policies. Do they insist on polishing out "ugly" guns? If so, find out the rate, and the average charge. Armed with policies, rates, etc, you can make an informed decision about polishing before you ship. For a discussion of polishing, review Chapter 6. Some gunsmiths do not send work to platers who insist on polishing. The gunsmith has already done the work desired, and created the level of matte, polish, sandblast, whatever, that the owner wants. Look your work over very carefully before sending it off with the instructions "do not polish." If you do not, you have no one to blame but yourself when your gun comes back with the scratch you didn't see highlighted by hard chrome.

You will see many handguns with a matte or brushed finish under their plating jobs, but not many with a mirror finish. Why? There are three reasons. First, the acids used to clean the parts prior to immersion in the plating

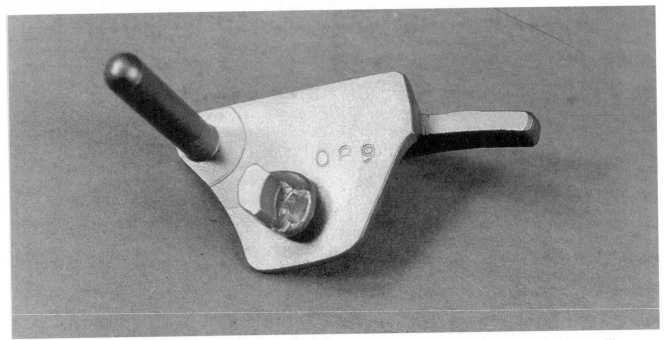

Mark your parts before shipping them. This safety has the last three digits of the serial number stamped on the back side.

tanks will slightly etch the surface. Even the brightest mirror finish will lose some of its lustre. Second, the plating will adhere better to a rougher surface. To reduce the possibility of the finish lifting, platers prefer a matte or brushed surface. Third, a mirror polish is not easy to do. It takes skill, practice, and time. Rather than charge twice as much money, (and not make twice as much) the plater might just say "no" to a mirror finish.

Ask if they want the handgun in pieces.

If you are plating the whole thing and the plater can disassemble it, ship the handgun assembled. This is the best way to ensure all the parts are there. If you are only having parts of the handgun plated, or you are polishing before you ship, disassemble the handgun first.

While you have the handgun apart, mark the major parts with your serial number. In case a tray of parts gets knocked over at the plater, there will be no problem figuring out what parts go with your handgun. On a revolver this is not a big deal, as the major parts already have either the serial number or the factory assembly number on them. On a pistol, I mark the parts to be shipped with the last three digits of the serial number, using a set of punches I keep in a drawer for just this task. An electric marking pencil does the same thing. Marking the parts also helps you if you have more than one handgun of a particular model. Yes, one may be blue and the other stainless, but often, matched pairs are just that, matched. Your backup may be identical except for serial number to your main competition gun. Having the precisely fitted parts numbered to the gun to which they are fitted only makes sense.

Separate the objects that won't, or can't, be plated.

Platers simply won't plate plastic parts, such as the mainspring housing on a 1991A1. The older Colt pistols had steel or aluminum mainspring housings. If you want your 1991A1 to have an unplated plastic mainspring housing, while the rest of the pistol is plated, fine. If you want the handgun to match all over, you will have to fit a steel mainspring housing before you ship the pistol.

Platers will not plate springs. Even if the spring survives the cleaning acid bath, and the plating process does not change the compression qualities of the spring steel, the extra layer of the plating can bind the spring.

Platers do not plate titanium or tungsten. If you send your pistol assembled, note what parts are titanium or tungsten. If you are shipping it in pieces, leave those parts out and note in your cover letter that you have retained them.

Unless you want your sights plated, take them off. The plater, before plating, can mask a staked front sight, but there is a better way. Have him plate the front sight. When you get it back, use a paint or epoxy to blacken it. For a three-dot set of sights, blacken the sight, then paint the dot back in. Or, remove the front sight and stake a replacement back on when the pistol gets back. If your front sight is in a dovetail, like the Novak sight, remove it before shipping the pistol. The rear sight should always be removed.

None of the radioactive night sights will survive the plating process. If you do not remove them, the plater must remove or mask them, and charge you for the extra work.

Write up a detailed list of all the parts being shipped. Everything goes on this list. Note parts that have been removed: "Sights removed, missing recoil spring guide rod," etc. Total the number of parts on the list, and count the number being shipped. If the plater receives a package, and there are not enough parts for a complete pistol, they have a puzzle. Without your note, they have a problem. You will receive a phone call, asking if all the parts you wanted plated are there, and is there a fax number they can call to send a detailed list of what you shipped? You will be charged for the time and phone call. Save the time and money. Send a list.

Type a letter detailing what level of polish and what finish you want. Keep it simple. As an example; "Enclosed, please find Colt Series 70 pistol #123, caliber .45 ACP, assembled, without sights. Two magazines, assembled. Please wire brush the surface and hard chrome all parts of pistol and magazines, excluding springs. Check enclosed. Ship UPS Next Day when finished."

In the letter, specify which parts are soldered, and what solder was used. Solder is softer than steel, and can be eroded by bead-blasting, or wiped out of the edge of a joint by a wire wheel. Some acids can attack solder. By telling the plater which parts are soldered you let them exercise due caution when stripping those parts. In this new age of digital everything, it is easy enough to take a digital photograph of your parts, laid out before you pack and ship them. You can include a copy of the photo for the plater, along with the written list.

You will rarely want to have the exterior of a pistol barrel plated. Instead, spend your money on a stainless match barrel. You'll gain accuracy and corrosion resistance.

For liability reasons, the plater will not plate the interior of the barrel. Your barrel was manufactured to a precise interior dimension. Plating thick enough to be durable in the bore would change those dimensions, increasing pressure. Plating thin enough to prevent pressure rises would not be durable. The chrome-lined barrels you read about for military rifles? The thickness of that plating is several times greater than the plating on your handgun. The barrel maker took into account the thickness of the chrome plating when broaching and rifling the barrel. In any case, I do not have pistol barrels plated. A pistol barrel spends its entire life banging around in the slide. I have seen a few, and heard of more, barrels that broke due to plating. The plating hardened the barrel just enough that the repeated impacts finally caused the bottom lug to break off.

Tell the plater how tightly the slide and frame fit. If you have made the fit so tight they cannot plate it and get the slide back on the frame, they will call you. Do you want them to lap the fit before or after the plating goes on? Or will you re-fit the slide and frame after the pistol comes back?

Once your package returns, open and count the parts. The same number you shipped? Great. Assemble, and have fun. If not, call immediately.

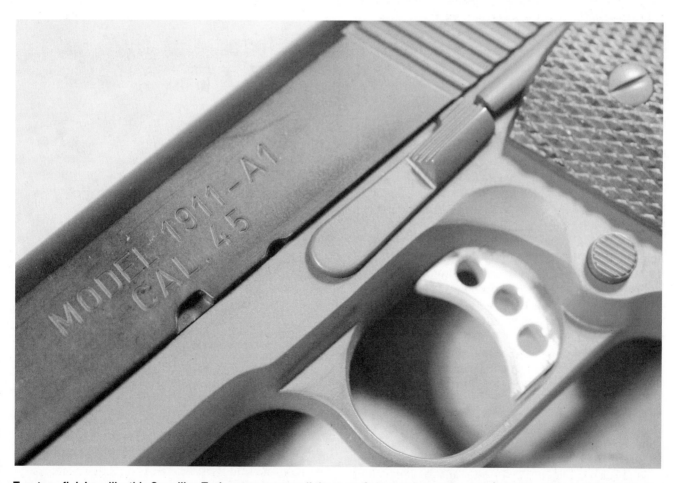

Two-tone finishes, like this Spradlins Tech-cote, are now all the rage. Color hardly matters, but durability does. And this finish is as tough as the rest.

CHAPTER

10

MALFUNCTIONS OF THE REVOLVER

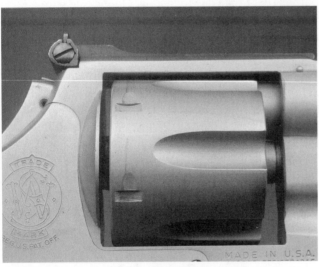

The drag line of the locking bolt against the cylinder shows that this revolver is working properly. Revolvers will get this ring around them, there is no way to prevent it except by not turning the cylinder. Where's the fun in that?

In the early days of practical competition shooting, the jockeying between pistol and revolver shooters was very interesting. The big advantage that revolvers supposedly had over pistols was their reliability. And for the most part, in the early days it was a real and not just theoretical advantage. As long as the revolver shooter stayed with factory ammunition, he could count on reliable function. (If the pistol shooter he was competing against had just undergone a series of home-gunsmithing experiments, the revolver shooter was assured of success. Pistolsmithing in the old days was as much voodoo as it was practical.) But on the rare instances of a malfunction, the revolver shooter usually found himself with a stage score of zero. A revolver malfunction usually meant the tools had to come out, and that ended the stage for the shooter.

But the rarity of malfunctions kept revolvers going for a number of years in the early days. Wheelguns can still be a lot of fun, and in the hands of a good shooter, competitive at many clubs.

What is a malfunction? Defined broadly, a malfunction is what happens when you were expecting something else instead. You could call a miss a malfunction, though

Abused or damaged cases can be rolled to the proper dimension with the Case-Pro from Image Industries. (photo courtesy Image Industries)

it's more a malfunction of your own personal mechanism than of the revolver's. And calling your miss "A malfunction of the optical/mechanical sighting system" will not help your standing at the gun club, or bring down that deer happily sprinting away.

As firearms instructor and authority John Farnam remarked in his book *The Farnum Method of Defensive*

Powder residue or unburned flakes of powder under the extractor star will keep the cylinder from closing. Brush them out to close the cylinder.

Handgunning, "The most common stoppage encountered in the revolver. . . [and] in the autoloaders is running out of ammunition." This wide casting of the malfunction net can give a focus to your panicked attempts at correction in a tactical setting, but does not do much for your gunsmithing efforts. When the handgun stops working, by definition a difficult situation, the first thing to ask yourself is: "Do I have ammunition left?"

We will only cover mechanical malfunctions here, and leave the Zen of hitting and missing for later books.

Most mechanical malfunctions are caused by lack of maintenance. If you keep your revolver clean you won't have too many problems. When you do have a problem, though, you will be in one of two situations. The first is the calm, collected and unstressed atmosphere of the shooting range or gun club. There is no need to hurry. Your target won't escape, or worse yet, turn around and attack you. At the range you have plenty of time to figure out exactly what went wrong, and how, and what corrective measures to take.

The second situation is a highly stressed one. You may be in the middle of a match, with time ticking away and have to figure out how to correct the problem. Or, you are deer hunting, and all of a sudden the handgun just doesn't want to work. You may not have another chance this season at your quarry. In the worst situation of all, you have attempted to use your handgun in defense of

yourself or another, and it won't work. In all of these instances, you have a very limited amount of time in which to take corrective measures, and then continue.

The second situation is actually the simpler, but under stress even the simple becomes difficult. Open the revolver, dump out the rounds that won't work, load fresh ones as quickly as possible, and continue. If new ammunition doesn't solve the problem, drop the revolver and draw your backup.

No backup? Now, you are in trouble. You will need to ferret out the exact cause of the problem, and may not have enough time.

In the first situation, you can take all the time you need to diagnose the problem.

When your car fails to start and you call your mechanic, the first thing he'll do is ask you a barrage of questions: When you turn the key, what noises does it make? Clicking? Whirring? Cranking but not catching? The answers to these questions give him clues about the probable solution; the simple statement that the car won't start provides only the roughest idea of what may be wrong. With your revolver, you are the mechanic. You will have to ask yourself the questions, and then supply the answers.

If, for example, the round won't chamber, you must ask yourself why. What, exactly, is happening to prevent chambering? Or if the revolver fails to fire, what is it doing, and what isn't it doing? Don't immediately jump into fixing the problem. Study the symptoms first. If you hastily assume a particular problem is the culprit, and make a quick fix, you may be setting yourself up for greater problems in the future. Use Chapter 4, How They Work and What to Look for, as a guide to troubleshooting.

With your non-functioning car, a quick and erroneous assumption could send you off to buy a new battery, only to find you have a nasty short in your electrical system. Likewise, if you make a quick assumption about your revolver's malfunction, you could end up fixing it two or three times, and, just like your car, paying each time for the right or wrong solution.

CHAMBER

When a round fails to chamber, it does not seat completely. Ask yourself why a round would fail to chamber.

First, did you load the correct ammunition? At first glance, the rounds may be so similar that you mistakenly picked up a wrong one. A single .357 Magnum in a box of loose .38 Specials will go unnoticed until you try to chamber it. Then it will stop, sticking .10 inch out of the cylinder. Likewise with .44 Magnum ammunition and a .44 Special revolver.

Second, are you using reloads? If so, were they correctly re-sized? The sizing ring of a re-sizing die cannot reach all the way down to the rim of a cartridge, so if you use stray brass picked up at the range you may run into a chambering problem. The previous owner of the brass could have had a larger chamber, or a larger sizing die. He might have fired much hotter loads than the brass could stand, bulging the bottom of the case where your sizing die can't reach. The result will be an incompletely chambered round. The long-term solution to this problem is to use the Case-Pro 100 from Image Industries to iron the case down to size all the way down to the rim. For now, you will have to set the round aside. It cannot be used.

Competition shooters will chamber-check every round before a match, to prevent this problem.

Third, is the chamber clean? Dirt in the chamber will keep the rounds from going all the way home. If you haven't cleaned your revolver lately, or have fired many rounds since the last cleaning (even if it was only yesterday), the chamber may be so gunked up with powder residue that the rounds can't drop in. A temporary fix is to push the stuck round in place with your thumb, but the real solution is more frequent cleaning.

If you have put fewer than 100 rounds through your revolver since the last cleaning and it is already having trouble chambering, you may have undersized chambers. An undersized chamber is already a tight fit; with just a little powder residue you can have a problem. To correct it you need purchase a chambering reamer, open the chambers up to the average range for your caliber, and polish the chambers again. Between doing the job yourself and having a gunsmith do it is a toss-up. The cost of the reamer will probably be close to, maybe a little more than, the labor of having a professional do it. And unless you expect to run into this same problem again, in the very same caliber, you'll never need the reamer again.

The bottom chamber is bulged, right at the notch for the locking bolt. A hot load that was over pressure has just cost this shooter a new cylinder.

Fourth, are there any nicks or burrs on the edge of the chambers? Nicks and burrs, more common on used revolvers, can bind a cartridge and prevent it from fully sliding into the chamber. Burrs and nicks should be stoned out with an extra fine synthetic round stone.

CLOSE

If the cartridges appear to have seated fully, check to see if the cylinder is closing. Don't bang on the cylinder, or force it closed.

If the cylinder fails to lock into place, start with a check for dirt. First look under the extractor star. Revolvers commonly end up with flakes of unburned powder and powder residue here. This gunk pushes the extractor star out from its seat by a few thousandths of an inch, and makes the cylinder assembly too long to fit into the frame. If this is your problem, remove the rounds, push the ejector rod to lift the extractor star, and brush the back of the extractor star and the cylinder clean.

You may wonder how those flakes got there. Occasionally, when an empty case is being extracted, powder residue and powder flakes will drop out. If the flakes fall at just the right moment, they can land between the extractor and the cylinder. Ironically, you can also cause this condition when cleaning the cylinder. If your chamber brush fits so tightly that when you pull it out it lifts the extractor star, the gunk the brush removed will end up between the extractor and the cylinder. Don't stop cleaning your revolver! Instead, when you finish brushing out the chambers, hold the extractor open and brush behind the extractor, too.

If the extractor star is not the problem check the front of the frame where the crane fits when closed. A buildup

of powder here can also keep the cylinder from closing. Scrub it out. Check the back of the barrel. If you have allowed powder residue to build up on the back of the barrel it can bind on the cylinder face. The powder residue on both the back of the barrel and the front of the cylinder will be crusty and burnished from the action of the cylinder. Scrub both areas clean.

If residues and buildups are not your problem, the next likely cause is reloaded ammunition. Check your cases. Look for one with a very minor bulge – not enough to keep from chambering, just enough to keep the cylinder from closing. A nicked rim will also keep the cartridge from fully seating. If your top round is the nicked one, you won't be able to close the cylinder. Similarly, a high primer will prevent the cylinder from closing. You'll have to be more critical in your reloading, and use the Case-Pro to iron your cases and their rims smooth and even.

You've checked for residue, and you're shooting factory ammunition, or perfect reloads. What next? Try closing the cylinder without any ammunition in it. If the cylinder closes but won't latch, press the cylinder with one or both thumbs. If it latches with a click, your crane is out of alignment.

The most common cause of crane misalignment is watching too many movies. The hero checks to see if his revolver is loaded, a rare and amazing cinematic moment. He flicks his wrist to the side, opening and closing the cylinder, and — even if he's doing it correctly — putting a lot of stress on the crane. Repeatedly imitating the hero while on the range, and forcefully flicking the cylinder of your revolver open and closed can bend the crane.

Some of you will be puzzling over my saying "even if

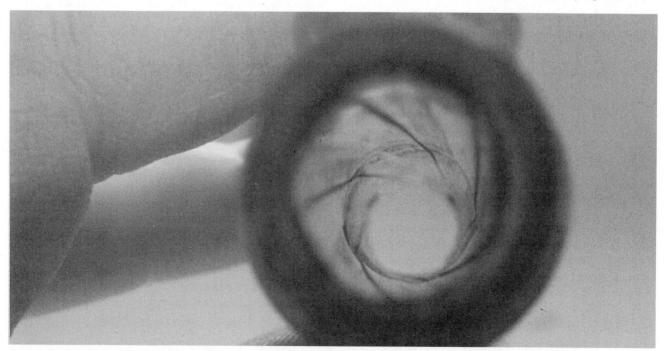

A bulged barrel may not be apparent on the outside. When you look down the barrel you may see a dark ring.

he's doing it correctly." You've probably been told never, NEVER, to handle your revolver this way. Well, sometimes you don't have a choice. When practicing one-handed drills for defensive shooting with a revolver, the quickest way to close it is with a flick of the wrist. Once your practice is done you'll probably need to realign your crane.

To align the crane, you'll need a plastic wedge, a plastic-faced mallet, and a crane alignment gauge. Look ahead to Chapter 15, where crane realignment is covered in detail.

Did you just detail strip and clean your revolver? Perhaps you replaced the sideplate screws in the wrong holes. On earlier Smith & Wesson revolvers the front screw is precisely fitted to hold the crane in the frame but let it swing freely. The other two screws are longer and will bind the crane. To check, back that front screw out half a turn. If the crane now moves freely, you need to switch the screws around until you find the short one. The next time you take the revolver apart, be sure to keep the sideplate screws in order, so you don't have to do this again.

Look at the ejector rod. A bent one will bind against the barrel and prevent closing. To check yours for straightness, open the cylinder and remove the ammunition. Hold the revolver in your right hand, braced against a padded vise. Give the cylinder a spin with your left hand. If you see the tip of the ejector rod spinning in a little circle, your rod is bent. The fix is easy only if you have the right tools. With the fixture, straightening the rod is a ten minute operation (see Chapter 15). Without a Powers centerpin/ejector rod alignment fixture, you are likely to make the problem worse.

ROTATE

Failure to rotate follows two paths. In the first, the cylinder binds and won't rotate. In the second, although the cylinder seems to be free from binding, it does not advance when you pull the trigger or cock the hammer.

A revolver that binds and won't rotate is useful only as an oddly shaped paperweight. To return the handgun to its intended function, check the same things that can keep it from closing. Examine the extractor star for powder residue. Look for a buildup of powder in the crane cutout, and on the back of the barrel and the front of the cylinder. Also inspect the rounds to see if any have high primers. A high primer will stop a cylinder cold.

Look under the cylinder, and see if the cylinder stop (or locking bolt) is disengaging properly. If the cylinder doesn't unlock, it can't turn. An incorrect trigger job can prevent the stop from unlocking. If the trigger or cylinder stop has been altered, you may have to buy new parts to get the revolver running again.

Check crane alignment. A bent crane binds the cylinder unevenly. The cylinder may move at first, stopping only when it rotates against the bent section of the crane.

Open the cylinder. Look at the tip of the centerpin that sticks out of the extractor star. Does it look centered? Push it into the extractor with a drift punch. Does it bind? Now release it. Does it return from the extractor sluggishly? The same wrist-closing and opening that can bend the crane can bend the centerpin. If yours is bent, you must replace it. A new one is inexpensive and easily fitted.

While you have the cylinder open examine the back of the frame opening. The firing pin passes through a hole in the frame and the recoil shield. The edge of this firing pin hole can become burred from dry firing. If it has, the rims of the cartridges may be catching on this burr, slowing or stopping rotation. Simply stoning the burr down will solve the problem, and it'll be another 10,000 hammer falls before one crops up again. Which is to say, keep up the dry fire practice. It's good for you.

If the cylinder rotates freely except for one chamber, remove the ammo. Recheck rotation. If removing the ammunition does not correct the problem inspect the cylinder from front to back, checking for each mechanical problem listed above. If all other causes come up negative, the extractor star ratchet may be damaged. Dropping a cylinder on the ratchet can burr or peen one of its studs. You will have to re-time that stud, a simple, but fussy job requiring a modified file. More on this in Chapter 20.

In the second type of rotation failure the hammer and trigger may seem to be working, but although the cylinder does not seem to bind, it simply will not turn. Or, it turns but not far enough to lock up. The hand may not be doing its job. To check a Smith & Wesson, point the (empty) revolver straight down. Try again. If the cylinder now rotates, strip the revolver and make sure you have the hand spring, found in the trigger, properly hooked over the pivot pin of the hand. Without the spring the hand flops around in its slot and will not push the cylinder. Gravity holds it in place when you point down, but pulls it away when you point up. If the spring is broken a replacement will solve the problem.

Check the sideplate to see that it is tight. Especially on the Colt DA revolvers, the sideplate holds the hand in place. If the sideplate is loose, the hand can drift away from the cylinder, and not fully rotate it.

On a used revolver, check the hand. A previous owner may have shortened it during a badly done trigger job. With the sideplate off watch the action as you cock the hammer and see if the hand stops short. Fitting a new hand will take an evening of work, but you may be able to get off easy. If the cylinder only fails to rotate and lockup on one chamber, you're in luck. You can peen the ratchet stud on which the hand fails to carry up, and get the cylinder to lock up.

If the cylinder fails to carry up on several chambers, you will have to fit an over-sized hand. This is also covered in Chapter 20.

One particularly disturbing reason for failure to rotate is a bullet stuck across the cylinder/barrel gap. A poorly reloaded round, usually one with no powder in its case, will still have enough power from its primer to launch the bullet from the case. If the revolver is clean, the primer can push the bullet an inch or two into the barrel, allowing the cylinder to rotate with the round stuck in the bore. Fire another bullet behind it and, at the very least, you'll bulge the barrel. In the event of that happening, a close inspection will reveal the bulge. Hold the revolver up with the barrel pointing towards the light, and look at the shadows running down the barrel. If your barrel looks like a snake with a big snack, it's got a bulge. Or look down the bore. A bulge will look like a dark ring. A bulged barrel rarely stays as accurate as it was before. A large bulge can be dangerous, bursting at some future, unknown moment when fired. Another cause of bullet jump (besides insufficient neck tension) is an ultra-light revolver. If you have one of the new Smith & Wesson Scandium, or Airlite revolvers, the weight (or rather, lack of weight) is great for carry. You probably found out right away in your first practice session that the recoil can be sharp; even vicious. The recoil can be so snappy that the inertia of the bullet is great enough to cause bullet pull. It can cause bullet pull in ammunition that would be fine in a regular-weight revolver. The only cure is proper ammo, factory or reloaded.

To remove the bullet (or bullets), use your range rod to find the location of the bullet's nose. Exercise some caution here, as there may still be loaded rounds in the other chambers. If the measuring shows you that there is only one bullet, you can heave a sigh of relief. Use the range rod and a hammer to pound the bullet back into the cylinder. Open the cylinder and remove the cartridges. Complain vociferously to your reloader.

If there is more than a single bullet in your barrel, you will probably have to replace the barrel. Try pounding the bullets back with the range rod, until you come to the joint of the nose of one bullet and the base of another. See if you can open the cylinder. If you cannot, you must cut through the bullet at the cylinder gap. Removing the barrel to open the cylinder will not work very well. Frame wrenches for unscrewing barrels are used on a revolver that already has the cylinder removed. You can't remove it until you can open it.

Resign yourself to cutting through the bullet. Take a spare blade for an X-Acto knife, and with the carbide cutter in your hand-held grinder, serrate the blade. With the serrated blade you can now saw through a lead bullet. While it is tedious, you will eventually open the cylinder, and the blade will not damage the cylinder as a hacksaw blade would. Once open, scrub the bore and inspect it closely. If the extra bullets did not bulge the barrel, consider yourself lucky. If they did, you'll need a new barrel, and a new source of ammunition in the future.

COCKING

A cocked hammer should stay cocked. If it doesn't, you may have a serious problem.

This ring is right near the muzzle, and the barrel might be salvaged if it is shortened.

First check the hammer spur and the grips. A dropped revolver will sometimes fall on the hammer, bending the spur. A bent spur can bind against the frame or grips. Exercise care when straightening a bent spur. Since hammers are usually very hard, if you try to bend the spur back cold it can easily crack and break off. Don't take this risk. Instead, use heat. Clamp the hammer in an unpadded vise, with only the spur sticking out. Use the mass of the vise as a heat sink, to protect the hardness of the rest of the hammer. Heat the spur to cherry red, and with a pair of pliers bend back to shape. Let it cool, and reassemble. Oversized grips can interfere with the path of the hammer spur. While it is rarely encountered, it can happen. If that is your problem, dress back the grips to clear the hammer spur.

Some shooters cut the spur off. If you are carrying your revolver for defense, you may want to consider this as a way to prevent the hammer spur from catching on clothing when you draw.

If your problem is not in the hammer spur or grips, you'll have to look inside for its source. Strip the revolver and examine the hammer notch. The surface of the hammer notch should be square, even and unaltered. If it isn't, you could have a big problem. Some previous owner may have tried to lighten the trigger pull by stoning the hammer notch. A hammer notch that's been stoned must be replaced. The hammer is surface-hardened, and stoning generally removes the hard layer of steel. If the first stoning hasn't, your corrective stoning certainly will. It should be obvious from this description that you must never stone a hammer. If you need a lighter single-action trigger pull (highly unlikely) the place to work is the trigger nose, or single-action sear (see Chapter 20).

If the revolver was dropped when it was cocked, the hammer notch may be chipped or broken. Again, the only solution to a damaged or altered hammer notch is a new hammer. A new hammer will cost 20 percent of the handgun's new cost, the trigger nearly that. If you have to replace both parts, your outlay will be over a third of the cost of a new revolver. The labor will run an additional 20 percent, bringing the expense to over half the cost of a new handgun.

Can you re-fit the parts yourself? On some Smith & Wesson revolvers, yes, with careful and detailed work. If your S&W is a Magnum, .357, .41, or .44, S&W will not sell you parts for it, for fear someone will try to turn something into a .44 Magnum that shouldn't be. They will gladly sell non-magnum parts. Try to get a hammer and trigger from them. If they turn you down, go elsewhere. If you have a Colt "V" mainspring revolver, send it back to the factory or off to Bill Laughridge at Cylinder & Slide. Trying to re-fit the hammer and trigger on one of these could drive the Pope to drink. The Colt coil spring revolvers are a piece of cake.

If the sear and hammer notch look fine, check elsewhere.

Modern revolvers have internal safeties intended to keep the action from working if the cylinder isn't fully closed and latched. To see if your latch is the problem, open the cylinder. Pull the cylinder release all the way back, forward, or out, whichever way it naturally moves when closing. Try to cock the hammer. Hold the latch closed. Does the hammer cock now? If it does, the latch is gunked up with old oil or powder residue. Clean it.

Smith and Wesson revolvers use a flat spring as the mainspring. If you have backed out the mainspring strain screw to make the trigger pull lighter, you could have caused your problem. When you cock the hammer you should be bending the spring. With the relaxed spring, at a certain point the angle of the spring lines up with the axis of the hammer. You end up compressing the spring. Called "knuckling," the problem is easy to fix. Just turn the strain screw in a half-turn. The problem goes away. If you still want a very light trigger pull, use another spring. This one won't cooperate.

FIRE

Failure to fire can be very embarrassing. Far worse, it can be very dangerous.

Open the cylinder or the loading gate, and check to see if the revolver is loaded. If it is, unload it and look at the primers of each round. Look for any sign of a firing pin strike. A full indent from the firing pin, but no "bang!" is an ammunition problem. A slight firing pin hit usually means weak springs. If there is no sign at all of a strike the firing pin had better be broken or you'll have one puzzling problem to solve.

Professional gunsmiths joke about the number of firearms, handguns included, they see with the same problem. As described by the customer, the story goes something like this. "It wouldn't fire. Must be a broken firing pin." Sometimes the tale is even accompanied by a lament about the size of the buck that was standing in the open. The firing pin is very rarely the cause of failure to fire. Even so, the first thing the pro checks, and the first thing you should check, is the firing pin. Is it broken? A broken firing pin is pretty obvious: there is part of it missing. Is it bent? A bent firing pin is more subtle, but with close inspection you can tell. A bent firing pin can bind in the clearance hole through the frame. Bent or broken, you have to replace the pin. You can try to straighten a bent one, but if it survives the attempt, it will break soon after. Save yourself the effort and just replace it.

If it is a frame-mounted firing pin, is it binding in its seat? Petrified oil or grease, or Loctite that has flowed into the firing pin hole from some other screw, can bind a frame-mounted firing pin. You'll have to remove the firing pin and its spring from the frame, clean them off and re-install them. Simply hosing oil into the hole will not correct the problem.

Sometimes the firing pin is just too short, the result of a "modification" to gain some unknown improvement. If you just got a great deal on a used revolver that doesn't fire, check firing pin protrusion. First measure the gap between the recoil shield and the cylinder with feeler gauges. Then dry-fire the revolver and hold the trigger back, to keep the firing pin forward. Use your feeler gauges again to measure the gap between the tip of the firing pin and the cylinder. Deduct the second measure from the first, and you have firing pin protrusion. The firing pin protrusion should be more than .040 inch and less than .050 inch. If someone has shortened the firing pin so the protrusion is less than .040, you will have to replace the firing pin.

Some Smith & Wesson revolvers will not let you measure protrusion so easily. Older Magnum revolvers were made with recessed chambers. Each chamber was reamed with a seat for the rim of the cartridge, leaving the firing pin protruding past the back of the cylinder. To check these, you must use Brownells protrusion gauge. Remove the cylinder. Measure the gauge in its closed position, with the locking screw unlocked. Then, holding the cylinder latch in the closed position, cock and dry-fire the revolver. Hold the trigger back. Position the gauge over the firing pin, which will push the center out. Lock the gauge with the locking nut. The extra length of the gauge over the previous measurement is the protrusion.

More likely than a shortened, broken, or bent firing pin is that someone has decreased the strength of the mainspring. If you've noticed light and insufficient firing pin strikes on the primers, check the mainspring. Modified springs as the problem in a misfiring revolver is so high a probability that after the firing pin, it is the second thing a professional pistolsmith checks.

When modifying a handgun some shooters just jump in, lightening springs until the action "feels good." What feels good, though, may not work so "good." The strain screw on Smith & Wesson revolvers is a favorite target of unenlightened experimenters. With a turn or two of the screw they can lighten their trigger pull remarkably. But now the screw is not secured. It is loose in the threads and vibration will further unscrew it. The light trigger pull gets steadily, but only very slowly, lighter until the revolver starts misfiring. Tighten the screw. In Chapter 20 you will learn how to smooth and lighten the trigger pull without causing misfires.

Some shooters clip a few coils off the mainspring on revolvers with coil mainsprings. Sure enough, the trigger pull gets lighter, and just as sure, the revolver starts misfiring. Replace the cut spring with a new one.

One of the oldest tricks to lightening the trigger pull of the Colt "V" mainspring revolver is to place a small-diameter rod in the "V" and cock the revolver. Cocking bends the mainspring over the rod and the resulting kink can lessen the force of the spring. If you bend in the wrong spot, however, either you don't lessen the trigger pull, or you make the spring too light, and have misfires.

A seriously worn revolver can have so much endshake that the firing pin can't reach the primer and strike it hard enough to fire the cartridge. See the buyer's checklist in Chapter 4 for the endshake test. Once you remove this much endshake you'll probably have to set back the barrel as well.

If, when you inspect the rounds for firing pin strikes, you find ones that are heavy enough, but in the wrong spots (say, on the rims of the cartridges), you have a cylinder out of time. It is skipping over the locking bolt, or falling off the hand and failing to carry up. In either of these cases the cylinder will not present the primer correctly for the firing pin. If the cylinder doesn't carry up you will have to adjust the hand. If the cylinder skips you must adjust the locking bolt. See Chapter 20.

RETURN THE TRIGGER

The trigger return spring and rebound block push the trigger back to its resting position. Unlike pistols, revolvers have very clean, crisp, light, single-action trigger pulls, right from the factory. I have rarely seen a revolver that needed improvement in the single-action pull. While you should leave this spring alone, because the trigger return spring (like the mainspring) affects the weight of the single-action trigger pull, it is the subject of a lot of poorly considered experimentation.

A shortened trigger return spring can cause such sluggish trigger return that in double-action shooting your trigger finger may move forward and back so fast the trigger will not be able to reset. The action will lock up tight. While light trigger return springs are common in PPC shooting, they are not useful for IPSC, ICORE or bowling pin shooters. With speed of fire an issue, the failure of the sluggish weak spring to return quickly enough can be enough of a handicap that the light trigger pull isn't worth the cost.

Even a standard-strength factory spring can be overworked if the mechanism is too dirty. Heavy grease or petrified oil, mixed with powder residue, dust, dirt and lint can bind the spring and rebound block. Cold weather can render a dirty revolver completely useless. Clean the gunk out. Use light oil, preferably a synthetic, and you will not have this problem.

The last source of trigger return failure is heavy-handed reassembly. The stud behind the return block is long enough to fit into a recess drilled into the sideplate. Forcing the sideplate during reassembly will bend the stud. The bent stud will bind the block and freeze it in place. This will require a return to the factory.

OPEN

Look at the front of the ejector rod to see if it has unscrewed. If it has, screw it back in. Once you get the revolver open and unloaded, lock the ejector rod down properly.

The cylinder latch may be binding. On the S&W there is a slot cut into the frame. The cylinder latch moves a bar that rests in this slot. The gap between the bar and the slot provides a large area in which oil can petrify, preventing the latch from moving the bar. Disassemble and clean the bar. Use a synthetic lubricant.

A bent centerpin that makes closing the cylinder difficult will also, when you are done shooting, make opening it difficult. A centerpin bent from swinging the cylinder open and closed will be difficult to push open and may stay wedged in the extractor star. You will have to replace the centerpin.

If the cylinder latch moves smoothly, but the cylinder won't swing out of the frame, check that pesky crane screw again. On the S&W revolvers, the crane screw is the front one on the sideplate. You may have the screws in the wrong order.

A cylinder that fails to open because of a bullet in the gap has already been covered.

EJECT

An empty has failed to eject, and not for the first time. Are your reloads too hot? Most failures to eject stem from a load that is too ambitious. A sufficiently heavy reload cannot only make ejecting these empties difficult, it can also make future ejection difficult.

Colt revolvers have their locking slots cut into the side of the cylinder, but slightly offset from the chamber. Revolvers with an odd number of chambers have the slots in between the chambers. On many revolvers the

locking slot is directly in line with the chamber. With these revolvers there is not much steel left between the slot and the chamber. A very heavy load can bulge the steel from the chamber into this slot. Even a small bulge can cause difficult ejection.

The bulge may be so slight only an experienced eye can see it. Whether obvious or not the cure is the same. You must replace the cylinder. A few hundred feet per second increase in the velocity of your reloads will cost you a third the cost of your revolver. Do not exceed the maximum limits of reloading guides! The upper limit on velocity is there for a reason.

Have you been shooting shorter cases in your revolver, say .38 Specials in a .357 Magnum revolver? As discussed in Chapter 5, in the section on specialized cleaning tools, the shorter cases create a buildup of powder residue and lead particles between the mouth of the case and the front of the chamber. When you switch back to longer cases, your empties may wedge against this buildup, defying ejection. The solution to this problem lies in better cleaning. Reread the pertinent information in Chapter 5.

When the cylinder is in the open position, the ejector rod sticks out with no support, and may become bent if you are not careful. A bent rod may only allow the empties to be pushed partway out of the cylinder before it binds and stops. To see if your ejector rod is bent, brace

Cracked or broken cases will prevent your handgun from working properly.

It doesn't take long for a professional pistolsmith to collect a box of damaged, bulged or broken barrels and cylinders. If you want more power than your caliber can deliver, buy a bigger one. If you hot-rod yours you may break something.

your hand and give the cylinder a spin. A damaged rod will be obvious. In an emergency, pluck the empties out of the cylinder, put new ones in and push the rounds and ejector star back into the cylinder.

In a non-emergency, unload the revolver and turn it over to a professional pistolsmith. To straighten the rod properly requires an expensive, specially made fixture. You can spend half the cost of your revolver for one, and never use it again. Even a professional pistolsmith may only pull it out of the cabinet a couple of times a year.

One rare reason for failure to eject is the wrong ammunition — rare because there are just a few combinations of calibers that you can mix up and escape with only a funny story to tell. At a Smith & Wesson Dealers' Seminar I attended some years ago the factory was showing off their then-new Mountain Revolver, a 4-inch barreled stainless steel .44 Magnum, with a round butt, skinny barrel and beveled cylinder. It was designed to be the lightest .44 Magnum revolver that could survive a steady diet of factory ammunition. (Little did we know that, years later, it would be a heavyweight compared to the scandium .44 Magnum!) After breakfast, the factory representatives let the dealers loose on the range, with free ammunition and plenty of new Smith & Wesson handguns to shoot.

After shooting the new Mountain Revolver and missing the target spectacularly, one dealer could not get the empties to eject. Much struggling ensued. Finally one of the factory assemblers who had come along on the trip banged the ejector rod against a tabletop to get the empties out. That's when we found out the dealer had loaded .41 Magnum ammunition into the .44 Magnum revolver. The two calibers were close enough in size that the shooter hadn't noticed he was loading from the wrong box. The cases had bulged and split horribly, but the revolver was fine. As you can imagine, accuracy with that combination was terrible. However, the shooter was such a bad shot no one thought anything of his six misses when he was shooting.

The only other calibers this easily confused are the .44 Magnum and the .45 Colt. The results of this particular mismatch are much more serious. Put .44 Magnum ammunition in a .45 Colt SAA revolver (or one of its clones), and you will not just split the cases, you will also damage your revolver.

If you own a pair of revolvers in these two caliber combinations (.41/.44 Magnum or .44 Magnum/.45 Colt), be especially careful not to mix your ammunition. Some shooters go so far as to mark all the brass in one caliber with a felt-tip pen so as to not get them mixed up.

SPECIAL CONSIDERATIONS OF THE SINGLE-ACTION

The single-action revolver is prone to many of the problems of the double-action revolver, and for many of the same reasons. A cartridge without powder in it will tie up the cylinder of a single-action, or bulge the barrel, just the same as in a double-action.

Unique to the single-action are centerpin problems. Since it has no crane, the single-action needs only a simple axle, or centerpin, for its cylinder. The very first Colt single-action cartridge revolver used a screw to keep the centerpin in the frame. Shooters who lost the screw quickly found their revolvers unusable. The centerpin would jump forward, and the cylinder would not rotate until you lined the up centerpin with its seat in the rear of the frame and pressed it back into place.

Probably because they were receiving a lot of complaints from shooters with lost screws, Colt changed to a spring-loaded cross-bolt. Pushing the cross-bolt to one side released the centerpin. The cross-bolt stayed in the frame. The method worked fine even with the stout recoil of a full-power .45 Colt cartridge, but is not so effective when subjected to the recoil of a .44 Magnum. Not a problem for Colt as they never offered the SAA in a .44 Magnum.

Ruger does. Their .44 Magnum single-action revolvers, the Blackhawk and Super Blackhawk, use the spring-loaded cross-bolt to keep the centerpin in place. Under the repeated recoil of Magnum loads, the cross-bolt can become battered and start failing to do its job. If yours is looking beat up, you will have to replace the cross-bolt assembly.

Under the stoutest of .44 Magnum loads advocated by J.D. Jones, the centerpin can batter right past the cross-bolt, tying up the action. These loads, using 290- to 315-grain bullets at up to 1,200 fps, are so heavy in recoil they aren't even any fun to shoot. Call me wimpy, but if I need that much performance I'll go get something with a shoulder stock on it. If you insist on using such loads, the only thing you can do is lay in a supply of cross-bolt assemblies and a couple of extra centerpins. Replace the cross-bolts as they become battered, and replace the centerpin when the recoil has battered its locking shoulder beyond repair.

On the original single-action design, both the two-leaf spring, which actuates the cylinder-locking bolt and the trigger, and the hand spring are fragile. If you plan to do any competitive shooting, or want to get lots of practice with your single-action, buy several replacements for each. Since neither requires fitting, replacing them is easy.

THE GAP WIDENS

In the early days of practical shooting competition, revolvers often held their own. However, every wave of advances in technology, ammunition, practice and technique has opened the gap. Now, it is a rare revolver shooter who can hold his own against the average pistol shooter. What with high-capacity magazines, compensators, optical sights and high-pressure medium-bore cartridges, the wheelgunner is hard-pressed to keep up. Even with an optic-sighted, comped revolver in .38 Super, the revolver shooter is still using an eight-shooter against a pistol shooter who has 28-round magazines at his disposal. As a result, revolvers are now in their own category at matches. What hasn't changed is the reliability. It isn't unusual for a squad of revolver shooters to go through a big match without a single malfunction. No failures to fire, no failures to eject, no need to clear feedway jams. In some ways, life with a revolver is good. And if you shoot a revolver that uses full-moon clips, you also never lose any brass.

MALFUNCTIONS OF PISTOLS

Police departments and firearms instructors who teach defensive shooting have plans for clearing a malfunction, or "reducing a stoppage." There are very simple two-step plans, and there are elaborate plans requiring flowcharts and days of classroom instruction.

In this book we aren't concerned with surviving a gunfight, but with the root causes of malfunctions and how to correct them once you are home from the range. Of course the best way to correct a malfunction is to prevent it from ever happening. You should not use a pistol for a match, hunting or defense until you have test-fired it and addressed any problems that may have occured. Once you have shot it at the range for hundreds of rounds without a single burp, you can depend on that pistol in a match, hunting or in daily carry. Change your ammunition brand or your magazines, though, and you have to re-test.

There are problems that cannot be solved, only puzzled over. And there are problems that cannot be fixed,

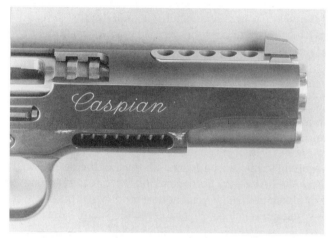

A cutaway pistol, such as this Caspian, is useful to show how a pistol works.

not on the range, not in the shop. My friend Jeff Chudwin presented one such insoluble problem to me. President

The two rounds on the right have bullets seated too deeply. The two on the left have bullets that are not deep enough. None will feed worth a hoot. If your reloads look like this, do not blame your pistol for not working reliably.

of the Illinois Tactical Officers Association, and a Chief of Polcie of a small city outside of Chicago, he does a large amount of firearms instruction for police officers. And he has fired even more rounds in training and competition than I have. He showed me photos of a pistol where the top round had flipped end-for-end on feeding, and went base-first into the chamber. What caused it? There is no way of telling. Perhaps the Officer involved simply loaded it backwards? Perhaps, but unlikely. If such a malfunction happens to you in a gunfight, there is no correcting it short of locking the slide back and finding a stick with which to poke out the offending cartridge. An unfixable problem happened to Jeff himself. His Glock burst while firing remanufactured ammunition. It doesn't matter how much training you have had at malfunction clearance, you aren't going to solve this one on your own. Except, of course, never using ammo that will detonate. However, the only way to test ammo to see if it will bust a gun in this way is to fire the ammo.

Solving problems with the pistol is much the same as with the revolver. You must study the malfunction, both in terms of what the pistol is doing, and what the pistol is failing to do. In what particular part of the operational cycle is the malfunction occurring? If, for example, the pistol fails to feed, you must determine what in the feeding cycle failed. What stopped the round from going

This case came out of an H-K MP-5 sub-machine gun. The flutes that aid extraction also crinkle the cases. This case can be reloaded once again, and then it will expire.

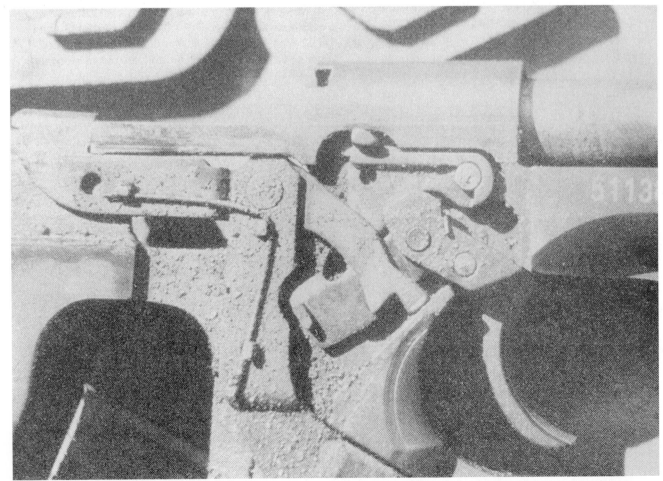

This H-K P-7 has digested more than 4,000 rounds at this point without a failure. With proper cleaning it may never fail. (photo courtesy Massad Ayoob.)

forward? Does the fault lie with the pistol, the ammunition, or the magazine?

Or perhaps your pistol fails to eject reliably. Before you go bending the extractor to increase extractor tension, or installing a longer ejector, study the problem. Does the slide show brass marks from the empty cases? Where are the cases hitting? Could that be preventing ejection?

You could jump in for a quick fix only to discover later the root cause of the problem is something entirely different, and thus, something you still have to fix.

As with the revolver, the most frequent reason for a malfunction in a pistol is dirt. While some pistols can go for an amazing number of rounds without being cleaned and still perform properly, there are limits to everything. The limit for your handgun may be a few hundred rounds, or a few thousand.

Curious about the functionality of one of his HK P-7 pistols, Mas Ayoob of the Lethal Force Institute tested it in his firearms training school by using it as a loaner. When a student showed up for class without a pistol, or with an unsuitable handgun, out would go the HK P-7 loaner. If a student's pistol broke beyond repair the HK P-7 would see service. When loaning the pistol, Mas always provided the same set of instructions to each student: "Don't clean it, and stop immediately if it malfunctions." He ended the test after 4,000 rounds. The pistol still worked perfectly. There had not been a single malfunction. Internally, it was so caked with powder residue that it was appalling to look at. But it worked.

I do not recommend this course of action, if only because that sort of treatment seriously wears the bore of a pistol and greatly shortens its accurate service life. But Mas' test does give you an indication of the level of reliability a properly tuned pistol can deliver. With regular cleaning, that HK P-7 might never malfunction, although a part could break. Even the best-quality parts break from time to time. If you own a pistol that performs very reliably, and after tens of thousands of rounds that one part in 10,000 breaks, box the part up, send it back and see if you can get a free replacement. If not, select the best part for your pistol, buy it and install it, even if it is from the same manufacturer.

It's a different story when you're breaking the same part regularly. Chances are, something you are doing is placing the part under much greater stress than it was designed to withstand. Study what you are doing to that poor part, and relieve its stress.

In addition to the grubby gun syndrome, pistols also malfunction because of poor-quality ammunition. Low-quality reloads, produced with tired brass, improperly sized or seated bullets, or improper bullets, cause a large number of headaches at the range. In a revolver, where you place the cartridges in each chamber by hand, when one doesn't fit you can just lift it out. In a pistol the slide has to chamber a round from the magazine. If the round doesn't want to go in, you may have

a struggle on your hands getting it out. It can be tightly wedged in place.

BE CAREFUL!

Trying to remove a live cartridge, one that didn't chamber and doesn't want to come out, is a very hazardous thing. At the range, or at home in your workshop, be very safety-conscious.

Remove the magazine. You are struggling with only the one cartridge. There is no reason to keep a ready supply of others in the pistol. If you do not remove the magazine, as soon as you clear the offending cartridge another round will be chambered. In the relief that follows clearing a stuck cartridge you may forget you still hold a loaded pistol. Not good.

Keep the gun pointed in a safe direction. At the range, you must keep the muzzle pointed downrange. In your home workshop, keep the muzzle pointed at something solid and hopefully inexpensive. Don't just point at the wall – think about what is on the other side of that wall. If, during your struggles, you end up fully chambering this round and firing the pistol, you want the bullet going in as safe a direction as possible.

To remove the round, find a wooden post or table. Place the front of the slide, next to the muzzle, against the edge of the post. Hold the slide to the post with your weak hand. Pull your shooting hand back a foot from the butt of the pistol and whack it, still holding with your weak hand. Grab the butt of the pistol as your hand strikes home. The impact should jar the cartridge loose.

This .45 barrel did not survive the combination of faults. Hot loads, a light recoil spring, incorrect fitting and lots of shooting combined to break this lower lug right off.

If not, strike again a bit harder. When you have freed the round, check the extractor. The banging can damage it.

Don't hold the pistol and bang the end of the slide against the post or table. Doing this bangs the muzzle against the wood, which doesn't help. It is the slide that must be freed. You may end up striking at an off-angle, and hard enough, that the pistol can turn in your hand, pointing someplace unsafe.

Save the round, for study to prevent this problem occurring in the future.

In a more stressful situation, such as hunting or competition, you must be ready to use your pistol as soon as you clear the jam. Leave the magazine in. Remove the round by striking your hand against the butt of the pistol, as above. When you are trying to clear the cartridge, do not point the muzzle at yourself. Once cleared, remember that your pistol is loaded, and you are now ready to continue the match or the pursuit of your quarry. Don't bother with the round you've removed. If circumstances permit, look for it later.

The next likely reason for a malfunction, and one unique to pistols, is use of a poor quality magazine. Saving a few dollars on magazines is a perfect example of being "penny wise and pound foolish." The worst deals are what I call "Two for $10 gun-show specials." I will occasionally see a customer in my shop who wants his 1911 pistol to feed reliably, but who insists on using tired, beaten, worn and heavily-used magazines he bought at a local gun show because they were "a bargain."

Getting such pistols to feed reliably with good-quality magazines is usually just a few minutes' work. Convinc-

The right case is severely swollen at the base. The center case is perfect. The left-hand case was swollen and the sizing die did not remove all of the swelling. The base still has a ring around it, just above the extractor groove. This ring will prevent the case from chambering, and wedge the pistol tight.

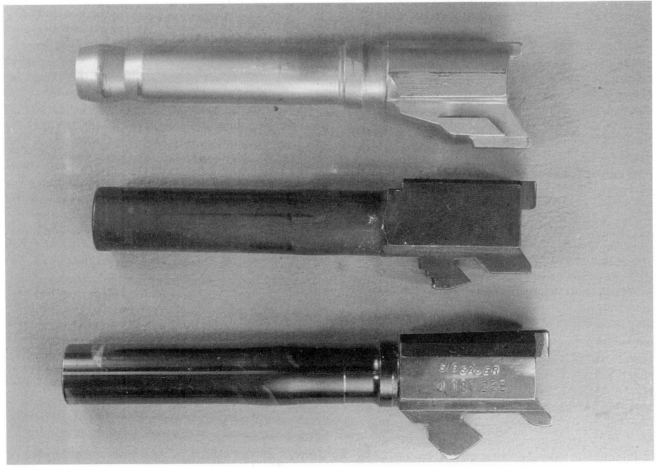

These three barrels were bulged by squib loads being followed with regular ammunition. Cheap reloads strike again.

ing the customer to pay five or six times as much for a good magazine as he paid for his "bargain" takes much longer. Without the proper magazines, the work I did (and you will do) is wasted.

Back when I started to shoot competitively, one of the fellows in our club was inordinately fond of his pistol. He was especially proud of the fact that as he shot most of his brass "went into a coffee can." His pistol did, indeed, eject very consistently. If you placed a coffee can on the ground an amazingly high percentage of the brass would be in the can when you were done shooting. Neat, right?

Except for two problems. The handgun wasn't particularly accurate, and the owner couldn't shoot it very well.

Too much attention paid to unnecessary details can blind you to more important things. A thought to live by.

When working on your pistol, you must separate the unimportant "fussy stuff" from actual problems. Ejection on a 1911 provides an excellent example. One of mine brasses the ejection port area. Although I have to scrub the marks off the slide with steel wool each time I clean the pistol, I haven't bothered to track down the reason. And why should I? The brass never fails to eject. It's never dented. Who cares if it's leaving a mark? As far as I'm concerned there isn't a problem

I shoot another .45 with a very wide ejection pattern. The brass can be found forward and back, near and far. I haven't worried about this one either. Unless the brass is coming back in my face the ejection pattern is of no concern to me.

On the other hand, if you have a pistol whose ejection pattern suddenly changes, and you haven't changed your ammunition, you may have a problem. If your pistol used to throw the brass three shooters to the right, and now it falls at your feet, you should check into things. And empties in your face? That deserves an immediate inspection. I've fired a Desert Eagle in .44 Magnum that ejected the empties into my face, hard. It was no fun.

You may find that the simple act of using your pistol creates a dilemma for you. The wear to the finish from shooting, cleaning, drawing and reholstering; the scratches to the frame from inserting magazines; the occasional rub mark from shooting next to a barricade all leave their reminders. If the wear to your pistol troubles you, investigate harder finishes. Keep in mind, though, that those annoyingly bright corners do not affect your pistol's function. Instead of investing heavily in cosmetics, you may want to save your money for more practice ammo or for true malfunctions that require fixing. The choice is yours.

While I will be going over the causes of malfunctions here, the detailed solutions will be in the chapters devoted to your particular pistol. For the 1911, see Chapter 19. For the Glock, see Chapter 16, and the Beretta see Chapter 17. Magazine solutions will be in Chapter 12. Many of the problems occur in all pistols. Even if you are working on a different pistol, reading about the others can provide helpful information.

Seen at an angle, the bulge in this barrel is obvious.

Ammunition problems are only generally covered. The proper reloading of ammunition is covered in other fine books available from Krause Publications, and you should obtain and study these if you have persistent ammunition problems.

FEED

In order to shoot, your pistol must get a round into the chamber. If it doesn't, and you've made sure there's a loaded magazine in there, start with the feed stroke. Like a well-crafted story, the feed stroke has three areas to check: the beginning, the middle and the end. Not highly technical, I'll admit, but there it is.

In the beginning the breechface of the slide hits the rim of the cartridge and pushes it forward releasing it from under the lips of the magazine. (See Chapter 4 for the detailed explanation of the functions of a revolver and a pistol.) Most malfunctions at the start of the feed stroke are magazine-related. If the feed lips have been abused or incorrectly modified, or if the magazine is of such poor quality that the lips won't hold their shape, the cartridge will not feed reliably. Magazine tubes that are poorly dimensioned can shift in the magazine well and affect feeding. If the mag catch slot is cut in the wrong location the magazine may sit too high or low and not feed properly.

When a problem occurs at the beginning of the feed stroke, you'll usually find a cartridge nose down in the magazine, wedged against the feed ramp. The magazine with abused feed lips may sometimes give up the ghost by "porpoising" the round, trying to throw it out the top before it can make the trip into the chamber.

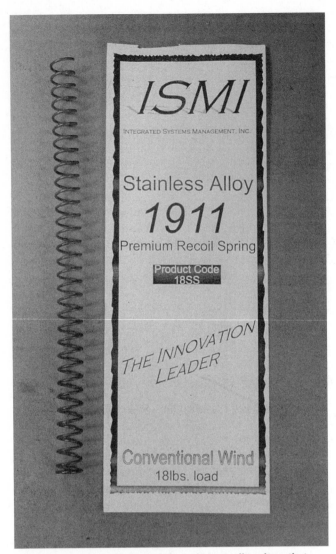

Integrated Systems Management makes recoil springs that do not seem to shorten with use. Preliminary testing has convinced me to switch.

Obtain ammo gauges and check your reloaded ammo. The rounds must drop flush, and fall out, or they don't pass.

To see if you have a faulty magazine, switch to a new one of known quality. In the 1911 I've had great success with Wilson, McCormick, Ed Brown, and Metalform. To test your Smith and Wesson nothing beats a new Smith magazine. For many other pistols I have had excellent results with Mec-Gar magazines. With factory ammunition in one of these magazines, you can be certain any feeding problems are not related to the magazine or ammo.

The middle of the feed stroke, like the middle of a story, contains all the heavy action. As detailed in Chapter 4, the front of the round must feed up the ramp, hit the chamber top and cam over the corner of the chamber and feed ramp junction. While this is going on the rim of the round has to slide out of the feed lips, and start going up the breechface. While the bullet nose is camming up and down, the rim has to slide into place under the extractor without binding. This is the trickiest part of the feed stroke to investigate, because so much is going on.

A feeding problem in the middle of the cycle will often send a new shooter to the feed ramp, which he will polish to a mirror finish in a hopeless attempt to solve the problem. The feed ramp must be at the right angle, and in the correct location on the frame for the pistol to operate properly. If these dimensions are correct the level of polish hardly matters. Don't be distracted by the ramp, or by "throating" the chamber. In my years of shooting and gunsmithing I have heard many explanations of just what "throating" is. None of them makes sense to me.

Malfunctions in the middle of the feed cycle are usually ammunition-related.

Carefully examine the slide for burrs or machine marks on the breechface or breechface sidewalls. Either one can bind the cartridge rim, preventing reliable feeding. The joint between the feed ramp and the chamber, called the cam-over edge, is sometimes a source of difficulties. If either part has been polished, the edge may now be too sharp, digging into the side of the cartridge. If the chamber has been reamed out, the edge will certainly be too sharp. The cam-over edge must be rounded, but only slightly. Too much, and you will leave the case unsupported. If you reload your ammunition to high pressures, an unsupported case can bulge. The bulge may not be entirely ironed out by your sizing die, and can cause chambering problems later. You will have solved one problem, but created another.

CHAMBER

At the end of the feed cycle the round fully chambers, and the barrel cams up into locking position. Years ago, the common advice for a round which failed to chamber was to smack the back of the slide. I have a very clear memory of the last time I did this. It was the summer of 1983, and I ended up bleeding all over my pistol and magazines. I had cut my hand on my Bo-Mar rear sight.

If your pistol fails to fully close, and you have some

time, stop and take a close look at the jam before clearing it. You will likely find that one of your rounds was not fully sized down. Failing that, the chamber is probably very dirty. Occasionally, you may run into a pistol with a rough, short or undersized chamber. When clearing the round, don't just smack the slide to close it. You'll only make the problem worse. Instead, work the slide and remove that stubborn round.

Get your finger off the trigger. Hold the pistol out from your body, with the muzzle pointed downrange. Grab the slide and try to open it. Do not try to gain more leverage by pulling the pistol close to your body and pushing your hands towards each other. You will end up pointing the muzzle to the side, the shooter next to you, or even worse, at yourself.

If pulling fails, find that post or bench top we discussed earlier and strike the back of the butt with your hand. Save the jammed round.

Once home, get a case gauge to check the round that failed to chamber. The gauge is a cylinder with a minimum-sized chamber reamed in the center. Drop the offending round into the gauge. If it drops in flush with the rear it passes muster. If the round sticks up out of the gauge it is too large somewhere. Spot check some of your other rounds. Do they also have sizing problems? Study your reloading and correct your ammunition. You may have to scrap your brass and start with a new batch. Try adjusting your sizing die, or, if it is already touching the top of your shell plate, consider buying a Case-Pro 100 from Image Industries, to iron your brass down. If you buy ammunition reloaded by someone else, think about finding a new supplier.

If your ammunition gauges correctly, even the round that wedged on feeding, you may have to open up your chamber. A rough, undersized, or out of round chamber can stop even a factory cartridge. You can purchase a

Use ammo gauges to check your reloads. These rounds have not been properly sized, and are too large for the gauges. They may or may not be too large for a pistol. Set such rounds aside and use them for practice.

chamber reamer in your caliber, cutting oil and a large tap wrench. We'll be covering this procedure fully in Chapters 16 and 19. Again, the cost of these tools may exceed the cost of having your gunsmith do the job, and you only have to do it once to each barrel. If you buy the tools you might never have to use them again.

LOCK

Once the round is fully seated, the barrel cams upwards to the locking lug or lugs in the slide and the slide moves to its fully forward position. Failure to lock is usually due to bad ammo or extreme dirtiness. To quickly establish which, determine how near the slide is to being fully closed. If the slide is held out of battery by just the smallest amount, and it can be pressed closed with a thumb, then the problem is dirt. If the slide is held out of battery an eighth of an inch and stubbornly refuses to move when you press on it with a thumb it is likely a bad round.

An extreme case of failure to lock comes from bad components. A soft barrel or slide, or a barrel that has been improperly fitted to a slide, can peen the locking lugs. The barrel in the photograph was both soft and poorly fitted. The front locking lug took the full brunt of the locking load, and was soon peened badly, interfering with the pistol's functioning. The owner "solved" his feeding problem with a heavier recoil spring. The increased forces that resulted peened the locking lug even more, building the ridge on top of the barrel to the point where it bound against the inside of the slide. The stress on the barrel cracked it on the bottom, and accuracy suddenly disappeared.

Miraculously, the slide was not damaged. Properly fitting a new barrel solved all the problems.

FIRE

The scariest sound in the world is not a roar or a scream, but a click when you were expecting a bang. Sometimes the reason for this failure can be quite subtle. The first thing to check is the power of the hammer fall. Have you clipped the hammer spring of your pistol shorter in order to make the trigger pull lighter?

Firing pins rarely break, but check anyway. While you have it out, scrub the pin, its spring and the tunnel in which it travels. Firing pin "failure" more likely stems from dirt than anything else. I have cleaned 1911s that were so dirty that pulling the firing pin from the slide created an audible sucking sound. In one pistol the firing pin and spring were so caked with petrified oil, powder residue, dust and lint, it was a miracle the pistol fired at all. On the Series 80 Colt pistols, check that the firing pin safety parts were correctly installed and that the trigger travel hasn't been restricted so much that the firing pin can't get past the safety plunger.

Installing a new target trigger with an over-travel screw in a Series 80 pistol can bind the firing pin safety. If you turn the over-travel screw in too far the hammer

The case on the left is really swollen. The one on the right couldn't hold out, and blew apart. The load was too hot and the barrel had been ramped too much. The ramping was to "improve feeding." The pistol feeds fine, but the cases don't survive to be reloadable.

can fall but the firing pin safety may not be pushed fully out of the path of the firing pin. When you take the firing pin and its part out, look at the firing pin safety. Does the corner of it have a large number of little "dings" in it? They are caused by the firing pin catching on, but pushing past, the safety. De-burr the safety, and turn your over-travel screw out at least half a turn.

UNLOCK

Rarely does a pistol fail to unlock, but when it does, the cause may be underpowered ammunition. Severely underpowered ammunition will leave a bullet in the bore. Firing another shot will then bulge the barrel. If

you fire a round and the pistol doesn't cycle, DON'T just work the slide and fire another shot. You MUST stop and investigate.

An underpowered round that leaves a bullet in the bore is easy to fix. Remove the magazine and lock the slide back. Slip your range rod in the muzzle and, with a tap, push the bullet back out of the bore. The rest of that batch of ammunition should be viewed with suspicion. Fire it slowly and make sure each round fired produces a hole in the target. Do not use the remaining ammunition for any high-speed practice. Once you finish the batch, study your reloading system to see how you could have produced a round without powder.

If you overlooked the squib round and fired another, you have a real mess on your hands. The barrel may be bulged enough to wedge the slide. Remove the magazine. You will have to bang the back of the slide hard enough to free the slide from the barrel, so you can disassemble the pistol. Use a plastic mallet or a piece of wood. Inspect the bushing to see if it was damaged. Striking the bulge may have bent or cracked the bushing. If so, replace it. Think about what barrel you will buy to replace the bulged one.

You must get a new barrel. Some shooters think they can file down the bulge and keep using the barrel. Doing this is asking for a very serious problem. The barrel will be thinner where it bulged and was filed. It may crack or burst if you continue to use it.

If the barrel is only slightly bulged, the slide will continue to work. You may not see the bulge for a few hundred rounds, or your next thorough cleaning. What you may have noticed is a drop in accuracy. On cleaning, you may find accelerated leading or copper fouling from the powder gases that have blown by the bullet as it passed the bulge. Consider yourself lucky to have gotten this far without further bad luck and look into buying a new barrel, soon.

Primers that look this bad are definite signs of either a load that is too hot, or excess headspace. Check your powder charge, and measure your chamber.

EXTRACT

Extracting is the act of yanking the empty out of the chamber. Do not confuse extraction with ejection, where the fired case is tossed overboard.

The failure to extract is usually an extractor problem, sometimes a chamber problem, and occasionally both. If the extractor fails to pull the fired empty out, the pistol usually tries to feed another round. Check the extractor tension first, and then look for broken extractor hooks. An extractor that is bound with petrified oil, grease and powder residue may be held away from the case, and unable to grab the rim. The only two pistols I have seen with chipped or broken extractors are Glocks and 1911s. The Glock extractors I have seen chipped are all in .40 caliber, and were all on high-volume police pistols. The 1911 extractors suffer the indignity of being experimented on to a much greater degree than any other pistol. Replacing an extractor on a Glock is simple. With a 1911 the operation is only a bit more complicated.

Even if you locate a problem in the extractor, checking the chamber to see if it is rough or undersized is a good idea. After all, the extractor lost tension for a reason, and hauling the fired empties out of the chamber against the additional friction of a rough, pitted, or undersized chamber can tax even a new extractor. A rough chamber can be polished, an undersized one can be reamed out. The only thing to do with a pitted chamber is replace the barrel.

EJECT

The empty is unceremoniously tossed away like last week's tabloid newspaper. Hot and dirty, it is left on the ground until you are finished. The causes of failure to eject are usually insufficient extractor tension, a loose ejector, and occasionally lightly loaded ammo.

Proper extractor tension ensures ejection. To check extractor tension you need a tension gauge in your caliber, and a trigger pull gauge. See the chapter for your particular handgun.

The original 1911 did not have a large ejection port, and the ejection was designed to be upwards, not sideways. A common modification on the 1911 (unnecessary on other pistols) is to lower the ejection port, which gives the empty more room to escape, and tosses it to the side. It is also very common on the 1911 to install an extended ejector to strike the empty sooner in the slide cycle when the slide has more velocity. The result is a more brisk and certain ejection. If you install an extended ejector on a 1911 without modifying the ejection port you may create a traffic jam. The extended ejector is designed to throw the empty to the side. The unmodified port is designed to let the empty escape upwards. Many times, the empty will not be able to climb out. Make sure your port is low enough, before you install that extended ejector. These are covered in Chapter 18.

Modern pistol designs have large, open ejection ports for the empties to escape. The Beretta is the winner here, having essentially no slide to interfere with ejection.

COCKING

Failure to cock rarely causes a pistol to "machinegun." Many people think that if the hammer follows the slide down, the pistol will fire. That is not the case. If the hammer simply goes forward with the slide, it won't have enough force to set off the primer. If the hammer stays cocked until the slide closes, and then falls, you'll have a double. In this instance, the delay in falling gives the hammer sufficient force to set off the primer.

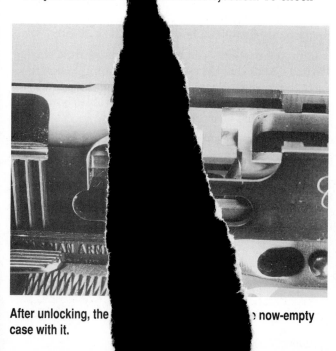

After unlocking, the [...] now-empty case with it.

Striking the ejector, the empty pivots out and is ejected.

Brassing on the slide is not usually an indication of a problem. However, if you've never seen brassing on your pistol before, and all of a sudden you start getting some, check extractor tension.

The hammer's failure to stay cocked can be caused by dirt, improper assembly, broken parts, or, in rare and mysterious cases, the shooter himself. I once spent an afternoon tracking down the problem of a pistol whose hammer followed the slide down, but only when fired left-handed. Cocked by hand, the hammer would not stay cocked. Cocking, then releasing the hammer, allowed you to fire the pistol, but it still wouldn't cock after it had fired this way. It turns out that the knuckle of the shooter's left forefinger was striking the bottom of the safety, and the bumped safety was binding against the bottom of the sear, keeping it from re-setting.

A broken or improperly modified hammer and sear can fail to cock. Look for hammer hooks that have been stoned too short. Or if the sear tip was stoned to the smallest possible point it may be fragile and prone to

breakage. If your pistol suffers fr[om] these "modifications," you will have to replace t[he] parts. If it is a used pistol you just bought, you may [hav]e recourse with the dealer from whom you bought [it. N]ot, replace both the hammer and sear. If the previo[us own]er worked on one, he probably worked on both.

Improper assembly can k[eep the ha]mmer from staying cocked. Check that the sea[r has s]pring tension to force it into engagement [with the ham]mer hooks. If it isn't, you have found you[r problem. A p]roblem you probably can't blame on a pre[vious owner.]

And finally, make sure [you watch] for every gunsmith's favorite proble[m. A hamme]r assembly so caked with gunk that t[he parts are s]luggish to keep the hammer cocked. T[his one is ea]sy to solve. Just keep the pistol clean[.]

CHAPTER

MAGAZINES FOR THE AUTOLOADER

The history of magazines, and their collection, is a subject that fascinates some shooters. And others view magazines as just tools, simply "bullet holders" needed for the task of shooting. Regardless of how attached you are or are not to yours, magazines are vital for proper performance, both for the performance of your pistols and your performance in the match. The great advance (and advantage) of pistols over revolvers was the magazine. As a more efficient storage and feeding device for ammo, it allows for greater capacity in a compact package. (Just try to imagine a 15-shot revolver in .38/.357!) However, as with all technological advances, in order to take advantage of the increase you must obtain, and maintain, the additional parts. The electrical starter for automobiles was a huge step forward when it was introduced (1912, the Cadillac brand) but in order to have that advantage, your mechanic has to keep the starter and its associated parts working. So it is with magazines.

In most cases, a pistol without a magazine is an awkward single-shot handgun. In the case of some Smith & Wesson pistols and others, with their magazine safety, they are not even a single-shot but only a clumsy club.

It follows, then, that you must have magazines for your pistol. And not just any magazines. You must have good-quality, dependable magazines, and enough of them for your needs. Once you have them you have to take care of them or your investment will be wasted through neglect or abuse. At some point you may want to modify them, to improve their function or reliability.

Manufacturers ship pistols with one or two magazines. When you buy a used pistol you may only get the magazine that is in it. While a pistol with a single magazine works, it can be a drag at the range. If you are going to shoot in competition, or want to have more fun at the range, you will have to buy more magazines. When buying, remember that pistols were once viewed as much less reliable than revolvers, mostly because of their magazines. The cheapest magazine is in many cases the worst bargain. The most expensive magazine is often the best bargain in the long run.

HOW MANY?

A question every buyer faces. How many magazines do you need? The snarky answer is "One more than the match or gunfight called for." A pistol used for defensive work should have at least three tested, marked and utterly reliable magazines. You'll want the one in the gun, and two spares on your belt. Someone who carries a hi-cap gun may feel one spare is enough, but I always felt that if you were in for a penny you were in for a pound. And the bulk of carrying two is not so much greater than carrying one that it should keep you from packing a pair of spares. Compared to what you're already packing that second spare is little enough weight and bulk. Single-stack pistol owners must have two spares. After

The old-style tapered feed lips on the left, and the newer, shouldered lips on the right. Generally, the newer style feed more dependably than the old. This is not an iron-clad rule, and you may get fine results from a magazine with the old style.

all, you've elected to carry something with less ammo to start with, you shouldn't skimp on spares.

Competition shooters need more. A single-stack 1911 shooter with only three magazines is on the line with 22 to 31 rounds, depending on the magazine type and capacity. (Even less for those electing to shoot a match with their carry gun, if it is an Officers' Model 1911 with six-shot magazines.) As it is not unusual for an IPSC field course to be more than 30 rounds, you'll need more. It is not unusual to see a competitor step to the line with six magazines on the belt. With a magazine in the pistol, that is up to 71 rounds. You may think that is too much, but I've seen shooters with that many magazines need all they had, what with misses, dropped magazines, and magazines lost when stripped off the belt by doorways.

GETTING GOOD ONES

It used to be that finding good magazines was a chore. Shooters did not lend magazines (still a good idea, by the way) because reliable ones were too rare a thing to part with even temporarily. As recently as the late 1970s I would sometimes buy twice as many magazines as I needed for a given handgun, so I could be sure of finding enough reliable ones in the batch I had just purchased. The rest? I sold them to other optimistic shooters after I had tested and kept the reliable ones.

The very first article I had published in a national firearms publication was on the selection, care and maintenance of magazines. It also has the distinction of being one of only two articles for which I have not been paid. The choices were a lot harder, and magazine selection rougher around the edges, in the "good old days" than they are today.

When police departments began switching to pistols from revolvers they absolutely would not tolerate unreliable pistols or poor-quality magazines. As a result, the quality of the magazines sold with police pistols is top-notch. Glock, Beretta, Ruger, SIG-Sauer and Smith & Wesson all make police pistols. If you want reliable functioning from these pistols, do what police forces do: buy the magazine the manufacturer makes. Aftermarket magazines have a poor, and in some instances deserved, reputation. Except for Mec-Gar, Millett, or Pachmayr, I would not depend on aftermarket magazines and prefer those made by or for the pistol manufacturer. The 1911 is the exception, where aftermarket magazines are actually better than some factory magazines. You are much better off feeding your Colt Series 70 or Kimber or Springfield pistol with Chip McCormick, Wilson, Ed Brown or other aftermarker mags than the ones that

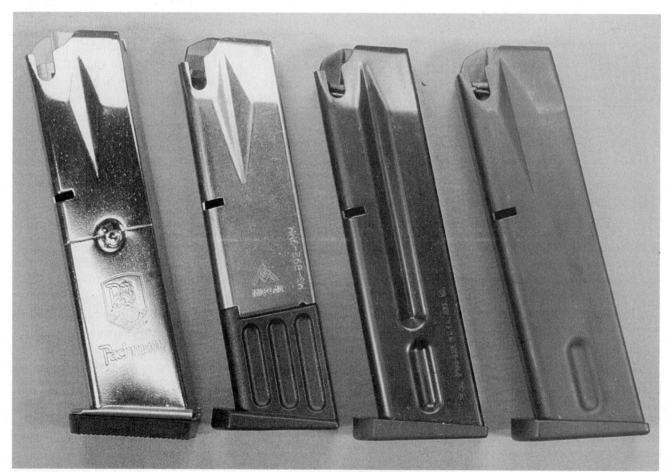

Not only must current-production magazines not hold more than 10 rounds, they have to be difficult to modify. The Pachmayr magazine on the left is split and dimpled. If you drill out the dimple the magazine will fall apart. The Mec-Gar has a short steel tube and a long plastic base. The Beretta has a large crease in each side. The magazine on the right is an older, fifteen shot one.

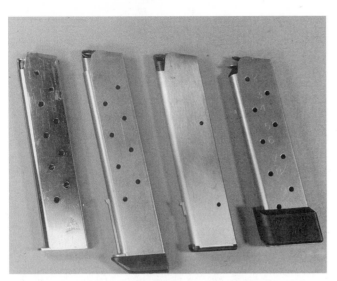

With the law limiting magazines to only ten rounds, it was a natural for 1911 magazines to expand up to the maximum. The Mec-Gar mag comes bare of base pad. The Ed Brown magazine has both a base pad and a front bar that limits upward insertion. The Wilson magazine has only two view holes, at five and 10 rounds. The McCormick magazine has a large rubber boot that acts as base pad and grip extension.

The patented follower on this Chip McCormick 1911 magazine increase the capacity to eight rounds of 45ACP without making the magazine any longer.

Colt left the factory with back in the 1980s.

For 1911s, the demand for improved magazine quality started with competitive IPSC shooters. The matches would not allow an "alibi," or re-shoot because of a malfunction. Once shooters became willing to pay anything for reliable magazines, manufacturers started making better magazines. One of the first was Bill Wilson, who started making .45 ACP magazines in 1980. I bought some right away, and more later. They have yet to give me any problems.

Soon after Bill Wilson, other magazine makers cropped up. Now, finding reliable magazines for the 1911 is simple. Buy from one of the "old" names – Wilson, Mc-

Cormick, Magpack, Ed Brown, Millett – and you will not have problems. All offer impressive warranties. If your magazine cracks or breaks and you haven't "improved" it with a pair of pliers, you'll get a new one. Chip McCormick even goes so far as to take samples from production and regularly test them to destruction. If Chip can wrestle a welded baseplate off of one of his magazines, someone was lazy in the welding department and will hear about it. (It wouldn't surprise me to hear of similar tests done by all the other manufacturers.) Chip tracks all production, and if he finds a deficiency in any batch, he corrects it. And he is not the only one. As a result, the current design of 1911 magazines are the best, most reliable and most durable magazines that you can buy. The old bias of "1911 bad, other magazines good" no longer holds. For pistols other than the 1911, your best bet is either buy the magazines made by the manufacturer, or from Mec-Gar or Para USA. In some cases, the "factory" magazines you buy will have been made for them by Mec-Gar.

If you are looking at a magazine out of its package, perhaps a used one, give it a thorough inspection. Each manufacturer has a distinct, if subtle "look" to its magazines. Sometimes, as in the case of the Wilson magazines, the look is not so subtle. Is the magazine a name brand one? Great. Check the magazine tube for hammer or plier marks. While you're at it, check for tire tracks, too. If you see none, then bargain for a good price.

If you see any of the above, especially marks from pliers, put the magazine down and forget it. Even if it was free, it would be too expensive to own. Magazines that have had the feed lips "adjusted" with pliers are always feeding headaches, and never work 100 percent.

If the magazine is not a name brand, look at the quality of its construction. Look especially hard at the weld. Most magazine tubes are formed by wrapping sheet metal around a form, and welding the joint in the spine. A good magazine will have a single continuous weld down the length of the spine. If the weld is ugly, uneven or ground down, pass. A magazine with the spine folded over and spot-welded should also be passed over. Tap the tube itself. Does it sound tinny, like it's made of soft or thin steel? If so, leave it.

There are enough good-quality magazines out there that you can afford to pass up a dubious "bargain." What costs you money is the cheap magazine that never really works well enough.

TREATING THEM WELL

Except for the Glock magazines, your magazines are made of steel and prone to rust. Even a magazine made of stainless steel, or one with an electroless nickel finish, has a carbon steel spring in it.

If you have been in the rain or snow, or your magazines have fallen onto wet ground or grass, you should wipe them off. Strip the spring and follower out of each of them one at a time, and wipe these parts dry. If you find the spring or follower rusted, use 0000 steel wool and light oil to scrub it clean. Leave the spring lightly oiled from the scrubbing, wipe the oil off the follower, and do not oil the inside of the magazine.

Do not let your magazines stay wet for any length of time. Many years ago, after shooting a match in a driving rain, I got home so tired I only had enough energy to pull my pistol out of my shooting bag and wipe it down. I left my wet magazines in the bag. The next time I went to the range, my magazines were crusty red lumps. It took a lot of scrubbing to get them clean. I had to learn this lesson again, after I had retired the magazines made of carbon steel and switched over to stainless. After that second rainstorm, I found my springs and followers red with rust, even though the magazine tubes themselves were fine.

This brush scrubs grit and dirt out of the magazine interior.

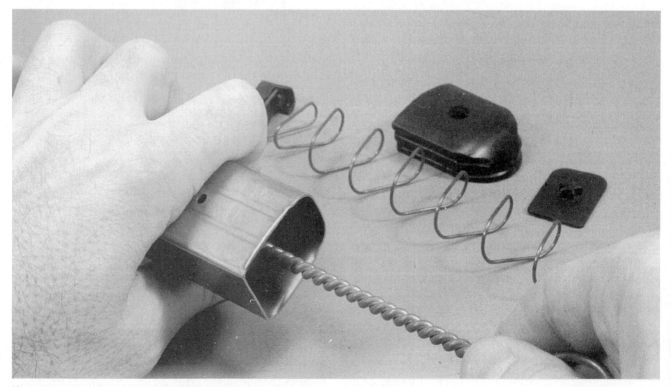

Keep your magazines in good working order by cleaning them.

Some shooters have an inordinate fear of dropping their magazines. Some even put plastic or rubber bases on their magazines to ease the shock of the magazine hitting the ground. Don't worry. A good quality magazine will not be damaged by dropping it onto the ground. Concrete may be a problem. I've used Wilson magazines for many years in my Colt .45, and have dropped each of them hundreds of times. They are still working fine. If you are shooting at an indoor range, and the floor has some sort of carpeting, then your magazines will be safe from the concrete. I have dropped magazines right onto concrete and, while I wince each time, I have yet to find a magazine damaged by the fall.

The basepads don't help in falling but are useful in loading.

MAINTAINING THEM

The only magazines made today without a removable baseplate are certain 1911 magazines. To disassemble the non-removable baseplate magazines, push the follower half-way down with a pencil or dowel. Take a drift punch that fits through the view holes in the magazine, and push the punch through the magazine. Select a view hole that will let you capture the magazine spring, but not the follower. With the spring captured, turn the magazine upside down and gently tap it until the follower falls free.

Hold your hand over the magazine lips, and pull the drift punch out. Before you remove the spring, make a note of its orientation. The top coil of the spring is designed to fit against the follower a certain way. You'll want to put it back that way when you reassemble it.

To reassemble, push the spring back and compress it fully into the magazine. Holding the spring down with one thumb, slide the follower into the magazine with the rear leg parallel to the feed lips. Once the corner of the follower is in the magazine tube rotate the follower to its upright position. Remove your thumb from the feed lips. Reach under the follower with a dental pick, and push the top coil of the spring until it correctly bears against the follower.

Except for Glocks (see below), magazines with removable baseplates are easier. On the bottom of the baseplate you'll find a hole. A retaining plate inside the magazine locks in this hole. Use a drift punch to push the retaining plate away from the baseplate. Push the now-unlocked baseplate off the rails on the bottom of the magazine tube. With the baseplate off, the locking plate, spring and follower will come out of the bottom. If you aren't careful, they will launch out. Again, note the spring's orientation. It is designed to fit only this way. If you swap it end for end, or turn it front to back, the magazine will not feed properly.

With the magazine apart, wipe or scrub the follower and spring. Brush or swab out the magazine tube. Do not oil them. You can prevent malfunctions of your high-capacity magazines by lubricating the interior of the tube, but not with oil. A spray silicone that dries on the surface can keep your cartridges sliding smoothly, without attracting grit or dirt. Most outdoor ranges have a large amount of dust or sand and the silicone will keep your dropped magazines from collecting too much gunk.

To reassemble, first place the follower, spring and retaining plate in the tube. Make sure the spring is oriented correctly. Compress the spring and retainer. While holding them in place with one thumb, slide the baseplate on. Look through the hole in the baseplate. If the retaining plate is not locked into this hole, tap the side of the magazine until the retaining plate snaps into place.

For Glock magazines, push the drift punch into the baseplate hole until the retaining plate snaps out of alignment with the baseplate. The Glock magazine tube has two little shoulders on its bottom rails, to keep the baseplate from sliding off. You must squeeze the bottom sides of the magazine to remove the baseplate. Reassembly of the Glock magazine is the same as other removable baseplate magazines. Again, you must squeeze the bottom of the magazine, this time to get the baseplate to clear the locking shoulders and snap into place.

To disassemble the Glock, press a punch into the bottom hole until the inside plate snaps to the side.

Squeeze the sides of the magazine and slide the floorplate off.

IMPROVING THEM

The first thing you can do to improve your magazines is buy the best. Having done that, mark them with your name or initials. Now you can decide what other upgrades you want: a basepad, plating, increased capacity.

Why mark your magazines? So you'll get them back, or at least be able to identify them. If you are shooting in a match that requires reloads, you and the other competitors could end up with a bunch of magazines scattered over the firing line. I used to shoot PPC with the local Sheriff's Department. The last firing sequence called for 24 rounds from four magazines from each of us. The indoor range was practically shoulder-to-shoulder tight. We would end the course of fire with over 30 magazines on the floor. Marked magazines were easier to sort out.

The simplest marking method is to use a stencil and spray paint. Use your initials or simply number your magazines. Heck, paint is cheap, do both. Between your initials, the number and the color of the paint, you should be able to find your own mags. At the end of a stage, you can take a quick count. If you come up short, you know and you know which one. "Hey, anyone got a magazine with 'PJS' and a green four on it?"

An electric pencil works too. If you are feeling particularly posh, you can find that booth at the local megamall that engraves gifts. You may be able to get them to engrave your name or initials on your magazines. Ask first, before you dump a bag full of magazines on the bench. They may call security over as they stall you asking for the correct spelling of "Smith."

You can also make your magazines easy to find, and separate them from other shooters' mags by using a particular color of basepad. They are available in colors that will sear your eyes. Color-coded baseplates also are a way to keep the capacities straight. If your basepads are all the same color, then you can stencil the capacity onto the basepad. That way you needn't try to memorize which is which. Lest you think it a theoretical problem, I have an example. My EAA Witness pistol is set up as a Limited IPSC gun. It has two uppers, one in 9mm and one in .40. Three magazines feed 9mm only, and three other magazines feed .40 only. One, as a very puzzling magazine, feeds both. Each of the three caliber-specific magazines has one that holds a round more than the other two. When deciding what order to use them in a stage, knowing their capacity can be useful. As they are all black-anodized aluminum basepads from CPMi, color doesn't help. But stenciled numerals do help.

PROTECTING THEM

If you have reliable carbon steel magazines you can protect them from rust by plating them. Robar will NP3 plate them and Accurate Plating will hard chrome them. With either method, your magazines will last much longer and work much more smoothly. The cost can run as much as a third of the cost of the magazine, but that is still less than buying a new stainless magazine.

As with your handguns, send your magazines for plating only after you have done everything else you want to them. Fire enough rounds through them to determine that they work 100 percent for you, mark them, then send them for plating. It would be most unfortunate to spend the money getting your magazines plated, only to then find they and your pistol do not get along.

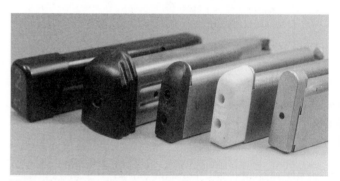

Magazine base pads come in a variety of colors and materials. The left one is black aluminum, the next is black plastic, the center one is black rubber, the second from the right is bright yellow rubber, and the right-hand one is brass. Only the first one increases capacity.

This is a CPMi magazine base pad for the EAA Witness. It increases magazine capacity by two rounds of 40S&W. The small screw keeps it from shifting.

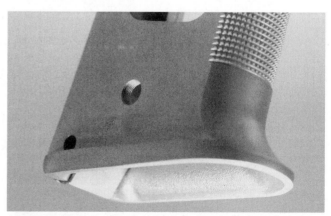

You can avoid the hassle of trying to solder on a magazine funnel, one piece or two. Just order a Caspian frame with integral magazine funnel.

MODIFYING THEM

Basepads or buffers make it easier to insert the magazine, especially if you have a magazine funnel. If you do not have a funnel, the extra length of the basepad keeps you from pinching your hand between the magazine and the magazine opening. Some magazines already have an oversized baseplate that acts as a basepad. The Glock and Beretta both feature oversized baseplates. The 1911 magazines with attached baseplates do not. However, many magazine makers provide a buffer pad and screws to secure the pad. To make it dead simple they even drill two holes in the magazine for you. The screws are euphemistically called "self-tapping." Don't count on it. The magazine steel is hard and screws are small. Rather than exhaust yourself trying to self-tap the screws, go to the store (or call Brownells) and buy a 4-40 tap. Tap the holes and then screw the pad on.

For magazines that are not drilled the procedure is still simple. Take your dial calipers and measure the width of the magazine. Divide this number in half, adjust your calipers and mark a line down the center of the baseplate. Measure the distance of the holes in the base pad from the front and the back and use the calipers to mark these distances on the centerline. Centerpunch the hole locations. Drill the holes with a #43 drill, and tap with your 4-40 tap. Install the basepads.

If basic black plastic is not what turns you on, the pads can be bought in a variety of colors, some not even found in nature. You can buy them in plastic, rubber, aluminum or brass. The metal basepads speed up your reloads a fraction of a second, as the extra weight gets the magazine out of the pistol a tad faster.

Wilson makes magazine buffers in various thicknesses in both slide-on models for their magazines and screw-on for others.

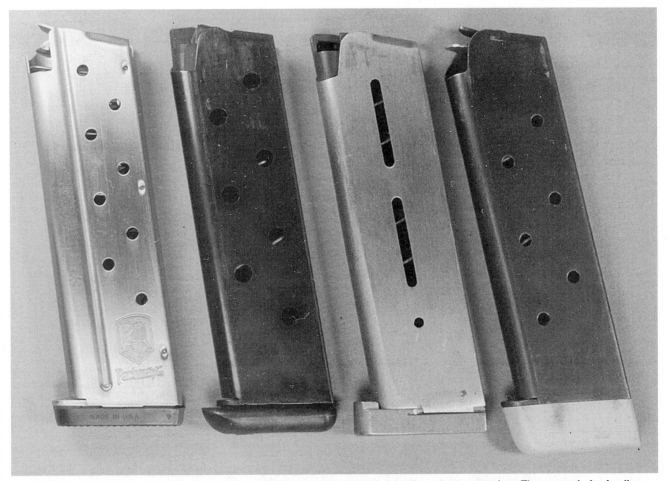

The Pachmayr magazine on the left came with a rubber base pad attached. It is also a 9mm magazine. The crease is for feeding, not to decrease capacity. The next magazine is a Mag-pack, eight rounds of .45ACP and an included mag pad, also black rubber. The Wilson-Rogers magazine has a brass base pad, and the McCormick magazine on the right has a CP Bullets bright green rubber pad screwed on. All the pads work, it is just a matter of taste which one you use.

Basepads are also available for magazines that have removable baseplates. The early Wilson basepads were made of a plastic that would crack after six months of hard use, and I ended up replacing my plastic ones with brass. The newest formulation of plastic Wilson uses shows no signs of cracking and comes in a variety of colors.

Those who feel that black is best, but do not like the idea of drilling and tapping their magazines, there is a secure but messy way of attaching basepads. The following method only works for magazines that do not have removable baseplates. If the plate comes off, you must use another method. You'll need a bottle of contact cement, some crepe rubber from a shoe repair store, and a belt sander. Carefully cut rough basepads from the rubber. Sand and degrease the bottom of the magazine. Apply contact cement to both magazine and rubber. Allow for drying time, and then attach the rubber. Now use the belt sander to dress the rubber even with the magazine. You should wear a mask, and you will fill the air with ground rubber dust. Once done, the pad will stay for years of hard use. Fair warning: twenty years after you do this, the crepe rubber you've glued onto your magazines will have hardened to a concrete-like substance, and you'll have to pry them off and do it all over again. So, in 2029 or so, don't say I didn't warn you.

CAPACITY

Current legislation prohibits manufacturers from making new magazines with a capacity greater than 10 rounds in some States. Thankfully, the Federal law that similarly restricted magazine production has since expired. Existing high-capacity magazines can still be bought, sold and traded in those States. Those of us living in free states can buy whatever we want. For a while during the Federal ban, prices skyrocketed. At the peak, a high-capacity magazine for a Glock went for one-quarter of the cost of the handgun itself!

As shooters became used to the idea of "only" 10 rounds per magazine prices stabilized. Some of the lesser-capacity magazines were re-designed to hold ten. The 1911 was the first. You can now buy 10-round magazines from Wilson, McCormick and Ed Brown. There are even 10-round magazines available for the little Colt .380!

The previously high-capacity magazines were redesigned during the Assault Weapons Ban of 1994-2004 to hold only 10 rounds. The redesign also made it impossible to increase their capacity. You should not try to circumvent this design limit. There is no longer a law prohibiting it, but the magazine designers did their jobs well: is just isn't mechanically or economically feasible to make them hi-cap again.

The ten-year Federal foray into the stupidsphere produced a large supply of 10-round-only magazines, which is actually a good thing. First, each of them acts as a reminder of that period, and second, they are also reliable magazines for practice.

It is now (2009) legal to increase the capacity of a magazine that already holds more than 10 rounds. To this end, the makers of basepads make over-sized, hollow basepads. Depending on the pistol, the caliber, and the extension manufacturer, you can increase your capacity an additional two to eight rounds. However, there is one limit you have to be aware of: extensions only work on magazine tubes with removable baseplates, and on those tubes that have the bottom lips bent outwards. Inward-bent lips to hold the baseplate make it impossible to increase the distance the follower can travel down.

To install one of these baseplates, strip the magazine. Pull off the old baseplate. Some extensions (such as the CPMi) use the old spring, others do not. If you use the

This particular Arredondo extension is for 9mm/40 Glocks, and won't work on other guns or Glock 10mm or .45 magazines.

Magazine extensions can add capacity. You need to make sure you have the magazine-specific extension, and a magazine legal to add. Even if the federal law expires, there are states that would prohibit extensions. And some competitions don't allow them. Check before you spend!

old parts, compress the spring, or spring and retainer, and slide the new extension onto the magazine rails. The CPMi extensions use a small screw at the back of the extension to keep the extension from sliding forward.

The Taylor Freelance Glock extensions use a pair of screws and an external retaining plate to keep the extension in place. The Glock +2 extensions sometimes pop off the magazine if they are bumped, launching bullets, spring and baseplate out onto the floor. The Taylor Freelance doesn't come off so easily, and you can get a +4 extension or a +8. The latter brings your Glock 17 up to a 25-round magazine! Other makers of magazine extension are Arredondo, Dawson and Grams. You cannot count on all hi-cap magazines having the option of a replacement baseplate to increase capacity. The most popular pistols, and those used in practical competitor, are most likely to have aftermarket extensions available. Also, as I mentioned, the magazine in question must be made so the retainer plate attaches to lips of the magazine body that are bent outwards. Inwards doesn't work. Basically, you can get extension for Glocks, the STI/SVI pistols, Beretta, CZ-75 and its clones, and a few others. By searching out the manufacturers catalogs you can find gems like magazine extensions for the Browning Hi-Power from CPMi.

A new magazine capacity increasing baseplate comes

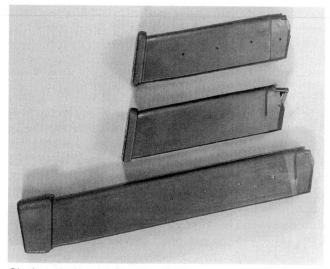

Glock magazines come in a variety of capacities. On the left, a full-size high-cap magazine, 15 rounds of 40S&W. In the center, a full-size magazine that holds 10 rounds. On the right is a 29- round magazine. While the high-caps are legal, they are also hard to find.

to us from Canyon Creek; made by Rich Dettlehouser, and are made for XD and XDm pistols. There, you can make the XD higher, and the XDm almost excessive in capacity.

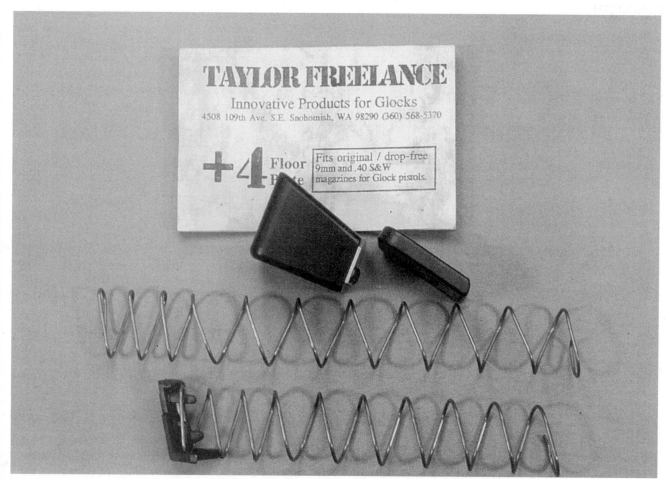

The Taylor Freelance floor plate for Glocks also includes a new magazine spring. This plate increases capacity by four rounds.

Unless there are enough people asking for extensions for any given model, the makers don't make them. If you own a model for which they are available, you can increase the capacity of your magazines.

In some competitions the extra capacity isn't an advantage, and in others it isn't allowed. In USPSA Limited-10 Division, for example, you can't have more than 10 rounds in the magazine. Ditto Glock Sports Shooting

matches. If you were shooting a bowling pin match, you could have an extended magazine for the 9-pin event, but having 20 rounds on tap isn't going to help much. If you need more than 11 or 12 rounds per run you aren't going to win the match. Single Stack Division shooters canot use more than 8-shot mags in .45 or .40, and not more than 10-shot mags for 9mm or Supers.

Also, if you're thinking that a higher-capacity magazine would be a good thing on a carry gun, give it some extra thought. A higher-capacity magazine is longer, and thus can be more difficult to conceal. Having more rounds is not so good, if the extra size got you "made" and put you at a disadvantage before the gunfight even starts.

If the conversion replaces the spring and retainer, pull the old parts out and save them in a plastic bag marked with the magazine type and number. The Arredondo extensions use a new retainer to keep the extension in place. Install this new retainer along with the new, longer spring.

If your high-capacity magazine becomes damaged you can replace the tube or have it repaired. You can buy replacement tubes for some brands. Other companies will repair or replace their tube, if you send them the

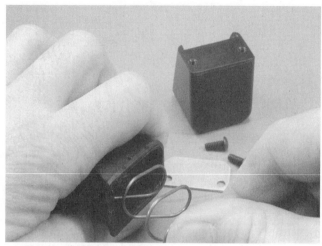

Compress the spring.

Screw the retaining plate on the Taylor Freelance, and your magazine now holds four more rounds.

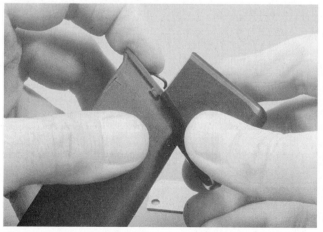

Keep the spring compressed while you slide the new bottom on.

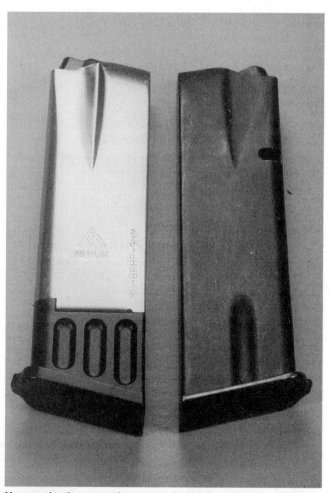

New production magazines can only hold ten rounds. This Mec-Gar magazine on the left is for the Browning Hi-Power. The one on the right is an older, 13-shot magazine. Both are the same size, and both work just fine.

old one. Brownells lists replacement tubes and whole magazines. Buy what you need, what you want, or what strikes your fancy.

The law once again allows manufacturers to make high-capacity magazines for all. There are old magazines made with high capacity that were made for law enforcement, military or export use only. They are clearly marked. The markings now mean nothing, unless you live in a restrictive state like California or New Jersey. Maybe not even then, but the peculiarities of firearms law in irrational states is not my concern. Similar markings may get you in trouble; if you find magazines marked as being owned by a particular police department, and not just generally marked as Law enforcement Only, they may still be that department's property. You never know, so do be careful.

MAGAZINE SPRINGS, LIPS AND LATCHES

There are three critical parts of a magazine: the spring, the feed lips and the magazine catch. A weak or bent spring can lift the cartridge stack late or crooked. Malformed or damaged feed lips can present the round badly to the chamber. And an incorrectly located mag catch slot can position the magazine too low or high, defeating an otherwise correctly made magazine.

The spring must be strong enough, but not too strong. It used to be impossible to get a spring "too strong." Such is not the case. If you rebuild a 140mm hi-cap magazine (such as is used for USPSA Limited competition) and use a spring intended for a 170mm magazine tube, you'll find you've just reduced capacity. The spring is too long. And, when fully loaded the spring tension

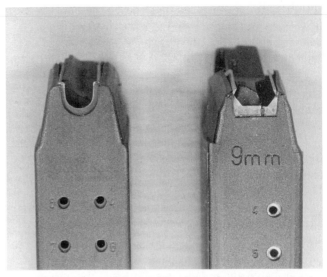

The old Glock magazines would not drop-free from the pistol. They have round notches on the spine. The newer ones do drop free, and they have square notches on their spine.

on the top round may be too much for the slide to strip a round to chamber it. When replacing a tired spring, get one intended for your application, not something "stronger to improve feeding." How can you tell when your springs are tired? One clue is that the slide doesn't lock open. If an otherwise reliable pistol, and magazines, starts not locking open when empty, your springs are probably tired. I ran into this situation in the early 1990s with my single-stack 1911 .38 super guns. My magazines were Chip McCormick 10-shot Super mags, and I had been using them weekly for nearly a decade. They were used in my Steel gun (which was also my PPC gun for

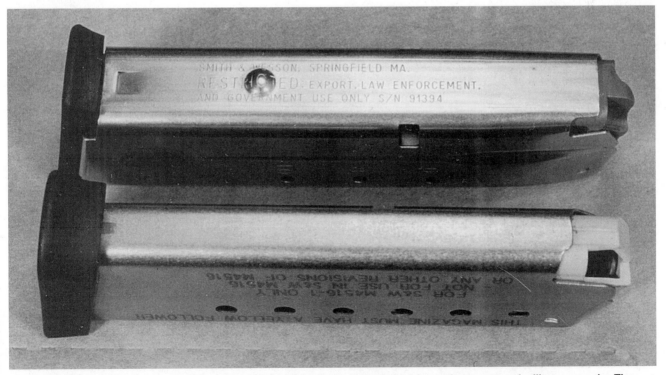

High-capacity magazines made after the Crime Bill was signed were intended for law enforcement and military use only. They are so-marked. Possession of one of these magazines used to be a federal felony. Now they are curiosities.

several years of winter league shooting) and my USPSA/ IPSC Open gun before I went to a hi-cap Super. They also got used as my 9-pin gun magazines for a week each June at Second Chance. In the early 1990s they started not locking open, even though they fed reliably. New Mc-Cormick springs solved the problem,

Another clue (especially for guns that never locked open when empty, even from the beginning) is the "bolt over base" feeding failure. Seen more often in AR-15 rifle, the bolt (in our case the slide) has over-ridden the rim of the cartridge, and struck it in the middle of the case. The spring is late in lifting the stack, and the bolt arrives before the top round has settled into the feed lips. Again, replace the spring to solve the problem.

Mangled or improper feed lips are a much tougher problem to solve. Many magazines that are unreliable are unreliable due to experimentation on the part of their owners. The experimentation usually involves a pair of pliers and the feed lips of the offending magazine. Let me begin the advice by suggesting that you not alter the feed lips of the magazine unless you are willing to scrap a few experimental magazines in practice. Preferably surplus ones from the gun show, and not brand-new Wilson or McCormick mags. Indeed, if you pull one of

the latter out of its plastic bag, test it and find it wanting, you should look first to the ammo or the pistol itself as the source of the problem. If the problem persists, send the mag back. If you try to "adjust" it, and then send it back, the plier marks will immediately void the warranty.

Unmarked Glock aftermarket magazines can be troublesome. They do not look so different that a quick glance will tell you which magazine you have. To be sure you need to measure the gap of the feed lips. A quick measure with dial calipers will uncover the info. Magazines with the following measurements serve only the rounds specified:

.325 inch to .335 inch are for 9mm

.360 inch to .370 inch are for 40, .357 SIG or 10mm

.425 inch to .435 inch are for .45

Some IPSC shooters spend a great amount of time and effort using padded pliers, tweaking the feed lips of their magazines. However (and here is the big qualifying quibble) they keep detailed records, they measure their work with dial calipers, they test extensively, and they are under no illusions that the manufacturer will correct or offer assistance on their mistakes. They are

Measure the spread of your magazine feed lips. Record the numbers and check your magazines periodically. If they start to spread you may have to have a wizard like Bevin Grams re-tune them.

When buying magazines, get ones with smooth, unaltered feed lips, like this one. Don't buy magazines with marks on them. Not unless you want an unreliable magazine that you'll spend hours fussing over to try to make right.

also working on ferociously expensive hi-cap magazines for specialized guns. Commonly they'll be tweaking a 29-shot magazine of 170mm length for .38 Super or a 22-shot 140mm magazine for 40 S&W. With $150 invested in the magazine, basepad, custom follower and spring, and their match performance riding on the result, they are intensely interested in the magazine's performance. However, detailed records are a must, as well as careful measurements.

Should you expend the same effort on a $30 single-stack magazine that is easily replaced? When the manufacturer will warranty its performance as long as you don't mess with it? (Is the answer clear enough? Don't do it.)

What you should do is this: Once you have tested your magazines to be sure they work reliably in your pistol, mark and number them. Then record the relevant statistics. Use a dial caliper to measure the gap between the feed lips at the rear, middle and front. Don't be surprised if the measurements vary a bit from magazine to magazine. (If it works there is no point is adjusting a working magazine just so its measurements agree with another working magazine.) Then check spring strength. Lay the pistol flat on the table, mag catch up. With the slide forward, lock a magazine in place. Then press the mag catch and see how far the empty magazine is pushed by the spring with the slide forward. Record the distance. At any time in the future you can check each magazine. If the feed lips have begun to spread, you'll know. If the magazine then begins to give feeding problems, you have exact measurement to give to the manufacturer when you request a warranty replacement. If the springs become weak, you have a means of measuring the change. At the point any one of them begins failing to lock the slide back, you have two choices: replace all the springs, or replace those whose decrease matches or exceeds that of the offending magazine. My

choice would be "All." Magazine springs are not so expensive that changing all the springs in your magazines will be an onerous expense. After all, we aren't talking of a bushel basket full of magazines, right? Right?

And what of the magazine latch slot in the wrong place? Warranty it back to the maker. I've repaired otherwise unreplaceable magazines. For the cost of welding, machining, testing and refinishing, you can buy two or three new magazines. For some pistols you don't have that choice (ever try to buy magazines for a French MAB-15?) but for current production pistols such magazine work is definitely in the R&D category: Do it only if you want to learn how it is done.

HOW LONG DO MAGAZINES LAST?

The magazine tube can last quite a long time. I have some Wilson .45 magazines that I bought soon after they came out (early 1980s) that are still going strong. I've replaced the springs several times, and the followers have all gotten replaced along the way, but the tubes are fine. Springs need replacing over use, not time. A magazine that has been sitting on the shelf for 20 years need not have its spring replaced simply due to age. Flexions age springs, not time. And a loaded magazine is probably good as long, too. It is the magazines in constant use that have their springs tire. Every now and then you see a magazine article about an old magazine found loaded, which is shot, and still works. I once left a bandolier of AR-15 20-round magazines loaded (I forgot about them) for nearly three years. They all worked fine. The record from personal knowledge was a batch of 1911, Browning Hi-power and .30 Carbine magazines. The shop bought a houseful of guns and gear. The widow and her late husband had both been Marine NCOs and he had died some 17 years before we bought the gear. (She had just gotten tired of tripping over all his stuff and brought it to us to buy.) There were ammo can full of loaded magazines. They had been loaded for not less than 17 years, probably longer. They all worked.

One shortcoming of the Wilson magazines are their polymer followers. The followers can get ground up by dust, dirt, lint and grit. (Of course, steel followers can rust.) Cleaning your magazines helps them last longer. One match at our gun club happened during a heavy rainstorm. We didn't stop, as there was no lightning. Andy stepped up to shoot a stage that was ankle-deep in soupy mud, and 42 rounds later we began searching the mud for his 10-shot 1911 Wilson magazines. We found the last one by getting a rake out of the tool shed and raking the mud looking for it. A clean water rinse later, they were ready to go for the next stage. But Andy (indeed, all of us) made sure to disassemble, wipe, silicone spray and reassemble those magazines after the match.

CHAPTER 13

SIGHTS TO STEER BY

Sights are essential for good shooting. This was not always held to be true. Even now there are still some writers who advocate "pointing" or "natural" shooting.

Before WWII, sights were very small, hard to see, and hard to use. Compared to today's sights, they were practically non-existent. Since most handgun altercations were (and still are) at very close range, it was easy enough to ignore the sights and fire away.

And fire away, and fire away, and fire away. . .

I mean, when you can read accounts of cowboys and gamblers literally running around a pool table shooting at each other, quitting only when they run out of ammunition, having hit no one — well, you have to assume that "pointing" had some drawbacks.

Sights have come a long way in the last 50 years. The surge of interest in handgun hunting and the heat of practical competition have proved the worth of sights. If you want to hit, you have to aim. What you aim with is your choice. Sometimes your choice is limited by the rules of the competition you are in. In USPSA/IPSC shooting for example, you can use optics if you want. However, if you elect to use optics, you are required to compete in Open or Modified divisions. You cannot use an optical sight and still shoot in Production, Limited, Single Stack or Revolver. In IDPA, you cannot use an optical sight at all. You may not be allowed to use a fiber optic sight in some competitions, or divisions. Be sure you know what the rules allow. And when hunting, be sure you know what the game regulations permit. It may well be that the regulations committee of your state was particularly behind the times, and thought a red-dot sight projected a red dot, and thus considers it an "illumination device." No amount of arguing that it isn't will get you off the hook with the DNR officer.

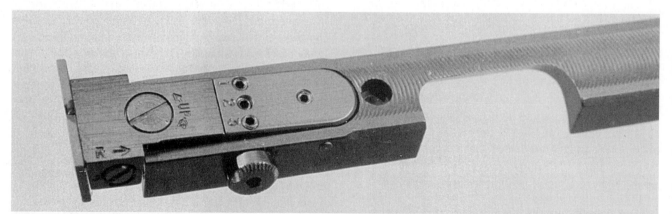

Ribs are allowed in PPC, in some categories. In many other competitions, they are either restricted or not allowed at all. Check before you go bolting an excellent rib like this Aristocrat to your handgun.

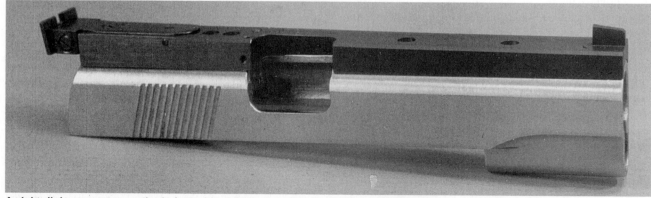

A sight rib is a common method of attaching sights to a slide for Bull's eye competition.

THREE TYPES

Sights come in three types: fixed, adjustable and optical. Fixed and adjustable sights are referred to generically as "iron" sights. Despite their name, fixed sights can still be adjusted, though they require filing or welding, and drifting with a hammer and copper punch, to adjust. Adjustable sights can be moved with just a small screwdriver, and you can easily make incremental changes. A lot of shooters wonder why they should use them, if the fixed sights are so hard to adjust.

The answer? Fixed sights are cheaper. They're also more durable.

The Caspian Race-Ready kit comes with two sights, one of which is their rear aperture/ front fluorescent bead.

Some handgun manufacturers give you a choice of sighting systems. Some models of Smith & Wesson and Taurus can be purchased with fixed or adjustable sights. On other handguns, such as SIG, Beretta and Ruger, if you want adjustable sights you'll have to install them yourself. Glocks can be found with adjustable sights, but these are a particularly fragile design.

Optical sights can be the traditional "scope," or a "red dot" scope, which reflects a dot of light onto the lens of the tube; or a laser, projecting a beam of light to the target.

The scope is used mostly for hunting, where a small amount of magnification is useful, and milliseconds do not matter. With a 2X or 3X scope, a deer at 50 or 75 yards turns into a deer at 25 yards. You can take a deep breath, aim, and fire easily enough.

The red-dot scopes are mainly used for competition. Most are 1X, or life-size; they offer no magnification. Since they require batteries, they are not as useful for hunting as traditional scopes. Sit patiently in a freezing cold hunting blind for a couple of hours with a red-dot scope and when you go to aim you'll probably find those batteries have quit. In competition, however, with limited shooting distances and severe time pressures, red-dot scopes really make a difference.

When I first wrote this book, lasers were used mostly in the movies. Who can forget the laser Ah-nold uses in Terminator? The tube was nearly the size of the slide on the long-slide 1911 he was wielding. (Quick: what brand 1911 was it?) Current laser technology creates a less-fragile sighting mechanism than in the past. The

If the competition rules allow it, you can install a compact sight like this (now out of production) Tasco Optima or a Docter sight right on the slide. You'll need a mill to do it right, but the work isn't very hard. This installation took less than an hour.

The Novak rear on a Glock. It uses the standard-height front, and is available in three-dot and night sights.

This Aristocrat sight rib has an adjustment button for quick-setting the sight to different distances.

This is a Millett fixed rear. The bar can be had in white or orange. If three-dot is your preferred style, that is also available along with plain black.

The Trijicon rear is marked in the same manner as the Glock rear. If you need to adjust your group vertically, you get a different height rear sight. Get a Trijicon marked the same as the Glock rear that is zeroed on your pistol.

usual arrangement for turning a laser on back then was wires wrapped around the outside of the laser and frame leaving your handgun looking like some sort of cyborg. Clamping the laser to the frame typically left it exposed to all bumps, any one of which will jostle it right out of alignment. The handgun-laser assembly would not fit into most holsters. Well, that has changed. Lasers are now compact enough to be out of the way. Crimson Trace now makes lasers built into the grips. If you want one, it is easy enough to install one. In fact, so easy it is now simpler than tasks that can be called "gunsmithing."

And if you have a handgun with an accessory rail, the picatinny rail under the slide but forward of the trigger, lots and lots of laser are made to clamp right on that rail. Instructions (and often the batteries) included, no gunsmithing needed.

Early sights consisted of a small, rounded blade up front and a narrow and shallow notch in the rear. The design offered the shooter a view of a little bump, the front sight, resting in a shallow divot, the rear. There were no straight lines or right angles. Right after WWII Smith & Wesson began offering a sight design known as the Patridge. Others soon followed suit. The Patridge design changed the front sight to a flat-topped blade with straight sides. The rear was modified to a rectangular notch.

The new design would not hang up on the draw. It was easy to see, and extremely durable. Nonetheless, it still took a long time before the majority of handgun manufacturers offered it.

Using a Patridge design is simple. Line up the sights so the top edges of the front and rear sights are on a single line. The vertical "light lines" between the front blade and the rear notch should be even. Keep that alignment and press the trigger. You'll hit the target.

The width of the light lines is a subject of some discussion. Bullseye shooters want the maximum precision available, and so prefer the smallest possible light lines. If their aim is off even the slightest amount, they can tell. Action shooters using iron sights will often ask for a rear notch that is wider than normal, and a narrower front sight. The result is larger light lines, but faster sight setup.

Sights used to come in only the same color as the rest of the handgun. If you bought a blued handgun, your sights were blue. If you bought a nickel handgun, your sights were nickel. Now, bars, dots and colors abound. Glock offers a white-dot front and a white-outline rear notch. Smith & Wesson has offered a red ramp front and a white outline rear for many years. Older handguns, or one that left the factory without these additions, can be brought up to date.

Today, even glow-in-the-dark radioactive night sights are available. In the daytime the sights seem to have simple white dots or bars on them. In darkness the dots or bars glow green, yellow, or red. You can still see your sights long after it has gotten too dark to identify your target.

As durable as your particular sights may be, they still are one of the more fragile parts of your handgun. Any handgun dropped on its sights will require repair.

MEASURING THE LOCATION OF YOUR SIGHTS

Any time you adjust your sights, you have to know where they were when you started, and where they ended up after you're done.

For pistols, the height of front sights can be measured by simply using the end of your dial calipers as a depth gauge. To find out if your front sight is centered, take the slide off the frame, and place it on its side on a flat surface such as heavy plate glass. Measure up from the surface of the glass to the edge of the front sight blade. Turn the slide on its other side, and repeat. If the two

measurements are the same, your sight is centered in the slide. If not, then take the difference between the two measurements and divide by two. The number you get is the distance for your adjustment, if you will be adjusting the front sight.

Measuring the rear sight height can be as easy as the front. If your rear is a simple blade, use the dial calipers as a depth gauge. To measure the height of adjustable sights such as the Bo-Mar or Millett, measure the height of the slide and the sight, then subtract the height of the slide, measured right in front of the sight. To find out if the rear sight is centered, use the same method as with the front sight.

Revolvers are not so easy. Though the front sight height can be measured with the dial calipers, using the same method as a pistol, the only way to find out if the front sight is centered is to shoot the revolver. If the sight is off-center, the group will be, too.

The height of the rear sight can only sometimes be measured. Many times there is just no place from which to check. Ditto finding out if the sight is centered. Again, you will have to take a revolver to the range, test fire it, and see if the sights are on.

This is a Trijicon night sight. If you drop the pistol, or send the slide through a bluing solution, the tiny vial will crack and lose its Tritium. The sights will no longer glow.

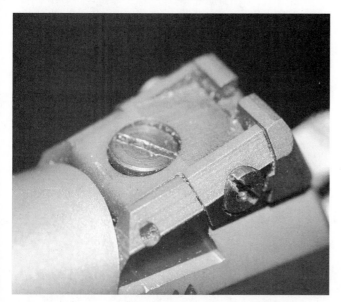

The new Caspian adjustable sight for Novak dovetails. The word is that it is highly thought-of by Marine Corps special units.

The standard Glock front is a small plastic pyramid. It can wear enough to change your point of impact. Change it to a steel sight for greater durability.

The standard Glock sight is plastic, and not as durable as the rest of the pistol.

RED RAMP INSERT

Your handgun has a plain front sight, and you want something different? First, look to see if the front sight is removable. Many are held in with cross pins, and some are built to fit in a dovetail on the barrel or slide. If you can remove your current sight, simply buying a new sight is the easiest way to upgrade.

When straightforward replacement is not possible, you will have to look into other methods of improvement. The simplest is paint. Degrease the sight. Use masking tape to protect the barrel. Select an appropriate color for your sight, but remember that whatever paint you choose will be darker on blue steel than it appears in the bottle or can. For many applications, I have found fluorescent orange works well. To keep the paint as bright as possible, first put on a coat of flat white. Follow this "primer" coat with a coat or two of your chosen color. If you use orange, which seems to be more fragile than other colors, protect it with a coat of flat clear.

Voila! You have a bright orange blade.

If you want just the surface facing you be a bright color, then the D&S Enterprise system of paints works better. In the standard kit, you get a selection of colors, some of which look brighter than you might think paint

can be, without batteries. Degrease the sight, and brush the paint onto the ramp facing you.

Tru-glo also makes sight paint, in an array of eye-searing colors. As with all paints, degrease, primer coat, color coat, sealer and you're good to go.

Both of these painting methods will produce a front sight that will stand up to quite a bit of cleaning, as well as most solvents. But the method is not permanent. To make a permanent red ramp front sight, you will have to file a dovetail into the ramp, and cast colored epoxy into the dovetail. The kit offered by Kings Gun Works has everything you need in one box.

Start by marking the location you will file. The top edge of the insert must be even with the top edge of the sight, or your aiming point will be slightly lowered. Use the extra narrow Swiss pillar file to file a notch in the sight. Then use a small safe-edge three-sided file to undercut the front and back edge of the notch, forming a dovetail. To give the epoxy casting greater strength, take a #48 drill and dimple the bottom of the dovetail you have filed.

Degrease the sight, and clamp the handgun in a padded vise so the notch is level. Clamp the Kings sight form around the front sight. Mix the epoxy, adding dye

Kings makes an epoxy kit that lets you replace a tired orange front sight insert. You can also file a dovetail into your front sight and cast the epoxy into place.

The Bright Sights sight paint is formulated to be bright, and adhere to your sights.

until the color looks right. Do not over-stir, or whip, the epoxy, or you will force air bubbles into the mix. They will not all escape, and be left as voids in the epoxy when you finish the job. Use a toothpick to place drops of the epoxy into the notch, pushing them into the undercut ends and the dimple until there is a slight bubble above the level of the sight. Let the epoxy cure overnight.

The next day, remove your handgun from the clamp. Use your Swiss pillar file, clean and unchalked, to file the dome of epoxy level with the rest of the sight. If you find

you have air bubbles, you can either clean the epoxy out of the dovetail and start over again, or use a flat clear paint to seal the epoxy.

You can clean the epoxy out and try again as many times as you want. While I have illustrated these methods with a Smith & Wesson revolver, all three will work on any pistol. They will also work no matter how your front sight is attached.

ADJUSTING THE SIGHTS ON A FIXED-SIGHT REVOLVER

There are two directions to adjust on a sight: Vertical and horizontal. Do not make vertical (up-down) adjustments until you have the revolver hitting on the centerline (horizontal, or left-right adjustments).

Adjusting horizontal is done by turning the barrel fractionally in or out of the frame. When you turn the barrel slightly tighter into the frame, you will move the bullet strike to the right. When you slightly unscrew the barrel, you will be moving the bullet strike to the left.

Before you start, examine the top of the barrel where it joins the frame. You need to record exactly how the two fit together before you make any adjustment. If the barrel is a smooth round cylinder, take a permanent marking pen and draw a straight line from barrel to

INSTRUCTIONS

1. Remove all gun oil and dirt from your sights using BRIGHT SIGHTS gun sight cleaner and a clean rag or cotton swab. Let dry for a few minutes.
2. Shake container to mix the coating.
3. If you have dot sights or want to create new sights, take a flat toothpick and dip it into the coating, getting a small amount on just the end. Carefully place this drop of coating on to your gun sight., Repeat to make the dot larger or higher.
4. If you have a bead or blade sight, use a small artist brush. Close the container, do not let the coating dry out.
5. Allow the coating to dry for 24 hours. Longer if possible.
   CAUTION. BRIGHT SIGHTS WILL NOT WASH OUT OF CLOTHING.

The Bright Sights paint comes in colors so bright you would swear there has to be a battery somewhere.

The Glock front sight and its wedge.

frame. With a barrel that has a rib, or grooves on the top, make a drawing of just where the rib or lines match up with the frame.

Take the cylinder out of the frame. Clamp the barrel vertically in a padded vise, or in barrel blocks in the vise. Secure a frame wrench firmly around the frame. Depending on which adjustment you need, right or left, use the wrench to tighten or loosen the barrel slightly.

The amount you will adjust the barrel is very small. Make your first adjustment so the mark you are using as an index on the barrel/frame alignment is moved only .010 inch. Take the revolver to the range and test fire it. Your group will be moved by the adjustment you have made. Use the difference between the unadjusted and adjusted groups to determine how much more additional adjustment may be needed, or what fraction of the correction you need to un-do. As an example: your bullets had been striking 6 inches to the right, and you loosened the barrel .010 inch. Now the bullets are only 2 inches to the right. A .010-inch adjustment corrected 2/3 of the error (4 of the 6 total inches). To correct the remaining 1/3, or 2 inches, you need to make another adjustment of .005 inch, or half the adjustment you already made. Setting up a simple proportion will help you calculate the adjustment with any set of numbers.

Vertical adjustment can be made only by filing the front sight to raise the bullets' impact, or welding more steel to the sight to lower the impact.

Except when you change barrels, you will rarely have to adjust the horizontal impact. You may have to "tweak" the new barrel back and forth a couple of times until the sights are dead-on. Filing the front sight for vertical adjustment is common only on single-action Colt or Colt clone revolvers. On these the barrel is often made with the front sight too tall. You file it to the correct height after adjusting horizontal impact. I have never had to adjust a Smith & Wesson barrel for vertical impact.

Old texts on pistolsmithing sometimes referred to a factory method, using lead bars, of adjusting point of impact on revolvers. The bars were made of a particular alloy, babbitt, and the factory assemblers would whack the frames or barrels of the revolvers with these bars, "adjusting" the point of impact as they hammered away. If you want to go whacking your revolver with heavy lead bars, you are on your own. I would never do that to mine, nor will I ever suggest doing it to yours.

ADJUSTING THE SIGHTS ON A FIXED-SIGHT AUTOMATIC

To make horizontal adjustments on most pistols you move the rear sight. Use a brass or copper punch and a hammer, or an adjustment fixture. To move the bullet impact to the right, move the rear sight to the right. Move the sight to the left to move the bullet to the left. Many modern pistols will have a front sight that is installed in the slide by means of a dovetail. Just like the rear, the front sight is pressed into the dovetail and left centered. If you have a pistol that strikes right or left of your aiming point, look first at the front sight as a check. Measure it. Is it centered? If it is, then you can proceed

The Hesco sight adjuster is so heavy and durable it makes some vises look flimsy. It is adjustable to handle a variety of handgun slides.

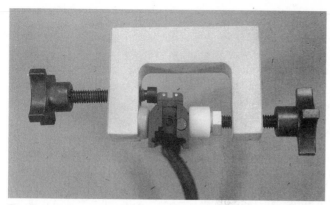

The Brownells sight pusher is not as heavy-duty as other sight pushers, but it gets the job done, and for a fraction of the cost.

to make your corrections on the rear. If it is not, plot the front sight offset, and how it affects your problem. If you find that you have a pistol that hits to the right, and curiously enough your front sight is left of center, perhaps the front is more of your problem than the rear? Center the front, shoot again, and see what happens.

Unlike barrel turning, you can calculate the exact amount you have to move your pistol sight without trekking back and forth to the range. The ratio of the sight radius to the correction needed is the same as the ratio of the distance to the target and correction on the target. This is the same formula in Chapter 3, using a mill to adjust your sights. The sight correction divided by the sight radius equals the target error divided by the target distance.

For vertical adjustment, file the front sight to move the bullet impact up. Install a taller front sight to move the bullet impact down.

Glock makes vertical adjustment very easy, by offering their rear sights in a range of heights. If you find that your Glock is off vertically, check the side of your rear sight and find the line or lines cast into the plastic. The

lines indicate the height of the sight. When you write to Glock for a replacement, tell them which model Glock you have, how far off your pistol is at what distance, and what your current sight says on the side. If you plan to own several Glocks, you can order one sight of each height, and then swap them around as needed.

ZEROING ADJUSTABLE SIGHTS

The great advantage of adjustable sights is that you can adjust them with a screwdriver instead of a hammer. If you are at the range, simply "click" the sight until the point of impact coincides with the point of aim. Move the rear sight up to move the bullet up, and move the rear sight left to move the bullet to the left.

If you are at home and cannot test fire, use the equation above to calculate how much the rear sight has to be moved. Measure the location of the rear blade compared to a non-moving part of the handgun, and then click the sight until you have moved the calculated amount.

SELECTING SIGHTS

The job of your sights is to direct your aiming at the target, not distract you from that aiming. Purists feel that plain black sights are best for the job in the majority of situations. Not all shooters agree. There are situations in which your eyes can lose track of plain sights. When hunting in deep cover, for example, with trees and bushes providing shade, you might want a red ramp front and white outline rear.

Do not assume that "perfect" sights are perfect for you. The handgun manufacturer ships firearms with sights that are great, but maybe not for you. The top shooter at your gun club may have selected the one, perfect, set of sights for his eyes, but they may be a poor choice for you and your shooting. In competition, especially, the color of the targets and the background can often dictate the best sight color.

Glock rear sights come in different heights. If you need to adjust your sights, get the next higher or lower sight and change the rear. The bars on the side indicate which is which. The standard sight has one bar. The shorter one has a smaller bar under the wide bar. The taller ones have shorter bars above the wide one.

The McGivern gold bead front sight is favored by Jerry Miculek.

This Smith & Wesson barrel does not have a sight cut of any kind. It can be milled to take either a S&W sight, or a Novak dovetail.

Mag-Na-Port offers front sight blades made of solid fluorescent plastic. Orange, yellow, blue, green and red.

So what are the choices out there?

Besides a red ramp, Smith & Wesson and Novak both offer a front sight with a Gold McGivern bead. Ed McGivern was a high-speed revolver shooter in the 1930s, whose times were neither matched nor surpassed until Jerry Miculek came along. Ed favored a plain black blade with a gold bead on it. While Jerry is faster than Ed ever was, he favors the same sights.

If you want color and lots of it, then Mag-na-Port offers replacement front sights that are all color. Made from a tough plastic, the whole blade is orange, red, green, blue or pink. You can shape the sight with a file, to make it a ramp or a post.

You can get sights in red, white and blue, with dots and bars (although no stars) and even sights that glow in the dark. Use what improves your shooting, and don't be afraid to ask to try someone else's handgun to see what his sights are like.

INSTALLING SIGHTS

There are four ways front sights are attached to a handgun: 1) forged as part of the slide or barrel, 2) fitted in a dovetail, 3) staked to the slide, or 4) pinned to the slide or barrel. Rear sights are a) attached as a permanent part of the frame or slide, b) fitted in a dovetail, or c) produced as part of an adjustable sight assembly. You must know how your sights are attached before you order any new ones.

A special note of caution when installing night sights: handguns with permanently attached sights must be shipped to the night sight manufacturer for installation. It is therefore especially important that you know how your sights are attached in order to purchase the correct replacements.

While you could use a hand file to low-mount some sights, a mill is by far the better tool.

FRONT SIGHTS

PERMANENT

Permanent front sights can be found on fixed-sight revolvers and some Smith & Wesson, Beretta and Taurus pistols. These can be painted, or if the blade is large enough you can send them off to the night sight manufacturer to have the blade drilled for the tritium insert. If your front sight is not .125 inch wide, it cannot be drilled.

If you are repairing a permanent front sight you can weld it.

Replacing a fixed front sight on a revolver requires a milling machine. You will have to mill the barrel for either the Clark or Novak dovetail, fit the sight, and then shoot the handgun to fine-tune the front sight height. (see milling chart).

When replacing a fixed front sight on a pistol, you can mill a dovetail, or on the case of the 1911, use the Millett Dual-Crimp system. To install the Dual-Crimp sight, use the fixture in the Dual-Crimp kit and drill a pair of holes through your slide. The two cups of the sight will fit these holes. With the Dual-Crimp tool, you then expand the skirts of the two cups on the sight, inside the slide. The older crimping tools would only expand the skirts of Dual-Crimp sights. The newer tools have replacement jaws, and can be used to stake regular 1911 sights.

Some pistols, such as the Beretta or Taurus, do not have enough metal at the front of the slide to mill for a new sight. You must either paint the existing sight or use a Millett Accurizer.

The Millett Accurizer sight fits over the regular blade, and is held on with a cross pin through a hole you drill through the old sight. The Accurizer has two set screws that bear against the barrel. As the action closes up, these two screws push the barrel into a consistent position in the front of the slide.

DOVETAIL

Dovetailed front sights are easy. If your handgun came from the manufacturer with a dovetailed front sight, then you order a new sight for that model.

Custom 1911 slides are commonly made with a Novak front sight dovetail. Measure your current front sight, and order one the same height or taller. Use the brass drift and hammer, or a sight adjustment tool, to remove the old sight. Check the new one for fit. If it is too tight, use a safe-edge three-sided file on the dovetail extension of the sight until you can start it into the slide. Do not over-file the dovetail. If you make the fit loose, you have to either tighten the slot on the slide, or buy a new sight.

A standard front sight, soon to be changed to a Millett Dual-Crimp front sight.

Clamp the sight and rotate the slide to one side or the other.

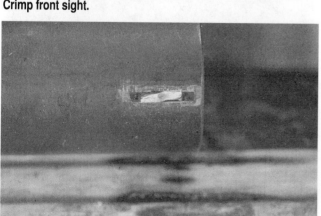

The front sight has broken free, sight is in the vise and the foot of the tenon still in the slide.

Use a narrow tapered punch to drive the foot of the tenon out of the slide.

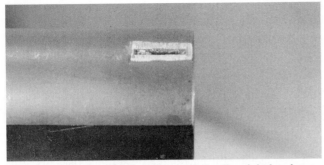

Here is the standard front sight tenon after the sight has been removed.

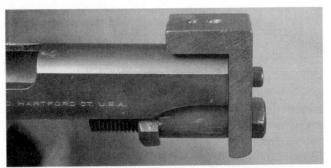

Clamp the drilling fixture to the slide, and drill the two holes with a carbide drill.

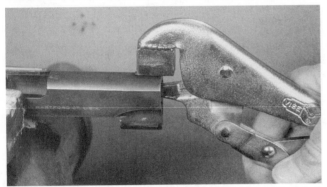

Use the crimping tool to crimp the sight skirts into the beveled holes in the slide.

Here is the Millett Dual-Crimp front sight attached to the slide.

To tighten the slot, use a centerpunch to punch a row of spots on the bottom center of the dovetail. If this is not enough to tighten the fit, use a steel drift punch and a ball peen hammer to bend down the top edges of the dovetail, ONLY in the center. The new front sight blade will cover the bends.

If this is still not enough, you must buy a new front sight and exercise more care in filing it to fit.

Once you can press the sight a third of the way into the slot, you are ready to use the hammer. Place the punch against the dovetail extension of the sight, and not on the sight body itself. If you pound on the sight itself you may bend it. In the case of night sights you may crack the tritium element in the sight, and lose that cheery nighttime glow.

Drift the sights until it is on the centerline of the slide. Test fire to determine that you have the handgun zeroed. If not, make the necessary calculations and then adjust.

If you have a slide that is not milled for the front sight dovetail, then you have found a job for your new mill. If you do not have a mill, find a gunsmith who does. Hand-filing the dovetail is not an option.

This is the Novak dovetail for a front sight.

File the sight until you can press it a third in with your fingers.

STAKED

In this category you will find all 1911s that still have their original front sight tenon arrangement.

The easy way to remove the old sight is to clamp it in

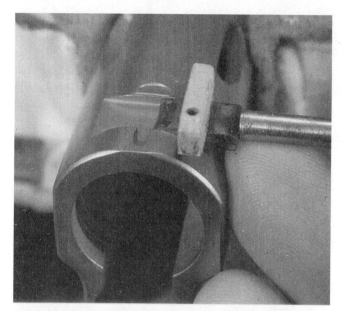

Once the Novak sight will finger-press a third or half of the way in, use a brass drift punch and a hammer to drift it the rest of the way.

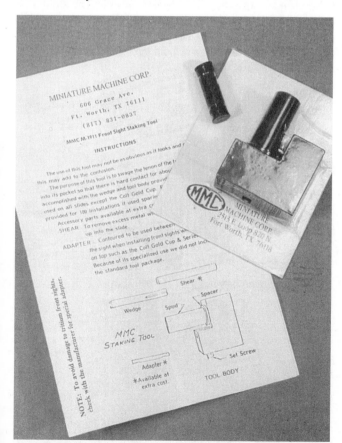

The MMC front sight staking tool comes with complete instructions and a tube of high-pressure grease. Use the grease or you risk wedging the shearing bar in your tool and will not be able to remove it.

the vise, and turn the slide to twist the sight, breaking it from the tenon. Use a tapered punch to drive the tenon out of the slide.

To put the new sight in, you need a front sight-staking tool. The MMC fixture, which is the best, clamps the front sight against the slide. Driving the staking bar into the fixture peens the foot of the tenon. The peened end of the tenon expands into its slot on the slide, holding the sight in place. As mentioned earlier, there are three tenon sizes. Measure yours before ordering a new one, or it will not fit.

When installing night sights, if you simply clamp the front sight using the standard locking screw and brass shim, you will crack the tritium element in the front sight. No tritium, no glow. To allow clamping without cracking, front night sights have two wings on them. If your staking tool pre-dates the introduction of night sights, you will have to make an adapter. File a small piece of steel so it fits into the tool. Then file a slot in this piece of steel, so it ends up in a "U" shape. The "U" takes the place of the brass shim. When you put the feet of the U on the wings of the front sight the bottom of the U must clear the front sight blade.

Clamp the sight against the slide with the "U" upside-down, holding the wings in place. You can now stake without crushing the tritium element.

PINNED

Some Smith & Wesson revolvers and Ruger pistols have the front sight pinned to the barrel or slide. To change it, drive these pins out. Check the new front for fit and file the extension if necessary. Check the size of the hole on the handgun, and select a drill of the same size. Press the sight in place in the slot, and then clamp the barrel or slide in your drill press vise. Drill through the sight using the pre-existing hole as a guide. Drift the pin or pins back in place.

The Novak-style sight on the right uses a cross-ways dovetail slot. The Clark-style sight on the right uses a dovetail in line with the barrel.

A selection of Novak front sights. From the left, an over-sized Glock sight ready to be trimmed down, a Glock dot standard-height, a 1911 oversized for filing, a dot front, a plain front and a gold-bead front.

REAR SIGHTS

PERMANENT

Installing an adjustable rear sight on a revolver with a fixed rear sight involves milling the rear of the frame. It is not reasonable, and in some cases not possible, to do this. The cost of obtaining the sights and either doing, or paying for, the milling can be more than the price jump to a revolver with adjustable sights. Many revolvers with fixed rear sights are rounded so much at the rear sight area of the frame that there is not enough steel in which to mill the sight slot.

This Smith & Wesson front sight is pinned to the barrel. It can be easily replaced. Some sights are an integral part of the barrel and are not easy to replace.

The traditional front sight on a 1911 has a tenon that sticks through a slot cut in the slide. The tenon fits into the slot and the bottom of the tenon, inside the slide, is swaged to wedge the sight into place.

Once the sight is inserted in the slot, the MMC swaging tool is placed on the slide, and the sight protector is placed onto the sight. Tighten the top screw to hold the sight in place.

Place the swaging bar into the fixture.

And drive the swaging bar through the fixture.

If you have a fixed-sight revolver, and want the same one with adjustable sights, trade the old one in for a new one.

Permanent rear sights can have night sights installed, but only by the sight manufacturer.

DOVETAIL

The dovetail rear sight is the easiest sight to swap. Drive out the old rear sight, fit the new rear sight by filing its dovetail, and drift it in place. Test-fire and adjust if you need to.

The King's and Novak Competition Hi-mount for the 1911 are fixed sights that will fit the dovetail with a little bit of filing, and still use the original front sight. That is, if the front sight is one of the latest production, at least .180 inches high. If you have one of the older Colt's with a narrow little sliver of a sight, you'll have to change the front sight, too.

If you want an adjustable rear sight that uses the current front sight, then a low-mount rear such as the Mec-Gar or Pachmayr sights are just the ticket. In addition to the 1911, these are available for your Glock, SIG, Ruger or Smith & Wesson.

The Bo-Mar BMCS-2 fits into the standard rear dovetail of a 1911. However, where the Mec-Gar and Pachmayr sights use the standard front sight, the Bo-Mar requires a front sight that is .280 inch high, compared to the standard sight at .180 inch.

Another adjustable rear sight that fits into the standard dovetail is the Millett. The Millett needs an even taller front sight, .312 inch. If experience shows you that this taller front sight will not stay on your pistol, Millett makes front sights in their Dual-Crimp configuration. These do not come off of a pistol.

If you want a full-size rear sight that is adjustable, but does not use a higher than normal front sight, you will have to mill the rear of your slide.

This modification began with the early IPSC shooters. Bullseye shooters didn't need a low-mounted sight.

A Kings low-mount sight fits the standard 1911 rear dovetail and uses front sights .180 to .200 inches high.

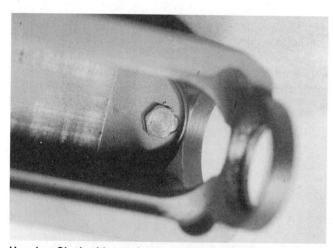

Here is a Glock with a replacement front sight, showing the sight nut. This nut must be tight, and locked in place with a thread-sealer, or it will shoot loose.

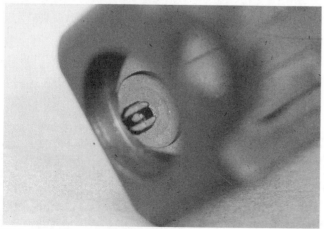

To remove the old Glock front, use a sharp dental pick to pry the wedge out of the sight.

A Bo-Mar "bar-dot" night sight. Standard three-dot night sights can be misaligned when shooting. If you place the dots 1-3-2 or 2-1-3 instead of 1-2-3, you will miss to the side. With the bar-dot, you place your front dot over the rear bar, and you will be lined up.

For shooters who do not want to have their slides milled, Novaks makes a high-mount rear sight. It fits the standard 1911 dovetail and uses a front sight from .180 to .200 inches high.

Their pistols sat in a hard pistol case until it was time to shoot at the range. The height of the sights, either in the case, or on the line, was not a problem. Unlike Bull's-eye competitions, IPSC shooters had to start each string of fire from the holster. Drawing the customary undercut (and large) front blade would often leave ribbons of leather on the front sight, making shooting difficult. By milling the rear of the slide and mounting the rear sight lower, IPSC shooters could then use a lower front sight.

Shortly after lowering, shooters also began "melting" the rear sight. By beveling, or rounding, all the sharp edges of their sights, shooters found they no longer bled all over their pistols just from handling them.

The Mec-Gar low adjustable sight uses the standard front sight.

A standard Bo-Mar BMCS rear sight on a 1911 slide. A lower, more durable and more elegant adjustable rear sight cannot be found.

The Pachmayr adjustable rear sight on a Glock. It uses the standard-height front sight.

Here we see the distinctive wedge shape of the Novak low-mount rear sight.

The Mec-Gar high adjustable requires a replacement front sight, higher than normal.

The Novak low-mount rear sight from the shooters viewpoint. You could almost use it as a hammer to drive nails, and not hurt it.

Use a safe-edge three-sided file to adjust the new dovetail for a sight.

Even though it is not adjustable, the Novak Low-mount rear sight requires milling. The sight itself is larger than a standard sight. Because it is lowered into the slide in a dovetail it does not require a higher front sight. The Novak rear dovetail was quickly accepted by shooters — so much so that Smith & Wesson had Wayne Novak design a set of rear sights for their pistols. These sights were proportioned to the slide of each series, so a small pistol would not have large sights, and vice versa. If you are replacing a rear sight of the Novak design with another Novak design, you must make sure you specify which handgun you have. Otherwise you could end up with the wrong one.

While they are strong, and can be drifted in their dovetail, the Novak sights are not adjustable. An adjustable sight that fits the Novak dovetail is the MMC. Rather than designing a new dovetail, MMC decided to take advantage of the wide acceptance of the Novak dovetail.

Another adjustable sight that requires milling is the Bo Mar. It uses a different dovetail than the Novak. The oldest adjustable sight still around for pistols, and used by many shooters, it requires more elaborate milling than the Novak dovetail does.

To low-mount the Millett adjustable sight you will have to mill a dovetail different from the others. You will be able to use a standard-height front sight with the Millett low-mount installation.

ADJUSTABLE ASSEMBLY

If your pistol or revolver already has an adjustable rear sight, you can simply swap it for another assembly. To change a Smith & Wesson revolver from a plain black rear sight to a white outline, you only need to unscrew the front locking screw, slide the assembly out, and slide in a new Smith & Wesson or Millett sight. Handguns do not all use the same height rear blade. Be sure and specify the model, caliber and barrel length when ordering.

REAR SIGHT REPLACEMENT ON THE SMITH & WESSON

Replacing the blade alone is less expensive than the

whole assembly. If your rear sight is not damaged, but you want to replace the plain blade with a white outline one, the details are in Chapter 6.

RECENT DEVELOPMENTS IN SIGHTS

Red-dot sights offer two great advantages over iron sights: much greater speed of shooting, and no loss of accuracy. These advantages are so great the organizing bodies of handgun competition have had to split their matches into two categories, iron sights and optical.

Being human, competitive shooters want sights that qualify as iron but afford them the speed of optics. One of the disadvantages of iron sights is that they obscure the lower half of the target, slowing down aiming. If an iron sight could be designed that would not obscure the target, it would be a faster sight. Creative minds have been re-visiting the idea of sights, looking for a better iron design.

D.R. Middlebrooks has a nifty offering: a rear sight with a large ring, and a front sight that's a tall post with a bead on it. Inside the rear ring is a clear plastic disk with a small circle on it. At close range, say during an IPSC match, you put the front bead inside the rear ring, and don't worry about the small circle. For a precise shot, you place the bead inside the small circle. While it is available only to fit a Bo-mar rear dovetail, D.R. Middlebrooks is working on other dovetail dimensions.

Matt Waki began by modifying the Bo-mar rear sight until he ended up with just a skeleton. The Matt Waki

On the left the Novak low-mount, on the right an MMC adjustable. They fit the same dovetail on a 1911 slide.

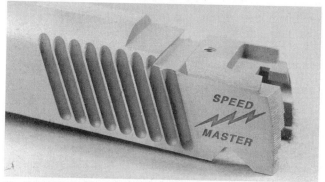

The Speed Master slide includes the vertical adjustment screw hole. Slide your sight in, screw it down and its off to the range.

The MMC adjustable sight for the 1911 fits in a Novak rear sight dovetail. Available plain, three dot or night sight, you have to mill your slide to install it.

If you drop your handgun you are likely to damage or break the sights.

The Bo-Mar rear sight dovetail requires several machining cuts. This "fenced" Bo-Mar cut is even more involved. The small rear sidewalls enclose the rear windage adjustment unit.

Combat sight has a rear blade that's been slotted, to let you see the target, but retains the edges needed to align the front and rear sight. While the Waki sight can be used with a regular front blade, you can gain even more speed by using a front sight with a dot or bead on it. Rather than slot steel blades for a Bo-mar sight base, Matt simply molds his sights out of a durable plastic.

To install either of these sights, simply unscrew the Bo-mar adjustment screw and lift up the hinged half of the sight. Unscrew the locking screw and slide the old sight off. Slide the new one on, and secure the holding screw. You will definitely need a higher front sight for the Middlebrooks sight. The Waki sight may not need a new front, unless you want to try a front sight with a dot for greater speed.

A development that has swept many other options away is the fiber optic sight. The fiber optic sight starts as a plain steel front sight blade. The blade is drilled lengthwise for a fiber optic tube. The center of the blade is notched or relieved to expose the tube to ambient light. The fiber optic tube collects light striking its surface. Because of its optical properties, light cannot escape through the sidewalls, only the ends. The result is a glowing dot in your front sight. The advantages

MMC adjustable sights are available for a variety of handguns.

Here a slide is locked in the mill, ready to have a dovetail cut for a rear sight.

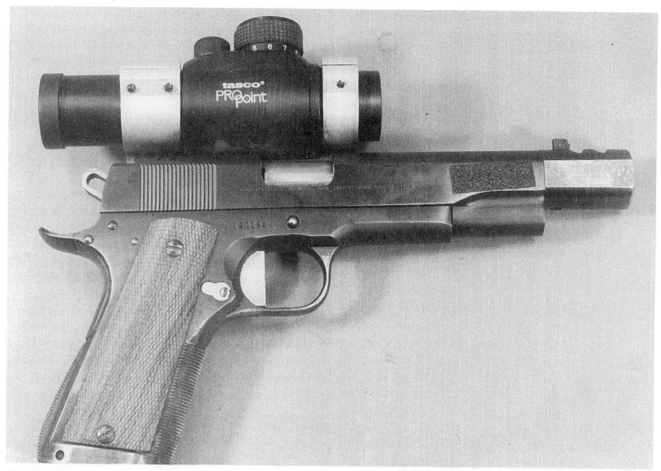

Red-dot sights are very popular for competition, but battery performance in cold weather limits their use in hunting.

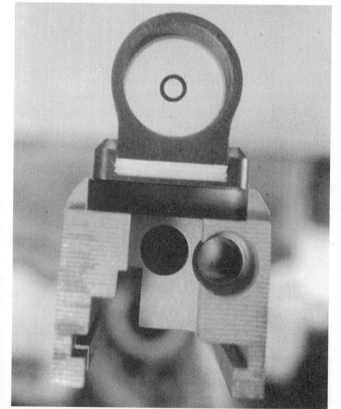

The shooters-view of the Middlebrooks sight. The front sight is a fluorescent dot. Place the dot in the ring, and your sights are lined up. Very fast, but still accurate.

The Middlebrooks sight fits a standard Bo-Mar dovetail cut.

The Waki Combat sight from Matt Waki. It fits the Bo-Mar dovetail without fences.

From the shooters viewpoint, the Waki sight is simple. Put the front dot at the center of the three bars and your sights are lined up.

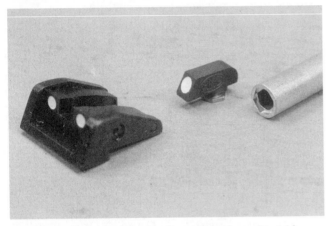

This MMC sight set for the Glock consists of an adjustable rear, a replacement front, and a special tool to turn the bolt that tightens the front sight nut.

are speed and automatic adjustment of brightness. At close range, or for a fast, wide-open shot, the dot itself is enough of an aiming point (that is, if your "index" is proper and you practice at it). As the ambient light changes, so does the dot intensity. You aren't faced with a non-adjusting dot if the clouds roll in or out.

Fiber optic sights have become almost ubiquitous on the practical shooting circuit, so much so that dinosaurs such as I who still use plain black iron sights are sometimes looked at pityingly by other shooters. That is, until we turn in fast times and high points scores on stages. Still, fiber optic sights have become so common in matches that they are now starting to show up on non-match guns, in catalogs and gun-shop counters.

The one drawback they have is fragility. If hit hard enough, the small fiber-optic tube can break. The sight still works as a sight, and you can replace the tube, but for the moment your dot advantage has gone away. Match shooters commonly have a spare section of fiber optic rod in their gear bags. It is the work of a minute or two on the range, in a Safe Area, to cut a new length off that rod, heat the tip, insert it into the sight, heat the other end, and get back to the squad as they walk to the next stage.

RIBS FOR SIGHTS

Bull barrels do not come with sights; you must install them yourself. Just as the barrels are precise, the sights must be precisely adjustable.

Most gunsmiths drill and tap the barrel and install a sight rib. Available from Aristocrat and Ron Power, the sight rib is a single bar containing both front and rear sights. Ribs commonly offer quickly adjustable specific sight settings and are useful in competitions with fixed

The Power rib has four settings for the rear sight.

Low-mount sights are milled into the slide, like these two Novak sights.

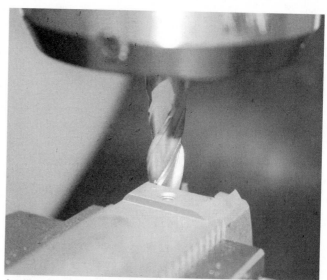

A mill makes short work of a Bomar installation, and is an absolute must if you want a "fenced" install, as here.

On the right is the original (now out of production) low-mount Novak sight, with its flat rear surface. On the left, the newer design, with a recess for the rear notch.

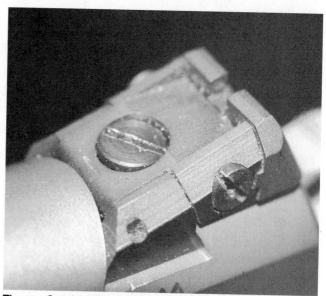

The new Caspian adjustable sight fits Novak dovetails.

This Smith & Wesson is a tack-driver, with a slicked-up trigger pull, Barnett barrel and Aristocrat rib.

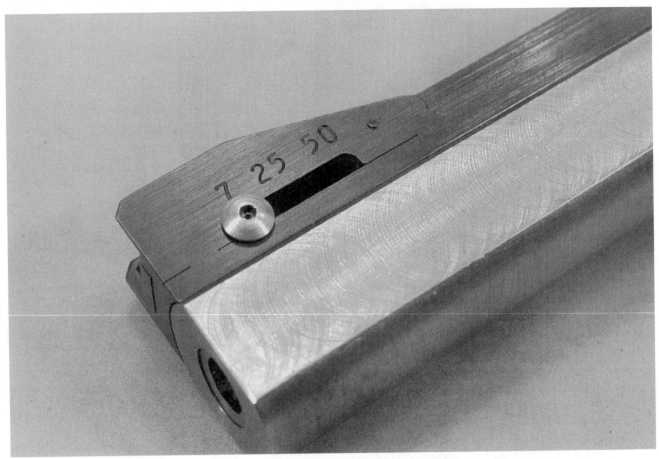

This Aristocrat rib uses a sliding button on the front to set the sight for 7, 25 and 50 yards.

firing distances. The Aristocrat Custom has a sliding button on the front left side that allows the shooter to select from three settings. The Power Double Grand Master has four settings in the rear. By moving a knurled wheel you can quickly set the rear sight for one of four different distances.

Bo-Mar also makes revolver ribs. Their design, however, fits over the standard barrel, not a bull barrel.

Ron Power offers some of his barrels drilled and tapped for his rib. If you want to install the Aristocrat rib you will have to drill and tap your barrel. You will need the correct size drill and tap for the sight rib screws, and a hole-centering locating punch.

Take the rib and center it on the top of the barrel. Make sure it is flush with the muzzle. With a piece of masking tape attach it to the top of the barrel. Hold the revolver up in your firing position, and look at the rib. Are the sights vertical? If the rib doesn't look right, it isn't. Adjust the rib and tape it again. Once the rib is vertical, mark the rib holes for drilling and tapping.

If you have used a Ron Power barrel that is already drilled and tapped, use one screw to hold the rib in place while you check its vertical alignment. If the rib is not straight up and down, you must adjust by turning the barrel.

On the untapped barrel, after you have marked your hole locations, use a #31 drill and a 6-48 tap. The holes do not have to be more than .150 inch deep.

Install the rib and tighten the screws. Your bull barrel is ready for shooting.

CHAPTER

GRIPS: SOMETHING TO HOLD ON TO

You have to have some part of the handgun to grasp when you shoot. Luckily, handgun designers are aware of this and have created grips. There is just one problem in all this: shooters still insist on having different sizes and shapes of hands. If we would all settle on a single hand size, the problem of correct grip design would solve itself. Not likely, I know. Even Glock, a company that managed to figure out a way to dispense with grip panels, found that they had to offer different size grips if for no other reason than to accommodate different calibers. As a result, you may find one frame/caliber fitting your hand better than another. It is far easier to

buy another handgun, or replacement grips, than it is to acquire different hands.

Faced with the dilemma of different sized hands, pistol designers have created many types of grips for many types of hands. If you are not the proud possessor of an average hand, take heart; the variety and availability of handgun grips is legion. Look at grip/hand variation as an opportunity, and feel free to change grips to whatever feels good or looks good to you.

The material used in making grips is limited only by the imagination and skills of the person making them. Some of the better-known materials are wood, plastic, rubber, pearl, ivory, bone, horn, metal and Micarta.

Easily shaped and modified, warm, durable, and comfortable to the hand, wood has always been the traditional grip material. Its many positives have only recently been overshadowed by cost and environmental considerations. Now, while some makers still turn out wood grips, many others have turned to rubber or plastic. Smith & Wesson, for example, no longer ships any handguns with wood grips. All their revolvers come with rubber grips. All their pistols have had plastic grips on them since the early 1980s.

When synthetic grips first came out, many shooters were cool to them. It was only after word spread about

The Miculek grips provide a smooth surface for a fast draw, while the filler behind the trigger guard protects your second finger.

The Navidrex grips for the Browning Hi-Power turn a 2x4-feeling grip into a comfortable and secure grip. At least for me, and everyone I've handed this gun to.

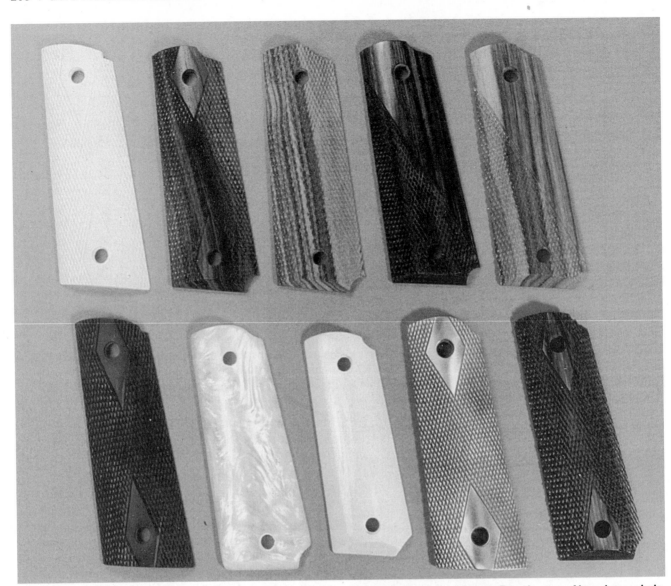

Top to bottom, left to right: An Ajax ivory-epoxy, Ahrends rosewood, Ahrends cocobolo, Ahrends French green, Ahrends cocobolo semi-checkered, Navidrex Ebony, Ajax pearl, Ajax smooth ivory-epoxy, Ajax pewter, Ajax rosewood.

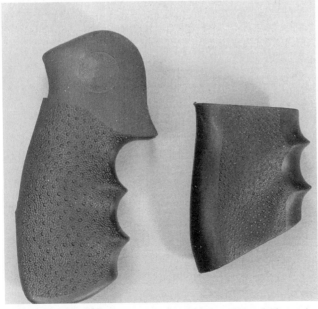

Hogue makes Monogrips in rubber, and also slip-on grip adapters for all the common pistols.

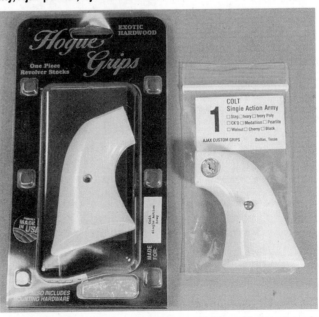

Hogue and Ajax both offer ivory-epoxy mix grips. They look and feel like the real thing, but at a fraction of the cost.

the comfort and recoil reduction of rubber that "basic black" grips gained acceptance.

Early wooden revolver grips were designed to be narrow at the top and wide at the bottom. The only way you could use them comfortably was by firing slowly with only one hand. Which, come to think of it, was the way most competitive shooters fired a handgun for the first eight decades of the 20th century.

The design was not useful or fun when shooting double-action, or using hard-kicking magnum loads. The grips tapered the wrong way. Heavy recoil caused them to slide right out of your hand, driving the muzzle upwards. When Smith & Wesson switched to rubber grips for their revolvers they reversed the taper. Now wide at the top and narrow at the bottom, with palm swells and finger grooves, most shooters can comfortably lock their hands to these grips.

If your grips don't fit you perfectly, there are minor variations in the dimensions and contours of the rubber grips from Smith, Pachmayr, Hogue and Uncle Mikes. It is worth investigation to see if other members of your gun club have these grips on their guns. If so, you should try them out. You will greatly improve your shooting enjoyment with properly fitting grips.

Pearl grips still suffer from the same social stigma that nickel once did. To quote General George S. Patton: "Only a pimp from a cheap New Orleans whorehouse would have pearl grips on his pistol!" (I guess the expensive whorehouse pimps used ivory, as did the General.) The stigma against pearl does not keep shooters from buying pearl, or synthetic pearl grips. In some applications I must confess that even I can find pearl attractive. Real pearl is expensive and fragile. Synthetic pearl is neither.

Ivory was always the socially acceptable fancy grip material. Where a gentleman a century ago would never be seen with pearl grips on his pocket pistol, ivory was considered perfectly proper. Today ivory cannot be com-

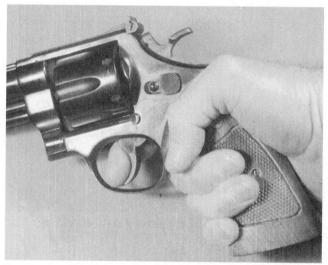

Traditional grips, flared at the bottom, push your little finger forward...

while the Miculek grip tapers down, so your little finger can get a grip. (Note the location of my little finger tip, compared to the next finger, on both grips.

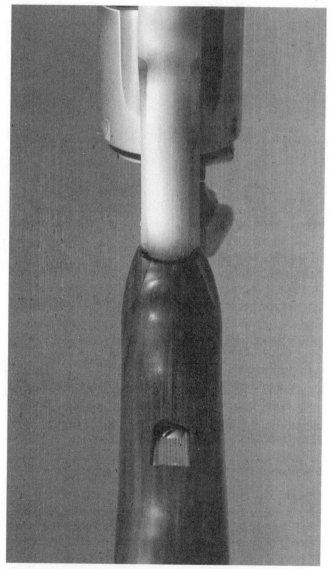

Here is the view underneath the grips, showing the shelf behind the trigger guard.

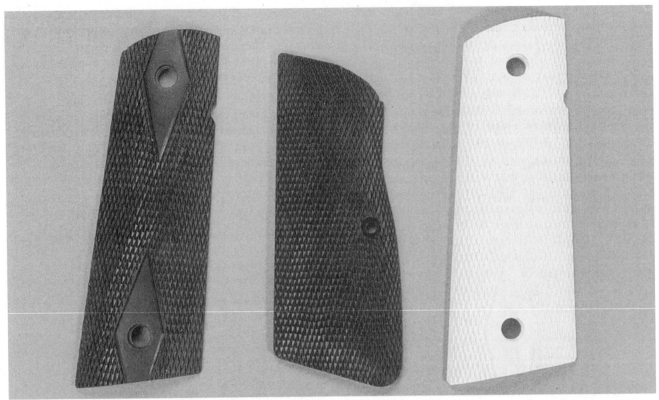

The black grips are Navidrex ebony grips, the white grip is an ivory-epoxy grip from Ajax.

The Navidrex grips make a big difference on the Browning Hi-Power. On the left are the standard, portly grips. On the right are the Navidrex grips.

Not only are the Navidrex grips thinner, they are sculpted. The Ebony Navidrex grips in front, compared to a standard pair of grips in the rear.

mercially imported into the United States. One of the few ways to get real ivory grips is to go on safari and shoot your own elephant. Have a part of the tusks turned into grips.

Manufacturers such as Hogue and Ajax offer ivory polymer. The sawdust and filings from ivory and bone are mixed with epoxy and cast into the shape of grips. It looks like ivory, it feels like ivory, but no one has to shoot an elephant to get it. With age and handling, real ivory will turn yellow. It will also crack, but not enough to weaken the grips. While the ivory polymer will yellow, it will not crack.

Made out of antlers, stag grips have been a favorite choice for single-action revolvers for over a century. The surface offers a non-slip texture and a rustic look favored by quite a few shooters. I am not particularly warm to stag grips, but some of them can be attractive, and when they are I prefer them on a single-action revolver. On a pistol I usually find them too thick for comfortable shooting, but if I could find stag grips thin

enough I would use them. Their non-slip texture is as effective as checkering, and less prone to wear. If you want your pistol to feel larger and rounder, stag will do well for you.

Grips made of metal can be steel, brass, aluminum or pewter. Metal grips add weight to the pistol, dampening recoil. They can be checkered, engraved, and even plated. Ajax offers pewter grips in several designs, and even plates them with gold on demand.

One new grips come from Techwell and Alumagrip. They are made of aluminum, and if you simply want aluminum grips to replace the grips on your 1911, then Alumagrips has them. The Techwell ones are Alumagrips with an integral mag funnel. Clamping the grips on also traps the mag well in place. As a means of getting sharp-looking grips out of a tough material and adding a mag well, Techwell is the option.

Micarta is the trademark name for a product manufactured by layering cloth or paper and saturating it with epoxy. The resulting product is tough, durable, and impervious to oils and solvents. It is easily shaped. By adding dye to the epoxy, or layering different colors of cloth or paper, Micarta can be produced in all the colors of the rainbow. In an off-white color, Micarta can look like ivory, with much greater durability. In a jet-black color, Micarta looks very much like ebony.

Some pistols do not have grips at all, or do not need the grips that are available for them. Many competition shooters remove the grips from their Para Ordnance or Caspian Hi-Cap frames, using only skateboard tape to provide a non-slip gripping surface. On the STI and Infinity guns, they even apply a belt sander or file to the plastic portion of the frame, and grind it until the shape fits their hand. All the models of Glock pistols, the Ruger P-95, and the STI/SVI pistols have polymer frames or polymer-steel composite frames, and do not need grips. The non-slip checkering that would be on grips is cast right into the frame. What appear to be grip screws on the STI and SVI frames are not. The lower ones, if they are present at all, are purely cosmetic. The upper ones hold the plastic magazine housing to the upper (steel) rails assembly.

The checkering cast into the polymer is not aggressive enough for some shooters. As soon as the Glock appeared, shooters experimented with rubber bands and sections of inner tube, looking for a stickier surface or a more comfortable grip. When grip manufacturers saw this new market, they began offering cast rubber tubing to slip over the "grips" of these pistols.

Also, the frames of some Glock models are too large, and there are manufacturers and gunsmiths who specialize in reshaping them to a more human contour.

WHAT TO LOOK FOR

When buying replacement grips you should look for four things: performance, comfort, appearance and pride of ownership.

The performance of a given set of grips can be measured by how much they improve your ability to shoot your handgun. I find the shape of the Browning Hi-Power extremely comfortable, but the hammer used to bite my hand so badly I could not shoot the pistol. With Navidrex or Spegel grips, the Browning Hi-Power became so comfortable to hold, and its pointing qualities were so improved that I solved the hammer-bite problem just so I could use the grips!

The World's Best Revolver Shooter, Jerry Miculek, has designed a set of revolver grips. Since Jerry can shoot a revolver so quickly, and so accurately, that most shooters with pistols cannot keep up with him, I thought it only prudent to try his new design the very nanosecond I heard of them. I was not disappointed. Like Navidrex

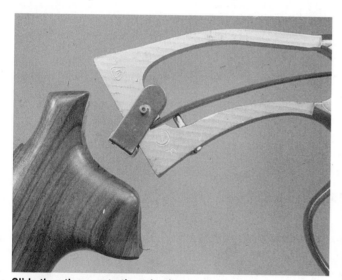

Slide the stirrup onto the grip slot.

Monogrips use a single screw on the bottom.

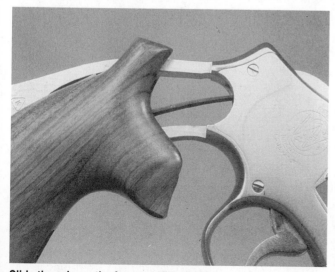

Slide the grip up the frame until it stops.

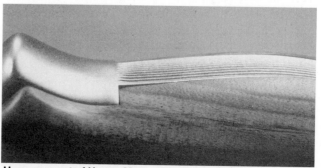

Here are a set of Hogue Monogrips that perfectly match the contours of the frame.

or Spegel grips do for the Hi-Power, Jerry's grips greatly improve the hand comfort and pointing qualities of the revolver. Gently curved, and without either taper or checkering, these grips have the curve behind the trigger guard filled with a wide, flat section. The filler protects your second finger from the trigger guard under recoil, and the width gives the grip stability in your hand. Even though the grips do not have an apparent reverse taper to them, they do not slide through your hand under recoil. The smooth surface keeps the draw as fluid and fast as possible, though you can checker it if you want. The most important thing about these grips? When I used them, my times improved noticeably. That's performance, and it's different for every shooter. I'd think it would be obvious, but it bears noting: when you find something that improves your performance, in a measurable way, use it.

In the search for comfort, many shooters select grips that are too large for them. A grip that is too large often feels comfortable at first, but holding an overly large grip will tire your hands quickly. Shooters with small hands have a particular problem — everything is too large.

With revolvers, shooters with smaller hands can select a model that has a round-butt frame. Smith & Wesson at one time had the idea to offer all their revolvers in a round-butt version. I thought it clever, and so did a lot of other shooters. But not all. S&W went back to offering models with square-butt frames, just because enough people wanted them, and were willing to demonstrate their desire by buying square-butt framed revolvers. Ruger revolvers offer an even better chance at finding the proper grip size. Since the frame inside the grips is just a post on some Ruger models, you can carve wood grips down without worrying about hitting the frame. Make them as small as you need. For the smallest size on other revolvers, select a "boot grip" design, intended for round-butt revolvers used in concealed carry. At first glance they appear entirely too small to be useful, but once you find the right size for your hand, the design works very well. The subtleties of contour on a boot grip are very important. When you go to buy one,

Grip thickness makes a difference in the pistols feel. The standard grips on the left, the Navidrex grips in the center, and the slimmest of all, the AFS Tech on the right.

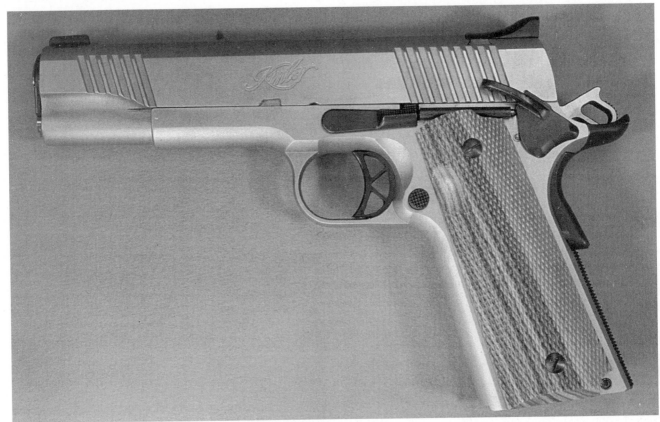

Nothing sets off an elegant pistol like a classy set of custom grips.

take your revolver along with you to the gunshop. Try every design available. Or, try other gun club members snubbies. If it is that important to you, organize a special snubbie-only match, and let everyone handle everyone else's snubbies.

For pistols, you can select smaller than normal grips, or select a smaller pistol. Slimline grips are available for the 1911 from AFS Tech and Navidrex. The difference in size between these and standard grips is quite noticeable. They can make the grip area so much smaller that I find it difficult to use a pistol with these grips; it doesn't sit quite right in my hand.

A smaller pistol usually means a smaller caliber. If you don't want to go to a smaller caliber, the only way I know to get a smaller pistol frame and keep the big caliber is through the Gunsite Custom Shop. They'll shave fractions of an inch off of the entire circumference of the grip area of the frame of a 1911, creating the Gunsite Custom Shop Slimline 1911. It is expensive and delicate surgery, and for most shooters slimmer grips will do nicely.

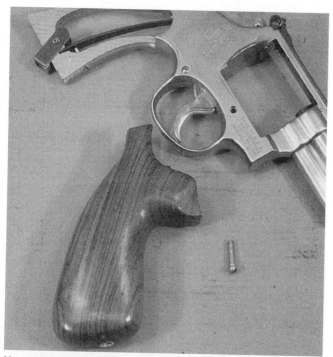

Hogue Monogrips are one-piece grips of wood or rubber.

If you are looking for recoil reduction in your grips, Pachmayr makes their rubber grips out of a synthetic selected for its softness. It's called Decelerator. On a rifle or shotgun recoil pad, Decelerator is amazingly soft and resilient. While the handgun grips are thinner than shotgun recoil pads, they work very well at taking the sting out of the recoil of magnum loads. The Decelerators are available for all the common designs and models.

And one benefit of rubber grips is the ease with which you can modify them. I found that I preferred revolver grips that were not round, but rectangular. Similar in shape to a pistol frame. I could get the shape I wanted by cutting the rear of the grips off, where they covered the backstrap of my ICORE revolvers. With the modified grips I could shoot faster, always important in ICORE shooting.

Appearance and pride of ownership are very important to some people, and not at all to others. I have gone through several shifts in my worldview, and find myself now seriously considering exotic woods and ivory as being entirely suitable for grip material. Before the 1970s such choices were not even available, unless you happened to know both a source of exotic woods and a craftsman who could make grips for you.

Now, you can get exotic wood grips from Bill Wilson and Kim Ahrends. Bill offers half a dozen different woods. Kim offers a dozen, and they are spectacular! Just reading the names gets you thinking about your handgun in a whole new way. There's Mayan Bloodwood, Pink Ivory, Snakewood, Lignum Vitae, to name a few. There are grip snobs, just as there are handgun snobs, finish snobs and ammunition snobs. If you have one or more at your gun club, you can easily keep up with the Joneses by getting some exotics grips from Kim and "letting" the snobs notice. For those interested in performance, and who cares about looks, the "Burner Grips" from Jerry Barnhart are slick. Well, actually they are the opposite of slick. Each grip base is coated with a special mixture of epoxy and abrasive. Instead of a sheet of skateboard tape that can wear, come loose when hit with solvents or curl at the edges, the solid coating of the Burner grips stay put. If they wear, the wear simply exposes a fresh surface of abrasive-containing epoxy. If the

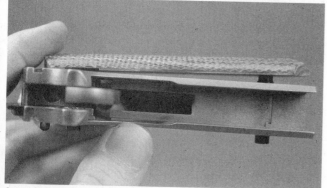

Sometimes your grips will not quite fit over the grip screw bushings. Use a carbide cutter in your hand-held grinder to provide clearance.

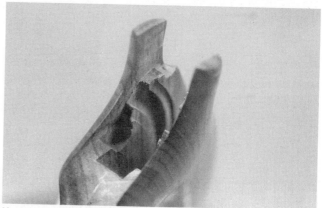

Here is the slot that the grip stirrup must follow to the bottom.

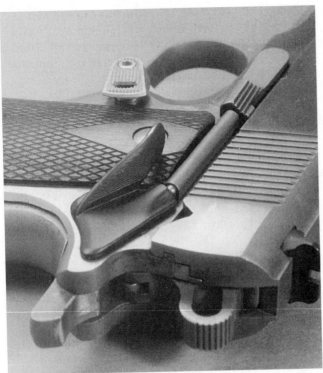

For small hands, a lowered thumb safety from Gunsite Custom Shop can make even a .45 manageable.

Once on the frame, the grips look like any other, except they are non-skid.

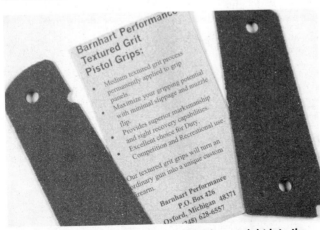

The Barnhart grips come with no-skid grit cast right into the surface. Even as it wears it still grips, as fresh surface is exposed.

grit gets loaded up with abraded skin, dirt, dust or other gunk, you can scrub the grips clean. And Burner grips are available for a variety of pistols. You could slather a mixture of grit and epoxy on your grips, but getting the application evenly applied would be a problem. And getting the mix evenly distributed, so you don't have slick spots from bare epoxy is not easy. I know, I tried. I'll admit it; sometimes I like to save money. So I tried mixing up epoxy and grit. I tried epoxy, and then sprinkling grit. I tried a lot of things. In the end, I concluded that it is simply easier to get the grips from Jerry. He figured out how to make it work, you wouldn't save much money anyway, and he deserves to profit from his R&D.

Last up in grips are the exotic synthetics. Various iterations of NASA-grade plastic, like G-10, are now very hot. Grip companies like VZ Grips make them, and make them in non-standard non-slip patterns. Instead of checkering, they make grips with vicious-looking slahes cuts across the surface, and the result is a set of grips that you practically have to have assistance to get off your shooting hand.

How do you fit your grips to your handgun? In many cases, very easily.

Fitting most rubber grips, including Pachmayr, is as simple as falling off a small log. Remove the grip screws that hold your grips. Use Pachmayr's replacement screw to bolt on the replacement grips. Check to see that your new grips do not interfere with the hammer spur of your revolver. If you've put Pachmayr grips on a pistol, check the magazine catch and slide stop to see that the grips don't interfere with their function. If they do, use a razor blade or X-Acto knife to slice away just enough rubber to provide clearance.

Pachmayr makes a line of grips that combine the comfort of rubber with the looks of wood. Fitting these, and other grips that leave the backstrap exposed, requires an additional step. After attaching them to the frame, check the fit of the grips to the backstrap. If the grips overlap the frame, the sharp edge will be very uncomfortable.

First, take a sharp pencil and mark the grips by following the edge of the frame, drawing on the exposed part of the grips. Take the grips off the revolver and clamp each panel in a padded vise. Carefully file the edges down to the pencil line you have drawn. There is no need to rush. Check the fit of the grips frequently, and gently file where needed. Once you have the grips almost fitted, use your 400-grit cloth backed with the file to sand the surface smooth and to a perfect fit.

You are done. Seal the wood.

All grips for the 1911, and many other pistols, must fit over the grip screw bushings. Do not force tight-fitting grips into place. Wood grips, especially, are thin, and the extra stress may cause them to crack. Take new, tight-fitting grips off the pistol. Place the grip screws back in the bushings. Flip each grip panel around, placing the outside against the frame. Check the grip screws against the grip screw holes in the grip panel. If the holes are so far off that the one of the screw heads won't even clear the grip screw hole, send the grips back with a note about your problem. Use your dial calipers to determine the distance between the grip screw bushing centers, and send this information along with the note. The grip manufacturer can tell if your pistol needs grips with the holes custom-drilled, or if his grips are off.

If the grips are very close to fitting, and only need a little help, then you can modify them. Use a candle or match to smoke the grip screw bushing. Press the grip on the frame, and then pull it off and look for the carbon deposited on the grip. Use a half-round needle file to open the hole, so the grip can fit over the bushing. Once the grip slides over the main part of the bushing, use your hand-held grinder with a carbide cutter to open the relief cut on the back of the grips.

Traditionally, grips have been two pieces, one on either side of the frame. Guy Hogue designed his one-piece Monogrip, wood or rubber, to slide up over the frame from the bottom.

Hogue Monogrips are much easier to fit than you might think. Remove your present grips. On Smith & Wesson revolvers there is a locating pin in the bottom

of the grip strap that keeps the wood grips from shifting. Your Monogrip attachment will go over this pin, but don't try to spread the attachment to fit. Instead slide the attachment over the frame from an angle. Once one side of the attachment has snapped over the locating pin, slide the attachment vertical to the frame to snap it over the other side of the pin. On revolvers that do not have the pin, Hogue provides one to fit over the bottom strap of the revolver.

Grips must not have sharp edges in the wrong spots. While sharp checkering can be an asset (once your hands become accustomed to the points), sharp edges never are. Hold the handgun in your firing grip. Look closely at the top of the grip near your thumb. Are the edges there sharp? Do they rub against your thumb? Look at the other side, where your trigger finger curls around to the trigger. Is the edge there sharp? Does it touch your finger? All these sharp edges have to be dulled, or knocked down.

While you are checking for edges of the grips that will interfere with your hands, check for function of the other parts of the pistol. Does the safety hit the grip? Extended thumb safeties on the 1911 can stop on the left grip before they have traveled their full downward distance. Ambidextrous safeties can do the same on the right-hand grip panel.

On double-action pistols, or pistols with a decocking lever, check the function of the safety or decocker. Does it travel smoothly, and snap back cleanly? Also check the magazine catch and slide stop.

To remove the sharp edges, use your Swiss pillar file. Once you have the sharp edges removed and the grips clearing the safety and other levers, use some 400-grit cloth with the file as a backer, and polish the edges smooth. If the decocking lever on a DA pistol is

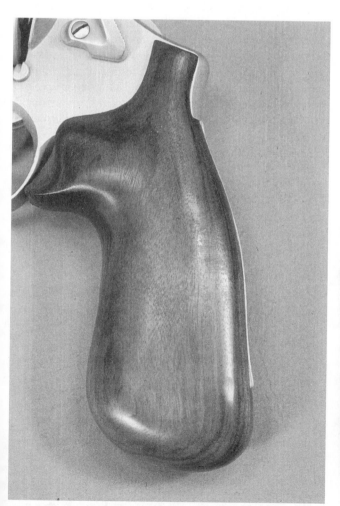

The Miculek grips do not have any checkering on them. The contours keep your hand in place.

Don't be afraid to experiment. These ugly Pachmayr grips met the belt sander and sharp knife, and have since gone on to win me much loot while shooting in ICORE and USPSA matches. One of these days I'll make them pretty. Or not.

You can see that the Navidrex P-35 grips are thinner even than the heavily-worn originals.

not functioning smoothly, use the cloth backed with a file to polish the surface of the wood the lever slides against. When it is smooth, switch to 600-grit cloth. If the grips are wood, seal with Grip Dip or other wood finish. Micarta, plastic, pearl, ivory or ivory polymer grips do not need a sealer. Rubber grips probably don't need the edges filed.

Many grips have a joint between the two halves. If the two sides don't line up perfectly, the gap or ledge can be very uncomfortable. Pachmayr solved this problem by molding the grips as one piece that you flex to fit on the frame. With other grips, check the joint of the two halves all the way around. File and sand the edges to remove any ledges. Grips that are much too large can be filed, see above.

Revolver grips either cover the backstrap or fit flush. Poorly-fitting flush grips can only be fitted if the grips are too high. File them as above. If the grips do not come up to the surface of the frame, you can blend them only by filing the frame. Don't. Instead, send the grips back to the manufacturer with a note about your problem. They can send another set that are up to the frame.

FITTING THE "RUBBER BAND" GRIP ADAPTER

All the grip makers who make rubber grips offer a slide-on grip enhancer. Some of these have finger grooves molded into them. Others are just a rubber sleeve. Both add a rubber non-slip surface to the molded polymer frame of Glocks, the S&W Sigma, Ruger P-95 and other pistols. They can even be slid onto pistols that already use grips, but sliding them over rubber instead of plastic grips is like gilding the lily.

The question on the minds of many shooters who buy slide-on grip enhancers is "How do I install this without destroying it or going crazy?" If you just grab the pistol and the sleeve and try to wrestle them together, you can tear the sleeve. Worse, you can hurt yourself. There is an easier way.

Clamp the pistol upside down, by its slide, in a padded vise. Take the sleeve, and heat it. Use a blow dryer if available, or a pan of hot water if not. The blow dryer is preferred because you can re-heat the sleeve after it is

partway onto the pistol. When you go to slide the sleeve on, work it on by alternating sides down the grip a little bit at a time. If you try to slide too far too fast, you will tear the grip. Don't go more than a quarter of an inch at a time. Don't try to grasp a lot of the sleeve when pulling it on. You will stretch the rubber too much and tear it.

You do not want to use anything under the grip to help it slide. No talcum powder, no Vaseline, no lubricating oil. Once the grip is on, you want it to stay. Lubricants that help you slide the grip on will allow the grip to shift after you are done.

Slide the grip up the frame (down towards the vise), checking the fit, until you get to a point where it feels comfortable. I find that a comfortable spot on the Glock frame ends up with the sleeve so high it interferes with the magazine catch. If this is true for you, too, don't worry. A sharp knife or razor blade cuts away just the part of the sleeve that interferes, allowing it to clear the magazine catch.

POLYMER GRIP REDUCTION

The high-tech grip change for Glock pistols is to fill the hollow rear of the grip section with epoxy or a filler block, and then belt-sand it down to a slimmer configuration. The process is not without its faults. First, the polymer from which Glock makes its frames seems to either have a solvent of some kind in the mix, or the release agent is quite persistent. Getting an epoxy that will bond to the polymer without melting it is not easy. Without a sufficient bond, your filler might break loose when firing or dropped. Second, the conversion voids the warranty. I do not usually worry about voiding a factory warranty. However, Glock pistols have an annoying habit that other pistols do not: they fracture when treated to an overload. I've shot, and seen shot, 1911 pistols that received a double-charged load. Of the bunch, the only one that required a new frame was the lightweight gun with an aluminum alloy frame. The steel frame guns sometimes needed a new magazine but not always, sometimes new grips, one or the other, or nothing but a cleaning. The 10mm that let go when I fired it

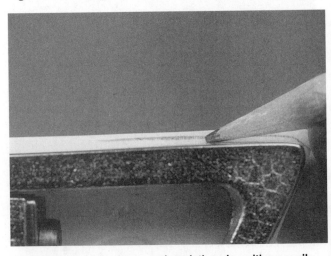

Hold the grips to the frame and mark the edge with a pencil.

didn't even need a replacement magazine. Glocks, on the other hand, fracture.

A modified Glock blown up by handloads is most unlikely to be replaced by the factory.

If you simply must reduce the grip on a Glock, contact Robbie Barrkman at Robar, and he can modify your Glock for you. He can guarantee that his epoxy won't release from the frame.

GRIPS FOR THE SAA

Back when I was first shooting single-action revolvers, our choices were limited. My brother and I would spend our summer vacations at the cabin Up North at our club, rolling tin cans on the rifle range (yes, we walked out to the full 100 yards and dropped them at the base of the backstop) with handguns. Dad made us stop when other club member showed up to sight in their deer rifles. "They don't need the distraction, and they sure don't need to know they can't hit the can you're rolling with their deer rifle, when you can with a handgun." We had our choice of the plain wood grips that came on our Rugers, the worn gutta percha grips on the Colt, or the imitation bone grips with the cast-in steer's head available at the local gun shop. Since we were using full-power .357 and .41 Magnum loads, we didn't want the then-new Pachmayr rubber grips. The gun didn't roll in recoil, and shooting was harder. (Did I mention we were

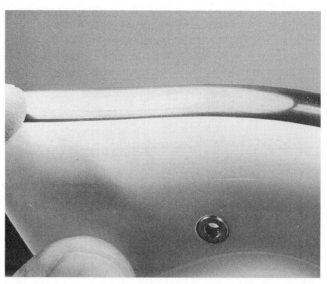

Once you have filed the grips to the line, they should not overlap the frame any more.

shooting one-handed offhand only? What did we know? We were young, IPSC hadn't been officially formed yet, and they were after all handguns)

Now the choices are greater. And the power is too. If you're shooting two-handed, roll is less of a requirement, and control is needed more. You can't just let a .454 Casull whip up in your hand. You can use the full-size Pachmayrs for grip and control.

Cowboy Action shooters have created a renaissance in SAA grips. You can now have someone custom-make them in just about any material you care to mention or can afford. Bone, ivory or Ivorex (an epoxy/polymer and ground ivory combination) rubber, gutta-percha, silver, you name it, someone makes it. Oh yes, wood too. You can get oversized ones and fit them yourself or send your single-action revolver off to someone like Mike Wallace who can custom-fit grips of whatever material you specify. And Cowboy Action shooters tend towards more ornate grips than other competition shooters, since part of their shooting is the dressing. It just doesn't do to have plain guns stuffed into tooled-leather holsters.

Clamp the grips in a padded vise and file to the pencil line.

CHAPTER 15

TIMING AND TUNING YOUR REVOLVER

The Smith & Wesson double-action revolver has been the basis for accurate and smooth-shooting revolvers for more than a century. In the last half of the 20th century the S&W revolver surged ahead of its Colt counterparts partly because S&W offered more support to police departments and competition shooters than did Colt. But also the S&W design is easier to work on than the Colt. As a result, by the late 1970s you could shoot a whole season of PPC, indoors and out, and not see more than a lone Python in the hands of a PPC competition shooter. Even rarer would be a tuned "Moran" Python, made buttery-smooth and light by Jerry Moran. The hundreds or thousands of shooters you'd be rubbing elbows with would all be shooting a K frame S&W.

Today, with less, almost no PPC but lots more IPSC, ICORE, IDPA and Steel shooting being done with revolvers than ever before, you won't even see those rare Moran Pythons. They're far too valuable to be on the range. The only place you'll see the hegemony of S&W broken is on metallic silhouette ranges, where Dan Wesson revolvers chambered in calibers suited to the game rule the roost.

Your hands provide all of the operating power in a revolver. In a single-action, your thumb and trigger finger do the work. In a double-action, your trigger finger has to "shoulder" the entire load.

The chief culprit making this work so difficult (aside from basic anatomy) is friction. The relatively rough

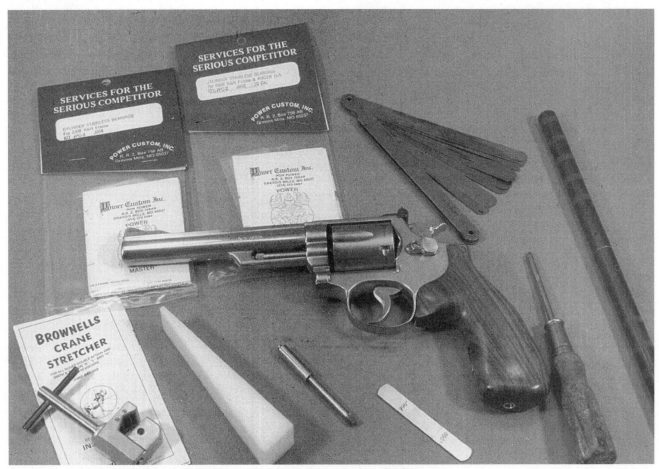

To remove endshake and align the crane on your revolver, you need a few simple tools.

The Ed Brown cylinder release makes high-speed opening a lot easier, is easy to install, and is allowed for almost any competitive class.

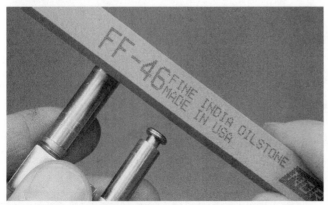

Check cylinder gap with the cylinder pushed back. Record the measurement.

This cylinder is chambered in .45ACP and has the extractor chamfered. Only do this to a .45 ACP revolver. On any other, the chamfered extractor may slip off the cartridge rim and cause a malfunction.

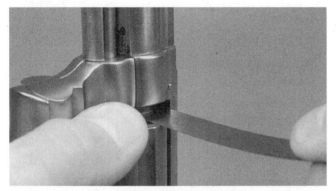

Use a stone to dress down the edges of the line if the crane will not re-enter the cylinder.

surfaces of the working parts and the slots in which they travel work against you in both directions. The friction of the surfaces moving past each other and binding against tool marks, which you may have barely noticed, not only make it tough for your finger to work the action, they also require greater spring tension to move parts.

Remove this friction, and you will improve your action. Here is an overview of the process.

In all revolvers, the main friction points are (1) the cylinder rotating on the centerpin or crane, (2) the hand advancing the cylinder, and (3) the hammer and trigger pivoting on their pins. Double-action revolvers have to reset the mechanism, a task handled by the rebound block. It also adds friction. For all the revolvers covered, there are reduced-power spring kits available; however, you must reduce friction before you can reduce the spring tension. If you reduce the spring tension on your revolver first, the roughness only becomes more apparent.

When you stone parts to remove tool marks and roughness, remember that you must not change the angle of any surface. Rounding off corners never improves an action, and in many cases if you go too far you will end up buying new parts to replace those you have been incorrectly stoning.

The crowning touch to any action job is lubrication. In addition to a synthetic lubricant to protect against oxidation and to keep powder and dirt from hardening on the parts, use a low-drag lubricant such as Chip McCormick's Trigger Job or Brownells Action Magic II on the bearing surfaces. The CMC Trigger Job is very persistent. Once on your parts, it stays, and even cleaning solvents will not entirely remove it. Both these low-drag lubricants can leave your parts so slippery you may not be able to pick them up easily when reinstalling them. They are available in handy form, the CMC Trigger Job in a syringe, the Brownells in a pair of squeeze bottles.

A timed and tuned revolver shoots better because it shoots easier. The idea is to make your job easier on the firing line.

GETTING STARTED

Detail strip and degrease the revolver. Start with the trigger, and use a fine or extra fine stone. On the front of the trigger, stone the bottom of the tip, where it bears against the cylinder bolt. Stone from side to side. Do not round the corner. On the rear of the trigger, polish the top, and the curve of the double-action sear. Move the stone from the center towards the rear of the trigger, following the curve of the double-action sear. Do not follow the curve all the way to the end. That end, or tip, is the single-action sear. I have never seen a Smith & Wesson revolver straight from the factory that needed improvement in the single-action trigger pull.

With these two trigger areas polished, go to the cylinder bolt. Stone the angled face of the bolt bright. The trigger pushes against this surface when it resets after firing.

On the hammer, polish the front end of the double-action sear. On re-set, the trigger must push the sear out of the way, and by polishing here you will smooth the feel of the trigger re-set. On the bottom of the hammer, stone the safety foot. The safety foot is cammed back by the rebound bar, forcing the firing pin away from the primer and keeping it there.

The biggest part of your action job will be working on the rebound bar. Unlike the other parts, the rebound bar does not pivot. It slides. Use a fine or extra fine stone to polish the sides of the rebound bar until they are mirror-bright. Use a round file or steel rod wrapped in 600-grit cloth to polish the inside of the bar, where the spring resides. Polish the cam lump on the top of the bar, which engages the safety foot of the hammer.

For the cylinder to move as smoothly as possible the crane must be aligned and any endshake removed. Get the alignment correct first. Put the crane alignment gauge in the crane, and close the crane. See if the alignment gauge slides smoothly and freely into the centerpin hole in the frame. If it does not, use a nylon wedge or crane bar to bend the crane in the correct direction. The wedge can only correct up and down. The bar can correct in all four directions. Do not try to make your correction all at once. Tweak and check in one direction (up and down or left to right), tweak and check. Once centered that way, make the other correction to get the gauge in the hole.

Once the gauge moves smoothly in and out, remove endshake (see Chapter 6).

With endshake removed, polish the bearing surface on which the cylinder rotates. Clean out the grit from

Stone all four sides of the rebound block.

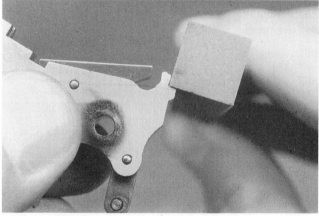

Stone the underside of the hammer. The single-action notch is that tiny little thing just to the left of the stone in the picture. Leave it alone!

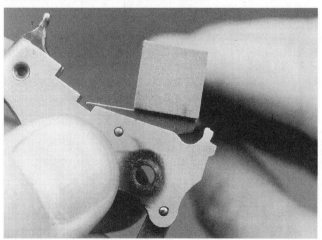

Stone the top of the double-action sear.

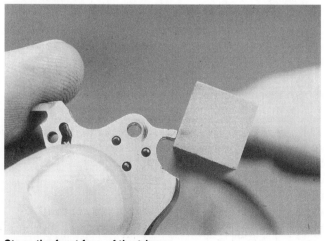

Stone the front face of the trigger.

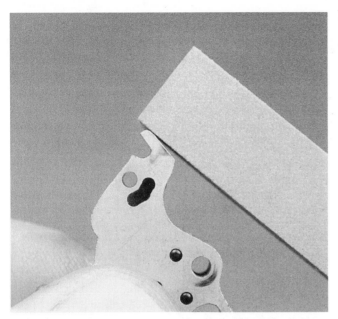

Stone the curve of the trigger, starting here with each stroke, and....

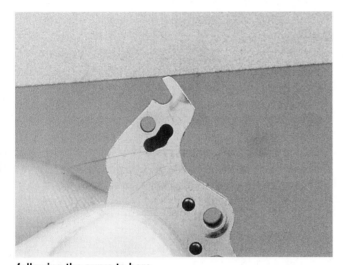

following the curve to here.

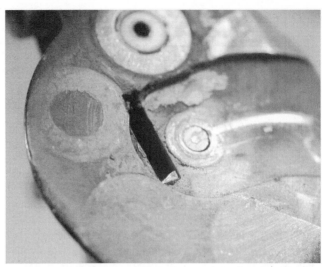

At the start of the firing stroke the hand is at the bottom of the slot, ready to lift the cylinder.

TIMING THE S&W REVOLVER: THE HAND AND RATCHET

The hand lifts the cylinder via the ratchet, turning it one sixth (or one-seventh, eighth, ninth or tenth) of a rotation. The hand must turn the cylinder so each chamber lines up with the barrel in time for the hammer hit. If it does not, you will have "shaving" where bits of the bullet are shorn off by the edge of the rear face of the barrel. Shaving is annoying and hazardous to the shooters beside you. It also hurts accuracy. (Shaving is sometimes confused with "spitting" where the cylinder/ barrel gap is uneven, and the gas jets out the larger side with sufficient force to strike nearby shooters. Shaving requires re-timing, while spitting requires setting back and regapping the barrel.)

The hand lifts with the top of the tip, and finishes rotating with the inside of the tip. You will, however, be doing most of your adjustments to the ratchet and not the hand. If the hand is too short or too thin you replace it. A short hand lifts late. A thin hand fails to carry up all chambers, not just some. A hand of correct length (and almost all will be in the correct range) fails to carry up due to a thin ratchet knob. Or, the opposite problem is binding as it finishes carrying up, from a fat knob. Use a grease pencil, china marker or felt-tip pen to number your chambers. Then double-action dry fire as slowly as possible. If the cylinder fails to carry up, note which one fails. If you feel binding as the hand is forced past the fat knob once the chamber has carried up, note that one. (A reminder: the knob behind that chamber is the one you are interested in. The knob closest to each chamber is the one driving the cylinder on the chamber before it. So, the chamber at 12 o'clock is driven by the knob at 2 o'clock.)

To deal with a thin knob you need a hammer and drift punch. You peen the shoulder of the knob that the hand cams against, to fill the gap between knob and hand as

stoning. Burnish these surfaces after polishing, using compressed air to spin the cylinder. Once it is spinning as fast as the air will drive it, remove the air and let the cylinder come to a stop on its own.

Reassemble using a synthetic lubricant. For extra smoothness apply Chip McCormick's Trigger Job or Brownell's Action Magic II. Both these lubricants are somewhat resistant to solvents, so you won't have to reapply them after each cleaning.

If you feel that you need a lighter double-action trigger pull, you can use a Wolff spring kit, or a Powers mainspring, to ease the spring tension. Before you go making the springs too light, let me remind you that Jerry Miculek uses the factory springs as Smith & Wesson ships them — unless he needs a heavier spring. Remember, lighter springs can make the action sluggish enough in double-action shooting that the trigger cannot keep up with your trigger finger.

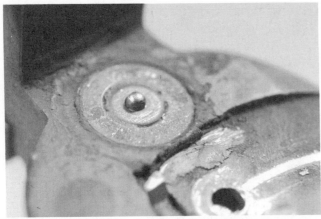

Firing pin protrusion is important. Too much and you get pierced primers and erosion of the firing pin boss. (The circular shield around the firing pin) Too little and you get failures to fire.

The end of the firing stroke. The hand is all the way up, the firing pin through, and the cylinder (missing in order to photograph the rest of the parts) locked in place.

The extractor ratchet is specific to the frame size and capacity. This Baumann custom cylinder (seven shots of .357 Magnum) needs seven teeth in the ratchet in order to work the cylinder.

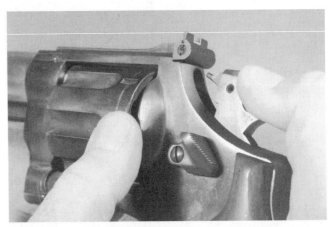

Thumb drag on hammer cocking uncovers a failure to carry up. If your revolver has it, you need to advance the timing

Notice that the teeth of the ratchet fall between the chambers. The tooth that controls timing of a chamber is the one to the right on an S&W and left on a Colt.

The corner on the tooth is important. The point begins the carry-up, and releases the hand at the right time to lock the cylinder.

the cylinder carries up. You need to move metal, so light taps will not do. Remove the cylinder and disassemble it. Place the extractor ratchet-up on your vise with the long tube down between the jaws. Place the ratchet so the vise jaws support it. You do not want to bend the legs, just peen one knob. Strike the knob, reassemble

and check timing. If you struck too little, there is no change. (Or not enough change.) If you struck just right, the chamber now carries up. If you struck too hard, you now have a fat knob and must file it.

An over-sized knob requires a special file. You can make one by using a bench grinder and a needle file. You must have a thin file with a safe edge and back. You must also be careful in grinding. A needle file is thin, and the least bit of over-heating on grinding and you'll remove the temper and ruin the file. You can just buy a file from Brownells for the job. File the trailing edge of the knob, where the hand presses against it last. (You can remove the hammer and internals, and turn the cylinder while looking through the hand slot, to see exactly what parts of the knob work when.) You do not have to remove the ratchet from the cylinder to file on it. File a couple of strokes, then reassemble and test. File only until you feel some or most of the binding is gone. Do not over-file, for if you do you may end up peening the knob to fatten from over-filing.

TIMING THE S&W REVOLVER: THE CYLINDER STOP

The cylinder stop locks the cylinder in place. It must be unlocked to start the cylinder turning. The tip of the trigger activates the lock. As you press the trigger (in DA mode) the tip of the trigger presses the lock down. The hand then begins turning the cylinder, and sometime after that the lock falls off the tip of the pivoting trigger, to be in place when the next locking slot comes along. The lock has a slot in it, where the frame pin sticks through. The slot allows the lock to move out of the way of the trigger tip when you release the trigger, resetting the mechanism for the next shot. Some of the actions of the stop depend on the hand. A short hand will fail to begin lifting by the time the stop is finished unlocking and is released, and the cylinder will re-lock before turning. Or, a long hand may start turning the cylinder before the cylinder stop is unlocked. Lastly, and cylinder stop may fail to lock, due to a weak spring. The solution to your problem is usually in the hand or the cylinder stop spring. Replace a short hand, shorten a long hand, or replace an old spring, depending on what your inspection finds.

You can create problems for yourself by overly vigorous polishing of the lock on your action job. If you polish the sharp tip of the lock, you shorten it, and make it fall off the trigger tip early. If you (for reasons no one can figure out) polish the sides of the lock head, you can decrease the rigidity of the lockup. Polishing the sides of the lock body seems reasonable, but is rarely called for. Lock work is simply this: polish the return face under the sharp tip. Make sure the spring is full-strength. Then leave the cylinder stop alone.

CHAMFERING THE CHAMBERS

In many types of competitive shooting, reloading must be done quickly. A second or two lost in reloading is that much less time available for shooting a disappearing target.

To speed up reloading, the edges of the chambers are beveled, or chamfered. This chamfering is allowed in all the modern revolver disciplines: Steel Challenge (al-

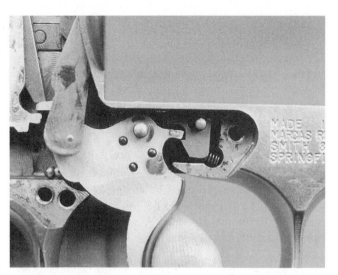

At the beginning of the action, the front of the trigger pulls the cylinder bolt down, releasing the cylinder to rotate.

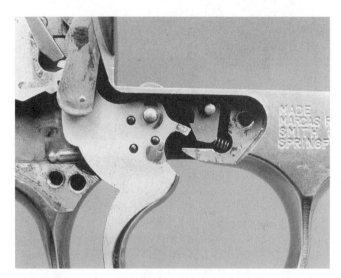

Once the hand has begun rotating the cylinder, the locking bolt pops back up, ready for the next locking slot of the cylinder.

On double-action shooting, the rear tip of the trigger pushes the hammer up.

though if you need a reload there against the clock, your scores will really suffer), USPSA. IDPA, and ICORE.

While chamfering can be done with files, stones, and a steady hand, the easier and less hazardous method is to use Brownells chamfering kit. You can get one caliber-specific to your revolver, or the larger kit that can do all calibers.

Remove and disassemble the cylinder. It is important that you remove the extractor star before chamfering. If you chamfer it the extractor will not hold your empties firmly. In such a situation an empty can slide off, and then under, the extractor before being ejected. It is difficult to remove an empty so positioned. The sole exception to that would be a revolver using full-moon

Use the Brownells chamfering kit.

This cylinder is not chamfered.

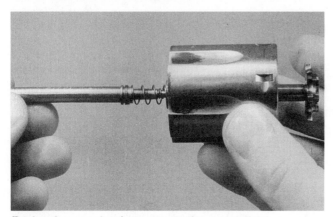

To chamfer your chambers, remove the extractor star.

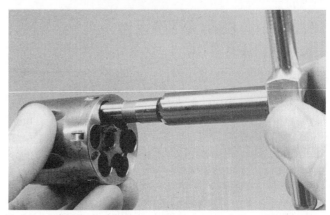

Put the correct pilot for your caliber on the cutting tool, and insert the whole thing into the chamber.

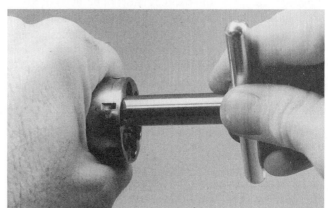

Turn the handle a couple of times and remove it. Check to see how much you've cut. Repeat if necessary. Go on to the next chamber.

clips. As the extractor star lifts the clip, and not the rims of the cases, you could so it. But it offers no advantage to chamfer the star, so take it off.

With the extractor star out, clamp the cylinder in your padded vise. Insert the correct caliber pilot into the chamfering tool. Put a few drops of cutting oil on the teeth of the tool and slide it to the back of each chamber. Take two turns, pull the tool out and look at the edge of the chamber. You want to bevel the edge and no more. After the chambers are chamfered, use an extra-fine round stone to curve the edges of your cuts.

Before reinstalling the extractor, use your pillar file to bevel the outside corners of each arm, and just the cor-

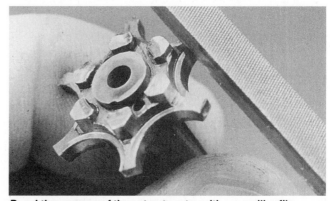

Bevel the corners of the extractor star with your pillar file.

You don't have to do more than knock the corners off.

The beveled corner of the extractor star will blend with the chamfered chamber mouth.

ners, to match the chamfer you made in the chambers.. The bevel keeps the extractor tips from forming a corner at the end of your chamfered edges.

Reassemble.

FULL-HOUSE TRIGGER JOB

It would be nice if all it took for a mighty improvement in shooting accuracy was a new, accurate, match barrel. Unfortunately for most of us, it is only the rare revolver shooter (the great Jerry Miculek springs to mind) who can get by with a match barrel and a standard trigger job. The rest of us need some additional help.

For this project you will need a spring kit from Wolff. The kit comes with your choice of a standard-power or a reduced-power mainspring and three rebound springs, with weights of 15, 14, and 13 pounds. The Wolff mainspring in the kit offers smoother compression than standard mainsprings. Use the standard-power spring if you will be shooting magnum ammunition, or reloading with magnum primers. For standard ammunition or primers use the reduced-power spring.

To obtain the lightest trigger pull you must remove the hammer spur for faster lock time. Clamp the hammer in your vise with the spur pointed out. Put a cutoff wheel in your hand-held grinder. Cut through the base of the spur on top and the sides. On the bottom of the spur, do not cut right at the radius of the lower arc. The bottom of this shoulder, which prevents the hammer from over-rotating and misaligning the action parts, must be left intact. When you cut through, remove and discard the spur. With the spur gone you have to make the hammer more attractive, and less like something Dr. Frankenstein

To ease the trigger pull and cocking force, use Wolff springs made specifically for your wheelgun and the job you want done.

would shoot. Move the hammer in the vise so the area you have just cut off is horizontal. Use grinding stones to polish the cut area smooth.

Since you will be adjusting the mainspring you need some way to lock in your adjustment with the mainspring strain screw. If you simply adjust the spring by backing out the screw, the vibrations of shooting will loosen it. At some point you will start to experience misfires. Instead, remove the strain screw. Drill through the bottom of the frame to the strain screw hole. Use a #31 drill and tap the hole 6-48. Replace the strain screw. Install a 6-48 screw in the new hole that is long enough to reach the strain screw. You now have a locking screw.

Reassemble the revolver to test-fire your spring tension. At the range, start with the strain screw fully tightened. Gradually loosen it, reducing spring tension until you begin to experience misfires. Now tighten the strain screw, increasing the spring tension until your rounds

You can recognize a Wolff spring for S&W by the spine forged down the center when the spring stock was fabricated.

The hammer spur should be removed to improve trigger pull. Leave the shoulder at the bottom of the spur to prevent the hammer from over-rotating.

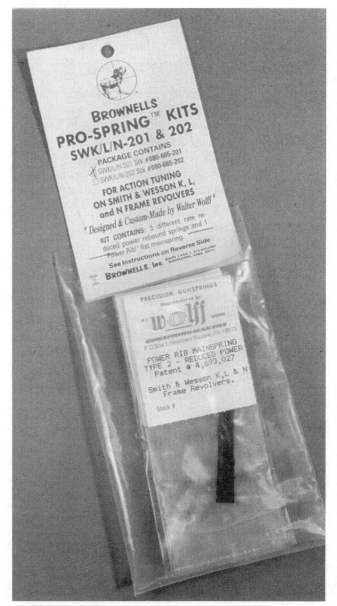

Wolff makes a spring kit to improve your trigger pull. You can get it from Brownells.

Here is the locking screw (bottom), keeping the strain screw from backing out.

all fire. Add a quarter-turn more to the strain screw, and mark the location. Tighten the locking screw to hold the strain screw in position.

Trigger pull is a matter of feel and speed. What works best varies from shooter to shooter. If a heavy rebound spring with a light mainspring feels awkward, install a lighter rebound spring. A 13-pound rebound spring doesn't work for me in fast double-action shooting, so my bowling pin, IPSC/USPSA and IRC revolvers all have heavier rebound springs. In the slower pace of PPC competition, I use the 13-pound spring without problem. You will have to experiment to see if what works best for your practice or competition.

CYLINDER & SLIDE ROLLER ACTION

In the standard revolver design the hammer and trigger slide against each other. To make the action even smoother, Bill Laughridge of Cylinder & Slide designed a hammer with a roller bearing located on the tip of the double-action sear. To fit the roller bearing, Bill re-designed the trigger.

The C&S kit is a double-action-only mechanism. You will not be able to thumb-cock the hammer. The spur is only for holsters with a thumbstrap.

The two parts start life as standard Smith & Wesson issue. Bill re-grinds the trigger so its curvature is better suited to the roller-action DA sear. He modifies the hammer to take the precision-ground DA sear and its roller tip.

To install, remove the factory hammer, trigger and rebound block. Set them aside. Take the hand from the factory trigger and install it on the C&S trigger. Install the C&S trigger and the factory rebound block with its spring. Observe the trigger function. It should pull the locking bolt down and release it cleanly.

Install the cylinder. Check that the trigger advances and locks up the cylinder each time you work it. If the front of the trigger is late in releasing the cylinder-locking bolt, the cylinder will rotate past locking. Do not adjust the cylinder-locking bolt or the revolver will have problems when you reinstall the old trigger. Instead, adjust the trigger. Use a medium fine stone across the front of the trigger. Keep the stone at the original angle of the trigger face. You will need to shorten the face only a few thousandths.

If the cylinder won't rotate, the cylinder-locking bolt is being pulled down too little or too late. Which is to say, the hand is pushing on the cylinder before it is unlocked. You must adjust the hand. Stone the top of the hand, shortening it only a few thousandths. Stone the tip for a few strokes. Try the fit. Repeat until the cylinder will advance. The shortened hand will still work with the old hammer and trigger.

Install the hammer. During manufacture Bill sets the DA sear "short," that is too close to the hammer. You must adjust it for your revolver. Drive out the sear

retaining pin and file on the shoulder marked with red ink. Reinstall and check the fit. Correctly adjusted, the DA sear will spring back into position when the trigger returns to rest. There will be only .005 to .010 inch of gap between trigger and sear when both are at rest.

Place some McCormick Trigger Job on the roller bearing, and in the hammer pivot hole. Your double-action trigger pull will now be smoother than before.

The Cylinder & Slide roller bearing action kit can make your revolver smoother than ever in double-action shooting.

REASSEMBLY TIPS

SMITH & WESSON

When putting an S&W revolver back together, a few steps seem to cause more trouble than the rest. One is the insertion of the cylinder-locking bolt, and its spring, into the frame. The bolt has to go down its shaft, while the spring has to be squirmed back into the tunnel drilled into the front of the frame cutout. (I have no idea how they drill that hole.) With the frame resting on a padded surface, place the spring into its hole in the locking bolt. Start the bolt partway down the shaft until the spring bears against the edge of the frame. Use a small eyeglass screwdriver to compress the spring enough to clear the edge of the frame and push the bolt and spring down the shaft. When you get to the frame hole, the spring will snap into place. Be sure the bolt is completely down the shaft, and pivots smoothly up and down through the cutout under the cylinder.

The second problem concerns the rebound block. The return spring is quite strong for its size, and resists efforts to push it in place. You will have to alter a screwdriver to fit the spring. Grind the tip so it is the exact width of the spring. Grind a shoulder on each side of the screwdriver to bear against the spring, leaving the center of the tip narrow enough to fit within the spring.

With the hammer and trigger already in place, slide the spring into the rebound block and the rebound block in behind the trigger. The spring will rest on the rebound block-retaining stud. With one hand, use your thumb to push down on the block enough to keep it from pivoting up. Use the screwdriver to compress the spring, push-ing it into the rebound block. When the spring clears the retaining stud, push the block down with your thumb enough to capture the spring. Remove the screwdriver and push the block the rest of the way down.

TAURUS REVOLVERS

Slicking up the Taurus involves much the same process as the S&W, as the mechanisms are quite similar. Polish the bearing surfaces of the Taurus in the same places you find them in the S&W.

Despite similarities to S&W revolvers, Taurus uses a different method to spring-load the hand. S&W has a wound spring in the trigger; Taurus uses a coil spring and plunger in the sideplate. The Taurus hand travels in a slot in the sideplate. The plunger pushes the hand forward against the extractor ratchet. Getting these parts reassembled can be a hassle. The obvious – and wrong – way is to assemble the hand to the trigger, and then attempt to compress the spring and plunger as you press the sideplate in place. The problem is that anything strong enough to compress the spring will be too thick to get the sideplate in place.

The best method is to assemble the action into the frame, omitting the hand. Compress the spring and plunger into the sideplate, and put the hand in place in its slot. Hold the frame in one hand and the sideplate in your other hand. Position the sideplate against the frame, while simultaneously aligning the leg of the hand with its trigger hole. Once the hand is inserted into the trigger, jockey the sideplate around until it lines up with the frame. Press in place. This method takes a fraction of the time, and has none of the aggravation, of the wrong method.

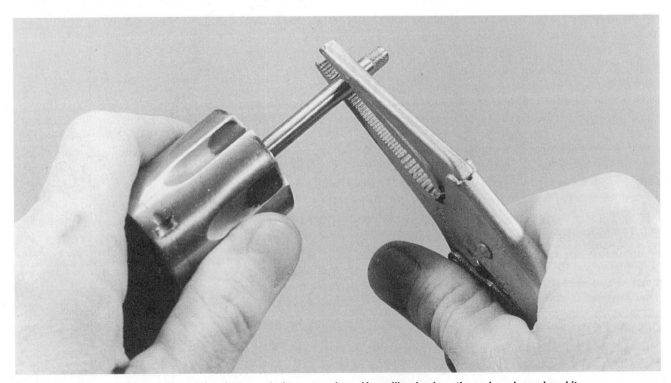

Do not use pliers to tighten or loosen the ejector rod of your revolver. You will only chew the rod, and may bend it.

RUGER REVOLVERS

Rugers slick up a bit differently than S&Ws and Taurus revolvers. Polish the top of the mainspring strut where it rides in the hammer. Polish the DA sear and cam face of the locking block. You will find that while S&W revolvers respond to polishing, Ruger revolvers respond more to lighter springs.

The Ruger double-action revolvers offer a couple of challenges all their own. The safety bar on the trigger assembly seems to catch on every interior edge inside the frame. To ease assembly, clamp the butt of the frame in your vise. Point the muzzle towards you. With one hand insert the trigger assembly from underneath. With the other hand use a dental pick to guide the safety bar past the cylinder latch and all other internal obstacles, until the trigger assembly latches into place. Do not pull the trigger while the trigger assembly is out of the frame. The assembly is designed to retain its springs when the mechanism is relaxed. If you pull the trigger you will launch three springs and plungers in three different directions.

The hammer of the Ruger goes in after the trigger assembly. With the trigger assembly in place and latched, pull the trigger back. Hold it. Lower the hammer into the frame until you can line up the hammer pivot hole with the hole through the frame. Insert the hammer pivot pin. Let go of the trigger. The hammer and trigger should work normally. To check, take the Ruger out of the vise. Point it down and dry fire it double-action. The trigger should work and the hammer should flop back and forth. Put the mainspring strut assembly in place, thumb-cock the hammer and pull out the capture pin. You really can't go wrong putting the hammer in after the trigger assembly.

RUGER DOUBLE-ACTION

Disassemble the revolver, and detail strip the trigger assembly. Carefully capture the springs and plungers from the hand, safety bar and cylinder bolt. They should be set aside or marked, so you can return each spring and plunger correctly in its starting place.

Stone the safety bar on the front and back. The hand (or pawl, as Ruger calls it) should be stoned on all four sides, but not on the tip. Stone the sides of the trigger. The top rear of the trigger, where it bears against the double-action sear of the hammer, should be stoned. Do not stone the rear face of the trigger, or single-action surface. You must use a fixture to stone this face, and only if your single-action trigger pull needs it. Few do.

On the hammer, stone the bottom of the double-action sear, and its front face where the trigger bears against it on trigger return. The hammer flats need to be polished. Start with a fine or extra fine stone. You want to polish the high spots, but you must not reduce the hammer thickness. Stone only the bottom, pivot section of the hammer. Stone the slots in the frame where the hammer rotates.

Stone the top of the hammer strut, where it bears against the hammer. Stone the sides of the strut, and slightly round its corners. The hammer strut is a stamped part, and the edges can be rough. Rounding the corners smoothes the spring's travel over the strut.

Unscrew the ejector rod from the cylinder. Note that Ruger uses left-hand threads. Clamp the ejector rod in a padded vise or in lead or copper vise jaws, and unscrew the cylinder counterclockwise. With the crane stripped, stone the bearing surfaces, treat with Action Magic II and spin the cylinder with compressed air.

When reassembling the trigger housing, do not be bashful with the McCormick Trigger Job. Use it, or Brownells Action Magic II on the hammer, safety bar and hammer strut.

DOUBLE ACTION REVOLVERS – COLT V-SPRING

The Colt V-spring action originated at the beginning of the 20th century, when steel was expensive and labor was cheap. The design, a marvel of complexity, requires years of practice and study to fully understand, fit and service. Few and far between are the gunsmiths qualified to work on it. The common models you will run into using this mechanism are the Python and the Detective Special.

You can slick up the action on your own, but serious problems must be referred to a professional.

Disassemble the revolver, and remove all of the internal parts except the cylinder bolt, which you will leave in place. On the trigger, stone the top of the double-action sear. Do not stone the tip in an attempt to lighten the single action trigger pull. Stone the three sides of the hand that are facing away from the trigger, but, again, do not stone the tip. Hand length is always critical to correct timing. As with Colt SA revolvers, stoning the tip can shorten the hand, and prevent carry-up.

Use a short, small-diameter punch to drift the pin of the double-action sear out of the hammer. Use a round stone to polish the lower front of the hammer's DA sear. The trigger rubs against this area during trigger return. Stone the inside of the DA sear, where the trigger bears against it during the double-action stroke. At the minimum, both of these areas must be polished to a 600-grit surface.

When you reassemble the DA sear to the hammer, be sure the pin is secure in the hammer, and that it is flush with the hammer. If you have to stake the pin to keep it in the hammer, stone down any high spots left by the staking.

Stone the safety bars enough to polish the high spots, but no more.

On the rebound bar, stone the underside of the forward tip, where it bears against the hand. Very carefully stone the shoulder that bears against the hammer. This shoulder cams the hammer back from the primer, and

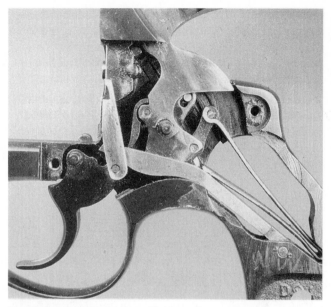

The Colt "V"-spring action. The large bar on the bottom controls everything.

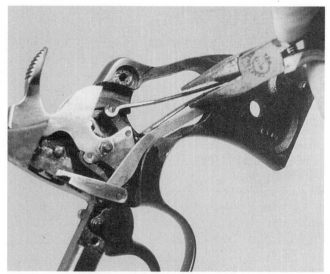

To disassemble, compress the mainspring with pliers and lift it out.

allows the safety bar to slip between the hammer and frame.

The most delicate stoning of all is the triangle found on the rebound bar. Do not use anything coarser than an extra fine stone on this triangle, and use a delicate touch. How delicate? Take a stack of new copying paper, and jog it so all the edges are flush. Pick only the top sheet off the stack, without disturbing the flush edges. That delicate.

The cylinder does not easily come off of the crane on these Colt revolvers. Rather than investing in a wrench and staking tool, slide the crane out of the cylinder without disassembling them. Clean and degrease the bearing surfaces, and treat with Brownells Action Magic II. Slide the crane back into the cylinder. Use compressed air blown at an angle into the chambers to spin the cylinder, burnishing the bearing surfaces. Repeat the Action Magic and spinning.

The traditional method of easing spring tension on these Colts, of sticking a rod in the spring and cocking the revolver, was necessary before the advent of reduced-power mainsprings. If you want a lighter spring buy a reduced power mainspring from Wolff. If you want to try the old method, buy extra springs to experiment on and keep your original one unmodified.

DOUBLE-ACTION REVOLVERS — MODERN COLT ACTIONS

Because of the need for years of training to properly assemble and tune the V-spring revolvers, Colt designed a different mechanism. Gone is the rebound bar, and its excruciatingly difficult to fit and time triangle. The improved mechanism is found in the Mark III, King Cobra and Anaconda revolvers.

After you disassemble and degrease the parts, start

Drift out the action bar pivot pin and remove the action bar.

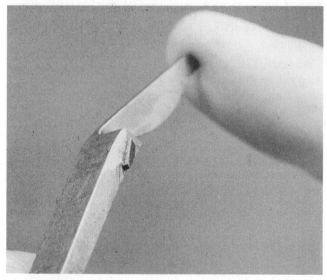

The small diamond on the right side controls the cylinder locking bolt. Do not do more than polish this diamond.

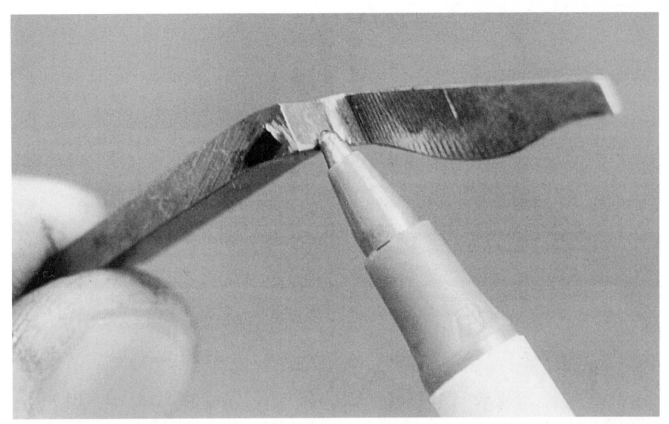

This is the hammer rebound shoulder. It cams the hammer back from the primer, and prevents the firing pin from reaching the primer until the trigger is pulled.

with the trigger. The front end of the trigger has a tip that looks like the beak of a small bird. It pulls down and then releases the cylinder bolt, letting the cylinder rotate. Stone the underside of this beak, but do not shorten the tip. On the back end of the trigger, stone only the top of the double-action sear. The rear of this end of the trigger is the single-action sear. Stoning the single action sear must be done with a fixture, if, and only if, your single-action trigger pull is too heavy. One revolver in several hundred leaves the factory with a single-action trigger pull that is too heavy, and that does not improve with dry-firing.

On the hand, stone the sides, but not the tip. Do not try to polish the hand pin. Instead, use McCormick Trigger Job on reassembly.

On the hammer, slide the double-action sear out of the hammer, and hang on to the spring and plunger that are behind it. Stone the underside of the DA sear, where the trigger picks up the hammer on the start of the DA stroke. Stone the top face of the DA sear, where the trigger rubs on its return stroke.

Polish the mainspring strut.

Unlike the Colt V-mainspring revolvers, the cylinder comes off the crane easily. The ejector rod threads into the extractor star, and is secured at the factory with a mild grade of Loctite. Clamp the ejector rod in a padded vise or one with lead or copper jaw protectors, and turn the cylinder to unscrew. Polish the crane, and when you reassemble use McCormick Trigger Job or Brownells Action Magic II on the bearing surfaces. When you screw the rod back in, use Loctite #290 and tighten lightly.

CHAPTER 16

THE vZ-52

When the Soviets rolled into town (so to speak) in the spring of 1945, they brought with them the ideals of socialist brotherhood. The Czechs and Slovaks took them at their word, and began working on making the future safe for the clearly superior form of government. Clearly superior by the oldest of tests, i.e., who had won the last

war. The Czechs, always good designers and engineers, set about making new small arms, new designs that took into account the lessons learned from that war. Primarily, the lesson that bolt-action rifles were passé, and that what an infantry squad needed most was lots of firepower, firepower that could be controlled and directed

The vZ-52, aka cz-52, is a hot number, just not as hot or strong as some would have you believe.

This little dot of red paint (which may or may not be on your 52) is all the indication you get that the safety is off.

Push the safety to level to make the 52 safe.

onto the targets most important to said infantry squad: the guys within the nearest 300 meters or so. As part of that, they designed a new handgun; the vZ-52, chambered in the eastern-european cartridge of ubiquity; the 7.62 Tokarev. Well, it had been designed for the 9mm Parabellum to start with, but with a little bit of "hinting" from the Soviets, it was re-designed to 7.62 Tokarev, an important point we'll get to in a bit.

OK, just to maximize the confusion, the descriptor vZ-52 (Czech: *vzor*, meaning "year") was also applied both to a rifle and a light machinegun as well. The rifle, the vZ-52, was a box-fed 10-shot self-loading rifle that had the trigger mechanism design essentially stolen from the M1 Garand (although, to be honest, John Garand stole it from John Browning) and weighed more than the Garand. It and the belt-fed light machinegun were chambered for a new cartridge, the 7.62X45, a round unique to the Czechs. The LMG was pretty cool: it was air-cooled, had a quick-change barrel, and could use either belt or magazines. (Sound familiar?)

What the Czechs quickly found was that to the Soviets, the Warsaw pact, expressing brotherhood with all socialist workers across the globe really meant to Eastern Europe was: "We're in charge, and you supply us with small arms and replacement troops." And those small arms were to be chambered in the standard Soviet calibers. (The attempted Hungarian Revolution in 1956 probably had a lot to do with the Czech "wake-up call." Try to leave, or stray too far from the policies of the

To decock, push the safety up – but do you really want to trust communist engineering and manufacturing? Point that thing is a safe direction!

Politburo, and you'll find a Red Guard Army camped on your doorstep.) So the LMG got dropped. The rifle was changed to the vZ-52/57, newly-chambered for the Soviet 7.62X39, while the handgun, since it was already in a "proper" caliber, was left alone.

The "52" as we'll call it, is an interesting handgun. Given the time period, it is clearly right out of the science-fiction school of industrial design. It is racy, high-tech, and given the period and use, more than a bit clunky to use. The long 7.62 Tokarev cartridge makes for a rather long grip, and that length limits it to a single-stack

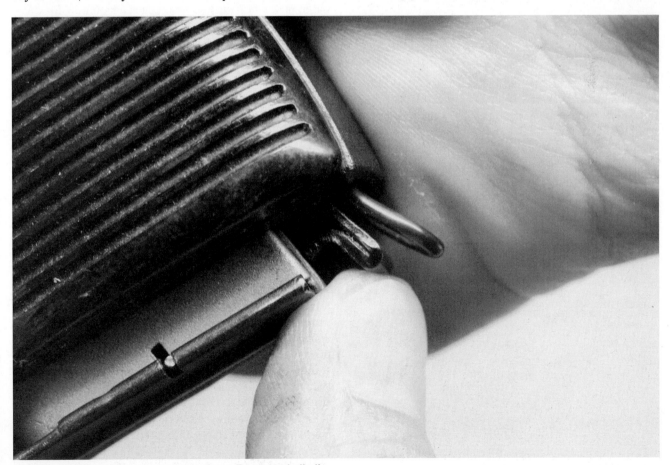

The magazine is held in with the ubiquitous European hell-clip.

The disassembly latch is paired, one on each side. Once empty, pull these down and your slide will pop forward.

This is how far forward the slide goes. Then you simply lift it up off the frame.

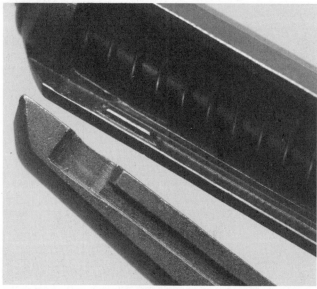

Here are the disassembly slots, where the slide lifts up off the frame. That's it, and it's kinda neat.

magazine. As a result, the grip is long front-to-back, flat and a bit much for those with small hands. It is hard to reconcile its grip shape and the similar one of the Tokarev with the stature or hand size of most conscripts in the Soviet system: short. Then again, the handgun would have been issued to officers, senior sergeants, and members of crew-served weapons. Mostly those from the upper classes (even though there were no classes in the Soviet system) and also keep in mind that Soviet war-fighting doctrine of the period had little concern for the individual.

But what really sets it apart from others is the locking system: the delayed-roller blowback system. When locked, the barrel has two rollers, one on each side, securely clamped into recesses in the slide. On firing, the slide and barrel recoil together for a short distance, before the rollers are cammed to unlock and allow the slide to continue on its own way. Yes, the exact same system used in the HK G3 and its derivatives. Which leads us to a very confusing situation: experts have asserted that the vZ-52 is by far the strongest pistol chambered in 7.62 Tokarev. When I first heard that, I figured, hey, they've looked inside one, I haven't, it could be true. Since then, I have looked inside one, and it is not true.

The G3 is the very definition of robust. However, there is plenty of steel in there (if you get a chance, pick one up, you'll see what I mean) to make it strong. The size of the rollers, the recesses they lock into, the mass of the bolt and carrier, all make the G3 anvil tough. The vZ-52 handgun is not nearly so large, even accounting for the smaller size of the cartridge. The standard pressure for the 7.62 NATO cartridge at the time was in the low 50,000 PSI range. The 7.62 Tokarev is probably in the high 30,000 to low 40,000 PSI range. To deal with the 25 percent increase in pressure of the bigger .30, you have more than twice the steel, and more than twice the brass case. The margins of safety are clearly far in excess for the rifle, over the pistol.

Also, many assert that as a result of this strength, the Czech ammunition for the vZ-52 was loaded extra-hot, for greater velocity, greatly increasing performance. Pish-tosh. Until the 1980s, we did not have readily-available chronographs to measure velocity. Calculating velocity by drop, noise, recoil or penetration is like measuring a new pair of shoes with an unmarked ruler: they're all the same size. Or they're any size you want them to be.

Low-cost commercial chronos for the average shooter weren't available until the 1980s, and the vZ-52 and ammo for it wasn't available until the 1990s. Given the production variances between ammo lots, arsenals standards, countries, propaganda and time, chrono-ing today ammo made in the 1950s and 1960s in Czechoslovakia is prone to confusion. There's no telling what velocity it was really loaded to, and if the storage conditions (or not) have conspired to make it more or less effective since then. No, we really don't have any way of knowing what they were loaded to, and what the

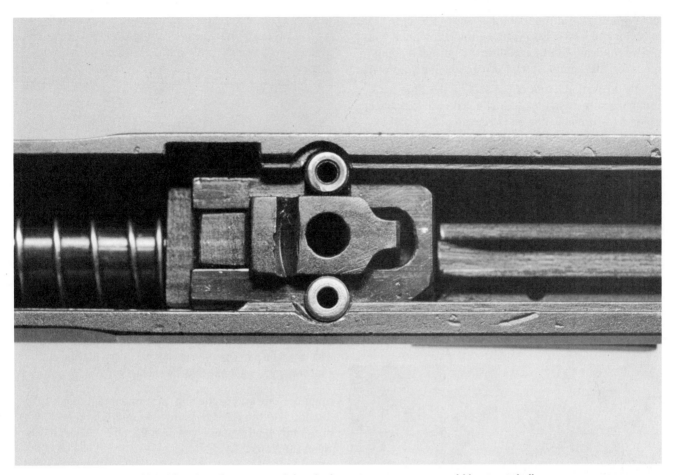

The action is all here, and it is hi-tech to the extreme. It just isn't as strong as some would have you believe.

reasons were. Heck, for all we know, the master plan in the Warsaw Pact countries was to gain extra velocity (100 fps or so) at the expense of long-term durability. In other words; trade a bit more performance for guns breaking sooner. After all, in an all-out war, the small unit leaders who would be using the pistols could have a life expectancy of 30 days or less. If a pistol lasted a couple of hundred rounds it would outlast its first two or three owners.

A friend of mine is a military historian and writer of military fiction. When we were discussing the vZ-52, he reminded me of his research into the Katyn Forest massacre in 1940. In the Katyn Forest, the Soviets executed captured Polish officers, policemen and intellectuals, nearly 22,000 in all. The NKVD executioners arrived with satchels and suitcases full of TT-33 pistols, which soon quit under the workload. (If one can use so prosaic a term for such horrific proceedings.) They switched to German-made pistols, which were able to continue functioning. When the Germans rolled East in the summer of 1941, they swept past the Katyn Forest. When the Germans heard rumors of the incident, they went to the location and proceeded to do a full forensic workup and published the results. One detail that caused some problems for them was the large number of German-caliber and German-marked empty casings found.

My suggestion to Dave (the other writer) was that the problem and comparison were not that the vZ-52 was

so much more durable, but that the indifferently-made and perhaps un-heat-treated TT-33s were so much less capable.

As a last point, and if nothing else to get you out of the "Czech *uber*-pistol" frame of mind, when we have your

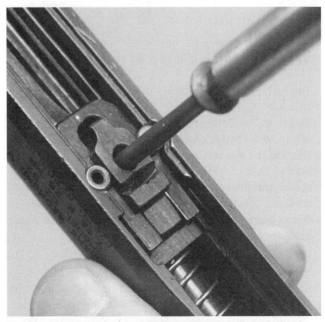

To disassemble, get a good-fitting drift punch in the hole (the mil-spec cleaning rod won't do) and pull the whole barrel towards the muzzle end of the slide.

vZ-52 apart, look at the wall thickness of the slide at the roller lock recesses. Eyeing that should convince you. You do not want to be exceeding the normal loading specs for 7.62 ammo, should you go loading your own.

Let's take a quick tour of the 52. Pull the slide back and make sure it isn't loaded. The slide will lock back, a useful feature not seen on European pistols half a century ago. Remove the magazine. It uses the European heel-clip, so lever that back and pull the magazine out. Run the slide forward. There is no external slide stop lever meant for your use. The lever is the flat bar on the left side, but there isn't a purchase for your finger, so just remove the mag and then pull the slide back slightly. Then ease it forward. Look on the left side. You'll see the safety lever and decocker. To put the 52 on safe, you rotate the little lever so the small red dot (if yours still has it) is covered. Up, in other words. Down is "Fire." You'll note that ergonomics had yet to arrive in the Soviet system by 1952, and the safety lever is easier moved with the thumb of your left hand, holding the pistol in your right hand to fire. Southpaws, you're out of luck here.

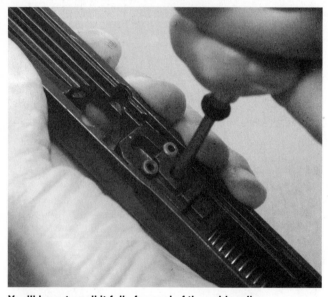

You'll have to pull it fully forward of the guide rails.

You can decock the hammer one of two ways, both with some slight hazard: you can get a thumb on the hammer and pull the trigger, controlling the hammer down to rest. Or you can push the safety lever up, activating the decock. However, I'm not sure I'd be fully prepared to trust 1950s socialist design, dimensional tracking and heat-treating. The safety does activate a firing pin safety, to pull the firing pin away from the hammer before it decocks. Nice idea, but I'm a belt-and-suspenders guy.

With the hammer down, grab the disassembly tabs, forward of the trigger guard. Pull them both straight down. You'll hear a click, and see the slide move forward an eighth of an inch or so. Now just pull the slide forward and up, and the whole top of the pistol comes off.

The grips are Bakelite, an early plastic, and are held on by the steel clip you see. Simply get a screwdriver

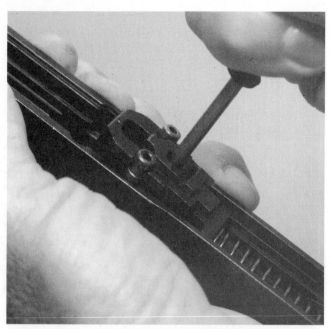

Once far enough forward, the barrel will tip up out of the slide. Well, it will tip out when you lever it out, using the punch. That's why you want one that fits snugly.

tip under one end of the clip, pry up enough to clear the notch in the grip, and pull the clip to the rear. That's pretty much all you need to do here, and you can easily clean the frame.

What if you want to do some work on the frame? I'd say move on, there isn't much to see here. The frontstrap and backstrap are too thin to checker, unless you're determined to show off. The hammer pin is held on by means of a staked nut. The right end of the hammer pin is threaded, and the nut screwed on and then staked in place. To remove it you'll have to either un-do the staking (easier said than done) or destroy the nut and replace it late. (Good luck with that.) Please also note that the hammer nut, along with the staked end of the trigger pivot pin, holds on the right side plate of the frame. That's right, it isn't one piece, it is a machined frame with a sideplate bolted on. Why? I can only surmise that I was needed to get the hammer and decocking parts in, and still allow for some means of assembly.

And you're going to remove the hammer, why? I've handled a couple of crates of vZ-52 pistols, and one thing I've noticed (besides the putrid grease some are packed in for shipping) is that the trigger pulls are all pretty nice. No, they wouldn't do for bullseye shooting at Camp Perry, but for a plinking and perhaps defensive pistol they have no drawbacks. They have all been pretty clean, reasonably crisp and not gritty at all. No, unless you are going to do an autopsy on a vZ-52, you really have no need to be taking it apart to that level.

The only thing I could see doing would be to remove the slide hold-open bar so you can silver-solder a tab on it to use as a slide stop, ala so many other, more-modern pistols. One advantage to such a simple layout is that when it comes time to clean, you can get access to everything, and can hose and air-clean easily.

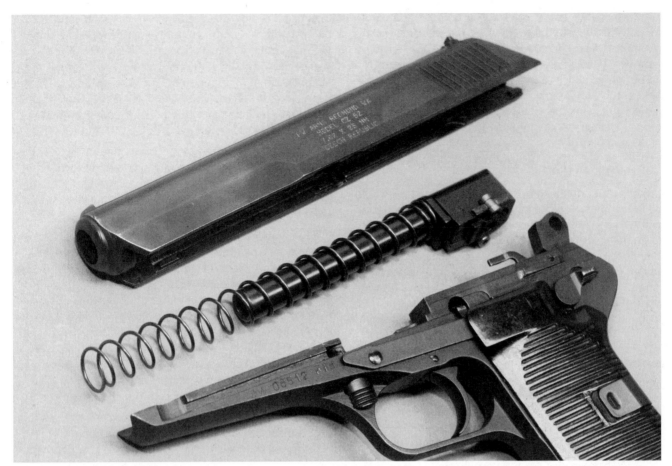

The disassembly latch is paired, one on each side. Once empty, pull these If all you want to do is a cleaning after shooting this is all you need. Remember, a lot of commie ammo is corrosive, despite that Ivan says. Scrub that bore.

To reassemble, hold the grip panels in place while you press the steel clip back on. Note that the clip is directional, and it does matter which end is up.

The slide and barrel now need your attention. Note the fit of the rollers to the slide. That's how it is locked. The block in the middle, with the hole in it? That is the locking wedge. When you fire the 52, the slide and barrel move to the rear. The wedge hits the machined rib you see on the frame, right in front of the feed ramp. The rib causes the wedge to move forward, creating clearance for the rollers. The rollers cam out of the slide recesses, and the barrel stops, while the slide continues to the rear.

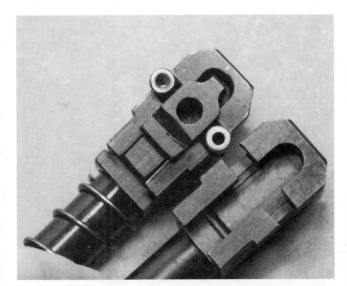

The roller locks get cammed in and out by the sliding locking cam. Your new barrel probably lacks these. You can either remove the old, or buy new – but if you buy new, make sure you buy hardened rollers.

The locking cam retaining pin is staked in place. You'll have to work to remove it.

To remove the barrel, stick a drift punch or cleaning rod into the hole in the wedge. Pull the wedge towards the muzzle, and once the rollers have had the tension removed, you can lever the breech end of the barrel up out of the slide. Careful here, as the barrel is being held in the slide by the recoil spring; if you slip at this point you'll launch the barrel four or five feet across the room. Perhaps you do not want to be doing this with the full-length bedroom mirror within range? While it is not a really strong spring, this is not something you can do with the tip of a ballpoint pen.

You'd think that a convenient item for this task would be the supplied cleaning rod, you know, the one that is in the issued holster? Guess again. It is just a bit too big to fit. Also, you'll read that the front lip of the magazine floorplate is the correct size to fit the notch in the wedge. That is correct, but it overlooks one important detail: once you've retracted the wedge, there's no way to tip the barrel out of the slide. Sigh. So in the end, you're left with a drift punch or a handled allen wrench. I realize that we're looking a half-century into the past, but was it too much to ask that the design proles of the socialist worker's paradise of Czechoslovakia make either the cleaning rod capable, or the wedge easier to remove? It does add a bit of background to one of the details the Austrians insisted on, in the pistol trials that led to the Glock: no special tools to disassemble.

Why is the wedge such an obstinate thing to move?

Because it is what the recoil spring bears on, not the barrel itself. So, you're compressing the recoil spring, without actually moving the barrel. At least not until you've moved the wedge enough to allow the rollers to fall out of their slide recesses. You also have to move the barrel far enough towards the muzzle to get the chamber block clear, and into the rail slot access grooves milled for disassembly.

As with all things there is a certain amount of learning the "feel" for compressing the spring and removing the barrel. Once you get it, the process comes easily. Until then, don't expect to impress your friends with your ability to strip the vZ-52 blindfolded.

While you have the barrel and slide separated, take a moment to look at the recesses in the slide for the rollers. Not too thick, eh? I slipped my digital calipers on my slide, and found something interesting: the wall thickness on each was 0.0695 inch. And yes, it was the same to .0005 inch between them. I'm impressed with that level of precision in machining. What I'm not impressed with is the ability of a pair of slots that deep, and .372 inch high, to take the load of a cartridge much more than 34,000 PSI. No, no super-pressure 7.62 loads for my vZ-52, thank you very much.

Once you have the barrel out, you can separate it from the recoil spring and get to the barrel cleaning. One detail you'll notice is that the rollers do not fall out when

Check the fit of your new barrel before you install it. It can't bind on the extractor, and the new roller slots have to line up with the slide recesses. Check before you get the tools out.

The slide hold-open lever is just asking to have some external ledge put on it. However, it is a flat piece of sheet metal, and may not respond well to your attempts to soldering.

The frame has the locking cam activator milled right into it. That rib in the middle is what stops the cam (and barrel) and allows the barrel and slide to unlock.

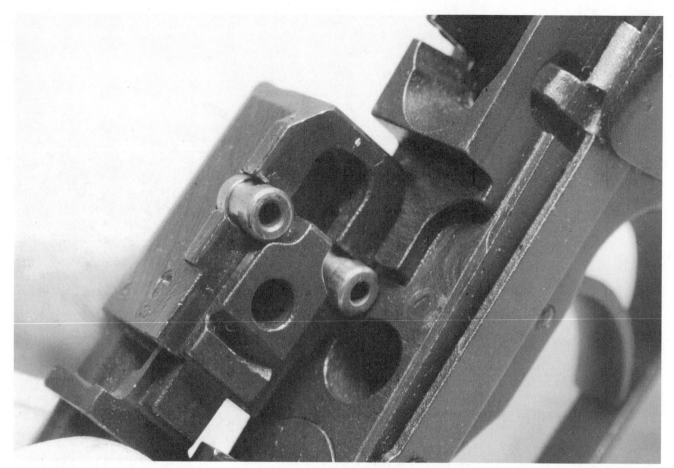

Tipped to the side, you can see how the barrel and locking cam stop relate. You can also see the slot that is supposed to allow you to use the magazine to remove the barrel from the slide. Oh, those wildly optimistic socialist workers!

you remove the barrel from the slide. I've got to give the designers credit there: they knew that if they didn't make the rollers a captured set, the troops would lose them the first time they cleaned a pistol. Look on the side of the chamber, below the bore line. There's a cross pin that is staked in place that keeps the wedge on the barrel. The wedge can't move enough to lose the rollers.

Why are we looking there? Because your new barrel, the one chambered for 9mm Parabellum, probably didn't come with rollers. In fact, it probably arrived without rollers and wedge. If you want to swap calibers, you have two choices: find new rollers and wedge, or swap out the ones existing, into the new barrel.

One slight drawback to new rollers: I've heard of shooters buying rollers that were not properly hardened. Ooops. Too-soft rollers can damage the new barrel, a shame, or the new barrel and the slide, which is catastrophic. Well, catastrophic to your investment in the gun. So while it is a bit more of a hassle to swap the parts, it is safer until you locate real-deal hardened wedge and rollers for your new barrel. Now, in researching the vZ-52, which many call the CZ-52, I find that my own terminology is perhaps incorrect. Then again, translated from the Czech, they could be called anything. The terminology I find (although not always the same) is "Roller cam" for wedge, and "Roller lock" for roller. When I began this chapter parts were rare. As I wrap

To take the grips off, slip a screwdriver under the retaining clip.

Once you get the clip started, pull it off to the rear, or get the screwdriver around on the other side and repeat.

things up to send to the editor, parts are much more common.

So, let's assume you have parts, either taken out of your barrel, or new ones to fit to your new barrel. How to fit? First, check the fit of the new barrel in your slide, without any other parts involved. The barrel has to pass through the muzzle hole in the slide, but not have too much slop. Too big? You can polish, file or lathe-turn. Too small? Oh, well. Unless you're willing to fit a larger sleeve to the barrel, and then re-fit it, you'll just have to live with some extra room. Also, check to make sure the extractor does not bind against or hit the rear of your new barrel.

The roller slots have to line up with the slide recesses. If they don't, return the barrel. You can't make it fit. To make your new barrel fit, you need the roller cam, a pair of roller locks, and the retaining pin. If you're taking the old ones out, us a tapered punch to start the pin. Once it moves, then select a close-fitting pin to drive it all the way out.

Remove the pin, cam and rollers. Now place the rollers in the new barrel. They are symmetrical, so it doesn't matter, but I like to keep things the way they were. That way, if the parts have burnished themselves to a certain fit, they come back to it with the new barrel. Slide the cam on, and press the pin in enough to keep things together. Make sure the cam still retains the rollers. If they don't, you're in trouble, as the dimensional mis-match will probably be more than you can overcome. However, that is unlikely. Drive the pin all the way in, re-stake it, and reassemble your pistol.

Here you can see the hammer pin retaining nut, staked in place. If you plan on doing trigger work (although you really don't need it) you'd better make sure you have spares handy. You may well destroy the nut or the screw threads in disassembly.

Why would we do all this? At the moment, 9mm ammo is very expensive, and 7.62 Tokarev is much less so. However, these things will not last. The price of 7.62 will go up, as the supplies of "surplus" dry up. The price of 9mm is bound to come down. If you plan to reload, reloading 9mm is a piece of cake compared to reloading 7.62X25.

In looking at the vZ-52, I wonder about what might have been. The trigger is liveable. The pistol is all-steel, and thus handles recoil well. I like flat-handled pistols. The magazine holds 8 rounds, but with the bottom lips bent out, it would be easy enough to make an extension.

With a 9mm barrel, fitted with a compensator I could increase the sight radius from its already useful, 6.5 inches to about 8 inches. As an inexpensive gun to build on, it might well have made a really neat 9-pin gun.

Still, as-is, it is a great plinker, and given the current cost of 7.62X25 ammo (a quick price check turns up a spread of $80 to $100 per thousand rounds of corrosive surplus ammo) it is nearly dirt-cheap to shoot.

Get one. They don't cost much to buy or feed, and as long as you don't over-stress those rollers, they will last a good long time.

Here you can see the joint of the sideplate on the frame. Why a sideplate? Beats the heck out of me.

Stripped for a thorough cleaning. To reassemble, work backwards.

CHAPTER

17

BASIC PISTOLSMITHING THE GLOCK

In response to a proposed pistol contract for the Austrian Army in the early 1980s Gaston Glock designed the Glock Model 17. Although his company had manufactured items for the military before, he had never designed a handgun.

Rather than re-hash old ideas, Glock started with a clean sheet of paper. The result was a revolution in handgun design, with an impressive list of firsts and unique features: 1) a polymer frame, 2) no external safeties, 3) three internal safeties, 4) a surface finish on the steel harder than anything available from any factory, 5)

amazing durability and reliability, and 6) a new benchmark for stark, utilitarian looks.

Police departments across the country and around the world quickly adopted the Glock Model 17. Once that happened, many civilian shooters had to have one, too. Each new model has been eagerly adopted, with few exceptions, and Glock now owns a large segment of the police market. In the war in Iraq, apparently any and all police, security and protection forces who were not regular US military forces were commonly armed with Glocks, either G-17s or G-19s. The US regular forces used

Big or small, all Glocks work the same way.

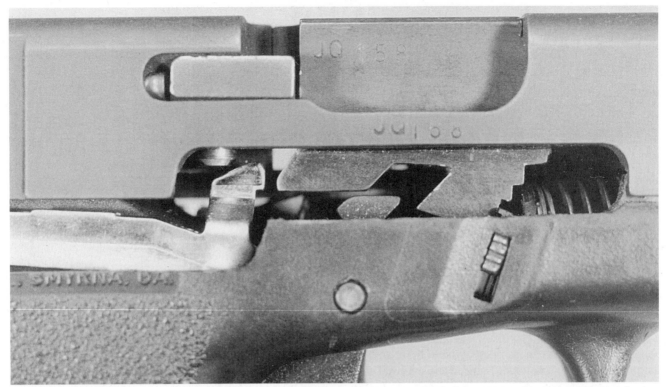

Underneath the ejection port is the locking block. The angles of the barrel cam the barrel up and down to lock and unlock it. Right behind the feed ramp of the barrel is the part of the trigger bar that pushes the firing pin safety out of the way as you pull the trigger.

You only need a single drift punch to disassemble the Glock for cleaning and service.

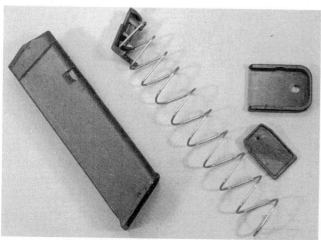

Glock magazine tubes are steel-lined, but encased in polymer. The follower, baseplate and baseplate retainer are plastic. If you want your magazine catch to last, use polymer magazines with polymer mag catches. If your magazines are steel, switch the mag catch to steel.

Beretta M9s, and the SpecOps people used whatever they wanted.

The very things that make the Glock unique and attractive — such as its easily installed replacement parts — also make it difficult to modify or work on. The areas that you can readily change are sights, barrel, slide stop and magazine release, trigger pull, and recoil springs.

GLOCK MODIFICATIONS

Some modifications may not be prudent. If you are going to shoot in Glock Sport Shooting matches, almost all changes from "box-stock" will put your Glock in the Open category. So, changing (for example) your connector to a 3.5-pound connector, if it puts you in Open, is not prudent. You'll be competing against Glocks with compensators and red-dot sights. If you're going to move up to Open, go all the way and not just part of the way.

The Novak sight is a very durable, all-steel unit that fits the standard Glock dovetail.

This Glock cutaway has been used to soothe distraught customers who had been told untrue things about the Glock. It allows you to see all the workings of the Glock, without being able to actually fire a round.

246 BASIC PISTOLSMITHING THE GLOCK

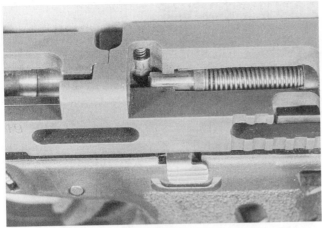

Here you can see the firing pin safety, just above the striker (firing pin). If the trigger has not been pulled, it will not move out of the path of the firing pin.

The Glock front sight and its wedge.

And any modifications that void the warranty (such as grip reduction) should be undertaken only after thorough consideration, and will also preclude you from shooting in a GSSF match.

SIGHTS

Glock sights are plastic. Unfortunately plastic, while inexpensive to manufacture, does not stand up well to hard use. With only a few weeks of draw and dry-fire practice your front sight can be visibly worn. The Glock rear is a plastic casting with a small steel plate at the bottom to engage the corners of the dovetail. If you drift the sight out you must be careful to put your punch at the bottom of the dovetail against this plate. Otherwise

you will damage the rear sight removing it. Glock rear sights are well known for their frailty.

The original front sight uses a small wedge to hold it in place. If you want to replace this plastic sight with a steel one, you will find your replacement comes with a small screw that threads into the bottom of the sight. Be sure to use Loctite to secure the sight and screw. Replacement rear sights slide into the rear dovetail, just like the originals.

The most durable replacement rear sights – available as plain, three-dot and night sights – are from Novak and MMC. With any of them you can keep your original front sight. You can also use a rear sight from Scott Warren, a top-notch practical shooting competitor and retired fed-

Glock makes a sight pusher to handle their sights. The angled sides of the rear sight, and its plastic composition make using other sight pushers difficult at times.

eral law enforcement agent. He has designed a rear sight that is compact and gives you a good sight picture. It must work, as he's done well on the competition circuit, well enough to kick me around.

If you want to replace your original rear sight with an adjustable one, the Mec-Gar or Pachmayr sights use the original front sight, or a replacement of the same height.

The Millett adjustable rear sight slides into the dovetail, but requires a front sight much taller than the factory original. Millett makes a screw-on front sight that uses the standard Glock oval. If the screw-on front sight comes off, (it's a big piece of metal, after all) buy a new Millett Dual-Crimp front sight and install it.

Sight changes do not alter the division in which you shoot in most competitions. Unless you go to a red-dot optic, any notch-and-post sights are the same as stock in a lot of competitions. However, check and be sure.

The international rules of practical shooting, the IPSC rules, can be quite particular in some Divisions. It would be very bad to spend a lot of money on travel, and time on practice, to arrive in a foreign country and find your pistol is not kosher for the match.

BARRELS

The Glock barrel does not use regular-style rifling. Traditional rifling is cut or swaged into the barrel's bore as a square-bottomed channel, or a square-topped rail. In swaging, a super-hard button that is shaped in the intended rifling pattern is pushed through the barrel. Whether cut or swaged, in cross section the raised portion, or "lands," and the lowered portions, "grooves," look like a gear.

The rifling on a Glock barrel is curved. Instead of right-angled lands and grooves, the Glock lands are gently rounded above the grooves, in order to minimize wear. As a traditional bore wears, the top corners of the lands become eroded, allowing gas to leak past the bullet. Called "blow-by," these leaks may harm accuracy. In a

This Novak front sight is taller than standard so it can be filed down to a perfect height after test-firing.

The standard Glock sight is plastic, and not as durable as the rest of the pistol.

The standard Glock front is a small plastic pyramid. It can wear enough to change your point of impact. Change it to a steel sight for greater durability.

A cut-rifling barrel for the Glock on the right, and the Glock barrel on the left. If you want to use lead bullets in your Glock you will have to install a cut-rifling barrel such as this Wilson.

The author's dependable assistant, Mike Clare, helping with the chronograph work.

The Wilson barrel and two groups, each just over an inch across. Groups this size are not rare with a match barrel in the Glock.

match-grade barrel, however, the steel is so hard that any erosion of the lands is so slow as to be nonexistent. I own cut-rifled pistol barrels with over 100,000 rounds through them that are still delivering match accuracy and show no signs of blow-by.

Although Glock barrels may not wear any better or worse than any other top-of-the-line match barrels, the rifling allows Glock to manufacture the barrels cheaply. The rifling on a Glock is also very easy to clean — with one big exception. Glock barrels hate lead.

The use of lead bullets in a Glock barrel will cause severe leading and loss of accuracy. As each bullet tries to push its way through the lead deposits left by previous bullets, chamber pressure soars. In the .40, the leading can push pressures past the physical margins of brass and steel. Several owners have blown up Glock .40 pistols — just by using lead bullets.

Intended as a pistol for use by law enforcement agencies and the military, neither of which use lead bullets, Glock rifling was designed for use only with jacketed bullets. What to do? Your first choice is not to use lead bullets in a Glock barrel. Buy jacketed ammunition, or jacketed bullets if you are reloading. Given the cost of ammunition, restricting yourself to jacketed bullets only

The standard Glock barrel is accurate. The Wilson barrel is even more accurate, and handles lead bullets too. The flier on the right-hand target is probably the shooter's fault.

Police never use lead bullets, so you rarely see anything but a Glock barrel in a Glock sidearm.

may not be financially prudent. Your second choice is not to use your Glock barrel. Replace it with one that has cut-rifling in the bore, allowing the use of lead bullets. Many barrels are available, from suppliers from Accu-match to Wilson (and just about everyone else in between).

For those who want to stick with their Glock a barrel, the question arises — is a Glock barrel accurate? Yes. With my Glock Model 22 in .40 S&W, I tested factory and reloaded ammunition using jacketed bullets. It shot as well as any other .40 I had along, and like any other pistol it showed distinct preferences for one load or another. It was not a tack-driver, but ten it was never intended to be one.

For those who want to stick with lead, there's another question — how cost-effective is swapping barrels? To figure this out, I compared the cost of lead bullets per 1,000 to jacketed bullets per 1,000. Using the least-expensive replacement barrel available, you would recover your investment in 3,000 rounds. The most expensive barrel would be paid for in 5,000 rounds. A serious competitor could recover the cost of a cut-rifled barrel in a few months. Less serious shooters could still recover it in a year.

FITTING A NEW BARREL

Disassemble your Glock and remove the factory barrel. The new barrel should slide into place. If it doesn't, take a close look and see where it is binding.

If the barrel binds on the sides of the hood, file them to provide at least .003 inch of clearance on each side. The clearance must be an equal amount. If you have it perfectly fitted side-to-side at .002 inch, leave it alone. But make them even. You can't have .001 inch on one side and .004 on the other. Well, if you erred and you have that much difference, perhaps you'd best leave things alone. Trying to fit it with .004, .005 or .006 of clearance on each side might not be such a good idea. Better to be careful nd sneak up on the fit.

If the barrel binds on the rear of the hood, apply Dykem and try to force the barrel into place. File where the Dykem has been rubbed off, and try again. Once you can force the barrel into place, switch to a medium fine stone and stone the end of the hood until the barrel moves smoothly into place in the slide, but bears evenly across its whole rear face.

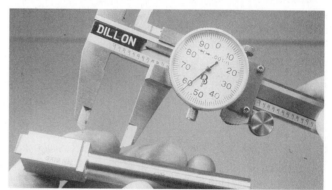

This 9mm chamber measures .757 inches, just over minimum and has proven itself to be ultra-reliable.

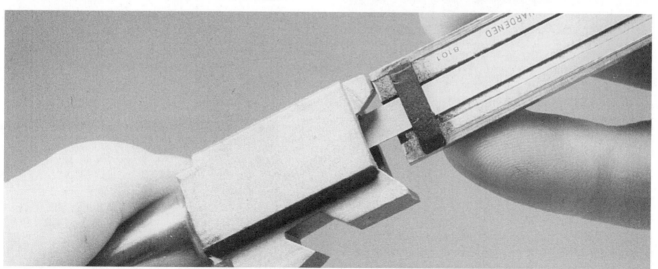

Once your new barrel is fitted to the slide, measure the chamber length. It should not be less than the caliber minimum length. If it is, ream it carefully until it is just at the minimum.

Measure the chamber length. If the chamber is now shorter than the caliber minimum, you must lengthen the chamber with a chambering reamer.

I did not need to file the Wilson barrel I tested and went right to the stoning. Many Glock replacement barrels are intended to be drop-in units. The Wilson chamber was the correct length and did not need reaming.

Carry-up and fitting in lockup in a Glock is easy. The bottom foot controls how high the barrel lifts, and all you need is for it to be lifted high enough to close firmly to the slide as the slide finishes its return. In most cases, you will not have to do anything to the foot. In some very few, you might have to gently file or stone the bottom of the foot so the slide can close without binding.

CALIBER CHANGES IN THE GLOCK

It is possible to change the caliber of your Glock. You can either change the barrel, or change both the slide and barrel.

Calibers that share a head size can be interchanged with the change of a barrel. For example, Glocks chambered in .40 can also shoot .357 SIG. Since the .357 SIG

cartridge is basically a necked-down .40 S&W case, by installing a .357 SIG caliber barrel you can shoot either caliber. The same process works for a Glock in .45 ACP, re-barreling it to .400 Cor-bon. Use the original slide and fit the new barrel.

To change calibers where the case head size is not the same, you will need an extra slide. You can get slides from Glock or Caspian Arms. Since you must use the same length slide that the pistol had when it left the factory you can't build a short-barreled pistol on a standard frame as you can with a 1911.

Soon after I bought a Glock Model 22 in .40 S&W, I lucked onto a source of cheap and readily available 9mm. Sometimes the ammo was jacketed, and sometimes it was loaded with lead bullets. I obtained a slide in 9mm from Caspian arms, and fitted it with an Olympic cut-rifling barrel.

Fitting the barrel to the slide took a little time (it wasn't a drop-in barrel), but was easy. Because the hood was longer and wider than the slide opening, I filed and

Press the rear retaining pin out.

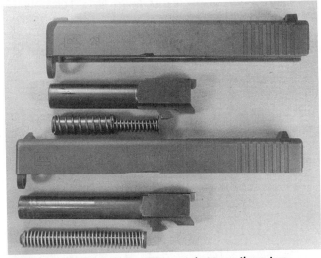

While it looks like the only difference between these two Glocks are the lengths of the slide and barrel, that is not the case. Some models have minor differences to preclude installing a shorter (or longer) slide and barrel on a particular frame.

When switching from a .40S&W upper assembly to a 9mm upper assembly, you will have to change connector housings. The 9mm ejector is longer, and bends slightly in towards the center. You cannot use a 9mm ejector with a .40 slide and barrel, or vice versa.

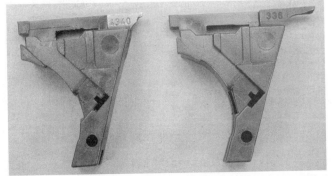

Not only are the ejectors shaped differently, but they have different part numbers.

then stoned the hood until the barrel moved smoothly into place. The chamber was short, so I reamed it to the minimum dimension once the barrel was fitted to the slide. Through test firing I learned that the slide would not always fully close; the minimum chamber size was too small for reloaded ammunition. I reamed the chamber .002 inches longer. Once I did that, by switching slide assemblies, ejectors and magazines I could shoot either 9mm or 40. I had a two-caliber handgun.

BARREL CHANGES AND COMPETITION

Don't bother to show up at a GSSF match with a non-Glock barrel fitted to your Glock. You'll find yourself

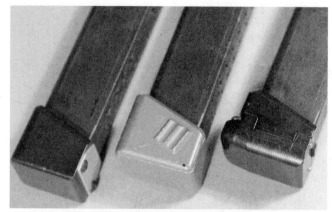

You can extend Glock magazines like any others. Left to right, Taylor Freelance, Dawson, Grams.

shooting in Open with the comped and red-dot sighted guns. (If they let you shoot at all.) A replacement barrel in USPSA or IDPA doesn't matter. And for Steel Challenge, American Handgunner Shoot-Off or other matches, no one is likely to ask unless they want to know what kind of accuracy you're getting. In IPSC, you can't make changes to a Production gun. So, unless your new barrel is another Glock barrel (and the same caliber as the original) you can't use it.

SLIDE STOP AND MAGAZINE CATCH

The Glock was designed as a combat pistol, long on toughness and durability, short on the touches that make it fast in a match. The slide stop is small and hard to use, and the magazine catch is sometimes so stiff you need both hands just to release it.

When the Glock first came out, the magazines wouldn't drop out of the pistol. After you pressed the magazine "release," you then had to wrestle the magazine out of the frame. Apparently it is not the custom in Europe to let expended magazines fall free to speed the process of reloading. When American consumers complained about needing three hands for a reload, Glock made changes. If you want a magazine that falls free, look for one with a square notch on the back. The old magazines have a U-shaped notch on the back. Both feed just fine.

It is easy to find and install a larger slide stop. They

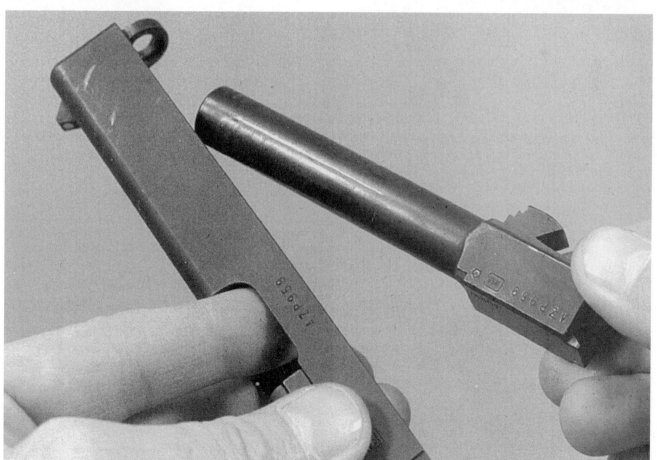

Push the rear of the barrel out of the slide.

are available from both Aro-Tek and Alchemy Arms. Remove the locking block pin as described in Chapter 5 and pull the old slide stop out. Slide the new one in, replace the locking block pin, and you are done.

The easiest way to get a larger magazine catch is to go

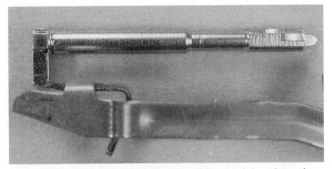

Here is the relationship between the striker and the trigger bar. The trigger bar pushes the striker back until the curved part of the trigger bar is cammed down by the connector angle. Then the striker is released, hitting the firing pin.

16-19   Here is the installed three-and-a-half-pound connector. The small tab attached to it is the disconnector. The slide presses this tab towards the centerline, allowing the trigger bar to slip off the connector, resetting the mechanism.

The trigger bar, from the front where it contacts the firing pin safety, to the rear where it contacts the connector.

with one from the next larger frame Glock. The only difference between the magazine catch for the 9mm/.40 pistols and that of the 10mm/.45 pistols is the length. Install a 10mm/.45 mag catch on your 9mm/.40, and you have an over-sized button. If you want to do the same for your 10mm/.45 you have to get a button from Alchemy Arms or Aro-Tek.

Changing the magazine catch can be a frustrating experience. Take the slide assembly off of the frame, and clamp the frame in a padded vise. The mag catch is held in by a wire. You will have to reach into the magazine well with a screwdriver and pry the wire out of its seat in the magazine catch. It will snap clear. Pull the old catch out, slide the new one in and use the screwdriver to flex the spring back into its seat in the new magazine catch. It's dark in there. You don't have much leverage. Use good lighting, a long screwdriver, and plenty of patience. The last time I changed a magazine catch the wire slipped off of the screwdriver seven times before I had it free. After that, the three attempts to secure the wire almost seemed easy. Patience is essential.

The difference between the connectors is the angle of the camming shoulder. On the right, an eight-pound, in the center a five-pound, and on the left a three-and-a-half-pound.

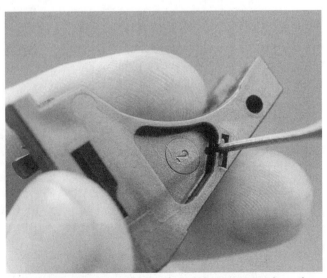

Use a small punch to press the end of the connector from the ejector side of the housing.

TRIGGER PULL

The Glock does not respond to the usual trigger-pull enhancement techniques. Because you will be pushing a polished stainless steel plate over plastic as you stroke the trigger of your Glock, stoning won't help. The engagement of the trigger bar to the striker tail has no bearing on trigger pull. The two things that will improve your trigger pull are changing the angle in the connector and replacing the spring in the connector body.

As the trigger bar moves back under your finger pressure, it cocks the striker. At the end of its stroke, the connector pushes the trigger bar away from the striker. The shallower the connector angle, the lower the apparent trigger pull. To change the angle you must change the connector. The standard connector is a so-called 5-pound connector. The target connector is a 3.5-pound connector.

If you want a new connector for your non long-slide pistol, send for one from Alchemy Arms or Aro-Tek. Disassemble the pistol and strip the trigger mechanism from the frame. On the trigger block, push the tail of the connector out from the other side, and then pry it free. Push the new connector into place. Use a dab of McCormick Trigger Job on the angle of the new connector. If the connector came with a new spring, and you are improving your trigger for competition, unloop the old spring and loop the new one on in the same direction. Reassemble and check function. Test fire and see if you

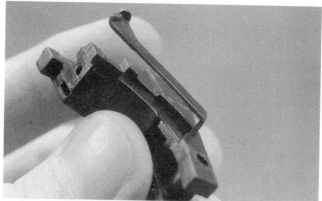

With the connector pushed up, you can grasp it to pull it out of the housing.

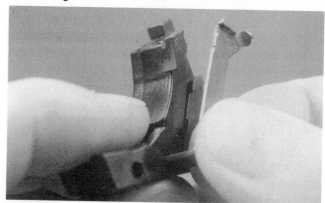

After removing the old connector, press the new one into the connector housing.

Unhook the trigger bar from the connector housing and swing it out of the way.

With all the frame pins out, hook the punch under the ejector and use the left side of the frame as your pivot point.

Lever the trigger assembly out of the frame.

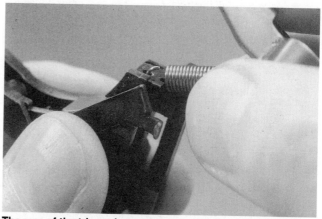

The rear of the trigger bar spring is hooked onto the connector housing. You have to remove this spring when installing a New York Trigger spring.

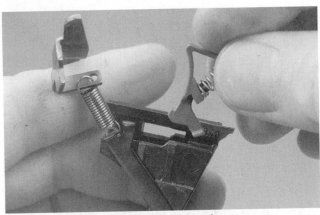

Press the spring into the connector housing.

When the little foot on the bottom of the New York Trigger spring snaps in place, the spring is installed.

Use the trigger bar to compress the top of the New York Trigger spring and install the trigger bar in the connector housing.

Here you see the New York Trigger spring installed, and the standard coil spring removed.

like the results.

If you want a connector for your long-slide pistol, you must send it back to the factory. They offer it on the 17L and 24L long-slide match pistols. Glock will not sell you a 3.5-pound connector to install yourself.

For competition, improve the trigger pull of your Glock by replacing the factory striker with one made of titanium. Titanium is lighter than steel, and the striker will get to the primer faster once it is released. This shorter lock time improves your shooting. Do not use the Ti striker in a carry gun. You're trading a bit of durability for a bit of increased scoring ability. Faced with a felon, you do not want any potential durability issues jumping up and biting you someplace tender.

If you carry your Glock for personal defense you may want to increase your trigger pull. The Glock's standard trigger pull, their 5-pound connector, is similar to the feel of a double-action pistol in the single-action mode. In the first half, when you are taking the slack from the parts, the trigger has a light pull. As you draw back the striker the pull gets noticeably heavier.

When police departments started turning in their revolvers for Glocks they wanted a trigger pull that felt more like a double-action revolver — the same weight all the way back. Glock's first attempt at a uniform trigger pull was to offer an 8-pound connector. While it made the second part of the pull heavier, the heavier connector did not change the initial light pull. Many police departments, including New York City, still found the pull unsatisfactory. It was just too light at the start. For them Glock designed the "New York Trigger." The "New York Trigger" is simply a replacement trigger return spring that makes the trigger pull feel the same for its entire distance.

Police officers spend much more time pointing handguns at suspects than they do firing them. While holding a group of suspects at gunpoint the hazard of a light trigger can be significant. A loud noise, a quick movement, an officer who stumbles — any one of these can lead to a suspect's being shot. Rather than spend millions on lawsuits, New York City spent pennies on a new trigger spring.

The New York Trigger is a prudent choice for anyone who carries a Glock for defense. Under the stress of a violent encounter, its extra weight and feel can keep you from a ruinous accident.

The New York Trigger spring is intended only for use with a 5-pound connector. Don't install both an 8-pound connector and a New York Trigger spring in your Glock. The combination generally results in a pistol that will not fire.

RECOIL SPRINGS AND GUIDE RODS

Originally, Glock designed their plastic guide rod with a separate recoil spring. Later they changed this to a guide rod with a captured spring. Now when you pull the rod and spring out the captured spring will not launch itself across the room.

To change the balance of the pistol and dampen recoil, you can install a steel or even tungsten guide rod. The spring will no longer be captured, but for many shooters that is a small price to pay to reduce the felt recoil of hot hollow-point ammunition. You can even replace the standard guide rod with a dual-spring guide rod from Sprinco. It will take the snap out of the recoil of hot ammo like Cor-bon.

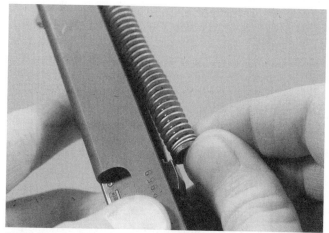

Catch the rear of the recoil spring assembly and lift it out of its seat in the barrel.

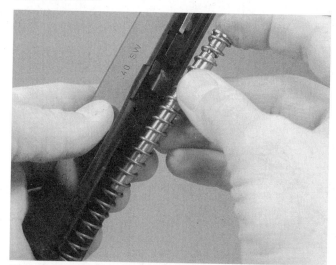

Place the front of the recoil spring against the slide and compress the spring.

Here is the Glock M-22 with the installed Sprinco dual-spring guide rod.

MATCH THE CATCH TO THE MAGAZINE

The Glock magazine catch, frame, and magazine body are polymer. The frame has a steel skeleton in its upper part. Parts of this skeleton stick out of the polymer to form the slide rails.

The magazines have a steel sleeve inside them, to stiffen the magazine tube. The old, non drop-free magazines had steel on only three sides, and the magazine was supposed to swell slightly to keep it from dropping out when released. The drop-free magazines have steel internally in all four sides.

Unlike the rest of the pistol the magazine catch does not have any steel in it. If you use a steel-bodied replacement magazine, you will ruin your magazine catch. In a choice between steel and polymer magazines for a Glock, always take the polymer. For all other pistols, always take the steel.

If you already have steel magazines for your Glock invest in a steel magazine catch from M.G.S. so the magazines don't chew your polymer catch to pieces.

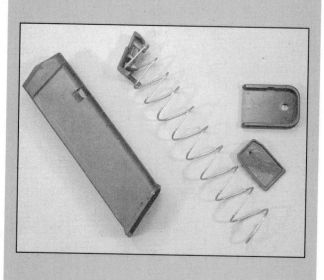

CHAPTER 18

BASIC PISTOLSMITHING THE 1911

When the Colt .45 Automatic was first called the Model 1911, planes flew more slowly than we now drive on freeways, cars had wooden frames and were started with a crank, and what illumination there was for houses mostly came from gas. (Yes, there was electricity, but Thomas Edison was still struggling to wire the cities of the East Coast with DC current. Luckily for us, he lost.) Titanic was growing in a shipyard. William H. Taft was President of the United States. Today all are gone, save the 1911 pistol.

Through all the decades there have been two distinct camps among those objecting to the 1911: those who fault its accuracy, and those who fault its reliability. There are also those who have complained of its heavy recoil, but in this age of magnum cartridges, the .45 is viewed as something of a pussycat. Besides, if the .45 really is too much for you, simply have your 1911 cham-bered in other, softer-recoiling calibers. You can convert yours to a smaller caliber, or exchange it for one smaller. A 9mm or .38 Super pistol is all the rage in IDPA for the Enhanced Service Pistol Division. A light-recoiling 1911 for use in Limited or Limited-10 USPSA Divisions is a great way to teach new shooters good habits. It is also a good way for an experienced shooter to work through carpal tunnel, tennis elbow or shoulder problems. And the cost of ammo can be so low that you get a lot more practice. And if 9mm is not cheap enough or easy to find, then a .22 conversion on your 1911 is easy to arrange.

The truth about the 1911 is simple: the longstanding objections to it have never been a response to the gun, but instead were reactions to decisions made concerning its use. Those "unreliable" 1911s? They were (but are not any more) hand-fitted target pistols used for seriously accurate bullseye competition, competitions

Les Baer offers parts as well as frames, slides and pistols. You can mix and match, or simply order a complete package.

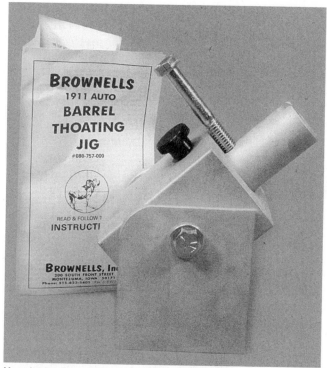

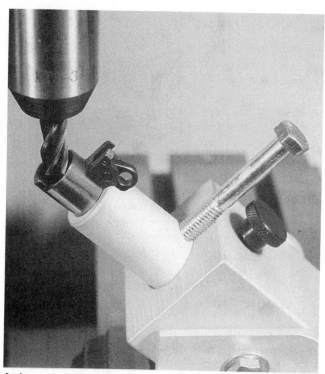

Here is the Brownells barrel ramp throating jig. It allows you to cut a new ramp without making a mistake.

A close-up of the barrel, fixture and end mill.

where a lack of reliability was not a serious impediment. Those "inaccurate" 1911s? Ultra-reliable, but so-loose-they-rattled military pistols selected because they shot well enough to hit the people they were aimed at. And surplus, to boot. The target shooters didn't care about reliability, and the military wasn't interested in more than "enough" accuracy. The pistols performed exactly as required in both uses.

The need for accuracy combined with reliability didn't come up until the development of IPSC. You can't win an IPSC match with an inaccurate pistol. Misses not only don't help you, they hurt you with penalty points. Nor can you win with an unreliable pistol. If you have a malfunction, you cannot stop and start the stage over again after you have solved the problem. You must continue. One extra second in the time of a stage can mean the difference between winning and losing. Lose 10 seconds clearing a malfunction and you have a disaster. Well, a match disaster. It has to happen in real life for it to be more than an annoyance.

The good news is simple: You can have both reliability and accuracy in the same pistol. Since improving reliability is easier, we will start with that and go to accuracy later.

Testing the reliability of your 1911 involves taking it to the range and putting many rounds through it. Use a top-quality, standard-length (seven- or eight-shot) magazine such as a Wilson, Brown, McCormick, Mag-Pack, Mec-gar, Para USA or Pachmayr. Start with factory hardball. Put 200 rounds through your pistol. If you have no problems strip and clean your pistol, reassemble and go to the next test. If you do have problems, go directly to the

section on performing a reliability package. Do not clean your pistol.

Some shooters like to brag about how many rounds they have put through their pistol without a cleaning, as if this was some sort of test of reliability. It isn't. All it really tests is how long you can go before your luck runs out and you cause some serious wear or damage. Whatever your intended use for your pistol, 200 rounds tests reliability. You are not going to be in a gunfight requiring anything close to 200 rounds. You are not going to shoot in a match requiring more than 200 rounds before cleaning. There are some matches calling for very high round-count stages: 50-75-100 round stages. Or at least there were, before ammunition became so expensive and hard to find.

If your pistol is intended for defense and has passed the first test switch to the hollow-point ammunition you have selected as your defensive ammo. All the current high-tech hollow-points perform admirably. Buy at least two brands and practice with each. Purchase 200 rounds of whichever brand feeds reliably and shoots accurately in your pistol. Repeat the 200-round reliability test.

If you are using the pistol for competition, you will probably be reloading your ammunition with lead semi-wadcutter bullets. Test fire at least 200 rounds of your match or practice ammunition.

If, when you switch to the hollow-points or the lead bullets, reliability suffers, then roll up your sleeves, for you have some work to do. Do not clean your pistol. You'll need to see the brass marks and the powder residue left behind by the cases.

RELIABILITY PACKAGE

The purpose of a reliability package is to ensure that your 1911 is operating correctly. There are minor problems of fitting and dimensions that the mechanical forces of operation can overcome. However, just because the recoil spring can force a round past a burr or toolmark doesn't mean it is a good idea to always depend on it doing so. For many pistols, the effort of a reliability package is mostly expended in looking at, but not needing to correct, the more common problems. The feed ramp is one example. If you take your 1911 apart, inspect the ramp, and find it correct, you have done your job even though you have not done anything but look. If a part, dimension or angle is correct, leave it alone. Don't go polishing, stoning or filing it just because its "part of the work." If your pistol is "accurate enough" then don't go changing things like the bushing just to gain an "improvement" that won't help you. Indeed, before you go spending a lot of time, money and effort chasing accuracy improvements, you should determine just how accurate your pistol and ammo are. Use a Ransom rest if available, and if not, then have the best shot at your gun club shoot your gun over sandbags. Use both your reloads (I assume you are reloading your ammo, if you shoot competitively and expect to be able to afford to practice) and factory match ammo. You might just find that you could gain a greater improvement in accuracy for less time, cost and effort by improving the reloads you produce, than by dropping a match barrel into your 1911 and continuing to use said reloads.

Disassemble the pistol and look closely at the breechface, the extractor and the tip-over edge of the chamber. Factory machining usually leaves toolmarks on these parts, and the marks cause friction. The friction rubs brass from your cartridges and leaves a noticeable deposit behind. You must remove the more egregious toolmarks and thus reduce the friction.

Remove the extractor and slightly round and polish the bottom of the hook. Polish the inside face of the hook, where the cartridge rim bears. Polish with a narrow strip of fine-grit cloth. On the slide, stone the side of the breechface under the extractor hole. Stone the sidewall of the breechface opposite the extractor. This second area is often the critical source of friction, and removing the toolmarks here promises to clear up 90 percent of your reliability problems. You want the extractor to slide smoothly onto the rim of the cartridge, and have as complete a "bite" on the rim as possible. You also don't want the rim dragging on rough spots on the breechface. Look at the breechface itself. If there are heinous tool marks, polish the breechface. Otherwise, leave it alone.

Should you polish the feedramp? Only if you want to. Unless the toolmarks are huge (HUGE!), polishing the feedramp has practically no effect on how well your pis-

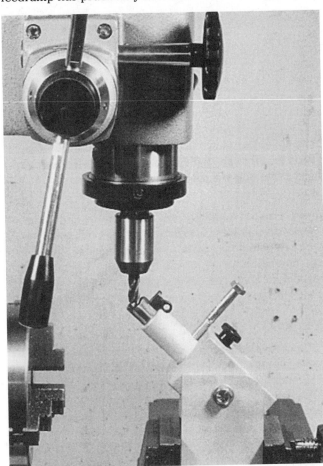

The Brownells fixture set up to cut the feed ramp on a barrel.

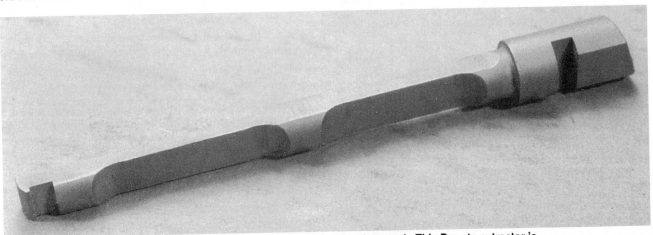

The extractor is meant to do a spring's job, and it should be made of spring steel. This Bar-sto extractor is.

tol feeds. If you must polish the ramp, do not round off the top edge of the feedramp in the frame. Doing so will instantly turn your pistol into a non-feeding 1911, in dire need of a weld and re-cut ramp job.

Very old pistols have narrow barrel ramps meant only for hardball. To feed hollow-points or semiwadcutters you must open the ramp or buy a new barrel. Base your decision on how well the pistol works.

If the current barrel is accurate, cut the ramp. If the current barrel is only average in accuracy (3 inches or greater at 25 yards), don't cut the ramp. Instead, spend your money on a better barrel. All currently-produced barrels come with the correct ramp configuration.

Cutting a ramp is best done with a ramp-cutting fixture. Lock your barrel in the fixture and clamp the fixture in a mill or drill press. Cut the ramp according to the instructions. What those instructions will do is guide you to clamping the barrel at the correct angle to produce a proper feedramp, and how widely you have to cut the ramp. The short form: the same angle it already has, and only slightly wider than the width of the ramp in the frame. If you have an experienced, steady hand you can do the job with grinding stones in a hand-held grinder, but you risk marring the angle between barrel and feedramp. Use of the fixture eliminates the possibil-

ity of this damage.

Once you have cut the barrel ramp use an extra-fine stone on the tip-over edge of the chamber. You want to reduce the sharpness of the tip-over edge, not round it into a smooth curve from ramp to chamber. Clean the slide and reassemble it. Use an extractor tension gauge to measure the tension of your extractor. Record the reading for future reference. Repeat the 200-round reliability test your pistol had previously failed.

If you still experience feeding malfunctions at this point in the process you should use the malfunction guide in Chapter 11 to hunt down the specific problem. Many more than 95 percent of 1911 pistols will feed perfectly after a reliability package.

FITTING THE EXTRACTOR

The 1911 has always had a small but persistent problem with the extractor. Take a flat piece of steel. Bend it. How much tension have you placed on the steel at the bending point? Good question. So it is with the extractor, which, after all, is just a flat piece of steel with a bend in it. The amount of tension this bend creates is critical. Is there a specific, single best amount of tension? No. There are upper and lower limits, and for each pistol there is an acceptable range.

To adjust tension on your extractor, slide the extractor out....

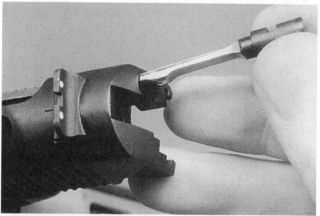
turn the extractor around....

When installing an extractor, make sure the lower corner and lower edge of the hook is rounded and polished.

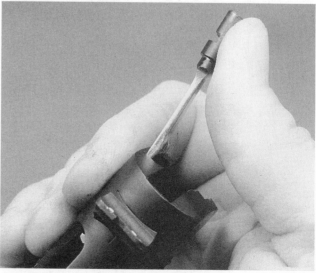
and press the end away from the slide.

More-modern pistols, such as the Glock, use a coil spring and plunge to pivot an extractor into place. The amount of tension the extractor has is easy to design, gauge and replace if needed.

The old method of "measuring" 1911 extractor tension involved taking the slide off the frame and removing the barrel. A loaded round was stuffed in the breechface to be held in place by the extractor. If the round fell out there wasn't enough tension. It wasn't what you'd call a precise test.

The new and better method is to use a Weigand extractor tension gauge. With the pistol disassembled, slip the gauge under the extractor. Pull it out with a trigger pull gauge as the "handle." The amount of force needed

Check extractor tension with a tension gauge and a trigger pull gauge. Slide the tension gauge under the extractor....

to slide the gauge out from under the extractor is your tension measurement. Record this, and save it with your pistol. Check the tension every 1,000 rounds or so, and if the measured value starts to decrease, increase tension (see below).

While the old way to "test" extractor tension was poor, the old way to increase tension on the extractor still works. Disassemble the slide and pull the extractor halfway out of its tunnel. Rotate the extractor 180 degrees. Bend it slightly with your thumb, pushing its tail away from the firing pin tunnel. Turn it back around, slide it into place, and with the firing pin and retaining plate in the slide, measure the extractor tension. If the tension is not back to its original value, repeat, pushing harder this time. You can also bend the extractor in your vise. Remove it from the slide. Open your vise jaws 1/2 inch and gently close them on the front of the extractor. Using the vise to hold it, bend the rear of the extractor. Better yet, use the Weigand extractor tension adjustment tool to tension the extractor. Jack Weigand made this tool specifically to be able to adjust the tension of an extractor in measured amounts. The ideal way to use it is at the range. Remove your extractor, use the tension adjuster to increase extractor tension by a small amount, and reinstall and test fire. If you need more, adjust the tool for more tension. The bottoming screw prevents over-adjusting the extractor. The adjustment knob flexes the extractor. As you need more tension, turn the bottoming screw more and more away from the adjustment knob. If you cannot range-test and adjust, the traditional adjustment specs are for the extractor to have between 12 and 20 ounces of hold, when tested with a Weigand extractor gauge and recording scale.

If your extractor becomes too troublesome, losing its tension every few hundred rounds, replace it. Irv

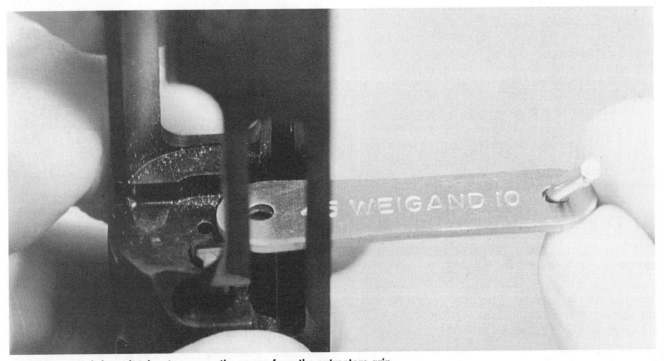

record how much force it takes to remove the gauge from the extractors grip.

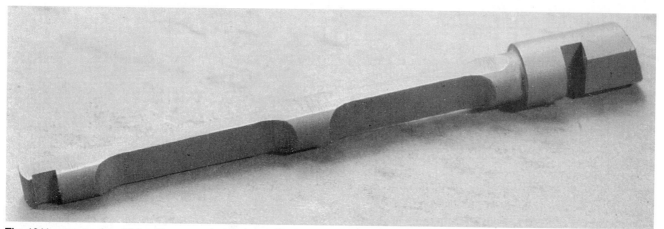

The 1911 extractor is criticized by some, but properly fitted and tensioned it will work 100% for a long time.

Stone III of Bar-sto believes that many problems with the extractor stem from the alloys used in manufacturing. He has a set of blueprints for the Match 1911 that date before WWII; the specifications for the extractor call for spring steel. Irv notes that many current extractors are made out of tool steel, an alloy that does not resist fatigue as well as spring steel. He makes his extractors out of spring steel. Other makers, such as Wilson, Ed Brown and Les Baer, don't tell us specifically what they make their extractors of, but do promise long life and reliable function. Whatever they make them from, their extractors deliver.

To fit a new extractor, remove the old one and clean out the extractor tunnel. Check the bottom of the new hook; it should be slightly rounded, just enough to smooth the extractor's trip over the cartridge rim. Round the hook too much and you decrease its gripping area. Polish the hook and the rim recess, as above.

Slip the extractor into the slide and check the fit of the retaining plate. Remember, it must hold the extractor firmly. A too-large plate can be filed along its edges until it will slip into the slide. A too-small plate will allow the extractor to wobble in the tunnel, called "clocking." While dimpling the plate's edge with a centerpunch or peening it can keep a too-small retaining plate from falling out of the pistol, it won't help support the extractor. Get an oversized retaining plate, and fit it to the slide and the new extractor.

Adjust the tension on your new extractor to match the setting the old extractor had when it was working properly. Test fire. If you see the cartridges feeding hard or even hesitating before camming over the tip-over edge, reduce the tension and test again. Do not reduce the tension too much or your empties will not eject well. Extractor tension has the potential of sucking up all your time, effort and attention, if you let it. The test of "proper" extractor tension is simple: do the empties eject cleanly, reliably and to pretty much the same angle and distance? At that point tension is correct. In my book The Gun Digest Book of the 1911, I had occasion to test the extractor tension of two dozen new and newly built 1911s. The measured extractor tension using

a Weigand gauge and Brownells recording trigger pull measure went from zero (no recorded extractor tension) to 40 ounces. All the tested pistols proved 100 percent reliable with the ammo used, factory and reloads. The problem is not the amount, but the change. If your pistol works 100 percent, then the extractor tension is within acceptable specs for that pistol. Should the tension change, you could be in for an unpleasant surprise.

Since then, I'm a whole lot less concerned with the absolute tension value of any given pistol. That is, I don't expect any one of them in particular to have extractor tension between "X" and "Y" ounces, or I "fix" it. If the pistol extracts reliably and ejects in a reasonably consistent manner, I'm happy.

If your firing pin retaining plate is loose and drops out, or it does not provide a firm fit to the extractor, replace it. The standard plate is .465 inches wide. This oversized one is .480 wide, and must be filed before it will slide into place.

INSTALLING THE NEW EJECTOR

Even with correct extractor tension, sometimes a new extractor combined with the old ejector can still cause weak ejection. Installing an extended ejector will increase ejection force and distance. Begin by measuring the sidewall of the ejection port. If it is higher than .480 to .490 inch, you may find that better ejection will dent your brass. You will probably have to lower the ejection port (see below). However, if what you have is a USGI 1911A1 or 1911, consider carefully any work you might do. At the current level of collector interest and market values, a clean USGI WWII 1911A1 could be worth as much as $1,000. Double that if there is anything rare about it. A WWI 1911 could start at two grand and quickly rise in value. Those are the pistols most likely to have very high slide sidewalls, and lowering the ejection port will remove any collector value. There is no such

The standard ejector below, is designed to toss empties up and out. The extended ejector above is designed to toss the empties to the side.

The magazine at rest is not supposed to come near the ejector.

Make sure your new ejector does not touch the magazine when the magazine is pressed up as far as it will go.

The ejector sits in two holes, the long leg goes in front.

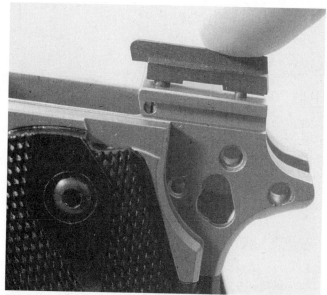

Press the ejector into place to see if it fits snugly.

Check the front leg first.

tors want them as original as possible.

Ejectors are caliber- and model-specific, with the slide slots in slightly different locations depending on caliber and slide length. You will not be able to fit a .45 ACP ejector into a slide for a .40/10mm or a .38 Super/9mm. Likewise, the Government Model and the Commander slides take different ejectors. When you order a new ejector specify both the caliber and the slide length.

To remove the old ejector, use a drift punch and drive the retaining pin out of the frame. Clamp the ejector in your vise, and tap the frame off of the clamped ejector. Discard the old ejector. Check the fit of the front leg of your new ejector to the frame, with the ejector turned at an angle to the frame. It should slide easily into the hole. Now press the ejector down into both holes. Don't worry if you have to tap gently with a hammer; you want the ejector to fit snugly.

If you have checked the fit of both legs of your ejector and found it slightly loose, remove the ejector and bend the front leg by tapping it with a hammer. Replace the ejector in both holes and recheck the fit. Continue your gentle bending until the ejector doesn't wiggle after you've pressed it into both holes.

With the ejector in the frame, but not secured, press a magazine into place. Check to see that the magazine is not touching the ejector, even when pressed up past the locking point. If your ejector is sitting too low over the magazine well it will get pasted every time you slam a magazine into place — bad for both the magazine and

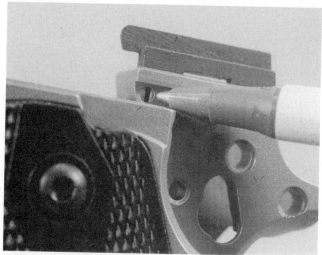

You have to measure the distance down and remove the ejector to file the leg. You cannot drill through the hole and the leg.

File the front leg of the ejector at the measured and marked location.

Once filed, you can replace the ejector and its retaining pin.

If your extended ejector comes to a point, leave it alone. If it comes with a square front, slightly bevel the edges of the tip.

ejector. If it hits the mag, remove the ejector and file the underside of the ejector until the magazine clears on subsequent checks.

Check the tip of the ejector. If the manufacturer shipped the ejector with a point on it, leave it alone. Most manufacturers, however, leave the tip square. You must profile it yourself. Gently bevel the corners. The beveled edges lever the brass out of the slide without putting extra stress on the extractor. Bevel to remove sharp edges, not to sharpen the ejector to a point that rivals that of the Washington Monument.

Now you fit the retaining pin. The retaining pin passes across a dimple in the front leg of the ejector, and keep the ejector in place. Do not think of simply drilling through the hole to create that dimple. Your drill is too small to withstand the lateral load, it will flex when it hits the ejector leg, and you will make a mess of your frame. You may even break the drill and then be in a real pickle.

Pull the ejector out of the frame. Measure the distance from the frame top down to the hole in the frame for the retaining pin, and use a round file to cut a clearance notch that far down on the ejector leg. Check the fit regularly. Once the pin will fit across your clearance notch or groove, drift it in. You can live without the retaining pin, but every time you clean the pistol you'll run the risk of losing the ejector down the drain.

Check that the slide, without its recoil spring or barrel attached, will fit over the new ejector. It should. If it won't, gently file the ejector sides until the slide clears.

Assemble the pistol and test-fire. Your empties will now eject with greater vigor. A note: you can, if you search, find an ejector that is too long. You need more, but not too much more. Resist the temptation ot hunt down and install the longest possible ejector, or make one yourself.

LOWERING THE EJECTION PORT

With your new extractor and new ejector briskly flinging the brass out of your pistol, you may find that your old ejection port is now too small, and the sidewall is too high. If you are seeing bent empties, brass marks on the lower rail of the ejection port, or an occasional empty that stays around to gum things up, you will need to lower your ejection port.

Ejection ports used to be much smaller than they are now. When first designed, the ejection was intended to be upwards, and the sidewall of the slide at the ejection port was as much as .550 inch high. Current production on many pistols leaves this dimension between .450 and .475 inch, still too high for brisk, reliable ejection. However, a lot more 1911s are leaving their respective factories with sidewalls that are low enough for clean, brisk ejection. If you have one of them, you need not bother with sidewall lowering except as theoretical knowledge.

A proper height for the sidewall is around .415 inch, but the steel of a slide is too tough to hand file to this measurement. You will have to use power, and for this job, a mill works best. It is possible to use a hand grinder such as a Dremel tool or a die grinder, if you are very careful, have a steady hand, and work slowly. However, a slip can mean a marred slide or an injured hand. If at all possible, use a mill. Borrow some mill time, trade favors, do what you have to. Take the slide off the frame. Remove the barrel, recoil spring system, and extractor. Lock your dial calipers to the final desired sidewall height, and use it to scribe a line below the current ejection port. Clamp the slide in the mill vise with the right sidewall up and level. I find a 3/8-inch cutter leaves the corners with a slightly smaller radius than the factory cutter — a look I like. If you don't, or feel this is too small, you can use a cutter up to 1/2 inch.

To save time later in hand-blending discrete mill cuts on the ejection port you will guide your cutter to travel in a "U" shape during its cutting path. You want a medi-

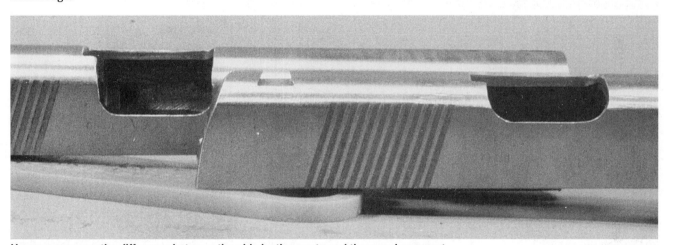

Here you can see the difference between the old ejection ports and the new, lower port.

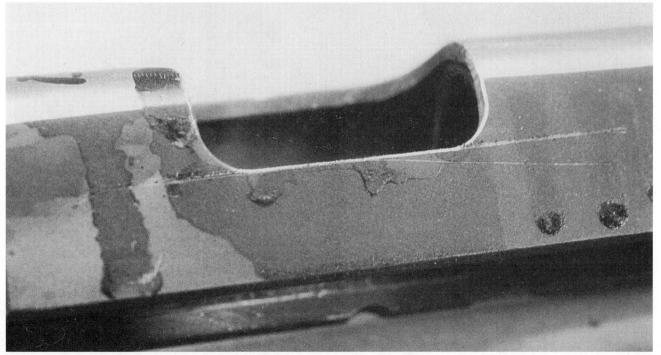

Here is another slide with the limit line marked in Dykem and the port cut to the line.

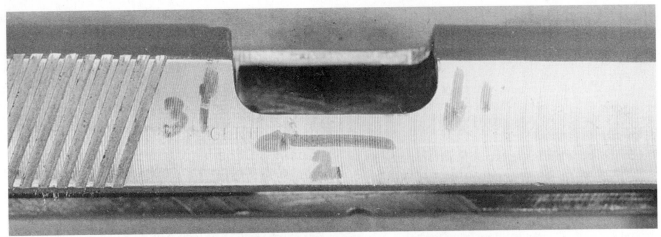

The order and direction of your milling cuts to lower the ejection port.

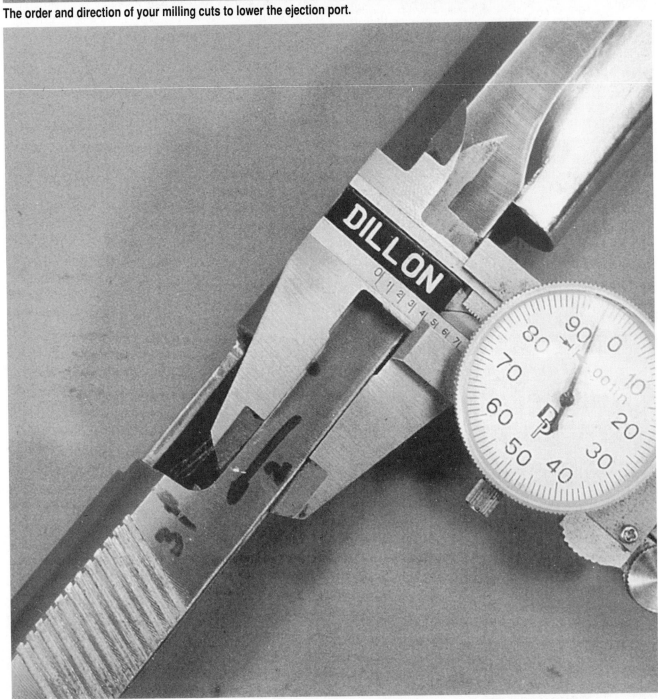

This port has had the sidewall lowered to .395 inches. This is more than is needed, but not so much it will be too thin.

um speed of rotation on your cutter. Carbide or tin-coated cutters would be best, as the slide is hard steel. You can do this with an HSS cutter, but it won't be fun. Lower the cutter it into the ejection port and run it towards the muzzle until it just touches the front edge of the ejection port. Move it towards the line you have scribed. When the cutter reaches the line, move it towards the rear of the slide. When the leading edge of the cutter gets to the rear edge of the ejection port, move it back towards the top of the slide. You have just completed your "U." Lift the cutter up out of the slide, stop it and inspect your work. If you need to remove a few more thousandths, follow the same "U."

Now, the theoretical and the actual can and usually do differ. In a production shop, the ejection port would be cut in one pass. It also would be bathed in a steady stream of lubricant while cutting and be guided by a computer. You will probably have to do the cutting in several passes. The front and back passes will be the same each time, but the bottom passes, the ones that actually lower the ejection port, might have to be done as two or even three passes. It depends on how hard your slide is and how new your cutter is.

The mill will leave the edges of the ejection port burred, and the lower rail square in cross-section. You must clean up these flaws. Remove the slide from the mill, and clamp the back half of it in a padded vise. With a carbide cutter or small stone in your hand-held grinder, bevel the inside lower rail of the ejection port. What you are putting a bevel on is the edge the brass will bang against on its way out of the pistol. Polish the bevel smooth with 220-grit cloth. Take your needle files and de-burr the outside of the ejection port edges. Move up to 600-grit cloth, and polish the filed edges and bevel. All this grinding and polishing will push a large amount of grit into the extractor tunnel. Scrub it before you reassemble. As a temporary protective measure, cold blue or heat blue the fresh edges.

If you do not have a mill, you can do the whole operation with a carbide cutter in a hand-held grinder. To prevent overheating the cutting tool, do not bear down

This is EGW's "The Plate" set up to mill a lowered ejection port on this 1911 slide.

Here is the slide set up in the mill, ready for the cuts.

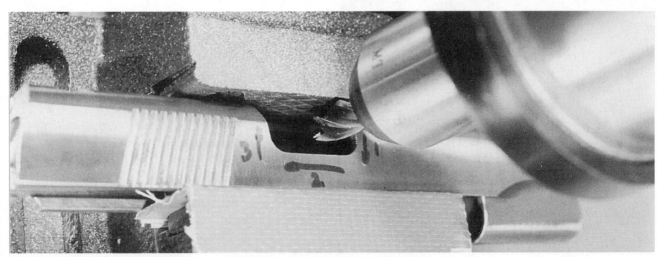

Bring the cutter to the right until it touches the ejection port, then down, left, and up.

heavily, and do not cut for more than 15 seconds at a time. Move the cutter in smooth, even strokes from front to back. Do not stop moving while in contact with the slide, for if you do the cutter will continue to cut, and you will be left with a divot to blend with the rest of your cuts.

Once you are down to the scribed line, clean the slide off. Use your pillar file to smooth and even the lower line of the ejection port.

With the hand-held grinder, bevel, de-burr, and polish, as above.

If, after this, you wish to have the "ejection port groove" in your slide, you need a special grinding tip from Brownells. The groove is a shallow relief behind the ejection port, and the intent is to reduce denting of the brass by angling that corner back. Me, I don't see it as a solution, but some want it. If you do, get the special grinding tip. Nothing else will properly make that cut.

MATCH BUSHINGS

To allow proper and reliable function in adverse conditions, the barrel bushing on military 1911s was made as a relatively loose fit. Wet, frozen, muddy, or even rusted pistols will continue to function and can be disassembled if their barrel bushings are loose; and since only a functioning pistol can save a life, loose bushings make sense for military applications. If you

Measure the inside of your slide when ordering a replacement bushing. It is easier to ream the inside of the bushing than turn or polish the outside.

If you are going to de-horn or melt your pistol, start by fitting a "melt" bushing to the slide. Bevel the bushing instead of the slide.

Measure the outside of your barrel, if you will be using the old one.

Sometimes the old staking on the front sight interferes with your new, larger bushing. Carefully grind it flush to clear the bushing.

Once ground flush, cold blue.

The Briley bushing ring rides on the barrel. Shown outside of the bushing.

This is a Briley ring bushing. The ring fits in the bushing and the barrel slides through the ring.

anticipate living in a hole, and needing your pistol in dire emergencies, you may want to keep this loose fit. Otherwise, replacing the loose bushing with a tighter-fitting one can improve accuracy without decreasing reliability.

How tight should the bushing be? The question has been asked ever since Browning designed the 1911. To check the bushing and barrel fit, remove the barrel and slide the bushing up and down on the barrel. If it is tight enough to bind, the pistol will not be reliable. Loose enough to feel play when you wiggle the bushing, and the pistol will lack accuracy.

The fit of the bushing to the slide is an argument that will rage on as long as shooters use the 1911. Bullseye shooters feel that the bushing should be so tight in the slide that it can be removed only with a bushing wrench and lots of muscle. Defense-minded shooters who favor the 1911 feel that if you can't remove the bushing from the slide with just your fingers, it is too tight and it's a hassle to take apart and clean.

I fall in the middle. I fit the bushings on my 1911 pistols to be tight enough that I can disassemble them with my fingers if I have to, but tight enough that a bushing wrench is a comfort to use. I like accurate pistols, but not if they are so tightly fitted that they become unreliable.

Before the abundant variety of after-market parts, your choices of bushings were two: the loose, military one, or an over-sized bushing that had to be machined to fit both the slide and barrel.

Not anymore. There are so many choices today that to fit a new bushing you only have to measure the inside diameter of your slide and the outside diameter of the barrel at the muzzle.

You can buy bushings for the 1911 with external diameters from .697 to .705 inch. They are available in increments of .001 inch. Measure the inside diameter of your slide and order a bushing at — or just under — the measurement. When it arrives, check the fit. If the bushing slips in place, you are done.

If the bushing needs force to slide in, set it aside and pull out your hand-held grinder. With a rubber polishing

With the standard barrel and a Kings match bushing, the Springfield showed improved accuracy, and greater consistency. Definitely worth the small amount of work.

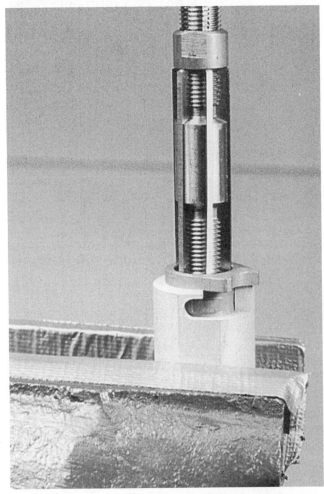

The Wessinger bushing reamer. The reamer is adjustable to ream the inside of the bushing to any diameter you need.

bob ground down to .600 inch, polish the inside of the slide, starting at the muzzle end and continuing for 1 inch back. While you are polishing off the high spots, do not round the edges of the bushing slot.

If you do not have a hand-held grinder you can use slide fitting paste or grinding compound to fit the bushing. Slather 600-grit on the bushing and into the slide. Force the bushing into place. Take a bushing wrench and rotate the bushing back and forth. Lap the bushing to the slide until it moves easily, pull it out and clean off the grinding compound.

The bushing will then slide into place. You will also have removed some of the finish from the face of your slide. Welcome to an unavoidable lesson in gunsmithing: few things don't remove finish somewhere.

Once you have fit the bushing to the slide, turn it all the way into the slide-retaining slot and check the fit. Sometimes the bushing lug binds entering the slot. Cover the lug with Dykem and check the fit again. If you have to, use a bushing wrench to get some muscle into it. When you have found the location of the binding, the place where the Dykem has been rubbed off, file the lug to clear the slot. File carefully! You do not want to file so much that the bushing is loose in the slot.

If you cannot order a bushing that is the perfect size both inside and out, then order a bushing that is the perfect size outside, and too small inside. It is easier to decrease the diameter of the barrel a few thousandths of an inch, or increase the inside of the bushing, than to adjust the diameter of the bushing exterior.

The easiest way to adjust a too-small-inside bushing is to chuck the barrel in a lathe and turn the diameter down until it fits the bushing. If you do not have a lathe but want a tight-fitting bushing, you have to ream the bushing out. You cannot do this in your vise. If you try to, you will either ream the bushing crooked, or squeeze the bushing into an oval shape trying to clamp it and then ream an oval hole. You may even end up with a crooked oval hole! Instead, buy a fixture to hold the bushing and an adjustable reamer.

The Wessinger fixture and adjustable reamer are both available from Brownells as a set. With it you can fit barrels and bushings to each other for a long time.

If all this fitting and adjusting seem like too much aggravation, use a Briley's bushing. Their bushing is designed and made as two pieces. The external piece looks like a standard bushing. Nestled inside the bushing is a ring that looks like a large wedding ring. The barrel rides in this ring. The bushing body comes in two diameters, while the rings come in six different diameters. You order the combination that fits your slide and barrel, and with it you get the performance of a fitted bushing.

How much do tighter bushings improve accuracy? I tested a Springfield 1911. Right out of the box, the bushing fit was typical for a factory pistol. While you could slightly wiggle the bushing in the slide and the barrel in the bushing, it wasn't too bad. At the range, the Springfield delivered 3- to 4-inch groups at 25 yards. After fitting the Kings bushing to the slide and reaming it with the Wessinger tool until the barrel fit properly, accuracy improved. While the best groups improved only slightly, the occasional 4-inch or larger groups disappeared. The average dropped from 3-1/2 inches to just under 3.

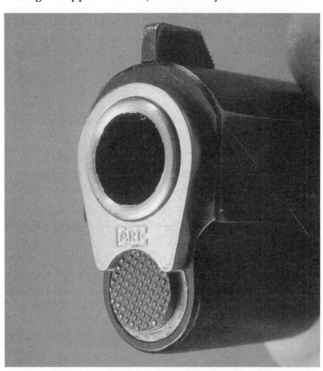

Here is the Kart match bushing included in the kit. With a properly fitted bushing up front and a tight fit in the rear, you will get the full benefit of a match barrel's accuracy.

Here the Springfield 1911A1 is in the Ransom rest getting ready to test the Kart barrel.

REMOVING SHARP EDGES: PART ONE

Shooting pistols can be hard work. Loading magazines, picking up brass, trying to hit the target with consistency, avoiding a flinch — these are more than enough to do, without adding pain to the problem. If you find that there is a sharp edge or spot on your pistol that makes shooting uncomfortable, do not ignore it. Remove it. If you are going to carry a pistol for defensive purposes, sharp edges can cut and tear your clothing as well as your hands. Trim your pistol and save your clothes.

In this section we will go over the restrained edge-breaking of a 1911. The more aggressive "melting" done to some carry pistols will be covered in the next chapter.

To locate the sharp edges, run your hands over the pistol. Mark with a felt-tip pen every place that irritates your hand. The lesson we just went over, about most processes removing finish somewhere? This one is going to remove it in a lot of places. Plan on re-finishing your 1911 when you are done, or shooting one that has white edges. Stainless 1911 owners, you won't have to worry or bother.

To de-horn your 1911, start with the straight edges and the outside of curves. Use the extra narrow pillar file. On inside curves use a fine half-round needle

When de-horning, a small bevel is your start.

file. Follow up with 400- or 600-grit cloth. In most cases you will file just enough to "break" the edge, and then remove the file marks with the cloth.

Look at the back of the frame, slide and safety. Many shooters find these edges the most irritating. I find the back corner of the thumb safety particularly bad. On almost every one made, I must take this corner down to a completely rounded surface. The one safety I have found that doesn't require this work is the Chip McCormick. Also used on the Kimber pistol, the McCormick safety is plenty large enough for competitive shooting and its

The grip safety pad rides out from the frame along its entire length, and is almost impossible to grab incorrectly.

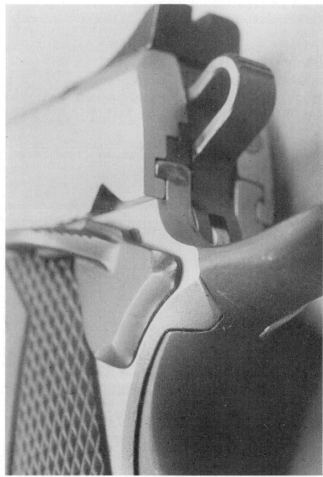

The McCormick thumb safety is sculpted on the rear, and does not present a sharp edge to the shooters hand.

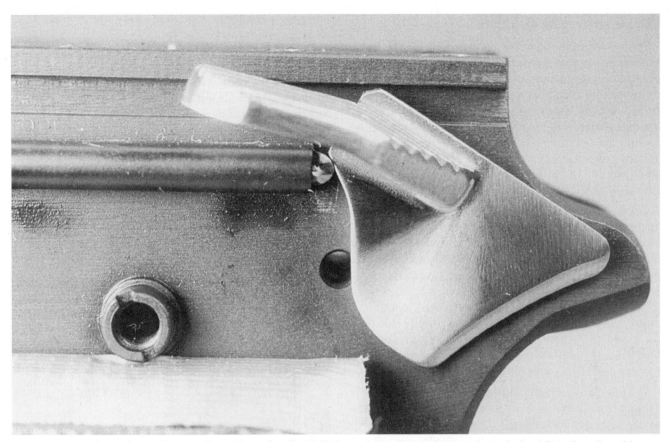

If your thumb safety comes off too easily, pull the dimpling drill through the plunger tube and attach the drill to the other side. Carefully drill the safety until it is harder to push off, but not too hard.

blended edges work great for concealed carry.

The standard grip safety can be uncomfortable. Some shooters think it is a pain because it is too small. You don't have to race out and install a larger grip safety, though.

When you bevel the lower edges of the slide, leave the edge of the hold-open notch its full thickness.

Just rounding the edges will make it more comfortable.

Now look at the bottom, outside edge of the slide. If you use a high hold on the pistol, or have large hands, they can get very close to this edge. If you shoot with your thumb over the safety the edge can shred your skin right off. I bevel this edge the entire length of the slide, except for the short section between the slide stop notch and the disassembly notch. While some shooters bevel this section, because it is already very shallow I prefer to keep it untouched.

Round the back edges of the slide to keep them from irritating your hands and your clothes.

The main sources of irritation on the top of the slide are the sights and the ejection port. Approach the front sight with caution. Round only the front edges. Since you use the top and rear edges for aiming, rounding these will cause you serious shooting problems. The same goes for the rear sight. Again, round only the side and front edges, not the aiming edges. If you have a Novak sight installed, you won't have to do any rounding. Novaks were designed and made already beveled.

On ejection ports the main culprit for pain or bleeding is the top edge of the right-hand breechface sidewall. This edge, lurking between the cuts for the breechface and the ejection port, often ends up as a needle-like point. Round it. Rounding will save you pain and bleeding the first time you have to clear a malfunction.

INSTALLING A NEW SAFETY

You've been shooting your newly rounded 1911, but the safety just isn't large enough. You want to fit a new one. Before buying one, try fellow club members' pistols to see if there is a safety particularly suited to your hand. There are many, and you may have to try quite a few. It is easier, and less expensive, to try the safeties on a whole slew of other 1911s, than it is to randomly install and try safeties on your 1911. Once you have an idea what you like, order that one. Your chances of getting the safety you want or actually need are much greater.

Once your new safety arrives, begin the fitting by checking it to the frame. Strip the frame down bare. Check the fit of the safety into the frame. Does the pivot pin slide in easily? If not, deburr the hole and lightly polish the new safety's pivot pin. Does the safety lug pass through the frame? If not, use your extra narrow pillar file to file the outside of the lug. Once the lug clears, does the safety press home flush to the side of the frame? If the hole in the frame was not sufficiently beveled at the factory, the safety may not go flush. Use an over-sized drill to bevel the frame hole.

You are ready for your final frame checks. Does the safety pivot when it is in the frame? If the slot cut on the safety lug is not deep enough the safety will be unable to pivot. With a flat needle file open this slot until the safety moves freely. Check the extension of the safety to see that it clears both the plunger tube and the grips. Check the safety against the plunger tube, and if there is interference, file the inside of the safety extension. Hold the left grip panel in place, and check the safety to see if it hits the grip. If so, file the grip to clear.

Ambidextrous safeties require additional fitting. Look at the tips of your hammer and sear pivot pins. They are designed to dome slightly above the right-hand surface of the frame. You must grind these rounded tips flat until they are flush with the frame. If you do not, the domes

will interfere with the right-side safety. The pins are usually too hard to file flat, thus the need for a grinder or dremel tool. Some ambi safeties are kept in place with a tab that sticks under the right-hand grip panel. If your grips are not cut to clear the safety, you must cut them with a carbide cutter in your hand-held grinder to provide clearance. Some safeties use an overly long hammer pivot pin, with a slot cut into it. The right-hand safety slides into or over this slot, keeping the safety in place. Check the fit of this pin and the right-hand safety.

Now you are ready to fit the safety to the sear. Assemble the frame with all of its parts except the grips, grip safety, and thumb safety spring and plunger. Cock the hammer. Slide the new safety into place as far as it will go and look at the sear through the back of the frame. You will see the safety lug striking the side of the sear. Pull the safety out, and compare the new safety lug against the old safety. Look at the small flat filed on the old safety lug. The tip of the hooked part of the new safety lug must be filed at this angle until it will just barely

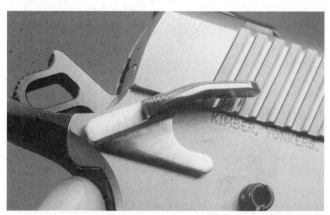

Here is the right-side ambidextrous thumb safety, in the up, safe, position.

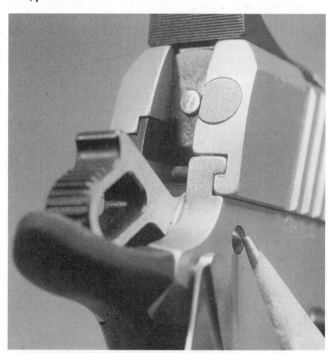

You will have to grind the dome off of the hammer and sear pins. If you don't, the safety will hang up on them.

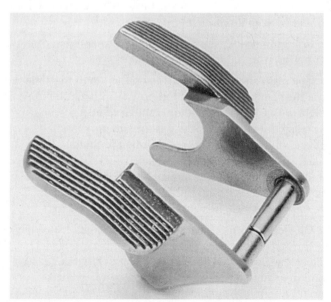

An ambidextrous safety such as this one from Ed Brown is a boon to left-handed shooters. (photo courtesy Ed Brown)

Here is the relief cut, on an Ahrends grip.

Ed Brown and Les Baer both make ambidextrous safeties.

slide behind the sear. As you get close, use a candle to smoke the safety lug and see exactly where it is hitting.

The last fitting is quite delicate. If you have to force the safety up into engagement, the fit is too tight. Look for the marks left behind on the safety lug by the sear, and stone them off. Re-install and press the safety into engagement again.

Once the safety presses into place without marring the safety lug, perform the safety check procedure from Chapter 4. If it passes the test you are done.

What if you went too far, and when you checked engagement you heard that little tink? You filed too much. It is possible to peen the safety lug, and have the gap filled with the upset metal. This is not a typical fitting step, but rather is a means to salvage a safety you have taken too much metal off of. Clamp the safety in a pad-

ded vise, safety lug up, and with your ball-peen hammer strike the safety lug at its engagement point. Install the safety and check engagement. You can whack the lug 2-3 times, but if you need to hit it more than that, you are moving too much metal. You have obviously filed more than just "a smidge" past where you needed to be.

If two or three hits are not enough to remove the "tink," you must either get the safety lug welded or you must buy a new safety. You're faced with an expensive choice — reason enough to go slowly when filing and stoning the safety lug.

SAFETY SECURITY

The safety and slide stop are kept under control by the plungers and spring in the plunger tube. Acting like a middle-aged chaperone, they keep the safety and slide stop from doing wild and crazy things while at the prom. In order to do their jobs, the plunger tube in which they ride has to remain securely attached to the frame. If it comes loose, bad things can happen. The slide stop can get trapped down, and not lock the slide open when the magazine is empty. Worse, the plunger can ride over the safety, trapping it up or down, and making the pistol either unsafe or unusable.

If it comes loose, what to do? Simple: stake it back on. The process is simple, if a bit fussy. The plunger tube

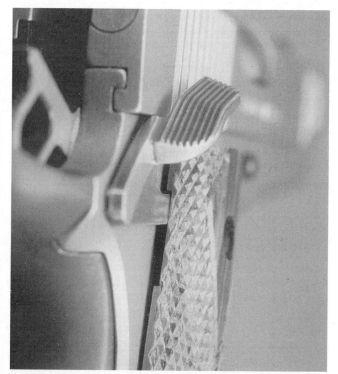

Some ambidextrous safeties are held in place by the right-hand grip panel. If the grip is not cut for the safety arm, you must relieve it with a hand-held grinder and carbide tool.

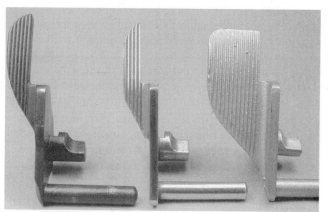

Safeties from mild to wild. The left is a Chip McCormick, the center an Ed Brown, and the right one is a huge safety from Kings. Missing this safety is cause for embarrassment.

is held on the frame by means of two studs on its back. The plunger tube studs protrude into the frame through a pair of holes drilled in the frame.

The two studs are machined hollow, and the holes in the frame are chamfered (or should be) on the end inside the magazine well. When installed, the studs are swaged, or upset, in the chamfer inside the magazine well. Once swaged, they aren't supposed to come loose. But they do. If yours comes loose (or you need to attach one to a new frame) the process is simple: You need the swaging tools, a vise and some Loctite. To re-secure, strip the frame. Press the plunger tube back flush to the frame. Clamp the frame in a vise and use the swaging tool to re-swage the stud. Simple, right? Simple, but tricky.

The first time I read the instructions for the swaging kit, I thought "That's not right, the mechanical leverage is all wrong."

First, if you do not have enough chamfer, you can't swage the stud, Look closely at the frame hole, and if it lacks chamfer, you may have to pull the plunger tube off completely and start over. However, it is worth trying to re-secure it. Degrease and apply Loctite to the gap between the plunger tube and frame. Second if you do not clamp the plunger tube securely, you're simply going to swage it securely onto the frame in the wrong orientation. So, when you go to clamp, use the plunger tube holding fixture, but clamp it directly to the frame. Use a block of wood or plastic to support the frame on the other side , and protect it from the vise jaws.

Third, insert your swaging tool (the bar with the pointed rod in it) down through the frame, with the short end up and the long end down. Once down it will be extending out of the frame. Hold the bottom end, and locate the pointed tip in the hole in the plunger tube stud. Lever the bar so it is pivoted to bear against the stud, with the long end against the mag well opening. The bar is now supported for the impact to come. With your ball-peen hammer, strike the bar just above the frame rails, in the direction that will drive the pointed tip into the stud of the plunger tube.

You're done. Reassemble, check fit and function, and get back to practice.

But what if the fix doesn't stick? Now, back in 1914 or so, when plunger tubes first began coming loose (or whenever it was) I like to think I'd have had the temerity to over-ride Browning. I'd have changed the design to add a third stud. Instead, the makers simply stuck with the two-stud design, and gunsmiths have been re-staking them ever since. Not that it is a national emergency, with plunger tubes flying off 1911s left and right, but how hard could it have been to change? Or, when the upgrades from the 1911 to the 1911A1 were made, in 1926, how hard would it have been to add an extra stud to the drawings?

There are two solutions: the traditional and the better. The traditional is to chamfer the back of the holes, so the swaged studs have a larger area into which they can swell, and hold on tighter. This does work. I've done it

to a number of 1911s, and the fix sticks, especially if you hose liberally with Loctite.

But better is better. Ned Christiansen to the rescue again. He makes a replacement plunger tube with four studs on the back. To locate and drill the extra holes, he makes a locating bar that uses the existing holes as the index points. Slap the locator on, drill the new holes, chamfer the backs of all four, and then install his four-stud plunger tube. Oh, wait, it gets better. Instead of whanging away with a hammer to swage the studs, he has figured a way to use a torque wrench to swage them.

Now, I'll admit that this is overkill if all you want to do is re-secure the loose plunger tube on your lone 1911. But if you have several, or you are building a carry gun, and you want there to be absolutely no chance of a problem with the plunger tube, this is a wise investment. And, if you are going to be a 1911 'smith in your area, you'll need these skills, and probably this tool.

Done correctly, a re-swaged plunger tube will not need to be refinished. However, if you put a new one on, old or Ned style, you probably will. Think of it as the first step to your new hard-chrome or other high-tech finish.

INSTALLING A NEW TRIGGER

Old-style triggers suffered from two faults: they were of all-steel construction, and they had no overtravel screw.

The all-steel construction made the trigger heavy, heavy in mass, not necessarily in pull. A heavy trigger, bouncing back and forth in its slot, will strike the sear. If you lighten the trigger pull by reducing sear and hammer hook engagement on an all-steel trigger too much, the sear will not be able to take this hit without being partially or completely dislodged from the hammer hooks. The hammer will fall to half-cock.

Without an overtravel screw, old-style triggers had no provision for stopping their rearward travel early. When the trigger had fulfilled its job of pushing the sear out of the hammer hooks, it just kept moving back. That movement, called overtravel, can disturb your aim.

To solve both of these problems, install a plastic or aluminum trigger with an overtravel screw. A lighter trigger strikes with less force during bounce, decreasing the wear and tear on the sear/hammer hook fit. The lighter weight will also increase the life of your trigger job. The adjustment screw allows you to remove most, but not all, of the overtravel.

Strip and clean the frame. First check the fit of the trigger bow in the frame by installing it backwards. If the bow binds, file the high spots until it slide into place. Deburr the edges of the trigger bow. Slide the trigger into the frame in the normal manner, and look into the slot to see if there is any daylight appearing around the trigger body. Pull the trigger out and use a candle to smoke the trigger body on its top and bottom surfaces. Press the trigger into place, pull it out, and file where the soot has been disturbed.

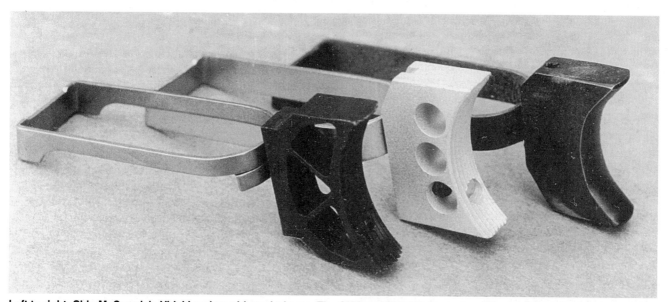

Left to right, Chip McCormick, Videki and an old steel trigger. The CMC and Videki triggers together are lighter than the steel one.

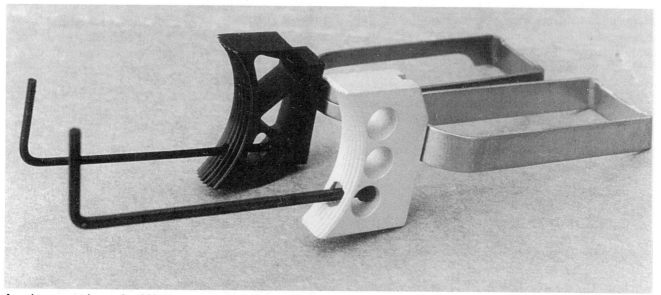

A replacement trigger should have an overtravel adjustment screw.

This is a lightweight trigger from EGW that is also longer. It is meant for shooters with large hands.

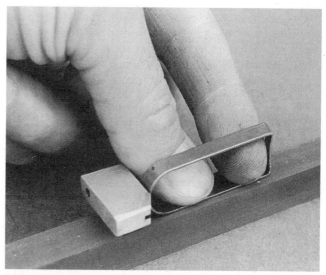

If the trigger will not ride smoothly in the slot, stone the sides and high spots.

Once you get close, you will be able to force the trigger fully into the slot. Go slowly from here, smoking and filing in small increments. The goal is a trigger that does not have up and down play in the frame, but will fall freely out of the frame when you turn it upside-down. Once there, deburr the outside edges of the trigger body where it travels in the frame slots.

Install the overtravel screw in the trigger body, and then reassemble the frame. Cock the hammer and hold it back with your thumb. Press the trigger and hold it back, too. Now ease the hammer down. The first step in correctly adjusting your overtravel screw will stop the hammer at the half-cock notch. If the hammer goes all the way forward, turn the overtravel screw in a full turn. Cock the hammer and repeat until the hammer stops at the notch.

Cock the hammer again, and turn the overtravel screw out of the trigger a half turn. Try lowering the hammer. Adjust the overtravel screw in and out until you can feel the hammer, on release, just brushing the tip of the sear. At this point turn the overtravel screw another quarter turn out of the trigger. You must not feel the sear brushing the hammer. To finish, disassemble, and use Loc-tite to secure the overtravel screw.

This is the minimum of overtravel you can set. Less than this and you risk interference with the trigger's function when the pistol gets dirty. However, some like to have more overtravel than this. Me, I found that when I tried to tune the trigger to the minimum of overtravel I created problems for myself.

For me, a trigger with the absolute minimum of overtravel is an invitation to "trigger clutch." This is where, in rapid fire, I don't let my finger go forward far enough to allow the trigger to reset. If I increase overtravel, I increase reset, and get my finger moving far enough to ensure reset. If it tighten the overtravel to the minimum, I trigger-cutch and shoot badly at speed.

If you have set your overtravel to the minimum, and find yourself doing the same thing I do, your solution is simple: add overtravel. However, if you've used Loctite to secure the screw, you'll have to strip the frame and remove the trigger, Then, carefully file the overtravel screw, reassemble, and practice some more. When you get to the point that you do not trigger-clutch at speed, you're done.

INSTALLING A NEW FRONT SIGHT

The traditional method of securing a front sight is to stake it. The sight tenon goes through the slide, and the foot of the tenon is peened to fill the slot, wedging the sight into place.

To install a new sight, first remove the old one. The quick and dirty way is to clamp the old sight in your vise and rotate the slide, twisting the old sight until it breaks off. Use a drift punch to drive the stub of the tenon out of the slide. If the thought of a twisted wreck of a sight lying on your bench troubles you, or you want to practice filing, you can file the old sight down to nothing and then drive out the stub.

In either case, once the sight is out prepare the top of the slide by filing a flat around the tenon slot. The bottom of the sight blade will bear against this flat. On the inside of the slide, use a carbide cutter or small stone in a hand-held grinder to open up the edges of the slot. This gives the tenon room to expand, securely locking it in place when you stake it.

Check the tenon for fit in the slot. You should be able to press it into place on the slide. If the tenon will not go into the slot, carefully file only enough to get the sight into place. Degrease the slide and sight. Use Loc-tite on the tenon and slot, and press the sight into place.

Slide the MMC staking tool into place, and with the brass protector on the sight, tighten the locking screw. If you are installing a night sight, use the U-shaped sight clamp. Do not be bashful in tightening the locking screw. If you do not have the sight firmly pressed into place it will lift when you stake it. Sometime in the future (no doubt at the worst possible moment) such an improperly staked front sight will fly off the slide. As you tighten the screw, check the front sight to make sure it stays straight up and down and is not tilted by the clamping tool.

If you're looking at your MMC instructions as you install your sight, you'll see my procedure differs at this point. Experience has taught me to grease the staking wedge and drive it completely through the MMC staking tool, until it drops free on the inside of the slide. Doing so fully stakes the sight, and makes it easier to remove the staking tool from the slide when you are done.

Remove the staking tool, wipe the excess Loc-tite off, and check the sight for straightness. If you paid proper attention to fitting the tenon and clamping the sight straight, you'll be pleased with your job. If you find that your new sight is tilted or crooked, however, use flat brass protectors in your vise, clamp the sight, and force it straight.

Take your bushing, and see if it will still fit the slide. If it does not, the excess tenon staked in the slide will have to be filed or ground down. Remove just enough to allow the bushing to go back in place without binding.

INSTALLING A DOVETAIL FRONT SIGHT

The Novak front dovetail sight is very popular, with good reason. You can adjust windage using both the front and rear sights. You can easily change to a sight of a differing height. You can install night sights or a three-dot system without a lot of fuss.

But you have to have the dovetail. And if your slide doesn't have one, then you also have to have a mill.

Strip the slide and remove the old front sight. Level and clamp the slide in the mill vise. For the Novak, install a .330-inch X 65-degree dovetail cutter in your mill. If you are installing another brand, be sure and read the dimensions the manufacturer lists for its sight. Different manufacturers' sights require different size dovetails.

Bring the cutter down almost in contact with the slide, and line up the tip of the cutter edge with the front edge of the slide. Move the cutter back from the muzzle .175 inch. This is your slot location. Bring the cutter down just enough to contact the slide. This establishes your vertical zero. Move the cutter to the side of the slide, and lower the cutter .075 inch. Slowly pass the cutter through the slide, using liberal amounts of cutting lubricant.

Remove the slide, deburr the slot, and fit the new sight. If your slide already has a dovetail, then fitting the new sight is a matter of filing the edges of its dovetail foot until you can press the sight a third of the way into the slot by hand. Drift it the rest of the way with a brass drift. Range test to determine if it is centered on the slide, and to correct its height.

MAGAZINE FUNNELS

Not all magazine funnels require silver-solder attachment. The Barrett funnel, from Clark Custom, is a painless bolt-on unit. With an unloaded 1911, lower the hammer. Drift out the mainspring retaining pin. Slide the Barrett funnel over the bottom of the frame. Take the longer retaining pin included with the funnel and press it through the holes in the funnel and frame. Use the included Allen wrench to tighten the positioning screws. Dab some paint or fingernail polish on the screws to keep them tight.

Another magazine funnel is a replacement mainspring housing with "wings." The wings form a funnel. Take your mainspring housing off and remove the retaining pin, mainspring and its plungers. To remove the spring and plungers, clamp the mainspring housing in your vise. Use a rod or drift punch to compress the mainspring. Push the retainer out, and slowly ease up on the mainspring. Pull it out, and clamp your new mainspring housing into your vise. Slide the mainspring and its plungers in, compress and install the retaining pin.

Last, bevel the inside of the new funnel to match the frame, and blend them as a smooth surface.

The S & A magazine funnel replaces the mainspring housing.

Here is the Barrett funnel, with adjustment allen wrench and replacement retaining pin.

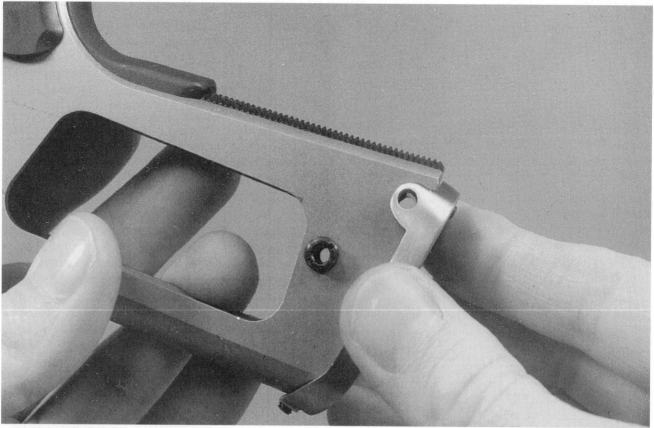

Slide the Barrett funnel onto the frame.

Press the replacement retaining pin in place.

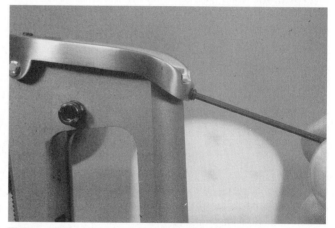

Tighten the front screw to hold the funnel in place.

Tighten the rear screw to pivot the funnel tight against the bottom of the frame.

With the Barrett magazine funnel secured, put your grips back on.

GET A GRIP

Sometimes the grip or frame of your pistol, 1911 or other, is just too slippery. Traditional improvements have included stippling or checkering (see Chapter 19). A less traditional choice comes from California. (Now there's a surprise!) It's skateboard tape.

For those who have never ridden a skateboard, the tape is a tough, adhesive-backed cloth with a very aggressive abrasive on the top surface. It's the same kind of tape you can use for non-skid stairs, but while the stuff for stairs comes only in basic black, the California tape seems to be available only in various neon colors.

Before I completely turn you off from this approach, let me assure you that it works very well. You will not be some sort of pariah at the range if you show up with a pistol festooned with this tape. In fact, you'll fit right in.

Skateboard tape will provide a non-slip hold, if you can stand its non-traditional looks.

Nonetheless, if you decide you just can't stand the stuff, soak your frame overnight in mineral spirits and the tape will give up the ghost. It will not come off if briefly exposed to cleaning solvents.

Competitive shooters who favor high-capacity frames without grips use large swatches of the tape. If you want to try some, take an old pair of smooth grips and attach pieces of the tape to them. Start with a narrow strip of the tape on the frontstrap. Your preliminary testing has begun.

If you find that you like the tape, you have two approaches to attaching it to your pistols. One is to use narrow tape, and cover the frame piece by piece until you have blanketed the gripping area. The other way is to get a larger sheet and trim it to the contours of the frame. Install it as a single piece.

One of our local shooters is so fond of skateboard tape in hot pink that he has all his competitive handguns, rifles, shotguns and their magazines treated to patches and swatches of the stuff. He has no problem picking his rifle out of a rack of otherwise identical black rifles.

If tape — black, green or pink — is just not your thing, you can use a pre-checkered panel on your 1911. Wilson and EGW both make panels that will fit right on your frame. The Wilson panel has extension tabs that fit under your grips. Take the grips off, fit the panel on the front of the frame and bend the tabs back to hold it in place. Tighten the grips down to secure the panel.

To secure the EGW, and for a better job with the Wilson, get Brownells Acra-Glas Gel. This two-part epoxy mixes up into the consistency of soft butter, which makes it easy to use. It will not run and end up someplace other than where you intended it to be. Remove the grips. Degrease the frame and checkered panel. Mix the epoxy, and spread an even coat of it on the frame. Press the panel in place, and clean off any excess that oozes out. Use large rubber bands to clamp the panel and keep it from shifting. Check it in a few minutes to make sure it hasn't moved on you. Let the Acra-Glas cure overnight. Clean off the excess hardened epoxy

This is a pre-checkered panel from EGW. You can epoxy or solder it onto your frame, or you can even cut the frame out and solder or weld this in the gap. That is very advanced pistolsmithing.

The Cominolli rod with its dual buffers. The impact of the slide is soaked up by the plastic buffers without either the rod head or the frame getting peened.

Left to right, a Wilson tungsten rod, a Cominolli tungsten rod with dual buffers on it, and a Harrts mercury recoil reducer. All will cut down the felt recoil of your pistol.

You can also tune the trigger pull by lightening the hammer spring. Just be sure to test to make sure you don't have light primer hits as a result of using a too-light hammer spring.

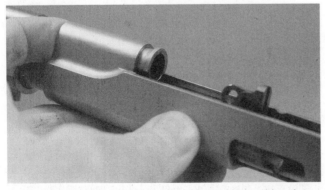

Reverse plugs on the 1911 must be removed by pushing them back out of the slide.

with a file or knife edge. Put your grips back on, and you are done.

If you want to make the bond even more secure, you can soft-solder the panel onto your frame. Although both epoxy and soft-solder will dissolve if sent through the bluing tanks, the soft-solder attached panel is less likely to quit if it is dropped or subjected to extreme cold.

SPRING TUNING

The subject of recoil springs is still one filled with myth, legend, misinformation and lots of wishin' and hopin'. The "standard" recoil spring for a 1911 Government model in .45 ACP is 18 pounds. I say standard because the standard had varied through time, and can vary according to what you are hoping to accomplish. Back in the old days, I heard of advice to increase the recoil spring strength in order to ensure reliable function. The recommended springs were 20 and even 22 pounds. For the Commander, even as high as 24 pounds!

Ahem.

First, if a pistol is so unreliable that you need a spring that heavy to force the round out of the magazine, up the ramp and into the chamber, you need to do a little work finding the spots where it binds. Second, a too-heavy spring can make a pistol unreliable when you can't hold it securely. A too-heavy spring can cause a "stovepipe," a failure to eject where the slide traps the spent case. Also, the 1911 is hard enough on its ammo, but using an extra-heavy spring to hammer them into submission can cause loosened bullets, setback, a loss of accuracy (loose bullets don't consistently leave the chamber) and even sharper pressures that can cause case failure. No, you don't want to be using extra-heavy springs for reliability, only for controlling recoil with extra-power cartridges. Save that 24-pound spring for use with your .400 Cor-bon or .460 Rowland.

If the 24-pound spring is for the Cor-bon, then what weight do you use? Many of you will have heard of

If you plan to do a lot of shooting, you'll need springs on a regular basis. Buy them in bulk from Wolff.

some shooters, competition shooters mostly, who use much-lighter springs. It is not unheard-of for some to be using springs at light as 12, 11 or even 10 pounds. The choice is not what is best, but what gives you what you need at a cost you can support. The heavier you go, the more you risk a malfunction from being too heavy. You also increase wear due to the slide and barrel crashing closed harder than designed to. The desire for a lighter spring is a competitive one: sight movement. When the 1911 (or any pistol) cycles, the front sights rises from recoil. The force of closing brings the sight back down. Where the sight stops depends on the force of the spring and the firmness of the shooter's grip. Generally, a too-heavy spring snaps the action closed farther "down" than a lighter one does. The pistol chambers a round, and the sights stop below the point of aim. The search for a lighter spring is an individual one, where each shooter selects a spring that brings the sights right back to the target when the action closes. However (and there is always a "however" when competition drives matters) there is no absolute. Each shooter is different. Each pistol is different. Each load is different. And each shooter may change. As a result, the top shooters are continually evaluating and adjusting their equipment. To add more complexity to the decision-making, shock buffers can change the feel of recoil. So some shooters are also always evaluating the effects of various brands, and their different durometer ratings. If you ask a top shooter what spring weight he is using, the answer may not be the same next week, next month, or the next (and perhaps different) match.

So you cannot compare (to take three extremes) the spring settings of a 1911 built for IDPA ESP Division, an IPSC Open race gun, and a tactical 1911 in .45 ACP built to be a SWAT sidearm. All must be adjusted to the task at hand, the shooter and the ammunition. Tuning is an advanced skill not because the job is difficult. It is easy to take a selection of springs to the range and try them. It is difficult because the effect is so subtle that for most shooters the effect doesn't exist. Just as an example (and not to use empirically derived figures) let's say changing from an 18-pound spring to a 16-pound spring alters the final muzzle direction by 5 degrees. Changing springs would have no measurable effect if the shooter who was firing brought the muzzle back after each shot to a random spot within a spread of 35 degrees. He or she has to refine their technique a lot more before they can begin to see the change spring weight would make.

A comparison I've made before, and will make again: agonizing over tires on a NASCAR vehicle, trying to decide whether to use the ones that let you take a turn at 215 or 225 miles per hour, is for naught if your skill only lets you take the turns at 150. If your skills are at a level where trying to take the turn at 160 puts you into the wall, the tires don't matter. For most shooters, fussing over a recoil spring that brings them on-target at closing is like the NASCAR question.

The recoil spring absorbs the force of the moving

You can also add weight to your 1911 by installing a tungsten recoil spring plug, or retainer. The extra mass under the barrel slightly dampens muzzle flip on recoil.

slide, and stores that energy to move the slide forward to chamber the next round and close the action. Ideally, it does not fully compress to stop the slide. You want the slide to bottom out on the frame, not on the compressed stack of spring coils. By bottoming out on the frame, the force of the impact is borne by the recoil spring tunnel of the slide. If the recoil spring "stacks" and stops the slide, the recoil spring retainer, and the bushing, take the brunt of the deceleration. In time, the bushing or retainer may fail.

To check if your spring is stacking, remove the slide and take out the barrel. Be sure to wear safety glasses, for you will be working with compressed springs on the next step. To hold the slide, clamp it muzzle down in a padded vise. Install the bushing, retainer, spring and recoil spring guide rod. If you do not use a full-length guide rod, be especially careful. Using the rod as a guide, compress the spring. If the spring stacks completely before you have pressed the guide into contact with the rear of the slide, you must shorten it. A few coils off the spring will not markedly decrease its strength. However, if you need to take more than three or four coils, start over with a spring the next step up in strength. Recoil springs can be cut with large sidecutters, but not easily. The steel is hard and strong. I found the easiest way to shorten springs was by carefully using the corner of the wheel on a bench grinder. Just go slowly, so you don't overheat the steel.

Why, if I've just told you not to go to over-strength springs, are we increasing spring strength in this adjustment? Simple: if you have to cut more than a few coils, you're reducing the strength of the spring. There is no point in starting with an 18 pound spring and then cutting so much off to make it fit that it becomes a 15 pound spring. In such an instance, we start with a 20 pound spring, and by the time we've trimmed it to fit, it is an 18 pound spring, more or less.

If you are going to use a shock buffer, be sure to knock any sharp edges or corners off your freshly shortened spring. Adjusting the spring to remove "stacking" is a good idea even if you are not to the point of noticing changes in weight. Having done so, you will be potentially adding to the longevity of your 1911.

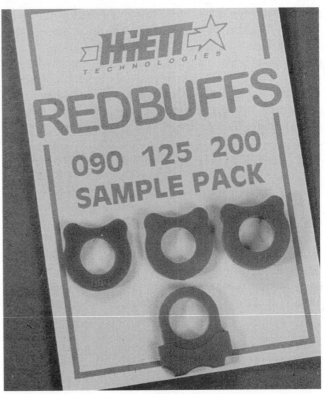

You can get recoil buffers in different thicknesses. The top three are .090, .125 and .200 inches thick. The bottom one is for the Beretta M-92.

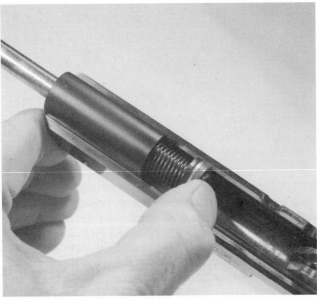

If you find that your spring collapses and stacks before the slide has bottomed out, you need to alter it. Test by pushing the recoil spring guide rod with your thumb. If it stops short, shorten the spring by a coil or two. Repeat.....

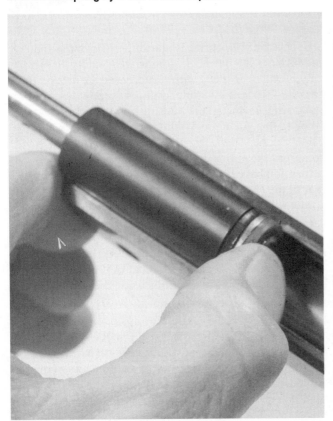

Until the guide rod bottoms against the slide.

If you plan to have a new barrel fitted (as Irv Stone of Bar-sto is doing here) decide if you will have the slide to frame fit tightened. If you fit the barrel, and then tight slide to frame, you'll have to re-fit the barrel all over again.

SLIDE-TO-FRAME FIT

I wasn't sure if getting the fit tighter was a basic or advanced part of 1911 work, but settled on basic for a simple reason: it is more nerve-wracking than skill-dependent. If you pay attention, and don't go trying to use muscle where a little thought is called for, getting a tighter slide-to-frame fit is not a problem.

What it is, is problematic. You see the accuracy of a 1911 pistol depends on a lot more than just how tight the slide fits to frame. As an example, my first prize gun, the one sent off to a 'smith, who welded the barrel. He also peened and lapped the slide-frame fit until it was tight, smooth and even. And the accuracy improved hardly at all. Not his fault. You can (as he did) go to all that effort and have not much to show for your time and sweat, if the accuracy potential of the barrel just isn't there. So realize that there are no guarantees.

To tighten the slide-to-frame fit, you have three options; 1) you can peen or swage the frame rails and then lap or fit them to the slide; 2) you can build up the barrel lugs and hood (by welding or silver-solder) to tighten the barrel fit and use the barrel as a wedge to force the slide and frame tight as the mechanism closes; or 3) you can replace the slide.

FITTING THE SLIDE TO THE FRAME

In order for manufacturers to make parts, they must leave a gap where any two parts are to be fitted. In order to assemble two parts made at any time over what can be years of production, this gap must be larger still. The measurements that allow assembly are called "tolerances." The larger the tolerances, the looser the fit. While a loose fit between the slide and frame can be beneficial to reliable function, or easy assembly by the manufacturer, it is not necessary for reliability. It is almost always detrimental to accuracy.

To improve accuracy, you should remove any play between slide and frame. Do you have to? No. You can correctly fit a match barrel to your loose slide/frame fit, and have a wonderfully accurate pistol. But it will never shoot up to its full potential.

You can remove the slide/frame play after you have fit a match barrel or bushing to your pistol, but the barrel will then have to be re-fitted. Better to do the work on your slide and frame first, and then buy and fit your barrel.

The simple method of fitting the slide and frame is to peen or swage the rails of the frame. Peening and swaging differ in how much metal is moved when you strike with your hammer. You will need your ball peen hammer, dial calipers, a rail forming bar or steel shim of the correct thickness, and some means of holding the frame without crushing it. For swaging you will need a swaging bar. For fitting the peened or swaged rails you need stones, your pillar file, lapping compound and either a

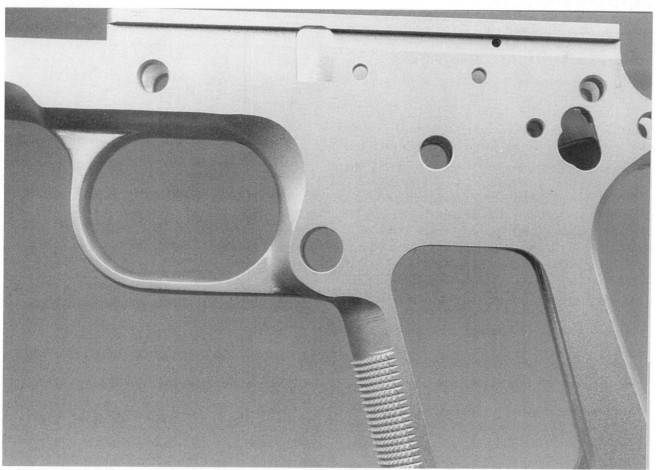

You can get frames with over-sized rails, to take up the slack of an old slide, or to cut and lap it to precisely fit your slide.

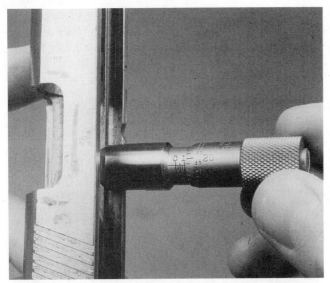

This Starrett rail micrometer is very handy for measuring the slide rails, to choose a set of forming bars. This is an over-sized slide and rail measures .119 inches. On some frames you may not need forming rails, just lap the slide to the frame.

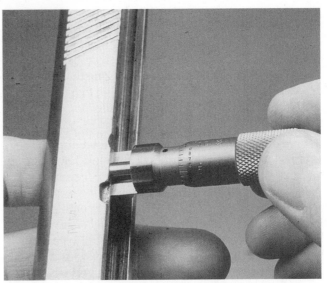

Measure the rails at several points, on both sides. Take the average and add .002 inches for your forming rail thickness.

The Weigand frame-holding fixture, for peening or swaging the frame rails. Made of aluminum, it will securely hold the frame while you fit the rails.

plastic faced mallet or a slide-lapping tool.

Check the face of your ball peen hammer. You must polish out any marks on it or they will be transferred to the rails when you strike them.

I have found it useful, even after years of performing this kind of job, to draw the fit. I transfer the measurements of the frame and slide rails to a sheet of graph paper, so I can see just where the fitting has to be done. By getting a better feel for the existing fit, I can judge where and how much I need to adjust, if at all.

Detail strip the frame and slide. Measure the height of the slide rail — that portion of the slide riding within the frame's machined-in slots. Select a rail forming bar or shim that is .002 inch thicker than the slide rail measurement and place it within the frame slots for those rails.

To keep the bars in place before peening, I recommend the Brownells dual forming bar holder. The holder will keep both forming bars in place while you are peening the rails. To avoid cutting yourself, re-install the grip safety and mainspring housing in the frame. Place the appropriate bars in the bar holder, the bars and holder in the frame rails and hold the entire assemblage in your off hand as if you were firing it weak-hand only.

Beginning with the rails forward of the magazine opening, use your polished ball peen hammer to strike the top of the frame, in front of the magazine opening. Do not strike the rails at the magazine opening. You may crack the frame or peen the rails into the opening, binding the magazine after assembly. When peening, a bigger hammer is better. You want to move the whole rail, not just peen a lip on the top of it. The more metal you move, the longer your fitting job will last. However, you can use too big of a hammer, and crack the rails by striking too hard.

Because the frame is positioned only in your hand, the simple method of fitting slide to frame requires greater striking force than is needed with a frame-holding fixture. The fixture allows you to lock the frame into your vise. With greater efficiency comes greater risk. It is very difficult to strike the frame hard enough to damage it, while holding the frame with one hand and while striking with the hammer in your other hand. However, in the vise-mounted holding fixture there is no give on impact. With both hands free you can use the rail forming bars one at a time and not need the special rail shim holding fixture and its shims. For extra rigidity and insurance against slippage while you are peening, place a hardwood block under the base of the frame.

Clamp the selected bars in the holding plate, and slide them on the frame.

Once you have fit the front rails to the slide, peen and fit the rear rails.

Holding the frame, peen the front rails.

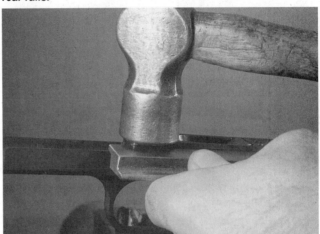

With only forming rails and a ball peen hammer, you can tighten the slide-frame fit.

Here are the forming rails and the holding fixture. With the holding fixture, you can peen the rails without a vise or vise-holding plates.

The frame holding plates should rest against the vise or a wooden block, to give support to your hammering.

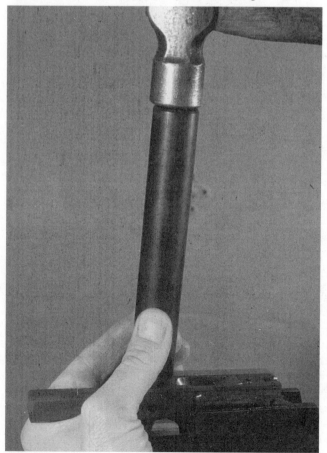

Strike the swaging bar to move the frame rails down to the forming bars.

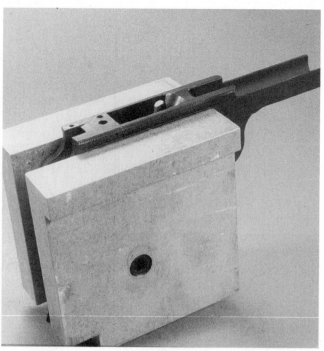

To swage, you must have frame holders like this Weigand set. You cannot swage while holding the frame in one hand, as you can peening.

The frame holding plates include a magazine filler bar. This prevents the vise and plates from collapsing the magazine tunnel.

The business end of frame rail swaging bars. The single on the left, the double on the right, press the rails down to your forming bars.

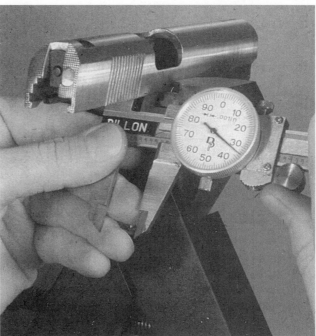

When squeezing the slide, measure the slide width before, during and after compression.

Once the rails have been peened down on the front corners, remove the forming bars and check the fit of the slide. You may find that it binds. Sometimes when the rails are being peened down they also get peened slightly out. Binding indicates you have widened the rails more than the clearance slot in the slide. The lazy way is to lap the fit with grinding compound. Don't take the easy way out. You want to end up with a free-running fit between the slide and frame, without loosening the peened fit you just worked so hard to obtain. Put Dykem on the rails, and try to install the slide. You will see the Dykem rubbed off on the high spots. Use a stone or fine-cut file to dress down those high spots on the outside of the rails. Once the slide will start to go onto the frame, Dykem the rails again and work the slide back and forth. Locate the high spots and stone again.

The price of a perfect fit is attention and patience. If you cannot watch for the details, and don't have the patience, then perhaps fitting slide to frames is not for you.

An occasional problem you may run into when checking the slide fit is interference with the recoil spring tunnel, or dust cover. The lowered slide may bind against it. Dykem the top of the dust cover and install the slide. If the Dykem is rubbed off, use a file to remove a few thousandths from the high spot. Repeat until the slide does not touch the dust cover.

Once the front rails are lowered and the slide moves smoothly, peen the rails behind the magazine opening and fit the slide to themwith the same process as you did on the front sections. This completes the rail fitting.

To swage, you must have a frame holding fixture and a swaging bar. The working end of the bar is shaped to press down the rail all at once, not just in the smaller area of the hammer blow. Place the forming bar in the

rail slot, and the swage on top of the rail. Strike gently at first, gradually increasing the force of your blows until you feel the rail move. To see if the rail has been fully swaged, check the forming bar for play. Swage until you can no longer feel any play.

Swage the front rails and check the slide for fit. If tight, stone the high spots as above. Swage the rear rails. If you feel the need for the extra speed, the swage is available in a double-sided face, so you can swage both the left and right rails in one step.

Peening and swaging remove the up-and-down play in the fit of your slide. You still may feel side-to-side play. If so, you need to squeeze the slide. You will need a slide-squeezing fixture. Measure the inside width of the slide and place the slide in the squeezing fixture in your vise.

Squeeze the slide until the inside of the slot is .020 inch smaller than your initial measurement. Let the slide sit in the vise this way for 30 seconds, then remove the slide and check the fit. The slide will now require force to move along the frame, but it should still move. If you overdo the squeezing and the slide will not move, you will have to reverse the fixture to expand the slide. Doing so is hard on the slide, and should be avoided. On the other hand, if the .020 inch squeeze didn't remove all of the side-to-side play, repeat the slide squeezing process, but this time reduce the slide slot width by a total of .025 inch. In the old days we approached slide squeezing with much trepidation. Soft slides (many of the military-production 1911A1s produced during WWII were essentially not heat-treated) squeezed easily but would not stay tight. Hard Colt National Match slides were so hard we risked cracking them. Commercial Colt slides squeezed with some difficulty, stayed squeezed, but their high polish sometimes showed the marks from

Squeeze the slide to remove side-to-side play.

The slide has to be squeezed at the rear as well as the front part of the frame rails.

squeezing. What can I say: life was sometimes hard in the old days.

With your peened and squeezed pistol fitting so tightly that you can barely move the slide, now is the time for lapping compound. Place a thin layer of 600-grit compound along the full length of the rails. Move the slide back and forth a dozen times, either rapping it with the plastic faced mallet or inserting the lapping tool and pushing and pulling the slide. If you use a mallet, expect to destroy the mallet during the production of three or four fitting jobs. In striking the slide (hard enough to move it but not hard enough to mar it) you will occasionally miss a bit and strike the rear of the frame or the front of the dust cover. The impact with the unmoving and sharp-cornered frame will gouge the mallet. Scrub the lapping compound out, lube the rails and check the fit. If the slide still does not move smoothly, repeat. Your goal is for the fit to pass the gravity test. When simply tilting your cleaned and lubed slide and frame makes the slide travel fully backward and forward you are done.

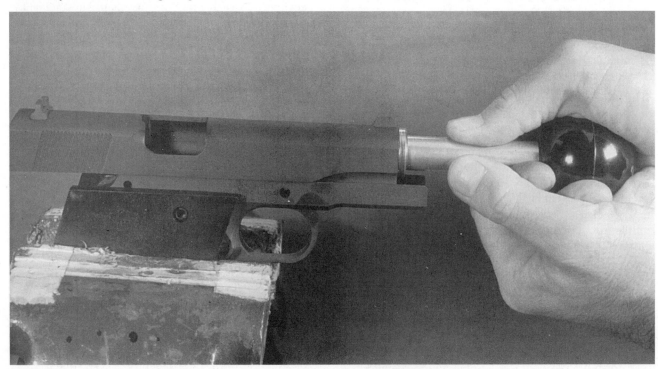

After putting lapping compound on the rails, move the slide back and forth to ease the tight spots and polish the surfaces.

BARREL FIT

Unless you are salvaging a known-quality barrel that someone has improperly-fitted but not otherwise abused, you will be "taking up the slack" with a new barrel. Accuracy in the 1911 can be achieved with a repeatable fit, even if in motion things seem sloppy. If every time the barrel closes, it does so in an identical orientation to the slide, your pistol will be accurate. (That is, if you are using the sights. A pistol with a frame-mounted optical sight will not show any improvements in accuracy using this method.)

The idea is simple; fit the barrel properly and tightly to the slide. And then fit the lower lugs to a "hard fit" using a lug reamer or a fitting fixture and an end mill. Every time the slide closes and locks up, it does so the same way, even if the slide rattles along the frame going back and forth.

The method does require a tight bushing fit, both to the slide and to the barrel. It does you no good to have the barrel locking up consistently at the rear, and still moving around at the front. In a pistol with a tight slide-to-frame fit, the amount of movement open to the muzzle of the barrel is greatly restricted. In the barrel-fit method, you must secure the barrel to the slide securely and repeatably, or the muzzle movement will defeat your efforts. You must also use the best barrel you can lay your hands on. Since the method is intended to eliminate the cost of slide fitting, it is penny-wise and pound-foolish to scrimp on barrel cost. Buy the best barrel you can afford, and even save some money to get a better one if possible. In the old days I would have reflexively said "buy Bar-sto." That is not my reflex today, not because Irv III makes poorer barrels than his Dad did. No, it is be-

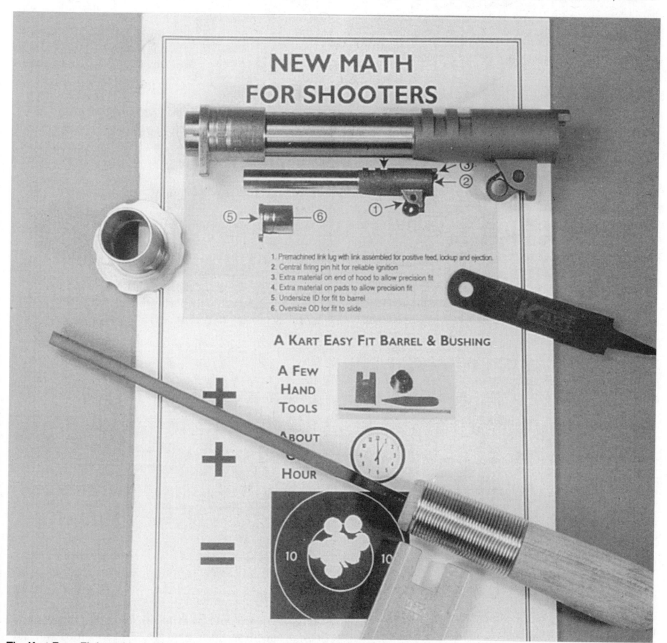

The Kart Easy-Fit barrel includes all the tools you will need for this and future barrel-fitting. Considering the cost of a match barrel, the tools end up coming for free.

cause are a lot of really good barrels being made today.

You may find that the barrel already installed in your pistol is not properly fitted. The problem could be someone at the factory was in a hurry (or being trained, and yours was the training gun) or the barrel is a replacement. There are a whole lot of older 1911s out there with barrels in them that were not the factory-installed barrel. For a long time there was a huge supply of corrosive

Clark makes accurate barrels in a variety of calibers.

You can re-barrel with other calibers, provided the breechface and overall length match. This .45 ACP 1911 has a .40 Super barrel fitted to it.

Fitting a barrel requires more than just fitting the hood. The barrel must rest firmly and evenly on the slide stop pin and not the link for support.

ammunition, for many years it was the only ammunition. Right through WWII and into the Korean War U.S. military production ammunition was corrosively primed. All that cheap surplus ammo that was blasted through cheap surplus 1911s had an effect: pitted bores. And during much of that time, a surplus spare barrel was just as cheap as the ammo and guns. So if the bore got too pitted, the owner might just plug in a "new" barrel. Fitting? What fitting? The parts were all interchangeable, and it was just an inaccurate 1911, wasn't it?

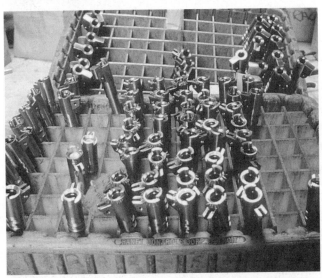

When barrel makers make barrels, they make a lot of them. These are Bar-Sto barrels awaiting shipment. (Photo courtesy Bar-Sto)

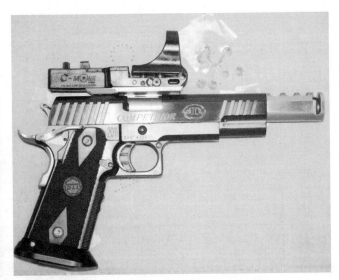

A properly fitted barrel (as in this STI Truebore Competitor) delivers superb accuracy. Here is a Fifty yard group with .38 Super Major ammo for USPSA/IPSC shooting.

FITTING THE MATCH BARREL

The heart of the 1911 is the barrel. An accurate and properly fitted barrel will deliver a level of precision to your shooting that might just astound you. Don't waste time or effort on an inaccurate barrel except as practice, or warmup to the expensive new match barrel. Likewise, don't bother with one that's been improperly fitted, or cut corners yourself when fitting a new one unless you want just the practice. An improperly fitted barrel is not only going to be unreliable but may well damage the slide.

Some would-be poets have labeled the task of properly fitting a 1911 match barrel as existing somewhere in the land between art and alchemy. Naw. You just have to keep track of the details.

What kind of accuracy should a match barrel deliver? Without any slide/frame tightening and using ammunition the pistol likes, the best you can expect from most factory barrels is 3-inch groups at 25 yards. I have seen stock 1911s that would shoot 3-inch groups with some ammo, and 6- or 7-inch groups with other ammo. A match barrel should deliver groups smaller than 2 inches with ammo it likes. With ammo it doesn't like the groups should still be less than 4 inches. Tightening

The EGW hood gauge makes a tough task easy: measuring the distance from breechface to front locking lugs on the slide.

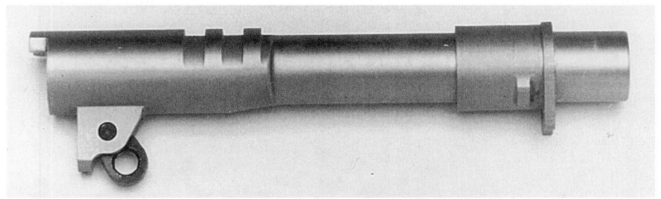

This Ed Brown barrel comes with bushing, link and pin. You can buy a drop-in barrel, or a "gunsmith-fit" barrel. Quite often the drop-in will shoot so well you won't need the tighter fit of the other. (photo courtesy Ed Brown)

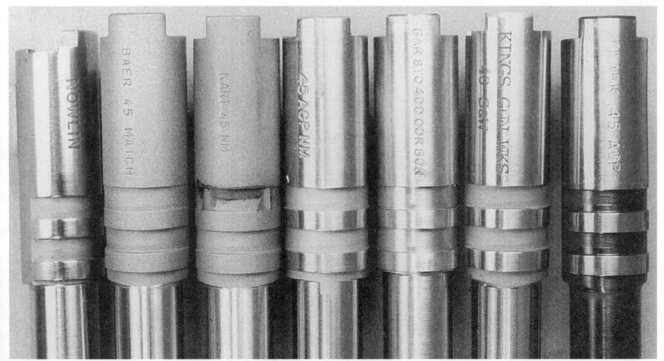

Unlike the old days, there are a number of top-quality match barrels available for the 1911. From right to left: Clark, Kings, Barsto, Olympic, Kart, Les Baer and Nowlin. And this is not an exhaustive selection.

the slide and frame will improve those numbers. I have a number of pistols, some with Bar-Sto barrels, others with Nowlin, Kart or McCormick barrels, that will deliver 1-inch groups or less at 25 yards out of the Ransom Rest.

I did not have to trade off any reliability to get that accuracy. I started with a match barrel, and then properly

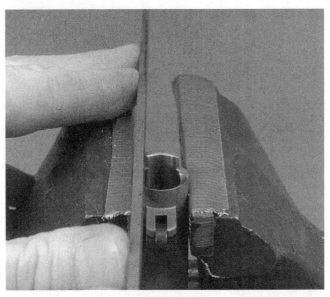

Carefully file the sides of the hood until you have .003 inches of clearance on each side.

The Kart kit comes with a fitting bushing. This lets you fit the rear of the barrel without worrying about false readings from a tight match bushing up front.

The EGW hood gauge informs us that this Springfield slide measures 1.318 inches from breechface to front locking lug. Now the match barrel hood can be shortened.

The lathe is very useful in precisely removing the desired amount of steel from a hood. And, in keeping the cut surface square to the axis of the bore.

fitted it to its pistol.

The 1911 barrel locks up in the slide by means of the locking lugs on the top of the barrel. It is supported in three other locations: the sides of the hood, the bottom lugs, and the bushing. Proper and consistent lockup and support mean consistent accuracy. Match barrels come in two categories, "drop-in" and "gunsmith fit." Although the drop-in barrel should do just that, not all pistols are identical. Even a "drop-in" barrel may require fitting. The gunsmith fit barrel is oversized in all of its rear dimensions, and you must adjust these to the individual pistol.

I have found Bar-sto drop-in barrels to be true to name in Colt and Springfield pistols. In many installations over the last few years not one of them has needed any fitting. Chip McCormick's drop-in also slides right into place, without any play or looseness, and without having to do any fitting. From opening the shipping box to the end of fitting takes 15 or 20 minutes.

Kart offers a barrel that takes a small amount of fitting. Shipped with instructions and its own fitting tools — including link, pin, bushing, feeler gauge, hood alignment gauge, fitting bushing and upper lug fitting file — the Kart requires about an hour to fit. Nothing in the kit is oversized except the hood length.

To fit a gunsmith-fit match barrel you will need the barrel, a spare bushing that fits the barrel more loosely than the match bushing does (or the Kart fitting bushing), your regular files, a barrel fitting file, a bottom lug cutting tool, a bottom lug file, a hood and locking slot gauges, a .003-inch feeler gauge, and a selection of barrel links.

Strip and clean your slide and frame. If you have a match bushing installed, remove it temporarily. If your barrel has a link installed, remove it, also temporarily.

Take your new match barrel and measure the width of the hood. It will be wider than your breechface opening. Install the barrel and your spare bushing in the slide. Put the hood gauge in the slide, and with a spare bushing in place, slide the barrel back towards the breechface. Hold the slide and barrel up to a light and see which side needs filing. Remove it and file with a few strokes. Repeat on each side of the hood until the barrel will

The Weigand fixture, and a barrel with some material being removed from the hood side. Once this side clears, then the barrel will be flipped over and the other side milled.

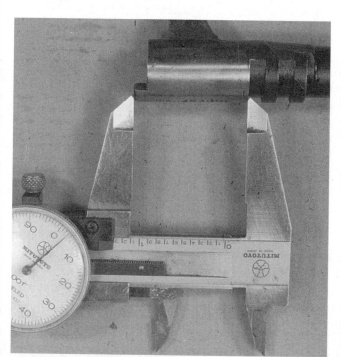

When fitting a barrel you have to measure your hood length.

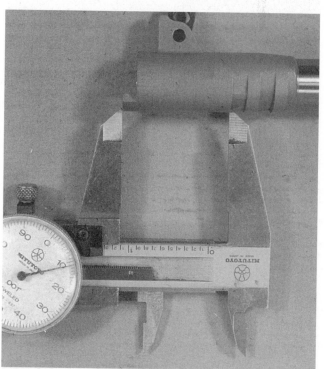

A gunsmith-fit match barrel will be longer in the hood than the distance from your breechface to your slide's locking lug.

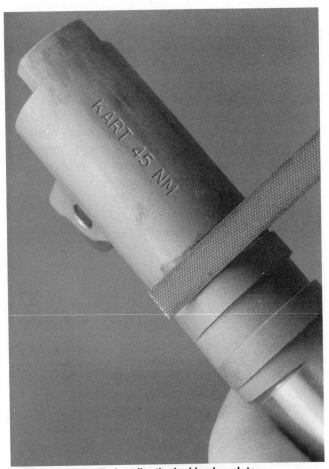

The barrel fitting file just fits the locking lug slots.

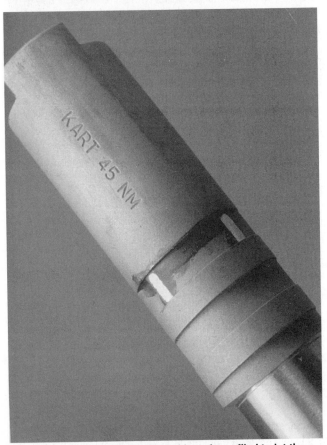

The fitting pads on this Kart barrel have been filed to let the barrel ride higher in the slide.

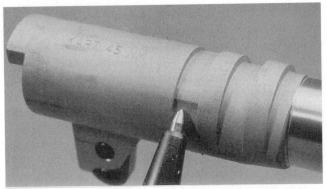

The Kart barrel uses pads machined in the slot to control upward travel.

You want the hood to clear and not bind, so milling the sides square and just free of the slide is your goal.

slide back to the breechface. Use your feeler gauge to determine that you have at least .003 inch clearance on each side of the hood, and that the area you have filed is parallel to the breechface sidewalls.

The barrel extension will be too long to lock in the locking slots. Use the EGW hood gauge to determine the length of your slide's locking slot to breechface distance. The easy way to shorten the extension is to chuck the barrel in the lathe. Take light cuts and measure the hood length until it is .002 or .003 inch more than your hood gauge measurement. Dykem the extension and check the fit. File only the binding areas until the barrel drops into place without pressure. There should be no back and forth movement.

You must next fit the upper lug engagement. Dykem the barrel locking lugs. In premium barrels upward movement is controlled by the rear slot. Place the barrel in the slide and press it into the lugs. Take a hammer and tap the bottom lugs of the barrel in the direction of the muzzle. Remove the barrel and measure the marks on the Dykem to see how much of the upper lugs are in engagement. You want to have a minimum of .055 inch of lug contact, and more is better.

On a Bar-sto the ends of the slot stop the barrel's upward movement. On the Kart pads in the slot stop the barrel. If you are below the .055-inch minimum, use a candle to smoke the stop points, and press the barrel back into place in the slide. Remove it and check these points. Filing the stop points allows the barrel to move higher in the slide, increasing upper lug engagement. The barrel-fitting file is just narrow enough to fit the slot. File where the smoke is rubbed off. Check the hood fit frequently with the hood gauge and feeler gauges, to make sure you are removing metal evenly.

Check the barrel spring with the match bushing. Install the match bushing and the barrel in the slide, and push the barrel into the locking lugs. The barrel should slide smoothly into place, and stay there. If you can feel

You can also use a marking pen to check locking lug engagement and fitting pad pressure.

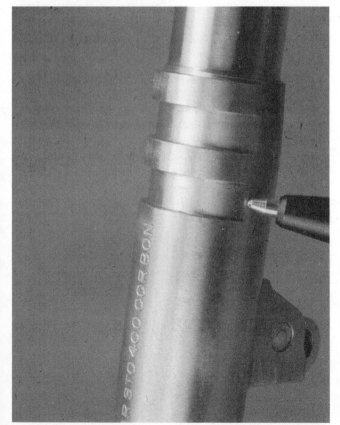

On Bar-sto barrels the ends of the rear slot control the upward movement of the barrel. If you need more upward travel, file here.

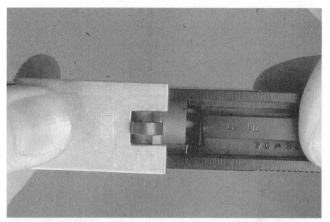

Use the bottom lug alignment gauge to keep the barrel centered and upright.

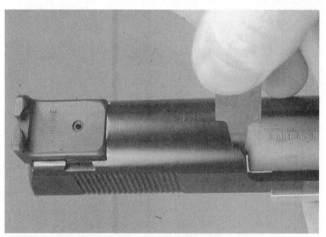

Use the feeler gauge to check hood sidewall clearance.

With the locking lugs coated with Dykem, smoked with a candle, or with a little blob of modeling clay in the slot, rap the bottom lugs. You can then measure locking lug engagement.

the barrel spring back out of locking engagement, it is binding on the bushing skirt. Use 600-grit cloth and polish the top inside of the bushing to relieve this binding.

Install the barrel with its looser bushing or the Kart fitting bushing, and use the locking bar of the lug-cutting tool to secure the barrel in place. Use the hood gauge and feeler gauge to make sure the barrel is centered. You need to fit the lower lug engagement.

Slide the assembly onto the frame, and insert the cutter through the slide stop hole. While pressing the slide

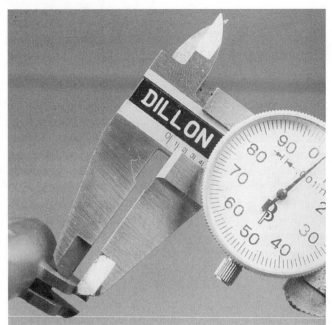

Measure the distance between the link pin hole and the just-fitted lower lug shelf.

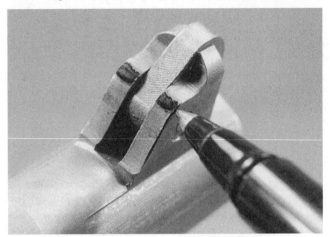

If the slide stop won't pass over the shoulder, file here.

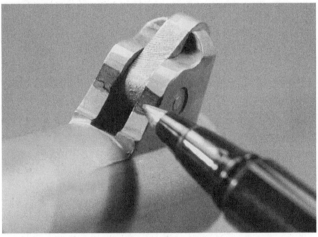

If the barrel binds on the slide after unlocking, the slide stop is probably hitting the front face of the bottom lug.

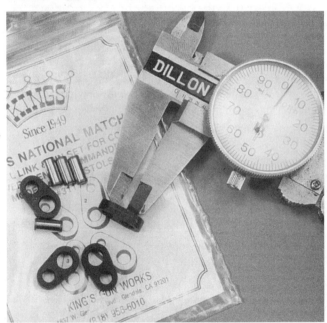

Select a link that is the correct length for your 1911.

Check the slide stop to make sure it passes over the front shoulder of the lower lug.

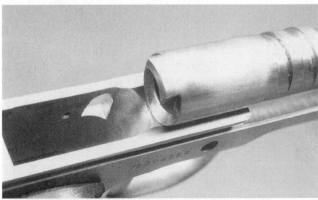

When your new barrel links back and is unlocked, there should be a gap between the top of the frame ramp and the bottom of the barrel ramp.

forward, use the cutter to remove metal from the bottom lug, stopping when the back of the slide is flush with the back of the frame. Strip the parts, remove the barrel-positioning rod, and clean the chips out. Dykem the bottom lugs. Replace the slide and barrel on the frame and put the slide stop in place. Push the slide forward until it stops. Pull the slide out of engagement and remove the barrel. Use your round fitting file to remove metal from the bottom lug where the Dykem is rubbed off. Use your feeler gauges to check that your work is even. The bottom lug must sit squarely on the slide stop, and the hood must ride centered in the hood slot. Repeat the process until you can press the slide home without any more force than you need to slide it on the rails. The bottom lugs are now properly fitted for locking.

Use your dial calipers to measure the distance from the barrel link hole to the just-filed surface of the bottom lugs. Measure the web between the holes on your link. This measurement cannot be greater than the barrel measurement. If your link is too short you can't install the slide stop. Too long and you won't be able to close the slide. If the link provided does not measure the same or slightly less than the barrel measurement you must select one that does.

With the proper link installed, check the fit of the slide stop to the front corner of the cut lower lug. During unlocking, the slide stop must clear this corner. Cutting the lower lug left it too sharp and too far forward. Now you must file it just enough to allow the slide stop to pass over it.

Install the slide and barrel on the frame. Install the slide stop. Run the slide back and forth, checking to see that it moves smoothly. If the slide hesitates during locking or unlocking, the front corner of the lower lug still needs to be filed. If the barrel rubs on the inside of the

The back end of this Wilson tungsten recoil rod has been beveled. If your recoil spring guide rod is not beveled this way, file it.

slide during movement the slide stop is hitting the front face of the lower lug.

Once the slide moves smoothly check the fit of the barrel feed ramp to the frame feed ramp. There must be a small gap. If the barrel is flush with or overlaps the frame, feeding will be poor. File the bottom of the barrel feed ramp until there is a gap between the top of the frame ramp and the bottom of the barrel ramp. Re-cut and polish the barrel feed ramp, but do not extend the top edge of the barrel ramp any farther into the chamber than it already is.

Completely reassemble the pistol and take it to the range for a test firing. After a box of ammunition, take the pistol apart and check to see whether the lower lug is banging against the slide stop. If it is, stone the contact spot to keep the parts from battering each other.

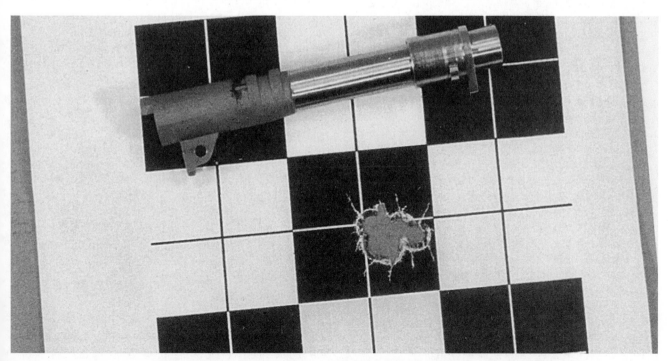

A correctly fitted Kart barrel delivers accuracy like this. Any better, and people would think you were fibbing!

MARINE CORPS HOOD?

If you peruse the barrel offerings by the makers, you'll come across the selection of 1911 barrels from Bar-sto noted as "Marine Corps hood" dimensioned. Your first reaction is likely to be something like, "Those wacky Marines, always trying to be different." Actually, it stems from the Marine Corps trying to get the job done with what the Navy gives them. The Marines are part of the Navy and have to obtain all equipments, supplies and materiel through the Navy procurement system. The end result is an upside-down economic system. The Marines Corps cannot get new 1911 pistols. Even if they were an item to be found in the supply system (choked with M-9 Berettas that no Marine wants) the budget would not exist to buy new ones. However, the Marine Corps has personnel on staff. So, the Marine Corps rebuilds 1911 pistols. The Pistol, Caliber .45, MEU (SOC) (1005-01-370-7353) is the star, but all 1911 pistols used by the Corps are existing frames that have been overhauled to keep them in service. Rebuilding an existing 1911 frame to the specifications desired by the MEU-SOC end users costs $2,000. (Or so I've been told.) A new pistol could be obtained for half that. However, there is no budget authority to buy new ones. There is, however, an existing system to procure repair parts. There is also a staff of MOS 2112 Match Armorers in the Precision Weapons Section, Quantico, Virginia to keep producing them so each pistol is "repaired" over and over again in order to keep them running.

The Marine Corps hood barrel that Bar-sto makes has hood and lower lug dimensions larger than even match barrels have. The extra steel is to ensure that the barrel can be properly fitted to any slide/frame combination that the armorer might encounter. (The locking lugs are also different, again to ensure they can be fitted to any slide/frame combination that the MOS 2112 staff might run into.) Yes, the armorers can mix and match slides and frames until they find a combination that works, but sooner or later you've got to build what the Gunny gave you. And with the frames and slides that are left after the "mixing and matching" it means using a Marine Corps hood barrel.

What with the recent fracas in Iraq, and the renewed interest and refreshed knowledge of what pistols are and need to do, the .45 is poised to make a comeback. There is word of the Corps being allowed to obtain new pistols, pistols built specifically for the job of waiting in holsters as backups. If and when that happens, the other services are not going to let the Corps be the sole purchasers. However, all the old frames will still be in the system for some time, and in order to rebuild them there will be a need for some USMC hood barrels.

If you need it, Bar-sto has it. But don't go buying one thinking that you're getting something "neat, cool and special." Oh, it is, but not for the reason you might have expected. And it will be a lot more work to fit.

MACHINE-FIT BARRELS

Those of us with lathes and mills prefer to do much of the grunt work by machine rather than hand. The barrel fitting can be simplified by using a lathe to trim the hood length to proper dimension. But the lathe can only cut the hood length. For the rest (and the hood too) a mill works wonders, provided you have a fixture to hold the barrel. Jack Weigand makes a fixture that is precise and repeatable. Repeatable in the machine tool industry means that when a part is removed to check fit (or measure the cut) you do not have to re-measure and re-position it when returning it to the fixture. With a small amount of care in positioning, you will have returned the part to the fixture within an unmeasurable amount of change: in the best fixtures in production, .0001 inch or less. Even a sloppy operator can get a part back to a thousandth of an inch.

The Weigand barrel fixture allows cutting the hood length and sides, and (the best part) the lower lugs. Using a 5mm carbide cutter, you can cut the bottom lugs until they are a smooth fit without play. You can adjust your cuts by .001 inch if you wish (and if your technique and machine are capable of such precision) until it is perfect. The Weigand fixture requires that you have a milling machine in order to fit the barrel, so I have placed the work description in Chapter 6, lathes and mills.

SLIDE REPLACEMENT

In the "not so good" old days, we modified everything because we had to. We made everything from scratch. Now, no one welds up and re-cuts a thumb safety. Why would you, when a perfectly good one can be had for 20 bucks? It may well be that a new slide is a cost-effective option. When Caspian began offering slides, we had few options; We could buy a Colt and build on it. We could buy a surplus gun and build on it. We could (if we had connections) buy parts out of the evidence room scrap program and build on a frame. If we could find a bare frame.

Now, it is different. Let's say you want to build a competition gun on a 1911. You could go through the work of peening and lapping, lowering the ejection port, milling for sights, and then fitting the slide to the frame. Or, you could buy a slide from Caspian with all the options you want, and do the work of fitting it to your frame. Or have Caspisn send you a slide/frame kit pre-fitted. If you are really into competition, or gunsmithing, you'll probably end up walking down both paths: modify the slide, and once practiced and with a better understanding of what it is you want, buy a new slide and fit it to the frame.

MEU-SOC: PART 1

When the U.S. armed forces went to the Beretta M-92 and its 9mm cartridge, there were many who were not pleased. The Marine Corps, as a whole, was not pleased.

Through diligent scavenging, hunting down guns in depots and warehouses and continuing to train their armorers in building and maintenance, the Corps managed to keep a number of 1911A1s up and running. The driving force was the desire of the members of the special operations community of the Corps to retain a reliable big-bore sidearm. When a bunch of Recon Marines keep telling their higher echelons that they need and desire something, they usually get it. The recent experience in Iraq has proven the decision to retain the 1911s a wise one. The single-stack, all-steel, big-bore pistol has proven more reliable in the dusty Iraqi environment, and the .45 more effective than 9mm. One change from the basic 1911A1 is the addition of a light rail.

The basic MEU-SOC (Marine Expeditionary Unit-Special Operations Command) is a state-of-the-art 1911A1 circa 1985: beavertail grip safety, large fixed sights, tightened enough to be accurate but not so tight as to be unreliable, fed with best-quality current style and production magazines. (We'll be building one in the next chapter.) But the light rail is the big change. In the mid 1980s we were still using big, inefficient flashlights that we had to hold with the off hand. A weapon-mount light is much more effective, and less cumbersome.

The only place available to mount a light is on the recoil spring dust cover. Luckily, Caspian makes just what you need. Available in three materials – steel, aluminum and titanium – the rail can be attached to your frame by three methods; the provided screws, soldered or welded. As a "belt and suspenders" kind of guy, I like to double my attachment methods where possible, If using just the screws, I'll make sure I finish the job with a liberal application of Loc-tite. If soldering, I use the screws as well as the solder. Welding doesn't need a double attachment.

If you don't like the looks of the Caspian, then Dave Dawson of Dawson Precision makes another rail. Be aware that rails are a lot more common on 1911s than they used to be. The Dawson is not the standard, but it is a known rail. The new standard for rails is not something you can attach to your existing frame, it must be made as an integral part of the frame.

DRILLING

The first thing you do with any part is check the fit. In trying the light rails, I've found some trigger guards are too large. If yours won't fit, adjust by filing the rail. It is the cheaper part and the easier method. The drilling presents a small dilemma: it is easier to measure and drill from the outside, but your screws enter the rail from inside the frame, and that is where the dustcover must be countersunk to clear the screw heads. With a mill and a drilling attachment it is easy: clamp your stripped frame, locate the centerline, and drill on the indicated spacing in the instructions. With a drill press, first find the centerline. Use your dial calipers to measure the thickness of the dustcover. Divide by half, set the dial calipers to that figure, lock them and use it as a scribe to mark the centerline. Then measure back from the front end of the dustcover the indicated amounts. Scribe a mark across the centerline. Now hold the rail to the frame and look to make sure the holes and your marks line up. If they do, great, use a centerpunch to indicate the drilling location. If not, figure out why. (Usually an arithmatical error from doing it in your head.) Clamp the frame bottom up and drill through the dust cover at the indicated points. Use a stone or file to clean the burrs off so the rail will clamp evenly.

The Kimber at the range, ready to consume 1,400 rounds of ammunition, testing the springs. The pistol gobbled all that ammo without a problem.

TESTING THE 1911 FOR RELIABILITY

The first thing to keep in mind is that the pistol you are shooting is a system, a system composed of the pistol, the ammunition being fired, the magazine feeding the ammo and the shooter. If any link is deficient, then the results will not be certain. Trying to determine if your efforts at improving reliability in your 1911 have worked, while using the cheapest reloads you could find at the gun show, is not reasonable. Always test using ammunition of known, 100 percent reliability. Ditto magazines. As for you, well, you can mitigate some shooter shortcomings but not all. Some people just seem born to cause malfunctions or parts breakages.

A preliminary test will require about 200 rounds. With the pistol and two or three reliable magazines to work with, put three or four magazines of ammo downrange. Does the pistol lock open when each is empty? Do all the empties extract and eject, and do they fall to the same location? A spread of 5 or 6 feet is good enough. Less is a sign of consistency. Greater spreads may not mean the 1911 in question is on the borderline of malfunctioning, but you might want to have a look again at the extractor and ejector. Once you've fired your initial batch, lock the slide open. Look at the ejection port to see if you have any "brassing" around the ejection port. Brass marks left by departing empties are not necessarily a bad thing. But heavy brassing can mean the ejection geometry is off. Or your sidewall is still too high. Look at the fired brass on the ground. Is it dented, creased, dinged or heavily marked? Even the best pistols bang the occasional empty against the slide. But if every empty looks hammered, you need to address the problem.

If you find nothing untoward, move on to the next test. Load up your magazines again and begin "wimpy" testing. Hold the 1911 as lightly as you can without dropping it. Fire a couple of magazines. Then do it all again with your weak hand. A "limp-wrist" shooting position can show you if your 1911 is oversprung or has a tight or excessive locking lug engagement. With your hand offering as little resistance as possible, if the recoil spring is too heavy the slide can't be energized enough to overcome the spring. You'll end up with the classic "smokestack" malfunction. It isn't unusual for a brand-new and not test-fired custom gun to smokestack in the first couple of magazines. Once the engagement surfaces are burnished and the sharp (microscopic) edges knocked off, it will probably function 100 percent. If it continues to smokestack on the limp wrist test after 200 rounds, you must decide if you will use a lighter recoil spring or return it to the custom smith who built it. If you are the smith, then check your work for proper barrel fit. If it is correct, lighten the spring.

If your 1911 passes the tests so far, it is time to have some fun. Expend the rest of the ammunition in one session, as quickly as you can and still get good practice in sight alignment and trigger control. The best test is a falling plate rack, with remote reset. You should be able to fire the ammo quickly enough to heat up your 1911,

The Kimber, in the Ransom rest, being checked for velocity and accuracy at the same time.

and get it good and dirty. If you have done your reliability work properly, the rest of the test session will be uneventful. If you are paying attention to building skills, it will also be fun.

The next step of testing takes some time. Once you have finished the test session, let your 1911 cool, and put it away dirty. (Yes, Sweeney the heretic: Don't clean it. Don't even oil it.) Leave it dirty and in its case until the next test session, where you will go through your regular practice session, whatever that might be. What you want is for the powder residue to set up and form a hard crust. The resistance of the crust will act to hinder the action of the 1911. If your pistol is on the borderline, the "grubby test" will uncover it. However, most 1911 pistols when properly set up will continue to work even after they are so powder-fouled and grubby that you don't want to touch them.

ACCURACY TESTING

Do not check the accuracy of your 1911 by standing there and shooting groups. If that is your test, you are testing yourself more than you are testing the pistol. Even a casually accurate 1911 is more accurate than most shooters can hold. You need, at the very least, a shooting bench with sandbags. Arrange the bags on the bench so the sandbags support the frame of the pistol, and your arms can lie flat on the benchtop. Sandbag supported prone can also work, if you don't have a bench. Make sure you are comfortable. There is no time pressure. Make each shot as perfect as you can, with full attention to sight alignment and trigger control. Take your time and make each shot not only perfect, but the same as the one before and the one that will follow. Whenever

accuracy testing comes up as a subject of discussion, the talk always ends up focusing on the details of how many shots, how many groups, and what do you do with the occasional flyers? More ammo is better, in any kind of testing. However, when people are involved, fatigue matters. You can be a great shot, but if you're tired, your groups will not be as tight as they would otherwise have been. Statistically, three-shot groups are nothing. Five is better. And three, four or five five-shot groups will give you a good base to determine the average. However, five shots of five rounds each, for each gun/ammunition combination, is a lot of shooting. And group shooting is tiring. By the time you've gotten to 200 rounds you've probably used up all the ammo, time and attention you've got for accurate shooting for the day. (Sooner, if you're testing some hot number like a full-house 10mm, .400 Cor-bon, .45 Super or .460 Rowland.)

And flyers? Recognizing that even the best shooters occasionally throw a shot, some advocate tossing the worst one or two shots of a test group. Me, when I test by hand I count all of them. Yes, I probably throw a shot now and then, but in the long run they average out.

The best way to avoid the problems of fatigue and flyers is with a Ransom Rest or Caldwell Hammer. The Ransom and Caldwell are mechanical shooting machines that hold the handgun in a consistent grip and provide a repeatable level of accuracy and mechanical delivery of recoil resistance. You can't use a Ransom or Caldwell rest to sight in a pistol (the "grip" of the two is not the same as yours, so the rounds will not print to the sights the same way they would when you fire) but you can use either to determine relative accuracy. The Ransom or Caldwell will not get tired, will not twitch on a shot and

The installation of a Kings bushing on this Springfield 1911A1 had a very satisfactory effect on accuracy.

Comments: RANSOM REST 3/4"

Used in the recoil spring tests, this Kimber fed 1,400 rounds without a problem. It really likes this Black Hills ammunition, shooting a 1-inch group with it.

throw a flyer, they don't learn a flinch from heavy recoil, and either gives you repeatable results. The Caldwell or Ransom are best used with a solid base. The more solid, the better. If you can get a large I-beam down into bedrock, then you're on the right track. Lacking that, a solid chunk of concrete or a sturdy post will do. In a pinch, a solid bench, with as much weight resting on it as possible, can serve. With the Caldwell or Ransom securely bolted to your stand, you must then learn to use them in a consistent manner.

When you tighten the clamping screws to secure your 1911 in place, do not overtighten them. It is possible to tighten the screws so much that the trigger does not return after firing. Once you've got your 1911 in place, check it by dry-firing it. If the trigger won't return, loosen the clamping knobs until it does. Once in place, you'll fire a few magazines to settle the frame in the grips inserts. When firing or returning it down from recoil do not touch the pistol. When loading, touch it as little as possible. You want to disturb it in the inserts as little as possible. One phenomenon I have noticed (much more so in .22LR) is that changing from one load to another can cause a momentary change in accuracy. If you change the powder or the bullet (especially if you go from jacketed to lead or vice versa) the new load needs to "blow out" the old fouling and re-establish its own fouling pattern and residues. If you are simply changing powder amounts, don't worry. If you (for example) move up from 4.4 of Vihtavuori N-310 to 4.6 under a lead 200-grain bullet in .45 ACP (both good loads, by the way) any accuracy changes will be a result of the loads themselves. If, however, you switch from an Oregon Trail lead

bullet to a Rainier plated or a Hornady XTP, you may find the first group or groups fired with the new batch of ammo are much larger than subsequent groups will be. Whenever I'm changing bullets or powders, I fired a "change group" or two to resettle the bore to the new load. Then, I shoot for record.

The Caldwell, being a newer design, has some differences. It uses springs to return the rest back to aim, instead of the ransom, where you have to press the machine back down. Also, the Ransom uses a lever to press the trigger, while the Caldwell uses a cable, much like the old-style photographic remote cable, to press the trigger back. They both work, and work well. Either allows you to test for accuracy without the need to absorb the recoil yourself, and keeps you from worrying about the effects of your own skills on the ammo and pistol you're testing.

When using the Ransom, once you've gotten through your settling groups or your change groups, record each shot. Don't throw out a group or shot because there is a shot out of the group. What you are seeing is a much truer representation of the accuracy of your 1911. Using a load that shoots "good groups except for an occasional flyer" is silly if you can get a better load. If you're going to go to all the effort of testing ammo in a machine rest, don't settle for less than the best results. Use all the data, and then only use the load that groups best of the ones you've tested. Provided, of course, that it meets all your other criteria. After all, the most accurate load in the world doesn't do you any good in an IPSC match if it fails to make Major. I know; I've been there.

CHAPTER

ADVANCED PISTOLSMITHING THE 1911

Going beyond basics on the 1911 requires more tools, more practice, and greater study of how the parts of your pistol operate. The rewards are great. You'll gain not just a better understanding of your pistol, but a pistol that operates just about perfectly and fits your hand beautifully.

You'll also be able to shoot better than ever before.

Before diving in, take a step back and consider your options, both in gunsmithing and in simply purchasing. There are three paths to a custom or super-custom 1911. If you want to work on a pistol you already own, you can do everything yourself. With your own pistol you can also shop out some, or all, of the work. If you want to create your own custom design, you can buy separate match-grade components and fit them yourself. But the continued interest in the 1911 has led us to this point: you can easily purchase a pistol that exceeds the specifications of all but the most skilled 'smiths of 20 years

ago. In the early to mid-1980s, gunsmithing the 1911 really took off. I look at photographs of custom guns from that era and I have to shake my head. The guns produced by big-name smiths could be, and often were, quite rough. So, before you go and build a 1980s-era 1911 (in quality and cosmetics) consider what you could buy.

OK, you want to build. Now that you understand the boundaries, let's go.

Buying and fitting your own parts was not always possible. In 1985, while still a sub-contractor to other manufacturers, Caspian Arms first explored the marketing of custom slides and frames directly to the consumer. Today, if you have a 1911 with a dead slide you can get a replacement from Caspian in any length, in blue or stainless, and with the dovetails already cut for your sights. You can order a frame to replace an over-experimented one, a barrel, and other components. If you want just the basics to build your own pistol order a frame and slide.

The Caspian Race-Ready frame kit includes everything but the springs and the grips. All you have to do is put it together.

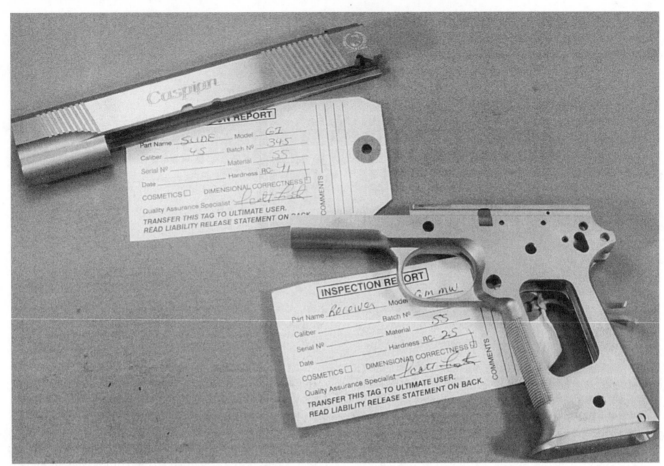

All Caspian frames and slides include an inspection tag showing who approved it, and what its score on the hardness test was. The frame came in at Rockwell C-25, and the slide at RC-41. Both are normal and correct. You may find that softer slides are cheaper, but they won't last as long under hard use.

This Wilson slide/frame combination is already fitted to a smooth sliding fit. (photo courtesy Wilson Combat)

When you order a Caspian frame, Race Ready or otherwise, you can get a custom serial number. It must contain at least one number, and it has to fit on the frame.

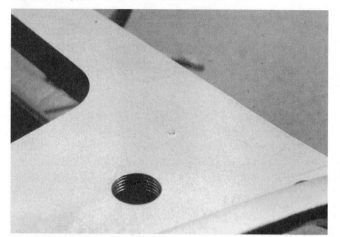

The little dimple on this frame is where Caspian tested it for hardness. It passed, or it wouldn't be shipped.

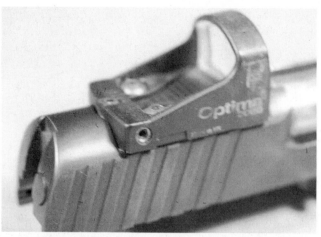

An optical sight fitted directly to the slide, for use in International IPSC matches, Modified Division.

A low-profile compensator on a Scheumann barrel. The stainless spine is part of the barrel, not the slide. The muzzle is canted to fit the size-box mandated by IPSC Modified Division

Or go whole hog.

Caspian offers a race-ready kit. The kit contains all the parts needed to assemble your 1911 except the thumb safety and the springs. The fitting and assembly are up to you, but with Caspian's close-tolerance machining, the work goes easily.

Where one goes, others follow. Chip McCormick was the first to offer hammers and sears that were held to such close tolerances that they did not require any stoning. Chip expanded his line of internal parts to include the whole pistol in the early 1990s. He became so busy with the components that he had to decide if he wanted to be a firearms manufacturer or a components manufacturer. He chose the latter, and while you can buy Chip McCormick magazines (first-rate) and parts (also first-rate) you can't buy CMC slides and frames. If you find a CMC pistol in good shape, buy it. There will be no more, it was made as top drawer components, and if someone did abuse it, a good gunsmith (maybe even you, with practice) can resurrect it.

Les Baer offers a very attractive deal on a slide and frame package. I received a frame already cut for a high-ride beavertail, with frontstrap checkering at 30 lines to the inch. The slide, dovetailed for a Novak front and a Bo-Mar rear, had extra cocking serrations up front. The fit of the slide to the frame was excellent — smooth and tight.

The best deal in a component 1911 is the STI "Short Block" kit. The STI is not a standard 1911 with a magazine capacity of eight rounds of .45 ACP but a high-capacity frame with a double-stacked magazine holding 15. The lower part of the frame is a durable polymer. The big advantage to the Short Block is that STI does the frame-to-slide fitting, installs a match barrel, and ships the kit with a recoil spring installed. All you have to do is install the frame parts behind the trigger, and put sights on the slide. Even if you were extremely particular fitting the parts, you would be ready to go to the range after an evening's work.

If you do not want to build a pistol from the ground up, but want to breathe some life into your tired 1911 with a new slide, then Scott Hunter of Speed Master can make a slide to your specifications.

As the market evolves and manufacturers adjust, the deals available shift. As tastes change, manufacturers shift with them. So keep an eye and ear out for the current deals on slide, frames, kits, etc. What was current now might not be in a short time, and what was unknown last week might be the hottest thing in a few months.

The STI Short Block has all the hard work done. The slide, frame and barrel have all been fitted. You need to put sights and internals in it. A great deal, and a great pistol.

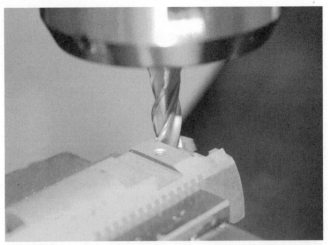

If your slide is "bare" or has only the original tiny dovetail, you need to mill it to low-mount a sight like the Bo-Mar. For that, you need to use a mill.

Purchasing match-grade component parts or kits is expensive. Buying just a slide, barrel and frame can easily cost you as much as a whole pistol out of the box. But the out-of-the-box pistol will not be as tightly fitted or machined to the close tolerances of the match components.

By customizing your 1911 by yourself, however, you can make your pistol fit almost as tight and its operation just as smooth as a match kit pistol, at a fraction of the cost. Even if you end up sending some of the work to a pro, a reasonable fall-back option for difficult jobs requiring special tools, you'll still save money (and learn more) doing your own work.

ADVANCED FRAME FITTING

Some slide-to-frame fits are beyond peening and/or lapping. If the frame is oversized by a few thousandths, you can lap the fit, moving the slide back and forth (with force) with a lapping compound in between the parts. You use each as the forming surface to shape the other. However, a slide or frame with rails more than a few

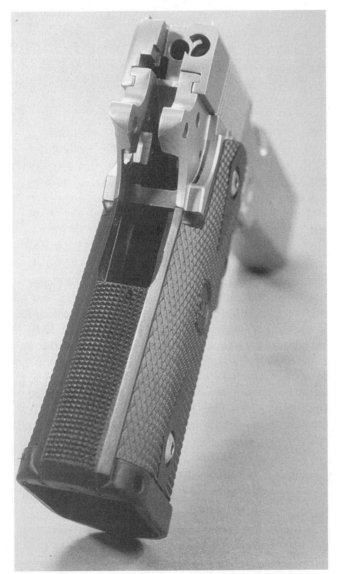

The checkering is cast right into the lower frame of this STI Short Block kit. It does not come with any internals besides the trigger. You have to install everything behind and above that.

After fitting the slide and frame you have to lap them to a smooth finish. This tool from Marvel and Brownells lets you push and pull the slide back and forth. You don't have to hit the slide with a plastic mallet.

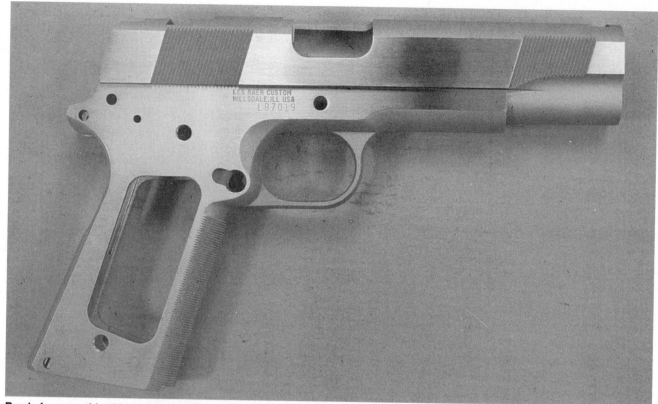

Ready for assembly, this Les Baer slide-frame kit has all the hard work already done to it.

thousandths oversized requires more work. You could file them to fit. However, that is a laborious process. Faster and far better is to mill or surface grind the parts to fit.

The fit is adjusted laterally (side to side) by milling/grinding the outsides of the frame rails to match the interior dimension of the slide slots. A surface grinder is fast, makes a clean and even cut, and can be cut in passes of less than a thousandth. A mill is not as fast, not as clean, and making a cut less than a thousandth is not always easy. (The tool can flex, your table may not be that precise, the moon may be in the wrong phase.) However, a mill is cheaper and has many uses, while a surface grinder is expensive and has fewer uses. Clamp-

ing the frame is done either vertically or horizontally. In the vertical position, the frame is in the position it would be when you are firing. However, if your vise does not have high enough jaws you can't hold the frame securely. Not-secure means not-precise, and there is no point in even trying the job if you know from the get-go that precision is not an option. And if the vise jaws are tall enough, you need to remove the grip screw bushings to clamp the frame. Clamping the frame horizontally is easier.

The vertical fit is adjusted by milling the bottom of the slide to match the vertical dimension of the frame rails. In extreme cases it may be necessary to remove a small amount of metal from the top of the frame, to get

The Weigand frame fixture, used carefully, can hold a frame to dress down the occasional too-wide rails. Again, easier than milling the corresponding grooves in the slide.

Tight slides can be milled (or surface-ground) to fit on the frame. It is far easier to dress down tight rails on the slide, than to mill out the corresponding groove in the frame.

the rails to fit the slide. While the Brownells/Yavapai slide-holding fixture is useful for many other slide milling operations, milling the bottom simply requires clamping the slide upside down and level in the machinist vise on your milling table.

Once the milling is done to the indicated dimensions, you need to stone the corners of the milled surfaces, and then lap for final fit. However, once finished, a cleanly machined and small-grit lapped slide to frame fit feels like the slide is running on ball bearings.

COMPENSATORS

Even though barrels are available with compensators attached (see photo) you must remove the comp when fitting the barrel. A compensator is fitted only after the barrel has been completely fitted and test-fired.

Screw the compensator on until it touches the slide or barrel bushing. Lock the slide back, turn the com-

This Clark barrel comes with the compensator already attached, and is meant to be a drop-in unit. Pull your old barrel out, put this one in, and check to make sure the new one links down properly. If it does, go to the range and shoot. If it doesn't follow the barrel fitting procedure to find out why.

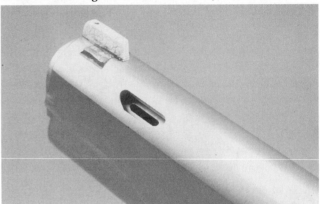

Mag-Na-Port also uses the EDM process to put ports on pistols, right through the slide. The hole in the slide is larger to allow the gases to blow out of the pistol.

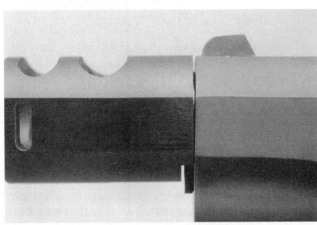

If this gap is too large for your tastes, you will have to screw the comp on a thread more and file the rear of the comp for clearance.

Some competitions allow, or even encourage compensators. Others do not. Check before you go to the expense and effort. Many authorities feel a comp on a defensive gun is a bad idea.

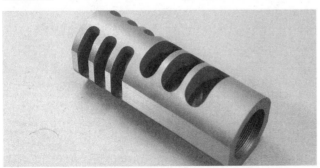

Compensators have to vent gas to be effective. The more vents, the greater the recoil reduction, provided you have enough gas to feed all those ports. This nine-port comp from EGW is effective and loud.

Filing the back of the compensator to clear the slide.

pensator clockwise until it is upright, and gently close the slide. Does the comp touch the slide? If it does, you must either unscrew the comp one turn, or use your file to remove the contact.

Try unscrewing first. Lock the slide back and turn the comp out one full turn. Close the slide. Can you live with the gap? If you can, mark the compensator's position. Unscrew it, and degrease the threads of both the barrel and comp. Apply Loctite to the threads. Screw on the comp. Wipe off the excess Loctite. Close the slide and check the alignment of the compensator. Open the slide to allow the Loctite to set. If you keep the slide closed the Loctite will wick between the barrel and bushing and lock it shut.

If the slide-comp gap is too large, screw the comp back down a turn. Use a candle to smoke the back of the comp. Gently close the slide. Open the slide and look at the marks in the smoke residue. Use your pillar file to dress down the high spots. Repeat until the smoke is not marked by the slide. Secure the compensator as above.

There can be no contact between the slide and the compensator. If they touch, every time the slide closes it will bang against the comp, driving it forward. You might only end up with a slightly peened comp. On the other hand you could crack the barrel in the threads from the stress of the repeated impacts.

The Brownells/Yavapai slide fixture makes it easy to hold the slide and mill the 1-degree back-angle you need on the front of the slide for compensator clearance. Again, you need a mill, but if you have one, or access to one, the fitting is a lot faster than smoking the surfaces and filing to fit.

IMPROVING YOUR TRIGGER PULL

Improving the trigger pull of your 1911 often has nothing to do with the trigger. You can perform a very good "trigger job" on your 1911 working only on the hammer and sear.

Lightening the trigger pull on a 1911 used to involve a great deal of work and a certain amount of hazard. If, after laboriously fitting the hammer to the sear the work was not quite perfect, the pistol would occasionally fire more than one round for each pull of the trigger.

Now, you needn't worry about the hazard or the work.

The easiest way to improve your trigger pull is to buy the right parts. All hammers and sears used to start life as little lumps of steel that were then machined into final form. Chip McCormick changed all that when he pioneered the use of the wire EDM process to create match-quality hammers and sears. Starting with precision-ground flat plates of already hardened steel, Chip used the wire of the Electrical Discharge Machining process to cut a perfectly shaped hammer or sear out of the plate. From the package, you can drop these parts

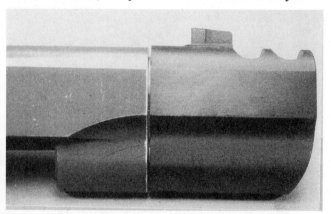

If this gap is too large for your tastes, you'll have to turn the compensator down another turn and file the back to provide just enough clearance.

If you will use a full length guide rod on your compensator, check clearance before the Loctite has time to set. Once the Loctite hardens, you aren't going to be able to adjust the comp.

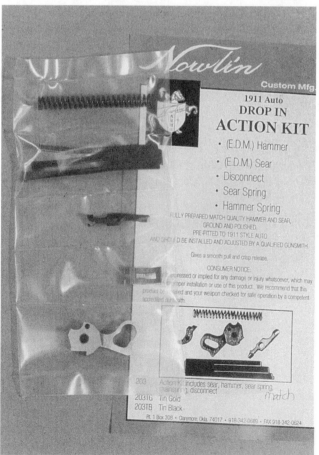

The Nowlin drop-in trigger kit. Everything you need for a match trigger pull in one package.

right into your pistol, check the operation of thumb and grip safeties, and enjoy your new trigger pull.

Stoning a hammer or sear from Chip not only wastes your time, it voids the warranty.

Chip is not the only one to make such golden parts. You can get hammers and sears from suppliers such as Cylinder & Slide, Wilson, Kings, Ed Brown and EGW. Nowlin offers a complete trigger job in a package, which has not only the hammer and sear, but the disconnector, hammer spring and three-leaf spring. My suggestion, if you are going to do the "CMC trigger job" as I started calling this process when Chip first offered his parts, is that you get the full suite all from the same maker. That is, hammer, trigger and disconnector all should be by the same company. Not an "X" hammer, "Y" sear and "Z" disconnector. Yes, they'll probably all work, but each company has made certain that their hammer-sear geometry is absolutely correct for each part as a team.

Swapping parts is not always an option. Precision parts can give you a trigger pull as low as 2-1/2 pounds, far too light for hunting or defensive carry. The lightness can also create problems for a relatively new competitive shooter. And if you are going to carry your 1911 for defense, do not install match parts that deliver such a light trigger pull. Stone your existing parts for a cleaner, crisper trigger pull, but one that is still 4-1/2 pounds or more.

Looking at this for the latest edition, I have to interject

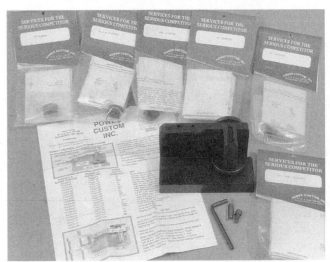

This is what you will be looking at.

The correct relationship of the sear and disconnector. The left ones are by Chip McCormick, while the right ones are by Cylinder & Slide.

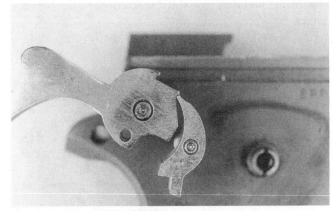

The Power custom stoning tool is adaptable to almost every handgun in existence.

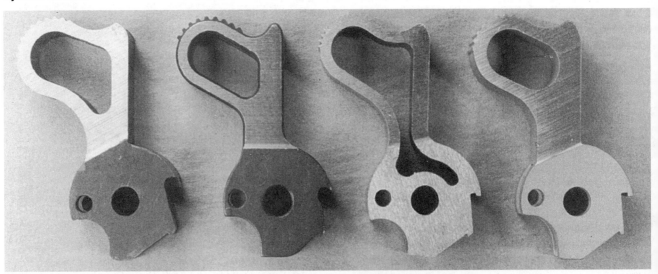

Replacement match hammers. Left to right: Wilson, Chip McCormick, Cylinder & Slide, Kings.

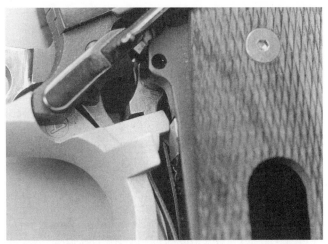

With the grip safety not depressed, it is pushed by its spring and interferes with the travel of the trigger.

Properly stoning the sear requires a fixture such as this Series 1 from Power Custom.

Here the grip safety has been pressed, and the trigger can travel under it to release the sear.

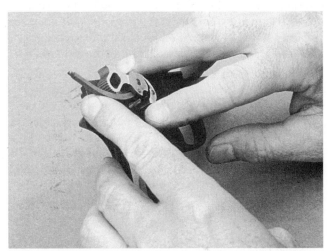

With external hammer and sear pins you can observe the hook engagement.

a comment here: stoning is probably not the best course of action. All us old farts will probably still be stoning parts for years to come. We'll also be re-building our existing guns all that time. As much as I love and respect Ron power, I have to advise you that for the cost of the stoning fixture, stones, and the time you'll spend practic-ing, you could have bought a hatful of hammers and sears, and installed them in all your 1911s. But if you too want to bring an old pistol back form use or abuse, and not exchange the parts, you'll have to stone, or use my secret method.

Proper stoning of hammer and sear requires a fixture. Ron Power makes the best. With adapter blocks, the same fixture can stone the hammers and sears of every handgun in common use. You will also need a magnify-ing eye loupe and external hammer and sear pins first to examine and then to check the engagement.

You stone the hammer hooks to make them square and to make their surfaces smooth. You must also shorten the hooks to a specific height. The hook height you select determines the weight of the trigger pull, the useful life of the trigger job, and the safety of continued sear engagement.

To stone the hooks square, set the fixture to work the hook flats and faces. Begin with a medium-fine syn-thetic stone, preferably a Brownells trigger stone. The faces and edges of trigger stones are precision-ground to be flat and square. Make a few even passes across the hooks. Dykem, and stone again. Continue marking and stoning the hooks until they are even across their full faces. Switch to the extra fine stone and polish the hooks with a dozen passes.

Adjust the fixture to stone the tops of the hooks. For hunting or carry pistols, where you want a trigger pull that is clean and crisp but not too light, adjust the hook height to .020 inch. For competition, where you need or want a lighter trigger pull, adjust the height to .018 inch. The .020-inch hooks should give you a trigger pull of around 4-1/2 pounds, while the shorter height can deliver a trigger pull of 3-1/2 pounds. Place your feeler gauge on the hammer flats, pressed up to the hooks. Stone the tops of the hammer hooks using the medium fine stone. Stop when the stone reaches the feeler gauge. To keep the now-sharp hooks from marring the sear tip, take one pass across their tips and break the corners.

Put the external positioning pins into the frame, and

The purpose of stoning the hammer hooks is to makes them square, polished, and a known height.

place the newly-stoned hammer and the sear on them. Adjust the hammer and sear so they are in contact, and examine the angle of the sear tip. It should bear evenly on the hammer hooks. Adjust the sear stoning fixture so you are stoning to maintain this angle. If the sear does not contact the hammer hooks evenly, adjust the sear fixture to compensate.

Stone the sear for four passes with the medium fine stone, and recheck hammer/sear engagement. If necessary, adjust the sear fixture again to the correct angle to the hammer hooks. With the correct angle locked in, stone the sear until it bears across the full width of the hammer hooks. Switch to the extra fine stone and polish the sear tip for half a dozen passes.

Remove the sear from the fixture. Place it against the medium fine stone with only its tip and foot making contact. Take two or three passes to stone the escape angle. By beveling the inside tip of the sear you create a surface for the hammer hooks to cam the sear out of the way, reducing wear on the sear and prolonging the life of your trigger job.

An additional method of creating perfect hammer hooks, my "secret" method, requires a mill. Clamp the hammer upside down, with the flats under the hooks dead level. Install a new, sharp, carbide end mill in your mill. (The size doesn't matter, really, as long as it is big enough, 1/4-inch or so.) Wipe layout die on the flats and hooks. Bring the cutter down until it just kisses the flats. Move it over to the hooks until it just cuts both hooks. Do not cut any more than you need to get a clean surface on both hooks. (Unlike many milling operations, this part is not a measurement-driven operation, but an observation-driven one.) Once you have cleaned the faces of the hooks, lift the cutter (or drop the table) .018 or .020 inch and cut the tops off the hooks. You now have perfectly square, even hooks that are precisely .018 or .020 inch high. Remove the hammer from the vise and stone the corner to remove any wire-edge left by the machining. Stone the release angle.

Clean and lubricate the hammer and sear, and install them in the frame. Perform the hammer and safety checks discussed in Chapter 4, and if necessary adjust your thumb safety to the new hammer/sear engagement.

Brownells offers the Brownells/Yavapai sear engagement fixture, where you can observe the sear and hammer hook engagement at 25X magnification. Using the Powers fixture and the Brownells/Yavapai optical viewer, you can make sure your sear is perfectly fitted to the hammer hooks.

Once you have done the safety checks, and now have a trigger job that is the weight and feel you want, you have one last task to perform: you have to "boost" the hammer. Strip the frame down again. Apply high-pressure grease on the hammer hooks and the sear tip. You don't need much, but you want an even coating on both. Reassemble the frame. Now, cock the hammer, and place a screwdriver under the hammer spur, using the grip safety as a cam point. Press the screwdriver down, using the screwdriver to force the hammer forward, the direc-

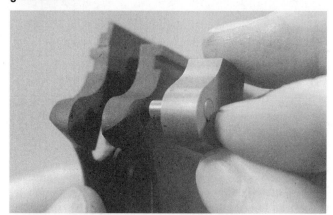

With the Wilson grip safety guide bolted on, you are ready to grind and file.

Press the right hand side onto the stripped frame.

Tighten the locking bolt.

tion it travels when you fire. You don't need, nor do you want, a lot of force here. A couple of pounds of force on a 6-inch screwdriver is plenty.

As you apply this force with the screwdriver, press the trigger to dry-fire your 1911. What you have done is burnished the sear tip and hammer hooks to each other. The grease is here to prevent scoring or galling, to keep an errant bit of grit from scoring your carefully stoned or milled surfaces.

Boosting saves you time. Generally, as you fire your

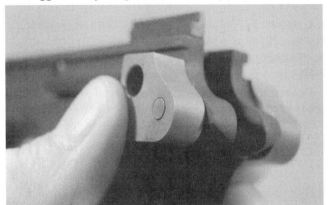

Slide the left side on and press the top edge flush with the slide rails.

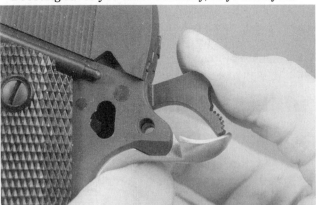

This Wilson drop-in beavertail grip safety will not work with a spur hammer. You must switch to a commander hammer.

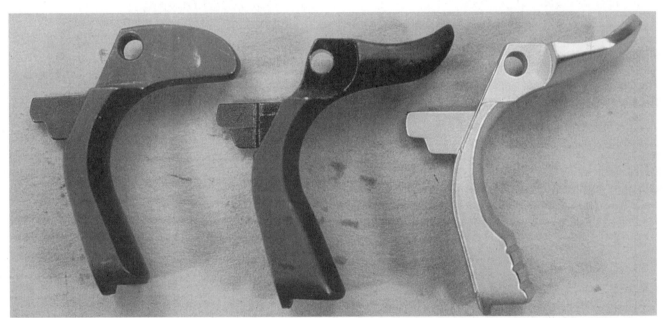

Three grip safeties. The standard on the left protects your hand, but isn't as efficient at aiding your shooting as the other two. The McCormick in the middle is much less sensitive to improper grip. The swelling goes far enough up that any hand will depress it. The Ed Brown on the right lets your hand get higher on the gun, but not everyone hits the pad on the bottom. If you don't push the pad, the grip safety will not unlock the trigger.

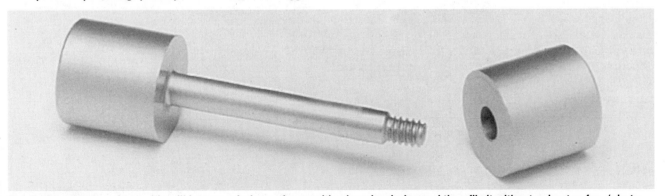

The Ed Brown grip safety guide will let you grind your frame with a bench grinder, and then file it without going too far. (photo courtesy Ed Brown)

pistol, the hammer and sear will burnish each other, and after a few hundred or a thousand rounds your trigger job will have gotten just that much smoother and a bit lighter. Boosting saves you time.

As with so many things, more is not better. If you operate under the assumption that "A little is good, so more is more good" then you will probably ruin your new trigger job. Too much leverage, or too much force will risk marring, chipping or breaking the sear or hammer hooks. If you do it, do it moderately.

INSTALLING A BEAVERTAIL GRIP SAFETY

Jeff Cooper once remarked that the beavertail name was wrong. The wider grip safeties looked like ducktails. Too bad "ducktail" is already in use to describe a haircut from the 1950s. We are stuck with beavertail.

The grip safety in the 1911 encloses the trigger and provides an additional safety mechanism that precludes the pistol's firing unless it is held. With its wider area the beavertail grip safety adds comfort and control by spreading out the recoil forces. It also keeps the pistol stable in your hand, speeding up accurate rapid fire.

Beavertail grip safeties change the way your hand fits the frame. When combined with a thumb-over-the-

The ground and filed frame tangs, smoked to check the fit of the grip safety.

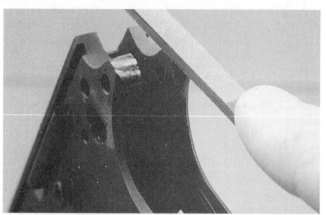

File the high spots rubbed bright by the grip safety.

Wilson makes beavertails and the fitting jig to get it on your frame correctly.

thumb-safety shooting style the grip safety does not always work properly. If your hand doesn't contact the grip safety at the bottom the safety won't unlock from the trigger. Your pistol will not fire. To prevent this problem, grip safeties are now available with a lump at the bottom. The lump fills the gap your hand leaves when you get a high grip on the frame. If you have trouble contacting the grip safety at the bottom, because of your grip or the size of your hands, you must get a beavertail grip safety with this lump.

The Chip McCormick grip safety incorporates this lump as part of the curve down the spine of the grip

safety. Called the "de-activator" it allows the grip safety to do its job regardless of how you hold the pistol. The Ed Brown has a large kind of rectangular pad at the bottom of the grip safety. Both work, and many others have one of these or other additions to aid grip safety function. If it matters to your grip which of these you have, then get the one that works. You might try a bunch of different grip safeties if yu can, to see what is most comfortable, and what works or doesn't.

Beavertail grip safeties come in two basic types. The drop-in does not require any frame modification. Simply remove the old grip safety, install the new one, check for

Here the cylinder and slide grip frame fixture is being used to cut a Springfield frame.

At 1,600 rpm, the carbide cutter makes quick work of the frame tangs.

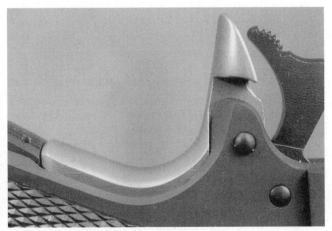

A side view of the Kings drop-in safety.

Simply rotate the frame around the pivot pin.

proper engagement of the grip safety to the trigger, and enjoy. Wilson and King both offer drop-ins available in blue or stainless. There are some minor design differences, and not all drop-in beavertails work with spur hammers. For the latter to work you must install a Commander hammer.

Drop-in beavertails do not fit snugly to the frame, and some shooters find the gaps objectionable or uncomfortable. The alternative is to modify the frame for a better fitting beavertail.

The sleeker beavertail grip safeties all require grinding, milling or filing the tang of the frame on a .250-inch radius from the thumb safety hole. Having done that, you face two more options: Ed Brown's style and everyone else's.

The Ed Brown grip safety is far more curved under

Here is the first cut.

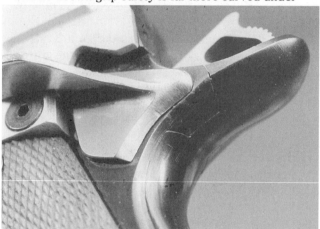

When you have finished, the thumb safety will fit the curve of the grip safety, but....

The next cut is deeper.

when the safety is on, the safety lug hole is partially uncovered. This is a cosmetic problem, not an operational one.

Here is the frame, ready for the safety to be lapped into place.

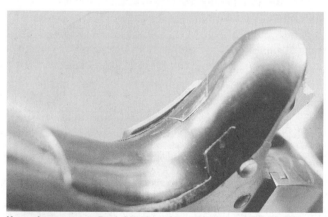

If you have a standard thumb safety on a frame with an Ed Brown grip safety, the thumb safety will hang over the back of the frame. You have to file or grind the thumb safety back, and polish the edge.

the tang than those from other manufacturers. To install a safety from Ed you have to file and polish the excess frame under the tang in order to blend the edges of frame and safety. Other grip safeties do not require blending under the tang. Why is the Ed Brown shaped this way? Simple. The greater curve lets you get your hand higher and tighter on the frame, affording many shooters greater comfort and added control. Other shooters see no improvement, and have no need to go to the extra trouble of fitting the Ed Brown.

The installation of a non-drop-in beavertail grip safety begins the same way regardless of the brand. You can grind and file or you can mill. If you intend to grind and file, when you order the grip safety also order a bea- vertail-fitting jig to guide you in your grinding. Strip the frame, install the jig, and fire up your bench grinder. Grind the frame down to the jig without touching the jig.

Use your pillar file to dress off the metal on the edges of the frame kicked up by the grinding wheel. With a candle smoke the freshly ground surfaces. Press the grip safety in place and remove it. File the contact points left bare of soot. As you work your way down, be sure to file the surface to a smooth radius. After a couple of smoke and file turns, start checking the thumb safety to see if it goes through the pivot hole of the grip safety. As you move down towards proper fit, each time you press the grip safety to the smoked surface, rub the grip safety against the frame, duplicating the rotating motion of the safety as it will pivot once it is installed. This will show you the high spots not just as the safety is pressed, but as it pivots, too.

When you get to the point that the thumb safety will insert, pivot the grip safety on the thumb safety pin to check for additional high points on the radius. Also check to see if the grip safety is binding on the frame opening. If so, file the safety until it moves smoothly.

Pull the thumb and grip safeties off and install the trigger. Reinstall the two safeties and look through the frame opening. Press the grip safety and attempt to pull the trigger. The trigger should pass under the grip safety extension. If it doesn't, file the bottom of the grip safety extension to provide clearance. Install the mainspring housing. Pull the grip safety up until ti stops against the mainspring housing shoulder. The tip of the grip safety should pass behind the trigger, preventing it from mov- ing back. If it does not, the grip safety tip is too long. Re- move the grip safety and file the tip, checking fit as you go. You want to shorten the grip safety tip enough that it passes down behind the trigger when pivoting, but not make it so short that the trigger can move when the grip safety should be blocking it.

As with so many things, power tools and the right fixtures make life easier. If you have a mill and are plan- ning to do more than one beavertail grip safety instal- lation, buy a grip safety fixture. Mine is from Cylinder & Slide. Other manufacturers make similar products. To use, clamp the fixture in your mill and install an end mill. Because of its speed and ease of use I prefer a carbide

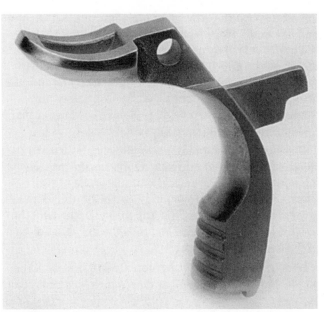

This Ed Brown grip safety will get your hand higher on the frame than a standard safety. (photo courtesy Ed Brown)

Here is an Ed Brown grip safety with the radius cut on the frame tangs, but no other blending done. You can see how much of the sides of the frame have to be ground and polished down to blend the edges. Once this is done, the frame will sit lower in your hand.

end mill. The thumb safety hole of your frame goes over the pivot pin on the fixture.

Position your cutting tool .185 inch from the fixture's pivot post. Wearing a pair of heavy gloves, set the frame on the pivot pin, turn on the mill, and rotate the frame against the end mill. When you are done de-burr the new cut. Check the grip safety for fit. The cut should be close, but the thumb safety will not yet fit through the frame. Move your milling table .005 inches in and repeat the process. Continue .005 inch at a time until the thumb safety fits.

Fitted this way the gap between your frame and the grip safety will be less than .005 inch. Usually the grip safety looks as if it grew out of the back of the frame. For an even finer fit, as soon as the thumb safety pin can be forced through the grip safety pivot hole, do not use the mill any more. Place lapping compound on the tang of the frame, install the grip safety and the thumb safety, and work the grip safety back and forth. Once the grip safety moves easily, clean off the lapping compound and check the fit. You are done when the grip safety moves freely. This attention to detail separates the Master pistolsmith from the good pistolsmith.

One last fitting and timing task. Take your pistol to the range and see if your grip fully depresses the grip safety. If it does not, you can solve the problem one of two ways: build up the "speed bump" on the bottom of the grip safety, or "sensitize" the grip safety. Of the two, the latter is a whole lot easier, and thus the one most-often performed when needed.

Look at the tip of the grip safety. The thickness of the paddle behind the trigger bar determines how sensitive

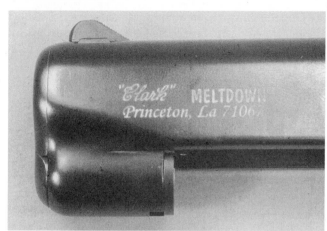

The Clark Custom Guns "Meltdown." The front of this slide has been fitted with an over-sized bushing, and rounded like a bar of soap.

The Clark Meltdown compared to a standard 1911.

The back of the slide has been rounded as well.

The Clark Meltdown, not a sharp thing in sight, except its bite.

The reverse-plug recoil spring retainer has been artfully blended to the bushing and slide.

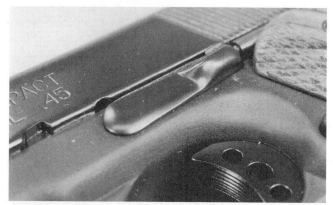

The slide stop has even been rounded.

the grip safety is. If the paddle is full height, the grip safety has to be fully compressed, or there is no bang in your future. If you take your file and remove some of the steel from the lower part of the grip safety tip, the grip safety will have to be depressed less to clear the trigger bow.

Clearly, if you file all of the tip off, the grip safety will not block the trigger at all. This is not a wise thing, so please do not do so. Instead, file the lower surface until the grip safety has to travel about one-third of its pivot into the frame, to clear the trigger bow. One-third is enough to keep the trigger locked in place if you should drop your gun (which is what the grip safety is all about) and yet will ensure that every time you want your 1911 to fire, your won grip safety is clear and won't prevent you from shooting.

THE ED BROWN DIFFERENCE

The Ed Brown grip safety requires more work. Fit as you would above, until the thumb safety will insert through the frame an dgrip safety. Install the thumb and grip safety. Press the grip safety all the way into the frame. Note that it will go past the edges of the frame. Since these edges are very sharp, you cannot shoot the pistol without blending them to the grip safety. Install the mainspring housing. You don't have to have the mainspring in it, and it is probably a good idea to remove them, as things are going to get messy.

Place masking tape across the bottom of the grip safety to hold it down. Put the frame on your holding

bar. Use grinding stones or a sanding drum in your hand-held grinder to reduce the edges of the frame, grinding them down towards he grip safety. You want them flush to the grip safety. Once flush, re-contour. You can't leave the new edges square, but you also can't get too radical in rounding them, as there is only so much steel there. Once you've blended the frame look at the thumb safety in its down, or fire, positon. You will have to grind its rear curve to match the curve of the frame. Once all the edges are blended, switch to 220-grit cloth and polish the frame, thumb safety and grip safety.

Unlike the installation of other grip safeties, once you are done installing an Ed Brown you will have to refinish the frame, as the whole rear, from the mainspring housing up, will be "in the white" or bare steel.

Which beavertail grip safety is the right one for you? You will have to try the pistols of other shooters at your club, with a variety of grip safeties on them, to find out what works for you. You may well find that while any beavertail grip safety improves your shooting, you notice no difference between the brands.

THE COMBAT MELTDOWN, OR DE-HORNING
PART 2

Shooters with tender skin hate sharp edges. Even without tender skin, those who must wear a pistol eight to 18 hours a day also find every sharp edge that exists.

Basic de-horning simply breaks edges and radiuses them. More is required for sensitive skin or daily carry. Every sharp edge must be removed. Every one. You

Stippling can be re-done and gone over. You can even use stippling to salvage botched checkering. This pistol had truly ugly checkering, with wavy lines at odd angles. Stippled, the ugliness is hidden, and the surface is non-slip.

The stippling was applied to provide a non-slip surface. Then, the pistol was given a Bearskin finish. Jet black, it doesn't slip and is easy to clean.

been sent to the bluer or plater.

GET A GRIP PART 2

Skateboard tape and clamp-on panels work to keep your grip from slipping, but they aren't quite permanent. To make a permanent change in the grip of your 1911 you must work on the metal of the frame. Once a frame has been altered, however, you are stuck with it. You can't go back and re-do it the other way. Before you begin, be sure of what you want.

Stippling has much to recommend it. To stipple the

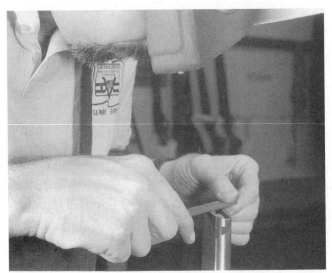

Magnifiers help you checker without going blind.

must be ruthless. You cannot look back. Ever seen the "Meltdown" by Clark Custom Guns? Except for being blued steel, it looks modeled after a bar of soap. Use this as your model.

Before you take the pistol apart, rub your hands over it. Mark the edges needing beveling with a felt-tip pen. These will be your guides to filing.

Start with the slide. File a .065 inch wide bevel on the back edges and bottom rail. On the front of the slide either file the slide itself, or install a bushing the same size as the slide and file the bushing flange. Clark combined the bushing flange approach with an extended recoil spring retainer, and rounded the retainer, too.

After you have beveled the edges go back and slightly round them with the file. Switch to 220-grit cloth and use a shoeshine motion until they are smoothly blended. Repeat with 320-grit and 400-grit cloth.

Do the same thing to the frame.

The sharp edges of the hammer will have to be rounded to keep them from rubbing you raw. Do not round the base of the hammer, which rests inside the frame.

Round any remaining felt-tip markings.

Before you have the pistol refinished, take it to the range and shoot it to make sure you've gotten everything. If you carry your pistol, wear it for a few days to be absolutely sure you've eliminated every nasty edge. It is expensive to address "one last" problem after it has

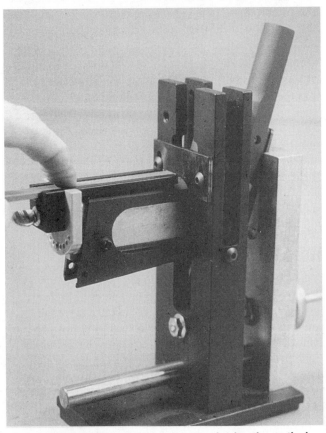

The Nowlin checkering fixture, set up to checker the vertical lines on the front of a 1911 frame.

frame you need a centerpunch and a ballpeen hammer.

If you are locating a spot for drilling, you hold the centerpunch directly against the metal and strike it. In contrast, to stipple you must hold the punch 1/2 inch away from the frame before striking.

Right-handers begin by holding the punch in your left hand as if you were trying to write with it. The point will be up, where a pencil eraser would be. Turn your hand over, resting the back against the frame or vise. From this position, the blow of the hammer drives the punch into the frame, leaving a mark, and your flexed fingers pull the punch back from the frame after the impact,

ready to strike again. Move the punch over slightly and strike again. Left-handers must begin by holding the punch in their right hand.

You do not have to swing the hammer very hard to make an impression. The harder you strike, the larger the mark. In the center of the area you will stipple, swing briskly. At the edges, tap the hammer, so you can precisely control the location of the strike. Once you have a feel for the technique, all you have to do is repeat it several thousand times. If the tip of the punch becomes dulled, stop and sharpen it.

It is not just the tip of the punch that will become

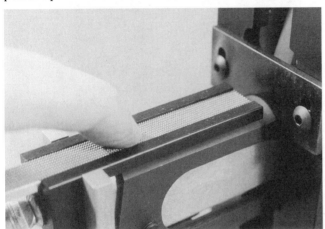

The guide bars keep the specially ground checkering file moving in a straight line. The top plate stops the checkering file at a consistent point.

The index holes tilt the guide correctly for the vertical lines to be properly spaced across the front of the frame.

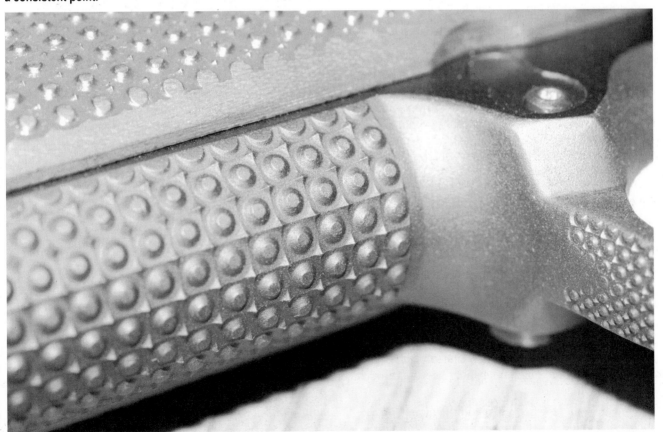

Exotic non-slip grip treatments, like these Conamyds from Ned Christensen, are the work of a true master. You cannot duplicate these with anything but the proper tools, and years of experience as machinist and gunsmith.

The Nowlin checkering fixture, cutting the horizontal lines on the front strap of a 1911.

Clamp the bar and slide in the vise.

Holding the checkering file against the bar, cut the lines at the bottom of the slide.

Follow the lines you've done up to the top of the slide.

dull. Stop when your arm gets tired. Don't hurt yourself swinging too many times in your first sessions. You may have to spend three hours or more stippling the front of your first frame. If you try to do all that in one day, your arm will be so tired you risk hitting things other than the centerpunch. You can also risk repetitive-motion injury. As you become more familiar and practiced with the technique you will speed up. The last time I stippled a frame, it took a little less than 45 minutes, but I've been swinging a hammer for many years now.

The beauty of stippling is that you can always go back and fill in with more stippling any areas that you didn't completely cover during the previous session. If you want to spread your stippling work over the course of several weeks and a number of trips to the range, no problem. If after you get a better feel for the technique you want to give the frame a coarser, heavier stippling, just stipple right over the old work.

CHECKERING, KING OF THE GRIPS

Checkering is hard and demanding work. Unlike stippling, in checkering it is impossible to correct any mistakes. The work requires a checkering file, with the number of lines per inch of the pattern cut into the file. To checker, work the file over the frame, keeping the lines straight, and filing parallel grooves.

Simple in description, checkering can be very difficult to execute. The beginning of the process requires a heavy but steady hand on the file, while the end requires a delicate touch and much time spent peering through your magnifying visor.

If you are going to checker, spend the money on a checkering guide. Nowlin makes the best. Without the guide, you have only your hand and eye to keep the lines of your checkering straight. You may feel like you're

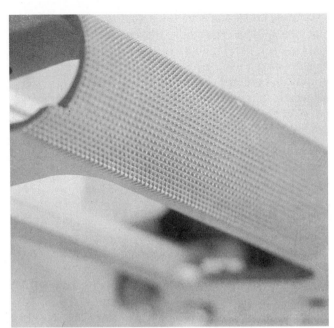

This Les Baer frame comes checkered 30 lines per inch. A beautiful job, and one you would be hard-pressed to duplicate without hours of work.

going crazy trying to keep the file straight, and until you learn the technique you will checker wavy lines. No doubt about it. If you cannot afford the checkering guide but must have a checkered pistol practice on mild steel bars. Buy one or two from Brownells, in .750-inch diameter, and checker these until you are happy with your efforts. Then start on your pistol.

To use the guide, strip the frame. Lock it in the guide. Set up to cut the verticals first. Establish the lines but do not cut them to full depth. Set the horizontal guide up, and make your first cuts near the bottom of the frame. Adjust the thumbscrew to move the guide up so your next set of lines just overlaps the first set. Continue up the frame until you have established the pattern.

Dykem the frame and go back over the horizontal lines until you have cut them to their full depth. Switch to the vertical lines and file them to full depth.

Pull the frame out of the guide, Dykem the checkering again, and put your frame on your holding bar. Take a three-sided needle file and follow each line across the frame, gently filing the Dykem out of the lines. The Dykem will show where the lines are too shallow or too deep. Use the needle file to adjust each line in depth until all of the points are sharp, and all of the bottoms of the lines are even.

Correctly executed checkering is beautiful. It is also very sharp. Correctly finished checkering will feel as if it could draw blood when you squeeze hard. For a very aggressive feel — large diamonds that can really grab your hand — checker your frame in 20 lines to the inch (lpi). This is relatively easy to checker. It is, however, very hard to shoot. Unless you work with your hands for a living, (and I don't mean at a word processor) 20 lpi checkering will be so sharp and aggressive that your

hands will object to the abuse. A less aggressive pattern is cut 30 lines to the inch. The lines here are shallower, and more difficult to cut. The file will wander if you are not extra careful. 30 lpi is also easier on your hands if they are office-soft. Shooting 30 lpi, you won't feel like you've been juggling cheese graters, as you would if you'd just finished a practice sessions with a 1911 sporting 20 lpi checkering.

Occasionally someone who wants to show off checkers a frame 40 lines to the inch. It is very delicate and exacting work, and must be done flawlessly to look right. Even finer than that are checkering files in 50 and 75 lines to the inch. All three of these smallest sizes are most commonly used on the rear of slides and the tops of slide ribs, applications that cut down glare when sighting.

To checker the rear of a slide, remove the slide from the frame. Take out the firing pin retainer, the firing pin, and extractor. Place a steel plate or bar against the bottom rails of the slide, and clamp the plate and slide rear end up. The plate will be your guide. Hold the checkering file against the plate and move it to the slide. Work the file back and forth, holding firmly against the plate to keep the file straight. Only a checkering file will cut in both directions.

After establishing your first lines, tilt the file down to follow the curve of the slide and cut a few more. Once you have a set of lines established, pick up the file and move it over. Position it so half rests over the lines and the other half over fresh slide. Use the established lines to guide you in cutting the next lines. Proceed until you finish moving up.

Unclamp the slide and rotate it a quarter turn, so the plate is now against one side of the slide. Follow the same procedure from one side to the other. Apply Dykem and use the needle file to clean up the lines.

If you really want to checker your entire 1911, go ahead. But there are easier paths. Custom frames come already checkered. You can have a professional gunsmith checker your frame for less than the cost of a checkering guide. The professional does it more quickly and less expensively not because he is so much better with a checkering file, but because he uses a fixture in his mill and lets power and computer control cut the checkering. It's almost like cheating, but no one complains.

OTHER FRAME TREATMENTS

Checkering is traditional, but there are other methods of achieving a non-slip grip. Interestingly, they all seem predicated on having a mill handy. Modern gunsmiths are both more likely to have one, and more prone to using it, than the older guys. Power has its advantages.

First up is simple: vertical lines. By milling narrow vertical grooves on the frontstrap, you get a better grip. You'd think that only horizontal ones would do anything and that vertical would be of no use. Apparently there is enough of a lateral component to recoil that vertical grooves work in our favor.

On the left, Stan Chen's exemplary checkering. On the right, a very useful and easily-added vertical grooves treatment.

Next are repeated patterns of horizontal end mill notches like Ed Brown Kobra or Chain link. While other gunsmiths can (and some do) copy these, if you want them from Ed Brown, you have to buy an Ed Brown gun with them on it.

Then there are repeated patterns of ball-end mill cutters, which are referred to as "golf ball" patterns, with good reason.

Stan Chen offers a diagonal checkering, with a skip-step cross pattern in the middle, that is distinctive, attractive and offers a non-slip grip.

Last, and unique, is a pattern Ned Christiansen came up with, one he calls Conamyds. Checkering is grooves at right angles, and the grooves form tiny pyramids. Ned figured a way to machine cones, and the flat-topped cones are "conamyds." The pattern is close enough to almost machine out all the material between the conamyds, but not quite. That leaves tiny tiger's-teeth between the conamyds.

Now, all these patterns (and more) are far beyond advanced gunsmithing of the 1911. They are proof of master-class ability. If you want to try any of them, you'd better be a first-rate machinist, a patient and detail-oriented gunsmith, and have lots of practice on plain old

steel bars. And if you want them, but don't have the machine or skills, you'll have to have one of the master-class gunsmiths who do it, do it to yours. However, the masters are either booked long in advance (get in line) or only do certain work. As I mentioned, Ed Brown does his treatments to his guns. Stan Chen only does full-house guns. No "this 'n that" work, but only a complete rebuild.

A lesson that even popes and kings in the renaissance learned: you want the work of a master, you commission work on his schedule.

RAMPED BARRELS

The feed ramp cut into a 1911 barrel removes steel from the bottom of the chamber. If the ramp is cut too far forward it may extend past the web, or strongest part, of the case. A hot load in an improperly ramped barrel will bulge the brass. A maximum-pressure or overload can blow out the side of the case. This usually trashes the magazine, occasionally damages the extractor and sometimes causes injury to the shooter. It is always startling.

To avoid this entirely requires that the chamber walls exist all the way around the case, all the way back to the extractor groove. Unfortunately this can't be done and still have a barrel ramp that matches up with the frame ramp. Somebody might design a pistol that accommodates a chamber like this, but it won't be on a 1911.

Both these barrels are in .40 S&W, but the Infinity barrel is the choice of many competitors because of the ramp. If you are not going to push your loads to (or past) the red line, the Kings barrel will be accurate, dependable and give a long service life.

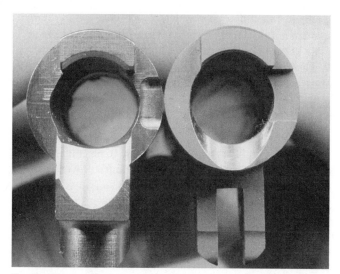

On the left, a ramped barrel, on the right a standard barrel. The ramped barrel offers more support to the brass for hot loads.

Therefore, barrel makers designed barrels where the ramp is attached to the barrel. The integral ramp barrel changes the geometry of the feed ramp, letting the chamber have support at the bottom futher back. Different barrel makers use different ramp dimensions. The three main types are Clark/Para-Ordnance, Wilson/Nowlin and Bar-sto. All the ramps work, but they are not interchangeable. As an example, you cannot simply fit a Bar-sto ramped barrel to a Para-Ordnance pistol. You must either modify the barrel ramp or the pistol frame. Installing a ramped barrel in a frame that is not designed for one requires milling a slot in the frame to provide room for the new barrel ramp. This can only be done with a mill. An enterprising machinist could do the work without a fixture. Because the fixture makes the work so much easier it would be foolish to attempt the work without it.

Cominolli makes one such fixture. The drawback to at-

The Cominolli fixture is so sturdy I'm not sure you could hurt it running it over with a truck. The frame is held here for one of the ramped barrel cuts.

The Cominolli fixture with the frame vertical for the second ramp cut. The tool can't wander, or be misaligned, as it has to pass down through the guide hole to reach the frame.

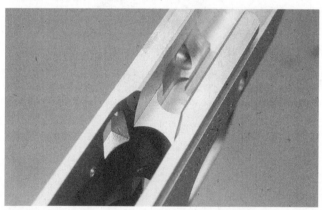

This 1911 frame has been milled for a ramped barrel. The bullet does not have to jump the gap from the frame to the barrel, as in the original feed ramps. Here, the barrel alone has the ramp attached.

tempting the work without a fixture is the low height of mill vise jaws. The fixture clamps the frame high enough to keep the frame rigid, and prevent tool chatter when cutting.

Complete with instructions, the fixture allows you to mill all the various ramped barrel configurations.

Oh, and for those of you who think that ramped barrels are a modern, IPSC-derived improvement, or came to us courtesy of the perfect Glock, guess again. John Moses Browning used the same ramped barrel design in his ground-breaking pistol, the Model 1900 .38 auto.

SLIDE TREATMENTS

Did you know that the 1911 slides had lightening cuts on the front end that are now referred to as "ball-end" cuts? Sometime in the 1920s, Colt changed the cut from a ball-end end mill, to a radiused Woodruff cutter. A ball-end cutter is a fluted rod, like a drill, that has a rounded end to it. A Woodruff cutter is like a wheel with teeth on the end. A circular saw blade would be a good comparison. Why the change? Speed and cost. A Woodruff cutter in this application would last a lot longer, cut faster, and could also have been (or probably is now) made as a two-bladed setup, cutting both sides at once.

But the ball-end cuts are cool. If you want to change yours, you can. It only takes a mill, a ball-end cutter and some patience. First, size. The ball-end cutter you need is a matter of cosmetics. Since the whole thing is cosmetic, you may have to experiment to see what looks good to you. (More use for that "dead" slide you bought.) 3/8 inch is a good starting point.

Ball-end cuts on the slide are a personal taste thing. If you like them, get them. If you don't, then don't get them.

The process is simple: first, mark your slide, the ends of the ball-end cuts have to end precisely at the front edge of the dust cover, or the job will look strange. So mark your slide. Due to the variations in slides and the differences between them (the manufacturers don't track the dimensions of the cuts as closely as they do other, more critical dimensions), you'll have to do all this by eye.

Clamp your stripped slide upside down in the mill vise, level and with the lower half sticking up out of the vise jaws. Secure your cutter in the quill, and set it for a medium speed.

Select the side of the slide to start on that will have the cutting edges of your ball-end cutter biting forward of the direction you'll be moving the cutter, and moving the cutter from the muzzle towards the chamber as your first cut. Bring the running tool down to the side of the slide, and bring the tool over until it is just kissing the existing surface of the lightening cuts. This is your lateral zero. Now, pull the cutter toward the muzzle until it is off the slide, and lower it a scosh. Bring it in (toward the chamber) and see how much of the old lightening cut radius it removes. If it does not remove all, pull the cutter back out past the muzzle, lower it some more, and repeat. You do this, a bit at a time, until the new cut removes all of the old radius. This is your vertical zero.

Now, with the cutter just kissing the old vertical wall of the lightening cut, and removing all the old radius, bring the cutter towards the chamber, until it reaches your mark indicating the dustcover edge. Note this on your dials or digital readout, as you'll need it on the other side.

Pull your cutter away from the slide, but do not change your vertical zero. Move the cutter out past the muzzle, over to the other side, and back towards the muzzle until your movement corresponds to the readout you noted on the other side. This will have you bringing your cutter into the slide exactly at the end-point of the dustcover. Bring the cutter in, cutting the slide, until it is just kissing the vertical portion of the lightening cut. Then make your cut from there out past the muzzle.

You've now done the machine work, and "all" that is left is the hand-stoning and polishing to remove the tool marks of the machine work you did. And then, refinishing.

PROJECT GUN 1
THE IDPA/CARRY SPECIAL

The International Defensive Pistol Association is an organization attempting to correct the perceived wrongs of IPSC. The IDPA founders, feeling that IPSC had strayed from its martial roots, determined that the new competition should not devolve into an equipment race or embrace full-speed hosing-style shooting. (At least not as they see it as "full-speed hosing.") They have only been partly successful in both, as equipment selection is always an integrally important aspect of any competition

A well-fit 1911 shoots like this, when you feed it what it likes. This is a ten-shot 30-yard target, from the Ransom rest.

The Caspian Titanium frames use a slightly different plunger tube. The tube has a slot milled for it on the frame, to ensure it stays tightly in place.

You can see the slot cut for the external, Paul Leibenberg-designed extractor, and the custom serial number.

You want a carry gun? My Ti Commander, a Wilson Combat IWB holster, spare mags, holder on my belt (not shown) and you have 28 rounds of 9mm goodness. Switch to the new Wilson 10-shot mags, and it bumps it up to 31 rounds.

that uses gear. And any shooting event that is timed to the last shot will always be won by fast, accurate hosing.

However, a good IDPA gun can be a good carry gun, and vice versa. So, I contacted Gary Smith at Caspian to find out what was new with their titanium (Ti) frames. Titanium is a hard, durable, light metal that has many useful properties. However, it is notoriously difficult to machine. That and its expense have kept it out of many uses. For a manufacturer willing to learn its machining properties, it has many positives. In strength, titanium is in between, but closer to steel, than aluminum. In weight, it is in between, but closer to aluminum than steel. The strength is great enough, and the lightness sufficient, that Caspian had planned to drop all aluminum frames from their line. Operationally, aluminum is plenty good enough, and they have not dropped aluminum due to high-volume shooting. Titanium is better for other reasons. "We haven't worn one out shooting it yet," was Gary's comment on the strength of titanium. "The problem was building." Apparently Caspian had regular discussions with customers who had tried to peen the rails of their aluminum frames, and cracked them, or crushed a frame clamping it in a holding fixture. No such problems with titanium. (Peening and swaging to take up the slack, on an aluminum frame, is not a good idea. Better to have your frame Acc-u-Railed if it is that bad.)

However, machining a Ti frame could be problematic. If you are in the position of attempting to machine one, a thorough reading of the ASTM specs, and a good machinist's manual, will give you some ideas. That, and according to one old machinist "...high cutter speed and lots of lubricant. Lots. Don't slow down or you'll work-harden the cut ahead of your tool."

You can solve that problem by simply ordering a frame and slide together from Caspian, and requesting a free-

The Caspian external extractor. When I started this project, external extractors were all the rage. Now, not so much.

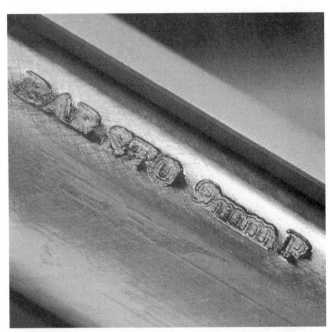

For tack-driving accuracy, and the option of "cheap as dirt" ammo, I used a Bar-sto 9mm barrel to build the IDPA Special.

The Caspian Titanium frame has an integral magazine funnel.

running fit. No lapping, filing, stoning or other fitting.

Well, the old motto that sys "life is what happens while you're making other plans" arrived in spades. Gunsmiths found Ti was a royal pain in the butt to work with. It could be done, but customers complained about the time and thus cost. But the real stumbling block was materials cost. You see, Ti was useful for other things besides making way-cool pistols. The price got bid up on the metals markets to the point where it was simply not rational to make or offer Ti anything to customers. Reluctantly, Caspian went back to aluminum, but if you abuse an aluminum frame by peening it (or trying) don't expect sympathy from Caspian.

I obtained a Commander frame and slide from Caspian, in 9mm breechface. As a carry gun I much prefer the shorter slide, as it is less likely to dig into me when holstered. In IDPA, with the closer distances and less-crowded shots than IPSC, I did not feel the need for a Government-length slide for that last iota of useable ac-

The M-guns Shield-Driver sight.

Here is the Virgil Tripp Carbidizing application. It looks rough, but the feel of the slide on the frame isn't. It also puts a stop to galling.

curacy. And for the IDPA Enhanced Service Pistol, a 9mm would work fine. I couldn't use a .45 and shoot ESP (that is only for Custom Defensive Pistol) and as a carry gun, a 9mm+P or 9mm+P+ load is plenty good enough for the street. To keep brass expansion under control with the hot carry loads (I can use powder-puff reloads for IDPA competition) I elected to use a ramped barrel.

The Bar-sto ramped barrel is accurate enough for any shooting, not just IDPA. In fact, Irv Stone of Bar-sto told me that given the choice between a 9mm and a .38 Super for tack-driving accuracy, he'd go 9mm.

All assembled, the 9mm IDPA gun weighs a few ounces more than an aluminum one would, but with greater strength. It is accurate enough to ring the 100-yard gong at my gun club 10 shots out of 10.

The stainless slide needs no plating to protect it, but I have coated it with a bake-on finish from Brownells. The extractor is Caspian's external 9mm extractor, designed by Paul Leibenberg. The original internal design works well, but can be fussy to fit and fragile in some applications. In 9mm, with the sometimes large variations between rim diameters, an external extractor should be less picky about working 100 percent.

Once it was up and running, I then did as many of you no doubt will with your projects, and turned it over to a pro for more work – in this case Ned Christiansen. Ned machined the slide to accept a Ted Yost rear sight, and

then modified the sight to his Nedster "Shield Driver" configuration. I can now use the rear sight to work the slide, if I have the simultaneous problems of a malfunction and also lacking the use of one hand.

He machined the frame and mainspring housing with his "Conamyds." Instead of the pyramids of regular checkering, Ned machines small cones, cones with flat tops, into the surface. The effect is striking, non-slip and non-abusive to your hands. He fit the thumb safety to be stiff to push off (no accidental un-safe pistols for carry) but even more difficult to put back on. Remember, you aren't timed on getting the gun back to safe. You do not want a carry gun on which the safety will pop up to the "firing is not permitted" setting.

In test-firing it, I ran into one of the drawbacks of titanium, and a reason it has fallen out of the limelight: galling. The surface of the slide and frame, at the rails, surfaces Ned had worked so hard to fit correctly, were rubbing themselves raw. What to do? Hard chrome? Electroless nickel? Both have drawbacks, and they have those drawbacks due to another aggravating aspect of titanium: fast oxidation. Titanium oxidizes so quickly, and so securely, that there is no time to get it from the prep bath to the plate bath. In the time it takes ot get it from one to the other, enough oxidation of the surface of the Ti has happened that the plating would be blotchy.

Arrgh! However, Virgil Tripp has a solution. Called

The muzzle end of the Caspian Recon, with light in place.
Where the light shines, the sights (and muzzle) are pointed.

The Caspian Recon Rail frame, with its integral tactical light rail.

The MMC adjustable low-profile sight fits the Novak dovetail and is tough as nails.

A well-blended magazine funnel speeds reloads greatly without adding much weight or bulk. Indeed, you might not even notice the added weight or bulk at a match or in daily carry.

As mentioned earlier, the Marine Corps is fond of the 1911. And as much of modern warfare is now conducted at night, or in buildings lacking illumination (there aren't any lights left when a 2,000-pound laser-guided bomb leaves a crater where the local switching station used to be), weapons need lights. Night vision gear is nice to have, but sometimes it is faster and easier to turn on the light on the gun than find, put on, turn on, and look through NVG.

The basis of Project Gun 2 is the Caspian Recon frame. Rather than bolt, solder or weld a light rail to an existing frame (which is what the Corps has done up to now) Caspian built the frame with the rail as an integral part. Their frames are so highly thought-of that Bill Wilson built his light-rail framed CQB pistols on Caspian frames for many years. And many other custom builders who put their names on their finished products begin with a Caspian frame.

On top I fitted an old 1911 slide I've had for years (waiting for just such a project) a surplus match slide marked "GENII" and finish-machined but not polished. After all, why polish a slide that will be parkerized, finished with baked-on resin, and then stuffed into a synthetic tactical thigh holster? A fine polish and deep blue would be wasted.

A spare .45 ACP barrel and assorted parts from the 1911 parts locker and the base Recon was finished. As with all project guns, until it is tested and has all the bugs wrung out, it does not get a final plating or other exterior finish. Thus, the various parts do not all match in color or finish.

An Insight M3 slides right on.

PROJECT GUN 3
A HUNTING 1911A1

At least one reader is wondering what kind of a hunting gun you can make on a 1911. After all, while the good old .45 ACP is plenty stout as a man-stopper (at least within the realm of handguns) it isn't good enough for deer, boar or, shudder to think, bear.

Wrong.

As a man-stopper it is not all that great. (It is just a lot better than anything else.) The problem in hunting is two-fold: energy and trajectory. More energy is a matter of more velocity, and that can be obtained several ways. One would be to switch from the .45 ACP to the 10 mm cartridge. At the top end of its performance, the .45 delivers a 200-grain bullet at about 1,000 fps and a 185-grain bullet at 1,150 fps. The 10mm can boot a 200-grain projectile to 1,200 fps, and a 175-grain hollow-point to 1,250. If you need more than that, you can have it. The .40 Super boosts 200-grain bullets at almost 1,300 fps, and 165-grain bullets to nearly 1,600 fps. .45 ACP+P and .45 Super loads exceed the standard .45 ACP. For weight and velocity, the .460 Rowland delivers true .44 Magnum performance (at least old .44 Magnum, not the new heavyweight bullet performance) with 230-grain jacketed hollow-points at 1,350 fps, and 185-grain JHPs at 1,450.

You must build a hunting gun with the hunting regulations in mind. Many jurisdictions have restrictions on what is allowed. Here in Michigan, a hunting handgun cannot be chambered in a bottlenecked cartridge. It must be a repeating action, and it cannot hold more than 10 rounds. Yes, that means you can't hunt in some areas with a T/C Contender in .35 Remington, but you can hunt with a Walter PPK/S in .380 Auto.

First, the barrel. A Clark Custom compensated barrel in .460 Rowland. The base gun? A single-stack Colt, and the scope mount an EGW mount.

The mount replaces the plunger tube on the left side of the frame and has provisions for the plunger and its springs in the mount. By using a one-sided mount I can minimize the work in drilling and tapping for the mount. Once drilled and tapped, the tapping ridge removed and the fit of the mount checked, I used Loctite to secure it. One note: be sure and check screw protrusion into the magazine well and the dust cover tunnel. It is easier to shorten a screw before you lock it in place on the frame. Once in place, wipe the Loctite that oozes out of the threads, and with a few strokes of your "perfect file" make sure the inner surface is smooth and clean.

In the mount I can put any optic or red-dot. I opted to mount an old Tasco I have on hand. It spent many years on top of my single-stack IPSC Racegun back before the capacity wars mandated 28-round magazines. As far as accuracy is concerned, it shoots better than I do. Five shots of Georgia Arms 230-grain Speer Gold Dot .460 Rowland ammo (230s at 1,350 fps!) go into less than 2 inches at 25 yards.

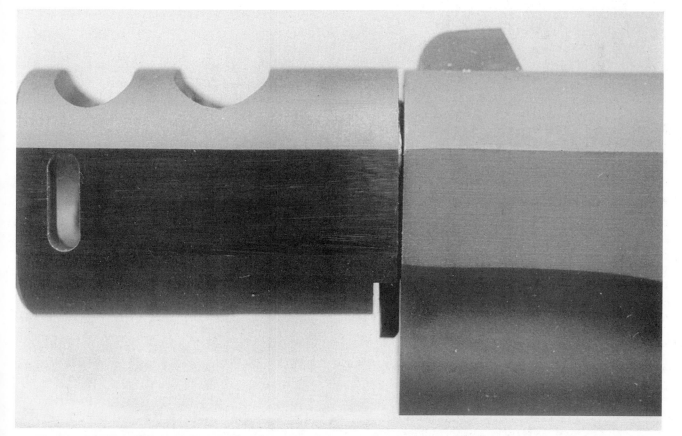

For hunting, a compensator lets you practice more without developing a flinch. It also affords you the opportunity to use a more powerful cartridge than you otherwise would.

PROJECT GUN 4
A STEEL GUN

The Steel Challenge is a match designed for speed. There is very little footwork involved, and if you have to do any reloads your time is not competitive. It is a draw and shoot game devoted to warp-speed shooting. An independent match for nearly 30 years, the Steel Challenge was purchased by the USPSA, and is now being run and promoted by them. The rules and attitude haven't been changed, but now the Steel Challenge has the promotion and organizational weight of the USPSA behind it.

To shoot in Open class at the Steel Challenge competition takes a specialized gun. While you can use just about anything and declare "Open," if you wish to be competitive you need competitive gear. You can just buy one. Call up STI and have them send you a steel gun. You may have problems getting one into California or some other nanny-state that treats its citizens like obstreperous little children. (I can only suggest either voting the bums out, or moving.) An Open gun is a compensated pistol with a red-dot optical sight. Since it is to be made for the Steel Challenge, you don't need hi capacity. A single stack will do. And, if you plan to go to the Steel Challenge, it is in California. Can you bring your hi-caps in? Maybe yes, maybe no. It all depends on what the legislators and Attorney General of Kalistan decide between when I write this and when you go. Generally built in some variant of .38 Super, a hi-cap with a "big stick" magazine will hold as many as 28 rounds. Single stacks will hold nine or ten, and a neutered magazine for your hi-cap frame will hold only ten rounds. If you can't get one from STI or another maker, you can build a gun. (Again, if the state will let you.) My project gun is built on a Caspian hi-cap frame.

Now, why would you want to use a hi-cap frame, if you are only going to load ten-round magazines? The frame shape. Many shooters find the slightly wider frame shape of the hi-cap guns is more comfortable. When you're trying to shoot at the maximum possible speed, comfort is a big deal.

The slide is a Colt that I picked up for a song at a match (the gunsmith who had it had taken it off of a gun he was building, and didn't want to take it home with him) and the barrel is a Nowlin. The comp is an EGW. The only part that was any work was the scope mount, as the Caspian frame pre-dated scope mounts. As a result, the frame was not drilled and tapped for the mount, and I had to carefully locate, drill and tap the holes for the frame. On this particular mount, the holes are all on the dustcover, so there is no need to change the plunger tube or modify the slide stop or safety. (Caspian, and

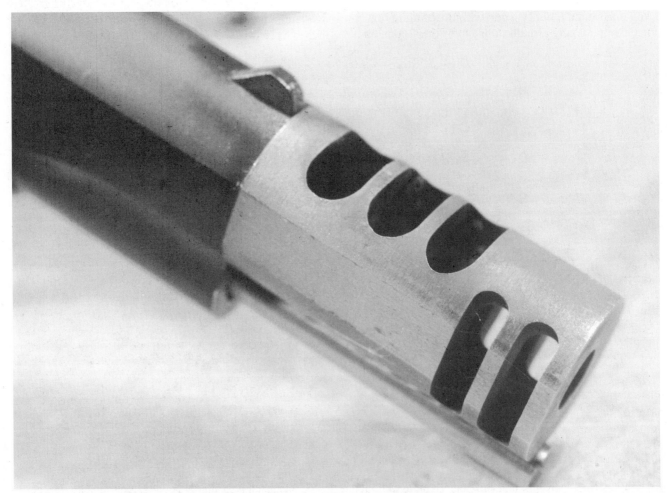

Any Open gun has to have an efficient comp. This EGW unit keeps the dot on target even when shooting fast.

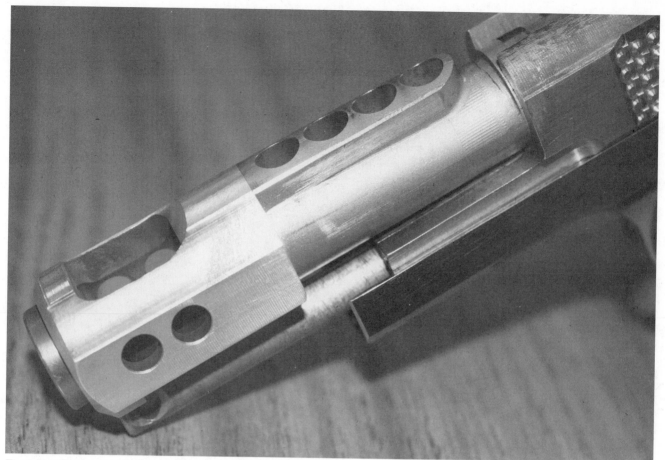

To make a Steel gun as light, responsive and quick-cycling as possible requires more than just weight reduction

all the other frame makers who can provide you with a frame for your Steel Challenge Open gun, can drill and tap the holes needed for whatever mount you wish to use. Take advantage of their offer. You will find that the modest sum they charge is worth saving the work of drilling and tapping the frame yourself. Let me repeat: do not be cheap. Pay them to drill and tap.)

The Caspian frame is steel and dimensioned for the .38 Super cartridge. As a result it is slightly smaller in circumference than the STI or SVI frames. (They were built to be hi-cap .45s, and thus slightly larger.) The Caspian is a good choice for someone who finds the larger frames a bit too large. Why is it not seen more in matches? Partly because of weight. For a while a lighter gun was all the rage. The Caspian, being steel, could not be as light as the polymer-frame guns. If you find weight helps in recoil (and some shooters have gone back to heavier guns) the Caspian works great. However, and we'll get into this in just a bit, recoil is not a big deal at the SC.

One modification I made to the mount was to provide clearance for the ejecting empties. On a scoped Open gun you need to ensure your ejector is as high on the frame and in the slide slot as the slide slot will allow. If the mount shows any brassing from the empties striking it, you should file/mill clearance for the brass. You also need to make the ejection port as low as you can without weakening it. I milled my ejection port so the sidewall was only .400 inch high and beveled the interior

edge. I have no problems with brass ejecting.

The need for speed at the Steel Challenge is encouraged by two things: the lack of a power factor, and the stationary targets. There is no power factor at all, other than the requirement that your handgun be chambered for a centerfire cartridge. And, the steel plates used as targets do not fall. They are painted at the beginning, and between shooters. If you scuff the paint, you are scored with a hit.

The process is simple: load up, and on the start signal, draw and hit the plates, leaving the stop plate for last. If you don't have misses, your time is your score. Misses call for added time penalties. That's pretty much it, in the broad strokes. There are seven stages, you draw and shoot each a number of times. (The stages are occasionally changed, but there are some that have remained unchanged for decades.) Your total times, for all the stages, with penalties added, is your score. Fastest man or woman wins.

So you do not need lots of power, but you do need enough to reliably work your pistol. And you need accuracy.

I was just talking to Robbie Leatham, the name in practical shooting. His steel load? A 115-grain 9mm bullet, traveling at 950 fps. That's a 109.25 power factor. Why not go lower? Simple: the lighter bullets are not as common, and usually not as accurate. And a slower velocity

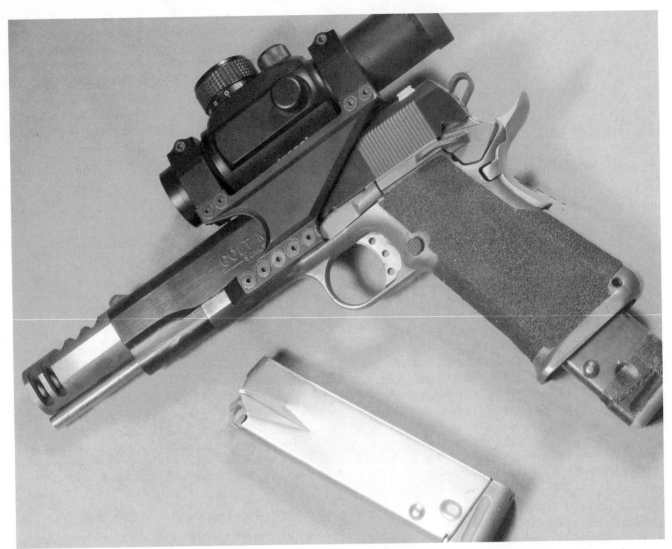

The Caspian hi-cap frame, built for USPSA/IPSC Open competition. With it, an 18-round magazine, and a 24-round magazine inserted.

risks an unreliable gun.

To increase reliability, you need to lighten the slide, and even the comp. However, taking weight out of a slide requires a mill and caution. You can weaken a slide if you aren't careful. This is definitely a place for planning and a practice slide. Also, you have to fit the slide to the frame before you do any weight reduction, as the lighter slide will be more fragile and might not withstand the forces of fitting.

The easiest way to get a significant amount of weight out of a slide can be done simply: you drill/mill cross-ways through the slide, behind the breechface. Two holes, not so large as to cut into the rails portion of the slide (and definitely not done to a Series 80-type slide) will take out a bunch of weight. They'll also expose your firing pin, spring and ejector to the outside, so you will have to do a lot more cleaning as a result.

More weight reduction than that wil have to wait on the 1911 Gunsmithing volume.

Last, peruse the Brownells catalog, A compensator or muzzle brake for your 1911, made of aluminum of titanium, will reduce weight while still reducing recoil.

CHAPTER

20

BARREL AND CYLINDER FITTING, S&W REVOLVERS

You can blame it all on Magnum Fever. Before the 1930s hardly anyone ever wore out a revolver barrel. Wear and tear on revolvers took an upward step when magnums arrived on the scene.

Pre-1970 someone who shot 4,000 or 5,000 rounds a year was consider a committed competitor. Today's serious competitor can easily shoot more than 25,000 rounds in one year. Around the late 1970s police departments upped their practice and qualification requirements. Part of that increase was a greater use of magnum loads. This came about as part of the Newhall Incident, where some police officers in Southern California found themselves in a shootout with bad guys. After the officers lost, the after-action reports highlighted some shortcomings with training. One of those shortcomings was the then-common use of light (and thus inexpensively-reloaded) .38 Special ammunition in .357

Magnum revolvers, and then issuing .357 Magnums for duty. As a result, many police departments changed their policy to: "If you carry a .357 on duty, you practice and qualify with .357 ammo." Barrels really took a beating. Then the advent of lightweight bullets just made it worse.

Magnum loads wear away the rear of a barrel. Police departments found their barrels cracking at the throat, next to the cylinder, from the combination of hot ammunition and lightweight jacketed bullets.

K-frames had been popular with police departments and civilian shooters for decades, in large part because their grip size was small enough for just about every shooter. The cylinder, barrel, and frame had survived the transition from low-pressure .38 Special ammunition to occasional use of hot .357 magnums. What K-frames couldn't take was high-volume magnum shooting.

Barrels are easy to swap, provided you have the right tools. This frame is ready to have a new barrel installed, once the measuring is done.

Rarely seen problems suddenly started appearing commonly. Forcing cones were eroding. Barrels were cracking. Cylinders were going out of time right after being tuned. Even frames were cracking at their thinnest point, under the barrel. When I began gunsmithing, my boss Dan had a project gun on the shelf. When the pre-hunting season rush slowed down, he was going to take the S&W M-19 with the cracked frame and weld the frame and re-fit the barrel. You know, I don't recall how that worked out, or if he even did it.

The problem became so serious that Smith & Wesson re-designed their K-frame revolvers. The design improvements grafted the grip size of the K-frame to a frame size close to the big .44 magnum. Called the L-frame, it was introduced just in time for the tastes of the shooting public and police departments to change to automatics. Nevertheless it is well suited to shooters with average or small hands. It sells well, and it should. Although offered only in .357 magnum, it is the toughest .357 you can get without having to stretch your hands over the grips of a .44 magnum-sized revolver.

Nowadays, the problem stems from another source: volume shooting. With the advent of IPSC and IDPA Revolver Divisions, *revolvoleros* have lots of places to get in range time. Add the Steel Challenge and ICORE to that, and you could easily spend every weekend

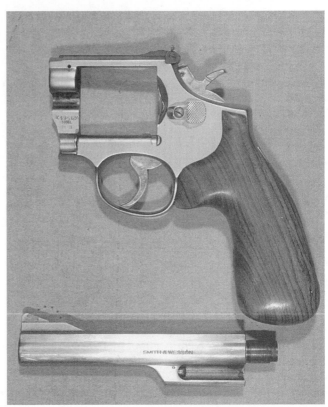

This Smith M-66 is all set to get a new barrel, or have this one set back.

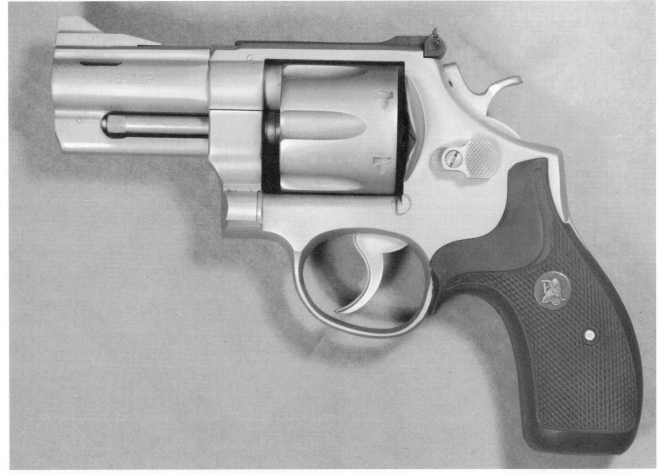

This revolver started life as a 6-inch .357 square butt N frame. It is now a round butt, .45 ACP snubbie. And it is plated with Armoloy and ported by Mag-na-Port. A complete transformation for a police trade-in.

shooting a wheelgun in competition. Some places, like the Phoenix area, you could spend three or four days a week, most of the year, shooting in matches.

That's a lot of shooting, and if you could afford the ammo and entry fees, you could easily shoot 50,000 rounds a year in competition and practice. Even if most of that is lead bullet ammo, that's a lot of wear on a barrel and forcing cone. One thing you won't be able to do easily is change barrels on an S&W K frame. S&W tells me that they have exhausted the supply, and unless or until they make a new batch in a run of Classics, there aren't any. So, if you expect to be wearing your barrel out anytime soon, start searching for a replacement now.

WHEN TO CHANGE BARRELS

The easy answers are when you a) have worn one out, b) when you find a bargain on a barrel you've always wanted, c) it will gain you an advantage in a competition or hunting, or d) when you just darn well feel like it.

You can wear a barrel out. Lots of high-speed shooting with hot magnums or jacketed high-speed bullets can wear a barrel, usually the forcing cone first. After you've re-cut the forcing cone and set the barrel back a couple of times, you'll find you then have to shorten the ejector rod and center pin to make the setback work again. Get a new barrel, instead. I've built new guns because of bargain barrels. My "pseudo 25-2" that has served me so well in nearly 20 years of bowling pin shooting started out that way. I was cruising a local gun show (back when they were full of strange and wondrous items, and not merely stocked with SKS rifles and beef jerky) and spied a barrel — a like-new S&W 25-2 6.5-inch barrel (who knows why it got taken off) for $20. I snapped it up. Even

if I had no use for it, I knew I'd easily find someone who wanted it for more than a mere $20. Later that week at the shop, I received a flier from the Jack First gun shop, back when they were still located in Lancaster, CA. They had police trade-in M-28 S&W revolvers for $100. My mind got to ticking. S&W had just discontinued the 25-2. I had the barrel. I could get the base revolver to build on. Could I get a cylinder? A phone call to S&W gave me an answer: Yes. As a non-magnum item it was not a factory armorer-only inventory stock number. For $58 and change I could have a cylinder and cylinder stop stud.

A week later I was puzzling out the sequence of caliber conversion and rebuild for S&W revolvers.

The last reason for a barrel change is to meet competition needs or requirements. Some years ago, IDPA changed the revolver rule. No longer were barrels over 4 inches allowed. All those S&W 625-2 shooters who had been shooting with their 5-inch guns had to change. I'm sure some simply switched to a 4-inch 625-2 gun, and stuck the 5-inch one in the safe. (Those of us who shoot

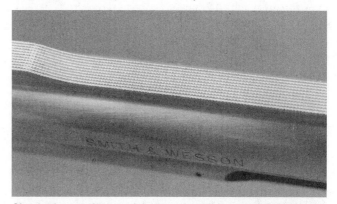

Checkering on the top of the barrel or slide cuts down glare.

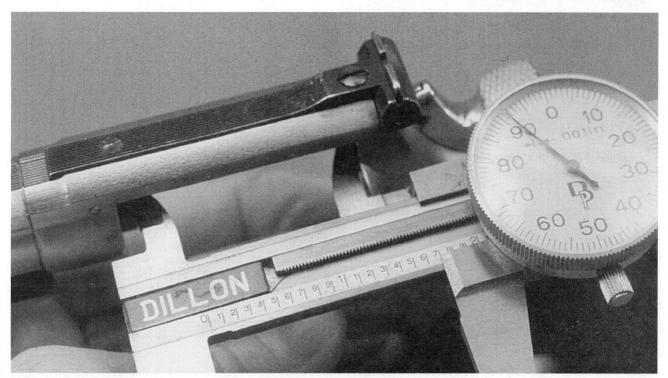

The barrel has been set back, and the gap is now .025 inches under barrel zero.

competitively in a serious manner usually have at least one gun for every category we might shoot in.) Others swapped to their 4-inch 610, and fed them .40 S&W ammo. But some changed barrels. In USPSA/IPSC, I went the other direction. I have a perfectly good 4-inch 625-2 (and the 5-inch barrel that used to be on it) but for practical competition where it is allowed, I prefer a longer barrel. In USPSA/IPSC shooting, any factory-configuration barrel is allowed. If I could lay hands on one of the

ultra-rare 8-inch 25-2 revolvers, I'd shoot that instead of a 6.5-inch. In many PPC competitions there are Service and Snubbie categories. Service is usually (some leagues have slightly different rules or interpretations of the rules) limited to a 4-inch standard-configuration barrel, and snubbie to a 2-inch or 2-1/2-inch barrel. Serious PPC competitors who wish to enter these categories will take an old, slicked-up competition gun and replace the bull barrel with a factory one. (The really serious will keep

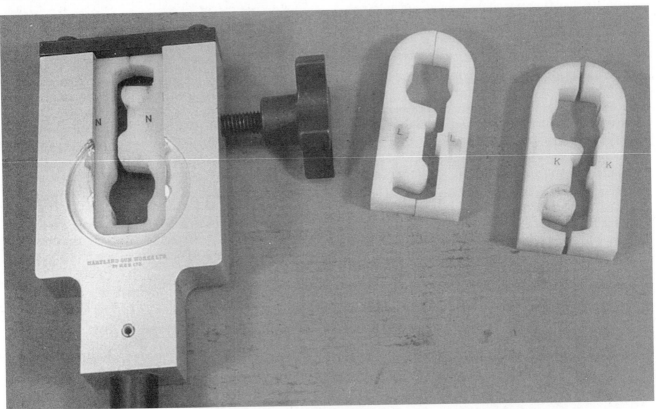

The inserts let you switch from one revolver to another, with one wrench.

Brownells makes a kit that squares the barrel face and cuts the forcing cone. It works on barrels from 9mm to .45.

swapping until they find an accurate barrel.) They then have a "Service" or "Snubbie" that feels like a competition gun (which it is, on the inside) that externally meets the rules.

With patience and attention to detail, changing barrels and even cylinders is no big deal.

SETTING BACK THE BARREL

But what to do with your revolver? If after your switch to magnum loads and your increased practicing you've been losing velocity and accuracy, you need to check the forcing cone and barrel. To restore accuracy you can set the barrel back and cut the forcing cone, or replace the barrel. If the barrel is cracked, you must replace it.

Any time you set back your barrel, or replace it, you should first remove any endshake in the cylinder (see Chapter 6).

To set back your barrel you will need a frame wrench,

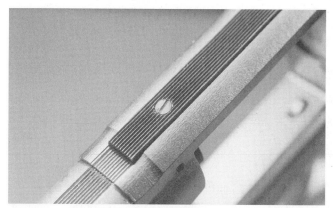

Or you can use the relationship of the rib to the frame. Make a drawing, so your memory does not cause you to worry.

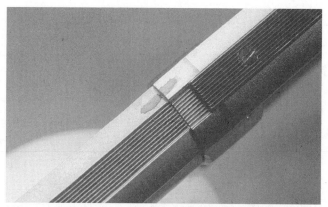

Use a permanent ink marker to locate the barrel to the frame. When you screw the barrel back in after setting the shoulder back, tighten until these lines match.

The Brownells set-back fixture, with cutter and pilots.

a shoulder cutter with the correct caliber pilot for your revolver, and a forcing cone and barrel-squaring cutter, complete with forcing cone gauge in your caliber. These are all available from Brownells.

There are a few preliminaries. You must mark the location of the barrel in the frame, and measure the distance between the rear of the frame opening and the rear of the barrel. We'll call this distance the "barrel zero" distance.

First mark the location. Use a permanent ink pen to draw a line across the top of the barrel onto the frame. If the barrel has a rib on top of it, carefully note where the rib joins the frame. When you replace the barrel you will tighten it to vertical using this line. Note: ink scrubs off, scribed lines gouged into the metal do not. Do not pick up a sharp piece of steel at this step in the process.

To compute the barrel zero distance, grab your dial calipers, pencil, paper, and a calculator. With your feeler

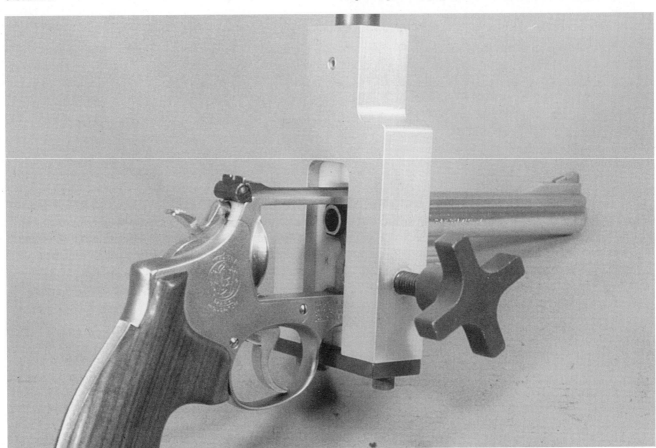

Here is the Maryland Gun Works frame wrench installed on a Smith & Wesson M-66.

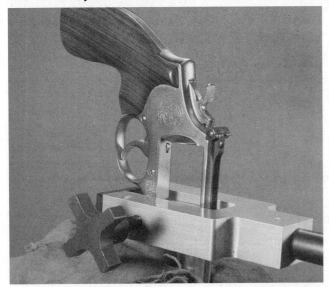

Use a frame wrench to remove your barrel properly. A hammer handle through the frame opening can bend the frame.

Rotate the barrel against the shoulder set-back cutter to remove steel from the barrel shoulder.

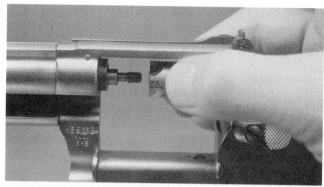

Install the cutter on the shaft.

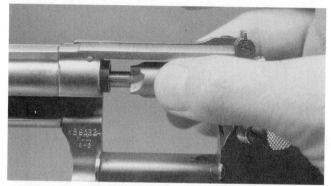

Tighten the cutter on the shaft.

Use the facing cutter to set back the rear of the barrel.

gauges, measure the cylinder gap. Open the cylinder and measure the distance from the rear of the frame opening to the rear of the barrel. Subtract the cylinder gap measurement from this amount to find your barrel zero measurement. This number is the maximum the barrel can protrude into the frame opening before it hits the cylinder. Save it. You will use it after setting back, or replacing, the barrel.

Use a frame wrench to remove the barrel. Maryland Gun Works has a good one. Do not, repeat, DO NOT use the barrel removal method advocated in old pistolsmithing texts — of clamping the barrel in your vise and using a hammer handle as a lever stuck through the frame opening — unless you want to bend the frame. A frame wrench comes with inserts to fit the frame of your revolver. It unscrews the barrel by holding the entire frame and not just parts of it. You cannot bend your frame using one.

Older Smith & Wesson revolvers have a locking pin in the frame's front, above the barrel. You must remove the pin before you can remove the barrel. Start with a small tapered punch to get the pin started without marring the frame, then switch to a longer one to drive it out. Newer revolvers do not have this pin, and the older ones probably never needed it. They do look a little strange to some of us old-timers without it, though.

Clamp the barrel in your padded vise, muzzle down, and slide the frame wrench onto the frame. Lock it in place. Unscrew counterclockwise.

Once you have unscrewed your old barrel you can gauge its "crush fit." Remove the frame from the fixture and the barrel from the vise. Hand screw the old barrel back in until it stops. You don't need to, nor do you want to, apply any force at this point. You're simply looking to see how much "torque-up" your particular barrel required, in your particular frame. Your ink line will be, or

The barrel has been trimmed to its barrel zero measurement. Now it is a matter of adjusting the cylinder gap.

The gap is set, but this dark and pitted forcing cone has to be re-cut.

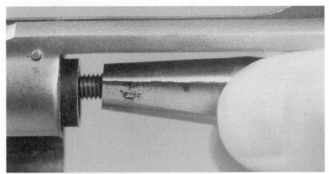

The cutters thread onto the cutting shaft.

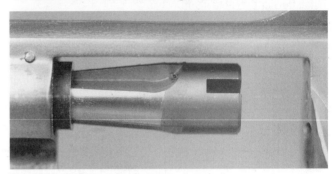

This is an 11-degree forcing cone reamer.

This forcing cone needs more cutting.

The forcing cone gauge shows that this forcing cone has been cut just right. If the upper shelf is in the cone, too much has been removed. If the lower shelf is not in the forcing cone, the cone is not deep enough.

should be, split into two lines, 45 degrees (or 1/8th turn) apart. Once you have properly set the shoulder back the barrel will hand screw in to this same position. The final 1/8 turn will squeeze the threads to lock up the barrel tight in the frame.

The 45-degree crush is important. You must be patient and get it right. If you set back the shoulder too much and can hand-tighten the set-back barrel this last 1/8th turn, the vibrations of shooting will loosen the barrel. If you set back the barrel too little you may over-torque it and crack the frame.

Depending on the amount of worn barrel you have to remove the barrel shoulder will be turned back the distance of a thread or two.

Clamp the shoulder cutter in the vise and install the correct pilot for your caliber. Put a couple of drops of cutting oil onto the cutting edge. Take the barrel, press it over the pilot, and turn it once against the cutter. Remove the barrel from the pilot and screw it into the frame. Repeat the cutting and checking until your barrel turns one full rotation farther into the frame than it did when you first hand-tightened it. You want it to stop at the same 45-degree (1/8th turn) point as before, but one full rotation farther into the frame. This is your new pre-torque point. Barrels with an underlug enclosing the ejector rod may require filing of the underlug to clear the frame. The barrel setback tool cannot cut the underlug.

Install the frame wrench. Re-clamp the barrel in your vise. Tighten the barrel all the way to vertical, back to your original pen mark, and remove the frame wrench. Unclamp the barrel.

Your next step is to trim the back of the barrel for cylinder clearance. You will also re-cut the forcing cone. Neither of these can be done with the frame wrench attached. Clamp the grip straps of the frame in the vise.

Measure the distance from the rear of the frame opening to the rear of the barrel. It will be less than your barrel zero figure. Slide the barrel-squaring rod through the barrel and install the cutter. Cut the rear of the barrel one turn of the rod. Remove the rod and measure the barrel zero gap. Repeat cutting and measuring until your measurement indicates you are at the recorded barrel zero you calculated at the start.

Although you should now be able to close the cylinder, you cannot shoot the revolver with zero cylinder gap. Powder residues will quickly bind the cylinder. Continue cutting the barrel and measuring the cylinder gap with your feeler gauges until you reach .003 inch.

With the barrel gap set at .003 inch you now must re-cut the forcing cone. Master Pistolsmith Ron Power

A freshly cut forcing cone, showing the clean steel.

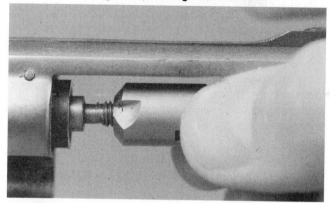

The 82-degree cutter breaks the edge of the freshly-cut forcing cone, removing any burrs that might be present.

has experimented extensively and found that wadcutter bullets give the best accuracy with an 11-degree angle on the forcing cone. For round nose, semi-wadcutters and jacketed bullets Brownells suggests an angle of 18 degrees. Brownells offers forcing cone cutters in both of these angles.

Replace the rod in the barrel and install the forcing cone cutter of your choice. Give the cutter two turns, and take it off the rod. Not all of the forcing cone will have been cut. Check to see how much metal two turns removed, and estimate the additional turns you will need. Repeat until the forcing cone has been fully cut. Use the forcing cone gauge to check the cone opening. Be patient and cut to the correct size. Stop when you have the gauge sitting correctly in the forcing cone.

Take the 82-degree edging cutter and run it once around the forcing cone, just to break the edge.

Your set-back barrel may now be a little too short to clear the tip of the ejector rod. Check by installing the rod in the cylinder without fully tightening it. Try closing the cylinder. If the tip of the ejector rod no longer clears the shoulder of the front locking bolt file the ejector rod down until it clears. While you're at it, check the centerpin. If it's too long, shorten it.

Before you replace the barrel-retaining pin you must go to the range and test fire your revolver. When you re-tightened the barrel you should have come very close to or have been on your witness mark. Test fire to see if you have to make any minor adjustments of the barrel

rotation to return your groups to dead-on. We covered the process of adjusting a fixed-sight revolver in Chapter 13. Use the fixed-sight adjustment process even if your revolver has adjustable sights. When your adjustments have the groups dead center, drift the retaining pin back in place.

Your revolver is good for another long series of magnum loads.

REPLACING THE BARREL — FACTORY REPLACEMENT

Sometimes a barrel is beyond repair and you must replace it. If the old barrel is so worn that it must be set back four threads or more, if it has already been set back once or twice, if is cracked in the rear, if neglect has left its bore pitted, you are best off replacing it. Or you may just want a different barrel.

If you are replacing the old barrel with a new factory barrel you will follow essentially the same procedure as you did in setting the old barrel back. If you are switching from a 4-inch barrel to something shorter, you may also want to replace the ejector rod and center pin. Snubbie barrels all use much shorter components. While you can shorten the existing ones it is much easier to purchase the appropriate ejector rod and center pin when purchasing your shorter barrel.

Measure and record your barrel zero. Unscrew the old barrel and set it aside. Screw on the new barrel by hand. If it stops 1/8th of a turn short of vertical, (the pre-torque point) you are in the catbird seat. Measure the frame-to-barrel gap. If it is equal to or less than your

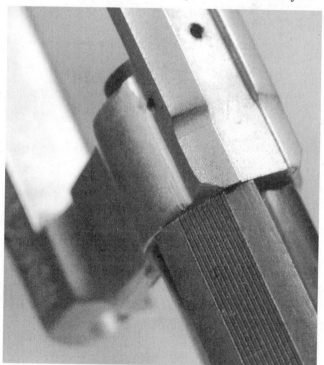

You want your new barrel to hand-turn one eighth of a turn short of center. Then you'll have the right amount of torque when it is snugged up.

barrel zero, tighten the barrel. If it is greater, you must set the shoulder back.

If the barrel does not reach, or rotates past, the pre-

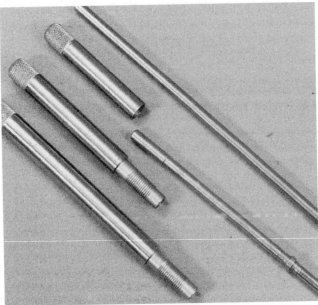

Snub-nose barrels use shorter ejector rods and centerpins. Keep this in mind if you change a four- or six- inch barrel to a two-inch one. Rather than shortening the old ejector rod and centerpin, buy new ones.

torque point you will have to set back the shoulder until it stops correctly. Once you have torqued the barrel in place cut the rear barrel face and forcing cone to set the new barrel to the correct cylinder gap.

Reinstall the old ejector rod and center pin and check them for fit. On a snubbie barrel install the new rod and pin.

Test fire to make your minor adjustments to zero the barrel, and you are done.

REPLACING THE BARREL — BULL BARREL

When shooting in matches like the National Police Championships, where triumph can be measured by one or two points out of close to 1,600 possible, and the NRA Bianchi Cup, where only a perfect score will guarantee a chance at the win, competitors cannot afford to give up a single point because of their equipment. Even a very accurate factory barrel will not be good enough here. For a competition barrel look to one of the big three: Clark, Power, and Barnett.

Installing a competition or "bull" barrel requires the usual barrel fitting equipment plus some special tools and parts. With a bull barrel you must deal with the pressure ring on the frame from the old barrel, provide

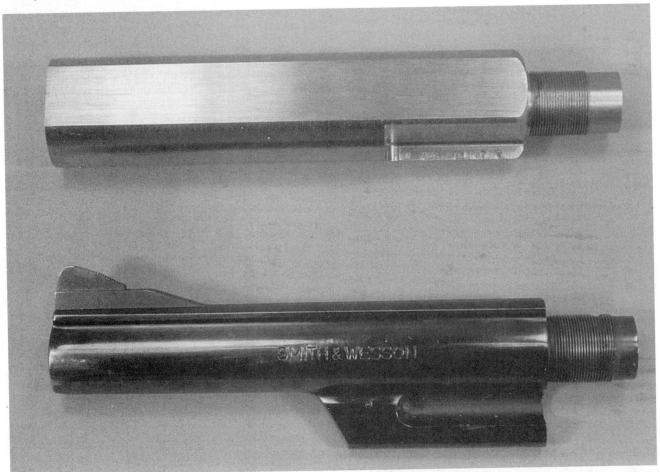

Replacing a worn factory barrel with a new match barrel can increase accuracy dramatically. The bull barrel will not have a front locking mechanism.

a means of locking the front of the crane, and install new sights.

BULL BARRELS AND THE PRESSURE RING

Regular S&W barrels measure .795 to .805 inch in diameter. Bull barrels are larger, ranging from 1 to 1.125 inches. Their increased diameter makes them heavy, which means more work for you when installing them.

Torquing a barrel into place pushes up a pressure ring on the front of the frame. The ring is a miniscule shoulder of steel pushed up outside of the diameter of the barrel, as the two shoulders get squeezed together. This pressure ring does not get in the way of setting the old barrel back, or replacing it with another barrel of the same diameter, because it is outside the barrel diameter. The larger diameter barrel, however, will touch the pressure ring before it can tighten flush against the frame. This contact can microscopically tilt or unevenly stress the barrel. As the revolver heats up from shooting, the tilted or stressed barrel may become inaccurate. Since the whole point of the new barrel is the utmost in accuracy, this pressure molehill assumes the proportions of a mountain. It must be removed.

After unscrewing the old barrel, Dykem the front of the frame. Let the Dykem help you with this delicate piece of work. Once Dykem'd, screw the new barrel in place by hand. See where it contacts the frame, where the Dykem has been rubbed off. Proceed carefully with your

This bull barrel has been "slabbed." The round barrel has been machined flat on the sides.

You don't need the barrel retaining pin, but the revolver does look a bit odd without it.

pillar file, using gentle strokes to remove the pressure ring without changing the barrel seat. You want the new, freshly-filed barrel seat to be perpendicular to the axis of the barrel. If you tilt the seat the barrel will not tighten evenly.

Once the ring is gone, apply Dykem again and screw in the bull barrel by hand again. Check to see that the bar-rel tightens to the 1/8th turn point as before, and that it contacts the frame evenly. Uneven contact will show up as uneven rubbing of the Dykem. If the barrel contacts unevenly but is almost to the 1/8th turn point, use a medium fine stone to dress down the tool marks that are first contacting the frame.

If the barrel is more than 1/4 turn short of the 1/8th

This is a good group, but not spectacular. The reason is, the forcing cone is cut to 11 degrees, for wadcutter bullets. Feeding it semi-wadcutter bullets isn't fair. Still, just over half an inch at 25 yards is plenty good.

This Smith & Wesson M-27 with a Power bull barrel and rib, shoots full-power .357 magnum ammunition as accurately as a bull's eye gun.

point, or turns past that point, use the barrel set back tool to remove some of the barrel shoulder until it will stop by hand at the 1/8th point.

Once the barrel is in full contact and turns by hand to the 1/8th turn point, tighten it with the frame wrench. Adjust the cylinder gap and forcing cone as above. If your revolver will see only wadcutter bullets, cut the forcing cone to 11 degrees. If you will be using it for NRA

Action shooting or the Bianchi Cup and you will be loading other style bullets or jacketed bullets, cut the forcing cone to 18 degrees.

CRANE LOCKUP

Your factory S&W barrel came with a front lockup. Since bull barrels do not, the crane must be locked in place mechanically. Commonly, one or two spring-load-

A bull barrel will have a larger shoulder than the factory barrel. You will have to remove the pressure ring from the frame for the new barrel to fit properly.

The crane in place, with the drill guide over it.

A single ball bearing is enough to hold the crane closed.

ed ball bearings are placed in the crane, riding against the inside of the frame and under the barrel. You must have a locating fixture to drill the holes in the crane and secure the ball bearings. I have used one from Maryland Gun Works for years. To allow the balls' purchase against the frame, you must drill small dimples in the frame, under the barrel.

Position the crane in the fixture. Drill the hole or holes. Place a drop of lubricant into the hole; insert the spring and the ball bearing. Place the staking rod on the ball and give it a tap. If you do not strike hard enough the ball will not be held in. If you strike too hard the ball will be locked down too far and not press against the frame. Since you can always strike again harder, start with light taps and build up in force, checking between hits.

Once the ball is locked in place, put Dykem on the upper inside of the frame cutout, under the barrel. Open and close the crane several times, until you see a line in the Dykem. Take your centerpunch and mark the frame at the end of the line or lines. With a 3-inch-long drill 1/8 inch in diameter, make a small dimple at the centerpunched locations. You want only enough of a divot to hold the crane. If the divot is too small the crane will not be locked. Drill too much and the crane will be loosely held.

This is the tip of the detent ball staking tool. It holds the ball in place while peening the edge of the hole.

These balls lock into the dimples.

The frame under the barrel has been dimpled to hold the crane closed.

The ball being staked.

CYLINDER REPLACEMENT

Replacing a cylinder can be necessitated by a number of things: You've gone over pressure in your reloading and have bulged the chamber at the locking slot. Or the cylinder has been neglected and is rusted, useless or dangerous. I know of one shooter who was safe enough to use blanks on News Year's Eve instead of live ammo. (Firing off live ammo in firearms to "celebrate" the arrival of the New Year is incredibly dangerous and irresponsible. But many do it. You should not.) However, those blanks were powered by black powder. He neglected to clean his revolver afterwards. The rusted cylinder could not be salvaged and was replaced.

You may not be able to change the cylinder yourself. Cylinders are usually only replaced when they must be. And for a long time S&W would not sell magnum cylinders. Magnum revolvers were difficult to get hold of for many years (especially the .44 Magnum) and the factory did not want enterprising people building magnums out of frames not built for the task. Yes, a .44 Magnum barrel and cylinder would fit the frame of your old surplus M-1917, but the old .45 was neither built nor heat-treated for the task.

Set the shoulder to provide a square surface, and timed to torque the barrel correctly in position. A minute's work with a lathe, an afternoon's work with a file.

Once the barrel is timed and correctly installed, measure, remove and cut the face of the forcing cone for correct cylinder gap.

So getting a cylinder may not be easy. But if you can, here is how:

You start from the rear and move forward. First, check the fit of your new cylinder in the frame. Take out the old cylinder, and mark it with an indelible felt tip pen. Then try to assemble the new cylinder into the frame. You'll probably find it doesn't fit, and if it does, the action will feel rough. If the new cylinder doesn't clear the rear of the barrel, then you'll have to remove the barrel to proceed.

Adjust headspace. Measure the gap between the firing pin bushing and the rear of the cylinder. For a .38/.357 it must be between .060 inch and .066 inch. If it is less, you have a problem. You cannot easily increase headspace. The only two ways are with a different cylinder, or by lathe-turning the rear of the new cylinder to create the headspace you need. For the former you need an understanding parts supplier (or the factory). For the latter you need a first-rate machinist who can set back your cylinder a few thousandths and keep the new face square to the axis. If the headspace if too large, you're fine. Carefully stone the center pivot boss of the ratchet, decreasing the headspace, until you get to the .066-inch mark. Then apply your Dykem to the center boss and stone the high spots to nudge the headspace down a couple thousandths more and keep it square. In stoning you've moved the cylinder off the crane, so you'll need to use your Power's shims to take up the internal slack. Unless, of course, the crane is too long the whole time, in which case you'll need to set back the end of the crane to allow the headspaced cylinder to fit into the frame opening.

With the cylinder headspaced and the endshake removed, proceed as if you were fitting the barrel anew. With luck, the new cylinder is longer than the old, and you can re-cut the cylinder gap and forcing cone. If the new cylinder is exactly the same length, then screw your barrel back in and get to shooting. If the new cylinder is shorter you'll need to set back the barrel, recut the gap and forcing cone, and re-zero.

If in the process you have also changed calibers (say, from .38/.357 to .45 ACP) you'll need to replace the cylin-

The barrel threads can only be cut with a lathe. If you try to use a hand tap there is no guarantee you'll get them centered on, and in line with, the axis of the bore.

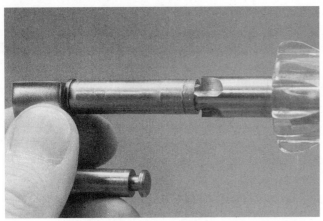

If you over-swage the crane, use a Power reamer to shorten and square the crane end.

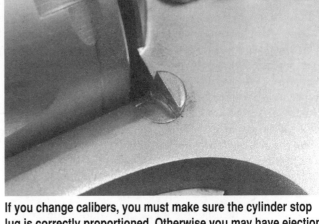

If you change calibers, you must make sure the cylinder stop lug is correctly proportioned. Otherwise you may have ejection difficulties

Sometimes the only way to hold the barrel and keep it centered requires a center in the forcing cone. Be sure to polish the forcing cone after your lathe work, to remove and marks you might have left behind.

The edges of the chambers on the cylinder can be beveled for faster reloads. Remove the extractor before beveling, so you don't cause extraction problems for yourself.

der stop stud. The stud keeps the cylinder on the crane when you press the ejector rod and eject the brass or rounds. The stud is staked in place on old models. On newer ones it is an integral part of the frame and cannot be easily changed. Drive the old stud out from the inside. Place the new one in place and stake the end of it using a blunt-pointed drift punch. (A dab of green Loctite is a good idea, too) Then carefully file the new stud to final dimensions: it must clear the rims of the rounds in the cylinder, but not allow the cylinder to come off the crane. A small amount of movement of the cylinder on the crane is permitted. File less than you think you need, and than range-test. If you feel binding, file more. Fitting a cylinder stop stud is not a critical process. If you over-file, you can drive out the filed one, replace it and try again.

Once the cylinder is in, correctly headspaced and the cylinder gap taken care of, then you can proceed to correctly rough timing and slicking up the new cylinder. Slick it up after it is correctly fitted, not before.

Another replacement cylinder that you'll have to go to the factory for is one made of titanium. Ti is a light, durable metal that oxidizes so rapidly that plating it is difficult unless you use a controlled atmosphere. Its advantage in revolver use is that it is lighter than steel, and thus is less prone to torque. When you snap a cylinder around double-action, quickly enough to do well in competition, the rotation and the stop can be noticed. The lighter Ti creates less torque. Also, repeated dry-firing and shooting can create wear on the locking slots cut into the cylinder. Ti is much more resistant to that than stainless,

As a final bonus, the Ti cylinders from S&W (what else is used in competition?) are machined on CNC machines, where many of the older guns were done on the prior tooling. They are more-precisley spaced, truer to the axis of the bore and have tighter control on the chamber throat dimensions.

When I had S&W replace the cylinder on my 25-2 with a Ti cylinder, I noticed an increase in accuracy and speed. Ask the S&W customer service department about it. The price of the conversion is very much dependent on the current market price of titanium, and it may just be uneconomical to do. It was a good price when I had mine done, and it is something to consider.

CHAPTER 21

THE MAKAROV

The Great Patriotic War is over, and it is time for all patriotic citizens of Mother Russia to prepare for the next war. Rebuilding must begin, and all obsolete things and ideas must be discarded, to be replaced with new ones. The Americans prepare for it by building lots and lots of houses, and sending their veterans to college. The Soviets prepare for it by designing new weapons, and keeping their troops in the occupied territories so they can ship back anything of value. Entire factories and their workers are boxed up and shipped East, where they will be used in the Soviet industrial rebuilding. Well, the parts and tooling are boxed up, the workers aren't, but it sure seemed like it at the time. Of course, this can all be excused (and to a certain degree, rightly so) when you consider that the Soviets lost perhaps 10% of their entire population in the war. The casualties among men of marrying age were so great that a huge percentage of the female population alive in 1945 will grow old and retire with no prospect whatsoever of finding a husband.

One change was in the issued handgun. Prior to the war, it had been planned to completely switch from the 1895 Nagant revolver in 7.62 Nagant to the Tokarev TT33 in 7.62X25. The Nagant, a Belgian-designed revolver, held six shots, and the interesting double-action mechanism not only rotated the cylinder, but shoved it forward. The result was a direct case mouth-to barrel fit that essentially eliminated gas leakage at the cylinder gap. However, by the 1930s revolvers were passé, and pistols were the modern thing. The Soviets first made the Tokarev TT-30, but soon improved it to the TT-33. They also made their submachineguns for the same caliber, 7.62X25, a hot number that launched an 86-grain bullet at 1,250 (handgun) to (1,600 SMG) feet per second. Then the Germans rolled East.

The Makarov is essentially a Walther PP in disguise.

The trigger guard hinges down, and you then tip it to the side to keep it in place while you take the slide off.

The pressing wartime needs for handguns meant that the Nagant continued in use (even as production was finally replaced by the Tokarev by the end of the war) and as pistols were easier and faster to produce, by the end of the war most handguns in service were "Tokes."

But the Tokarev had its drawbacks. It was large, heavy, overly powerful, and while the commonality with the submachinegun ammo was useful, it wasn't needed. And with the post-war plans to phase out SMGs, who needed a handgun that took the ammo no longer to be issued for SMGs?

So, they needed a new handgun. What they made was an existing one. Oh, you'll get all kinds of objections, but the Makarov wasn't so much "designed" as the Walther PPK was modified to accept the 9X18 Makarov cartridge. And why not? The PPK had an enviable service record, and the Russians were very familiar with it, having captured many of them in the four years of the war. So without devolving into a "yes, we designed it/no you didn't" argument, let's take a look around.

Made in Russia, Germany, Bulgaria and China, the "Mak" is a traditional, DA/SA pistol, with a slide-mounted decocking lever and a heel-clip magazine release. The action is blowback, and the magazine holds eight, 10 or 12 rounds, depending on the particular model. It was originally made to hold eight, but later variants were made with double-stack magazines to increase capacity. The caliber is 9X18, but the bullet diameter is not the standard 9mm of .355. Instead the bullets are 9.2mm, .363 to .365 in diameter, depending on where and when made. Why? Beats the heck out of me. The only think I can conceive of was that it was simply too much, having simply "appropriated" the PPK design, to simply adopt the ballistically equivalent 9X17 Browning, aka .380 Auto. Stuck with a blowback design (a locked-breech design would have been more expensive to make) the design bureau could not do much more than make it a 9.2mm, and lengthen the case just a smidgen.

Pull back and then up, and you remove the slide. Then ease it forward, as you're working against the not-weak recoil spring.

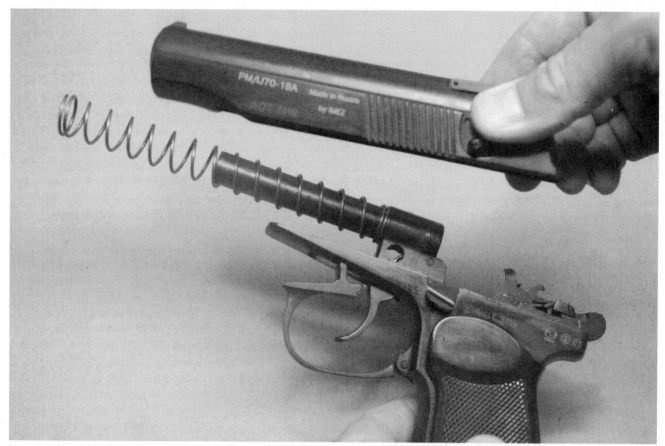

Here is a field-stripped Makarov.

However, the pistol itself is quite durable, while not being exactly a target-grade pistol. The Soviets had no need for a match-grade handgun, as they wanted something that was good enough for minute-of-target inside of 20 meters. The Soviets, along with almost everyone else save us crazy Americans, did not see the pistol as a fighting weapon. They saw it as a badge of office, a piece of emergency equipment, and a necessary evil. Hence, the low power, casual accuracy (by American standards) and limited capacity.

Takedown is easy. Make sure it is unloaded. Remove the magazine. With the slide forward, grab the trigger guard and pull it down. It will pivot at the point where it joins the frame. Notice, while you have it yanked down, that it "wobbles" a bit from side to side. That's to aid you in stripping it. Wobble the trigger guard to one side or the other, and ease it up. The edge of the slide stop shoulder will catch on the frame, keeping the trigger guard in the down position. Now pull the slide all the way back. Once fully to the rear, tip the rear of the slide up and above the barrel, then ease the slide forward with the recoil spring. The slide will come off the front, and the spring will usually stay on the barrel.

To remove the grips, unscrew the single screw you see at the rear of the frame. The grips are made as one piece, in a "U" shape, and it/they will slide off to the rear once you remove the screw.

That's pretty much it. The trigger on the Makarov is a double action first pull, and then single action as the

To remove the grips, unscrew the grip screw. Those clicks you hear and feel? That's the sheet-metal retention spring, to keep the screw from working out over time.

slide cocks the hammer for each repeat. The safety lever on the side of the slide is pushed up to decock and put on safe, and down to fire.

The trigger pull is not all that great. Get used to it. The whole idea of the pistol is compactness, and the smaller operating space for the trigger parts means you have a stiffer trigger pull. If you want, for example, a DA/SA like that of the Beretta M9, you have to allow for larger parts and a more advantageous geometry. I'm sure a Makarov could be improved, but that would be a graduate exercise for a professional gunsmith, not a home project.

That said, there is one project we can undertake. The Makarov was mostly made in 9X18 Makarov, and that is currently an inexpensive cartridge. Surplus ammo is at the moment running around $200 to $225 per thousand rounds. A year or so ago, I'd have thought that was extortion, but with today's prices that is not a bad plinking price. If course, it is extortion if you compare it to the cost when the Chinese were looking to pocket some cash, and were selling 1,600 round cases of ammo for $79. And that was the retail price. But that was then, and this is now. The 9X18 can be reloaded, there are dies, shellplates, bullets and cases to be had. But someone will ask, "Can't I make my Mak a .380?"

Yes, you can. It will, however, cost you more than simply shooting 9X18. First, you'll need a replacement barrel. Federal Arms makes them, among others. Then, you'll need the tools. You'll need a bench vise, drift punches, dremel tool with polishing bobs, perhaps some crocus cloth, and a barrel press. Before you undertake this job, take a look at your Mak. Mine is a Made in

Russia, after the fall of the Soviet Union, and came with adjustable sights. Most of the Maks you'll see will have come from China, then Russia and Bulgaria. The relatively rare ones will be marked with Soviet or East German proofs, but there really isn't that much of a Mak collectors market yet.

Take the slide off and look at the barrel. Underneath the barrel you'll see a cross pin. That, and the friction fit of the barrel in the "chamber hood" is what keeps the barrel in place. This is not going to be like swapping barrels on a locked-breech pistol, where you fit the barrel to the slide. No, you're going to have to break the mechanical bond between the barrel and chamber hood, after you drive out the cross pin. Those won't be easy.

Having swapped barrels, you may have to tend to some reliability issues between the old 9x18 and the new .380 in feeding. Worst-case, you may have to re-contour the feed ramp or barrel lug, and remove it from the frame to do so. Me, I'd leave a Mak in 9x18 in 9x18 (which is what I've done with mine) but if you have to change calibers, here's the broad strokes:

Take down the Mak, remove the recoil spring and grips, and place the frame on a solid backing block. Use a tapered punch and start the crosspin out. It may take a tap, it may take a solid blow, and it may take as much muscle as you can call on. There's no way of knowing until you try. Now, hose the barrel and chamber hood junction with the most aggressive penetrating oil you

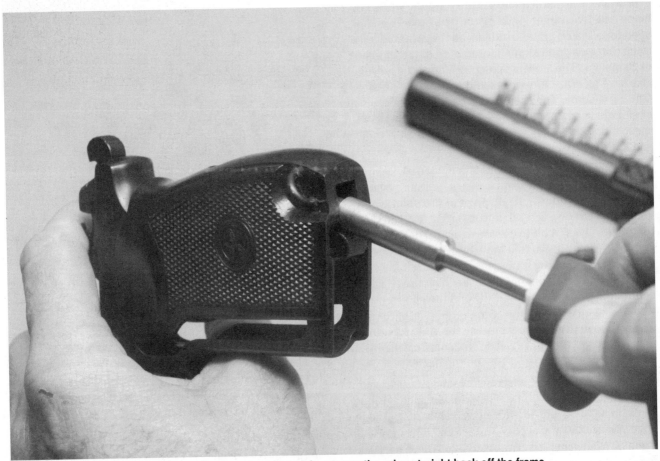

Sometimes the grips fit so tightly you have to use a screwdriver to pry the grips straight back off the frame.

Here it is, ready for cleaning.

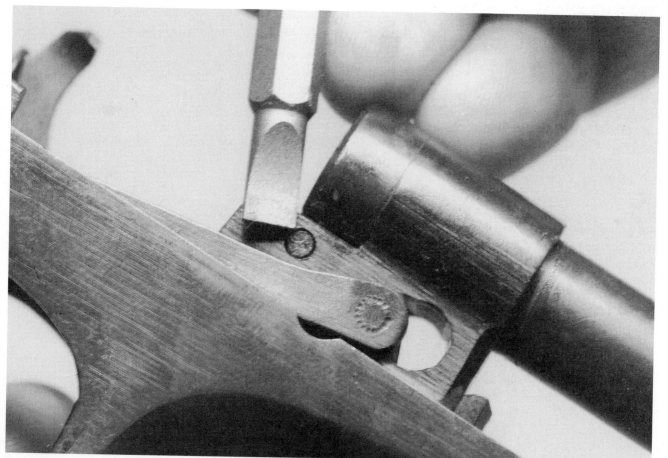

If you wish to remove the barrel, you have to drive out this pin first. Consider your options carefully, as the new barrel is likely to require fitting, and you are actually going to a more-expensive ammo choice.

have on hand. Install the barrel press so it is arranged to remove the barrel (it does double duty: removal and then installation) and see if tightening the press moves the barrel. If not, you have more work.

The barrel may simply be a tight fit. If Vladimir Ilyich Johnson and his buddies were working with the proper tooling when they made your Mak, the fit is snug but not excessive. If, however, the lathe operator who turned the barrel section made it too thick, or the reamer operator who reamed the chamber hood hole was working with a worn reamer (and the reason the lathe guy should have been making barrels just a bit thinner) then the fit will be all the hydraulic press operator could manage. If, since your Mak left the factory there has been some corrosion going on in the joint, the fit of barrel to frame may be tighter than it should.

Throw your Mak in the freezer and leave it there overnight. The next day, prepare before you pull it out. Have a propane torch ready. Yank the Mak out, heat the chamber hood (but not the barrel) and hose the joint with more of your penetrating oil. Back in the freezer. (Obviously, bachelors have an advantage in this operation.) Do that a couple of times, and then prepare the vise setup. Have the barrel press ready. Yank the Mak out of the freezer, install it in the barrel press, heat the chamber hood and tighten the barrel press. If it does not come free, that barrel is not going to be changed. Admit defeat, oil, reassemble, put it back in the safe, and move on.

If/when the barrel does come free, then you need to remove it. Some Maks will allow this simply stripped,

others require a detailed disassembly. Personal luck rules here.

Check the new barrel for fit. Measure the diameter of the bearing section of both the old and new. If the new barrel is larger in diameter than the old, or they are the same and the old barrel was a beast to remove, you want to polish down the barrel bearing section on the new barrel. You can use a lathe, if you have one, or coarse cloth to "shoeshine" the section smaller. Remember: smaller simply means an easier install, until the barrel bearing diameter becomes less than the inner diameter of the chamber hood, and then you start losing accuracy. So sneak up on the right diameter and fit.

Reverse the barrel press, line up the new barrel, and tighten to press the barrel into place. Once there, drive the crosspin through.

Check feeding. If yours will not feed with .380, figure out where it catches and apply the needed polishing.

Not to be too cynical about all this, but congratulations: you've taken a $200 pistol, and after buying a new barrel for $80, and a barrel press for another $80, and after an hour's work or ten, you've now got a pistol that shoots ammo twice as expensive as what you started with. I'm the last one to discourage gunsmithing or gunsmith experimentation, but take a moment to look at the situation. And, with surplus for plinking and hi-tech defensive ammo readily available in 9x18, as well as reloading components, I just don't get the point.

Of course, my experimental 6.5/9X18 bottlenecked cartridge is just about ready to go. . . .

If you install a new barrel, you may well have to do some polishing at the feed ramp. The design involves a lot of corners and sharp edges, and if they don't all fit, you won't be happy with the feeding reliability.

THE SPRINGFIELD XD AND XD^M

When it first arrived in the US in 2000, the Croatian-made XD was viewed as just another Glock wanna-be. Just another striker-fired polymer-framed pistol, one that would soon be left on the heap of other contenders. Yes, well, that didn't happen. It was successful enough that Springfield Armory, always on the lookout for good products, moved in and worked a deal. Springfield is the exclusive importer of the XD. And since then Springfield has driven design changes and improvements. So much so that the XD was in 2008 joined by the XDM, a pistol that takes the polymer pistol competition beyond contention between equals, and makes it another category entirely: Glock-killer.

The original XD is, well, let's be kind and just say it is like a comfortable old car: it works, but it won't win any beauty contests. (Unless, of course, your "old car" happens to be an AC Shelby Cobra, a split-window Corvette, or a Gran Torino.) The XD^M is a lot better looking, and has other advantages besides, which we'll get into in a bit.

The big advantage of the XD was that it had what the Glock did not: an external safety. Of course, the external safety was a grip safety, but that counts for a lot in many circles. The XD^M went one step further and added a disassembly method that does not require you to dry-fire the pistol. The big disadvantage so far for the XD has been an inability of Springfield to keep up with demand. As a result, there aren't any factory spare parts to be had. Not because, as one cynic put it to me, "Springfield wants to keep us from working under the hood" but because they simply can't keep up with demand. They are working on improving that, and there will be parts available.

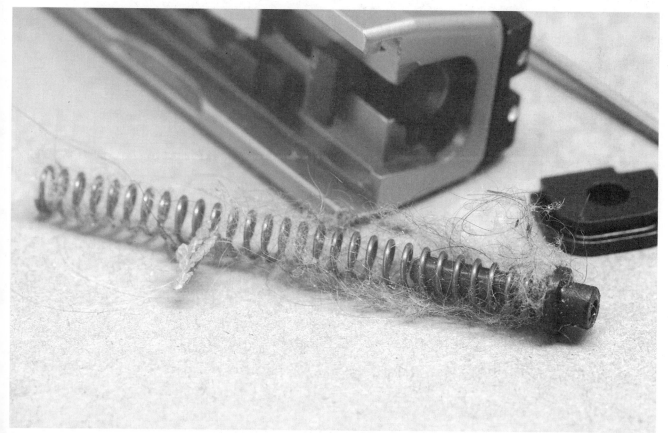

If you don't keep control of the striker spring and retainer, when you finally find them under the furniture they're likely to look like this.

The XD and XD^M are Springfield's striker-fired pistols for the hi-cap wars.

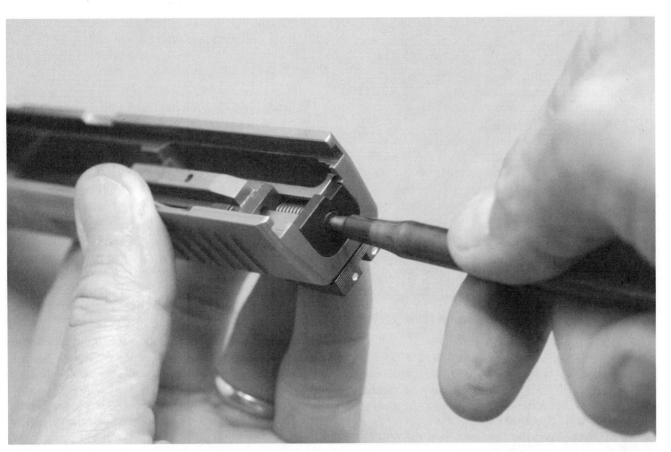

To strip the slide, depress the cocking indicator guide sleeve. Yes, you can use a ball-point pen for this, but the pen is not going to like it. In fact, it may be the last thing the pen is good for.

FIELD-STRIPPING THE XD

Simple, really. Unload. Remove the magazine. Lock the slide to the rear. Push the disassembly lever on the left side up, through the notch conveniently machined through the left-side slide "pontoon." Release the slide and ease if forward. Once it stops, dry-fire, and then run the slide off the frame.

Reach under the slide and pull the guide rod out of the retaining notch in the bottom of the barrel. Now pull the barrel down and to the rear, removing it from the slide. That's it.

FIELD-STRIPPING THE XD^M

A lot easier. Unload. Remove the magazine. Lock the slide to the rear. Pivot the disassembly lever up. Release the slide, and remove it to the front and off the frame. That's it, no dry-firing needed. Recoil spring and guide rod removal the same.

While the striker-fired pistol design has benefits, there is one drawback: gunk in the striker channel. The channel is well protected from the intrusion of dirt and gunk, so not much gets in there. But you have a cylinder running in a tube with (relatively speaking) lots of surface area and a relatively weak spring to drive it. Yes, it works, and works very well, but there isn't the margin of operating power that you'd see in a hammer-driven pistol like a 1911 or Beretta 92. So, you want to keep the

striker and channel clean. Start at the end of field-stripping. Look at the back of the slide. The rear panel, where the cocking indicator shows its tiny head? That plate has to come out.

Once depressed enough, the indicator sleeve clears the retaining plate, and you can slide the plate down.

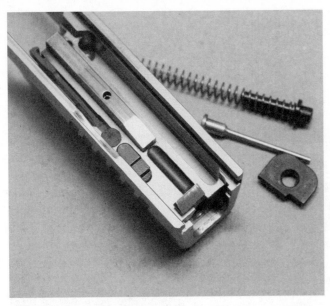

Once the plate is down, you can remove the sleeve, cocking indicator and striker spring.

Push the indicator sleeve into the slide, toward the muzzle. Now push the rear plate down, but be careful. Once the plate clears the indicator sleeve, the sleeve will be pushed by the striker spring. If you aren't careful, you'll launch the sleeve and spring across the room. If

you're lucky, you'll find it, albeit with a clump of lint and dust from its hiding spot under the dresser or desk. If you're unlucky, you'll have to use a magnet to find them. Now lift the striker indictor out.

Look at the middle of the stripper rail, on the bottom of the slide. There's a roll pin there. Use a 3/32-inch punch to drift the pin up, that is, out the top of the slide. The hole is tapered, and if you drive the pin down, towards where the magazine would be, you'll damage pin (and perhaps slide) for your efforts. Unless you're going to move on to some sort of machine work on the slide, you need not fully remove the pin, just drive it far enough to clear the firing pin.

Now you can remove the firing pin and firing pin dampening spring. If all you want to do is scrub things clean, then do so and reassemble. One aspect of the XD and XD^M (they have identical slide disassembly procedures) is that there is no plastic here. You can use light oil to resist corrosion.

To remove the firing pin safety and extractor, depress the firing pin safety and hold it in place. The safety retaining pin has a notch on its end. Use a small screwdriver as a lever, catch the notch, and pull the pin out. Now lift the safety and its spring out of the slide. Use the safety hole as your access point, and lever the extractor up out of its seat.

Now, to remove the striker you have to move the retaining pin. It will require some hammer work, but not much, so don't get out the 5-lb. sledge.

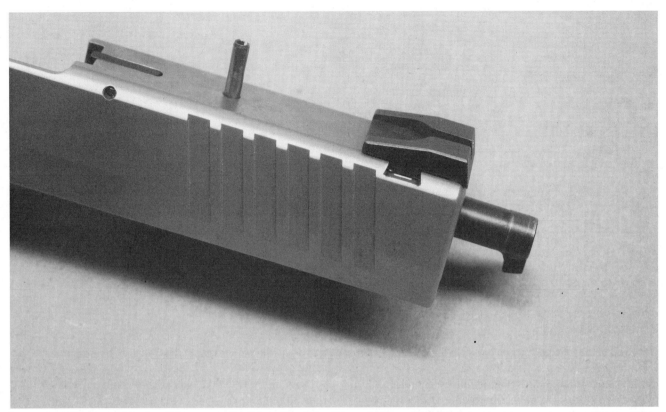

Leave the roll pin stuck in the slide, so you don't lose it and don't have to force it back in later.

You now have a fully-stripped slide. The assembly process is the infamous "reverse the previous steps." There are a few things worth pointing out. The extractor has to go down flush with the slide slot. If it won't go flush, find out why, don't just bash it with a hammer. The safety has an "up" and a "down." The safety goes into the slide with the spring end of the block towards the muzzle, in the hole drilled in the safety block, and the spring up towards the top of the slide. The safety retaining pin (which also retains the extractor, too) has to go into the slide solid end first. The notched end has to be at the back of the slide, or future reassemblies will be problematic.

Frame disassembly. OK, first we have to ask why Springfield does not have a lot of parts available. Your current source for new parts and upgrade parts is Canyon Creek Custom, owned and run by Rich Dettelhouser. From him you can get a lot of stuff, but nothing like the torrent of parts available for the Glock. (Hey, give it time; the Glock has been in the US since 1986, the XD since 2000.) You can get XD and XD^M barrels from Bar-Sto Precision: drop-in, semi drop-in and gunsmith fit. The

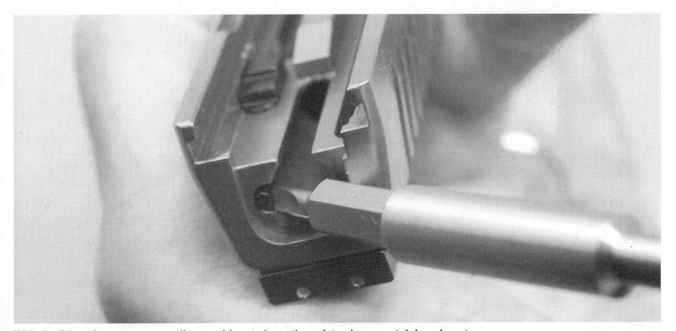

With the firing pin out, use a small screwdriver to lever the safety plunger retaining pin out.

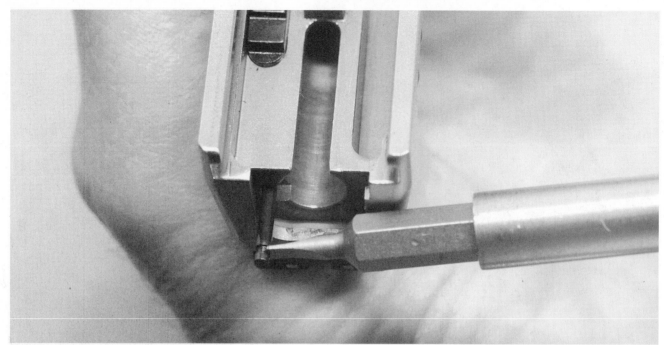

Once you get the pin partway out you can put down the screwdriver and pull the pin the rest of the way with your fingers.

main parts available, however, are barrels, guide rods, magazine extensions, mag funnels and replacement sights. But not so much for frame internals.

Lacking much in the way of replacement springs, trigger and other parts, I'd be hesitant to go stripping the lower to polish and "improve" the trigger. I figure by the time we're ready for the all-new 4th Edition of this book there will be parts galore (assuming we still have guns) and we'll have two chapters on the XD and XD^M.

Besides the non dry-firing aspect of the disassembly process, the XD^M has a few other changes that make it "better" than its predecessor. The frame of the XDM was redesigned to give a better gripping surface, and it has replaceable backstraps, so you can make it the size you want for your hand. Also, Springfield changed the magazine tubes. They proportioned them for proper stacking of .40 S&W rounds, and then crimped grooves on the sizes for proper stacking of 9mm rounds. As a result, the capacity of the 9mm is 19 rounds, and that of the .40 is 16. It holds more ammo than the comparable Glock, and in the high-capacity pistol competition, bullets are like processor speed used to be in the old days of computers: more is better.

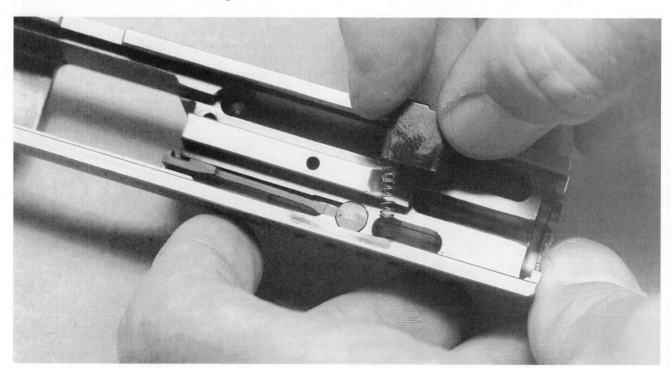

Remember this orientation. When it goes back in, spring in the safety plunger hole, towards the slide, flat face of the safety outboard.

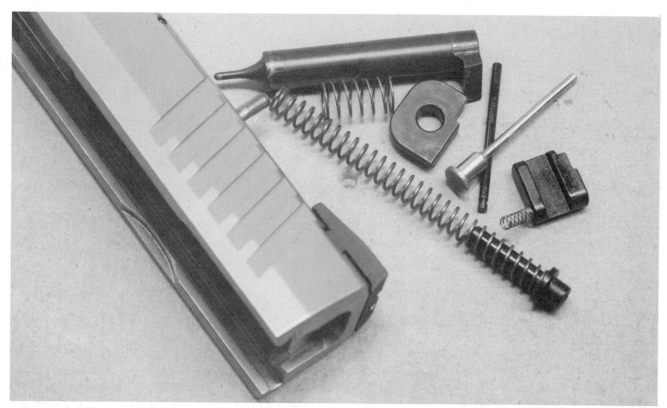

Even when grubby, you don't have much need to use a dental pick to pry the extractor out. And you may not even need to do this much once a year.

As a result, the XD is now a highly-competitive pistol for USPSA shooters, especially in Limited Division, where lots of .40 bullets are desired. In production, where the 9mm resides, everyone is held to 10-shot magazines anyway, so no big deal, except the frame is so well-shaped and comfortable that it offers a distinct advantage over the Glock.

So, in the XD and XD^M, we're looking at two things to gunsmith: barrel and guide rod, and the magazines.

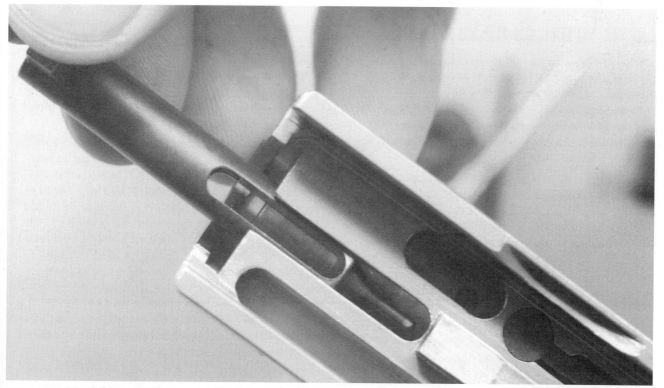

When you re-install the striker, remember: cocking tab on the same side as the safety bar, and push it far enough forward for the retaining pin to catch in the slot.

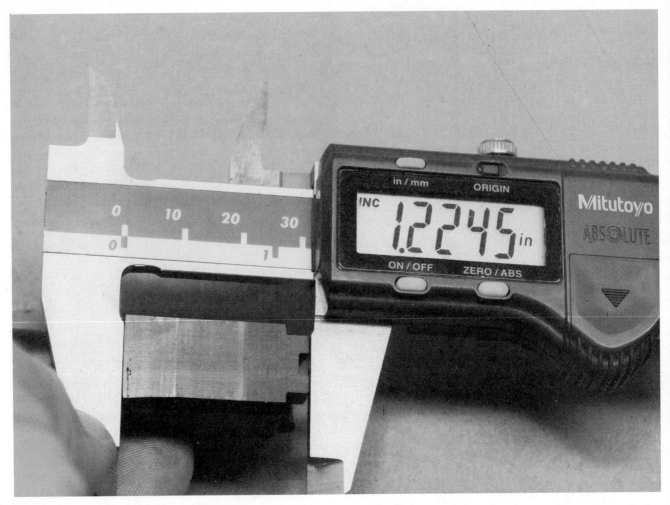

When you're fitting a new barrel, measure the old. On this one, I would not trim the new barrel shorter than 1.227 inch or so, before starting the hand-fitting.

BARREL FITTING ON THE XD AND XD^M

When it comes to barrels, the process is the same between them, even if the barrels have some small differences. Looking at them, they do not appear interchangeable. The cam surfaces have subtle differences, and the recoil spring seats differ, too. I'd be careful to specify which one I had, caliber, length and model, when ordering a barrel.

In talking to the guys at Springfield, I discovered that the above is a good idea for any model and caliber. Yes, the individual parts look the same or very close, but there are subtle differences between them. So if you plan to go fitting a new part to your XD or XD^M, make sure you supply all the particulars to the company you're getting them from. You don't want to hear, "No, you said standard XD, and that part is not the same for the standard and compact. You've got a compact, so why didn't you say so?"

One of the improvements of the XD^M over the XD was the barrel. The tolerances are kept to a narrower span, and the XDM barrels are marked as match barrels. You may well find that you need not change barrels on an "m" to get the accuracy you need. It may simply be a process of tuning your ammo. However, many shooters want more. Thus, replacement barrels. Also, it is possible, on a .40 S&W pistol, to fit three barrels: .40, .357 SIG and 9mm. Also, depending on the particular rules of the competition you may (or may not) enter, changing barrels may be allowed and it may not. Check before you show up only to find yourself bumped to Open.

We're assuming your new barrel is not simply a drop-in replacement. If it is, install, test-fire and get to practicing. First, check to make sure it is indeed what you asked for. Length, caliber, model. Then check the fit of the barrel to the muzzle opening in the slide. It should slide smoothly into the slide, even if it is too big to fit in the rear. Re-install your old barrel, without the recoil spring. Check to see how much play there is, front to back. Remove the barrel and measure the length from front to rear, over the chamber. This is your "not less than" measurement. Now measure your new barrel. It is probably longer. File or mill the rear of the hood to leave it a couple thousandths longer than your no-less-than measurement from the old barrel.

Try to fit it in the slide. If the hood bangs on the sides, you'll have to file them down until the hood slips in. Also, note that the loaded chamber indicator and extrac-

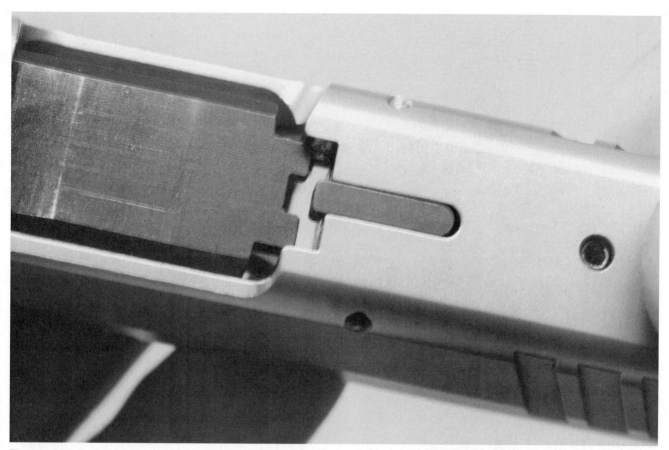

The hood has to fit in the slide clearance, and also has to not bind the loaded chamber extractor.

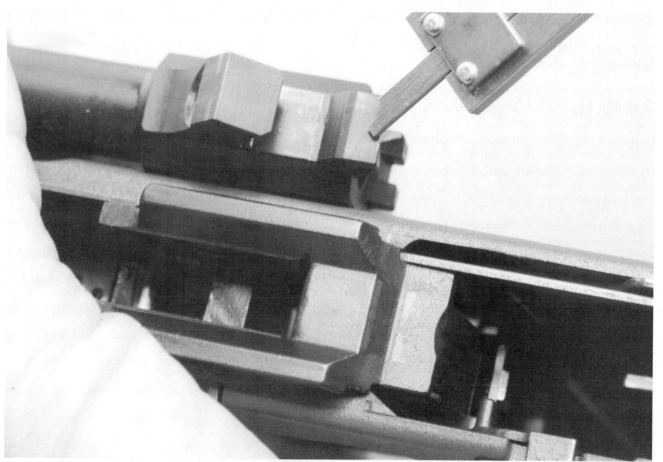

The locking cam (the surface you're interested in is marked by the dial indicator) lifts the barrel up to lock in the slide. You want it tight, but not binding.

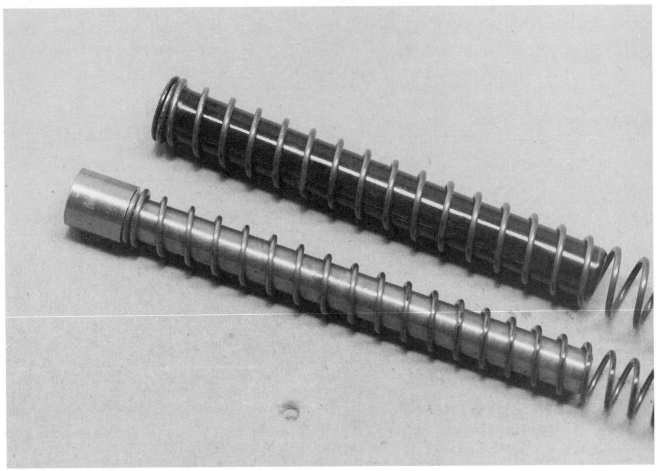

For competition, a new tungsten guide rod adds weight and dampens recoil. Useful on the street? Not so much.

tor cannot be allowed to bind on the barrel. If they do, they will suffer.

Once the hood slides in smoothly, you have to finish-fit the rear engagement. Get out the Dykem or a candle, and Dykem/smoke the rear surface of the hood. Press the barrel into place, then pop it out and see where the Dykem or smoke have been rubbed off. (Smoke is better for this purpose, as the Dykem may not be rubbed off much in the small movement of a barrel lockup.)

Where the smoke is rubbed off, file/stone to relieve the high spot. Repeat, repeat, repeat, until the barrel goes into engagement smoothly, and the barrel hood has smoke rubbed off evenly across its width.

With the barrel smoothly but freely locking into place in the slide, you now have to work on frame fit. The rear lug on the barrel, the one that also has the feed ramp, cams up on the locking block in the frame to close and lock the barrel. Install the barrel in the sldie without the recoil spring, and install the slide and barrel on the frame. Then use your thub to push the slide forward and see if the barrel "carries up" and cams into locking position. On the XD, you'll be doing this against the resistance of the striker spring, on the XDᴹ, you won't. If it lifts and locks, you're done, the barrel is fitted. If the lug is too large to fit between the locking block and slide, you have to carefully file the bottom foot of the cam lug. Again, smoke or Dykem, press and file/stone the bright

spots. Once the barrel will cam up and lock, without binding, you're done. Strip, clean, oil, reassemble and go to the range to test-fire.

The XDᴹ has replacement backstraps of different sizes, so you can adjust the gun to your hand.

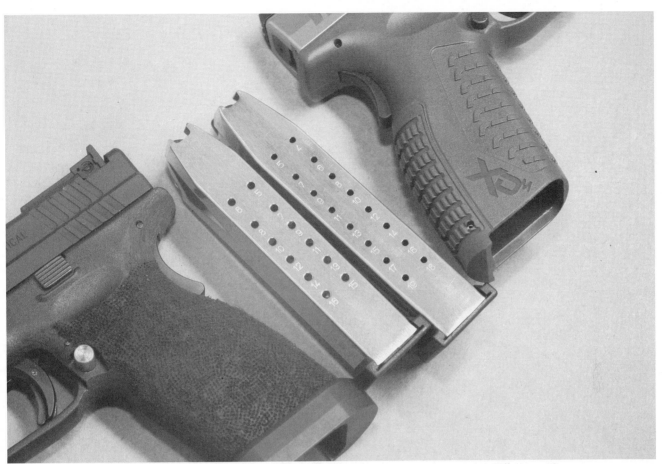

The XD^M uses different magazines, and the new style means more rounds. 9mm, XD, 16 rounds, XD^M 19 rounds.

It is unlikely that you'll have to do anything to the feed ramp for reliable feeding. If you do, however, that is a standard "find the problem and polish the surface" operation.

As a final option, you can replace the existing recoil spring guide rod with a tungsten one. The extra weight helps in controlling recoil. Well, it helps in a competitive environment. For daily carry, I'm not sure it makes much of a difference.

MAG CAPACITY

For Limited, you can't have too much ammo. What you can have is a magazine that is too long. A magazine tube extension that adds capacity, but does not run afoul

Alas, the XD^M, for all its advances, presents a problem when trying to put a magazine funnel on. Currently it requires a frame mod and an epoxied funnel. Technology will no doubt change that.

If you start with an XD or XD^M in 40, you can have extra barrels fitted for .357 SIG and 9mm.

The Canyon Creek mag extension for the XD^M uses a small set screw to hold it on.

Here is a standard XD^M frame with mag extension.

Here's an XD^M set up for Limited Division competition: mag extension and funnel.

of the USPSA stricture of 140mm in length, is what you want. Canyon Creek has that. Installation is simple: take off the old floorplate, pull out the spring and follower. Install the new spring (or spring and follower) in the tube, slide the new extension on, and lock it down with the pin or screw. It is as easy as it is with the Glock, hi-cap 1911s or others. What you get is 21 rounds of .40 S&W, and 24 rounds of 9mm. You can shoot your XD^M (the XD doesn't gain as much) in Limited and keep up in capacity. There is no advantage in Production, since all mags are "ten-shot capacity" per the rules, but if you carry an XD or XD^M, you can have a whole lotta bullets on the reload.

On mag funnels, the options are not so much fun. The XD^M magazine funnel installation requires that you (actually, Rich at Canyon Creek) modify the frame and then epoxy the new mag funnel on. For a competition gun, I can see a one-way mod that increases match utility, but

it does make it then a competition-only gun. If you want a carry gun, you'll have to have a second XD^M. Still, as a Limited Division gun, an XD^M (40 or 9mm Minor) with hi-cap, funnel and a nice trigger has a lot to offer.

SIGHTS

OK, this is simple: the XD and XD^M both have front and rear sights that are in cross-ways dovetails. If, by the time you get to Chapter 22, you can't drift sights out and replace them with new sights, start over on page one and begin again. For competition, the hot setup is now fiber optic sights, where the front and rear have light-gathering plastic rods in them. You end up with "nuclear" dots in your sights. Many competition shooters use just a front blade with fiber optics as a no-battery red-dot sight. On close targets, if the dot is on the target, you get a hit. On farther targets, you apply traditional sight

If you know how to run a mill, installing a rear sight like this is not a big deal. If you don't, it is.

But since both the XD and the XD^M have dovetails for the sights, you can easily slide in a replacement like this.

Currently the vogue for competition front sights is to have a fiber optic rod in the blade. It gathers light and glows, making high-speed sight alignment even faster.

alignment and break the shot.

The sight makers have a much easier time of it, as all they have to do is ask Springfield what the dovetail dimensions are, and then adjust their current sight designs accordingly.

If what you want is an adjustable sight, then the task is either simple or deucedly difficult: if you're already conversant with a mill, and/or have milled other slides to take a Bo-mar (alas, now no more) or other sight, then the XD and XD^M will offer you no surprises. It is a relatively simply matter to select a location (you can't cover the firing pin retaining pin and you can't cut into the rear plate) and calculating the depth of cutting so the rear sigh tends up at the correct height above the slide.

If you are not already familiar with mill operations, then you should be practicing your cutting on a dead slide or plain old bar of mild steel. Once you've milled half-a-dozen sight installations into a 1-1/4 inch steel bar, you can consider carving up an expensive pistol slide.

To close the Springfield XD/XD^M chapter, I'd like to make a few predictions: that the XD^M will muscle a lot of other striker-fired pistols out of the way. In USPSA and IDPA competition, unless the rules are rigged against it, it is going to rudely take over a big part of the Glock share. Unfortunately, it is not allowed in IPSC (international) competition in the Production Division. Something about the trigger not being "double action" enough. That's a shame, because with a magazine extension that fit the box, the XD^M in 9mm would be a smashing good Production gun.

As a carry gun, it offers a whole lot of advantages, and I think it will do well there. By the time we can get back to do the 4th Edition of this book, there will be a slew of parts, accessories, upgrades and other items we can spend much time installing. See you then.

CHAPTER 23

GUNSMITHING MISTAKES

Mistakes in gunsmithing fall into two categories: those you can fix with money or effort, and those that require paperwork to fix. Both happen because you jumped in without thinking things through. Before you tighten the vise, before you start cutting, drilling, filing or you fire up the torch, think about what you're going to do. A moment spent visualizing the process, and reminding yourself what is about to happen, can save you a lot of hassle.

The American Gunsmithing Association does not require you to be a professional gunsmith to join. You can learn many useful things.

GENERAL CONSIDERATIONS

Don't make a change that can't be reversed for a competition gun unless you're sure it is an allowed change for the competition in which you plan to shoot. For example, you can't shoot a 1911 with a coned barrel in IDPA or Single Stack Society matches. Installing a comp on your Glock moves you to Open in GSSF matches (and just about everywhere else, too.) If you go to the trouble of building a long-slide 1911, be aware that you can't shoot it in International matches for IPSC matches, where it won't fit into the Standard box. Hunting regulations matter. My .40 Super is a very good selection for deer hunting, but for a pesky part of the Michigan regulations: The handgun-allowed areas specifically disallow bottlenecked cartridges. (They don't want hunters using T/C Contenders in .30-30 in the "handgun" areas, and rightly so.) Be sure of what is allowed before you build something. If you plan to build a .460 Rowland as a hunting handgun, and your state has requirements about cartridge energy, pack some advertising proof with your hunting gear. (Not exactly a gunsmithing mistake, but still prudent.) The DNR officer you meet may not know or recognize it as anything but a .45 ACP, and he knows for sure the .45 ACP doesn't have enough energy.

You may also have to take into consideration bizarre and even idiotic national or local laws. A friend of mine shoots in Italy. He shoots 5-inch S&W 625-2. He cannot rebarrel it to a 4-inch gun. Were he to do so, he would be "making it more concealable" and thus violate Italian Law. (I kid you not, I mean, could I make this stuff up?) You may live in a state that insists on sample bullets as a requirement of sale. Changing barrels might also require a sample bullet. It may require a sample bullet from a "certified testing laboratory" or someone certified, bonded, inspected or approved. (God only knows what goes on in some states.) You can write to your state representative, senator, or state wildlife commission (whoever seems most receptive) and get the volume of state regulations on firearms. Some of the construc-

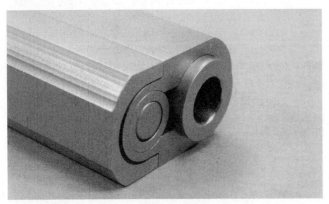

Some pistols are designed without barrel bushings. This STI pistol uses a tapered barrel that fills the slide. The recoil spring retainer is a reverse-plug. It must be removed from the rear.

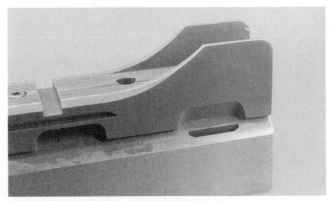

This revolver is Mag-na-ported, and death on bowling pins. But it isn't allowed in a PPC match, as the rules forbid it. Don't go paying for an advantage the rules don't allow.

Video tapes are a good way to add to your knowledge of a particular firearm or tasks performed on it.

tion may make your head spin. It seems that lawmakers cannot construct a simple, declarative sentence. Every statute apparently must be written as a triple negative, with "except as noted in 17(a) sub/3" inclusions.

Make sure you know what is allowed.

Some of the tales I'm telling happened to me, some happened to others, a few I'm speculating on, and some I can't say who they happened to, but trust me, they happened.

The Loctite episodes. Some thread-locking compounds fix quickly. One of the fastest-setting is my favorite, 680 Shaft and Bearing locker, the dark green stuff. It fixes in the absence of oxygen, and when friction stops. You can keep turning while it is on the threads, and it won't set up, but don't stop. My introduction to its setting speed came when I was using it to secure a compensator to a barrel. The phone rang, and I stopped turning long enough to pick up the phone and answer it. When I turned back to continue turning the comp a few moments later, the comp was locked in place. I ended up having to use a torch to break the bond, spin the comp off, clean the threads and re-do the job of installing it. Trust me, after that, as soon as the Loctite-treated part started turning, nothing would distract me from getting it installed except perhaps the fire alarm.

Loctite wicks. Every gunsmith in the country has bonded a trigger assembly together at least once. Once it starts wicking you cannot control where it goes. Use it sparingly, and use gravity to control it. Then check everything again after the Loctite has set. I once had to chip the Loctite off a rifle trigger mechanism (and detail strip it to do so) from an errant few drops of Loctite that were meant to keep the scope mounts in place.

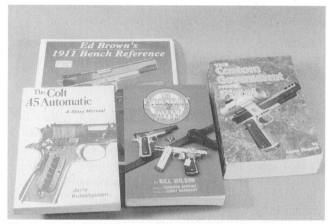
You can build your library around a single firearm, like the 1911.

Loctite does not work through oil. My first few scope mounting jobs (Jimmy Carter was President, in case anyone is burning to know) came loose because I did not sufficiently degrease the threads. If you plan to use Loctite, degrease the threads.

PARTS IS NOT PARTS

Keep track of what you're doing, and work on one firearm at a time. I once had a customer come in with his fully tricked out, super-custom competition 1911, that had suddenly "lost its accuracy." I was puzzled at first, but upon inspecting it discovered that the barrel was a loose fit. I stripped it and looked underneath, and sure enough the barrel was marked with a different serial number than the frame and slide. (Many custom gunsmiths number-match major and minor parts to each gun to make sure they don't get misplaced.) The barrel in his custom gun was the barrel from his carry gun. The match barrel was such a tight fit in his carry gun (which he had on at the time) that it would short-stroke if fired. In all, a very bad combination of barrel-fittings. He had decided to clean them both the weekend before, at the same time, and mixed the barrels up upon reassembling them. Luckily, he'd gone for practice with the competition gun before he needed the carry gun at work.

If you do own identical firearms and are in the habit of working on them at the same time, it might not be a bad

The Kuhnhausen series of books is very detailed, and firearm-specific.

idea to get an electric marking pencil and marking the last three or four digits of each serial number in unobtrusive places.

We all know about poor-quality magazines, but there are other parts that can be poor-quality too. Like the fellow who invested in a cheap replacement barrel at a gun show for his 1911. Too bad the barrel was made of soft steel and the locking lugs on the barrel peened. Once they'd peened enough, they started chipping the locking lugs on the slide. The end result of "saving" $50 at the gun show was a new slide and barrel, and the labor to fit them. Back then, about $300. More, if he'd gone ahead and had the Bo-Mar sights installed that the gun came in for, before we discovered the trashed barrel and slide.

Cheap slide stops can peen and break. Replacement barrels (pistol and revolver) that are "too good a deal" to pass up usually are "too good" for a reason.

Buy good stuff. If you buy from Brownells, or one of the independent makers with name recognition, you can be sure of getting good stuff. Yes, a barrel from Ed Brown costs more than one from "Billy Bob's Barrel Blank Emporium" but it will almost certainly be worth it.

MILLING AND DRILLING

I'm sure you've all heard the old carpenters adage: measure twice, cut once. Is the location you're about to drill the real, actual, place you want that hole to be? Once drilled it is difficult to re-drill. Yes, you can tap the hole, secure a threaded plug in place and re-drill, but even then there can be problems. What if the new plug is a different hardness than the surrounding metal? The correct, offset hole may wander when drilled. (Then you're really up the creek) The plugged hole may show after you've installed whatever the part is.

A gunsmith of my acquaintance once did not secure the dovetail cutter tightly enough in the chuck before proceeding to mill the dovetail slot in a slide. The force of cutting pulled the cutter down out of the collet, and into into the slide as it fed across. He was halfway across the slide before he noticed. Luckily the customer wanted the slide hard-chromed after all the work was to be done on his expensive and super-custom 1911. The solution was to file a piece of steel to fit in the mutant sight dovetail, solder it in place, machine the slide correctly, finish filing the edges of the plug to match the slide, then machining French borders to hide the plug, polish, beadblast and plate. The customer loved it, and showed all his friends the extra work he'd gotten as a make-up for the delay in delivery. The gunsmith ended up spending an extra five hours of time on the job because he failed to spend 30 seconds making sure everything (including the cutting tool) was tight and correctly positioned.

Why not just replace the slide? It was a Colt Delta Elite 10mm, and had already been fitted to the frame. There was no way to replace it, let alone replace it without being noticed.

Or another gunsmith, who couldn't find his calculator,

The other end of the Steel gun, with a radically lightened slide. Be sure you really want this before you go and do it. The cost of a mistake is a new slide.

divided his measurements in half in his head, and drilled the rib-mounting holes down a slide off-center? When the rib was mounted it was visibly tilted. The holes were not far-enough off-center to allow new ones be drilled without overlapping the old. He ended up using his end mill to mill out over-sized holes, thread them, fit plugs, contour them to match the slide, then drill the holes in the correct locations in the new plugs. Once the rib was on, it covered the plugs. The owner was happy and didn't care about the plugs even when told. After all, the gun did shoot 600s on the indoor PPC course, and that was all that mattered. (Competition shooters have a different focus than other shooters.)

Then there was my "oops." I drilled a scope mount on a rifle and "kissed" the barrel threads. (I mis-measured the stop gauge on the drill press by .010 inch.) No problem, as the customer never intended to change the barrel. Well, you guessed it. That hunting season was a very snowy one, his muzzle ended up in the snow, and he split the muzzle on firing it. And wanted a new barrel. I had a hell of a time getting the old barrel off, what with the drilling burrs I had created.

One big "oops" that I had the displeasure to see was a beautiful old European service revolver from the end of the 19th century. (I forget if it was French, Belgian or German.) It was essentially unfired, with a beautiful deep bluing and the slightest bit of holster wear. It showed up with the instructions "make work with ammo." It had arrived on my day off, thus the cryptic note. The revolver was cryptically marked ".44" by the arsenal that had made it a century before, and the present owner had obviously tried and failed to get it to work with the .44 ammo he had on hand; .44-40. He had attacked the rear of the cylinder with what looked like a die grinder, until he could get his .44-40 ammo to fit. Well, they all went more or less all the way forward into the individual chambers, but they each went a different distance forward. Headspace? What's headspace? Unfortunately, the rounds were longer than the cylinder, so he then ground

This weird compensator, on a Steel Challenge gun, doesn't do much to tame recoil. (Steel guns don't have much anyway.) But the holster the shooter used needed a comp to keep the gun secure. So everything not needed was cut away to speed the gun up. Not a mistake, but you can never sell a gun cut like this. Who would want it?

off the barrel where it stuck out from the frame to provide clearance for the rounds, poking out of the front of the cylinder. Luckily, it still would not fire. Had he brought it in before all this, we could have pointed him to the correct ammo. But a lack of forethought reduced a pristine collectors piece to a scrapped bad example.

PARTS IS PARTS

If at all possible, do your filing, stoning, fitting and other work on the cheaper or more easily replaced part. Sometimes you can't avoid it. You have to cut the frame to fit a beavertail grip safety. But if you need to fit a bushing on a 1911, fit the bushing and don't go cutting on the barrel or slide if you can avoid it. If your trigger is too large to fit the 1911 frame, file the trigger and not the frame.

Practice fitting on old parts bought for the purpose. Improving your trigger by stoning the sear that came with it goes much easier if you practice beforehand on one bought at a gun show for a dollar. Buy a rusted barrel and have it welded to learn to fit barrels. Unless you're a working gunsmith you won't have the luxury of practice guns to work on, but old parts are cheap, and bar and round steel is cheaper still. Practice takes time, and if you are working for yourself time doesn't matter. A pro has to bill his time, and practice is time he can't bill. (But a necessity regardless of cost.) You aren't billing your time, and are working on your own handguns. Get it done right by working your mistakes out on practice parts.

And if you do make a mistake on a "good" part, don't be cheap. So you stoned a Chip McCormick sear to death? Or a Wilson? Spend the less than $20 and buy a new one and learn from your mistake.

THE EARLY PLATE JOB

Hold off getting your gun finished, especially if you are a competition shooter. You may find that there is a sharp edge or corner you hadn't noticed at first. Or the safety chafes once you've gotten some practice with it. Or the sights just aren't all you'd hoped they'd be. But now the plating you so eagerly had applied has to come off before you can get the extra work done. Most plating cannot be treated like paint, "spot-sanded" and retouched. It all has to come off. The plater will charge you to remove the old, and charge you again to plate anew. If you want to shoot your new custom gun for a while before getting it plated, you can have it blued. Or you can treat it to a bake-on finish from Brownells. The finish will last long enough to let you determine that you are ready for plating. The temporary finish will also protect the surface until you can have it finish polished and plated.

Heck, you can even give it a quick application of spray paint. After all, you're shooting it to score points, right? I mean, points on target, and not social or cosmetic points. I don't know of any shooting match that give bonus points for the best-looking blaster.

One aspect of plating you need not worry about: porting. Chrome, nickel and other metal platings are all electrically conductive. Mag-na-Port will not have any problem porting your barrel (or slide) through the exterior plating. If you have a non-conducting finish like a bake-on epoxy, they can scrape enough of the finish off for the electrodes to find a conducting surface to work with, and then port through your finish. But the final finish will be better served if you port first, then finish.

PAPERWORK ERRORS

Well, there was the fellow who was so taken with the idea of turning his old surplus M-1917 S&W .45 ACP revolver into a snubbie (he'd gotten a barrel for a bargain at a gun show) that he didn't measure the location of the serial number. He used a pair of round-butt wooden grips as his grinding template, and ground the backstrap and butt to match the grips. Only when he went to have it polished for bluing did he discover he was missing a digit and a half. Luckily for him, the serial number was also stamped on the frame in the crane cutout. However, even with a pre-existing, valid serial number in place on the gun in a different location, it is a technical violation of Federal law to alter or obscure a serial number. Learn from his lesson. I did. I was just going to do the very same thing to my project gun when I heard of his problem, and measured my own. Lucky for me, the serial number was offset enough that I didn't have a problem in round-butting mine.

One prospective paperwork error is the crushed frame. If you attempt to clamp your pistol frame in the vise without a clamping block in place, you may crush the frame. It is very difficult to restore the interior to a size that will accept a magazine. (I know I've tried on a total of three frames brought to me. None could be

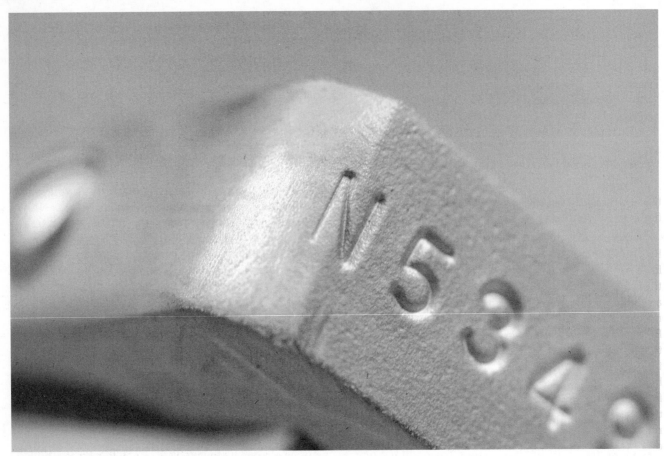

The frame was rounded, and the serial number survived. Measure yours before you go cutting, or you may have a slight problem.

restored.) If you are lucky, the factory will replace the frame with a new one bearing the same serial number (and destroy the old one). They will charge you dearly for it. If they cannot or will not send it back bearing the same serial number, you must then go through the paperwork process of proving the old one scrapped and then registering (safety-inspecting, state's attorney-approving, whatever the name is) your "new" firearm. The simplest way to do so is to turn it over to a professional gunsmith and his Federal Firearm License. He can enter the old one on his books, then show it sent to the factory and be retained by them. (You can then keep the work order showing the disposition of your "old" firearm.) You then "purchase" your "new" firearm from him, conforming to all the state requirements. All in all an expensive lesson.

Apparently the prospect of replacing a busted frame with one of the same serial number is now not as easy as it used to be. I was just discussing the subject with a big manufacturer, and had the following story related to me: apparently manufacturers get regular government inspections. On one of these, the BATFE agent being escorted around passed a door and asked "What's in there?" Answer: "Oh, that's where we keep the un-numbered frames for repairs." Well, not any more, they don't. Now, if that company wants to replace your frame with

one of the same serial number, they have to have an employee intercept a correct frame at the serial-numbering station, walk it to the custom shop, where it is stamped with your gun's number right after the frame of your gun is destroyed. That's a lot more cost, and may mean the end of the courtesy of same-numbered replacements.

One out that will not avail you is a new, replacement frame from a third source. For example, perhaps you are a clever guy and figure you can replace your crushed Colt frame with a new one from Caspian. Caspian is too clever for you. First, they won't ship a frame except to someone with an FFL. (That pesky paperwork requirement again.) And if you ask for a custom serial number, your request may tip your hand. Asking for "70S123456" clues them in that you are replacing a Colt frame. Sorry, Charlie. Even if you manage to slip one past them, there is the pesky requirement all manufacturers have of putting their name on the frame. So, you replaced your Colt, serial number 70S123456 with a Caspian, serial number 70S123456. Hmm, somehow I don't think that is going to pass un-noticed if it ever becomes something official-dom has to look into.

No, if you destroy a frame your best route is to take your lumps and correct it all legally.

Think twice, measure twice, then start the job.

CHAPTER
24

SOURCES FOR YOUR LABORS

For parts and tools, you have three kinds of sources: those who market it, those who make it, and those who find it.

The single biggest source for both parts and tools is Brownells, a gunsmithing supply house in Montezuma, Iowa. Not only can you obtain the tools you need to do the work you desire, those tools come with instructions and help on the other end of the phone. If you just can't make heads or tails of the instructions you can call up Brownells and ask one of the gunsmiths there just how the gizmo works. All of the guys there have been full-time gunsmiths, some with their own shop, for years before signing on with Brownells. (Modesty does not forbid me from mentioning that I was offered a position at Brownells on more than one occasion. For one reason or another that I can't recall right now, I declined on both occasions. Sometimes life takes the path you'd never expect.)

You can also get factory parts via Brownells. Many of the manufacturers do not want to deal direct with gunsmiths and individuals. Keeping track of 24 distributors and 1,000 police departments is hard enough. Add 10,000 gunsmiths and hobbyists and you have a night-

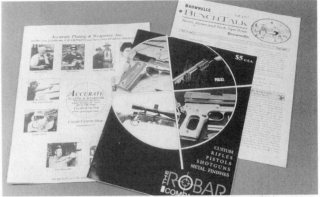

If you are thinking of getting a handgun refinished, get catalogs. If you buy anything from Brownells you will get their brochure "Benchtalk," relating to things gunsmithing in general.

mare for the billing department. By selling parts through Brownells, manufacturers such as Colt, S&W, Ruger and the rest can keep gunsmiths and customers happy, and keep their shipping and billing staff from munching Tums like breath mints. And lest you think that you are paying more because Brownells is the middleman, guess again. Because the parts leave [fill in the blank] in one

The owners manual, NRA publications and manufacturers catalogs all contain a wealth of information.

Scan the magazines for articles on pistolsmithing. If you subscribe to them all, you will be buried under a tidal wave of coated paper.

big box, the manufacturer doesn't have to assume the overhead of an order department, shipping department, packaging, etc, etc. If the part costs more than it theoretically would straight from the manufacturer, well, that's part of the cost of having such a kick-ass catalog as the Brownells catalog.

Quit your whining, man up, and reach into your pocket for the extra nickel or buck that the part costs. You're getting the deal of the century on it.

Brownells is a marketer (and a very good one, too) but not all tools and or parts are available from Brownells. A special tool may be something a gunsmith or retired tool and die maker makes and markets himself, and Brownells just hasn't talked him into joining their family. Or it might not sell in enough volume for Brownells to stock. You may find that a particular tool that is stocked by Brownells is the only one they have from a maker, and when you ask the manufacturer direct you find he has a whole slew of other items.

You can count on anyone I've mentioned in the book to come through with good stuff. Ron Powers, Jack Weigand, Bill Wilson, Chip McCormick and the rest all make great products, be they tools or parts. (My apologies if I've left anyone out.)

Bill Wilson, Chip McCormick, Ed Brown, all make things. If you want something from them you can go directly to them. You might find, however, that you cannot get a better price than Brownells. Then again, you might. A little comparison shopping can go a long way. What you will find are items not carried in other catalogs.

The Finders are companies like Jack First Gun Shop

and The Gun Parts Company. If you want a blue, K-frame crane for a Smith & Wesson that dates back to before the model number designation, don't go to S&W. Don't go to Brownells. Ask Jack, or write to Gun Parts. They have parts from old guns, surplus parts, parts taken off destroyed guns, and parts from I-don't-want-to-know-from-where. If they don't have it, you have to be patient. I had to write to Gun Parts three different times to find a sear for a Savage M-1907 in .32ACP. I got my trade-in M-28 that I turned into a "pseudo 25-2" for bowling pin shooting from Jack First when they were still in California. (They, as much of the rest of the firearms industry, have moved to South Dakota.)

When I first wrote this book, the internet was still a curiosity. Yes, you could go rooting around for a lot of stuff back then, but the internet had not gotten to the point now: every company on the face of the planet has a web page. Well, things have changed. I recently did a web search for pearl grips, to find that there was a maker of them. A maker in Vietnam. You had to be kidding me, right? A guy in a building in Vietnam has a web page, devoted to the sales of his custom pearl grips, and it took less than two miniutes to find him?

Web searches to produce the results you want can be an art. I know of people who can find what is desired in a few minutes, and others can't find squat. So, unless you have the knack, it can take some searching. But, once you find the web pages of dealers who sell parts, new, used, modified, rare, whatever, bookmark them.

It's a brave new world, and you have to keep up or it will simply forge on without you.